Looking at Lovemaking

Looking at Lovemaking

Constructions of Sexuality in Roman Art
100 B.C.–A.D. 250

John R. Clarke

University of California Press

Berkeley Los Angeles London

The publisher gratefully acknowledges the contribution provided by the Art Book Endowment Fund of the Associates of the University of California Press, which is supported by a major gift from the Ahmanson Foundation.

University of California Press
Berkeley and Los Angeles, California

University of California Press, Ltd.
London, England

First paperback printing 2001

Library of Congress Cataloging-in-Publication Data

Clarke, John R., 1945–
Looking at lovemaking : constructions of sexuality in Roman art, 100 B.C.–A.D. 250 / John R. Clarke
p. cm.
Includes bibliographical references and index.
ISBN 978-0-520-22904-4 (pbk. : alk. paper)
1. Art, Roman—Themes, motives. 2. Erotic art—Rome. 3. Sex in art. I. Title.
N5763.C58 1998
704.9′428′0937—dc 21 96-40380
CIP

Printed in the United States of America

17 16 15 14 13 12

10 9 8 7 6 5 4 3

The paper used in this publication meets the minimum requirements of ANSI/NISO Z39.48-1992 (R 1997) (*Permanence of Paper*). ∞

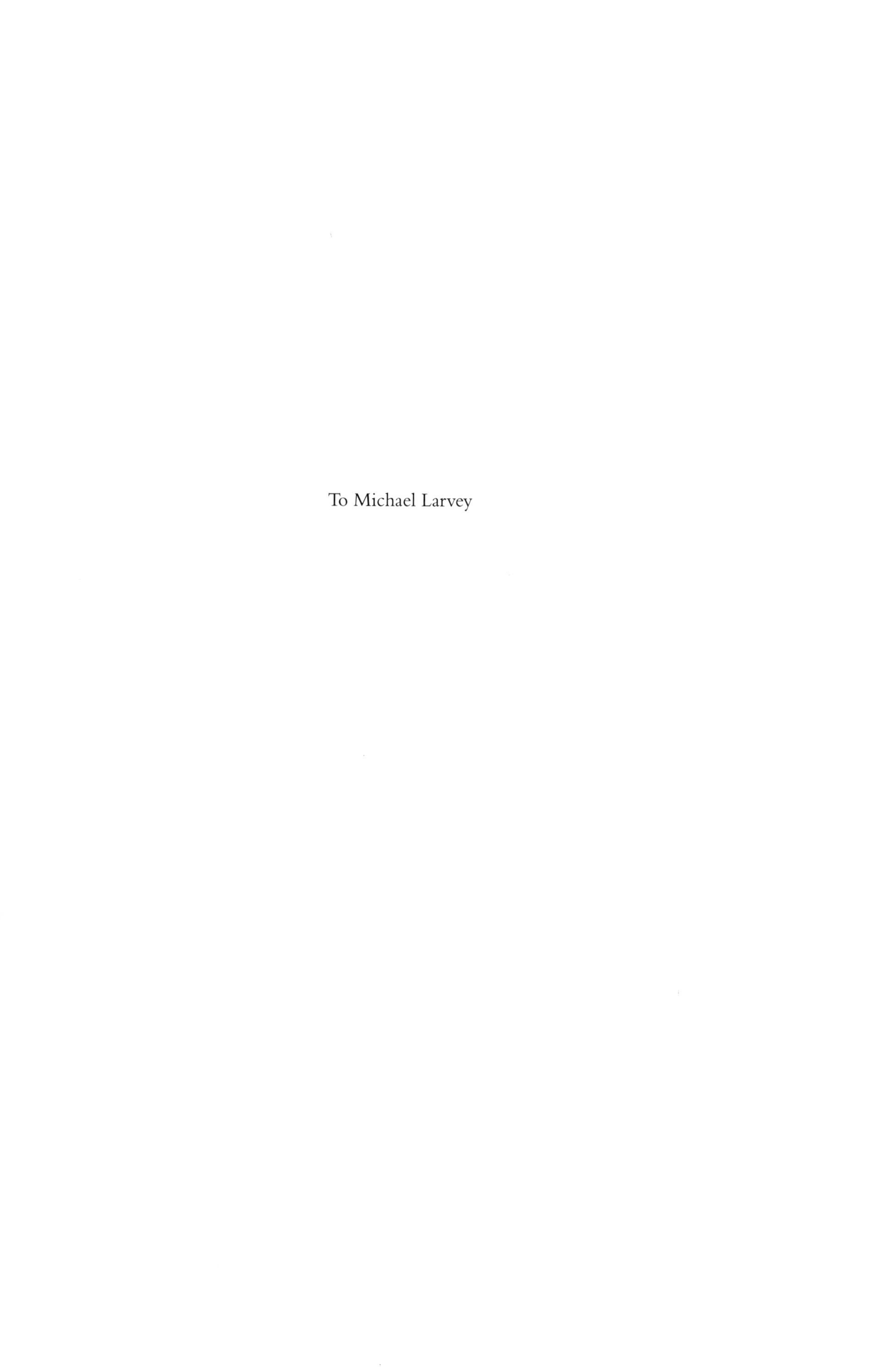

To Michael Larvey

Contents

Illustrations

Unless otherwise noted, all drawings and plans are by the author.

MAP

PLATES

(*following page 142*)

FIGURES

Acknowledgments

I greatly enjoyed writing this book, not the least because it needed to be written. The more research I did on Roman and Greek art with sexual subjects, the less satisfied I became with the conventional assumption that so-called erotic art needed no explanation. Most of the objects themselves ended up hidden from view in museum storerooms or in private collections. I soon found that studies on visual representation had not even begun to catch up with the important work being done on gender and sexuality in ancient texts. I had a big void to fill and few precedents for the project.

I discovered almost immediately, when I began work in 1992, on a grant from the University of Texas Research Institute, that many scholars were eager to help me and enthusiastic about the project. It was gratifying to have experts read and criticize my work. I have gained everything from these wonderful colleagues and friends, and I feel that I have given them quite little in return. I offer them this book, and my thanks here.

My biggest debt is to the scholars who read this manuscript for the University of California Press: Anthony Corbeill and Natalie B. Kampen. I have benefited much from their advice and erudition. Other scholars read the manuscript when it was nearly complete, offering suggestions and subjecting it to the healthy criticism it needed. Thanks, then, to Andrew Riggsby, Brian Rose, and Eric Moormann. Others kindly read parts of the manuscript, helping me shape it as I worked out individual chapters or ideas: Richard Brilliant, Ann Kuttner, Amy Richlin, and Richard Shiff.

Luciana Jacobelli generously shared with me her valuable insights not only on her excavation of the Suburban Baths but also on the complexities of Roman sexual representation. I also got timely help on specific issues from Malcolm Bell, David Halperin, Thomas Hubbard, Irving Lavin, Archer Martin, Jenifer Neils, Holt Parker, Andrew Stewart, Carolyn Valone, and Karol Wight.

I am privileged to work with exceptionally bright and talented graduate students and colleagues here at the University of Texas. In particular I want to thank Margaret Woodhull, who performed miracles as my research assistant on this project. Margaret also helped in the field, as did Michael Thomas. Sarah Benson, Charles Cramer, Megan Granda, Saundra Goldman, Marianne Kinkel, Nancy Hahn, Joe McElrath, Lynn Ransom, Lisa Schrenk, Lauren Petersen, Emily West, Blair Whitney, Margaret Woodhull, and Khris Villela, as members of my graduate seminar, "Constructions of Sexuality in Greek and Roman Art," offered excellent insights on this project. Melissa Kepke's thesis on the paintings of the Suburban Baths at Pompeii provided me much food for thought. Kimberly Cassibry, Tracy Chapman, Anne Collins, John Erler, Edie Gibson, Annette LeZotte, Julie Levin, Eileen McKiernan González, Lauren Petersen, Susan Richmond, Katie Robinson, Gwynn Thayer, and Michael Thomas all took part in a critique of the current manuscript in my seminar entitled "Pompeii: Art as Index of Acculturation," and I offer them my profound thanks.

This book involved extensive fieldwork, made possible because of the kind permissions granted first by Baldassare Conticello, superintendent of Pompeii, and later by his successor, Piero Giovanni Guzzo; by Stefano De Caro, superintendent of Naples and Caserta; and by Anna Gallina Zevi, superintendent of Ostia Antica. Antonio D'Ambrosio facilitated our work at Pompeii, as did Mariarosaria Boriello our study and photography in the National Archaeological Museum in Naples.

I completed the manuscript while a resident at the American Academy in Rome in the spring of 1995. I have warm memories of the hospitality of the academy, graciously offered by the director, Caroline Bruzelius, and her able staff. Christine Huemer and her staff in the library facilitated my research, and the lively company of the fellows and visiting scholars and artists made my stay there a season in heaven. Support for this research came not from heaven but from a National Endowment for the Humanities Fellowship for University Teachers, with additional funding from the Annie Laurie Howard Regents Professorship, and from Jon Whitmore, dean of the College of Fine Arts at the University of Texas.

Production of this book required making new drawings and plans, and without the help of Kirk Tuck to digitize them, this would have been a much more difficult and time-consuming task. Antonio Ortolan in Rome printed Michael Larvey's black-and-white photographs, and our friends David and Wesley Tobey generously provided much-needed photographic equipment.

Friends in Italy, especially Jeffrey Blanchard, Pamela and Larry Christy, Fabio Pignatelli, and François Uginet, made our work there all the more enjoyable. Friends in Austin, especially Frank Fisher and the Rankins—Susan, Jim, Jonah, and Zane—kept things running smoothly during long absences from home.

Many institutions provided access to their photo archives: I thank them all, but in particular Karen Dalton, Laura Gadbery, Catherine Johns, Elizabeth Milliker, and Carlos Picón.

I thank Mary Lamprech, Classics Editor at the University of California Press, for having faith in this project, and Deborah Kirshman for her encouragement. Suzanne Samuel oversaw the many details of production, and Edith Gladstone proved an astute and impeccable copyeditor. I must also thank two very special staff members here at the University of Texas: Gwendolyn Barton and Mario Bermea.

Last and most important, I owe a deep debt of thanks to my partner, Michael Larvey, who not only offered his enthusiastic support of my ideas but produced most of the wonderful photographs that illustrate this book. He was, and remains, an inspiration. It is to him I dedicate this book, and to love: AMORI AMICOQUE OPTIMO.

INTRODUCTION

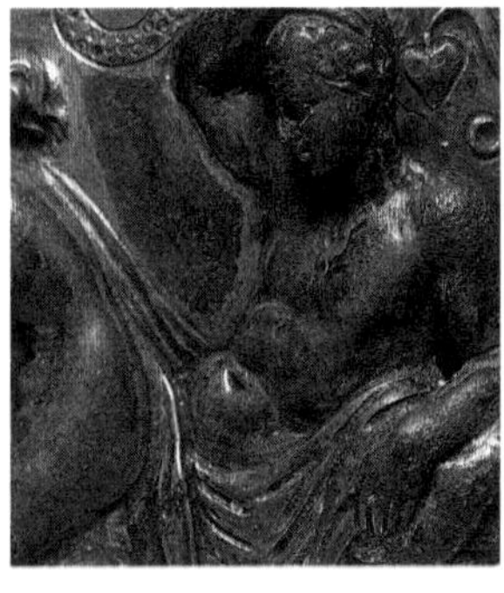

Why a book on Roman "erotic" art? The images are familiar enough by now, published in large and elegant picture books. They show artists' renditions—in paint, ceramic, silver, cameo glass, and gems—of human beings copulating. What can I say that's new about these images? Isn't human sexuality so familiar, so constant, that its meaning is self-evident? Why belabor the obvious?

What I've discovered in trying to understand these images as the ancient Roman viewer did is that almost *nothing* about them fits into our late twentieth-century conceptions about sex. Roman sexual images are not self-evident. What is more, they have the power to reveal a sexual culture that operated under rules completely different from our own. It turns out that such elegant books do us a great disservice. They cut the sexual images off from their original contexts. Seeing these images in glossy photos in a book means *not* seeing them as the ancient Roman did. Imagine drinking from an elegant silver cup with scenes of male-to-male intercourse on it, or holding a fine gemstone in your hand with a scene of lovemaking accompanied by an erotic inscription, or visiting someone's house and seeing fresco paintings depicting sexual activity on the walls of the best room. Or imagine entering the dressing room of a luxurious public bath and seeing sexual vignettes that showed much more daring sexual acts than the ones you saw in the local bordello. Every one of these experiences engages a whole gamut of sensations that glossy photos cannot call up. Sexual representations were embedded in specific Roman social practices, from entertainment at a banquet to the daily ritual of bathing. The key to understanding these images of lovemaking is to sweep away our experience of the picture book and try to see them as the ancient Roman did.

Such efforts bring us remarkable new discoveries, both about the artists who created these images and the people who looked at them. Visual artists were much bolder than the Roman poets and satirists who wrote so much about sex. Artists delighted in upsetting the norms of proper sexual relations by showing behavior that broke the codes set by the elite. If, for instance, the Roman writers tell us that an adult male could have sex with a woman or a boy as long as he was the one doing the penetrating, what does it mean when Roman artists represent two adult males having sex with each other? If these same writers tell us of the shame that descends on someone who engages in oral sex, what do images of men and women engaging in both fellatio and cunnilingus mean? Exploring these code-breaking images in context reveals a variety of attitudes toward sexuality that the writers never account for. Why? Because they are writing for and about the elite. The writers' values are those of the class they belong to. Not so visual representations.

We have, in effect, the standard attitudes presented in the writings and the nonstandard ones popping up in the visual art. The repercussions of this disparity are enormous. Study of the visual art expands the scope of ancient Roman sexuality far beyond the elite class. Visual representations of lovemaking had much larger and much more varied audiences than verbal representations. Take the mass-produced ceramics manufactured in Italy or the Rhône Valley and exported throughout the empire. Roman soldiers, and their barbarian allies, drank from them in far-flung outposts and proudly included them in the burial offerings in their tombs. Or the tiny gaming pieces called *spintriae:* their sexual imagery circulated in much the same way as the images of the emperors circulated on coins.

This diffusion of sexual imagery across class boundaries opens up the possibility of seeing new faces—the faces of people who had no part in writing the ancient texts. They are women of every class, non-elite free citizens, slaves, and former slaves. They are also people who were outcasts because of their sexual practices, such as prostitutes of both sexes. By investigating fresco paintings still in their original architectural contexts I reconstruct some of the attitudes that these excluded Romans had toward sex. It is clear that artists who created such images were addressing these non-elite people in ways that were dear to them. In some cases they placed sexual fantasies in luxury and physical beauty—a kind of "trickle-down" system in which elite representation found its way to the humble house of a freedman or even to a bordello. In other cases artists raucously overturned elite standards: the passive woman becomes dominatrix over the elite man who licks her vagina; two women parody male-female lovemaking; groups of men and women enact all manner of taboo sexual acts in threesomes and foursomes. In these parodies we finally get a glimpse of the non-elite and hear them laughing—at sex.

This book gains much from recent archaeological discoveries. I had the privilege of studying art that remained buried until very recently. Most dramatic of all are the paintings of the Suburban Baths at Pompeii, uncovered in 1986 and first published only in 1995. The Leiden gem, the Ortiz flask, the Warren cup, and the Metropolitan glass dish are all Roman luxury objects of the Augustan period that have only recently come to light: here I give them their first full studies, and they add considerably to the project. Even well-known objects yield surprisingly fresh information. In particular, when I match the paintings of lovemaking—cut from their walls at Pompeii by prudish excavators—to their original architectural settings, they reveal new dimensions of Roman culture.

What emerges, first and foremost, is that—contrary to our expectations—the Romans are not at all like us in their sexuality. The acts that artists depicted are familiar to us, but the meanings that these representations had for the viewers are far from the ones we would like to superimpose on them. Here was a world before Christianity, before the Puritan ethic, before the association of shame and guilt with sexual acts. And it is a world that had many more voices than the ones we hear in the ancient texts that have survived. There is no way that elite attitudes toward sexuality embodied in classical literature can explain these images, created as they were by anonymous artists for the whole spectrum of Roman society. The great surprise of my study is discovering many different Roman sexualities within a society that was anything but homogeneous.

In exploring how the art of the Romans reveals their sexualities, we find that our own concepts of what is pornographic, sinful, or shameful have little or nothing to do with what the Romans thought: they bought and enjoyed objects, or even commissioned paintings for their homes, that frankly represented sexual intercourse in many different forms. We see images of men and women making love, but also men making love to boys and sometimes to other men, women pleasuring women, and sexual threesomes and foursomes. Artists represented sex in many different ways, not only varying positions but also picturing practices such as fellatio and cunnilingus. In studying these images in context I came to the conclusion that the ancient Romans, rather than consider these images "pornographic" and hide them away, usually associated them with luxury, pleasure, and high status. Looking at these images of lovemaking with the eyes of the ancient Roman allows us to enter a world where sexual pleasure and its representation stood for positive social and cultural values.

My hope is to set up an arena large enough to allow these works of art, from the humblest to the most exalted, to recover meanings that are in some sense *proper* to them. By looking at these images of lovemaking with unbiased eyes, a modern viewer can learn at least some of what they meant to the ancient viewer. I want to make the modern experience of looking come as close as possible to the ancient one. Only in this way can doors open to reveal the values that sexual imagery held for ancient Roman women and men.

In the next chapter I explore in greater detail the problems of methodology inherent in this project and define terms that I use in handling sexual representation throughout the book. The following chapters deal with works of art in specific chronological periods because the visual evidence demonstrates great changes in sexual acculturation over time. Within this chronological framework I look at specific sexual themes and try to give them the fullest possible contextual reading. The second chapter is a review of the centuries of tradition that Roman artists—or Greek artists working for them—had access to. The three chapters that follow focus on art of the Augustan and early Julio-Claudian period, from about 30 B.C. to A.D. 30. Because the era offers such a wealth of material, each chapter takes up a different kind of representation. Chapter 3 examines images of male-to-male lovemaking; chapter 4 looks at male-to-female lovemaking; and chapter 5 considers seemingly sexual representations of the black African.

The following two chapters focus on wall painting from Pompeii dating from about A.D. 30 to the eruption of Vesuvius in 79. Chapter 6 looks at images that decorated private houses, while chapter 7 turns to paintings in public buildings.

The final chapter covers the broadest chronological and geographical range and analyzes diverse objects, from the coinlike spintriae of the first century to terracotta vessels produced in the Rhône Valley in the second and third centuries, to a painted room in third-century Ostia Antica.

CHAPTER 1

The Cultural Construction of Sexuality

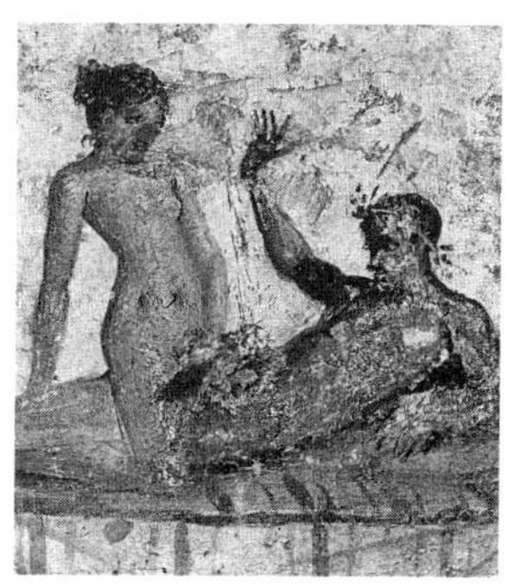

Sex and sexuality fascinate human beings. Whether we associate sex with extremes of pleasure—including the exalted emotions of love, passion, and romance—or with pain and suffering, as a species we tend to give sex a great deal of importance. It is not surprising, then, that the history of sexuality abounds with systems that regulate both sexual intercourse and procreation. Regulation of sex has resulted in lists of practices that a society finds "taboo," "indecent," or "sinful," with punishments for transgressors ranging from social ostracism to the eternal pain and suffering of hell. In addition to these negative strictures, even the presumably positive concept of love itself causes a great deal of turmoil in human lives.

The pursuit of love remains one of the most important themes in art, from the celebrated expressions of high art to the pop lyric. The concept of love is one fairly satisfying way of explaining the sexual commotion that often proliferates in our lives, whether it is the frustration people experience in finding satisfying sex, the obstacles between them and a sexual partner they desire, or the difficulty they experience in trying to maintain a sexual relationship.

Analysis of sex and sexual acts has led to the modern concepts—all tied together—of sexuality, heterosexuality, and homosexuality. As we will see, these concepts arise from a desire to consider sexual activity in a psychological and self-reflexive way. The very words—sexuality, heterosexuality, and homosexuality—and the notions that they express, make it difficult to understand people like the ancient Romans who, as this book will demonstrate, did not have a self-conscious idea of their sexuality.

Even the word gender, a term that in common parlance indicates one's being a male or female by virtue of sexual organs and secondary sexual characteristics, is far from obvious in its implications. Contemporary feminist, gay, and lesbian studies have made it clear that gender—far from being a biological given—is learned.[1] People define gender by a set of attributes and actions that go far beyond any biological givens.[2]

The Cultural Construction of Sexuality

The subtitle of this book, "Constructions of Sexuality in Roman Art, 100 B.C.–A.D. 250," announces my conviction that sexuality and sex—as we understand them in the late twentieth century—are notions that have little or nothing to do with those of people in other historical periods. Sexuality, rather than being a universal, a given, differs from one community to another and from one epoch to another. It follows that concepts like heterosexuality and homosexuality express social attitudes that arise within human communities that historians have designated as distinct in their culture. Geographical boundaries, common languages, belief systems, religion, and art characterize such communities as cultures.

The historian's assumptions about the past have come under great scrutiny in recent decades, and nowhere more pointedly than in the study of sexuality in different historical periods. Particularly relevant for the focus of this book are the pioneering—but diametrically opposed—studies by Michel Foucault and John Boswell. Foucault's ambitious project, *History of Sexuality,* although unfinished at the time of his death in 1984, foregrounded the various ways that the ancient Greeks and Romans "constructed" their sexuality.[3] Foucault's investigation of ancient texts showed little correspondence between Greek ideas of the body, love, and the uses of sexual pleasure and those of nineteenth- and twentieth-century Europeans. Boswell's project in his *Christianity, Social Tolerance, and Homosexuality,* to chronicle "gay people" from Roman times through the Middle Ages, announced his belief that homosexuals and lesbians (as we understand them today) lived in past historical periods.[4] In the ensuing debate Foucault became the champion of the "cultural constructionists," Boswell of the "essentialists." Although I explore the two sides of this methodological debate, my study of both Greek and Roman works of art with sexual subjects suggests to me that their meanings are almost entirely specific to the cultures—a clear corroboration of Foucault's position. In other words, our late twentieth-century views of sexuality are bound to distort their meaning. If I am to understand ancient Roman sexual representations, I must learn how to bracket out my own attitudes toward such representations, since my ideas are the product of my own acculturation.

What, then, do we—as late twentieth-century persons of Euro-American acculturation—want to know about sex in ancient Roman societies? Or better, how can we learn what sex meant to ancient Romans? The logical place to begin would seem to be Greek and Roman writings about sexual matters. They fall into four general categories: legal texts, medical texts, poetry, and public political discourse. What the texts reveal is an uneven mixture of legal rules and opinions, instructions on the care of the body, accounts of love-hate relations with the poet's boy- and/or girl-love, and the attribution of depraved sexual acts to individuals. Fortunately, the last twenty years have seen a veritable explosion of work on these texts by classical scholars. Much of what they have to say will help propel this book along. And much of what they show us is the blank page, for without exception the writers of these texts were men, and they were men either of the Roman elite class or men who worked for elite patrons.

So it comes as no surprise that a large number of ancient Romans have no voice at all in the preserved literature. We look in vain for the voice of one woman of any class, whether elite matron or poor slave.[5] The men put all the words in their mouths—and attribute to them all the deeds they are supposed to have done. Similarly, in all this literature no freedman or slave speaks out in anything other than the utterances constructed by these elite male writers.[6] Where are the marginal people? The many foreigners—who ranged from the redheaded northern German or Slav to the black-skinned Ethiopian? The same-sex lovers?[7] We find them where we would expect to find them—considering the sources; they are at the margins, where the "white" male elite set them.

Without texts from people at the margins, we turn to works of art that represent lovemaking to elucidate what sex meant for ancient Romans, for the visual record is much richer than the textual record. All social classes—and both male and female consumers—viewed works of art and used artifacts that featured representations of lovemaking. Many sexual acts and many sexual scenarios absent from the texts find expression, and often considerable elaboration, in works of art. The reasons for such wealth of sexual representation will emerge from this investigation: they include the conditions surrounding patronage, creation, and consumption of imagery. Artists working for a broad range of patrons created the objects I will consider here. It was the artists' job to please patrons or consumers who ordered or bought their products. Whether they created fresco paintings for the villas of the rich or crude decorations for the owner of a bordello, they had to please the person who paid for their work. By extension, artists had to create a representation of lovemaking that appealed to the intended viewers. Particularly in the case of wall paintings still in place it is possible to hypothesize what might have been the reactions of different viewers who saw them (a freedman or an elite citizen, a man or a woman).

The artisans who made portable objects, such as vases, lamps, coins, small stone reliefs, and mosaic panels, also had to please their customers. When excavation data are available, it is often possible to build a context—that is, a maker, a patron, a consumer, and even the conditions of viewing the sexual imagery. When there is no way of knowing where the object came from, it is difficult to assign the creation of its sexual content to a particular audience. But since these objects exhibit an enormous range of quality, from cheap pottery to outrageously expensive cameo-glass vessels, their relative costs point to different target audiences. In this book, then, I employ a variety of strategies in my attempt to recover the contexts for Roman sexual imagery. It is all the more important to explore such context in view of the fact that there exists no entirely satisfactory study of *any* of the objects listed here, from the still-in-place wall painting to the lamp of unknown provenance in a private collection.

What do exist are compendia of photographs lumping together all the genres of sexual imagery in Roman art. These typically are large-format picture books; some are catalogs of exhibitions. On facing pages or woven into the catalog commentary are ancient texts dealing with sex and love. This pattern, set up in Marcadé's books in the sixties, persists today.[8] Is the reader to believe that this or that passage from Ovid's *Art of Love* illuminates a painting, created a century later as part of the decoration of a house in Pompeii? If the text is one of Martial's invectives against men who like to be anally penetrated by other men, does it explain the elevated images of male-to-male lovemaking on a fine silver cup of the Augustan period of one hundred years before? If we want to know how the ancient Romans thought about themselves with regard to sex, we must use responsibly all the information about each visual representation of sexual activity to build the fullest possible context.

The rules for a meaningful and fruitful study of Roman sexual imagery are simple. In every case, with every object, I ask: who made it? (artist); when was it created? (date); who paid for it? (patronage); who looked at it? (intended audience); where did people look at it? (physical context); under what circumstances did people look at it? (use and purpose of object); what else does it look like? (iconographic models).

Asking these and related questions saves us from the interpretive impossibilities that have characterized many books on Roman sexual representation. For one thing, these rules will keep the art objects within their temporal and physical contexts. If a work of art belongs to the Augustan period, it will reveal information about sexual constructions of that period, or previous periods, but not about the future! For another, rules like these focus on the unique value of visual evidence, as opposed to texts. Notice that the artist, patron, and audience all find representation here. Furthermore, these visual representations—unlike the texts—appear at every level of society. Their potential for revealing the full range of Roman sexual acculturation is much greater than that of the texts.

The underlying premise of books that promise to unlock—in photographs and ancient texts—the erotic life of the ancient Romans is that "the Romans were just like us" in matters of sex. Careful study of the visual imagery underscores the great differences in sexual acculturation between "us" and the ancient Romans. It is the modern writer or reader who wants to make the Romans "just like" him or her. I believe that sexuality is a cultural construction. The ancient Romans' culture, defined broadly as the aggregate of social management strategies that shaped their behavior, taught them how to judge and classify sexual behavior. Of course not all Romans accepted what their culture wanted to instill in them, just as in America many people resist the dominant construction of sexuality with its center in the monogamous, heterosexual marriage. Rather than finding a single Roman "sexuality," we will discover a variety of Roman sexualities.

Postmodernist accounts of cultural constructions have shown us the many ways that the reader or writer deprives history of its validity by projecting his or her culture onto past societies. It is the aim of this book to demonstrate that among the wide range of different constructions of sexuality current at any specific time in ancient Roman society, very few correspond to what we think sexuality is.

Even this very sentence, however, fails to describe the complexity of the situation, for who is the "we" I have been speaking about? Is it a Euro/Anglo-American "we"? And if that "we" is "American," does it include Native Americans, African Americans, Mexican Americans, Asian Americans, and the many other racial and ethnic minorities who are Americans? Does it include people marginalized because of their sexual orientation or beliefs? There's bound to be a great a deal of ambiguity in both the transmission and reception of ancient sexual imagery, for just as there was no unified "we"—an average Roman—in ancient times, there is no unified "we"—an average American—right now. In this study I must content myself with a constructed "we" defined by my own culture: white, middle-class, American, male, academic. Each reader will make my readings more polyphonic and democratic, seeing them through her or his own eyes and experiences. Whatever the difficulties, something of great value can result from looking anew at ancient Roman sexual imagery. It is nothing less than learning about our own selves as sexual beings who, even as I write, construct and deconstruct—and continue to reconstruct—what we call sexuality.

How "Erotic" Is Roman Art?

The reader will notice that up to now I have not used the adjective "erotic" to describe representations of sexual activity in Roman art. It is probably already clear that the proper question to ask when someone describes a work of art as erotic is: erotic for whom? The word erotic qualifies representations—whether images, movements, sounds—by their ability to arouse someone sexually. Obviously the erotic impact of a representation depends not only on the representation transmitted but also on the condition of the receiver. Erotic stimulation may even change over time for the same individual: I may find an image sexually stimulating on one viewing but not on another. When applied to Roman art, the term erotic is even more slippery, for it implies that texts or visual art that might stimulate the modern reader or viewer sexually were sexual stimuli for the ancient viewer. If a modern author produces a book that collects Roman visual erotica, it may carry very mixed messages. The book may focus indiscriminately on images that picture humans in sexual acts; humans in scenarios such as drinking parties or banquets that may lead to sexual intercourse;[9] gods and goddesses in the preliminaries of lovemaking; hybrid creatures such as satyrs or pans, copulating; sexual parts such as phalluses and vaginas; phallic deities such as Hermaphroditus and Priapus. Considered in their cultural context, all these images probably did not produce sexual stimulation in the ancient viewer and become therefore erotic. Scholars have amply demonstrated, for instance, that images of the erect phallus, ubiquitous in the Mediterranean even to this day, are apotropaic—that is, their principal purpose has always been to ward off harm from the Evil Eye.[10] Hybrid creatures from mythology with exaggerated sexual appetites are the stuff of ribald humor and parody, not inducements to sexual arousal.

In this book I concentrate on representations of lovemaking between human beings, rather than interpret the meanings of apotropaic phalluses, the couplings of gods and demigods, or drinking parties. My focus is the visual representation of what Otto Brendel called the "factual and freely variable portrayals of sexual situations as a theme of art."[11]

Instead of analyzing twentieth-century reactions to these visual representations, I attempt to reconstruct the reaction of the original viewer. This reaction could range from our meaning of "erotic" (that is, sexually arousing) to side-splitting laughter at sexual humor whose meaning escapes us—as always, it depends on the individual, on who's constructing what to be erotic. When I use the word erotic in what follows, the reader should understand that it denotes a representation of lovemaking rather than my judgment that an ancient viewer found a particular image erotic. In each case I try to specify the conditions governing both the creation and the use of visual images of sexual activity.

"Sexuality," "Homosexuality," and "Heterosexuality"

It is for similar reasons that I avoid using the words "sexuality," "heterosexual," and "homosexual" in this book. Current scholarly debate focuses on these words, and their even more abstract derivatives (see the discussion in chapter 2); the central question here is whether my use of these words projects my own attitudes toward sex onto the ancient representation I describe. Foucault and the cultural constructionists believe that any use whatsoever of such modern terms brings anachronistic distortion to the past, whereas Boswell and the essentialists assert that sexuality existed in every society throughout history and that people of both sexes were heterosexuals, bisexuals, or homosexuals—even if they lacked terms to describe these ways of being. My work convinces me that contemporary terminology distorts the ancient contexts as I reconstruct them. Instead of using the word "homosexual" to describe images of lovemaking between two men or a man and a boy or two women, I use the terms male-to-male lovemaking, man-boy lovemaking, and female-to-female lovemaking. Similarly, rather than call scenes of a man and a woman copulating "heterosexual" scenes, I prefer the term male-female. As baldly descriptive as this language might seem to some readers, it has the advantage of bracketing out modern conceptions of homosexuality and heterosexuality that can only keep us from understanding the cultural conditions that surrounded sex in the minds of the ancient Romans.

"Lovemaking" and Alternatives

Perhaps the most problematic word of all is the word "lovemaking" itself; not only does it loom large in the title of this book, but it appears repeatedly where other, more direct terms seem appropriate. Colleagues seriously suggested that I escape the trap of applying contemporary constructions to ancient Roman representations by using the word "fucking" or "copulation" or "sex"—or even the most neutral of all expressions, "sexual activity." After all, the term "making love" is a euphemism in modern American English, and in this book it could suggest that ancient Roman images correspond somehow to our cautious, bourgeois framing of sexual intercourse in general. "Lovemaking" runs the danger of displacing meaning just as the words "erotic," "erotica," and "sexuality" have done in so many publications of Roman sexual art. It is indeed true that many of the images we will consider have very little to do with the mutual pursuit of sexual pleasure as an expression of an emotional bond that we call "love." The depictions of the use of prostitutes of both sexes are not properly scenes of "lovemaking," nor are the representations of hypersexual black servants (considered in chapter 5) who are sexually aroused but not making love with anybody. Yet there seems to be no blanket term general enough to cover the myriad representations of what we call sex or evoke the spirit behind these Roman creations.

To look at lovemaking is to look at the enactment of physical pleasure. Many images of sexual intercourse evoked symbolic meanings in the Roman viewer's mind, such as the goddess Venus in her guise as she who bestows the pleasures of physical union. In the end, lovemaking was the most neutral and open-ended expression I could find, and I use it in this book to avoid defining beforehand the meanings that any particular representation had. I hope the reader will accept its neutral and noncommittal sense rather than take the word as an anachronistic attempt to pull Roman sexual representation "into line" with contemporary notions about lovemaking.

Comparative Anthropology on Sexual Acculturation

Writers on sexual acculturation (Foucault and the cultural constructionists) make interesting use of anthropological work on sex and gender to underscore how far from universal the widely accepted notions of sexuality in modern Euro-American culture really are. Within the discipline of classical studies, John Winkler comments on the potential usefulness of comparative anthropology and ethnography. Although these disciplines hold a certain degree of inspiration, he disclaims using their methods systematically.[12] Other authors cite isolated cases to underscore how difficult it is for us to understand practices of other cultures that seem to be sexual in nature.

Several randomly selected examples will clarify aspects of this way of thinking. Jeffrey Henderson, in his overview of sexuality in ancient Greece, asserts that the words "prohibition," and "sexual behavior" are culturally defined terms. To illustrate his point, he cites a passage in Aristophanes' *Wasps* where the character Philokleon, in discussing various fatherly pleasures, mentions that he routinely enjoys letting his daughter fish small coins from his mouth with her tongue. Even though we know that tongue-kissing was a sexual behavior in fifth-century Athens, this practice falls outside the Greeks' notion of improper, even incestuous, conduct.[13] His second example comes from anthropological studies. In the Manchu tribe, a mother will routinely suck her small son's penis in public but would never kiss his cheeks. Among adults, the Manchu believe, fellatio is a sexual act, but kissing—even between mother and infant son—is always a sexual act, and thus fellatio becomes the proper display of motherly affection.[14]

In New Guinea the adult males inject young men with their semen through homosexual intercourse in the belief that they are transmitting their spiritual powers to them. Their semen makes the next generation good hunters and warriors.[15] David Halperin chronicles the uses that classical scholars have made of this ethnographical information in trying to explain pederasty in antiquity.[16]

Within the closed tribal culture of the Gypsies, Euro-American sexual constructions find few parallels. Concepts of purity and impurity focus on the woman who is sexually active (the woman who is married): she can make a man ritually unclean by throwing her skirts over his head and—as in Jewish law—is not permitted to prepare food while menstruating. In contrast to the danger associated with her genitals is the complete lack of taboo or even sexual associations with her breasts. Since breasts are for feeding babies, the upper body cannot be a source of shame or pollution.[17] Anthropologist Anne Sutherland notes that Gypsy women regularly pinch each other's breasts in jest or to punctuate a story.[18]

In addition to the abundant evidence that anthropology and ethnography provide for the ways that human beings often construe the same physical acts to be either sexual or nonsexual, there are many reminders that societies construct gender and gender roles quite differently. To take one example, many Native American tribes assign the role of woman and wife to the *berdache,* a male who is penetrated by men. The *berdache* maintains his special status through marriage to a warrior and performs duties that the tribe usually assigns to women.[19]

Although I attempt no comparable approach here, comparative-anthropological studies convince me that the only rigorous way to study Roman sexual acculturation is to take nothing for granted. We must enter Roman sexual territory with the full realization that we are entering a completely foreign domain where images that we think are self-evident—because they show sexual acts that we have done or have seen before—are not self-explanatory at all. If we are to begin to understand what these visual representations meant for the ancient viewer, we must learn to look at them as the ancient Roman did. We have to learn, in other words, how to look at lovemaking with Roman eyes.

Literature and Visual Representation

The misleading, or even false, connections between visual images and texts made in the glossy large-format books mentioned above arise from the assumption that any text—as long as it's ancient—might be used to "explain" any visual representation of lovemaking. In this book I restrict my analysis of texts to those found on the object itself. In discussions where I cite a Greek or Roman author to define attitudes toward sexual practices that appear in visual representations, I try always to foreground the author's own context: the period in which he is writing, his patron, his audience, and his own biases. Of particular use here is the work of contemporary scholars on Greek and Roman texts that deal with love, gender, and sexuality. Although Greek texts from the archaic through the late classical period furnish some background for understanding the cultural construction of sexuality, the most striking parallels with the works of art considered in this book begin with the Hellenistic period and continue through the fourth-century church fathers. Yet even here we must use caution. For example, the Hellenistic novel preserves scenarios that put forward a certain ideal of romantic love, comparable to—but essentially different from—nineteenth-century or late twentieth-century notions of love.[20] There are abundant visual representations from the Hellenistic period, particularly in the terra-cotta vessels, that seem to present monogamous, tender love between a man and a woman. As we will see, these images probably have nothing to do with the scenarios of the Hellenistic novel.

In contrast to these romantic portrayals of love, the Hellenistic period saw the proliferation and elaboration of sex manuals—often illustrated—that in turn become the butt of early Roman imperial parody in Ovid's *Art of Love,* completed after 1 B.C. The love poetry of Catullus offers a glimpse at the elite man's sexual passions in the first century B.C.; Martial, writing in the last decades of the first century of our era, frequently targets what he considers his victims' sexual excesses in some of his epigrams. And if Martial comes across as an cynical moralist, Juvenal's heavy-handed satires present us with a professional prig. It is only in Petronius' *Satyricon* (written by A.D. 65) that the author manages to stay out of the business of condemning or praising sexual behavior. Much later, Apuleius' *Golden Ass* takes us into the realm of the sexual fairy tale with little moralizing or invective. Taken together, these texts hold quite biased and fragmentary evidence for understanding Roman attitudes toward sex. For one thing, they represent—even if we add even more fragmentary material, such as selected comedies from Plautus, the *Priapea,* legal, and medical texts—a very small and rather random sample of a much greater body of literature that failed to survive.[21] For another, their writers—a point I underscore repeatedly throughout this book—were by and large elite men or men whose patrons were of the ruling class. Absent are the voices of all the others, including women, slaves, and foreigners.

In this study I touch on a few texts where they seem particularly relevant, but always with the realization that their proper contextualization requires extensive interpretation that is both beyond my powers and outside the scope of this book. Here I take up only those aspects of the texts that I can show have more or less direct bearing on visual representation, leaving more sophisticated exegesis to the specialists. My focus on visual representation offers scholars new perspectives that may in turn inspire further textual interpretations.

CHAPTER 2

Greek and Hellenistic Constructions of Lovemaking

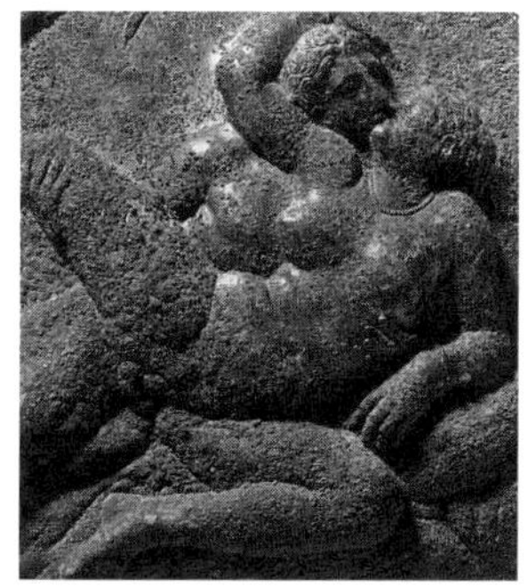

Roman visual representations of lovemaking owe much to the abundant imagery of sex that was integral to Greek culture(s) from the sixth century to the first century B.C. A rapid survey of its important categories of subject matter points up the enormous variety of imagery available both to the artist and to the consumer. Because I believe that the primary line of transmission was from Greece to the Italian peninsula, I set aside the thorny problem of Etruscan erotic art.[1] By 100 B.C. Rome had full command of the ancient Mediterranean and had just as fully embraced Hellenistic culture.

Lovemaking in Classical Athens

To its Roman conquerors, "captured Greece that held Rome captive" was the Greece of the great Hellenistic centers of culture—especially Alexandria, Pergamon, and Athens—yet Greece of the Golden Age, and especially Periclean Athens, held a prominent place in the minds of educated Romans. This was the Athens that institutionalized pederasty, or boy-love; this was the Athens of the drinking party where proficient female sex-workers known as *hetairai,* as well as prostitutes and boy slaves, provided entertainment.[2] Both sexual practices find ample illustration on painted vessels. In recent years scholars have amassed an extensive literature on painted vases that depict sexual acts, enriching our understanding of the construction of sexuality and love in the classical period and offering valuable insights into Roman sexual acculturation from this Greek evidence of the late sixth and fifth centuries B.C.[3]

Kenneth Dover's treatment of Greek homosexuality takes as its primary materials the text of Aeschines' *Against Timarchus* (346 B.C.) and the earlier black- and red-figure vases that depict sexual acts between males.[4] On the basis of this evidence Dover demonstrates that for adult elite Athenian men to court and (if successful) have sex with pubescent boys carried no stigma, as long as the men pursued only preadult boys. It was a matter of unequal love between an *erastes* (a lover, the "active" adult) and the *eromenos* (the beloved, a "passive" adolescent). The adult man was not to engage in either penetrative or receptive anal sex with other adult males. For an adult man of elite status, exposure as the receptive partner in anal intercourse could lead to civic censure.[5]

Dover claims that the preferred (and socially approved) sexual act between *erastes* and *eromenos* was not anal penetration at all, but rather "intercrural" intercourse. To engage in intercrural intercourse the man and the boy faced each other while the man inserted his penis between the boy's thighs.[6] Here I question Dover's interpretation of the visual evidence: just because all the representations of pederastic sex on extant vase paintings show intercrural copulation, it does not mean that Athenian men did not engage in anal intercourse.[7] Representations of intercrural sex constitute an artistic construction, not a documentary photograph of what Athenian elite men and boys did in the fifth century. There are many reasons for avoiding the artistic representation of anal sex between men and boys. For one thing, profile views of standing men facing each other are easier to draw. They also reveal the beauties of both men—buttocks, muscle development, and genitals—while allowing the artist to show facial expressions and tenderness. Even when, as in the Hellenistic period, artists began to represent pederastic scenes where the subject is clearly that of a man penetrating a boy anally, the artist often stopped short of showing actual insertion, preferring to emphasize the intimate setting: the couple alone in a bed piled high with pillows and covers. Dover, in short, makes the common mistake of taking artistic representation as documentation of historical act, or taking the part for the whole.

The vase paintings do hold significant evidence for another related aspect of the construction of sexuality: how artists depicted ideal—and nonideal—body types for men and boys. In the *Clouds,* originally produced at the City Dionysia of 423 B.C., Aristophanes defines both positive and negative body types in the words of his character Better Argument, who is trying to persuade young men to abandon the Sophist school: "If you do these things I tell you, and bend your efforts to them, you will always have a shining breast, a bright skin, big shoulders, a minute tongue, a big rump and a small prick. But if you follow the practices of the youth of to-day, for a start you'll have a pale skin, small shoulders, a skinny chest, a big tongue, a small rump, a big dick and a long-winded decree";[8] here Aristophanes uses the word "ham" with the clear meaning of "dick" or "prick." Dover discusses the "ingredients of the 'approved' male figure," including the right (small) and wrong (large) penis size.[9] In addition to these characteristics, artists depicted beautiful men with little or no body hair and liked to represent the penis with a long and tight foreskin. Circumcised men—Egyptians, for instance—were the butt of parody.

In vase painting the setting of sexual encounters between men and boys is either outdoors, implying perhaps the gymnasium, or an interior set up for a drinking party, with dining couches, tables, and drinking vessels. Women used as sex partners also appear in this interior setting or with no particular setting, but never in the bedchamber. Male-to-female lovemaking is a one-way experience in which the man inserts his penis into the vagina, anus, or mouth of the woman. No elite or freeborn women would appear in this artistic construction. The women are hetairai who hired themselves out as entertainers and often for sexual use at drinking parties, or symposia.[10] In Fig. 1 we see a detail of a vase where two men are debasing the hetaira in several ways. One is forcing her to fellate him, while the other prepares to smack her with a slipper while inserting his penis into her vagina. Although artists often depict these and other hetairai as unattractive, with sagging breasts or folds of skin at the bellies, many of these women fit what Greek men held to be the body type of the desirable female: she is broad-shouldered, thin-hipped, and resembles nothing more than a female version of the beautiful boy. An alternative to the boylike woman is the ideal of the goddess-matron: hers is the full figure of the grown woman, with large but firm breasts, wide hips, and rounded contours. Artists always depict her body beneath modest but clinging drapery: this is the body that Pheidias chose to depict the three goddesses of the East Pediment of the Parthenon.

With the end of the fifth century and Athens's loss of power, the sexual imagery

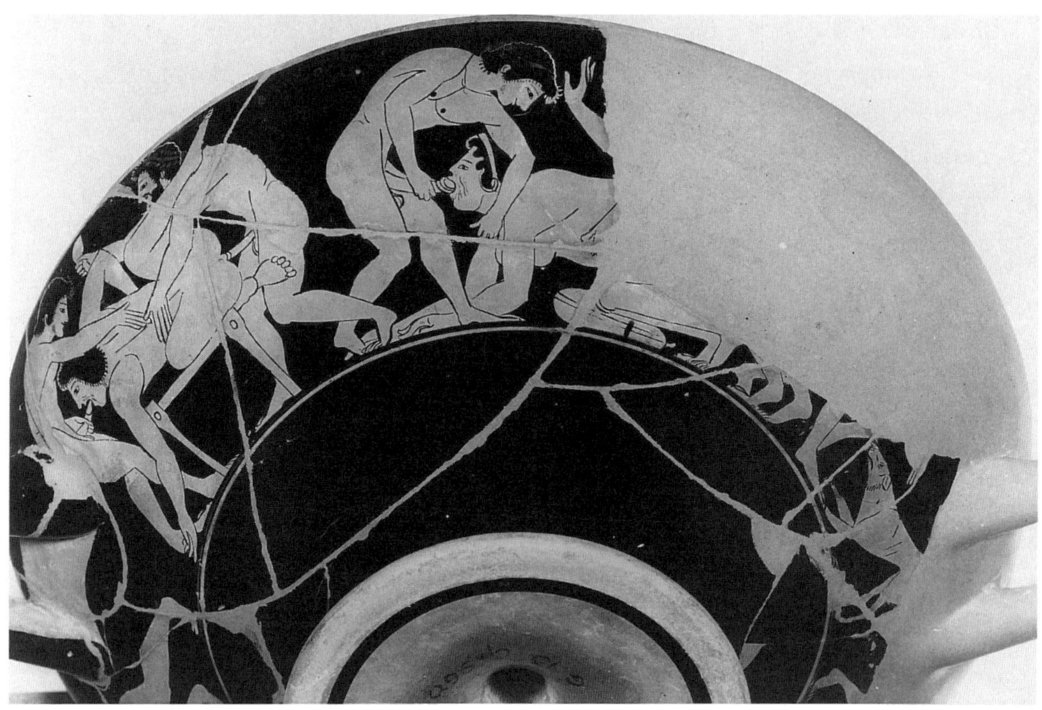

Figure 1. Men and women at a symposium, red-figure cup by the Pedeius painter (late 6th c. B.C.). Paris, Louvre, inv. G 13. © RMN. Photo Chuzeville.

of the orgy at the symposium dies out of vase painting. During the subsequent century artists began to produce very different images of sexual activity featuring a male-female couple, alone on a bed. This new conception may reflect a change in attitudes toward sex that finds parallels in the waning of the collective democratic city-state; the couple replaces the group orgy just as the cult of the individual overtakes that of the community.

Ardor versus Reluctance in Fourth-Century Reliefs

The most frequent scenes decorating bronze mirrors feature the loves of the gods and goddesses, yet the artist who created the bronze mirror cover in the Boston Museum of Fine Arts chose—or received a commission—to decorate both sides

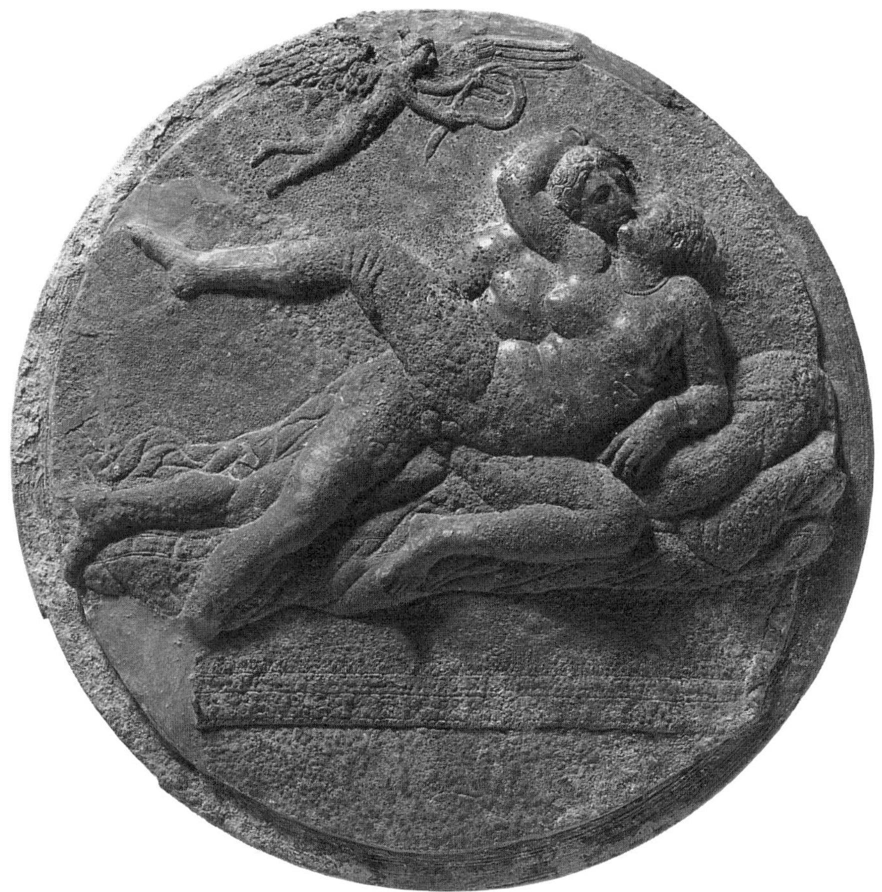

Figure 2. Male-female couple with Eros, exterior of mirror cover from Corinth (ca. 320 B.C.). Boston, Museum of Fine Arts, inv. 08.32c. Gift of E. P. Warren. Courtesy, Museum of Fine Arts, Boston.

with scenes of intercourse between a man and a woman (Fig. 2).[11] E. P. Warren gave the mirror cover to the museum in 1908, noting that it was from ancient Corinth. Scholars date it on the basis of style to between 350 and 300 B.C.[12] Bronze mirrors begin to appear among the grave goods of women's burials in the sixth century B.C. They were more than just items of utility, for in addition to creating a highly polished surface to reflect the owner's face, the artist often conceived elaborate decorations for the back of the mirror and its handle to reflect her beliefs and fantasies—or those of a man who gave it to her. In some cases mirrors had hinged covers that provided further fields for figural and decorative imagery.

The artist worked the exterior in bas-relief: the surface is pitted, yet the viewer can appreciate the couple's complex pose as well as the artist's attention to details. Although the artist did not indicate the precise setting, the couple's isolation on a bed and the absence of serving tables and vessels suggests that they are alone in a bedchamber—a major departure from the crowded symposium settings common in sexual representations of the sixth and fifth centuries. There is an intricately bordered coverlet on the bed, and several ample pillows support the woman's left elbow. With her other arm she draws her lover's head to hers to kiss him. This arm's somewhat awkward reach counterbalances the limpness of her relaxed left arm. But her legs express the most spectacular acrobatics in the composition, for she must hold her right leg high in the air, her foot almost at the level of her head, while she folds her foreshortened left leg under her to expose her vagina to her partner's penetration—and to the viewer's gaze. The man's pose is relaxed by comparison: his left leg rests behind him while he pushes upward with his right leg. The ankle and foot of this leg are missing, but his pose implies that this leg, clearly not in the bed, must be braced against the floor or the outside edge of the bed. The man "opens" the woman by holding up her leg with his right hand while grasping her beneath her left breast with his left.

Everything in this scene, as athletic as it is, bespeaks passionate and intimate lovemaking. It is important to note that this is an early representation of human, rather than divine, lovemaking. There is a messenger from the world of the gods, however: it is the tiny winged figure who flies above the couple. He is Eros, son of Aphrodite, whose arrows inflame mortals and divinities alike with love. It is unlikely that his appearance here designates the lovemaking couple as Ares and Aphrodite, since artists always represent the divine couple in the preliminaries to lovemaking, still fully clothed, and Ares' armor is usually included in the scene. Here it is a human couple, blessed by Eros, who extends a fillet to adorn the man's head. Such fillets are common in late sixth- and early fifth-century symposium scenes. There, however, lovemaking is a matter of several couples having sex in a group, not an intimate twosome.

On the inner side of the same mirror cover the artist engraved an equally athletic scene of lovemaking, this time using the bed as a background (Fig. 3).[13] The fact that we can see the top of the bed as well as its side indicates that the artist depicted it in an almost bird's-eye perspective, all the better to provide an interesting

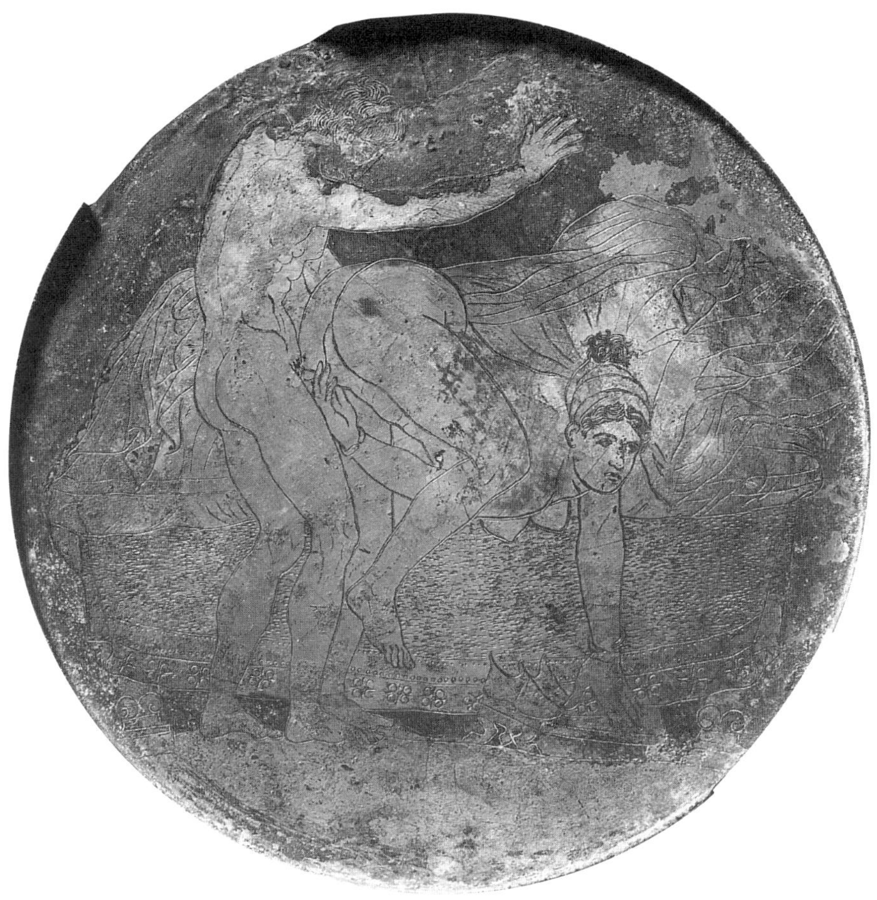

Figure 3. Male-female couple, interior of mirror cover from Corinth (ca. 320 B.C.). Gift of E. P. Warren. Courtesy, Museum of Fine Arts, Boston.

foil to the figures in front of it. Masses of drapery cover the bed and heaped-up pillows are on the right. The artist contrasted this tumultuous top surface with a field of stippling to indicate perhaps a heavy woolen sham, bordered, like the bed on the outer side, with a double band.

Against this background the artist froze the couple in a moment yet more dramatic than that on the outer cover, for although this is also the moment of entry, the woman's position is even more difficult. Supporting the whole weight of her body with only her left leg and left arm, she bends forward to receive the man's penis. In fact, the artist emphasized her acrobatic virtuosity in several details. Even though she supports all the weight of her torso with her left arm, only the fingers of the hand that carries that weight touch the footstool. (Partly effaced, the slippers on the back part of the footstool are still visible.) The balance is just as delicate for her lower body, since while standing on her left leg she is able delicately to lift her right leg so that she can pass her right arm back to grasp the man's penis and to help guide it into her vagina. Even here the artist emphasized the woman's effortless command of the situation. With her hand cupped toward her genitals she lightly grasps the man's penis between forefinger and middle finger. Finally, the woman's expression is calm and composed, if not to say complacent and bored. What must she be thinking about?

In contrast to the woman's calm demeanor in handling the athletic requirements of her position, the artist emphasized the man's relative agitation. He firmly plants his feet on the floor, while his right arm shoots up in the air, fingers apart. Although it is difficult to read his facial expression because of surface abrasion, his head inclines forward while his torso is upright, suggesting that his engagement in the process of penetration is still at the tentative stages. It is the woman who is taking the initiative here; she is in control and she instructs the man.

The Boston mirror cover raises important questions about the cultural construction of sex in the late classical period, most of them unanswerable. Who would have owned—much less have commissioned—such an object? It seems likely that the owner would have been a woman of the elite class—or at least a woman wealthy enough to own such an object. Who is the woman depicted? Who is the man? Were the two scenes meant to instruct a young bride in "advanced" lovemaking positions? Stewart offers two hypotheses, both of them attractive. The owner could be one of the accomplished hetairai or courtesans who flourished in the period between the mid-fourth and the mid-third century—perhaps even Leaina, The Lioness, a Corinthian hetaira who was the favorite of Demetrios Poliorketes. She was particularly adept at a position called "the lioness"—precisely the one the woman assumes on the mirror's interior engraving. Stewart's alternative scenario is that the mirror belonged to a woman who was not a courtesan but a married or unmarried Corinthian woman. If so, the representation of the woman's active participation and sexual prowess would reflect the Hellenistic notion that in marriage a woman should play an active role to achieve sexual pleasure for herself and for her husband. In this reading, Eros symbolizes the rewards of the woman's efforts.[14] In

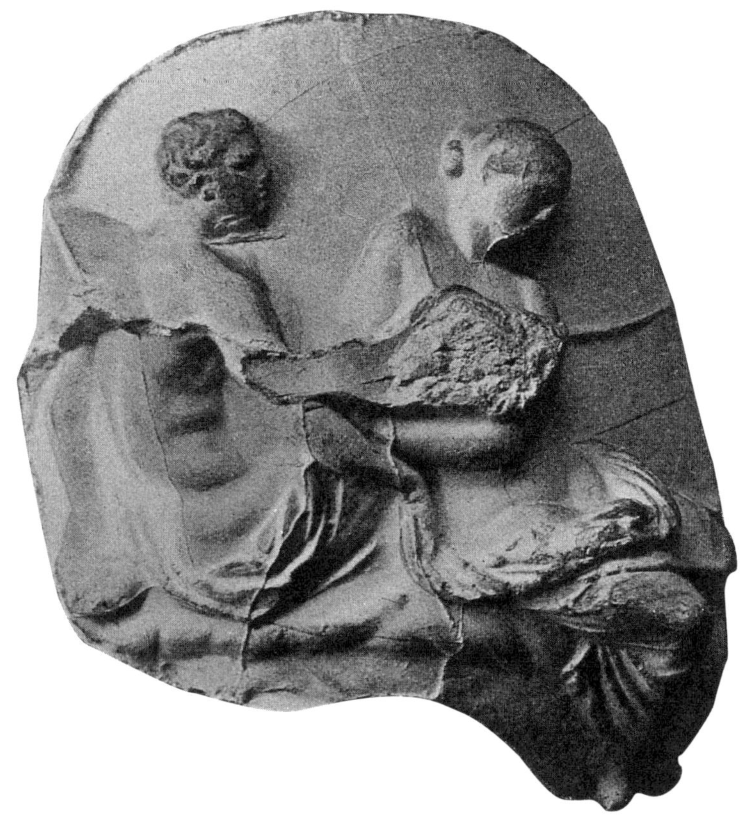

Figure 4. Male-female couple on bed, terra-cotta mold, Hill of Philopappos, Athens (350–300 c. B.C.). Athens, National Museum, after Brückner, *Anakalypteria* (1904).

either case, it is likely that the intended viewer understood the two images as reflections of the arts of lovemaking as practiced by accomplished women—whether hetairai or not. They present an ideal to strive for—for some a fantasy, far removed from everyday experiences of lovemaking.

A terra-cotta mold found in the region of the Hill of Philopappos in Athens and also dated to the second half of the fourth century B.C. is as reticent and modest as the Boston mirror cover is explicit and bold (Fig. 4). Scholars interpret the scene as the wedding night.[15] The young man sits on the left of the bed, nude to the buttocks. He has pulled the woman's chiton down to reveal her pubes and upper thighs, but she emphatically turns away from him. Not only her turned-away head, but also the way she places her left arm across her belly—and between her torso and the man's arm—suggests closure. She is far from relaxed as she sits on the edge of the bed, ignoring her partner's imploring gaze.

It is indicative of modern attitudes that scholars call up tender ancient texts on marriage ceremonies to explain this image—but offer none for the Boston mirror case. Must the one be the "proper" image of marriage and the other "improper" sexual debauchery? It may be more accurate to see the two objects as opposite poles in a range of acceptable sexual representation. At one extreme would be the man persuading his unwilling partner; at the other, the man surprised at the sexual inventiveness of his more-than-willing bedmate. Different artistic goals, rather than different moral standards, may be at the root of these differences in representation. It is fortunate that we are able to establish the coexistence of the coy with the brazen at this early date, in the 300s B.C., because it provides a foundation for explaining artists' conceptions of lovemaking in the Augustan age. These were the kinds of models they were looking back upon and, as we will see, they too created images that negotiated the two extremes.

In terms of physical ideals, the mirror and the mold underscore a new, more feminine image of woman. In place of the broad-shouldered, thin-hipped boy-woman of the sixth and fifth centuries, the artist depicts a full-figured woman—closer in type to the goddesses of the Parthenon. Both the courtesan and bride types have larger breasts and hips than the boy-woman type. The women's hair is carefully coiffed, and they wear body jewelry in the form of anklets and bracelets.

Otto Brendel's extensive analysis of the Boston mirror (bas-relief only), highly perceptive in some regards, is problematic in its avoidance of larger art-historical and social-historical problems of sexual representation in antiquity. He sees in the Boston mirror a new, late classical social attitude that would limit sexual representation to images of two people of opposite sex, always coupling in secluded quarters and on a comfortable bed. He attributes this change to the demands of a new urban bourgeoisie.[16] It is the new fashion of making love. Brendel also finds in the Boston mirror echoes of the originality and artistic virtuosity of fourth-century painters who created erotica. He specifically mentions Pauson and Parrhasios.

The evidence is scanty and not very convincing. Aristotle recommends that "the young must not look at the works of Pauson, but those of Polygnotos, and of any other moral (*ethikós*) painter and sculptor."[17] Examination of the context of Aristotle's use of the word reveals that it is highly unlikely that he is accusing Pauson of making sexually explicit paintings; the adverse reaction to them that Brendel posits on the basis of Aristotle's remark is far-fetched. As for Parrhasios, the mentions are in Roman authors, Pliny the Elder (A.D. 23/24–79) and Suetonius (born ca. A.D. 69). Pliny mentions that Tiberius fell in love with Parrhasios' painting of a high priest of Cybele—which may or may not have been indecent—and continues to point out that Parrhasios took pleasure in painting smaller pictures of an immodest nature.[18] Suetonius mentions a painting of Parrhasios owned by Tiberius: its subject was Atalanta fellating Meleager.[19] Although these Roman texts establish that at least one important master created sexually explicit paintings, Pliny and Suetonius have nothing to say about the sexual and artistic culture of Parrhasios' time, since they are Romans writing four centuries later.[20]

Although Brendel correctly defines the new representation of lovemaking as domesticated and romantic, his claim that these fourth-century representations set the model for both the Hellenistic and Roman periods is too sweeping and general. He did not know—or chose to omit—the many representations of male-to-male lovemaking that appear in the Hellenistic, Augustan, and Flavian periods. A second problem with his thesis is methodological. Brendel would define a single period style on the basis of the Boston mirror and the scanty information provided by ancient texts. We have already seen the coexistence of two different approaches to representing lovemaking, one energetic and highly illustrative (Boston mirror), the other restrained and allusive (Athens mold). The inventiveness of the couple's pose and the artistic virtuosity necessary to carry off the tour de force of the Boston mirror seem to carry on a tradition of vase painters who prided themselves in twisting hetairai's bodies in daring ways—sometimes to accommodate two penises at a time. The calm scene of the Athens mold has all the classical artistic tradition behind it, from graceful pederastic courting scenes to the recumbent goddesses of Pheidias. Rather than argue that artists changed style and content in response to bourgeois demands, I maintain that individual patrons—bourgeois or not—commissioned artists to create representations of lovemaking in the mode that fit their wishes. In arguing for a plurality of styles and content in lovemaking scenes I propose that already by the year 300 several styles and iconographies coexisted. Artists of later periods, fully aware of this broad choice of representation, freely borrowed from past forms while inventing in the style and the spirit of their own times.

Romantic Love in the Late Hellenistic Period: The Delos Rhyton Fragment

An exception to Brendel's rule that artists of the Hellenistic period consistently represented lovemaking on a bed is the rhyton found on the island of Delos, dated to the second century B.C. (Fig. 5).[21] The woman is squatting down to take the man's penis into her vagina. Her back is to him, and yet the two bodies twist so that their lips meet in a tender kiss, their eyes exchanging a loving gaze. To achieve this double contact of genitals and lips, the woman grasps the man's neck with her right hand, her arm hugging his shoulders, while the man leans back, his right arm crooked behind his head with his left hand just below and to the right of the woman's left breast. She steadies her torso by extending her left arm to her thigh. The woman's hair frames her face in thick locks that bunch and curve along her neck to a sort of bun in the back; she has adorned her body richly: a large necklace, an armlet, two triple bands on her upper thighs, and a strap—could it be the Amazon's baldric?—between her breasts.

It is hard to imagine how one would drink from the vessel. Remains of a broken spout between the man's legs suggest that the horn or container part of the rhyton was behind the couple. If so, a drinker would place his or her lips to the spout just below the man's penis and would see the couple up close as he or she drank. This intimate physical relationship with both the spout and the imagery might elicit laughter from the ancient drinker despite the tender nature of the sexual representation. It is also possible that the Delos rhyton was meant as a conversation piece rather than as a vessel that one would regularly drink from.

A Miniature Compendium of Lovemaking for the Wealthy: The Metropolitan Glass Dish

The Metropolitan Museum's recent acquisition of a tiny fragment of an opaque white-glass dish (2 ⅛ in. [5.5 cm] in length) raises a series of questions about patron and audience for serial images of male-to-female lovemaking.[22] To make the original dish the artist had to carve molds that incorporated the imagery of both its inner and outer surfaces (Fig. 6). By pouring molten white glass into the two halves of the mold, he was able to produce a dish with relief decoration on both

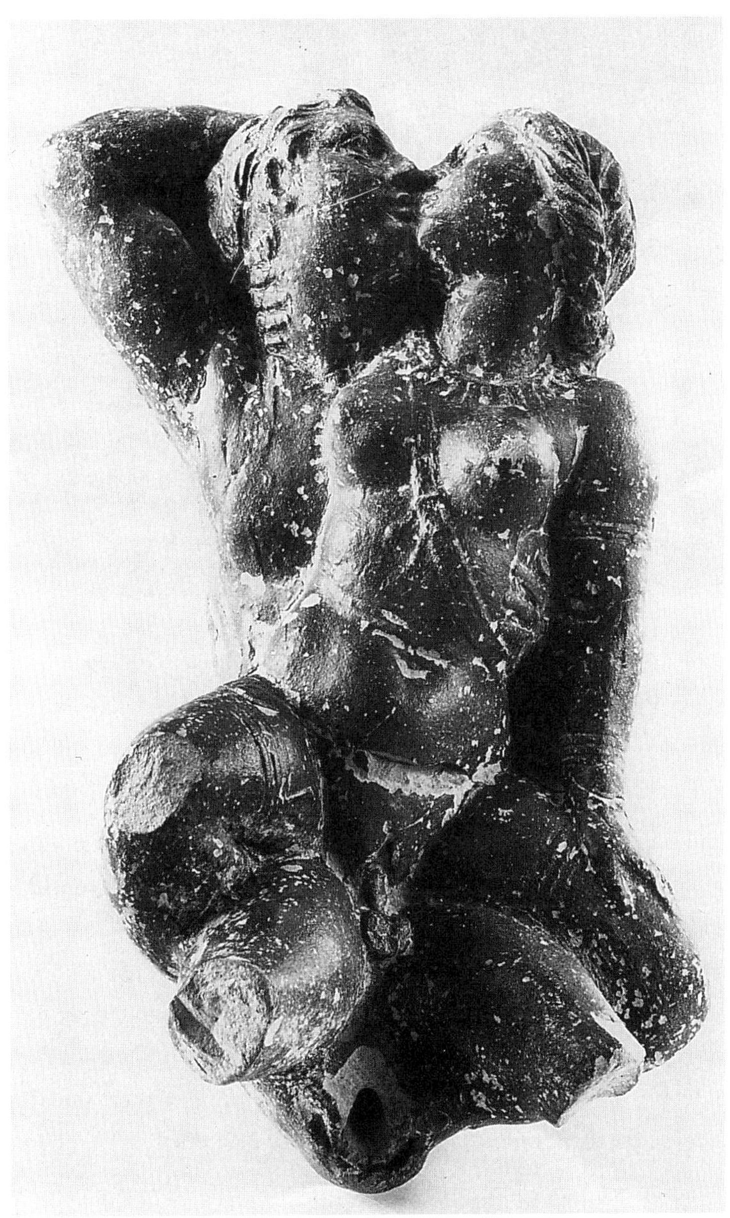

Figure 5. Male-female couple, fragment of rhyton (2d c. B.C.). Delos, Archaeological Museum. inv. B 7461., H. 15 × W. 12 cm. Photo, Ecole française d'Athènes.

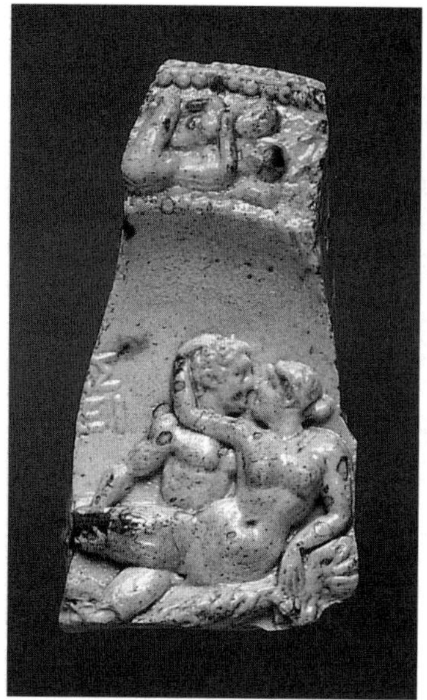

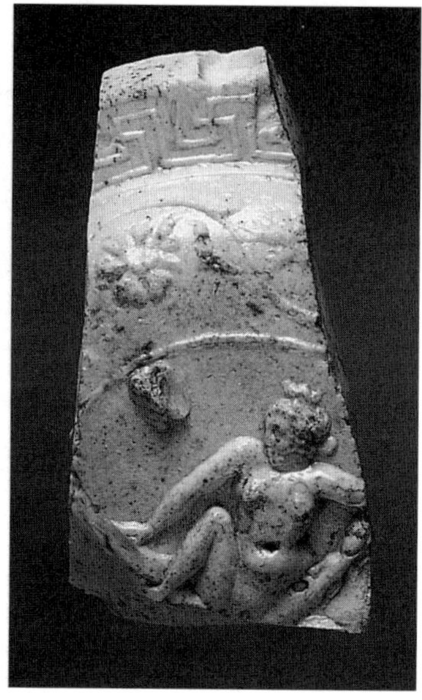

Figure 6. *a* (interior): Two male-female couples; *b* (exterior): squatting female. Fragment of opaque molded glass dish (1st c. B.C.). New York, Metropolitan Museum of Art, inv. 1995.86, L. 5.5 cm. Gift of Nicolas Koutoulakis. Photos courtesy of museum.

sides. After removing the dish from its mold, the artist polished it to produce a lustrous surface. Based on the size and shape of the Metropolitan fragment, the whole dish would have been only about 4.5 inches in diameter. The difficulty of the technique, the precision of the miniature sexual vignettes, and the remains of a Greek inscription indicate that this was an object meant for a wealthy patron. The fact that the artist produced the dish from complex and intricately carved molds suggests that he was able to create a number of replicas. None of them survives, to tell us whether the fragment of this dish was but one of a set. Analysis of the fragment's imagery does allow us to hypothesize the meanings that visual representations of male-to-female lovemaking had for the wealthy viewer.

On the basis of style and technique Carlos Picón dates the fragment to the first century B.C., perhaps fifty years after the Delos rhyton.[23] On the dish's inner surface are two areas that feature sexual vignettes: the center and the border. One vignette from the center survives (there may have been space for four). It depicts a couple in a position quite close to that of the lovers on the exterior of the Boston mirror (see Fig. 2). Instead of the mirror's three-quarters rendering of the man's head and the backward tilt of the woman's, on the Metropolitan dish the kissing couple is in straightforward profile. Although the woman raises her right leg to open herself to the man's penis, she does not hold it at such a high angle, and the man extends his right arm to support that leg. The hairstyles have changed: the woman has her hair pulled back to form a distinct bun at the nape of her neck whereas the man wears his hair in short curls. Comparison with the Boston mirror suggests that there was a bed, or at least piled-up cushions in the missing parts. It also appears that instead of folding the woman's left leg under her, the artist had her extending it beneath the man's right thigh and along the bed to the viewer's left.

These details of the couple's pose on the Metropolitan dish give the image a cool, detached air that contrasts with the passion of the Boston mirror. Since the vignette of a couple that decorates the rim of the vessel is much smaller, it is difficult to comment on the nuances of expression. The woman lies on her back and draws her left thigh up at an acute angle while the man, his torso pressed against hers and his head poised to kiss her, appears to be entering the woman. If this scene formed the rim's frieze decoration, there were probably eight such vignettes in all. The frieze format would have necessitated images that were, like this one, wider than they were tall, so that one imagines a series of couples lying down in various sexual positions rather than sitting up on the bed like the couple in the center of the dish.

The artist used a different decorative strategy for the vessel's exterior. He outlined the center with a circle that touched the outside edges of small protruding wedges of glass that served as feet for the vessel to rest on. The strategy was necessary because within that circle were several sexual vignettes in high relief, of which only part of one remains. A woman, her torso facing the viewer frontally as she sharply pulls up her folded right leg, turns to her right while extending her right arm, probably to grasp her (missing) partner's left arm. She pulls back her left arm, to grasp, it seems, her lover's right knee. Her head is in near profile as she looks to her right, presumably at her mate. She wears her hair in the same fashion as the woman on the dish's interior center, with the difference that some sort of crown (or garland) tops her head. Her position is clearly that of the woman "riding" the man, squatting over his penis.

The artist employed a body type for the women on the Metropolitan dish that has nothing to do with the tall, slender females with small heads who dominate late Hellenistic production (see Fig. 52). Instead he represented her with a substantial body reminiscent of the women on the Boston mirror and other early Hellenistic images. Her head is large in relation to her body, and she has ample breasts and a full, fleshy abdomen. As we will see in chapter 4, hers is the female body type that artists preferred in representations of the Augustan and early Julio-Claudian period.

The artist finished the exterior of the Metropolitan dish with carefully executed ornamental bands. On the convex surface between the circle and the rim he depicted a floral frieze, complete with birds. The rim itself received a fine meander.

Most important for determining both artist and patron is the fragmentary inscription visible on the inside of the dish. Only three Greek letters remain:

Σ
E I

Their large size in relation to the size of the whole dish indicates that this was probably the only writing on the dish. Otherwise we would have to dispense with the idea of other figural groups on the inner surface of the dish in symmetrical arrangement, with perhaps eight little vignettes around the rim. Fortunately, we can guess at the writing in the limited space on the Metropolitan dish. Numerous inscriptions recording the artist's name read *epoiei,* meaning that the artist "made" or "created" the work. A variety of Greek artist's signatures using this formula occur in mosaics found around the Mediterranean in the second and first centuries B.C.[24] It is logical that the fragmentary ends of two lines would record the artist's signature here. Less likely, but possible, is that the artist wrote short sayings in between the sexual vignettes.

What were the meanings of the images of sexual activity for the first-century B.C. viewer? Scholars tend to see in serial imagery of lovemaking in this period the influence of illustrated sex manuals (discussed fully in chapter 8).[25] Such an influence, however likely, is difficult to prove, since only fragments of written sex manuals remain;[26] the dish, too, exists only in imaginary reconstruction, since the Metropolitan fragment would constitute at most only one-eighth of the original. We cannot know for sure if the little reliefs of sexual couplings reminded the viewer of illustrated manuscripts, but it is certain that they reminded him or her of other art, especially the ubiquitous and inexpensive terra-cotta vessels decorated with serial images of male-female lovemaking. (A good example from the same period is that of a fragmentary vessel from Delos, dated to the late Hellenistic period.)[27] A theme common to these terra-cotta vessels and the Metropolitan dish is variation of pose: even when the artist makes fairly modest changes from one relief vignette to another, such variations seem to have been important to both artist and viewer.

It is difficult to say whether the Metropolitan dish, in its whole state, would suggest a narrative or even mimic the literary forms of the sex manual. What it does indicate is the taste, in the late Hellenistic period, for expensive vessels decorated with miniature vignettes of explicit sexual unions between men and women. It is clear that the patron and the guests who would see the dish were meant to pick it up and examine it at close hand, since the object was small and the images themselves tiny. What would the Greek or Roman woman see in the emphasis on the woman's active role in lovemaking: would she see in her the accomplished hetaira or the proficient married woman? In either case, finding these scenes on a dish—a kind of "novelty" dinnerware—would probably amuse her: no "proper" mythological scenes these. The presumably equally cultivated Greek or Roman man who gazed at the Metropolitan dish had very likely experienced the services of an accomplished female sex-worker; her representation would remind him of those sexual encounters. Perhaps he had the good fortune to experience such pleasures in marriage as well.

The Metropolitan fragment adds considerably to our knowledge of late Hellenistic visual representations of sexual activity because it is a luxury item, presumably signed, meant for the contemplation of the elite class. It suggests that interest in sexual representation extended to both sexes of this class, who delighted in contemplating a multitude of sexual positions no less than the consumers of less expensive, mass-produced terra-cotta objects.

Male-to-Male Lovemaking Scenes from Pergamon: A New Artistic Conception of Pederasty

In 1939 Otfried Deubner published a now-lost terra-cotta medallion from Pergamon, proposing that it represented male-to-male lovemaking (Fig. 7).[28] Until re-

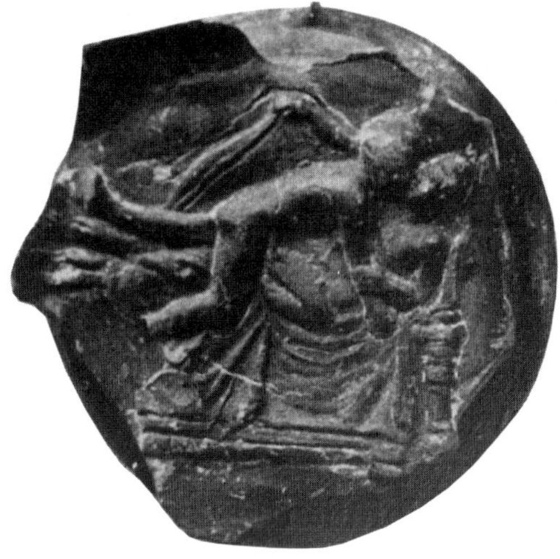

Figure 7. Man-boy couple on bed, terra-cotta vessel fragment, from Pergamon (late 2d c. B.C.). Formerly Berlin, Antikensammlung, inv. C. 7630 (lost in World War II). Photo after Deubner, *Archäologischer Anzieger* 54 (1939): 348, fig. 10.

cently Deubner's claim went ignored. In 1968, for example, Schäfer interpreted all examples of this type as scenes of intercourse between a man and a woman.[29] It was only in 1993 that Gerhild Hübner recognized another, more fragmentary replica of the same composition in her publication of the appliqué ceramics from Pergamon.[30] Despite the many evident breaks and losses of details throughout, the old photograph of the lost medallion reveals that the subject is clearly male-to-male, not male-female lovemaking, for the figure on the bottom lacks female breasts.

The subject is tender sexual intercourse between a man and a boy. On Greek vases of the classical period, artists represented the man and boy standing, facing each other, the man often fondling the boy's genitals; here, instead, the couple is on a high, heavily draped bed with a conspicuous bedpost on the right. The artist emphasized the boy's readiness for anal intercourse by having him turn his lower body to his right so as to expose his buttocks to the viewer's gaze. He extends his legs along the bed behind the man, who leans forward to kiss him. The man's pose is unstable, as if to emphasize his ardor. Although he straddles the boy's outstretched legs, supporting part of his body on his folded left knee, his right leg, slightly bent at the knee, is off the bed. The boy responds to the man's passion by grasping his right arm at the elbow; he lifts the covers high with his right.

A remarkable find from Sardis represents another related version of this image of man-boy lovemaking. It is not a fragment of a vessel but rather a finely detailed

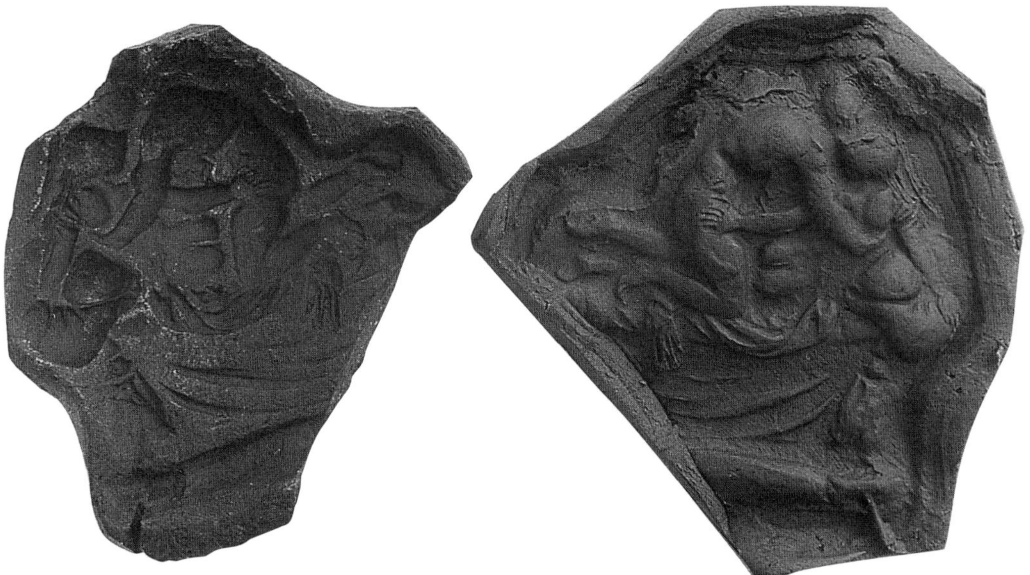

Figure 8. *a* (interior of mold): Man-boy couple on bed; *b* (positive made from mold): man-boy couple on bed, Sardis (late 2d c. B.C.). Sardis, inv. P79.6/T79.3: 8426. Photo courtesy the Archaeological Exploration of Sardis.

mold (6.5 × 7.4 cm) used in the manufacture of terra-cotta vessels (Fig. 8).[31] Like the Pergamon fragments it dates to the late second century B.C. and must have been imported from Pergamon to Sardis for use by local pottery workshops.[32]

In this composition the artist turned the boy completely on his side; he tightened the framing of his buttocks by drawing the man's knee closer and by extending the boy's left arm. A viewer could read this arm's gesture, pushing out to the man's massive thigh, either as the boy's last attempt to resist the man or as his desire to pull him close. In contrast to this active left arm, the boy's right arm dangles, relaxed, resting on two big cushions at the right. The boy twists his head to kiss the man, a difficult task since his entire body rests on his right side, so that the viewer sees his shoulders and upper back. The man's legs straddle the boy's. Consistent with the boy's pose—lying with his back and buttocks facing the viewer—the artist delineated the soles of the boy's feet, rather than their profiles.

The Sardis mold represents an even more passionate moment than the Berlin medallion; the artist also depicted this moment with more nuance and grace. For one thing, he effectively contrasted the man's massy musculature with the boy's small size. He showed off the man's bulky thighs, buttocks, and torso by having him kneel upright to the waist, only to bend down heavily over the boy. The boy's vulnerability comes through in the Sardis mold far better than in the Berlin medallion because the artist contrasted the man's powerful body and ardent stance with the boy's diminutive body; he also framed more effectively his most vulnerable part—the small buttocks that the man wishes to penetrate.

We see in the following chapter how artists of the Augustan period used this and similar compositions of man-boy lovemaking for a whole range of objects, from unique cameo-glass and silver vessels to mass-produced ceramics. We also trace the remarkably long afterlife of this particular composition in chapter 8.

A Late Hellenistic Gem with Male-to-Male Lovemaking

The fact that gem cutting represents perhaps the most expensive kind of visual art available in antiquity helps to explain the unique representation of male-to-male lovemaking on a gem now in the Royal Coin Cabinet, Leiden (Fig. 9).[33] The artist decorated this large banded agate (3.1 × 2.15 cm) with an especially daring scene of two nude, beardless men making love on a bed. A man lying prone raises his body up on his folded right arm and turns his head around in profile (an anatomical near-impossibility) to gaze at the man who is penetrating him. The man on top returns his gaze while he reaches down with his right arm to lift up his partner's right flank. He is kneeling, his right knee between his partner's legs, the tip of the left knee visible below his belly. The element in this representation that finds no parallel in either contemporary or later representations of male-to-male lovemaking is the large, erect penis of the man being penetrated. As we saw, and as will be apparent in discussions of Roman representations throughout their history, the man or boy being penetrated, while he can show affection by kissing or embracing his penetrator, never registers that pleasure in the most obvious way. The "passive" partner must be the object of the phallic male's penetration and must not respond with an erection.[34] From classical Greek times through the entire Roman period, artists maintained this distinction between man as phallic penetrator and boy as passive orifice by assiduously resisting the temptation to show the boy's gen-

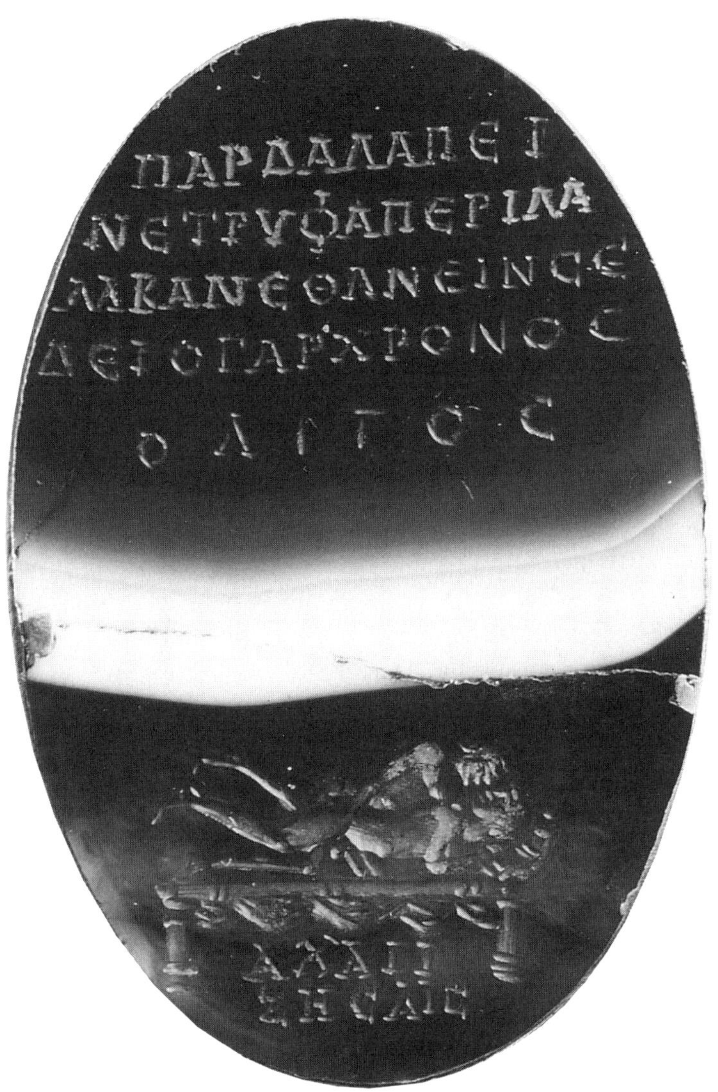

Figure 9. Male-male couple on bed with Greek inscription, agate gemstone, unknown provenance (1st c. B.C.). Leiden, Royal Coin Cabinet, inv. 1948, 3.1 × 2.15 × 0.4 cm. Photo courtesy of museum.

ital excitement. It comes as a surprise, then, that the artist of the gem in Leiden took special care to represent that excitement.

He constructed the couple's unusual pose precisely so that the viewer could see the erect penis of the man being penetrated. He had to raise up the torso of the man on the bottom to leave a clear space to represent the penis and testicles in profile. Foreshortening also aids in this illusion, for the viewer notices that the entire right side of the man being penetrated is larger than that of the man on the top. In this way the viewer reads relative body size as spatial depth: the next layer in, represented by the torso and right leg of the penetrator, reads as spatially farther away. This man's left leg, represented by the tip of his knee next to his partner's erect penis and—with a stretch—the calf, ankle, and foot of that leg kicked up in the air, is also the smallest and therefore farthest back in space.

This foreshortening also has the effect of making the man being penetrated seem at least as large the man who penetrates him; in this way the artist broke another aesthetic code of male-to-male representations. Rather than being the boy with the aesthetically beautiful small penis, he is another man of the same age, visibly excited by what is happening to him. As we will see in chapter 3, both transgressions make the Leiden gem unique.

An inscription takes up three-fourths of the pictorial field:[35]

ΠΑΡΔΑΛΑΠΕΙ
ΝΕΤΡVΦΑΠΕΡΙΛΑ
ΜΒΑΝΕΘΑΝΕΙΝCΕ
ΔΕΙΟΓΑΡΧΡΟΝΟC
ΟΛΙΓΟC
ΑΧΑΙΙ
ΖΗCΑΙC

Leopard—drink, live in luxury, embrace!
You must die, for time is short.
May you live life to the full, O Greek!

The inscription combines a command to enjoy wine, luxury, and sex with a memento mori—a trope common in Greek and Latin poetry. It is a popular variation of the Epicurean philosophical stance. One must seize the day (*carpe diem*), take life's pleasures when they offer themselves, for soon both pleasures and life will be gone. Since this is a small object meant for one person's use and contemplation, might the "leopard" be his bedroom alias? Or a nickname his beloved liked to use? Considering the ways that the artist transgressed cultural constructions of male-to-male lovemaking that appear in the texts of the late Hellenistic period (and for that matter, in Rome of the late Republic), it seems clear that his patron custom-ordered this gem. The representation, particularly considered with the inscription, emphasizes both tenderness in the couple's mutual gaze and—quite exceptionally—the sexual pleasure of the penetrated male.

What is more, it is not entirely clear that the male being penetrated is a boy. As we noted in the Pergamene terra-cottas, artists always made the male being penetrated smaller to indicate that he was a boy, since representing the "passive" male as an adult countered accepted cultural constructions of male-male lovemaking (more on this issue in chapter 3). All of its features, taken together, mark the imagery of the Leiden gemstone as unique. It expresses the special desire of an individual patron to possess an image that conveyed the mutuality of pleasure between two adult males. This patron instructed an artist how to represent that sexual reciprocity. The value of this unique object rests in its ability to peel away, for a moment, the visual conventions that established male-to-male lovemaking as a man penetrating a boy (pederasty), the mentality expressed in nearly all the preserved objects. In place of such conventions we find a surprising, highly original representation that goes against the dominant constructions in the late Hellenistic and early Roman period. That it is a tiny, expensive object comes as no surprise. It was not meant for the masses but for the owner himself, and probably his lover.

The Leiden gem, then, seems to give us insight into the sexual mentality of an individual—a rare occurrence in the visual representation of sexual activity in antiquity. If the person who commissioned it identified with the man on the top, we witness his interest in penetrating full-grown men who are unashamed to show their excitement at being penetrated. If the owner identified himself with the man on the bottom, his pleasure in looking at the man being penetrated again goes against the grain of late Hellenistic constructions of the ideal passive partner. Or it may be that the owner simply liked both roles and had access to an artist who was able to create a satisfying visual representation of his preferences. The owner could also have been a woman who found such unusual—even outrageous—representations of male-male lovemaking enjoyable to contemplate.

In comparison with the inexpensive and highly circulated representations of man-boy sex in the terra-cottas, the Leiden gem, as a unique object, raises some further questions about patronage and place of origin. Marianne Maaskant-Kleibrink, who dates the gem to the second or more possibly the first century B.C. on the basis of technique, would attribute it to a gem engraver working in Asia Minor or one trained there but working in Rome.[36] Considering the transfer of power and money to Rome in this very period, it seems likely that the patron was a wealthy Greek or Roman, whether living in Rome or in one of the captured capitals of Hellenistic culture. As for the artist himself, in addition to reflecting his high degree of skill, the Leiden gem underscores his willingness to create new imagery at his patron's instructions. Certain fine objects from the Augustan period, in particular the Warren cup, reveal the continuation of this kind of patron-artist relation in the creation of unique sexual imagery.

Sex and Otherness: Sexual Antics of Pygmies

Thus far we have considered a range of representations of human lovemaking, from the groom and his shy bride to unusual male-male penetration. Another feature of the Hellenistic age that introduces new representations of lovemaking hinges on avid interest in a particular nonideal type: the pygmy. Artists and patrons delighted in depicting life on the Nile; often they chose pygmies as chief protagonists in various antics meant to amuse the viewer: battling crocodiles, boating, picnicking under canopies spread between trees along the delta. Inevitably artists depicted pygmy men with enormous penises (as macrophallic) or with erect penises (as ithyphallic). They engage both in anal intercourse with other males and in vaginal intercourse with females.

Unfortunately it is difficult to pinpoint the origin of Nilotic lovemaking imagery in place and time, since nearly all the evidence comes from Roman Italy, beginning in the late first century B.C. and continuing through the end of the second century of the common era. The archaeological sites of Pompeii and Herculaneum brought to light a considerable number of wall paintings and mosaics depicting life on the Nile, many of them enlivened by the sexual antics of pygmies.[37]

In an effort to construct a scenario for the invention and diffusion of Nilotic imagery in the Hellenistic world, scholars focus on ancient Alexandria, center of learning and the arts under the Ptolemies.[38] Even though excavations in and around Alexandria yield little archaeological corroboration for the city's role in the development of the many Hellenistic innovations in the visual arts, both the location of the pygmies' picnics on the Nile and the overt parody that these scenes communicate point to Alexandria as the center of origin.

The constant in visual representation of pygmies is not their color. It is their short stature and nonideal proportions. Central to understanding why Alexandrian artists chose to make pygmies act out scenarios of fighting, feasting, and lovemaking on the banks of the Nile is their parodic content: artists required actors whose body types separated them from the body types of the intended viewers. They had to represent these scenarios in terms of the Other.

A central new feature of Hellenistic art is the interest in nonideal body types, manifest in paintings and sculptures of infants, low life (the drunken old market woman, the fisherman, the actor, the dancer), and deformed people (dwarfs and hunchbacks). Patrons, it seems, valued such novelties precisely because they contradicted classical Greek ideals of beauty. Wealthy collectors, in addition to owning originals by the classical masters, purchased contemporary works that parodied the very conventions of classical art. In place of the body that expressed the Greek ideal body, they embraced artists' representations of the extreme opposites of that ideal. In general, the ideal classical body type (somatotype) for a man or woman is that of the Caucasian race but of Mediterranean stock. The ideal body is also youthful. The female must be fully mature but not yet a mother; the male either a beardless adolescent (ephebe) or a young man. The body must conform to proportional systems to assure the consonance of all the parts. Classical art departs from these somatic norms only when representing wild hybrid creatures such as centaurs or satyrs.

Pygmies, as Hellenistic and Roman artists depicted them, represented the maximum possible contrast to classical body types: they are short and have disproportionately large heads, the males conspicuously macrophallic, the females with overly large breasts (macromastic) and with protruding buttocks (steatopygic). By having them carry out sexual acts in open nature, artists created a comic foil to the elegant couples on beds who represented "bourgeois" lovemaking. The viewer of the

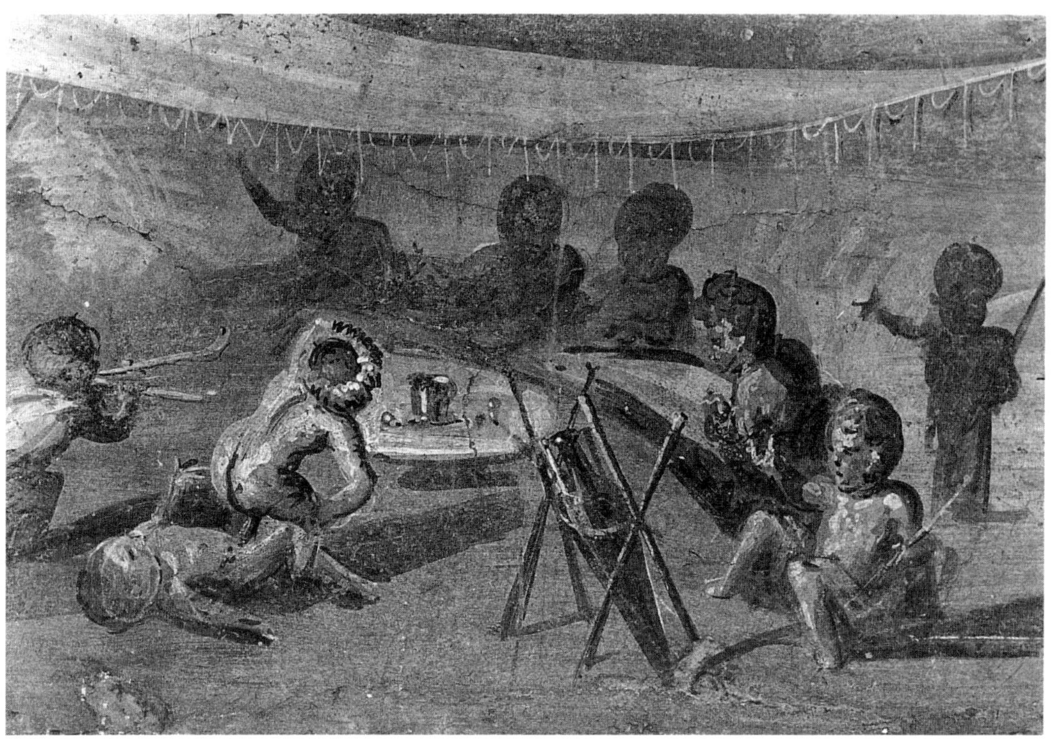

Figure 10. Pygmies at an outdoor banquet, detail; from Pompeii, House VIII, 5, 24 (House of the Doctor), peristyle (A.D. 45–79). Naples, Archaeological Museum, inv. 113196, whole scene W. 2.17 × H 0.56 m. Photo Michael Larvey.

Hellenistic period could identify him- or herself with the refined representations, but the expected response to the crude pygmies' acts would be laughter.

It is impossible to reconstruct the original placement of Nilotic scenes involving coupling pygmies within the picture collections or architectural decoration of the Hellenistic world. The numerous examples from the Roman world, carefully considered by Cèbe and others,[39] appear in areas of the house outfitted for entertainment rather than for business: these include the rooms around the peristyle, the walls of the peristyle itself, and the masonry couches of garden dining areas.

A brief analysis of one of these Nilotic representations offers reflections of this Hellenistic model of sexuality of the quintessential Other, the pygmy. This is a painting removed from the peristyle of House VIII, 5, 24 (House of the Doctor) at Pompeii, where it adorned the low walls between the columns (Fig. 10).[40] A parody of the Judgment of Solomon with pygmy actors also comes from this peristyle decoration. Vignettes to either side of this long, horizontal panel detail the Nilotic setting. At the upper left sails a boat with an ass's head adorning its prow, while in the lower left a crocodile devours a pygmy despite the efforts of his compatriot to extract him from the animal's mouth. Another pygmy, riding the crocodile, strikes it ineffectually with a short sword. The vignette with a scene of sexual activity takes place beneath an enormous canopy stretched between trees that shelters diners reclining around a curved couch.[41] It is a drinking party, clearly signaled by the amphora poised between a holder made of two pairs of crossed sticks—and by the entertainment: a pygmy couple copulating to the music of the double oboes.

The man lies on the ground, his right knee flexed, the fingers of his left hand lightly touching the woman's left buttock while she squats over his large erect penis. We see her from the back, her head so lavishly garlanded by a floral wreath that it resembles a large sunflower.

The artist painted this scene rapidly, paying little attention to refinement of details. He blocked out the figures and their shadows in a dilute brown, then picked out the lighted areas of the figures in flesh tones, reserving a light pink for the woman's body. He then sketched in facial features and anatomy with black daubs for deep shadows and white for bright highlights. Here the artist did not depict the pygmies as black- or brown-skinned (as they are in some depictions): instead he followed the conventions that artists used for light-skinned types—a warm flesh tone for the men and pinkish white for the woman.

Although the painting dates to the late Fourth Style, several centuries after the creation of Nilotic subjects in painting, it offers useful perspectives on a new artistic construction of sex in the Hellenistic period. For one thing, pygmies, as human beings from a far-flung area of Ptolemaic Egypt's Hellenistic empire, take the place of the entirely mythical satyrs and maenads created by artists to enact wild sexual scenarios in the sixth and fifth centuries. The satyrs, pans, and centaurs who aggravate, assault, and penetrate maenads (and each other) are all hybrid creatures, half man and half beast. Pygmies of both sexes, standing far outside the somatic norms of the Hellenistic Greeks, are still human beings. Artists could exaggerate their reportedly short statue by increasing the size of their heads and of their sexual parts. They were perfect subjects for the physical hyperbole that is caricature, and the Alexandrian viewer could look and laugh with impunity.

The pleasure that a Hellenistic Greek or a Roman of the late Republic found in viewing artistic representations of pygmies copulating was not—as we might construct it—a sadistic or racist pleasure. For citizens of Hellenistic kingdoms, all human beings outside the ideal body type, regardless of the color of their skin or their racial or ethnic characteristics, were curiosities. A citizen might speculate, in rather naive ways, about the origins of their strange appearance, but did not debase, enslave, or otherwise show ill will toward them because of their difference. If they spoke Greek—the essential characteristic that denoted a nonbarbarian—they often became integral parts of the sophisticated multicultural society of the large centers. The contrast in the concept of Otherness between inhabitants of these Hellenistic cities and classical Athens could not have been greater. Being a citizen of Athens in the fifth century meant being a white male of the citizen class: within the Hellenistic cities people had ever-more exotic racial, ethnic, and religious origins. In these cosmopolitan centers of luxury and learning, attitudes toward the increasingly diverse population tended to be both accepting and nonpunitive.

Figuring Human Sexuality: Aphrodite and Her Offspring

In the realm of myth and religion, the cultural construction of sexual love in the Hellenistic period would perplex late twentieth-century Euro-Americans. On the one hand is the sacred, or at least cultic, significance of sex: there is the worship of Aphrodite, goddess of love; the invocation of Hermes, Priapus, Dionysus; the invention of Hermaphroditus. Furthermore, countless sanctuaries of female fertility deities, such as Demeter, witness women's desire to bear children, the fruit of sexual union. On the other hand, as the Boston mirror, the Athens mold, and the mass-produced terra-cottas reveal, is the representation of sex divorced from these religious dimensions.

The birth of the romance novel in this period is also significant evidence for a new sexual acculturation. Long stories of boy meets girl, loses girl, and then gets girl drive home the point that sex and romantic love for its own sake—rather than merely for procreation—had become important for a sector of the population. These romances, either as written or as presented in readings and plays, must have had just as wide a diffusion in the Hellenistic world as the inexpensive terra-cottas that figured lovemaking—lovemaking of both the romantic and the explicit variety.

Although it is outside the aims of this study to investigate the lovemaking of mythological beings, Aphrodite and several of her many offspring populate the art of the Roman period. Eros, Hermaphroditus, and Priapus are particularly widespread in the sculpture and wall painting of the cities buried by Vesuvius in A.D. 79. In the Hellenistic era—and in Roman constructions as well—Eros, Hermaphroditus, and Priapus articulate different yet often overlapping aspects of sex; they embody, in turn, irrational sexual passion, ambiguity of gender and gendered experience, and male potency. We put aside the sociological and psychological aspects of the representation of these mythological beings to sketch their Hellenistic artistic identities and explore the visual precedents for their manifestations in the period that is the focus of this book.

Uncontrollable Passion: Eros

According to the earliest literary sources, the cosmos itself gives birth to Eros as a primary force of love, "fairest among the deathless gods, who unnerves the limbs and overcomes the mind and wise counsels of all gods and all men."[42] Sappho is the first to make Aphrodite the mother of Eros, but with Ouranos, rather than Ares, as sire.[43] By the Hellenistic period Eros' range of representation in art and literature had expanded: he lights his torch of love, unveils the person to be loved, or pushes the potential lover toward the object he should desire. Eros strings his bow to shoot arrows of love toward his hapless victims. He also symbolizes difficulties of unhappy love; we find him being sold or even whipped.

Eros becomes Amor or Cupido in Rome, beginning with his introduction into Italy in the fifth century B.C. At first the Romans contrasted Amor and Cupido as the good and bad aspects of love, but by the Imperial period they are indistinguishable, although Amor is his more frequent name, and an echo remains in the modern Italian *amorino.*[44]

In the Boston mirror (see Fig. 2) Eros arrives at the moment of sexual penetration. He embodies the irrational, uncontrollable sex drive that has reached the point of inevitability. Arguably the artist was articulating the male's feelings, since his penetration of the woman seems to be the "victory" that the fillet-carrying Eros symbolizes. It is also the victory of sexual passion over restraint. Perhaps from the perspective of the modern Christian tradition, with its emphasis on monogamy and control of "base" sexual drives toward pleasure rather than procreation, the outcome could not be a victory. But for the artist and audience of the Boston mirror achieving the pleasure of sex is a triumph—at least for the man—and a blessing of Eros.[45] With such a positive message—no matter how phallocentric—it is little wonder that Erotes populate so many Roman representations derived from Hellenistic art.

The Threat and Failure of Male Potency: Priapus

Originally an agricultural deity of Near Eastern origins, Priapus protected gardens from would-be thieves. In the Hellenistic period, writers and visual artists made him the offspring of Aphrodite and Dionysus.[46] In art Priapus has much in common with the ubiquitous stelae of Hermes, vertical stone pillars topped with a head of the god and figuring his erect phallus on the shaft below. The herm is a redundant image, for the vertical pillar itself could be seen as an erect phallus, yet the carved phallus is always present, sometimes in the form of a bronze attachment.[47] Hermes, a very old god, gives the newer god Priapus some of his functions. Priapus is a protector of gardens and agriculture just as Hermes is a guardian of the crossroads. As patron of commerce Hermes stands for wealth and plenty; Priapus also stands for abundance: he usually bears the fruits of the land in his mantle, lifted to reveal his enormous phallus.

The Romans, too, had myths and probably images (although none have survived) of a phallic agricultural deity and of the genii who protected the fields and orchards. Liber Pater, too, a rustic fertility deity, parallels Priapus' role as protector of the household and guarantor of male fertility. Yet in the abundant Roman Priapic poetry, Priapus "can himself be construed as a talking phallus."[48] He embodies both male fantasies of the omnipotent phallus and men's fears of impotency. Priapus' threat to those who steal the fruits of the garden is forceable penetration of the vagina, anus, or mouth.[49] He articulates the widespread notion that sex was the act of a man inserting his penis into someone's orifices—be that someone boy, girl, woman, or another man. Yet he is also, unlike the beautiful Olympians, a homely, rustic deity that one can laugh at. As Richlin points out, the Priapus of the Priapic poems "violates not only the sexual territory of men, women, and boys but the boundaries between serious poetry and the obscene, between the ethereal religion and the reverence for the sexual."[50] In the representations of Priapus that we will encounter in first-century Pompeii the god's dual nature becomes evident.

Embodying Male and Female Sexuality: Hermaphroditus

Scholars characterize the image of Hermaphroditus in literature, painting, and sculpture as yet another expression of Hellenistic curiosity about the different sexual experiences of men and women.[51] The myth of Tiresias, much earlier than that of Hermaphroditus, emphasizes that women take more pleasure in sex than men. Tiresias came upon two snakes coupling. To punish him for witnessing this event, Zeus turned Tiresias into a woman for seven years. When called to settle an argument between Zeus and Hera about which sex felt more pleasure in sexual intercourse, Tiresias responded that the woman did. Hera, enraged, blinded him; Zeus, to lighten this punishment, gave him powers of the seer.[52] It is likely that the myth of Tiresias expresses the classical Greek male's construction of woman: she lives for sex and finds it more pleasurable than a man does.

The myths of Hermaphroditus reveal a different attitude toward the sexual differences between women and men. Hermaphroditus first appears in Greek literary sources in the fourth century B.C., but it is Ovid's story that fully establishes his identity.[53] Hermaphroditus starts life as the male child of Aphrodite and Hermes—or, in the Roman version by Ovid, Venus and Mercury. The nymph of a spring called Salmacis falls in love with the boy, who rejects her advances; when he swims in the spring Salmacis surrounds Hermaphroditus with her embrace and begs the gods that the two might never part. The gods grant her wish and fuse the boy and girl together, thereby creating a new person with both male and female sexual characteristics. Rather than stand for a single human consciousness like Tiresias, who was able to distinguish his experience as a male from that as a female, Hermaphroditus is biologically both sexes at once and forever, a sign of gender confusion. As I mentioned in the introduction, contemporary gender studies and medical research on sex determination underscore the inadequacy of both the concept and the term "hermaphrodite" to describe a person whose gender is unclear. Rather than male, female, and male-female (hermaphrodite), Fausto-Sterling suggests that there are five sexes.[54]

For purposes of this study, however, we need to ask why Hellenistic artists constructed Hermaphroditus. Ajootian catalogs four main types for artistic representation of Hermaphroditus in painting and sculpture, each divided into subtypes.[55] The main types include Hermaphroditus alone, nude or semidraped; Hermaphroditus alone, draped; Hermaphroditus sleeping; and Hermaphroditus with others. These last two types offer the strongest evidence for the artistic construction of sexuality in the Hellenistic period, because they address the problem of the viewer's reaction to Hermaphroditus' unusual sexual characteristics.

The artistic creation of representations of Hermaphroditus must have responded to a demand on the part of patrons and other consumers. Although we cannot know exactly the nature of that demand, two constants appear. One is the mechanism of the double take; the other is the portrayal of sexual frustration.

In the most famous rendition of the sleeping Hermaphroditus, originating in the second century B.C., he/she rests, belly pressed into a mattress, head turned to the right side (Figs. 11 and 12). Hermaphroditus' torso twists just enough to the left to reveal his/her left breast and his/her genitals. Most scholars believe that the viewer was meant first to take pleasure in the beautiful "woman's" hair (ornately dressed), back, buttocks, and legs. Moving around the statue, the face, equally beautiful, would appeal to the (male) viewer. But with the revelation of the creature's combination of female breasts with penis and testicles come shock and surprise.

Although the extant representations of the reclining Hermaphroditus all date to the first or second century A.D., many scholars attribute the original creation of this image to the second century, some citing Pliny's mention of a bronze *Hermaphroditus nobilis* by the Greek sculptor Polykles.[56]

It is equally difficult to suggest a clear Hellenistic prototype for Roman replicas of another, equally revelatory image of Hermaphroditus: his struggle with a satyr. Even though scholars disagree whether this image was first created in painting or sculpture, it is clear that the element of surprise at identifying Hermaphroditus' dual sexual nature was central to the artist's intent. At Antioch excavators found two mosaic panels in the colonnade of the House of the Boat of Psyches; one showed a front view of the group, the other a view from the rear. Levi suggests that the mosaics drew on two sculptural groups, one meant to be viewed from the front, the other from the back.[57] From the angle represented in the painting from Pompeii

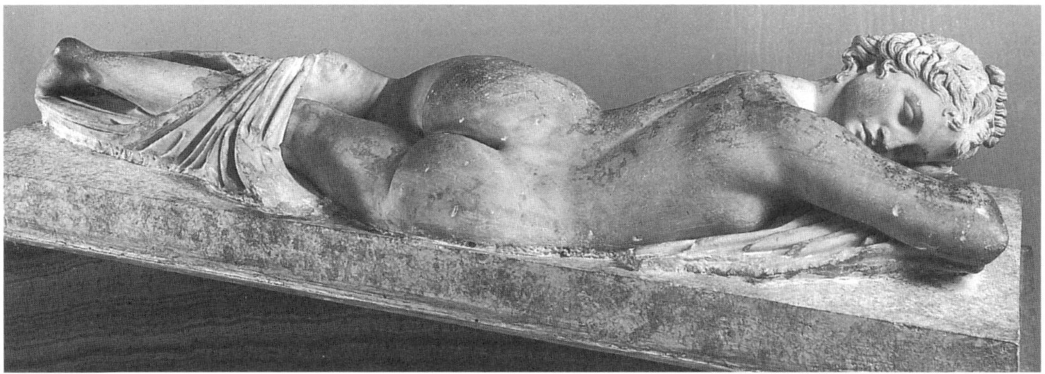

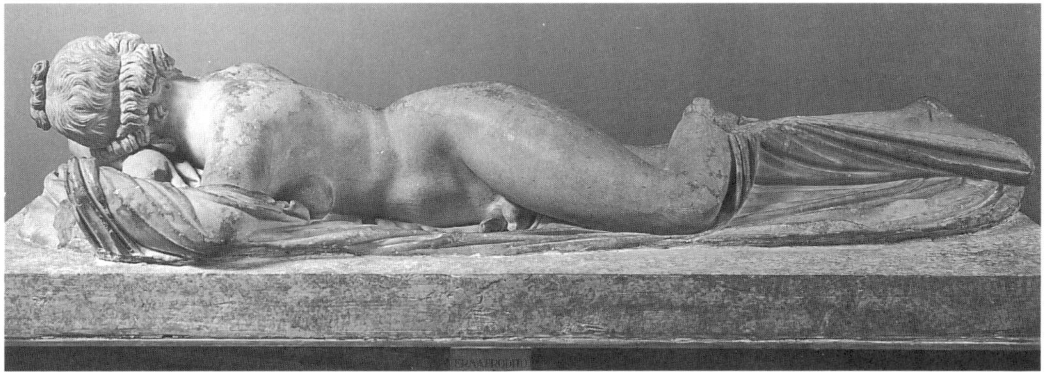

Figure 11–12. Sleeping Hermaphroditus, rear and front views (Roman copy of an original of the 2d c. B.C.). Rome, National Museum of the Terme, inv. 1087, L. 1.48 m. Photo Deutsches Archäologisches Institut, Rome, inst. neg. 54–97 and 54–99.

(now in the Pornographic Collection of the Naples Archaeological Museum), a viewer has no way of knowing that the nymph who violently stiff-arms the satyr with her right arm as she grabs his foot with her left hand is in fact Hermaphroditus (Fig. 13). Another view, available only in another painting of the same subject from a different angle or in the experience of walking around the free-standing sculptural group, will reveal Hermaphroditus' real identity (Fig. 14). Is the viewer experiencing the sleeping Hermaphroditus the victim of a deliberate sexual tease? If so, it is because the artist exercised considerable skill in making Hermaphroditus such an attractive—and passive—female to the viewer who approaches the statue from the rear. In the group of Hermaphroditus struggling with the satyr the strategy is different. It's an all-out battle between a nymph who calls up exceptional strength

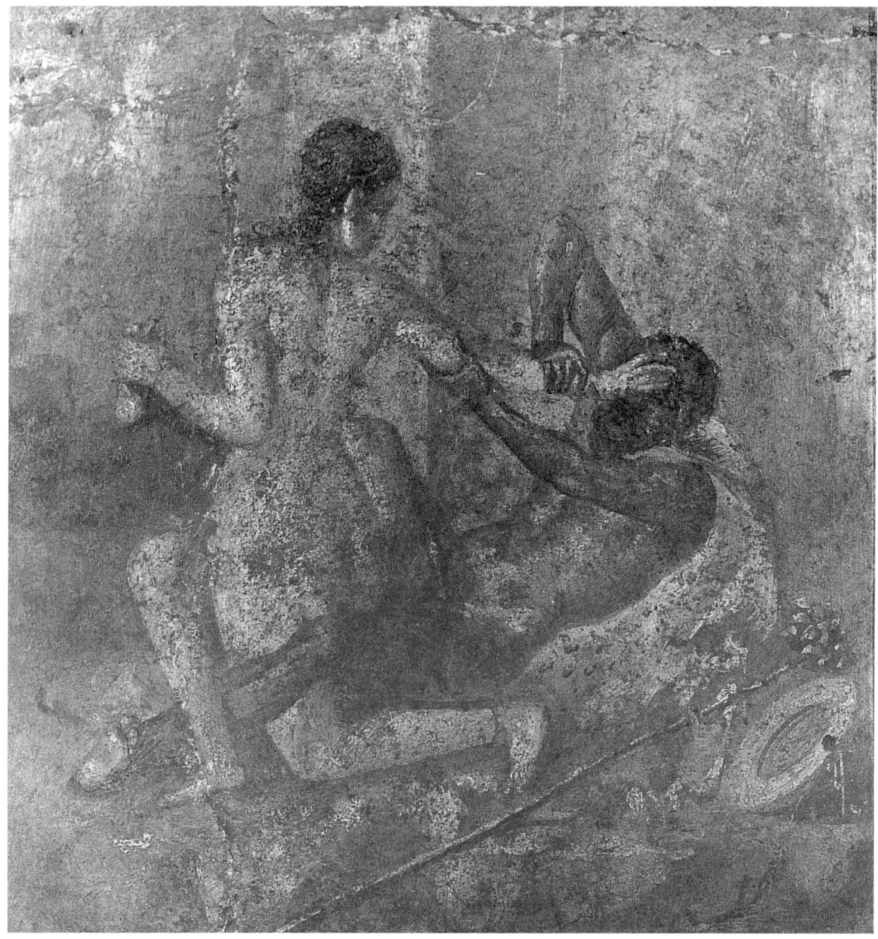

Figure 13. Satyr and Hermaphroditus, from Pompeii, unknown location (A.D. 45–79). Naples, Archaeological Museum, inv. 27699, W. 35.5 × H. 38 cm. Photo Michael Larvey.

to get the better of her randy aggressor—and then the viewer discovers that the "nymph" has the phallic power necessary to overcome the strong, bestial satyr.

The surprise of the double take is the stuff of all humor, revealing both the dual nature of Hermaphroditus and the sophistication of the Hellenistic audience for these representations. On the one hand Hermaphroditus, along with Aphrodite and Priapus, was a divinity associated with fertility. On the other, Greeks and Romans once feared sexually androgynous creatures and even destroyed them; in the Hellenistic

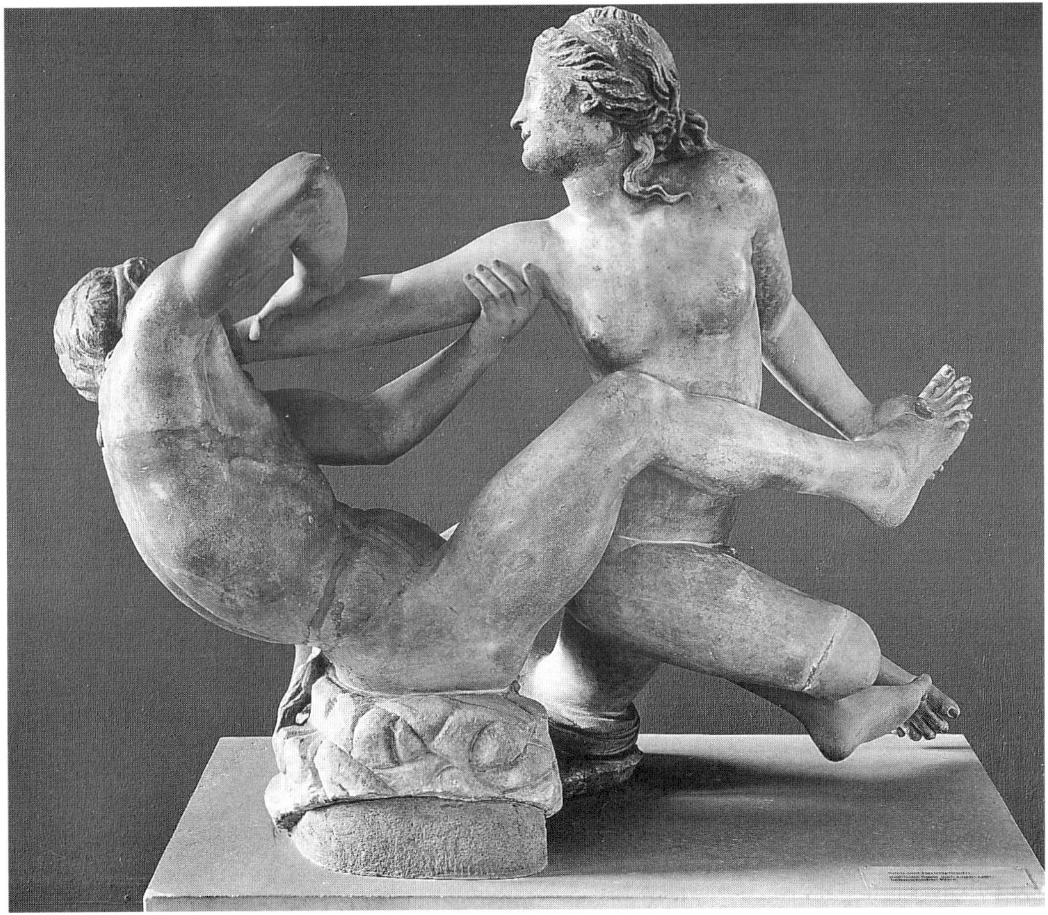

Figure 14. Hermaphroditus struggling with satyr, from Rome (Roman copy of 2d-c. B.C. original). Dresden, Staatliche Kunstsammlungen, 155, H. 90.6 cm. Photo Klut, courtesy Staatliche Kunstsammlungen, Dresden.

age they gradually came to accept them as amusing (if we are to believe Pliny).[58] Paintings representing yet another side of Hermaphroditus, as the sexually excited man-maiden imploring Pan or Silenus to initiate lovemaking, are common in Pompeian wall decorations of the first century A.D. (Fig. 15). Here the Hellenistic conceit of making the viewer the dupe of the sculpture's or painting's programmatic machinery undergoes a radical shift: now the viewer sees the male's surprise enacted within the picture itself. The active viewer becomes an omniscient, and passive,

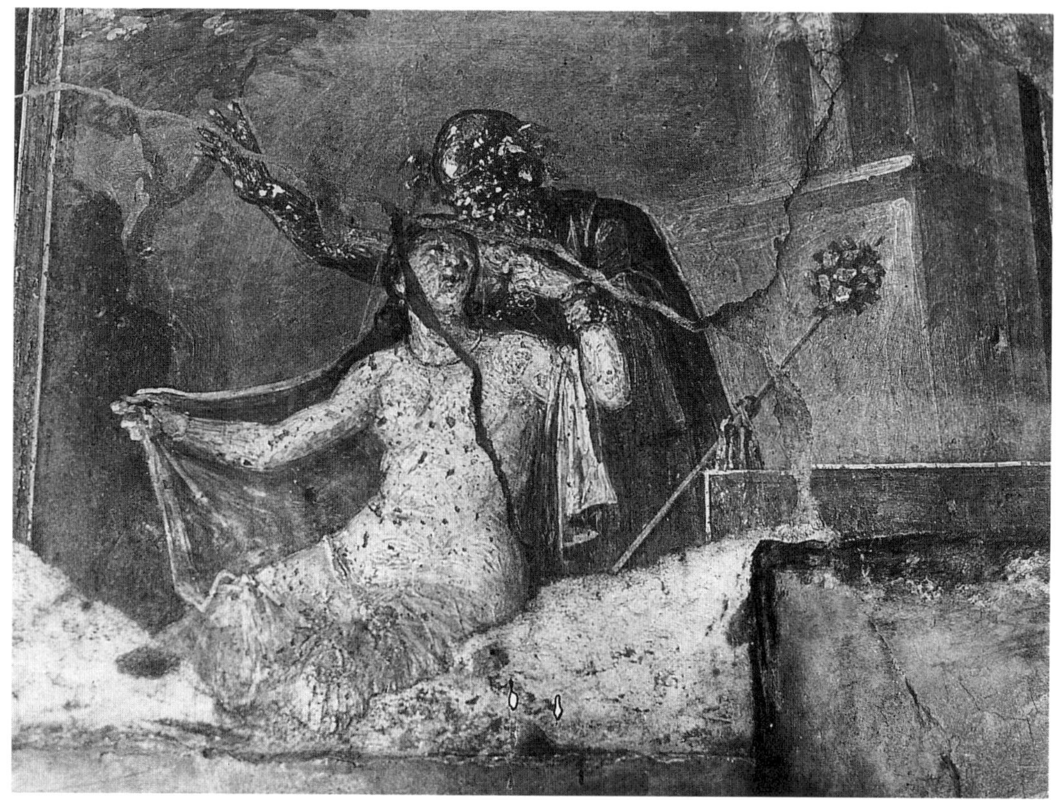

Figure 15. Silenus and Hermaphroditus, Pompeii, House of the Vettii (VI, 15, 1), room *q*, south wall, right part (A.D. 62–79). Photo Michael Larvey.

voyeur, since he or she can see Hermaphroditus' combination of male genitals with a woman's body and breasts. We return to this invention of the first century A.D. later on, when we consider Roman artistic representation of sexuality in that era.

If the struggle of the satyr and Hermaphroditus, or the unveiling of Hermaphroditus by Pan or Silenus were to end in lovemaking, the dilemma would really be the male's. For what can the satyr or Pan or Silenus do with Hermaphroditus? If rape is on the male's mind, will he be violating a man or a woman? Since Hermaphroditus is not a boy, the act would be neither pederasty nor male-female intercourse. Artistic representations of Hermaphroditus bring to the fore the ambiguities in sexual differences between women and men as well as the ambiguities in all sexual acts. Hermaphroditus remains a disquieting visual reminder that things are not always what they seem. If the myth of Tiresias is about clarity and distinction between the sexual experiences of men and of women, Hermaphroditus gives an eternally ambiguous answer to a man's curiosity about a woman's sexual experience—and vice versa. Hermaphroditus is the embodiment of that ambiguity of experience. The fact that artists always treat Hermaphroditus in terms of the viewer finding out his/her actual sexual identity (whether Hermaphroditus is sleeping and passive or actively struggling) points to a construction of gender as curiosity about a person's genitals. Gender confusion, I suggest, is only part of the construction here. It is also curiosity about the experience of the woman's sexual pleasure that a man cannot know and the feelings that a man has in sex that the woman cannot know. It goes even deeper, for in every sexual encounter, regardless of the sex of one's partner(s), the questions nag: what did you feel? did you feel what I did? are our feelings and thoughts as united as our bodies?

Hermaphroditus stands for both the physical and, more important, the psychological impossibility of ever understanding the feelings of the beloved. Hermaphroditus is a highly sophisticated representation, invading the boundaries between the sexes that seem so clear in classical thought and representation. Hermaphroditus for the Greeks of the Hellenistic period, and as we shall see for the Romans also, is the psychosexual enigma of feeling pleasure in sex.

Taken together, all the evidence for the cultural construction of sex and gender in the three hundred years that span the period from Alexander the Great to Augustus, despite the obvious gaps, indicates an extremely rich visual and textual tradition for Roman artists of the Augustan period to build on. Especially important is the fact that by the end of the Hellenistic period artists had established both a full repertoire of motifs figuring a man and a woman engaged in sexual intercourse and several explicit motifs of male-male intercourse. With the beginning of the Roman empire, when Augustus consciously engaged the arts in his largely successful attempt to create the image of a new Golden Age, artists turned to this established repertoire to produce an great number of works of art that figured human sexual activity. Artists of the Augustan period at once revived Hellenistic sexual representation and invented images to meet a large new demand.

THE AUGUSTAN AND EARLY JULIO-CLAUDIAN PERIODS

27 B.C.–A.D. 30

CHAPTER 3

REPRESENTATIONS OF MALE-TO-MALE LOVEMAKING

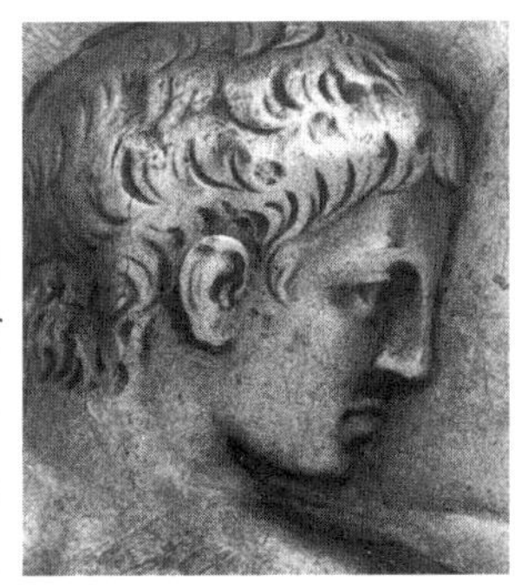

The political and social chaos from the mid-second century B.C. to the end of the first century B.C. makes it difficult to trace the reasons for the changes in visual representations of sex during the reign of Augustus and his early successors. Unlike the plentiful Augustan art with sexual themes in all the media, the best evidence for late Hellenistic art is an atypical yet expressive gemstone, along with humble terra-cottas from Pergamon and Delos. Grateful as we are that at least these survive, many other, finer creations in painting, relief sculpture, and silver existed and served as models for their poorer cousins in terra-cotta. Doubtless they also inspired artists of the Augustan period to create refined representations of lovemaking like the Warren cup or the Farnesina paintings, to be considered in this and the following chapter.

Even as war and pillage destroyed much of the evidence in Hellenistic centers, it brought both artists and famous works of art to Rome. The artistic booty of Rome's sweeping conquest of the Mediterranean filled both private and public collections in the city.[1] Pergamon, Ephesus, Carthage, Alexandria, Syracuse, Tarentum and scores of other wealthy cities saw their masterpieces of painting and sculpture hauled out of their temples, libraries, and picture galleries. Along with the transfer of artistic patrimony and liquid capital came the exodus of the artists, poets, playwrights, actors, and philosophers—the creative minds that had to seek patronage where the wealth had gone: Rome.

During the grim and bloody civil wars of the first century B.C., the Roman elite had plenty of money in their hands but little opportunity to enjoy it: survival was preeminent in everyone's mind. With Octavian's victory at Actium in 31 B.C., his assumption of the title of Augustus (27 B.C.), and the founding of an imperial dynasty came peace and prosperity for the survivors. A veritable explosion of artistic production in every realm—literature, drama, and visual arts—gave the Augustan period its special luster. Rome, as the powerful center of economic and political power in the Mediterranean, became center of intellectual and artistic production. Suetonius reports that Augustus beautified the city and so utterly remade it that he could justly boast that he found a city of mud brick and left it a city of marble.[2] This physical transformation was only the most obvious aspect of his thoroughgoing cultural transformation of the city and its inhabitants.

Recently there has been great scholarly interest in the role that the arts played in Augustus' new Rome.[3] Paul Zanker's excellent sociohistorical account demonstrates how the leader used art and architecture to propagandize his program of cultural renewal.[4] Other work focuses on specific genres or monuments of the Augustan period.[5] Yet accounts of sexual representation in the visual arts are sadly lacking. Scholars include lovemaking motifs in their dry catalogs of ceramics and, predictably, arrange the different figural motifs into typologies. Many studies are too general: the usually astute Brendel, for example, lumps together late Hellenistic representations with all those of the Roman period under the rubric of the "numbers game," meaning mass-produced art for the masses. He notes that "there is little need to discuss them in strict chronological order," since the objects repeat, with little variation, motifs set up in the late Hellenistic period. Brendel believes that what requires explanation is their lack of variation over time since regional and chronological differences are secondary.[6] Brendel would hope to find the variety of sexual narratives and scenarios that characterize Greek vases of the archaic and classical periods; instead he laments that artists of the Hellenistic and Roman periods used stamps depicting self-contained lovemaking scenes to create the relief decoration of terra-cotta vessels.[7]

Brendel's argument has several flaws. For one thing, the style of scenes of lovemaking—even within the medium of terra-cotta when artists use stamps—changes considerably from the late Hellenistic to the Augustan period. Style is a marker of Augustan classicism, and the style of sexual representation takes part in that classicism. For another, although narrative is absent from the stamped terra-cottas, it is very important to the compositions of two other media that depict lovemaking: silver vessels and panel paintings.

Zanker takes a different approach to the representations of lovemaking in the Augustan period but, like Brendel, ignores the silver vessels and paintings. He considers Arretine terra-cotta vessels under the rubric of "Atticizing" compositions: "Whether designing a mythological genre scene for a wall painting or an episode of Homeric inspiration for a silver cup, artists invariably tried to create the simplest and most lucid compositions and thus evoke a meditative mood. This even extends to the popular erotic subjects, which appear already in Hellenistic relief pottery. While the earlier scenes depict a more immediate intimacy, those on early Arretine bowls show couples in positions that could almost be called dignified." In the style of these new representations of lovemaking, in their purity of line and classicizing proportions, Zanker sees a new model of morality.[8] He would have Augustan classicism—even in sexual representations—express the moral probity that Augustus promulgated! Interestingly, he explains the lack of storytelling that troubles Brendel—both in the Arretine ware and in the mythologically framed scenes of love and desire on the Portland Vase—as examples of how artistic form takes precedence over narrative content.

As a challenge to these notions, I begin with an object near the top of the spectrum of production, rather than the mass-produced terra-cotta vessels that these and other scholars consider to be the major bearers of artistic representations of sexual intercourse in the Augustan period. Its high quality and originality point to contexts of patronage and sexual attitudes that go far beyond the modest interpretations that other scholars offer.

Male-to-Male Lovemaking for Wealthy Patrons? The Warren Cup

The Warren cup gives us a unique opportunity to explore questions of context because of its high quality and relatively secure date.[9] It is ovoid, made of silver, and measures about fifteen centimeters in height including the foot.[10] Two scenes of two male couples making love constitute its principal relief decoration. The viewer

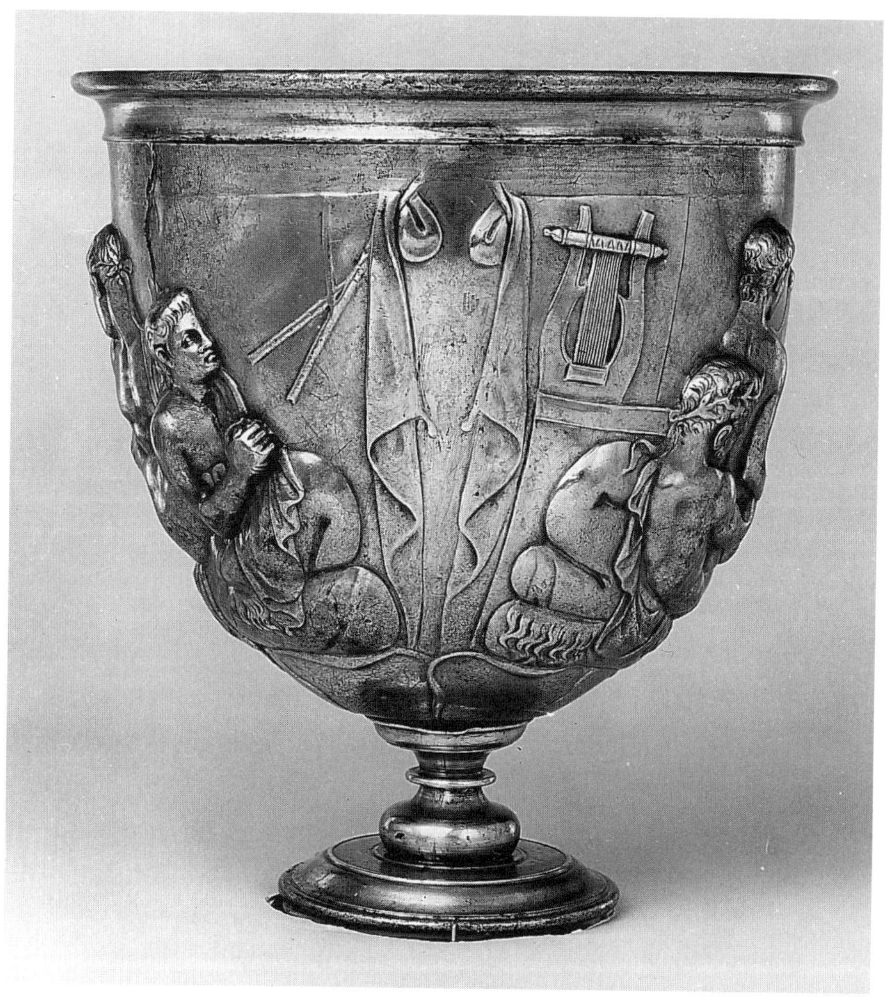

Figure 16. Two panels of drapery falling in symmetrical folds, Warren cup, detail (30 B.C.–A.D. 30). New York, Metropolitan Museum of Art, anonymous loan L.1991.95. Photo courtesy of museum.

can best understand the setting where the lovemaking takes place by examining the areas of the relief between the two scenes; here the artist suggested interiors by constructing a background from cloth, furniture, and a door. On one side two panels of drapery hang over their ties and fall in symmetrical folds (Fig. 16). A double oboe hangs from a strap over the drapery on the left while a lyre rests on top of a tall box or shelf on the right. On the other side the artist constructed a more com-

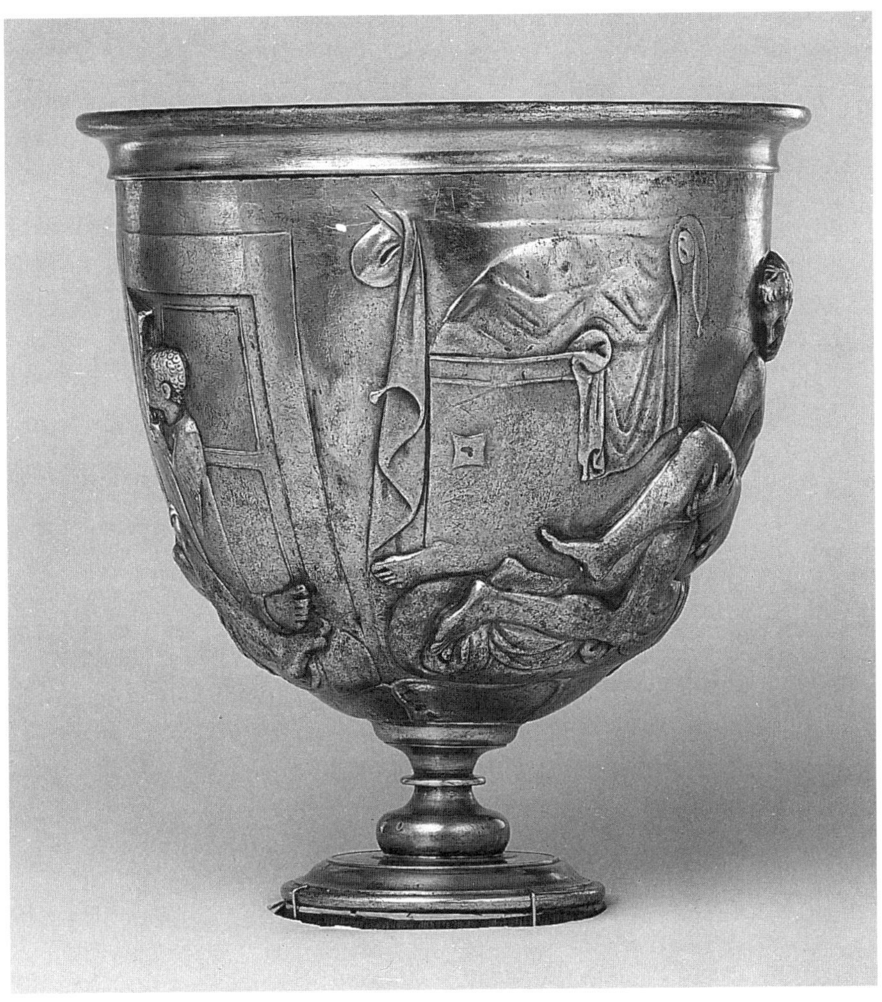

Figure 17. Double-batten door and clothing resting on furniture, Warren cup, detail (30 B.C.–A.D. 30). New York, Metropolitan Museum of Art, anonymous loan L.1991.95. Photo courtesy of museum.

plex background: on the left is a double-batten door with a wide frame whereas on the right piled-up clothing rests on a boxlike piece of furniture in front of the drapery (Fig. 17). Beneath both pairs of lovers the artist depicted heavily cushioned and draped beds, without including their wooden framework (a feature present in the Arretine vessels and wall paintings discussed below).

The side framed by the lyre on the left and the doorway to the right (side A)

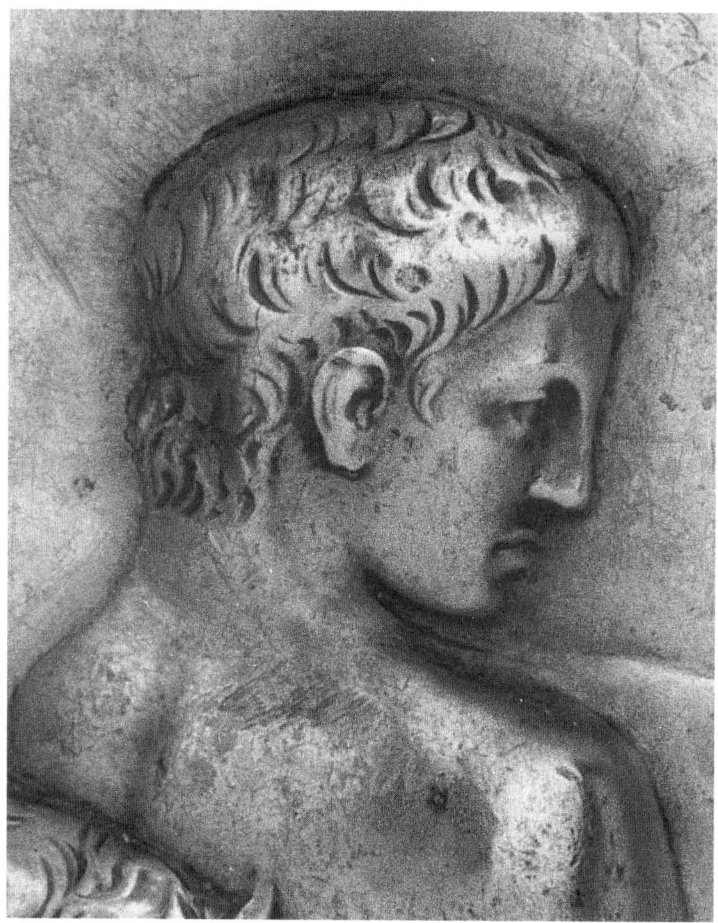

Figure 18. Head of man on top, Warren cup, side A, detail (30 B.C.–A.D. 30). New York, Metropolitan Museum of Art, anonymous loan L.1991.95. Photo courtesy of museum.

pictures two males on a bed (Plate 1). The young man on top is easing himself onto his partner's penis while holding on to a strap. He is clean-shaven (Fig. 18). Flowing drapery conceals the arm that holds the strap, parting in a gentle curve to reveal his right hip and buttocks but concealing his legs and feet, which disappear at an oblique angle into the picture plane (Fig. 19). The man beneath him has a close-cropped, curly beard and wears a laurel wreath tied with a fillet at the back of his head (Fig. 20). The drapery that coyly conceals and reveals areas of his lover's body covers almost none of his; it falls in a scallop above his right knee, partially masks

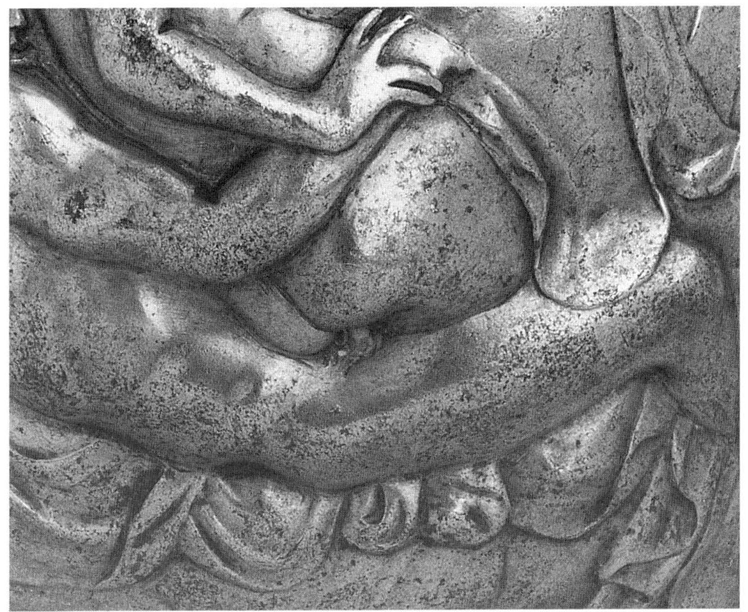

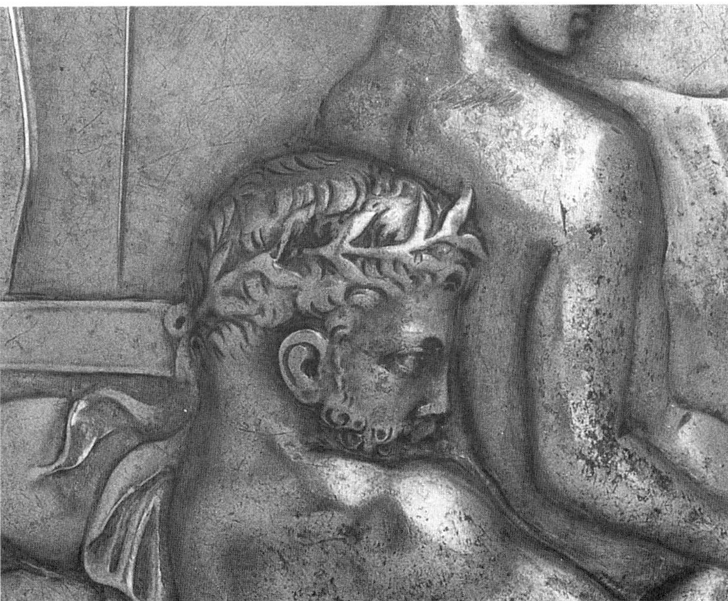

Figures 19–20. Above: Midsections of the two men. Below: Head of man on bottom. Warren cup, side A, detail (30 B.C.–A.D. 30). New York, Metropolitan Museum of Art, anonymous loan L.1991.95. Photo courtesy of museum.

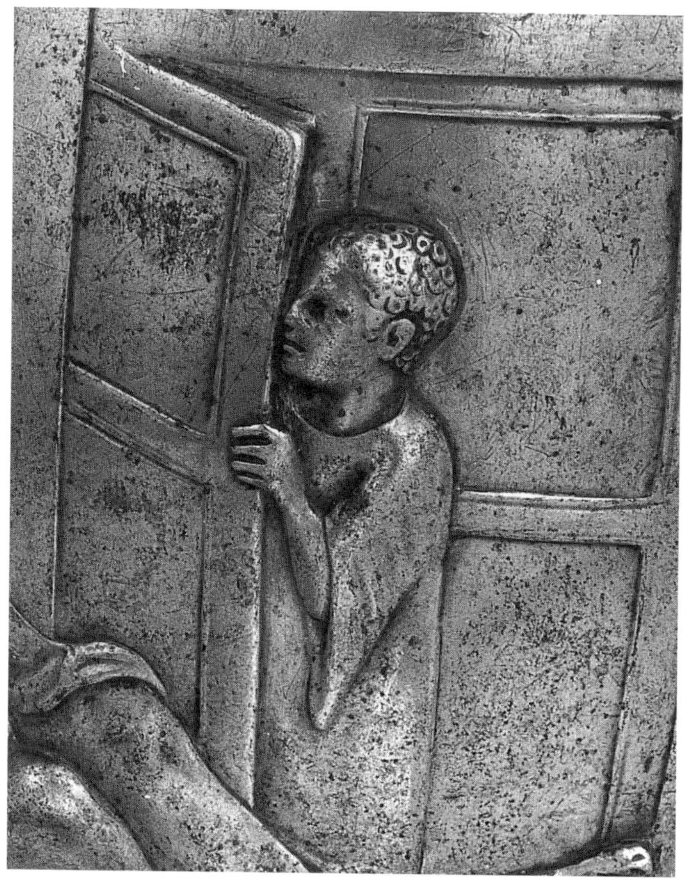

Figure 21. Boy onlooker, Warren cup, side A, detail (30 B.C.–A.D. 30). New York, Metropolitan Museum of Art, anonymous loan L.1991.95. Photo courtesy of museum. All rights reserved, The Metropolitan Museum of Art.

the awkward juncture where his left knee crosses over his right, and flows over his right foot.

The couple is not alone. To the right a boy opens one of the battens of the door—either to peer in or to glance back while quietly exiting (Fig. 21). He has tightly curled ringlets and wears a simple tunic. Both the boy and the door are quite small in relation to the couple on the bed, whether because of the limited space available or because the artist wished to suggest their distance from the couple or their secondary roles in the scene.

On side B, in contrast, the two males are clearly of unequal age (Plate 2). The

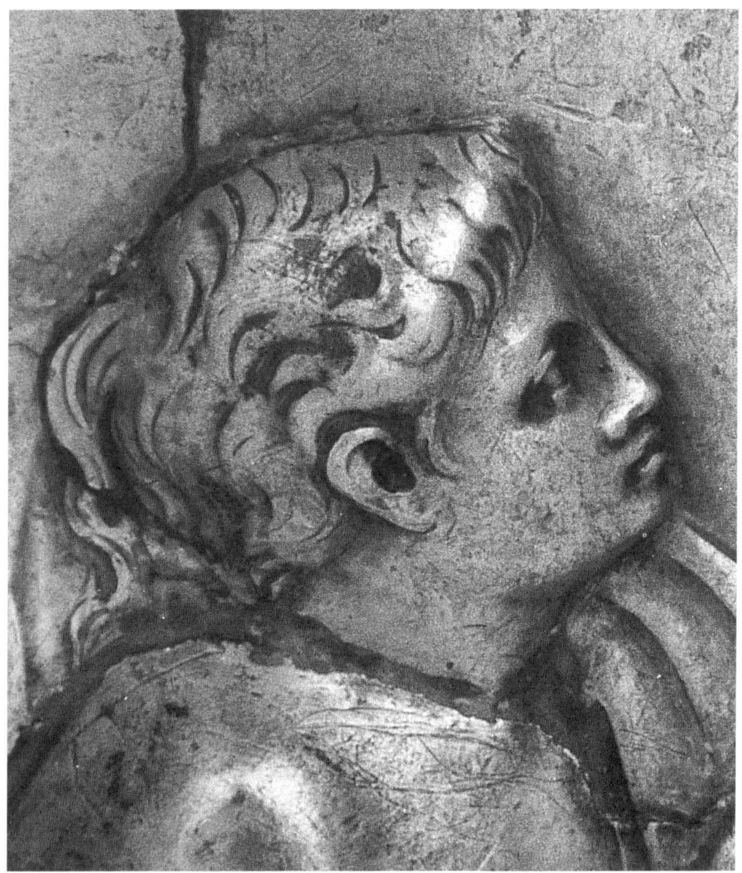

Figure 22. Boy's head, Warren cup, side B, detail (30 B.C.–A.D. 30). New York, Metropolitan Museum of Art, anonymous loan L.1991.95. Photo courtesy of museum.

long locks of hair of the male in front—as well as his smaller size—indicate that he is a boy (Fig. 22). His beardless lover, who wears a laurel fillet in his short hair, supports himself on his right knee while parting the boy's thighs with his right hand. His left leg extends beyond the edge of the mattress, his toes touching the bottom of the framing drapery (see Fig. 17). The artist represented one of the man's testicles directly behind the boy's, indicating that he is entering him. Rather than gazing at his partner, the man looks to the viewer's left, his head slightly lowered. Two details of the drapery in this scene take notably phallic forms: the folds ending in a drapery weight that hang from the mattress beneath the boy's left side and the similarly weighted drapery end that curves over the furniture at upper left resemble an uncircumcised penis.

A survey of Roman silver vessels reveals a broad range of subject matter that sometimes includes sexual representation.[11] Those closest in style to the Warren cup date to the reign of Augustus (27 B.C.–A.D. 14). In particular, two of the cups found at Pompeii in the silver hoard of the House of the Menander reveal that some Romans used vessels with scenes of lovemaking in their homes. Maiuri identifies both as picturing the loves of Venus and Mars.[12] The cups' elongated ovoid form closely parallels that of the Warren cup. Although the backgrounds' carefully wrought grapevines set the scenes in garden bowers rather than in bedroom interiors, each cup presents a pair of male-female lovers on each of its sides. In both cases side A pictures a seminude male on a couch entreating a modestly dressed female with diadem who sits near him, fully clothed; she seems to resist. The other sides of both cups are much more sexual, picturing close physical contact. In particular, side B of cup number 6 clearly pictures a very intimate moment, when the nude woman seems to be either rising from or sitting back in the nude man's lap (Fig. 23).

Particularly significant for the ancient Roman viewer would be the man's gesture, with right arm crooked over his head. This gesture has a long history. It appears on the standing figure of the Apollo Lykeios, exhausted after fighting the Python,[13] but then comes to signify drunken exhaustion in images of Dionysus.[14] It indicates troubled sleep in the Barberini Faun,[15] and innocent sleep in the sleeping Ariadne type.[16] Beginning in the early second century of our era, artists use the "crooked arm" gesture in representations of the sleeping Endymion on Roman sarcophagi. What does this gesture have to do with sex? Hellmut Sichtermann, in his discussion of the gesture on Endymion sarcophagi, points out its sexual meaning in representations of both Endymion and Ariadne, where the arm over the head signals an "opening up" to love.[17] Such a sexual interpretation is convincing, since the gesture occurs in conjunction with the motif of baring the body (either with the clothing falling away by itself or with cupids pulling it aside) so that the god or goddess can gaze at his/her mortal beloved. The arm crooked over the head, indicating sleep, underscores the fact that this readiness for love is innocent or unconscious. The Roman viewer would understand the man's gesture on the House of the Menander cup as a less innocent sexual readiness. The artist of the contem-

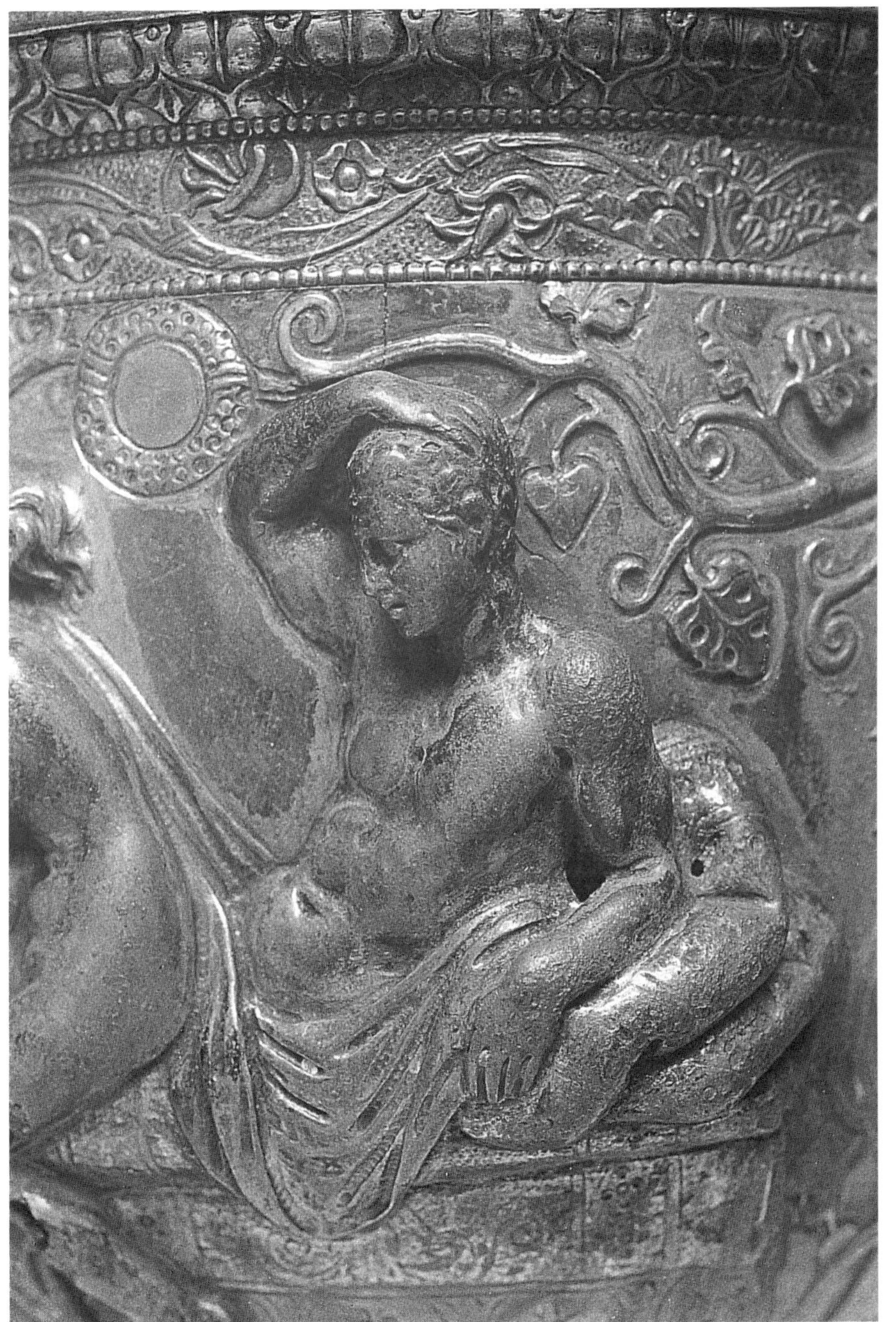

Figure 23. Reclining man and his female partner, detail of silver cup no. 6 from Pompeii, House of the Menander (I, 10, 4; 30 B.C.–A.D. 30). Naples, National Archaeological Museum. Photo Michael Larvey.

porary paintings of the Villa of the Farnesina, discussed in chapter 4, employed this gesture to indicate a woman's sexual availability. Many compositions in all media employ the motif of the man's or woman's right arm crooked over the head in highly charged sexual situations; in this study, including the image on the Menander cup, we discuss seven.[18] This easy crossover from the realm of mythical lovers to that of flesh-and-blood humans corroborates Sichtermann's interpretation of the gesture as a sexual one. (In discussions of images with this pose, I use the conventional term "erotic repose," although "sexual torpor" and "erotic readiness" would also convey its meaning.)

On the Menander cups, it is true, there are allusions to the deities Mars and Venus. The ancient viewer might link Venus to the woman's diadem and Mars to the arms that the cupids play with in the scenes under the handles. Yet the more intimate scenes on the Menander cups seem far removed from mythology: they picture ordinary mortals enjoying love.

Although the Warren cup depicts actual sexual contact, it is not far in spirit from the House of the Menander cups. In both cases they are silver drinking vessels that guests of both sexes would drink from, and in both cases they are meant to entertain the guests with their engaging imagery and fine craftsmanship. In particular, the secure archaeological context of the cups from the House of the Menander—found intact as their owner left them, together with 116 other silver articles—implies that such silver vessels with sexual representations could belong quite usually with the serving ware of a wealthy household.[19]

Unlike the many silver vessels found buried by Vesuvius, the Warren cup lacks an archaeological context, and our analysis of its style must supply its approximate date.[20] In addition to the analogies in subject matter, the two Mars and Venus cups from the House of the Menander share certain stylistic traits with the Warren cup: the Augustan hairstyles and body types, the clear separation of figures from ground, and the taste for fine details and textures—most of them added after the artist had used the repoussé technique to form the whole composition. Close examination shows the chasing: on the Warren cup, details of hair, beards, and drapery; on the Menander cups, particulars in the embroidery of the coverlets and in the petals and leaves of the vegetal ornament.

There are differences as well: figures on the Warren cup are larger in relation to the whole pictorial field. The tendrils and leaves of the bower crowd that same field on the Menander cups. Furthermore, all the figures of the two Menander cups are in higher relief, so that in side view a full three-fourths of the arms and limbs is visible. The proportions of the figures themselves also differ: whereas the artist of the Menander cups favored the elongated bodies with thin limbs and relatively small heads common in the late Hellenistic repertoire, the artist of the Warren cup constructed more solid, compact figures with Polycleitan proportions and high relief. The head of the reclining male figure on side B of Menander cup 6 is considerably smaller in relation to his torso and arms than that of the male on top on side A of the Warren cup (see Fig. 18). Whereas the similar male on the Menander cup has relatively soft facial features and unarticulated hair, the precisely combed short locks of the men on the Warren cup, coupled with profiles emphasizing the heavy jaw, straight nose, and union of nose and brow line, announce a typically Augustan, neo-Attic style. In fact, the Warren cup heads all compare closely with the male heads from the south frieze of the Parthenon. The modeling is deeper and simpler in the Panathenaic frieze, yet there is a surprising correspondence of all the facial features, even down to the so-called Parthenon pout, the men's fleshy yet downturned little mouths.[21]

Closer to the Warren cup's Polycleitan proportions are the figures on the Augustus cup, one of 108 pieces found in 1895 in a villa near Pompeii at Boscoreale.[22] The cups' common inspiration in Greek art of the fifth century B.C. is especially clear in the standing figures. Furthermore, the overlap of individual figures, rendered in differing degrees of relief, allows a sophisticated rendering of space on both cups—a characteristic largely absent from the Menander cups as well as from the two roughly contemporary cups found in a hoard at Hoby, in Denmark.[23] The Warren cup's complex overlap is also like that of the upper register of the cameo known as the Gemma Augustea, particularly in the complexities of placement and drapery in the figures of Augustus and Roma.[24] A similar layering occurs by necessity in the image of lovemaking on side A, with the added problem of suggesting an architectural interior, with strap, opening door, and lyre on ledge.

The facial types and hairstyles of the males on the Warren cup conform to the fashion established by Augustus at the beginning of his reign; he based his image on models from fifth-century Greece, for he wished to evoke the golden age of classical art. His own portrait establishes the iconography of the entire Julio-Claudian dynasty that he founded.[25] Gone is the exaggerated realism of so-called veristic portraiture of the Republican period in favor of a youthful idealism. Although Augustus was a toothless old man in his seventies when he died, throughout his reign he appears as a youthful, Apollo-like deity with Polycleitan features and smooth skin. He has a strong jaw, a small mouth, deep-set eyes, and short ringlets combed forward over his unwrinkled brow. These very features characterize the male heads on the Warren cup, so that it reflects the style of Augustus' visual propaganda even while its subject matter—as we will see below—seems to subvert the ideals that he promulgated.

Mass-Produced Images of Male-to-Male Lovemaking: Arretine Ceramics

Both the precious metal that the Warren cup is made from and the care taken in its figural modeling indicate that it was a luxury item intended for the wealthy class. Fortunately, the Arretine wares greatly enlarge the context for the Warren cup's style and subject matter, providing abundant evidence that persons of slenderer means also enjoyed drinking from vessels adorned with sexual scenes. These glazed terra-cotta cups, bowls, and vases come from the Roman city of Arretium—modern day Arezzo. Because they imitate the forms and decoration of expensive vessels in silver and gold, appear in modest archaeological contexts, and were mass-produced, scholars see them as products meant for poorer consumers.[26] Potters used fired clay molds for the exteriors of the vessels. To make these molds, they first turned them on the wheel. They then used stamps or punches in relief to create the negatives of the figural and ornamental designs. After firing, the molds were ready for use. The potter would press wet clay into the mold to make the vessel itself, producing its smooth interior by turning the whole thing on the wheel. When the molded clay bowl shrank in drying, the potter removed it and fired it.

The earliest description of Arretine wares comes from a thirteenth-century Tuscan chronicler, who marveled at the perfection of the human figures.[27] Figurative designs on Arretine pottery must have inspired generations of artists during the Renaissance, but it is not until the late nineteenth century that scholars or collectors took much notice of them. The first photographs of designs with male-male couples appeared in 1943 in a volume on Arretine ware in the Metropolitan Museum in New York,[28] followed by the publication in 1968 of the holdings of the Ashmolean Museum, Oxford.[29]

When the Boston Museum of Fine Arts reprinted Chase's 1916 catalog of the Arretine ware in 1975, the editors illustrated the pieces with sexual scenes from the collection of E. P. Warren that had only been described—but not illustrated—in the earlier work.[30] Although Porten Palange questions the authenticity of the molds with male-male lovemaking in New York and Oxford, indisputably authentic fragments of actual vases and molds in Boston, Oxford, and Arezzo demonstrate that there were at least two such compositions available to the Roman buyer.[31]

Both compositions alternate images of male-female with male-male copulation. In the first composition a statue of Eros standing on a fluted column separates the four scenes of lovemaking (Fig. 24).[32] The second composition is similar, but more complex and detailed: here herms sporting huge phalluses hold garlands that festoon behind the couples (Fig. 25).[33] The artist who created this composition exerted great care in details of modeling and fashioned beds with headboards ending in satyr's heads. He enlivened the herms by representing them in contrapposto and by having them actively gaze at the couples making love while grasping their own buttocks with their right hands. Rather than passive spectators, they seem ready to leap out of their decorative roles and join the lovers. It is clear that this artist's originality rests in his depiction of the herms and the creative use of satyr headboards, for both male-male and male-female couples are in essentially the same poses as in the first composition.

The scene of male-female lovemaking in both compositions is the most graphic of such erotic types on Arretine ware, picturing the female about to squat on the male's erect penis. She wears a breast band (*strophium*), a feature of many scenes of male-female lovemaking.[34] Although the positions of the male-male lovers are approximately the same in both compositions, there are two variants. In the first variant the two males, one an adult, the other a boy, gaze at each other on a bed (Fig. 26). The man prepares to enter the boy while supporting himself on his flexed right knee, which appears below and behind the boy's right knee. The boy's left arm rests on the edge of the bed, while his right hand touches the man's right arm near the elbow. In a modified version of this pose the man seems more relaxed; rather than kneeling bolt upright, he inclines toward the boy, who reclines as if floating or swimming, all the while locked on his lover's gaze. One fragment shows the man

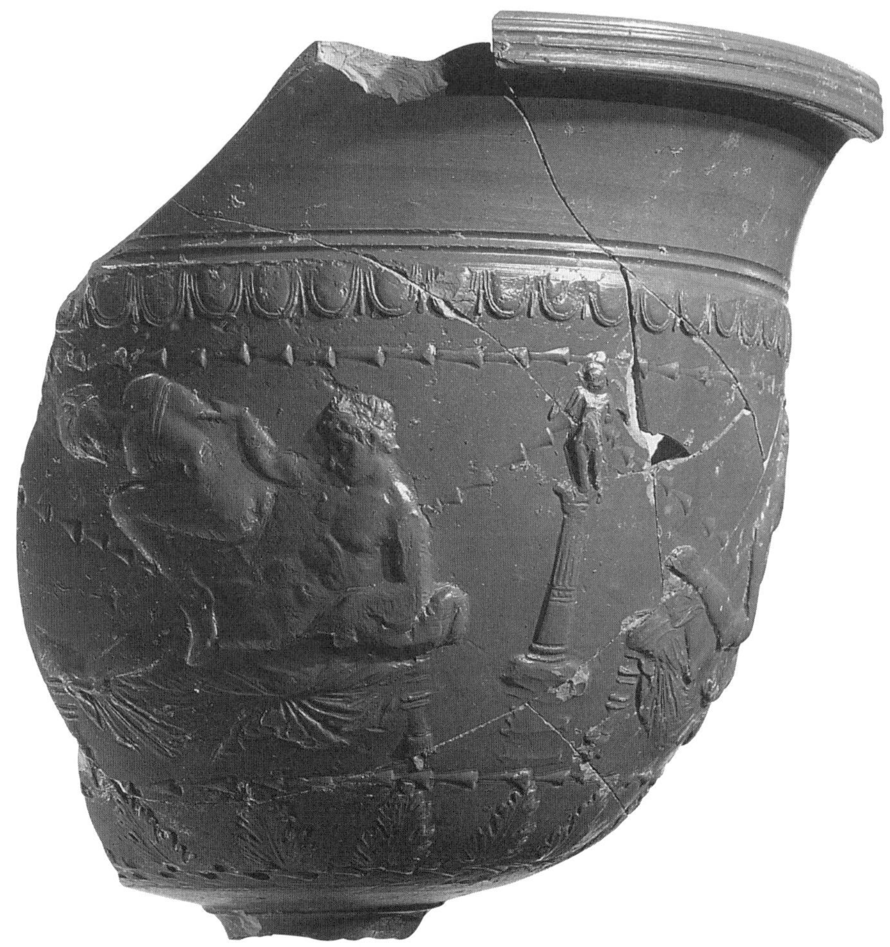

Figure 24. Male-female couple with Eros on column, detail, Arretine bowl fragment (30 B.C.–A.D. 30). Boston Museum of Fine Arts, inv. 6.13.109. Gift of E. P. Warren. Courtesy, Museum of Fine Arts, Boston.

kissing the boy (Fig. 27). These two variants of the male lovers can appear in either of the two compositions. A fragment of a vase in the Ashmolean, discussed below, may represent yet another variant.

This whole class of erotic cups and bowls produced in Arezzo during the Augustan age establishes an artistic context for the Warren cup, on a sort of "trickle-down" model. Because Arretine ware was an affordable—and widely exported—substitute for silver and gold vessels, examples have been found as far away as London

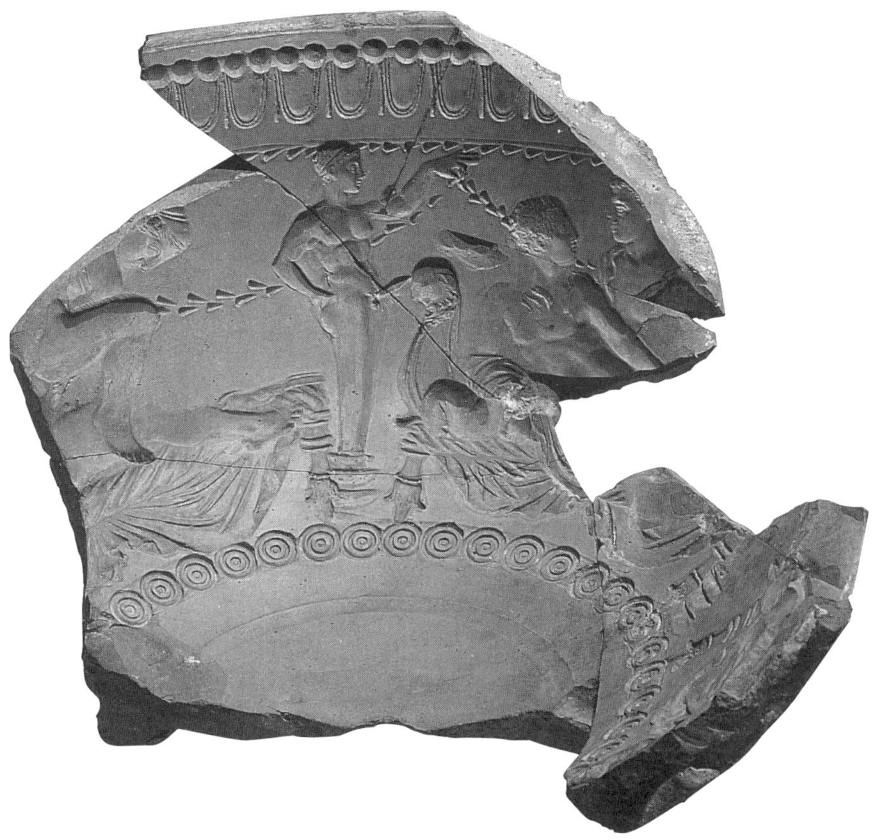

Figure 25. Male-female and male-male couple with ithyphallic herm between them, Arretine mold fragment (30 B.C.–A.D. 30). Boston Museum of Fine Arts, inv. Res. 08.33c. Gift of E. P. Warren. Courtesy, Museum of Fine Arts, Boston.

and Asia Minor. Although sexual scenes form only a small part of the imagery, their sources must have been in the decoration of the expensive objects. After all, it was Arretine ware's ability to mimic the style and subject matter of expensive silver that made it so attractive to consumers. On the evidence of the style and erotic subject matter of the Warren cup, the cups from the House of the Menander, and cameo-glass vessels considered later in this chapter, we must assume that wealthy Romans of the Augustan period had cultivated a taste for expensive vessels with scenes of explicit sexual activity. These vessels were part of the artistic fashions of the time, along with the more usual scenes from classical mythology and the theater. And if the Warren cup is a reminder of an aspect of upper-class taste, the sexual compo-

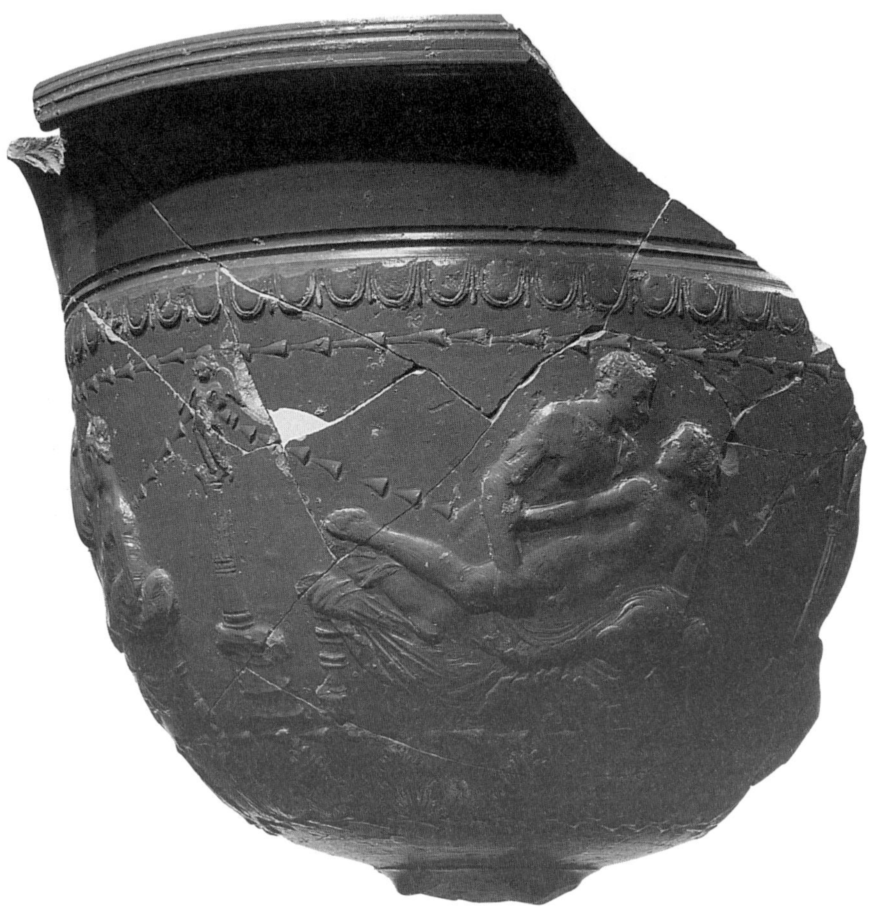

Figure 26. Man-boy couple, detail, Arretine bowl fragment (30 B.C.–A.D. 30). Boston Museum of Fine Arts, inv. 13.109. Gift of E. P. Warren. Courtesy, Museum of Fine Arts, Boston.

sitions on Arretine pottery show how the poorer classes embraced that taste throughout the empire.

Whereas the imagery of the Warren cup and other expensive vessels is idiosyncratic, the combination of male-male and male-female imagery, as well as the straightforward compositions of the Arretine ware, appears to simplify upper-class conceptions to appeal to less wealthy buyers—who were nonetheless eager to keep abreast of current artistic and cultural fashions. For one thing, the artist created a situation of absolute visual equivalence between the scenes of lovemaking that in-

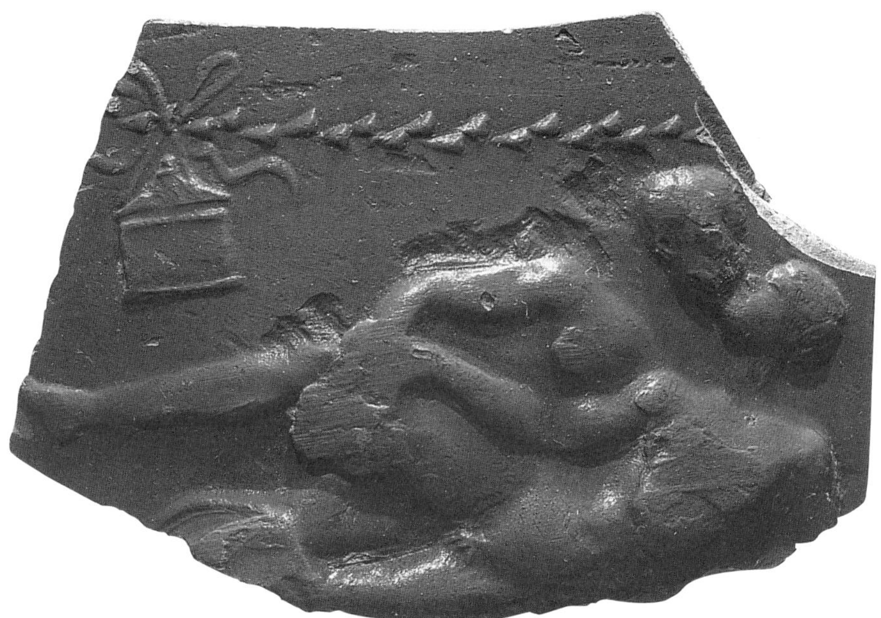

Figure 27. Man-boy couple, Arretine bowl fragment (30 B.C.–A.D. 30). Boston Museum of Fine Arts, inv. Res. 08.33f. Gift of E. P. Warren. Courtesy, Museum of Fine Arts, Boston.

volve males and females and those showing male-male intercourse. He used familiar and popular icons of sexual love, the winged Eros and the ithyphallic herm, both to separate and to frame the four scenes. Furthermore, the representations of lovemaking themselves are quite conventional and therefore easy for the neophyte to understand. By placing the female in a squatting position over the male's erect penis, the artist left no doubt about the act. And for the representation of male-male intercourse he modified a type from the male-female repertoire that displays the greatest portion of the front of the female's body. By removing the female breasts, breast band, and by adding a penis, the artist telegraphed the boy's sex to the viewer in the most direct possible pose; clear display was uppermost in the artist's mind.[35] It is less subtle, for instance, than the late Hellenistic compositions discussed above, where the viewer sees the boy's buttocks but not his genitals (see Fig. 8). With the Warren cup, meant for a more sophisticated audience, the artist could afford to be more inventive in his depiction of male-male sexual acts.

Although the scene on side A of the Warren cup has no equivalents on the Arretine vessels, that of side B closely parallels the Arretine in both pose and in the pairing of an adult male with a boy (Plate 2). The boy's position on the Warren cup is closest to the fragment in Boston (see Fig. 26), but here, as with the other Arretine vessels, the man and boy are locked in each other's gaze. The artist of the Warren cup created a much less intimate mood by turning the man's head sharply away from the boy's. The viewer who sees the man's elegant profile on the left and the boy's on the right could read detachment, disengagement, and distraction in these poses. Reinforcing this sense of isolation is the arrangement of the figures' arms. The boy turns to touch the man's arm as it crosses over his right leg—presumably to begin entry—on the Arretine vessels, but on the Warren cup the man's forearm passes under the boy's right thigh so that his hand is outlined against it. The boy, in turn, uses his right arm to prop up his torso on the cushions. The Warren cup's artist added a note of psychological estrangement and the strain of bodily torsion to the simple and easily legible versions of the pose on the Arretine cups.

Despite the differences of artistic quality and originality evident between the Warren cup and the Arretine vessels, it is important to note that the artists presented the act of lovemaking between males in a romantic, elevated manner. As we noted in the previous chapter, Dover's examination of archaic and classical vase painting demonstrates that depictions of rear-entry intercourse between two males is quite rare in Greece. The Greek artists focused their romantic notions in scenes of courting; when they depicted intercourse it was almost invariably the act of the older male rubbing his penis between the boy's thighs, so-called intercrural coitus.[36]

Not only are there no known examples of intercrural copulation in these Roman representations of male-to-male intercourse, the Roman artists infused images of anal intercourse between males with the same tender intimacy that pervades the images of male-female lovemaking on the Arretine ware and the House of the Menander cups. The artists went to great pains to make the male who is in the receptive position as dignified and attractive as the insertive partner. Whereas representations of rear-entry penetration of boys and women by males on Greek vases emphasize male domination and power over his (unwilling) and often unattractive partner,[37] these Roman depictions make *both* males as attractive as possible and show them mutually attracted to each other, even though in most cases one is a man and the other a boy.

Male-to-Male Lovemaking on the Costliest Vessels: Cameo Glass

If it is difficult to place the Warren cup precisely in terms of the wealth of its owner, it is because scholars are not in agreement about the relative value of silver in the Roman period. Was it a product of great luxury, available only to the wealthy few? Or did the great influx of artisans from the Hellenistic east, added to the flow of capital into Rome, make silver tableware affordable to Romans who were well off but not plutocrats?[38] The case is different with cameo glass. Both its rarity and the specialized labor needed to produce even small vessels in this medium make them very costly objects meant for the wealthy patron. The fact that scenes of male-to-male lovemaking decorate two cameo-glass vessels suggests that such imagery found favor with the elite consumer.

Cameo glass vessels are extremely rare: only sixteen survive, all produced in Rome between 30 B.C. and A.D. 50.[39] Although there was a dramatic increase in the manufacture of all manner of glass vessels in Italy during this period, those made in cameo-glass technique required extraordinary skills to produce. A master glassmaker would create a blank in the shape of the vessel through blowing or casting. To achieve the layers that resembled cameo stones such as onyx, the glassmaker would anneal successive strata of different colored glass to each other. Some of the most complex have five differently colored glass layers. Once he succeeded in making a perfect blank, the glassmaker would turn the work of carving the relief decoration over to a gemcutter. This artist expended considerable time and labor removing the unwanted layers, carving the figural and decorative motifs, and polishing the surfaces of the vessel. He would use the same tools and techniques needed to cut semi-precious stones.[40] Scholars conclude that cameo-glass vessels were very expensive and highly prized artifacts in the Augustan and early Julio-Claudian period, the best of them—like the Portland Vase—made for the emperor and his circle.[41]

An extraordinary cameo-glass perfume bottle (14 cm [5 ½ in.] tall) from Ostippo (Estepa) near Seville, found in a tomb in the Roman necropolis some time before 1986, is now in the collection of George Ortiz.[42] It offers dramatic evidence that the wealthiest patrons in the Augustan and early Julio-Claudian period—like the buyers of the Arretine vessels—enjoyed vessels decorated with scenes of both male-female and male-male couples making love. On side A the artist composed the couple in a manner very close to the mold from Sardis (see Fig. 8), with the difference that the partner on the right is a woman rather than a boy (Plate 3). Although, as on the Warren cup, the artist omitted the bed's legs and headboard, he indicated the bed with a heavy mattress at the base of the pictorial frame and several cushions piled high under the woman's right elbow. Like the boy in the Sardis relief, she rests her right side on the bed as she turns her torso toward the man, her left arm touching his right upper thigh. Her head is in profile, all the better to show off her fashionable hairstyle. She wears her hair rolled under and back toward a bun in the back, in the manner of many portraits of Julio-Claudian women. A band of cloth crosses her back, indicating that she is wearing the breast band.

The man kneels, his legs straddling the woman's upper thighs. The toes of his right foot touch the mattress, while the woman's right foot, in keeping with her pose, rests on it. She is wearing an anklet. An unexpected touch is the man's left leg below the knee, raised at an uncanny angle to suggest that he is slightly unbalanced. In fact, he bends deeply at the waist to grasp his partner around her waist with his right hand. Despite the ardor of the man's lunge forward, the artist maintained an air of coolness by keeping the couple from kissing. The woman's expression, seen in full profile, seems somewhat detached, while the man's profile head passes behind the woman's, not only keeping them from kissing but hiding his features from the viewer. Perhaps he is whispering entreaties in her ear!

On such a small object one would expect the artist to concentrate exclusively on the figures, rather than on the setting, yet the artist added nuance to the scenes of lovemaking by suspending two garlands above the lovers. The fact that the garlands include a variety of fruits and leaves, and that small ox-skulls swag the garlands at their midpoints, might remind the viewer of similar garlands on the masterpiece of Augustan sculpture, the Ara Pacis in Rome.[43] On the Ortiz flask the garlands decorate the altar of love, as it were.

Beneath the garland on side B (Plate 4), the artist produced an elegant version of the male-male lovemaking composition familiar from Arretine ware; the scene also has several striking parallels with side B of the Warren cup. The closest compositional parallel in Arretine ceramics is that visible in Fig. 26 (Dragendorff's Type XIV 8a), where the boy, lying on his left side, faces the man, who kneels between the boy's parted legs. The man has his right hand on the boy's right thigh, close to his genitals, while the boy grasps the man's right forearm with his extended right arm. The artist of the Ortiz flask added careful touches absent in the more summary versions of the composition on the Arretine bowls. For instance, the drapery over the boy's left arm gracefully outlines his youthful body, revealing his genitals and then disappearing between his thighs and the man's right knee. His beautifully articulated hand emerges from under the cloth, languidly holding a wreath—the same trophy of sexual love that appears in many of the painted representations of lovers, such as those in the Villa of the Farnesina.

The artist also paid particular attention to the boy's long hair—an important detail on the Warren cup as well. It falls in a pronounced S that starts at the back of his head and rests along the nape of his neck. The boy's long hair is probably an indication of his status as a slave, since in this period boys of the elite classes appear with short-cropped hair in the style of adult men.[44] It would be unthinkable—for reasons that we will explore below—for an artist of the Augustan period to represent an elite youth making love to a man.[45]

Further evidence that this particular composition of male-male lovemaking was fashionable among very rich Romans of this period comes in a remarkable fragment of multicolored cameo glass now in the British Museum (Plate 5).[46] Although the shape of the vessel that it came from is impossible to know because of the fragment's small size, it equals, if not surpasses, the quality of the Ortiz flask. The wall has five overlays, beginning at the deepest level with opaque white and progressing through translucent deep green, opaque white, deep green again, and opaque red. The artist carefully revealed these layers in this polychrome composition. Color greatly enhances the setting by articulating the bed's platform, mattress, and coverlet. The artist expended considerable effort on the decoration of the bed's platform. He carved down to the lowest white level and then represented the platform decorated with low relief bands consisting of a repeated diamond band framed by two vine-scroll bands. The thick mattress and heavy rolled cushion under the couple is in the highest relief and is therefore deep porphyry red, while the drapery that curves beneath the boy's left side is green. It may be that the artist sacrificed depiction of the boy's left arm and hand to these polychrome bedcoverings, since his upper arm disappears behind them. Virtuoso effects of figural three-dimensionality more than make up for this omission, since the translucent green layer shows through the white at the edges of the figures to give them a sense of three dimensionality. The shading also clarifies the positions of the figures' limbs and their gestures. The artist convincingly carved the man's right hand (damaged on the Ortiz flask) to articulate the fingers' firm grasp of the boy's thigh; his rendering of the boy's hand pressing into the man's upper forearm is equally fine.

Since artists represented scenes of male-to-male lovemaking in a variety of mediums—from extremely precious cameo glass to inexpensive, mold-made terra-cottas—it seems that a broad range of consumers bought them. All these works of art taken together—of varying quality but all dating to within the same fifty-year period—establish that buyers from every economic class—super-rich, wealthy, and of modest means—bought vessels decorated with representations of male-to-male lovemaking. This fact takes on further dimensions when considered against the textual evidence of the period for the cultural construction of male-to-male intercourse.

The Significance of Artistic Representations of Male-to-Male Lovemaking

What did Roman people living in Augustan society think of the male-to-male sexual contact pictured on these vessels? What would representations of same-sex lovemaking mean to their owners and their social equals? Was it shameful, naughty, and taboo—or was it amusing, exciting, or even routine? Was the artist recording fact, representing fantasy, or simply copying fashionable motifs from Hellenistic art for fashion-conscious buyers? Examination of ancient texts, coupled with their modern interpretations, can help answer these questions.

In the recent literature on same-sex relations in the ancient world there is considerable disagreement about using the word "homosexual." David Halperin points out that the word "homosexuality" is only one hundred years old and—like the word "sexuality" itself—describes a culturally determined concept. Following Foucault, he contends that the concept of sexuality, and especially homo- and heterosexuality, are cultural constructions of recent western, capitalist, bourgeois society.[47] Halperin and other cultural constructionists maintain that a person's society determines what sexual acts he or she might perform, and indeed the sexual feelings one person might have toward another. Applying the concept of "homosexuality" to history is bound to force modern concepts of self and other onto the ancient world. Whereas plenty of Greek and Latin words denote what two people of the same sex might do in bed and define the role a person might have in sexual activity and in a sexual relationship, no Greek or Latin word denotes a *state* of being homosexual—or even corresponds to our modern term "sexuality."[48] Can we call the couples on the Warren cup, the Ortiz flask, or the Arretine bowls "homosexuals?" Using the language of Augustan Rome, we cannot. No Greek or Roman word approaches our modern concept of the "homosexual," and any attempt to fit the practices of twentieth-century homosexuals with male-male representations in ancient art or text is certain to be anachronistic.[49]

The problem with such strict constructionist stances is that they make it very difficult to explain the positive signs of a homosexual culture in Roman society—signs that include not only the visual images of male-male lovemaking that we are considering but also a number of poems addressed by poets to their male lovers.[50] Amy Richlin argues that if ancient texts reveal Roman homophobia, they also reflect what could be called a homosexual subculture:

> What is to gain from a model that says there was no "homosexuality" in antiquity? Such a model allows us to stress the difference between ancient societies and our own, to explore what they did have in their own terms. This move, however, when it comes up against Greek and Roman invective against male-male love, emphasizes its political use, its quality of "bluff"; homophobia tends to disappear along with homosexuals. And this model makes it very hard to talk about real *cinaedi* [men who like to be anally penetrated by other men]. What, on the other hand, is the gain from a model that uses "homosexuality" as a category for analyzing ancient societies? A gay-history analysis . . . , which stresses continuity rather than difference, would emphasize what ancient invective has in common with homophobia, and would focus on real *cinaedi,* both on their oppression and their possible subculture.[51]

Along with the wealth that poured into Rome in the century before Augustus came to power came a passion among the rich to import Hellenistic Greek art, customs, and people into Rome. Thus it comes as no surprise that wealthy Roman gentlemen adopted the fashion of buying slaves to satisfy their sexual whims. Upper-class people took it for granted that the elite male would have his pretty boy to make love to. He would probably also have his female love toys—all under the same roof with his wife. Such sexual usages, rather shocking to modern bourgeois morality, constituted no problem for the Roman elite, since it was love between unequal partners, strictly speaking, between the owner of the property and his or her property. Rousselle sees sexual relationships between male master and slave in terms of power: "the inferior, servile position of defeated Greeks in Roman households must have helped to impart an aspect of power to the sexual relationship obtained in a partnership involving two men, one of whom was master, the other slave."[52] Roman law did not forbid another kind of lovemaking between males, that provided by homosexual prostitution, since male prostitutes paid taxes on their earnings and celebrated their own holiday like the female prostitutes.[53]

Modern authors repeatedly point out the "phallic" construction of sexual activity in ancient Rome: all the texts that come down to us frame sexual experience in terms of the freeborn, elite male who inserts his penis into the body of another, whether that other be male or female.[54] We look in vain for records of the feelings of the receptive partner of these phallic acts, whether male or female, of equal or lesser status. Texts tell us only of the desires of the elite male and his fulfillment of those desires with the sex object. But one rule seemed universal for the Roman elite male: he must not have sex with another freeborn male, whether a boy or an adult. It was easy to know the status of people in Roman times because of their dress: a freeborn boy, who was off-limits for sex, wore a golden amulet around his neck and a special toga.[55] It seems that the axiom voiced in the mid-second century B.C. by a slave in Plautus' *Curculio* still held in Augustan Rome: "Love whatever you want, as long as you stay away from married ladies, widows, virgins, young men, and free boys."[56]

In addition to prescribing the inferior status of the love object, the whole of Roman literature—from poetry to the law—made it clear that the elite male's role must only consist in inserting his penis into the love object. Words such as *pathicus* and *cinaedus,* denoting the male passive partner in insertive sex, carried great stigma.[57] Whereas the "active" or insertive stance carried no blame, the Romans scorned and sometimes penalized freeborn men who voluntarily had sex in the "pathic" or receptive position; Richlin details the range of these penalties as indicated in legal, rhetorical, and literary texts.[58] A scarcity of evidence in ancient texts for socially established homosexual relationships between freeborn men of the same age may simply mean that being a *cinaedus* (like being a woman in ancient Rome) was incompatible with the act of writing.[59] Richlin concludes that with respect to the social status of the passive male homosexual "we need not be surprised to see that law and anecdote and literature gives us not only differing but conflicting views of reality."[60]

My premise is that works of art tell a different story from the ancient literature because both readers and writers construct sex from the point of view of the elite male. Standard interpretations of Roman love poetry addressed to the beloved boy state flatly that the poets are simply imitating Greek fashions in lyric;[61] Griffin and others argue that the Roman poets are articulating a social and sexual reality.[62] Part of the problem rests in determining the extent to which Romans of the late Republic and early Empire adopted the Greek institution of boy-love, or pederasty.

As noted above, Dover's *Greek Homosexuality* turns to both legal texts and images in vase painting to articulate the practice of pederasty among the Greeks of classical times. The social institution of boy-love expected adult elite males to be attracted to, court, and engage in insertive intercourse with adolescent boys of the same class. For the elite Greeks in some city-states as in Thebes or Athens before the late classical period, such love was institutionalized and carried no stigma—as long as the "passive" partner was younger, generally under eighteen.[63] The only trouble came if the former beloved grew to maturity and refused to take his new, socially prescribed role—if rather than become the active partner and find his own new beloved, he preferred so-called passive sex.

Scholars, basing their arguments on textual evidence, disagree on the extent to which Romans of the late Republic and early Empire espoused Greek boy-love of any sort. Veyne believes that the Romans had an indigenous tradition of pederasty (and therefore no need of the Greeks to "teach" them its practices);[64] MacMullen, mostly on the evidence of the plays of Plautus, argues that most Romans abhorred "homosexuality."[65] Lilja, carefully considering a larger body of evidence than does MacMullen, concludes that many socially approved forms of male-male sexual activity were present in the late Republic and early Empire.[66] Cantarella's somewhat sketchy overview argues for a pattern of increasing social acceptance of male-male love in the same period.[67] Craig Williams's recent doctoral dissertation, the most extensive treatment of the subject, argues convincingly that the fundamental concerns of Roman society were to protect the sexual integrity of free persons and to distinguish between the active (penetrating) and passive (penetrated) roles. The sex of the partner whom a man chose to penetrate was unimportant; therefore acts that we would term "homosexual" remained undefined in Roman culture.[68]

Although some Romans of the late Republic publicly decried the institution of pederasty among elite Greek males and their equally elite young lovers, they shared with the Greeks certain attitudes that shed light on the artistic representations that we are considering. The prime question in the ancient viewer's mind—whether Greek or Roman—would not be *what* the couples were doing but rather *what status* the individuals had. Given the overwhelming testimony in literary texts for social approval only of phallic, unequal love, all the artistic representations of male-male intercourse that clearly indicate that one of the males is a boy remain unproblematic. These include the Ortiz flask, the fragment in the British Museum, and the mold-manufactured Arretine vessels. Although side B of the Warren cup presents the greatest variations, the pose is quite standard. The boy's long hair, represented on side B of the Warren cup, on the Ortiz flask, and on a fragment of an Arretine crater in the Ashmolean,[69] helped the Roman viewer understand his status as a slave: it separated him from the freeborn boys who were off limits.

The image on side A of the Warren cup is much more problematic. Despite the fact that the man on the bottom has a close-cropped beard, the two partners seem to be about the same age and size. In fact, the sheer weight of the man on top keeps the viewer from seeing him in a typically passive role. He uses a strap to lower himself onto his lover's penis, yet his lover seems to be working hard not be crushed. Although this awkwardness may not be entirely intentional, there is no doubt that the artist strove to make the two as equal as possible in age, size, and activity. There are several artistic precedents in Greek vase painting for representing lover and beloved as near equals.

Some vase painters depicted both partners as being the same size and age, making it difficult to distinguish man from boy. Dover notes a number of these compositions,[70] and Hupperts challenges the long-held assumption that black-figure vases always depict the "ritual" of pederasty between an older male and a boy. His many examples argue for the existence of a variety of sexual activities between males of the same age.[71] The red-figured psykter by Smikros (530–500 B.C.) in the J. Paul Getty Collection shows males courting and kissing.[72] For two of the couples, no beard or larger size or degree of activity distinguishes one youth as older than the other. These individuals appear to enjoy a relationship of equality. Is it possible that either patrons or artists deliberately designed such "nonstandard" representations?

Although there are no other representations of male-male lovemaking in the exact pose found on side A of the Warren cup, two of its features have clear ancient precedents. The use of the strap in the lovemaking chamber may have a long history, to judge by the red-figure cup by Onesimos (500–475 B.C.), where a female spreads her legs in anticipation of titillation while grasping a strap with her left hand.[73] Furthermore, the act of one male lowering himself onto another's penis appears on a vase by the Dinos painter, although he uses a staff, rather than the strap, as an aid.[74] Yet in both of these representations the person in the receptive position is also of inferior status to the male whose penis he or she accepts. Nothing in the body size, facial type, or hairstyles (aside from the "active" lover's beard and laurel wreath) differentiates the two men on side A of the Warren cup. If we did not know the overwhelming evidence adduced from the literature against the possibility of lovemaking between males of the same age and class, we would be inclined to read this image in terms of the late twentieth-century definitions of reciprocal "gay" or "homosexual" lovemaking.

Who are these men looking unusually equal in their lovemaking activities? Vermeule, the only scholar who attempts to identify them, believes that they are princes of Augustus' family. His thesis is that the cup is a degrading satire on the dynasty that Augustus founded. "On one side [side B] an elderly man with the features of the Pheidian Zeus is coupled with a Julio-Claudian prince. On the other side, the scene involves two princes, one older than the other, with faces like Tiberius and Drusus Jr. . . . Needless to say, this type of cup was produced for private viewings by a very limited, extremely sophisticated audience."[75] Although this is an interesting notion, we note that the boy's long hair on side B disqualifies him as a Julio-Claudian prince. The likenesses Vermeule proposes for the men on side A simply are not there. Rather than being Augustus' heirs to the throne, Drusus the Younger and Tiberius, these are generic Augustan males—faces, haircuts, and bodies.

Perhaps the Warren cup presents a satire that is not politically specific. Other features of the scene may yield clues to the lovers' identities. We might question the meaning of the accessories in the room once again. In the red-figure vase picturing the strap as a lovemaking accessory, the woman is clearly a prostitute. Other details on side A of the Warren cup could indicate that this is a room specially outfitted for lovemaking. The lyre, instrument of the muse of love poetry, Erato, seems calculated to establish a refined, cultured atmosphere in the room. Had love songs been a prelude to the lovemaking pictured here? It is also useful to note what accessories commonly found in scenes of lovemaking are absent: aside from the wreaths that the two penetrators wear, there are no signs of the symposium that so often constitutes the narrative framework of sexual imagery on Greek vases: there are no drinking vessels or tables. Nor did the artist include the erotic panel painting that sometimes appears above the couple's bed.[76]

The detail of the boy in a tunic who enters the room is more difficult to interpret. He may fit into the broad category of the so-called onlooker.[77] Grappling with the ubiquitous onlookers who seem to intrude into mythological scenes in Pompeian painting, Michel argues that their purpose is to bring the viewer into the mythological event; they are stand-ins for the viewer, placed there to make the event more theatrical.[78] On the Warren cup, the boy-voyeur of side A would be a surprised onlooker placed there to heighten the humor of the scene. He is the unwitting intruder on a delicate moment—the moment of penetration itself. His surprise at the two men making love would be all the greater if he is a potential partner for the man on the bottom. Someone else—and someone much older—has taken his place. As we will see in chapter 4, where many paintings figure the bedroom attendant looking out at the viewer, or in chapter 7, where people look out from the scene of lovemaking to address the spectator, artists often exploited the comic potential of sexual scenes by including onlooker figures.

Another possibility is that the scene takes place in a brothel, and that the entering boy is an attendant—or another possible partner for one of the men. Or we might interpret the onlooker as the bridge figure in a narrative that circles the cup from side A to side B. In such a scenario side A pictures lovemaking between two adult males, one of whom then makes love to the boy who enters on side B. The obvious problem here is that the boy in the tunic on side A has close-cropped curly hair and in no way resembles the boy on side B. I considered the possibility that we are looking at a scene in a hotel for gay men, where two men of equal age and status have rented a room in an establishment that countenanced, and even encouraged, same-sex lovemaking, yet the very notion of a "gay hotel" is, I now realize, naively anachronistic.[79] Jenifer Neils, taking her cue from the presence of the double oboes and lyre, recognizes the loaded meaning they would have for the Roman viewer who knew (as any elite citizen would) classical Greek culture. They designate the pairs of lovers as costly, cultured, musician-prostitutes, male counterparts of the hetairai who entertained gentlemen at symposia.[80]

Brian Rose suggests that the Warren cup is an image of Roman power.[81] At this time Romans did not wear beards.[82] The man with a beard on side A must be eastern Mediterranean, and he is penetrating a Roman man. On side B it is a beardless Roman man who is penetrating an eastern-Mediterranean boy. In this reading, the artist would be connecting the opposites of dominant versus submissive sexual behavior to the eastern and western halves of the empire. This kind of sexual and geographical contrast makes the scenes relate to each other quite closely; as we will see in the following chapter, artists in the Augustan period were fond of contrasting body type and sexual roles in their representations of male-to-female lovemaking as well.

Finally, it is possible that all the imagery on the cup is designed to evoke not the everyday world of the Roman elite who looked at it, but rather a world of sexual fantasy. In that world the individuals making love were not fixed in time, place, or social status—this in spite of the clearly contemporary, Augustan style of the figures.

As we saw, literary sources from the time of Augustus dealing with matters sexual offer a contradictory interpretative apparatus for the Warren cup. Because Augustan Rome comes as a chilly, somewhat reflective epilogue to the wholesale importation of Hellenistic luxuries in the late Republic, we would expect a rather sober tone in both art and poetry. On the one hand Augustus heralded a new Golden Age, to renew the virtues of the old Republic. He revived antiquated Roman rituals that had gone out with the influx of glittering, sophisticated Hellenistic religions.[83] He tried to get Roman elite women to bear children—a task male authors say they abhorred. And on the other, Augustan art belies moral rigor. Poets sing the praises of the boys they love, frequently alternating love poems to them with ones to their mistresses;[84] artists create images of male-male lovemaking for buyers of extravagant or slender means (and these, images in mass production). It is instructive that the images of sexually explicit couplings of males display the very neoclassical style that Augustus favored as the vehicle of his Golden-Age propaganda. Obviously these portable objects meant for private use reflect personal, not official, standards. They show actual fashions of private life rather than the constructed moral probity of official public life.

The Romans left us very little in writing about sexual activity between males in the Augustan period yet they bought, looked at, and used vessels whose images reflected their own sexual fantasies. We cannot know whether such an abundance of vessels displaying images of male-to-male lovemaking means that many Roman men liked to make love to boys. If poets praise their boy-loves in the same breath as their women-loves, it does not mean that all the men who could read those poets liked both kinds of lovemaking to the same degree. But what these vessels and their imagery do convey is the artistic representation of cultural attitudes toward sex that are quite far from those of the late twentieth century. These images encode the pleasure of looking at lovemaking, a pleasure open—and affordable—to people of most classes and to people of both sexes. That these Roman people living in the age of Augustus found pleasure in looking at male-to-male lovemaking depicted on vessels they drank from is remarkable, for their pleasure in looking gives us a glimpse of a society innocent of the notion that all male-male intercourse was shameful or even sinful. Artistic representation is not life, nor a snapshot of everyday practice, but these images of lovemaking do give perspective on a society that regulated sexual pleasure in ways quite different from our own. The fact that images of male-to-male lovemaking fail to fit commonly held modern notions about Augustan moral probity is a very good argument for studying them.

CHAPTER 4

REPRESENTATIONS OF MALE-TO-FEMALE LOVEMAKING

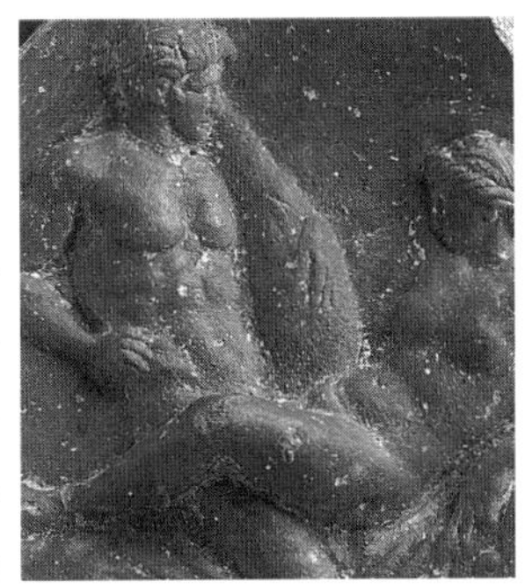

So far we have examined but one genre in Augustan art, that of vessels decorated in relief, focusing on those that depicted male-male lovemaking. What kind of paintings of lovemaking did the elite class enjoy? Fortunately there exist fresco paintings from this period to help us answer this question. Equally fortunate is the unusual circumstance that the literature of the period brings us several references on owning and looking at the explicit paintings of sexual intercourse. In one letter to Augustus from exile on the Black Sea, Ovid uses the word *tabella* to denote a small picture with illustrations of sexual positions. The words *concubitus varii* (various forms of copulation) and *figurae veneris* (sexual positions) leave no doubt about the subject matter of this painting. The setting he creates is one of a fine picture gallery hung with masterpieces from the Greek classical and Hellenistic periods:

> Surely in your houses, just as figures of great men of old shine—painted by some artist's hand—so somewhere a small picture depicts the various forms of copulation and the sexual positions. Telamonian Ajax sulks in rage, barbarian Medea glares infanticide, but there's Venus as well—wringing her dripping hair dry with her hands—and barely covered by the waters that bore her.[1]

Ovid's comments clearly indicate that for the upper class it is the norm, not the exception, to own and display little paintings that showed couples illustrating a variety of sexual positions. It seems that such pictures belonged in the proper elite citizen's art collection; they fit his image as a connoisseur of Greek art.

In the two places in his *Art of Love* where Ovid describes the *figurae* he does so not without irony, emphasizing that women were quite adroit in inventing positions that went far beyond the paintings; they also knew how to show off their best physical features while engaged in lovemaking.[2] The woman with a pretty face should lie on her back, whereas one with a good back should position herself to be seen from behind. Ovid recommends the "woman riding" position for someone with a petite figure, but a tall woman should kneel on the bed, with her neck slightly arched, and so on. Even though this second passage reads as advice for the woman, Ovid is clearly providing us with the man's point of view. It is the woman, not the man, who receives instructions on how she should look: she must conform to the expectations of the male gaze.

In Ovid we recognize the voice of the cultured elite man of the Augustan age. In Suetonius' accounts of looking at depictions of sexual acts we pick up a harsh tone that distances him from his subject and makes him an indifferent source on how elite men and women employed sexual images in their houses in this same period. For one thing, Suetonius (ca. A.D. 69–ca. 140) is writing over a century later; for another, his general intent is to discredit the whole Julio-Claudian dynasty (especially Tiberius, Caligula, and Nero). He takes the usual route for Roman writers: he accuses them of sexual turpitude. Nevertheless, the very form Suetonius' smear campaign takes is highly visual.

He has Horace (65–8 B.C.), one of Augustus' favorite poets, using mirrors to reflect sexual acts: "They say that he [Horace] was immoderately lustful, for it is recounted that in a room lined with mirrors he had whores so arranged that whichever way he looked, he saw a reflection of copulation."[3] This passage, from his *Lives of the Poets,* suggests that some wealthy Romans enjoyed seeing their own or others' sexual acts reflected in mirrors. In his biography of Tiberius, Suetonius takes a different tack in describing artworks—paintings and sculptures—that the emperor used for sexual stimulation.[4]

As we noted in chapter 2, Suetonius has Tiberius placing a painting by Parrhasios in his bedroom: it showed Atalanta performing fellatio on Meleager. Suetonius goes on to say that Tiberius had pictures illustrating sexual positions placed throughout bedrooms used for copulation: "He decorated rooms (*cubicula*) located in different places with images and statuettes reproducing the most lascivious paintings and sculpture, and he equipped them with the books of Elephantis, so that no position he might order would fail to be represented."[5] In addition to mentioning one of the famous sex manuals, this passage adds to the evidence (considered more fully in chapter 8) that artists may have illustrated the sexual positions detailed in them. The written descriptions or instructions of Elephantis' sex manuals were not enough—and in Suetonius' judgment perhaps not as reprehensible—as the painted images and sculpture that illustrated the sexual acts.

Both Ovid's apology for paintings that illustrated sexual positions and the indictment by Suetonius of Tiberius' use of them—placed among a variety of means for illustrating copulation—point to various conditions surrounding their display and use. Ovid puts the erotic *tabella* into the picture gallery; the context is that of the man of taste looking at high art. Suetonius has the evil Tiberius using these pictures as part of an obsessive project to fulfill his immoderate lust. Both literary constructions reveal the widespread existence of such paintings and their use both as high art and as base sexual aids.

Representations of Male-Female Intercourse: The Farnesina Paintings

Although none of these panel pictures remains, we do have painted depictions of them in frescoes from a villa in the heart of Rome itself, dated with certainty to the early years of Augustus' reign. This is the Villa of the Farnesina, so called because in 1879 workers discovered it while cutting through the garden of the Renaissance villa to construct the Lungotevere Farnesina, a broad avenue that today runs along the right bank of the Tiber. Excavators hurriedly detached and removed the painted walls and stucco ceilings of the Roman luxury villa. Its position took advantage of its view of the Tiber but made the villa susceptible to frequent flooding, so that it seems to have been abandoned shortly after its construction. The fine quality of its wall painting makes the villa central to the study of the chronology of the so-called Four Styles of Romano-Campanian painting; some scholars believe that the villa belonged to Augustus' own daughter Julia, married to his right-hand man, Agrippa.[6] The decorations date to around 20 B.C.

Painted representations of panel paintings are the building blocks of the rich decoration of the three cubicula that survived. Six of these panel paintings represent couples engaged in lovemaking. But before examining these paintings in detail, we need to consider the possible uses of the rooms where they appear; we also need to understand how these representations of paintings fit into the all-over decorative schemes that the artist designed for these rooms.

The Roman house, particularly that of an elite citizen, was anything but a private retreat from the public world of business. Because the owner had to conduct daily business in the house, it probably had no rooms that we today would consider "private." In the mornings the ritual of *salutatio* brought all the paterfamilias' clients into the front part of the house surrounding the atrium. At other times the rooms of the house arranged around the enclosed garden or peristyle would find use as reception spaces for the owner's peers, and on many occasions he could have an intimate business discussion in a cubiculum.[7] It was the status of the individual who entered the Roman house that determined her or his access to its rooms. Living barriers, in the form of household slaves, controlled access. In fact, Romans often named slaves in reference to the room where they served. The *cubicularius* was a servant who oversaw all the functions of the cubiculum, from the business tête à tête to lovemaking and sleeping. He guarded the cubiculum as well, sleeping at its entrance on a mat.[8]

At the time when the Farnesina cubicula received their decoration, architects worked with mosaicists, painters, and stuccoists to create an ensemble of decoration that differentiated the space for circulation, where the cubicularius would wait on his master or mistress, from the space for the bed. A photograph of the left wall of cubiculum B reveals how the wall painter's design differentiated the anteroom from the bed-alcove (Fig. 28). A gold pilaster placed three-quarters of the way into the room, proceeding from left to right, is the only element that divides the wall from top to bottom. It marks the point where the mosaic pattern on the floor changes and where the ceiling turns from an elaborately stuccoed vault over the anteroom to a flat ceiling over the bed-alcove. The decoration of the anteroom is more complex than that of the side wall of the alcove, since its lower parts would be obscured by the bed when it was in place. The right-hand wall followed these divisions in mirror reversal.

Within the differentiated scheme, predominantly painted in vibrant cinnabar

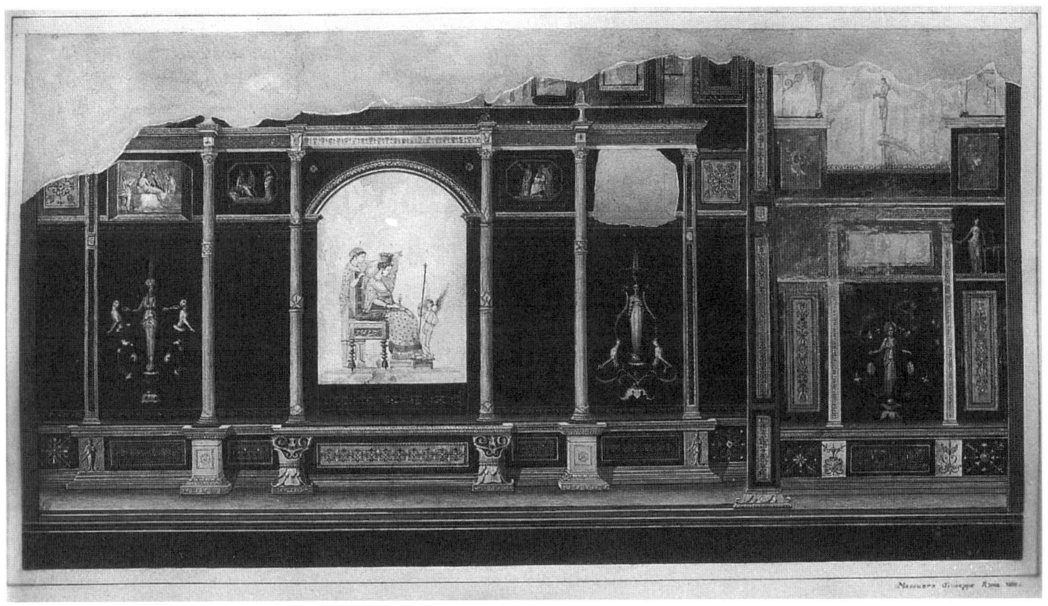

Figure 28. Rome, Villa under the Farnesina, late Second-Style scheme of left wall, cubiculum B (ca. 19 B.C.). Rome, National Museum of the Terme, inv. 1128. Photo Deutsches Archäologisches Institut, Rome, inst. neg. 37–1390.

red, the painter privileged the centers of the anteroom's walls, each occupied by a large white-ground painting. It is immediately apparent that hierarchies in the size, shape, and framing of the five pictures on this wall were important to the designer. Most elaborate is the central picture's setting, framed by the representation of a little pavilion called an *aedicula.* It consists of columns to right and left that carry an arched roof. There are four pictures in the upper zone of the wall. Symmetrically placed to either side of the curved frame are two black-ground paintings in octagonal frames. Also symmetrically placed, but farther away in this same upper zone, were two paintings with scenes of lovemaking (one was stolen).[9] The artist depicted these with movable wooden shutters seen in perspective. The Romans used the Greek word *pinakes* (*pinax* in the singular) for these shuttered paintings. The word *tabella* (*tabellae* in the plural) seems to refer to paintings that lack shutters. Although a modern perspective might tempt us to hypothesize that the shutters were for paintings that the owner might want to cover—for instance, so that children would not see the imagery—it turns out that artists also depicted shutters on quite neutral images, such as landscapes.[10] Uppermost in the mind of the wall painter was creating the notion of a real picture gallery on the flat wall, where the owner would display paintings with a variety of frames, including the shuttered pinakes.

Style and subject matter present further nuances. The large central picture depicts Aphrodite, seated in a golden throne with her maidservant behind her, looking down at Eros. The white ground, the emphasis on outline rather than color and shading, and the insistent profile views would signal to the astute Roman viewer the artist's revival of Attic painting of the fifth century B.C. Attic white-ground lekythoi reflect the qualities of these lost masterpieces. The black-ground paintings, fully rendered in color and shading, would recall fourth-century painting techniques, as would the pinakes.[11] Subject matter changes from the entirely mythological center picture to the mixture of theatrical figures with muses and poets in the black-ground octagons, to human beings making love in the pinakes. Analysis of the other lively elements of this wall—and especially the rear wall of the alcove—would further underscore its deliberate stylistic eclecticism: the artist is recalling a picture gallery or *pinacotheca,* where the wealthy collector would arrange paintings of different styles, periods, and subjects to show off both his wealth and his knowledge of the history of art.[12]

Two pinakes of the original four remain in cubiculum B. The one on the left wall (Fig. 29), presents five figures in all: the couple on the bed and three female servants. The woman sits on the bed with her back to the viewer, her head turned in profile to her lover. She wears a pink chiton tied at the waist and has a yellow cloak draped over her midsection and legs. Her hair is pulled back and gathered in a bun at the nape of her neck. The man sits, pressing close to her as he turns to look in her eyes. His head is profile and he is nude. The woman leans back on the blue cushion behind her back, while he sits upright, his hand on the bed near the woman's knee. Behind the bed and to the right the artist depicted two servant girls, one in profile and the other in three-quarters view. Like the girl at the extreme left of the picture, they do not look at the couple. Perhaps they are crossing the back of the room, having just arranged the white covers on the bed. Their small size in relation to the couple on the bed signals to the viewer that they are servant girls, rather than grown women. Whereas these two mark the back spatial plane of the picture, the girl on the left marks the foremost plane. The artist positioned the table holding the basin very close to the lower edge of the picture, and the girl stands right behind it, in frontal view with head turned slightly to her right.

The artist's mastery of color and shading gives this pinax unusual grace. Even though the light source is from the right, casting the servants' and the man's left side into shadow, the right side of the painting is relatively dark. It is the left side of the painting that the artist suffused with pastel light, using delicate lavender, violet-blue, and light blue in effective contrast with the bright lemon yellow of the woman's robe.

These compositional and pictorial effects comment on the tranquil, unaggressive sexual dalliance that is unfolding. The position of the woman's body tells the viewer that she is contemplating the pleasure of making love with the man, but without haste. The man's fervent gaze, his body language, and the fact that he is nude at least to the buttocks all suggest that he may be a bit impatient; yet finally he, too, seems ready to take his time. The water will be poured, the other two servants will perhaps leave, and love will take its course.

Early in this century Rodenwaldt noted the similarities of this painting to the mosaic excavated in 1865 near Rome, and now in Vienna (Fig. 30).[13] Although the mosaic is considerably cruder than the wall painting, it is clear that both looked back to a common model that was available to both mosaicist and wall painter. The painter understood nuances that eluded the mosaicist: he carefully reduced the size of the two servants to the right to make it clear that they were behind the bed, whereas the mosaicist rendered only one of the servants and had her touch the mattress. Instead of the man being clearly on the bed and touching the woman's right knee, he seems to be standing next to the bed and rather obviously staring at her. The other major difference is that the mosaicist confused the setting: he suggested the outdoors by, creating a kind of rustic canopy with a big swag of cloth tied to a tree, and by placing a statue, perhaps of Artemis, in the upper left corner.[14] Such free copies from a single source must have been common in the period; other instances of nearly exact copies of the same composition, especially at the site of Pompeii, point to the existence and circulation of copybooks for the use of painters and mosaicists.[15]

Excavators were able to retrieve only half of this cubiculum's right wall, and only two-thirds of the pinax in the attic story survives. This pinax, opposite the one just described, presents a moment of greater passion (Fig. 31). Although the woman

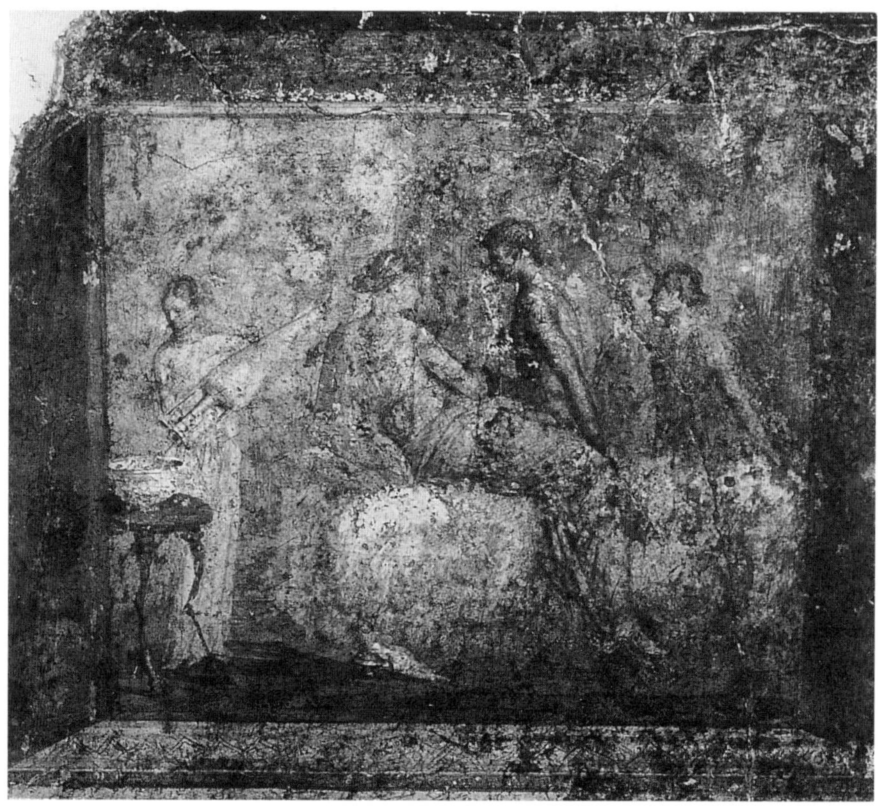

Figure 29. Male-female couple on bed attended by three servants, Rome, Villa under the Farnesina, cubiculum B, left wall, attic zone, to left of central aedicula (ca. 19 B.C.). Rome, National Museum of the Terme, inv. 1128. Photo Deutsches Archäologisches Institut, Rome, inst. neg. 77–1305.

is fully and even voluminously clothed, she dangles her feet off the edge of the bed with jaunty abandon as she turns to kiss the man. Like the man in the pinax opposite, he is nude to the waist, but here he needs to lean forward only very slightly to return the woman's kiss. His hair seems disheveled, but paint loss makes it unclear whether we see his hair or a leafy crown. Again the artist concentrated on the details that allow the viewer to "enter" this bedroom: his use of foreshortening places the bed convincingly in the space, complete with its decorated bedspread and cushions. Again the artist manipulated light and shade in the background, but this time to suggest the walls of the bedchamber on the left, the jamb of a wide door behind the woman, and the open space of a peristyle garden behind the man.

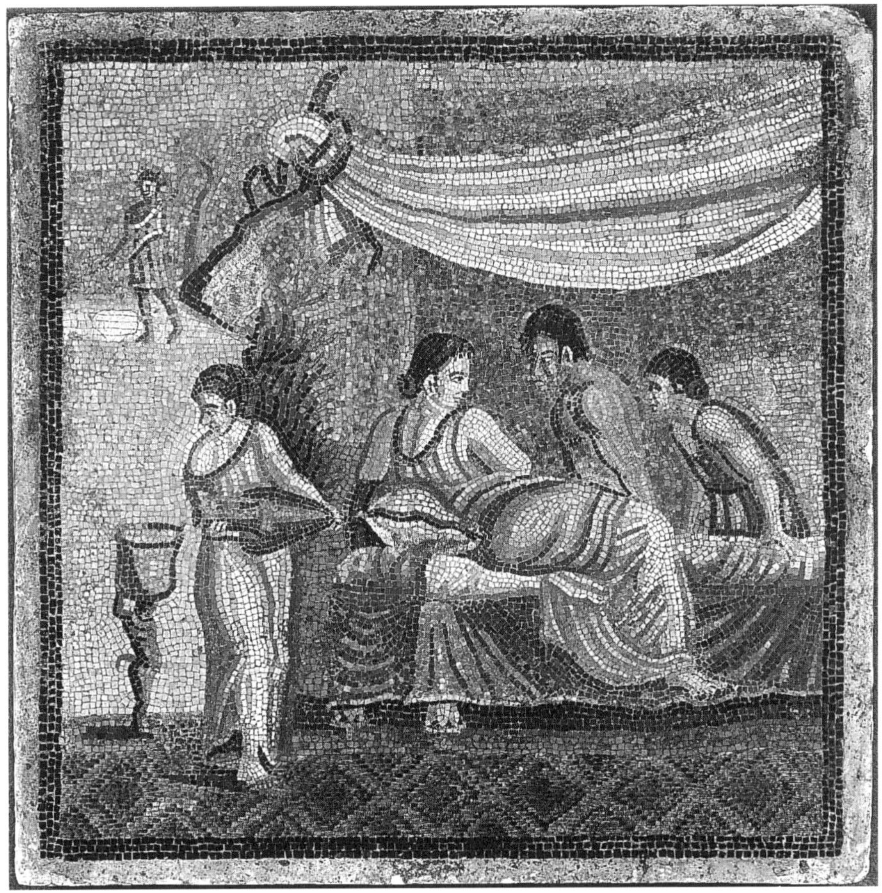

Figure 30. Male-female couple on bed attended by two servants, polychrome mosaic *emblema* from Rome, Villa at Centocelle (20 B.C.–A.D. 20). Vienna, Kunsthistorisches Museum, inv. AS II 9. Photo courtesy of museum.

Although the missing right-hand corner had space for the figure of a servant, it is impossible to know whether the artist included one or not.

Cubiculum D, although a wider space than B, otherwise is its mirror reversal in the villa's plan. Its wall-decorative scheme closely follows that of B as well, with similar architectural features dividing anteroom from alcove, and symmetrically arranged pictures taking pride of place at the centers of the anteroom walls right and left. Although the frames differ, the styles and subjects of the three ranks of paintings—white ground for the aediculae, black ground for the upper story pictures closest to the aedicula, and polychrome for the erotic tabellae—remain the

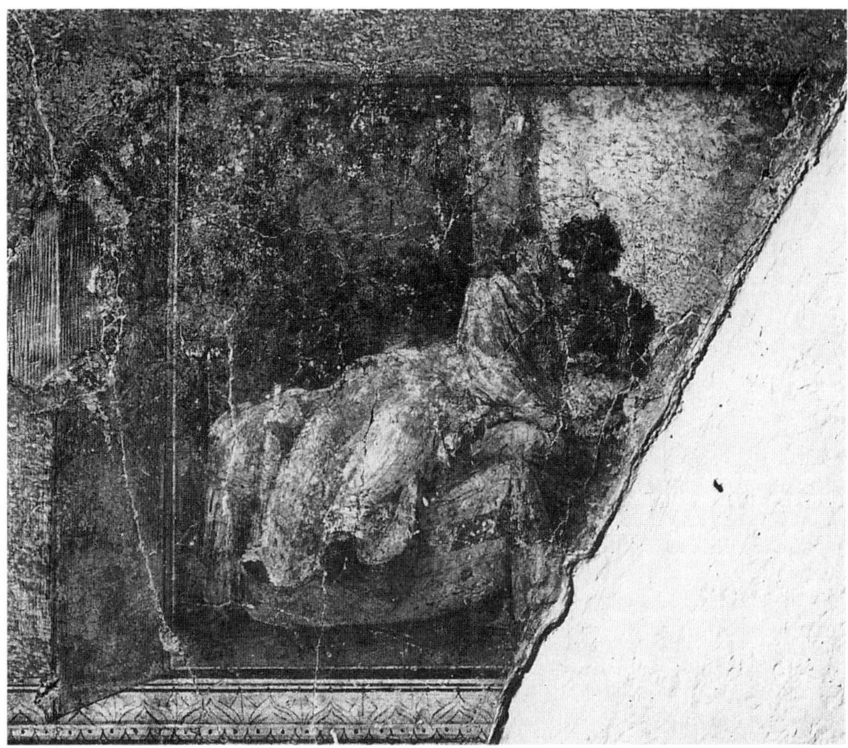

Figure 31. Male-female couple on bed, Rome, Villa under the Farnesina, cubiculum B, right wall, attic zone, to left of central aedicula (ca. 19 B.C.). Rome, National Museum of the Terme, inv. 1127. Photo Deutsches Archäologisches Institut, Rome, inst. neg. 77–1263.

same. Interestingly, instead of shuttered pinakes the artist framed the sexual scenes with the so-called eight-pointed square, formed by the crossing of two vertical bars of the frame with the two horizontal ones.[16] The picture to the left of the aedicula on the right wall seems to depict a serious moment between the couple on the bed (Fig. 32). Not only is the woman fully clothed from head to foot while the man is nude to the waist, but this time the woman wears a veil. The artist further heightened the contrast between the two in their poses: his legs (under the covers) stretch out the length of the bed, and he leans his left elbow on the cushions while attempting to place his hand on the woman's thigh. She sits upright, her head bowed demurely while she grasps the man's forearm to keep it from resting on her thigh. In the background a boy stands, expressionless, an object (perhaps a shield) between him and the man's foot.

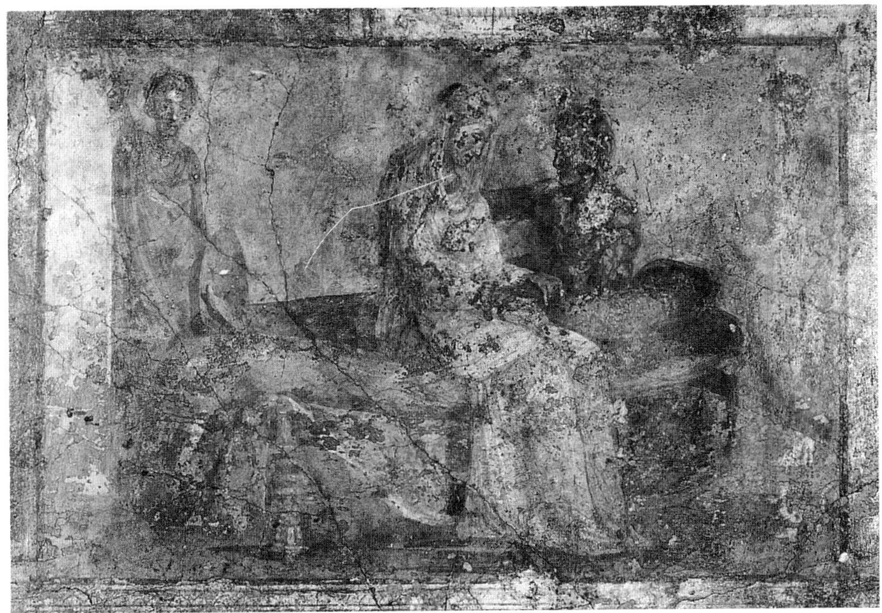

Figure 32. Male-female couple on bed attended by a servant, Rome, Villa under the Farnesina, cubiculum D, right wall, attic zone, to left of central aedicula (ca. 19 B.C.). Rome, National Museum of the Terme, inv. 1188. Photo Deutsches Archäologisches Institut, Rome, inst. neg. 77–1295.

Similarities of the woman's dress and pose to the figure of the bride in the painting known as the Aldobrandini Wedding,[17] cause Andreae to see this picture as a young married couple on their wedding night.[18] It is significant that scholars date the Aldobrandini Wedding to the same period as the Farnesina paintings, hypothesizing that it was part of a frieze in a room painted in the early Third Style.[19] Scholars propose many hypotheses for what must be an idealized representation of marriage ritual, perhaps alluding to Dionysian or other mythology. In any case, the Aldobrandini Wedding is a truncated and very free interpretation of the rituals that would occur at an actual wedding. If the pose of the couple on the bed in the Farnesina picture alludes to the wedding night, then, it does so borrowing even more loosely from the visual sources available to the artist of the Aldobrandini Wedding. Both paintings are creations of the Augustan age, graceful confections in the neo-Attic style.

If this painting from cubiculum D represents a woman—whether a bride or

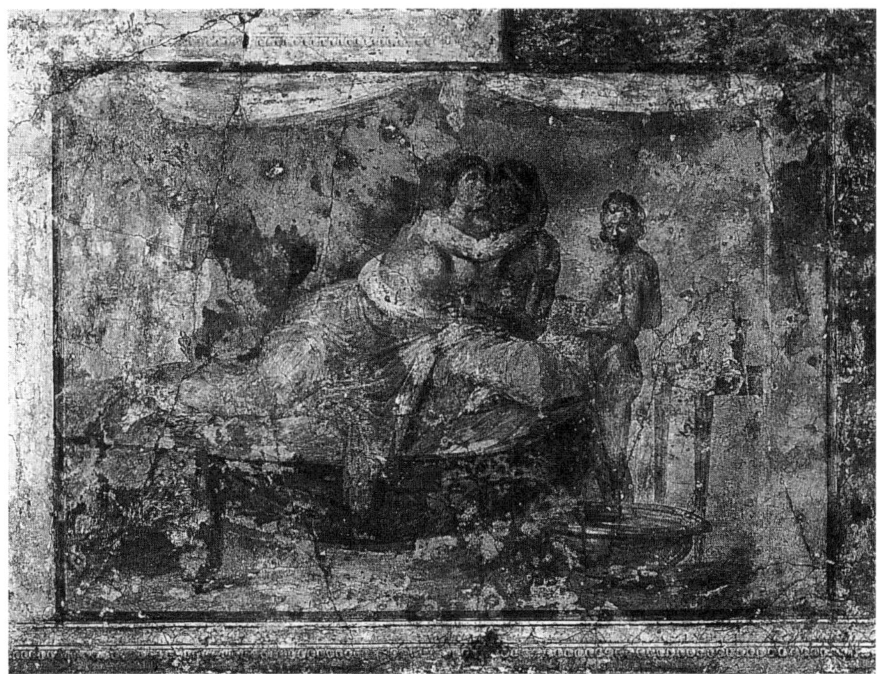

Figure 33. Male-female couple on bed attended by two servants, Rome, Villa under the Farnesina, cubiculum D, right wall, attic zone, to right of central aedicula (ca. 19 B.C.). Rome, National Museum of the Terme, inv. 1188. Photo Deutsches Archäologisches Institut, Rome, inst. neg. 77–1290.

not—as modest and resisting, the painting that formed its pendant, to the right of the central aedicula, constructs the woman as unrestrained and aggressive (Fig. 33). The artist stretched out her body on the bed and presented her nude to the waist as she reaches her arm around the man's neck to pull his head toward her. It seems that she wants to kiss him, but her mouth is at the bridge of his nose. The man, nude also to the waist, has his right arm around the woman's neck and shoulder; his fingers are just visible on her left shoulder. His right hand makes an ambiguous gesture: whether he has just disrobed the woman or is about to touch her breast is difficult to say. The artist created a contrast between the woman's expressive gesture and the man's wooden posture. The eye follows the sweep of her body from the toes that rest on the bed, through her voluminous yellow robe to her gesture of reaching around the man's neck. He seems disengaged, or perhaps stunned by the woman's passion.

Because the woman appears unrestrained, Andreae construes her as a hetaira, or prostitute. He rules out the possibility that the woman could be the chaste bride turned by passion into a eager sex partner. Why did the artist put these two representations of sex—one chaste and tentative, the other passionate and explicit—in juxtaposition? If the one woman is an elite bride, the sexual roles that her society constructed for her included sex with only one man (her husband) for the purpose of producing legitimate heirs. The prostitute's role is that of the sex worker: a slave or a freedwoman, bought or hired to provide sexual recreation for male clients of various classes. Yet prostitutes do not wear such voluminous clothing, nor do they wear the veil. By law they wore togas or were dressed for quick sex under the arches of the city (Martial mentions the arches); Catullus 55.11–12 has them wearing clothing that allows them to "flash" potential clients. Many Roman texts recognize the wife's erotic interest in her husband.[20] And in the Farnesina cubiculum it seems certain that Roman matrons would have looked at these paintings, perhaps recognizing themselves there as young brides. The woman of the left-hand painting must be a reluctant bride (a type attested both by the Aldobrandini Wedding and in literary sources) and the right-hand painting must represent a bride inflamed by passion.

An unusual feature of the right-hand painting that features the passionate woman is the nude boy servant gazing directly out at the viewer. The artist of cubiculum B took pains to keep the servants busy with their own work, unaware of either the couple on the bed or of the viewer. Here in cubiculum D the boy is obviously ministering to the couple—he has poured the water into the large gilded basin and holds a wine vessel—yet seems to be aware of the viewer's gaze at him and the couple. This device of having a figure within the pictorial space look out to address the viewer, discussed in reference to the Warren cup, appears with greater frequency in the latter half of the first century. Here the figure seems designed to heighten the viewer's awareness that he or she is a voyeur, looking in on the couple's sexual intimacies. The servant belongs there, his gaze seems to say, but you, the viewer, do not. Behind the bed to the left are traces of another figure who, like all the others in the Farnesina paintings, goes about his business without paying attention to either his owners or the viewer. At the top of the picture the artist represented a white curtain, knotted in the center and swagged to right and left.

If the painting is a vignette of the wedding night, as I believe it is, it is a narrative of the modest bride becoming the immodest lover—perhaps fulfilling a rib-

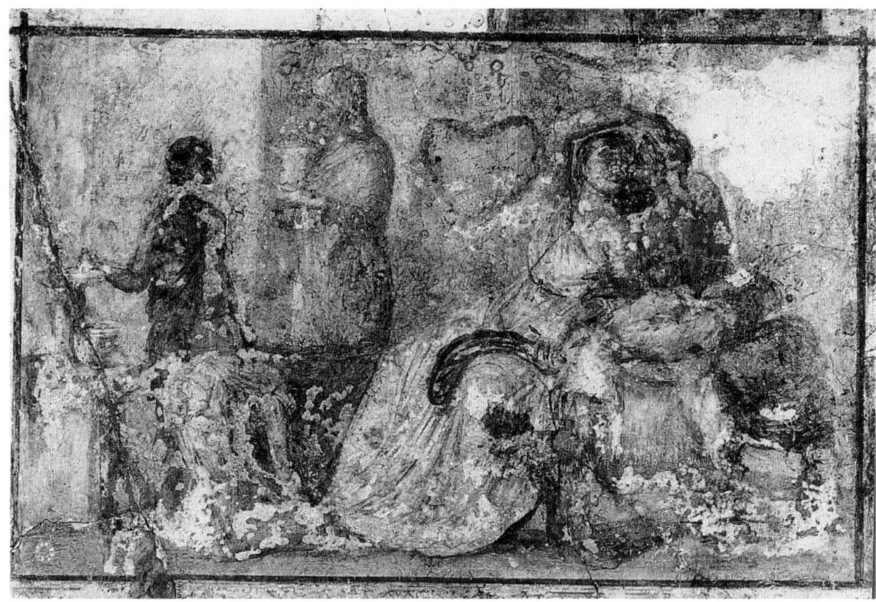

Figure 34. Male-female couple on bed attended by three servants, Rome, Villa under the Farnesina, cubiculum D, left wall, attic zone, to right of central aedicula (ca. 19 B.C.). Rome, National Museum of the Terme, inv. 1187. Photo Alinari / Art Resource, New York.

ald male fantasy. In this reading the slave who looks directly out at the viewer fills the role of bringing the viewer in on the joke; he is even more explicitly gazing at the viewer than the onlooker figure of the boy on side A of the Warren cup. What is more, the artist of these two juxtaposed paintings also created a deliberate contrast between two kinds of lovemaking scene, similar to the two contrasting scenes of lovemaking on the Warren cup, the Ortiz flask, or even the Arretine vessels in chapter 3.

On the opposite wall—to the left of someone entering cubiculum D—only one erotic picture remains (Fig. 34). Although it is directly opposite the chastest of these paintings, it is as passionate as the painting just considered. The couple is about to kiss: this time the artist aligned both their gazes and their faces to leave no doubt. The woman raises her right arm over her head, in a variation of the gesture of erotic repose discussed in chapter 3. Her arms frame her own head while her fingers rest on the top of the man's head. Her face is in three-quarters' view, as is her body, clothed in a chiton that billows at her knees. The man, his face and torso in profile, is nude to the waist. He rests his fingers loosely on the woman's left arm above the elbow.

This, too, is a bedchamber full of busy servants. A small girl at the lower right bends deeply to loosen the woman's sandals. Behind the bed are two servants. A small boy dressed in a tunic is touching a vessel as he turns to an adult woman servant who carries a wine vessel while moving toward him. Like all the other servant figures—with the exception of the nude boy looking out at the viewer in the painting on the opposite wall—they busy themselves with their duties and ignore the lovemaking couple.

The two red-ground cubicula, B and D, mirror each other in architectonic structure, symmetry of picture placement, and differentiation of picture style. Cubiculum E reveals a different approach. The architect, realizing that this room had much less natural light than B and D, instructed the wall painter to create a white-ground room. The central pictures present effects of atmospheric perspective that fade into a foggy white, and the neo-Attic panel pictures of women are elegant, white-ground compositions. It is only in the two representations of pinakes, to right and left of the back wall of the alcove, that the artist used bold color effects. Only the pinax to the left has for its subject the couple on a bed. Its pendant, on the right, is a scene representing three women; scholars disagree on its meaning. Andreae, perhaps following Helbig, gives a narrative reading to the two pictures together: on the right a woman consults a female panderer; on the left she gets her wish—a male prostitute. At best, this interpretation rests on flimsy visual evidence; at worst, it reveals Victorian notions that prostitution must be at the root of any representation of a man and woman enjoying sex.[21]

Although the painting of two lovers is much damaged, in the simpler arrangement of the figures and in their greater size relative to the setting (Fig. 35) we see the hand of a painter distinct from the artists of cubicula B and D . The man and woman, both crowned in ivy, sit on the edge of a bed. The man wears a yellow tunic that is open to reveal his left leg and his right shoulder. He embraces the woman, whose blue mantle has dropped below her shoulders. The simple setting includes a table to the right with a bronze basin in front of it and a white drape covering most of the wall behind the bed.

By dispensing with the servants and enlarging the figures, the artist emphasized the couple's kiss. His much more modest talents, compared with the artistry of the

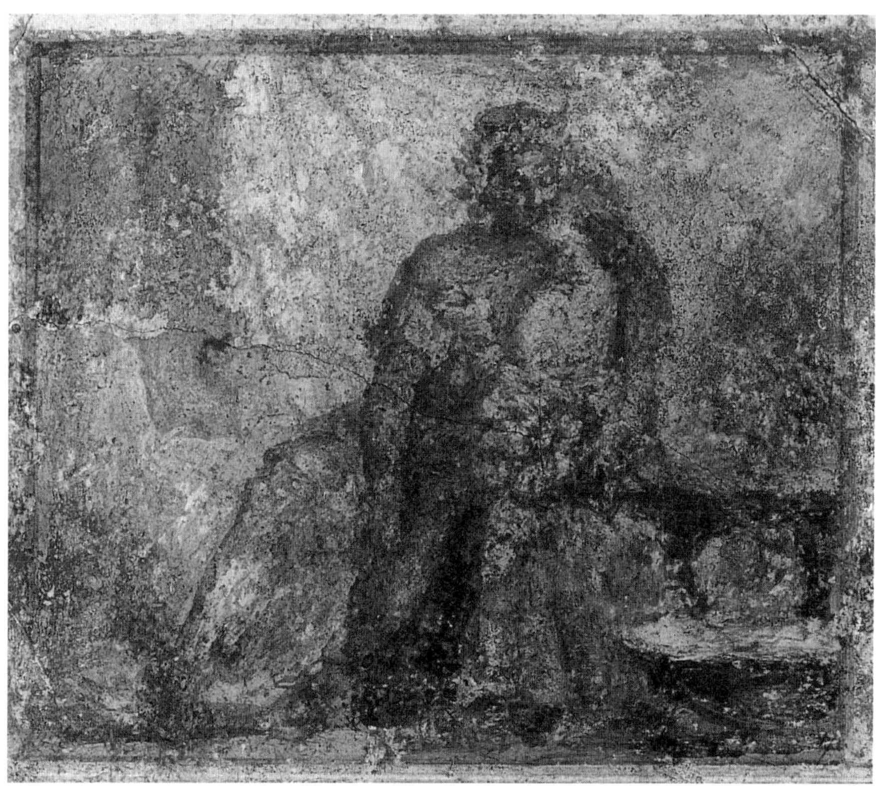

Figure 35. Male-female couple on bed, Rome, Villa under the Farnesina, cubiculum E, rear wall, attic zone, to left of central aedicula (ca. 19 B.C.). Rome, National Museum of the Terme, inv. 1174. Photo Deutsches Archäologisches Institut, Rome, inst. neg. 77–1322.

other two cubicula, may account for this simplification. As we will see, compositions that isolate the couple on the bed and minimize the background are common in the lovemaking reliefs on inexpensive Arretine vessels.

The Farnesina lovemaking paintings raise several important questions for the cultural construction of sexuality in the early Augustan period. Consideration of Ovid's *parva tabella* at least partially answers the most important question: why the patron would want erotic paintings represented in his or her bedchambers along with other nonsexual subjects. Such paintings belonged with the decoration of a stylish room. We are left with the question of the Roman viewer's relation to such pictures. Did the viewer see him- or herself in their scenarios? Or did the subject matter of the paintings belong in the world of art, not in that of the viewer's experience? Given their context, we must assume that these were not paintings meant to represent scenes from the viewer's life. They certainly were not illustrations of the sexual positions that Ovid discusses, for they are about the preliminaries to lovemaking, not about actual copulation. Given the emphasis on the *style* of representation in all the paintings in these rooms, content must be a secondary consideration. The erotic pictures stand out as much for their bold use of color and their illusionism as they do for their representation of sexual dalliance; they contrast strongly with the simple outlines of the archaizing panels and the pastel profiles of the pictures that imitate fifth-century white-ground lekythoi. Furthermore, it is hard to make a case for the subject matter being a commentary upon what went on in the bedchamber when mythological paintings or landscape paintings are the really large ones that take pride of place in the central aediculae. The very eclecticism of subject matter and style that characterizes the cubicula's decoration constitutes their primary meaning for the ancient Roman viewer, who would identify with the connoisseur of the treasures of Greek art in appreciating the enormous temporal and iconographic leaps between one picture and another. If there is a cultural construction of attitudes toward sex between men and women in the pictures, it is one of sophisticated appreciation—of their rich setting (signaled by the appointments of the chamber and the numerous servants) and of the unhurried pace of the couple's lovemaking. These are not images that "document" in any sense the acts of lovemaking that might take place in these rooms. Their role is decorative, not instructive or documentary.

Finally, what was the culture of the men who painted these pictures? On a column in cubiculum D is a graffito, *Seleukos epoiei* (Seleukos made this), causing Bianchi Bandinelli to attribute the work to an artist from Asia Minor.[22] Others consider it a product of artists from Asia Minor or Alexandria. Bragantini and de Vos point out that the Farnesina decorations take part in a repertoire of late Hellenistic painting that finds workshops of equally high levels in the area around Naples.[23] As our overview of Hellenistic pottery revealed, artists from centers around the entire eastern Mediterranean, including Athens, Pergamon, Ephesos, and Alexandria, had access to models in high art with representations of lovemaking. So too did the artists within the workshops who, in creating decorations in painting and stucco like those of the Farnesina, were able to revisit the entire history of Greek and Hellenistic art.

Male-to-Female Lovemaking in Mass-Produced Arretine Ware

If the refined paintings of the Farnesina give a full context for the uses of paintings of male-to-female in the picture galleries of the elite, the mass-produced Arretine ceramics of the Augustan and early Julio-Claudian period show how analogous images of lovemaking found their way to poorer consumers. We have already seen how one figural type within Arretine ceramic production put male-male and male-female copulation on an equal footing (see Figs. 24 and 25). The two, or possibly three variants on this type show the couple on a bed, the man tenderly embracing the boy while preparing to enter him. It was also clear that rather than an isolated phenomenon peculiar to Arretine ware alone, this representation embraced the high art models of much more expensive products like silver vessels and even super-expensive cut cameo glass. We must reconstruct a similar model for the male-to-female lovemaking representations on Arretine vessels.

Brendel emphasizes that the artists of the Arretine ceramics placed the lovemaking couples in settings that correspond to the symposium or banquet compositions in Greek red-figured painted vases; their fastidious formal design is an effort to recapture the Greek past through a romantic, neoclassicizing lens: "For once, a group of Roman artists tried to raise the social standing of erotic representations; and their way of accomplishing this was to recall the Greek paragons. In this somewhat esoteric undertaking the ease and naturalness of the prototypes went by the boards, to be replaced by a new and impeccable formal elegance."[24]

With the Farnesina paintings as a context (Brendel omits these from his brief discussion), it becomes clear that the Arretine representations of male-female lovemaking range from the elegant amorous dalliance of the Farnesina panels to the explicit insertion of the penis into the vagina (see Fig. 24). Their variety indicates that artists wished to present buyers with a choice—or that buyers demanded a choice of representations of male-female lovemaking.

From Amorous Dalliance to Sexual Penetration: Contrast or Continuum?

The scenes on the Arretine ware go far beyond the passionate gestures of the couples in the Farnesina paintings when they show actual intercourse. Arranging them in a hierarchy of increasing explicitness brings me to another important question: did the Roman buyer rank the images by degrees of explicitness? If I accept a late twentieth-century construction of sexual representation that differentiates between soft porn and hard-core porn, did the ancient viewer do so? Educated Romans certainly believed in different levels of verbal obscenity, as Richlin's discussion of Cicero's letter to Paetus makes clear.[25] Yet the Arretine ceramics were, first and foremost, decorated vessels that were mass-produced and in the hands of people, both women and men, of less than elite status. To divide up the Arretine representations in explicitness of sexual penetration is probably anachronistic. Rather than a contrast between suggestiveness and explicitness, I believe that the Roman viewer would see all these acts of lovemaking as part of a continuum. These were the blessings of Venus, the joys of sexual passion and release.

In purely artistic terms, however, arranging these images of sex allows us to examine the choices artists made in composing a scene and arranging the figures. What emerges—from our far from exhaustive treatment—is the artists' careful manipulation of stock figural groups to create variations in the emotional and physical relations of the couples. In this way they gave viewers variety in the illustration of sexual positions and in the range of emotional responses from the partners. Comparison of two bowl-fragments, formerly in the Warren collection and now in Boston, clarifies this point. In one (inv. Res. 08.33g, which I call "Warren g") the man reclines to the viewer's right, supporting himself on his heavily draped left forearm (Fig. 36). In the other ("Warren h") it is the woman who reclines, entirely nude and supporting herself with her left elbow and forearm resting on the bed's headboard (Fig. 37).[26] At first glance, we might imagine that the artist simply switched the figures' positions, having the woman sit on the man in one and having the man kneeling between the woman's parted legs in the other. But consideration of each figure's body language reveals expressions of different states of mind, and perhaps different emotions. The artist emphasized the relaxed pose of the re-

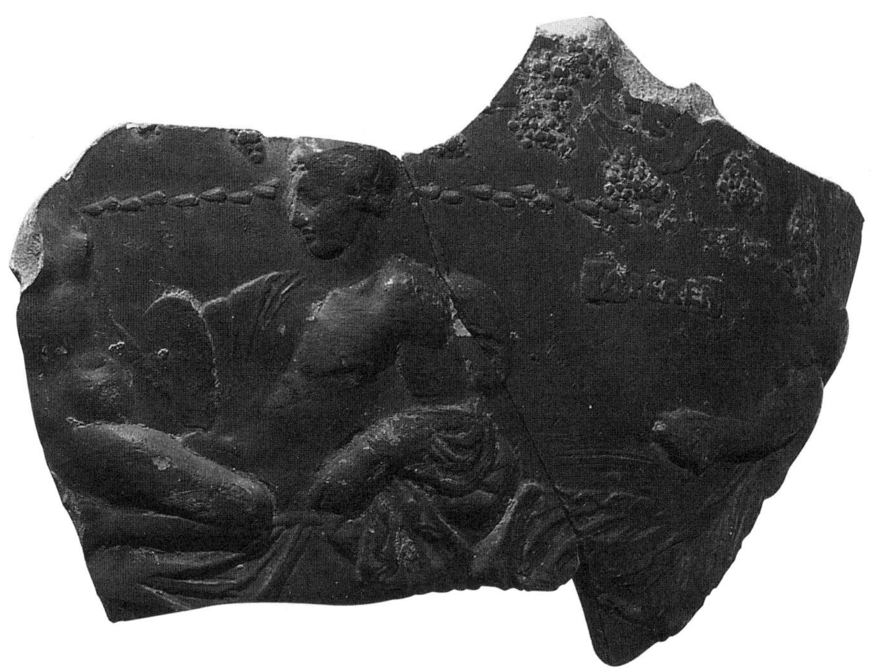

Figure 36. Male-female couple, Arretine bowl fragment, Warren g (30 B.C.–A.D. 30). Boston, Museum of Fine Arts, inv. Res. 08.33g. Gift of E. P. Warren. Courtesy, Museum of Fine Arts, Boston.

clining man in Warren g in much the same way as he expresses the woman's relaxation in Warren h. Yet in Warren g the artist represented the man's head in profile, so that he does not engage the woman's glance. His bodily repose and avoidance of the woman's gaze become signs of mental reverie and detachment, qualities that we noticed in the older male on side B of the Warren cup.

The reclining woman on Warren h, the other hand, wraps her left leg around her partner's knees while turning her torso in three quarters, so that while her upper body is in repose, her lower body actively seeks what is happening. The artist also created a dialogue between the reclining woman and the kneeling man in Warren h by emphasizing the twist of the man's torso—turned in nearly frontal view in contrast to his profile head. The man is directing his gaze at the beautiful woman's face even as he enters her. He seems about to speak. Another kind of balance between activity and repose appears in his hands: his right on his hip communicates the tension of his upright body and perhaps the act of entering the woman while

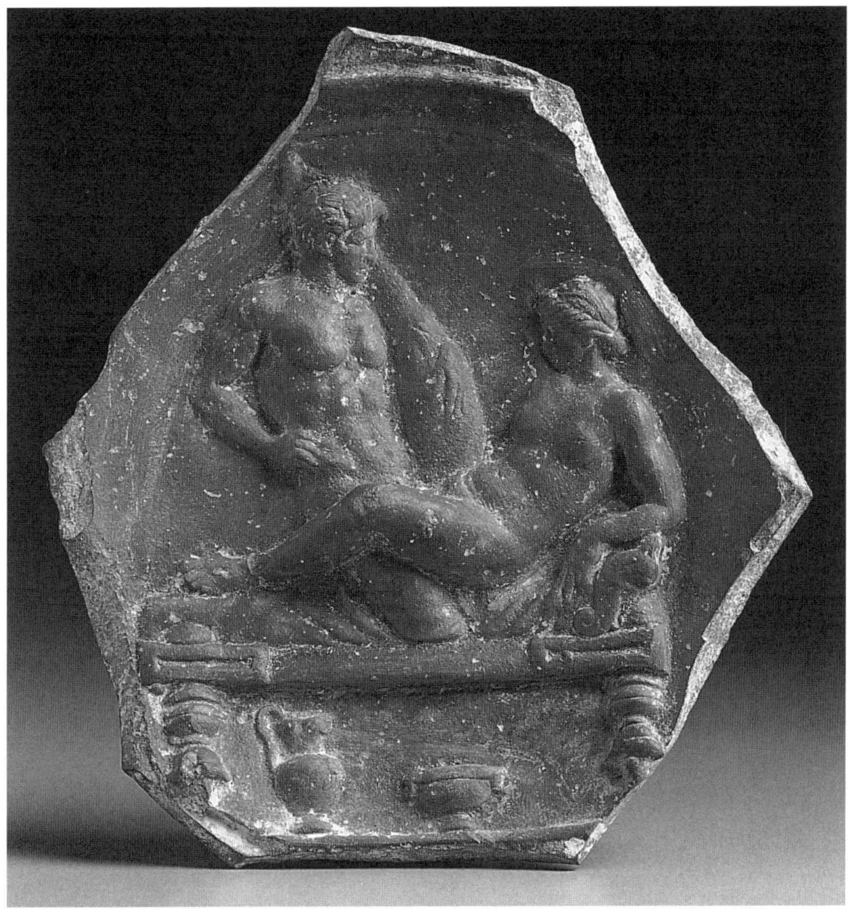

Figure 37. Male-female couple on bed, Arretine bowl fragment, Warren h (30 B.C.–A.D. 30). Boston, Museum of Fine Arts, inv. Res. 08.33h. Gift of E. P. Warren. Courtesy, Museum of Fine Arts, Boston.

his left drapes loosely on the woman's right thigh as she rests her raised leg on his left shoulder.

In Warren g the woman kneels very deeply, suggesting that the man has already inserted his penis in her vagina, and she leans backward perhaps playfully. Again it seems that counterbalancing both the physical positions and the emotional states of the couple is uppermost in the artist's mind. Both lean back, away from the point of genital contact, but he seems as distant from the sexual act as she seems to be engaged.

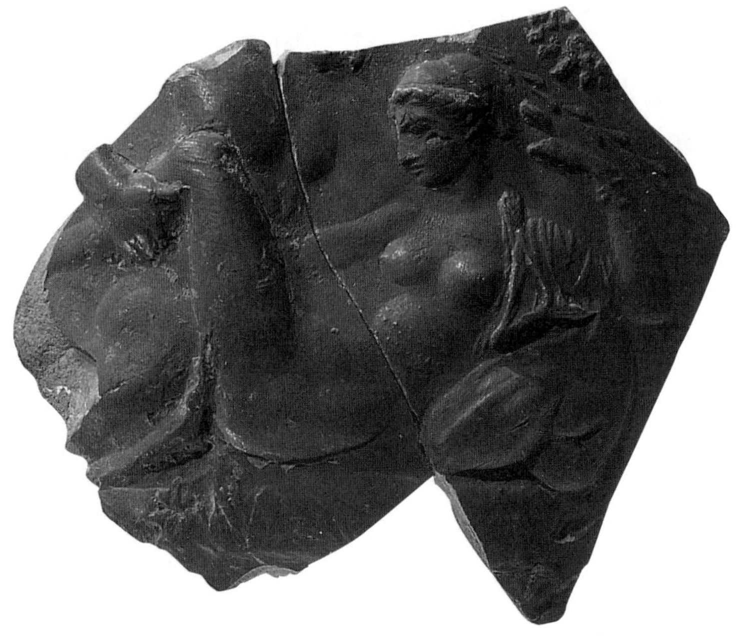

Figure 38. Male-female couple on bed, Arretine bowl fragment, Warren d[1] (30 B.C.–A.D. 30). Boston, Museum of Fine Arts, inv. Res. 08.33d. Gift of E. P. Warren. Courtesy, Museum of Fine Arts, Boston.

The artist's cunning use of variation within the very same composition is the foremost quality emerging from close comparison of two other fragments that originally decorated the same vase (Fig. 38, inv. Res. 08.33d, here "Warren d[1]" and Fig. 39, here "Warren d[2]"). In both the woman reclines to the viewer's right, raising her left leg sharply while the man presses into her from the right. His right leg extends out along the bed and his chest and head near the woman's. Once again, from this general scheme the artist built very different physical and psychological nuances. In Warren d[1] he turned the woman's head and breasts toward the viewer. Her left shoulder and upper arm are hidden in drapery while she limply raises her forearm and hand, bent at the wrist, from the cushions it rests on. Her right arm, in low relief, seems to reach for the man's penis. The man in Warren d[1] is farther from the act of penetration than the man in Warren d[2]; he is also physically farther from the woman, since he grasps her left shin as he nears her. By contrast, the man in Warren d[2] is much closer to the woman. He grasps her upper thigh just below

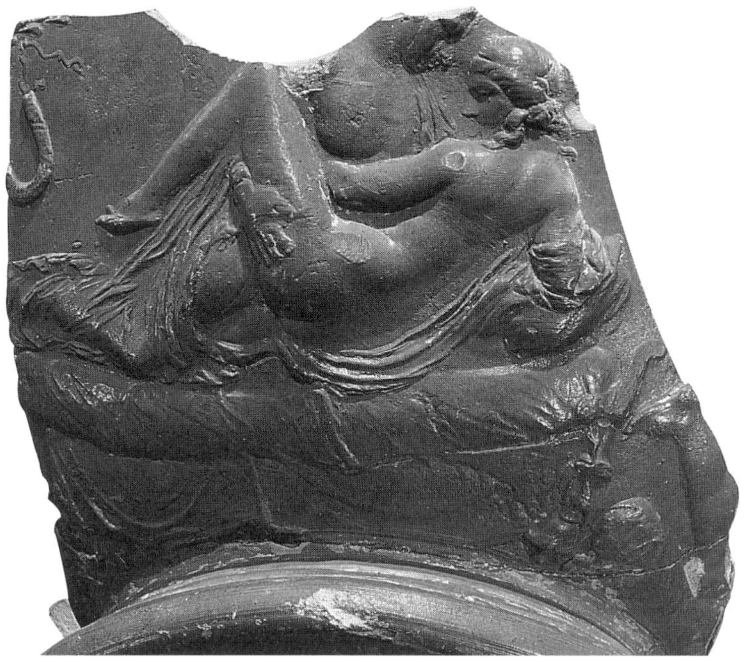

Figure 39. Male-female couple on bed, Arretine bowl fragment, Warren d[2] (30 B.C.–A.D. 30). Boston, Museum of Fine Arts, inv. Res. 08.33d. Gift of E. P. Warren. Courtesy, Museum of Fine Arts, Boston.

the buttocks. If the woman's pose in Warren d[1], head slightly inclined, hand dangling, suggests detachment, that of the woman in Warren d[2] suggests engagement. The artist turned her body so that the viewer sees her shoulders and back; she turns her head toward the man and lowers it slightly in what seems to be her aggressive grasp of the man's torso with her outstretched left arm. He, in turn, pushes into her, his head very close to hers. Her hair is in disarray, having fallen from its bun into massy locks upon her neck and shoulder.

Would the ancient Roman viewer find some sort of message in these two variations of pose? Seeing the two images as pendants, a viewer might notice the contrasts between the two couples, especially in the different levels of engagement in the two women. Or perhaps the viewer was meant to see a kind of narrative, to read a progression in the couple's contact. Both representations illustrate essentially the same position yet one seems to show the initial stages, the other deep engagement. Supporting both the pendant and the narrative readings of this vessel are the enormous differences between the gestures of the two women: one detached and the other engaged; one in self-absorbed reverie, the other focused on the sexual union.

Contrast this vessel to the Arretine bowl decorated with four scenes of lovemaking that we considered in relation to the Warren cup (in Figs. 24 and 25). The artist there juxtaposed two identically repeated scenes of a man copulating with a woman with two of a man penetrating a boy. Within the context of the present discussion of nuance in variation, this bowl has little further to offer, aside from the point—already noted—that the artist constructed the scene of boy-love by adding genitals and removing breasts from a representation of male-female intercourse. But it has much to say about our primary question, that is, whether the differences between the Arretine wares with images of amorous dalliance and those with outright penetration were important to the ancient Roman viewer. In relation to the other images of male-to-female lovemaking considered so far, this bowl emphasized the contrast between the man and the woman to the greatest possible extent. The woman, her weight on her toes, bends her knees deeply to position her vagina over the man's penis. She leans forward, twisting her back to her right to accommodate her right arm's reach down to the man's penis, erect between her legs. The man steadies her with his outstretched left hand on her back, but this effort does little to break his restful composure; the artist emphasized this by having the man languidly rest his right arm on a cushion while inclining his head slightly. If one could read emotional engagement in some of the scenes where the man and woman face each other, here the focus is on the woman's task of aiming the man's member—almost in spite of any effort on his part—into her vagina.

If there is a common thread in these representations of sexual coupling on the Arretine vessels, it is the balance of opposites. It is an equilibrium won through many different means, from the composition of individual bodies to the juxtaposition of scenes. In the few examples we consider the artist took care to counterbalance the tense limb with the languid one, torsion with uprightness, a dreaming countenance with an alert one. This visual balance informs the relation of the couples—one body to the other, one couple to another. He is relaxed, she strains; she holds back, he presses forward. Within the context of their place in the overall composition of each vessel, each pair of lovemakers counterbalances another. At times, as in two Boston fragments, the variations are slight and suggest successive moments in the lovemaking of a single couple. At other times, as in the alternating images of boy-man and man-woman, the balance is between different positions and the man's use of sexual partners of different sex.

These various aspects of balance account for the "almost dignified" air that Zanker finds in the Arretine representations. The ideal body types, Polykleitan for the men and Pheidian for the woman, carried the educated Roman viewer right back to the Parthenon frieze and canonical sculptural types of the 440s B.C. Seen in the context of the other subjects of Arretine vases, such as divinities, dancers, myths, and the hunt, the vessels with lovemaking belong to a real or imagined culture of Hellenistic luxury interpreted in Augustan neoclassical terms. Absent are the gladiatorial combats and caricatured figures that come to crowd the medallions of later terra-cotta vessels—the so-called *terra sigillata* produced in Gaul and Germany. The artists who made the Arretine vessels with scenes of lovemaking on them were looking to models in high art close to the Farnesina paintings; their products share with those paintings a construction of sexuality characterized by a fundamental unity of style and intent in all its variety—from dalliance to frank penetration: all stages belong within the same sphere of sexual pleasure.

The answer to our question—whether the different degrees of explicitness of the representations on Arretine ware corresponded to socially constructed boundaries or taboos about what was "permissible" and what was "taboo" in Augustan society—is that the visual evidence argues strongly for there being no significant difference for the ancient viewer. The vessels construct human lovemaking as a gift of the goddess of love. Venus brings carnal pleasure in love, and all stages of lovemaking are pleasurable. This essentially positive conception of all manner of lovemaking extended to elite society. If the male-female lovemaking paintings in the Farnesina show slightly more restraint than the imagery of the Arretine vessels, it is clear that they express a similar embrace of sexual pleasure. And the male-female scene on the Ortiz flask (Plate 3), considered in the previous chapter, not only forms a pendant to man-boy lovemaking, it also speaks for the tastes of the very wealthy.

One question, however, suggests another: who is the person receiving the pleasure? Can we identify these representations as strictly phallic constructions, a one-way experience for the insertive male—or are there indications that the object of that insertion, the penetrated woman or boy, also finds pleasure in looking at these scenes of lovemaking?

We have already reviewed what texts say. Written by male elites or men working for them, they celebrate the pleasures of phallic, penetrative sex, that is, of inserting the penis into the vagina or anus of the beautiful beloved.[27] We cannot argue for the equal status of the receptive partner in any of these acts as pictured in Arretine ware. The women in these scenes are dignified and perfectly coiffed, and the Roman viewer could see them as he or she wished. The Roman man could see in the women either a beautiful wife or servant; the Roman woman could read them in the same way. Most noteworthy, particularly if we compare the Arretine images with those of the late Hellenistic period, is that the Arretine stands out by its emphasis on signs of subjectivity in the penetrated partner.

An example from the same medium but dated to the late Hellenistic period helps clarify this difference. The terra-cotta fragment in Berlin (Fig. 40) presents a couple on a bed with vessels from the symposium beneath the bed (vessels like these also appear underneath the bed in Warren h; see Fig. 37). The couple's pose closely resembles that of the exterior of the mirror cover from Corinth, dated over three centuries earlier (see Fig. 2). The woman reclines on her side while parting her legs to reveal her vagina. The man presses energetically against her body while grasping her upper right thigh with his arm. She crooks her arm around his head to crush his face into hers. Probably the artist who carried out this terra-cotta lacked talent for nuance. Yet central to the image, even imagining a much more refined and skilled execution, is the representation of the woman as orifice to be opened, to be viewed, and to be penetrated by the strong male. The woman's surrender follows from this phallic model of male as penetrator—and also from the fact that the artist represented an advanced stage of the lovemaking process. How far this is from the counterpoised figures on the Arretine vessel, especially the woman's relaxed pose as she, too, raises her right leg high in the air. Would a Roman woman looking at the Arretine cup see her own subjectivity reflected there? Could she identify—not with the status of the prostitute but with her relaxed attitude—with the woman at the moment when the man *looks* at her?

What of the subjective experience of the penetrated boy as represented in Arretine vessels? Here we are on shakier ground for, as we saw, the penetrated male had to be of inferior status to the man who penetrated him. How do we understand the feelings of the penetrated male, if he was the ancient Roman looking at Arretine (or other) images of male-male lovemaking? Would he be a former slave,

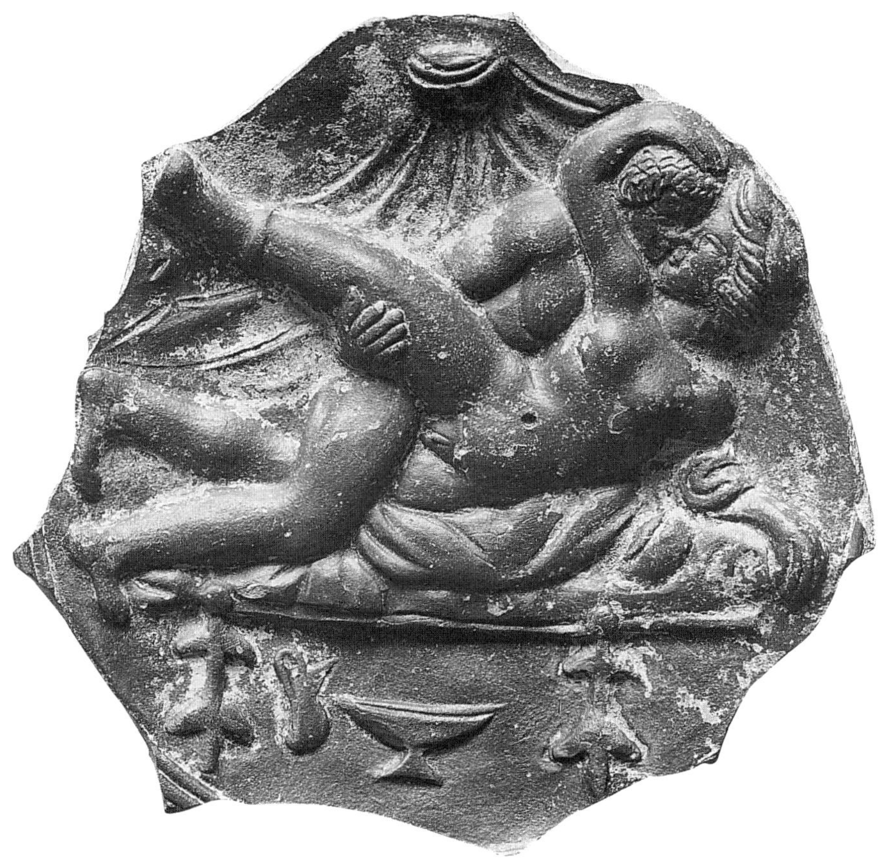

Figure 40. Male-female couple on bed, fragment of terra-cotta vessel (2d–1st c. b.c.). Berlin, Antikensammlung, inv. V.I. 4991. Photo courtesy Antikensammlung, Staatliche Museen zu Berlin, Preussischer Kulturbesitz.

now a freedman of some means, who could look back at himself as a boy performing a duty that was expected of him in no uncertain terms?[28] Or simply a freedman or a foreigner, that is, a man of any class but that of freeborn? The central aspect that makes the Arretine representations different from late Hellenistic ones is the tenderness of the male-male couple's contact. In the Berlin fragment of male-male lovemaking (see Fig. 7) as well as the Sardis mold (see Fig. 8), the key aspect is the man's domination of the boy: both his lunging body and the artist's efforts to display the object of the lunge—the boy's buttocks—emphasize the man's superiority and his aim to insert his penis in the boy's anus. In contrast, the Arretine scene of male-male lovemaking emphasizes not the boy's buttocks and the man's assault on his anus but the kiss—and it seems the boy's tender willingness to make love in this manner (see Fig. 27). Although we could attribute this condition to the adaptation of an existing male-female type, the artist had a choice that would include the less romantic representations of the late Hellenistic period. If these Augustan-period images spoke to a man who liked to be penetrated or had been penetrated as a boy—and there would be many such viewers—it is clear that they underscored the romantic and pleasurable aspects of that union. The fact that it is possible to project the same positive quality of subjective experience for the penetrated males on the Warren cup and on the Ortiz flasks argues for a deliberate change in the representation of such acts in the Augustan period.

Artists in the Roman world rarely invented a new representation without stimulus from the patrons who paid them. It follows that the depiction of varying, but always tender, physical and emotional relations in the Arretine vessels must be an artistic response to new social attitudes toward sex on the part of some Romans. The audience for these new artistic representations of sexuality belonged to a variety of classes and included both men and women. Whether, when looking at such images, they saw themselves or some aspect of their sexual fantasies is a moot point. One thing is certain: looking at new images of lovemaking brought them pleasure.

CHAPTER 5

Sex and the Body of the Other

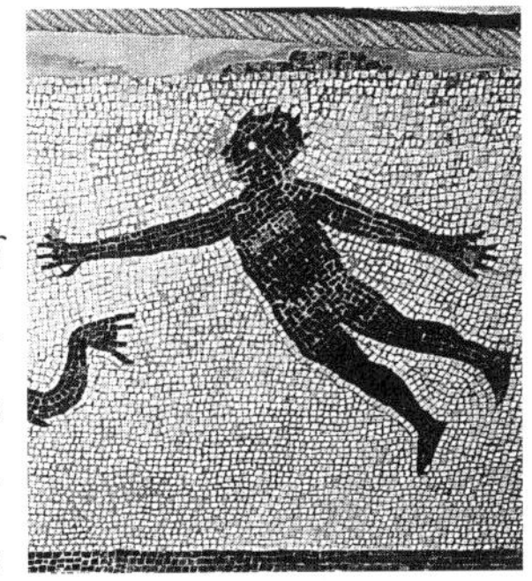

So far our investigation of the construction of sex in the art of the Augustan period has focused on representations of somatotypes that were ideal in the minds of art-buying Romans of the time. Yet our brief review of Hellenistic art emphasized the fascination of artists and patrons with people who did not fit the preferred body type. Of particular interest to this study is the fact that Hellenistic artists tended to portray the racial and ethnic people known as pygmies in caricatural images that had them performing outrageous sexual acts as part of their life on the Nile (see Fig. 10). As we would expect, artists continued to employ these Nilotic scenes with lovemaking pygmies in wall decorations and other art of the Augustan period; in fact, these representations live on—more or less unaltered—well into the third century. However, their very stability throughout the period in question indicates that they have little to tell us about new constructions of sexuality that arose in the Augustan, Flavian, and Antonine periods. It is a quite different case with another category of the Other. Whereas the pygmy belongs to the realm of caricature and appears as light- or dark-skinned, artists created a type of African with reference to a specific geographical location and race. This is the representation of the black African from Ethiopia.

Hypersexual Blacks in Mosaics of the Augustan Period

In three houses of the Augustan period at Pompeii appear mosaic images of black men that might appear highly sexual to some modern viewers.[1] These large houses belonged to individuals of some wealth; as patrons they were deeply engaged with earlier Hellenistic Greek culture and most likely understood the models and sources that the artists working for them used. Why, then, did these artists choose to represent black Africans with huge penises or prominent erections? Outside Pompeii, but in mosaics of about the same period, black women also appear, with exaggerated breasts and hips. Were these features meant to arouse the viewer in a sexual way? The two figural motifs that feature these black Africans are the bath attendant and paired swimmers; both motifs present the black person—not engaging in sexual intercourse—but as hypersexual. By "hypersexual" I mean that artists depicted the black men either with unusually large penises (macrophallic) or with enormous erections (ithyphallic); they represented the black women with large breasts (macromastic) and prominent hips (steatopygic). As we saw in chapter 2, artists also gave the more or less mythical pygmies these same physical characteristics.

Because the houses at Pompeii where these two motifs occur emerged from careful modern excavations, we can reconstruct the ancient contexts that might hold the key to their meanings. The motifs appear in the mosaic floors of small, private baths in the House of the Cryptoporticus (I, 6, 2–4), the House of the Menander (I, 10, 4), and the House of Caesius Blandus (VII, 1, 40; see map, p. 146). Associated wall painting dates all these pavements to the period of the late Second Style (40–20 B.C.).[2] There are indications that these houses belonged to the local elite: they are among the small group of exceptionally large houses at Pompeii.[3] Epigraphical evidence suggests that the owners of two of the houses belonged to noble families.[4]

At least one motif—that of the heraldic swimmers—spread throughout the Roman world through some sort of sketchbook tradition, since close parallels occur in two other bath contexts of the first century of our era: one at Este, in northern Italy, and the other at Cirta, in modern Algeria. The motif of the bath attendant is also widely diffused, although the preserved evidence skips the first century of our era: he appears—still macrophallic—in second-century mosaics at Ostia and in many North African mosaics of the third century.

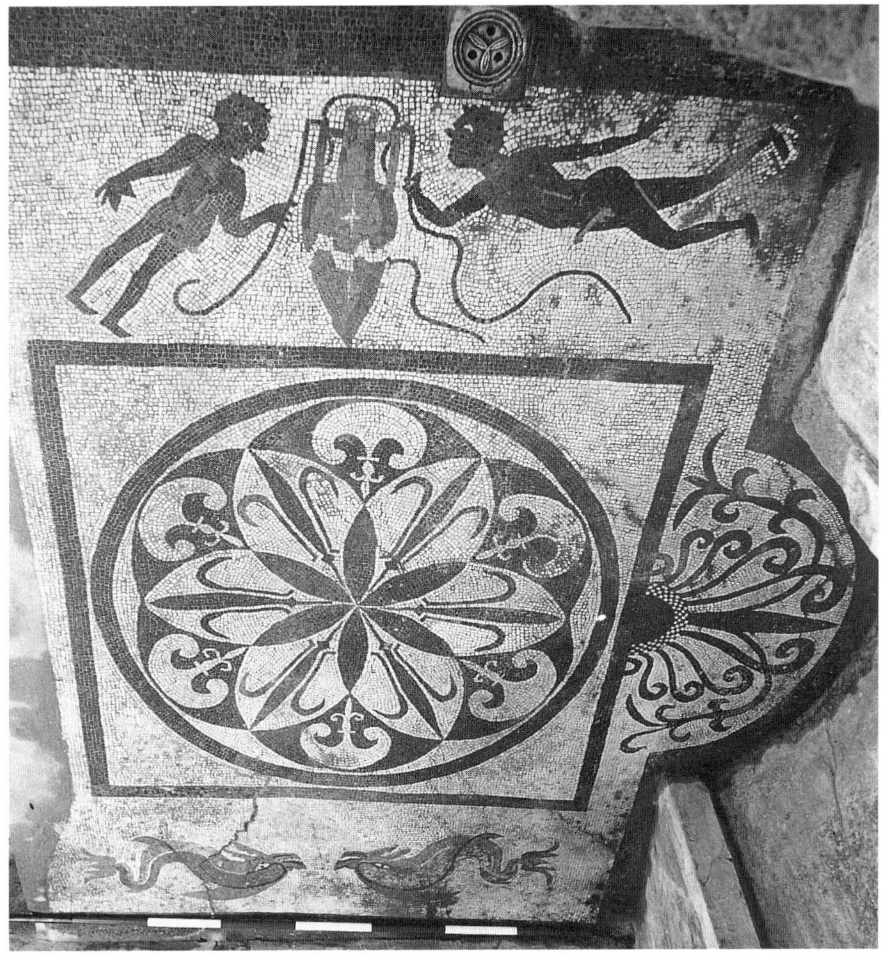

Figure 41. Ithyphallic black swimmers flanking broken amphora, Pompeii, House of the Cryptoporticus (I, 6, 2), mosaic pavement of *sudatio* (40–20 B.C.). Photo Michael Larvey.

In the three houses at Pompeii, all the images are of hypersexual black men, and seven of the eight images depict swimmers with huge erections. At the House of the Cryptoporticus, in the little heated room isolated from the rest of the bath in the southwest corner of the cryptoporticus, two such figures swim toward a broken amphora (Fig. 41), while heraldic dolphins swim on the opposite side of the central rosette. A similar composition appears twice, again on either side of a central decorative rosette; here the mosaic adorns the circulation space of the *caldarium* (hot room) in a two-room private bath in the House of Caesius Blandus. Each swimmer pair flanks representations of bathing equipment, the men facing outward with their backs to each other and to the object between them (Fig. 42). On one side this object (today partly destroyed: note the large lacuna) is a ring with two strigils (or scrapers) and an ointment jar hanging from it;[5] on the other, a round-bodied water pitcher.[6]

Two contiguous mosaic compositions in the elaborate three-room bath complex of the House of the Menander present interesting variations on the theme of the ithyphallic black man. One is a single swimmer—identical in figure outline, position, and size to the right-hand swimmer in House of the Cryptoporticus mosaic—that occupies the northwest corner of the complicated caldarium mosaic (Fig. 43).[7] In the opposite corner of that central picture another black African man appears, this time a fisherman who spears a mythical sea-dragon familiar in the repertoire of Hellenistic and early imperial art.[8] Since he is neither ithyphallic nor macrophallic (in fact, the mosaicist did not represent his penis), I postpone discussion of his contribution to the iconography of the whole mosaic.

In addition to swimming figures, the mosaics of Pompeii offer the image of the black macrophallic man. He occupies the entryway to the caldarium in the House of the Menander (Fig. 44). The composition of heraldic strigils framing an ointment jar on a chain—similar to that of the House of Caesius Blandus—fills the outer side of the entryway composition, so that it was the first image the visitor saw as he or she passed from the dressing room (*apodyterium*) to the caldarium. The macrophallic man's iconography separates him from the swimmers because the water vessels that he carries identify him as a bath servant; he wears a kind of short kilt that rides above his enormous penis. A laurel wreath crowns his head.

Confusion clouds the explanation of these images of black men. Maiuri, who excavated the House of the Menander, incorrectly characterized all three figures as pygmies,[9] an identification repeated by Spinazzola for the swimmers in the House of the Cryptoporticus.[10] Modern authors differ about the number of physical types of Africans depicted as black in Roman art,[11] but the pygmy is not difficult to distinguish from the *Aethiops,* the Ethiopian.[12] Following the Hellenistic models discussed above, Roman artists depicted pygmies as short, with exaggeratedly large heads; their skin color can be pale white or black; and the males appear with huge penises. In contrast, the Ethiopian is the adult black African, of normal height and

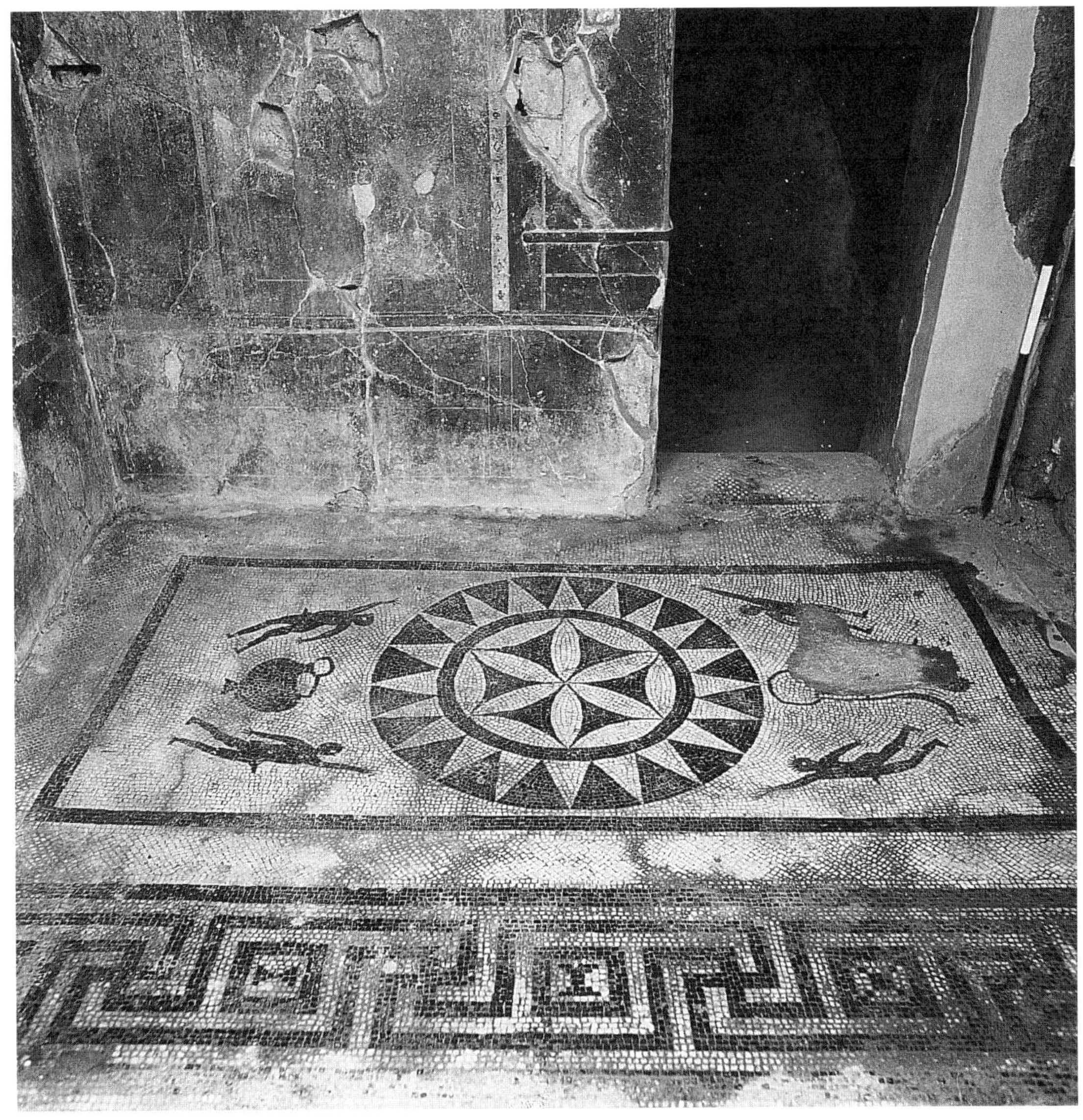

Figure 42. Four ithyphallic black swimmers, Pompeii, House of Caesius Blandus (VII, 1, 40), mosaic pavement of antechamber to caldarium 16 (40–20 B.C.). Photo Michael Larvey.

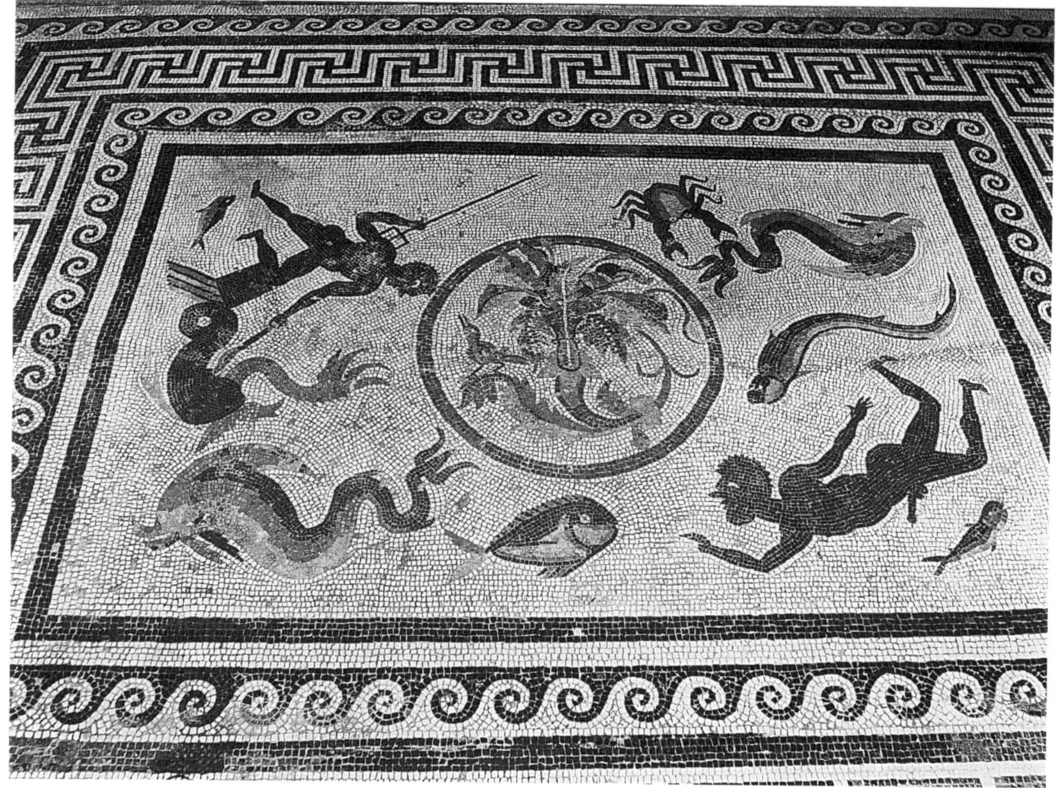

Figure 43. Black swimmer, black fisherman, sea fauna, and acanthus roundel, Pompeii, House of the Menander (I, 10, 4), mosaic pavement of caldarium (40–20 B.C.). Photo Michael Larvey.

usually beautifully proportioned in comparison with the pygmy. Ancient Roman imagery representing the Other of African origin covered a broad spectrum, from finely wrought sculptures of the often exotically beautiful Ethiopian to burlesque paintings of pygmies; Greek and Roman artists were concerned to depict their physical differences quite accurately.[13]

Since mosaicists working in the black-and-white medium, popular from the first through the third centuries A.D., used the silhouette convention for all figures, including humans, it seems reasonable to ask whether the figures in these Pompeian baths are black-figure depictions of whites, similar, for example, to the conventions of Greek archaic black-figure vase painting.[14] However, one consistent detail shows that artists meant to present Africans: they set the mosaic cubes (tesserae) to make

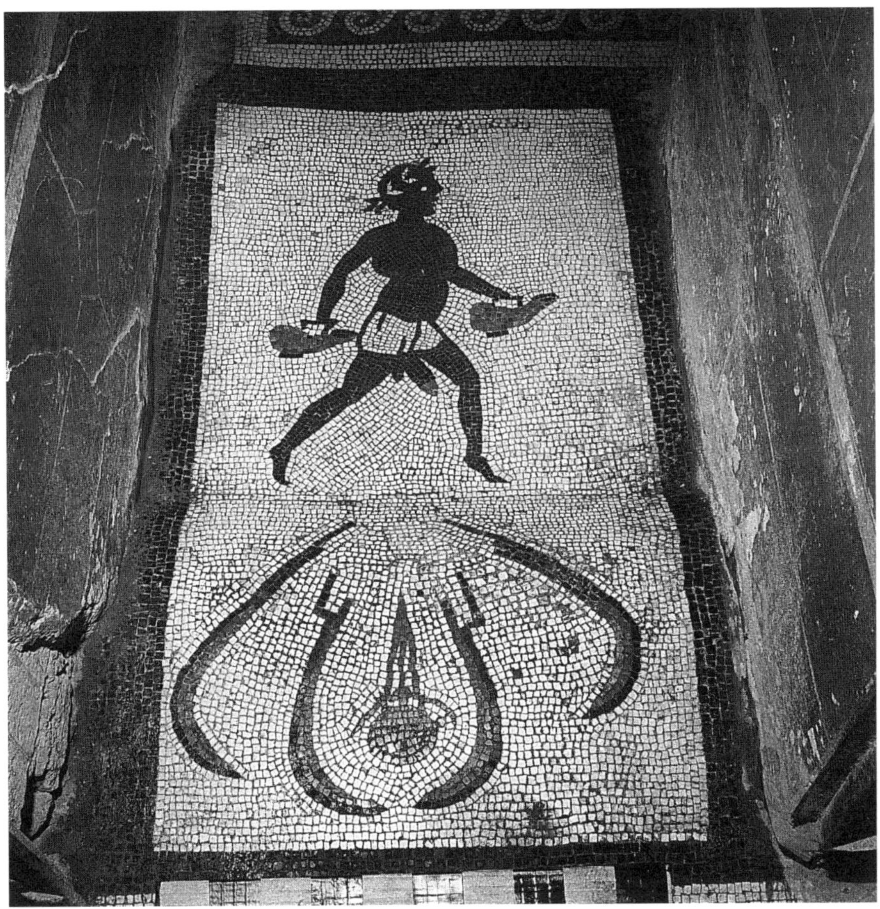

Figure 44. Black bath attendant, Pompeii, House of the Menander (I, 10, 4), mosaic paving entryway to caldarium (40–20 B.C.). Photo Michael Larvey.

a sawtooth silhouette for hair and thus indicate that it is tightly curled.[15] In later polychrome mosaics this detail would be plainer, as in the mosaic of a bath attendant from Timgad, dating to around A.D. 200, where the mosaicist delineated not only tightly curled hair but used a mixture of dark brown and black, rather than exclusively black, tesserae to denote skin color (Fig. 45).[16]

The artists' concern to distinguish the black male Ethiopian from pygmies or from black-figure representations of white men invites further speculation about their meaning, for deeply embedded in Roman aesthetic consciousness, and expressed frequently in the literature, is the notion of an ideal body type and of the

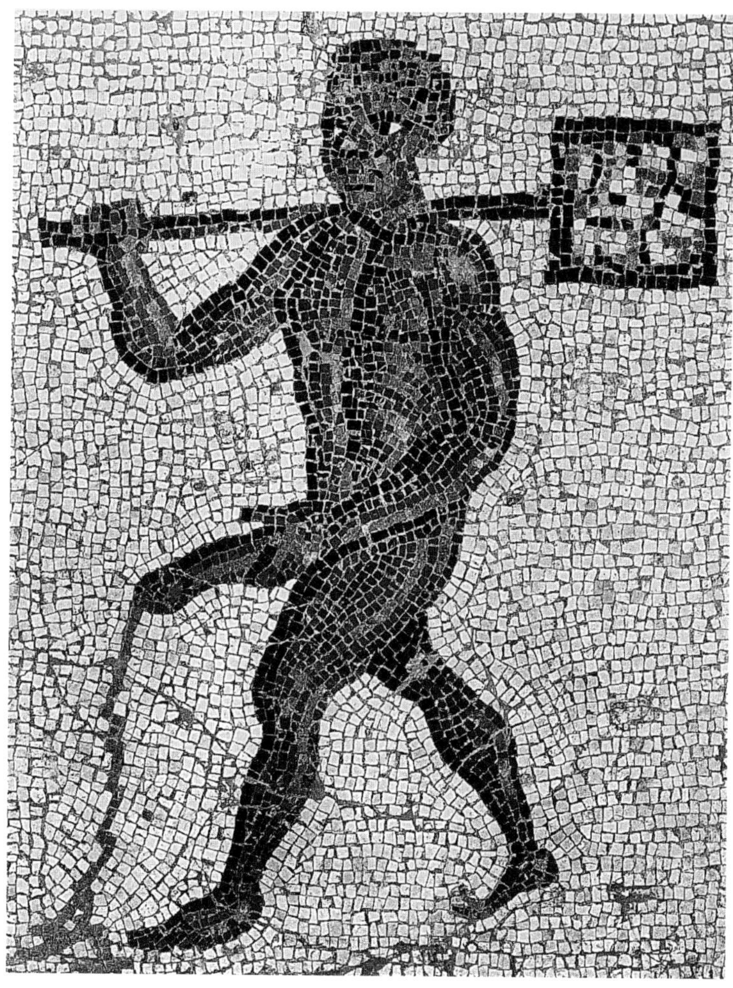

Figure 45. Black man with fire shovel, Timgad, Northwest Baths, mosaic pavement (ca. A.D. 200). Timgad, Archaeological Museum, W. 70 × H. 80 cm. Photo courtesy Menil Foundation, Houston/Mario Carrieri, Milan.

ethnic variants from that ideal. We have already considered the question of ideal somatotypes in the Hellenistic period and their relevance for artistic representation. Thompson, in his recent work on Roman attitudes toward the Ethiopian, also uses the term somatotype in his discussion of the literary representation of the Ethiopian, pygmy, and other body types that were nonideal for the Romans. He convincingly argues that late twentieth-century conceptions of the black person diverge greatly from those of ancient Romans. Central to his argument is the observation that our notions of "racism" and "prejudice" toward the black African stem from Euro-Americans' recent history of black slavery linked with imperialism. Greek and Roman slaves were predominantly nonblack. Modern authors looking at the ancient literature confuse Roman ethnocentrism with racism. Ethiopian means "burned, or sun-darkened, face," a usage that the Romans inherited from the Greeks;[17] it was the black African's *visual* appearance rather than his social status that made him the object of what might best be called an "aesthetic prejudice"—or more simply an aesthetic preference. The Romans put no legal constraints on blacks solely on the basis of their skin color; there are no Greek or Roman scientific treatises on race as an immutable category. Roman society apparently acknowledged the somatic differences of Ethiopians without using the racist social structures familiar to modern Euro-American culture.

In the Farnesina paintings we saw evidence for ideal somatic types of the Augustan period. A man appears with tanned skin, wavy brown hair, and brown eyes. A woman is fair, indicated by the use of pinkish-white pigment for the skin and reddish brown for her slightly wavy hair. Augustan neoclassicism valued Polycleitan—or more generally, fifth-century—proportions for the man. For the depiction of a woman artists also borrowed from classical statuary, taking as their model the young female type found on the Panathenaic frieze on the Parthenon and on fifth-century grave stelae. The tall woman with willowy proportions and tiny head that characterizes the late Hellenistic period disappears in the Augustan period.

The black skin, tightly curled hair, flat or broad nose, and thick lips of the Ethiopian distance him from this Italian-Mediterranean ideal somatotype, but no more than would the pale whiteness, red or blonde hair, and blue eyes of the Celtic and Nordic types. Other physical characteristics, such as pronounced buttocks in a man or woman, or large breasts in a woman, enter into the artistic construction of the Ethiopian. The Romans, like the Greeks, viewed both the Ethiopian and the Celtic–Germanic European with equal disfavor in the sense that they remained outside their ethnocentric canon of artistic beauty.[18] Roman satirists like Juvenal and Martial could mock any of these divergences, whether of the Ethiopian, the Egyptian, the Syrian, or the German, indiscriminately.[19]

From this very Roman point of view, the representations of the Ethiopian in these three Pompeian baths are stylish images of a group they considered exotic.

But are they also erotic? Considerable visual and textual evidence demonstrates that the Romans attributed extreme sexual proclivities and/or exaggeratedly large genitals to a large group of comic types, including white slaves, low-life types, dwarfs, pygmies, and the Ethiopian.[20] Within this general comic mode appear two black-skinned types—the more-or-less fictitious pygmy and the real-world Ethiopian. We see all these types—those with black, those with white skin—in painting, mosaic, and sculpture of the Augustan period, when artists followed late Hellenistic fashions even while fashioning neo-Attic conventions. There is especially abundant visual evidence for the continuation in the Augustan period of the Hellenistic predilection for pygmies, who act out a variety of comic scripts: fighting cranes or crocodiles or each other, or performing outrageous sexual antics on the Nile.[21] Often the pygmies (both men and women) appear with pink, rather than black, skin. Sexual representations featuring pygmies include sexual couplings, both male-male and male-female, in open-air settings or on boats. The male pygmies invariably are macrophallic and often sport erections.[22]

Could it be that the representations of the pygmies' sexual antics in so-called Nilotic landscapes carried over to the Ethiopian, a case of fiction informing, or adding to, the stereotype of the Ethiopian's potential hypersexuality? The literary evidence is inconclusive, offering no relation between the hypersexuality of pygmies and that of the Ethiopian. On the one hand, Thompson notes that the stereotype of the hypersexual black African had considerable currency among Romans of all social classes, adding that "the fact that the macrophallic black is a traditional theme in Roman iconography also underscores the image of black sexuality which attributed to blacks . . . the possession of a sinister fascination for nonblacks of the opposite sex (and in some cases, even of the same sex)."[23] On the other hand, Greek and Roman literature also holds the opposite stereotype, that of the virtuous, pure, and noble Ethiopian. Philostratus, for example, writing in about A.D. 200, admires the learning of Memnon, the protégé of Herodes Atticus.[24]

The visual evidence also indicates that artists conceived of the Ethiopian (of either sex) in terms quite different from those reserved for the fictional pygmy. In contrast to the more-or-less constant caricatural representations of the pygmy, they produced a range of imagery for the Ethiopian that included both the beautiful and the grotesque. The hypothesis that artists sometimes represented him as hypersexual because they associated him with the pygmy does not explain why hypersexuality is not a constant trait of the Ethiopian, as it is of the pygmy. Under what circumstances do artists make the Ethiopian hypersexual? Fortunately, it is possible to answer this question—at least in part—by considering the mosaics of this hypersexual figure that are still in their original architectural contexts, positioned prominently in private baths of Augustan-period houses at Pompeii.

The Bath Attendant

Consideration of the macrophallic bath attendant's context—both his specific appearance in an aristocratic house and more generally his association with a bath complex—explains his seemingly erotic qualities in terms quite unfamiliar to the late twentieth century (see Fig. 44). The fact that he appears in the House of the Menander, one of Pompeii's grandest, suggests that the owner(s) found nothing indecorous in his representation.[25] The owner who enlarged the house between about 40 and 20 B.C., when the mosaic was executed, added an enormous peristyle to the existing atrium house.[26] Rooms along the peristyle announce his elite self-image: the reading alcove with an image of the playwright Menander; a room of the Muses; and the largest dining room to be found at Pompeii. And there is a bath, with its own little atrium flanked by a dressing room, with a narrow passage leading from the dressing room to the hot room. The bath attendant graces the narrow entryway to the caldarium. He marches along briskly to the right, in the direction the bather will take after stepping on him or over him to enter the caldarium proper.

It is difficult for us to understand the full significance of baths in Roman life. Recent studies begin to emphasize the enormous extent of their social and cultural dimensions.[27] Five centuries of Greek tradition informed the Romans' conception of bathing, and the Romans extended and refined that tradition to create architecturally daring and magnificently decorated buildings as emblems of the civilizing values of *Romanitas* throughout the Mediterranean. The public baths of Republican and imperial Pompeii and Rome constituted the locus of a daily ritual of exercise, washing, and entertainment, open to all classes. Several aristocratic houses and villas at Pompeii and elsewhere had private baths. To engage in the bathing ritual meant to be Roman.

Study of the texts concerning bathing, including inscriptions found in bath mosaics themselves, reveals that both Greeks and Romans clung to beliefs that made it necessary to take special precautions in the baths.[28] There were of course the very real dangers of falling, drowning, being burned by hot pavements and walls, or even suffocating in overheated rooms. But even more compelling in the minds of Greek and Roman bathers were the dangers of *phthonos* or *invidia,* best defined as grudging envy that directs ill will against another person who possesses beauty or good fortune.[29] Ancient writers suggest that the envious person could cause illness, physical harm, and even death by focusing his or her eye on the person he or she envied. Although there were many theories on just how such harm could come to a person without physical contact, most believed that the owner of an Evil Eye was able to focus this grudging malice through her or his eye: it emanated particles that surrounded and entered the unfortunate victim.[30]

The bath, as locus of the pleasurable recreation of all Greco-Roman society for over a thousand years of history, was bound to accrue considerable lore about the dark forces that lurked there, not only the workings of the Evil Eye against the beauty of the individuals who bathed and promenaded there, but *invidia* directed against the beauty of the baths themselves. Both the numerous inscriptions and texts, thoroughly reviewed by Katherine Dunbabin,[31] suggest that people feared that demons inhabited the baths, that magical rites took place there, and imagined other terrors. How to guard against these dangers?

Individuals took the precaution of wearing apotropaic amulets, and mosaic artists often created apotropaic images at particularly dangerous spots.[32] The doorway—whether to a house or a potentially dangerous space in the bath—often required apotropaic images in the pavement that would ward away the Evil Eye of the envious individual as well as the collective potential harm of demons that might inhabit the space.[33]

Dunbabin opens the possibility that some mosaic representations of bath attendants might be intended to ward off the Evil Eye. As part of this project, she lists five images of bath servants found in Africa that may have an apotropaic function; four of them are black and macrophallic.[34] Her list takes in the images of bath attendants found in Roman Italy and discussed in greater detail here.[35] Although most of these bath servants have the physical characteristics of the Ethiopian, there are also a few with white Mediterranean somatotypes. Was the Ethiopian more efficacious against the Evil Eye than the white, and if so, why?

To the ancient Roman an Ethiopian would appear more effective against the

Evil Eye than the white because his un-Roman body type caused laughter—all the more so when he had an enormous phallus. Levi points out that in antiquity people believed that *atopía* or "unbecomingness" dispelled the Evil Eye: "Beings with a funny appearance or in which some obscene details are accentuated are good *apotropaia,* as well as normal beings represented in indecent attitudes, making vulgar gestures or noises. . . . Laughter is the opposite pole of the anguish produced by the dark forces of evil; where there is laughter, it scatters the shades and the phantasms."[36] Levi, and more recently Barton,[37] explains that the deformities of dwarfs, pygmies, and hunchbacks make them powerful charms against the Evil Eye. Central to their "unbecomingness" is the grossly exaggerated phallus. In fact, whether attached to the hunchback, the pygmy, or the Ethiopian, whether presented in isolation or in combination with other symbols, the phallus is the most ubiquitous apotropaic image in ancient Roman floor mosaics.[38]

Seen from this point of view, the bath attendant in the House of the Menander is a kind of aestheticized apotropaic image, loaded with meaning for the ancient Roman. This image has various levels of significance, including that of an anecdotal genre figure, representative of real-life Ethiopian bath servants the viewer might see. The visual evidence suggests that Ethiopians found employment in a number of domestic roles, including those of groom, cook, and bath attendants; but artists also depicted them as jockeys, circus performers, and musicians.[39] Beardsley, on the basis of visual and literary evidence, concludes that the bath slave was frequently an Ethiopian.[40]

At a less obvious level of meaning, the bath attendant's black (sunburned) skin symbolizes the dangers of the heat of the caldarium, reminding the viewer to put on sandals or other protection. There is ample evidence that many Romans believed that the Ethiopian was black because his entire people had been burned by the sun.[41] A different type of bath servant, the furnace stoker or *furnacator,* appears carrying the fire shovel, another obvious reference to the heat of the bath. Although there are no representations of this genre character exactly contemporaneous with the bath attendant in the House of the Menander, he appears at Pompeii in a mosaic from the Praedia of Iulia Felix (II, 4, 6–7), where the mosaicist portrayed the *furnacator* in the black-and-white technique (Fig. 46). De Vos has recently shown that this figure, dated to A.D. 62–79, came from the private bath of the Praedia, most likely from the caldarium, where the reference to heat is clear.[42] Because this

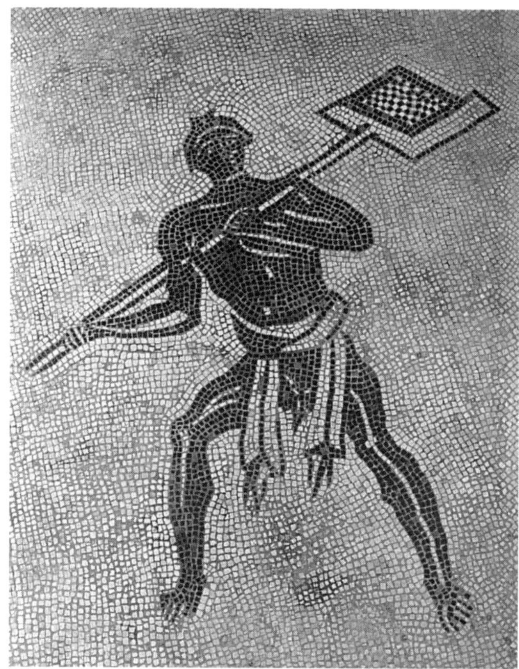

Figure 46. Black man with fire shovel, Pompeii, Praedia of Iulia Felix (II, 4, 6–7), mosaic from bath (A.D. 62–79). Naples, National Archeological Museum, room 132, figure: W. 79 × H. 93 cm; framed field: W. 87 × H. 104 cm. Photo Michael Larvey.

individual wears a turban, it is impossible to tell whether he is an Ethiopian, whereas the mosaicist took great pains to emphasize the curly hair of the early third-century African from Timgad introduced earlier (see Fig. 45). Located on the threshold between two heated rooms, this *furnacator* also carries a fire shovel. A tool that was both practical and symbolic, the fire shovel's primary symbolism is that of fire, here warning the viewer of the heat of the bath.[43]

Mosaicists used other images to carry the same warning about the heat of the baths; an analogous representation is that of a pair of sandals. At Pompeii they appear on the threshold to the caldarium of the private bath in the Villa of Diomedes, dating to the same period as the mosaic of the bath attendant from the House of the Menander.[44] This image, like that of the *furnacator,* has a long subsequent history. Around the beginning of the third century heat-warning sandals appear, for instance, at the entryway to a caldarium in the baths attached to the Grande Maison au Nord du Capitole at Timgad.[45]

Further levels of meaning, even more obscure to the modern viewer, concern the image of the bath servant as an *apotropaion.* His position outside the somatic norms of the ancient Romans makes him a curiosity, like the hunchback; he is a kind of being who represents an extreme that could elicit laughter and so counteract the workings of the Evil Eye. Corollary to the Ethiopian's somatic difference is the fact that his skin is black, a color that could have strong negative associations in Roman antiquity, adding another dimension of apotropaic power to the bath servant's representation.[46] Especially telling in this connection is the ill-omened Ethiopian who met Brutus' standard-bearer before Philippi and the Ethiopian who frightened Septimius Severus before his death.[47]

The most obvious apotropaic aspect of the image to the ancient Roman, and the one most easily lost on the twentieth-century viewer, is his hefty phallus. Representations of the phallus, whether in floor mosaics, stone or terra-cotta reliefs, or freestanding sculptures abound in and on the buildings and streets of Pompeii and other ancient Roman cities. From an early period the ancient Romans were also familiar with boundary stones, or *termini,* in the shape of the phallus. All these phallic representations were apotropaic in one way or another, serving the specific needs of the place that they guarded.[48] The mosaicist who designed the depiction of the bath servant in the House of the Menander was appealing to this understanding of the apotropaic phallus when he isolated the penis, making it unusually large and comically detailed (see Fig. 44). It immodestly hangs, perhaps partially engorged, below the kilt that cannot conceal it. The artist comically framed it between the Ethiopian's spindly legs and emphasized it by using purple tesserae to detail the exposed *glans penis.*

It is possible that the artist created another reference to the apotropaic phallus, this time within a vagina, in the arrangement of heraldic strigils on either side of the ointment jar on a string that immediately precedes the image of the bath attendant. In a visual pun, the ointment jar becomes the phallus, and the strigils the labia of the vagina. A striking parallel for this representation comes from Sousse in Tunisia, where two pubic triangles representing vaginas flank a fish-shaped phallus.[49]

There is a parallel for the comic treatment of the Ethiopian figure itself in the skillfully rendered image of the *furnacator* from the Praedia of Iulia Felix. Both his costume and pose recall the bath attendant from the House of the Menander: the two ends of the long sash that girds his waist fall in front of either thigh to frame and emphasize his genitals, and he strikes a spirited pose, legs apart, arms heaving the shovel upward. The artist who created the bath attendant from Timgad emphasized the figure's huge penis by representing him in the act of urinating even as he strides from right to left.[50] His penis becomes apotropaic by virtue of its exaggerated size and the exaggeratedly vulgar act of urinating. Will he douse the fires under the floor with that prodigious stream?[51] The ancient Roman, in laughing at such comic images, was well aware that their unbecomingness was an excellent protection against the evil eye. In both the House of the Menander and at Timgad—and arguably in the Praedia of Iulia Felix—emphasis of the figures' genitals constitutes the principal raison d'être of the image.

Further parallels to the mosaic of the bath attendant from the entryway to the caldarium of the House of the Menander underscore the workings of the apotropaic phallus. Although it dates to about A.D. 120 and represents not the Ethiopian but a black-figured representation of a white man, the mosaic of the Baths of Buticosus at Ostia Antica is close to the House of the Menander mosaic in both form and function (Fig. 47). Once again it is the phallus—this time in combination with large testicles—that dominates the picture. The mosaicist has named the servant by inscribing EPICTETUS BUTICOSUS by his left shoulder, and has made it clear that he is a bath attendant by giving him the attributes of water-pail and strigil. But his erect phallus signals his principal function, as guardian of the doorway, in this case a corridor leading to the heated plunge-baths.[52] Despite the less than elegant draftsmanship and figural conception, the figure of Buticosus is legibly a white man, with hair and beard arranged in gentle waves, straight nose, and wide, thin lips. Although Buticosus, because of his white ethnicity, may seem less exotic to the ancient Romans than the Ethiopian from either Pompeii or Timgad, his erect phallus performs the apotropaic function.[53]

These examples of apotropaic, phallic bath attendants demonstrate that the Roman viewer would see their large penises as most effective charms against malice but probably not as sexually stimulating. Outside the context of the apotropaic representations, in both Greek and Roman art there exist images of men with large or erect penises that are meant to be humorous or grotesque, not sexually stimulating. Dover makes this point abundantly clear through his 1978 survey of Greek vase painting.[54] Roman art and literature corroborate and continue the Greek aesthetic distaste for men with large penises; as late as ca. A.D. 400 the author of the *Historia Augusta* vilifies the emperor Heliogabalus by elaborating on his taste for men with large penises.[55]

This is not to say that for some ancient Romans the male Ethiopian (as opposed to these phallic representations of bath attendants) was not an object of sexual fan-

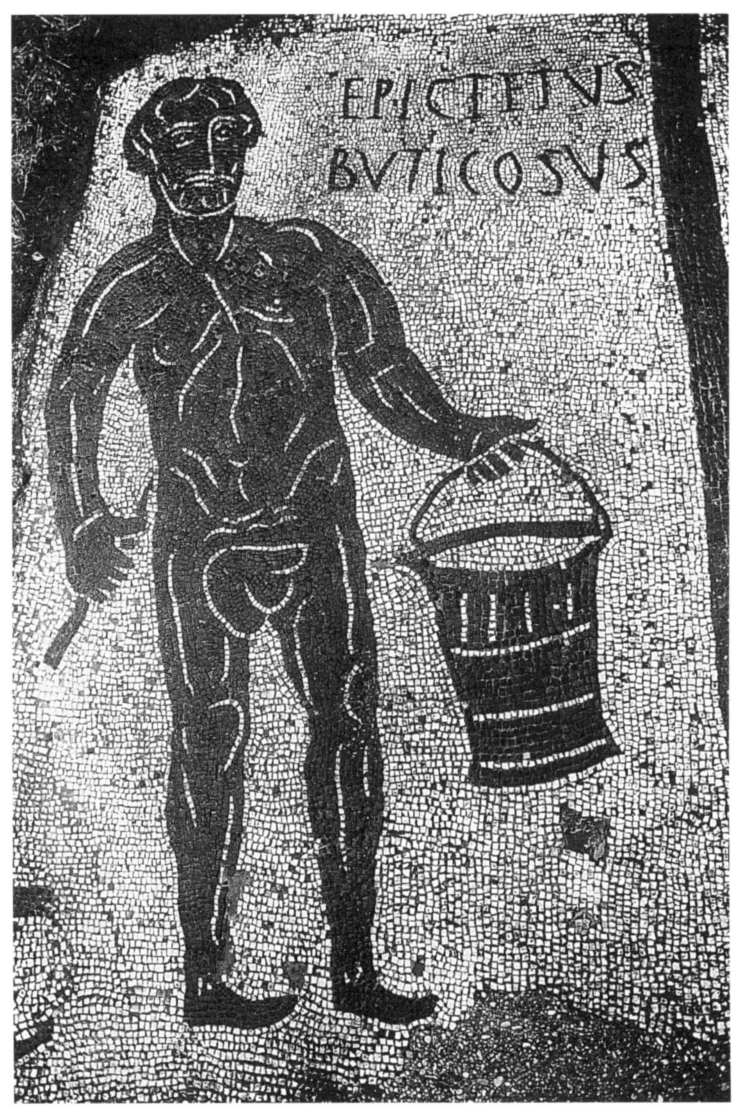

Figure 47. White male bath attendant with inscription, Ostia Antica, Baths of Buticosus (I, 14, 8), room A, detail of figure, north part (A.D. 130–140). Photo Michael Larvey.

tasy and desire. Considerable evidence, cited by Thompson and discussed more fully in chapter 7, reveals both fantasy and desire, at least in the minds of some of the white male elites who—aside from a few anonymous graffitists—are the only ones to leave a written record.[56]

Finally, these representations of bath attendants contrast sharply with the representations of the Augustan period that show couples, either demigods or humans, engaging in sexual intercourse. In fact, a mosaic featuring the coupling of a satyr and maenad decorates the floor of cubiculum 21 in the House of the Menander.[57] No such images have been found in the baths of private houses at Pompeii, where the man appears alone and has a large, apotropaic phallus rather than the aesthetically acceptable (small) penis; furthermore, he is a full-grown man, not the ephebic boy who was the usual object of sexual desire.

Pairs of Heraldic Swimmers

If these single figures of macrophallic men symbolize and warn against the heat of the bath while guarding the user from the Evil Eye, what is the meaning of the pairs of ithyphallic Ethiopians in these Pompeian houses? They are not servants, like the bath attendant, for servants never properly swam in the owner's swimming pool. Rather than refer (at least ostensibly) to everyday life, as the bath attendant does, they evoke another, exotic world. They are appropriate to their surroundings in baths in that they call up the image of a body of water, even though none of the mosaicists depicts a single wave on the pavement. Instead, the viewer must suspend disbelief to imagine the white-tesserae ground as water.[58]

Unlike the single-figure compositions of bath servants, in the mosaics that feature the swimming Ethiopian the artist took care to establish relationships both between the swimming figures and between the figures and images of dolphins and containers. The constancy of such relationships in the various versions of the paired-swimmers motif might prompt the viewer to ask whether the artist alluded to a specific incident. Could the swimmers belong to a narrative, an episode in a story, or even a genre familiar enough to the ancient Romans to be understood even when presented in reduced form?

To reconstruct this putative narrative we need to review all the mosaic compositions of the swimming Ethiopian, to find ones with the most relational imagery,

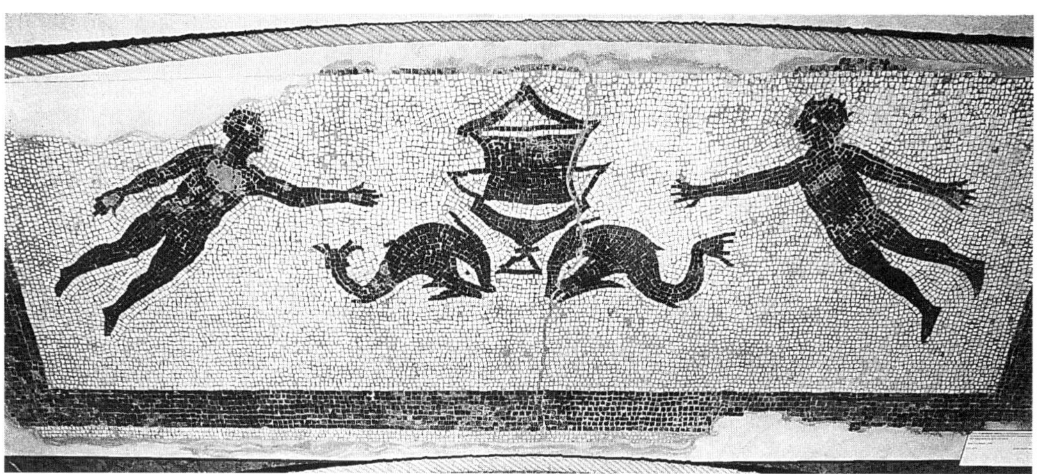

Figure 48. Black swimmers flanking crater, mosaic excavated at Este, 1915 (20–1 B.C.). Este, Archaelogical Museum. By permission of the Ministero per i Beni Culturali e Ambientali. Photo Michael Larvey.

ones we can read as narrative. The composition from the House of the Cryptoporticus holds the most information (see Fig. 41). The two swimmers flank a broken amphora. Although the artist depicted each in a different pose, both relate to the amphora in an unambiguous fashion. A line curving downward to the right from the break stands for the contents flowing out.[59] A second, serpentine line that curves upward from near the left-hand figure's knee, through his left hand, around the handles and mouth of the amphora, and through the right-hand Ethiopian's hand must be a cord attached to the amphora's two handles—a common method for lifting these vessels.[60] The amphora's pointed foot and thin mouth is of a type most usually associated with the transport and storage of wine.[61] The amphora itself implies a story in that it has "just" broken. Furthermore, the black swimmers are ithyphallic, and they appear directly opposite a composition of heraldic dolphins.

Casual excavations at Este, in northern Italy, turned up a close replica of the composition in the House of the Cryptoporticus; it is now in the National Archaeological Museum in Este (Fig. 48).[62] In the absence of associated wall painting or other reliable dating material, I would date it on stylistic grounds to the last two decades of first century B.C. Rather than represent the same two ithyphallic males of the House of the Cryptoporticus—but without the erect penises—the

Este mosaic pairs a man and a woman. The man, on the left of the crater, swims with his back turned to the viewer. The woman, on the right, swims with her chest and abdomen turned toward the viewer. The careful rendering of their tightly curled hair, flat noses, and large lips—these last emphasized by the use of ocher tesserae—leaves no doubt that both figures are of the Ethiopian type. Furthermore, the artist used ocher tesserae to pick out the palms of the swimmers' hands, no doubt based on his observation that black peoples' skin is often lighter on their palms. A final use of ocher tesserae delimits the areas of the breasts on the female swimmer to the right. The mosaicist was not particularly skillful here, since the breasts remain rather formless; he also erred in depicting the left palm of the left-hand swimmer in the ocher tesserae, since the silhouette of the fingers indicate that the hand is clearly turned palm away from the viewer. Despite these infelicities, the artist did differentiate the bodies of the swimmers sufficiently for the viewer to determine that one is a man and the other a woman: the figure on the left has broader shoulders and thinner hips and thighs than the one on the right.

It is interesting to compare the mosaic from Este with the Cryptoporticus mosaic to see what details the two mosaicists included or excluded from the model that must have provided them with the basic composition. That prototype must have included heraldic swimmers (two ithyphallic swimmers at Pompeii; a possibly ithyphallic Ethiopian with back turned and an Ethiopian woman at Este); a central vessel (at Este a lidded crater; at Pompeii an amphora), and heraldic dolphins (under the vessel at Este; on the opposite side of a rosette at Pompeii). The equal degree of care that the mosaicists lavished on details, especially their use of colored tesserae for special emphasis (the ocher-red outlining of the phalluses in the Cryptoporticus mosaic, the delineation of lips, palms, and breasts in the Este mosaic), contrasts with the other, less detailed mosaics of paired swimmers and leads me to believe that these two mosaics best reflect a lost prototype. Before hypothesizing what this visual prototype might have been, it would be useful to examine the other, less detailed, variations on the paired-swimmers motif to chart its diffusion and mutation.

The two pairs of swimmers in the House of Caesius Blandus communicate less narrative information than these first two: the artist simplified the representation by using the same cartoon for the poses of all four swimmers (see Fig. 42). Furthermore, he placed them with their backs to the centralized objects, so that they appear to swim up and away from them toward the central rosette. One of the central objects is a round-bodied pitcher, associated with the bath, but not with consuming wine; it shows no sign of being broken or spilling its contents. The other central object is a stylized pair of strigils, associated with cleaning rituals and not with drinking.[63] There are no dolphins. Despite these simplifications, the mosaicist took care to represent the figures as ithyphallic and of the Ethiopian somatotype.

In the mosaic with black swimmers from Cirta (modern Sidi M'Cid in Algeria), the mosaicist also took care to show that the swimmers are black men.[64] They are ithyphallic but not macrophallic like the swimmers from the House of the Cryptoporticus and the House of the Menander. The artist showed them swimming toward each other but omitted the central vessel entirely. Whatever their purpose, the artist put the figures of the ithyphallic, swimming Ethiopian into a new context whose meaning is unclear, despite considerable scholarly debate. The mosaic must date to the beginning of the first century of our era, rather than to the second or third century, as originally proposed.[65]

Finally, the swimmer from the caldarium of the House of the Menander, although closely related in design and workmanship to the right-hand swimmer from the House of the Cryptoporticus, lost his narrative context nearly entirely (see Fig. 43). He swims alone rather than with a mate; there is neither central vessel nor other association with the twin dolphins that appear in opposite corners of the pictorial rectangle of the mosaic. The mosaicist seems to equate him with the other figures in the mosaic—flora (the central medallion featuring a bird in an acanthus), fauna, and the Ethiopian fisherman—all pulled from wildly disparate sources.[66]

Both the constancy of relationships in these compositions featuring the paired-swimmers motif and their chronological concentration in the period between 30 B.C. and A.D. 30 suggest that this enigmatic composition might represent for the ancient viewer what Weitzmann terms an epitomized narrative, specifically a monoscenic representation that depicts a section of a narrative. If this is the case, the composition was comprehensible to the ancient viewer because he or she knew the whole narrative of which it was a part and was able to—in fact took special pleasure in—supplying the parts of the story that came before and after.[67] An artist who epitomizes the narrative must choose moments in the textual narrative that lend themselves to visual representation. Optimally, the scenes he chooses to depict should bring together the threads of the story and, if possible, suggest its final outcome. In the case of visual narratives surviving from lost texts, the art historian must try to determine the original relationships between the existing image and the lost text. He or she must try to understand how the artist conceptualized the text, for his conceptualization caused him to represent a specific scene or scenes that seemed representative of an entire story.[68] Even when the artist inscribed texts beside a set of images, as in the group of reliefs known as the *tabulae iliacae,* the historian often discovers that the image does not bear a strict relationship to the text(s); often the image does not even illustrate the contiguous text(s).[69]

What sort of narrative could cause the mosaic artists to extract for epitomization the elements of the Ethiopian swimmers (both the ithyphallic men and a woman with large breasts), the wine vessel (whether broken amphora or whole crater), and the heraldic dolphins? It seems to be a kind of fable or moral lesson rather than a long tale, for the representation, even in this epitomized form, is filled with easily understood signs. Foremost among them is the centralized action of swimming toward (not away from, as in the House of Caesius Blandus) the broken amphora. Although only in the House of the Cryptoporticus does the amphora spill its contents, only this incident explains the attention and alarm expressed by the black swimmers; the right-hand swimmer swims rapidly, while the one on the left seems to be gesturing in dismay. An analogous image carved on a sardonyx of the first century B.C. leads me to believe that the amphora is spilling out precious wine. On the tiny gem (1.4 cm high) two skeletons flank a similar amphora, holding it upright, while the skeleton on the left extends a reveler's crown to his counterpart. The skeleton–wine stewards, like the black swimmers, are exotic types. They remind one of death, a sobering (or amusing) memento mori for the wine drinker.[70] The Ethiopian-swimmers, holding on to the remains of a wine amphora that they have either broken or are trying to salvage from a shipwreck, could fit into a similar interpretation: the wine is lost, flowing into the water they are swimming in. Despite the shock that one could read in the left-hand man's gestures, and despite the haste of the right-hand swimmer's swift stroke, the damage has been done. The party—if not life itself—is over.

Other imagery in these three Pompeian private baths supports my interpretation of the bath attendant as primarily apotropaic and the heraldic black Africans as primarily narrative epitomes. Although the wall painting in the small heated room of the House of the Cryptoporticus and in the bath in the House of Caesius Blandus consists of plain, late Second-Style architectural elements, Maiuri and others detail the rich remains of mosaics, wall painting, and stuccoes in the three rooms making up the private bath of the House of the Menander.[71] Several aspects of this decoration are particularly relevant to the images of black men and women. In the caldarium's apse, stucco dolphins on the ceiling mirror their representation in the mosaic floor, while the river scenes with ducks navigating greenish waters painted at the bottom of the wall suggest a Nilotic setting. Caricatures of the gods and goddesses, depicted (like pygmies) with huge heads, form the frieze in the bath's little atrium. Although such caricatures are relatively rare in preserved painting, their presence in the House of the Menander—arguably a house of rather refined taste—indicates that in the early Augustan period elite patrons enjoyed such irreverent, comic send-ups of the Olympians.[72] Like these caricatures, the choice of the eager bath servant, the ithyphallic swimmer, and the energetic fisherman underscores the patron's desire to impress the visitor with his or her knowledge of current fashions in the art of decoration. For in addition to the narrative and apotropaic associations they bore, these images of the Ethiopian expressed the late Hellenistic interest in exotic physical types translated into early Augustan terms. The association of the Ethiopian with Egypt, and the great artistic interest in all things Egyptian, spread in Roman and in Roman Italy in the wake of the triumph of Augustus and Agrippa over Egypt. In the late first century B.C., Egyptophilia ruled supreme in Rome—a fashion with ample resonance in Pompeii.[73] Little wonder, then, that the Ethiopian finds such an important role in this fashionable private bathing complex.

Modern viewers cannot hope to comprehend fully the impact that the images of the ithyphallic and macrophallic black men in these Pompeian mosaics had on the ancient viewer: we carry a cultural baggage that gives these artistic representations of the body of the Other meanings particular to the late twentieth century. Yet consideration of their body type, their apotropaic powers, and their roles in lost narratives removes some of our twentieth-century (mis)constructions.

In chapters 2, 3, and 4, the rich documentation of sexual representations permitted us to explore how many Romans living in Italy during the Augustan and early Julio-Claudian periods thought of themselves in regard to sex. To some of these artistic representations that reflect the culture of the period we can assign specific dates. For several images among them—the Farnesina paintings and the mosaics—thanks to a specific architectural context, we can posit the social class and therefore the probable cultural biases of the patrons and viewers. For the vessels with scenes of lovemaking on them, information about production techniques lets us rank them according to their expense for the ancient buyer. Although this is not the most direct—or most certain—means for determining the class and social status of the persons who bought the vessels and looked at the images on them, it is clear that images of both male-female and male-male lovemaking enjoyed considerable popularity among all classes.

All this sexual imagery taken together—whether it reflects actual practices, commonly held sexual fantasies, or merely fashions in house decorating—greatly amplifies the voice of the Roman living in Augustan times. If the voice of the poet and jurist is undeniably that of the upper-class, that of the visual artist encompasses a chorus of voices never heard from in existing texts.

In chapters 6 and 7 we explore sexual imagery dating, for the most part, from the period between Nero and Domitian (A.D. 54–79), with a special focus on the many objects and wall paintings found in the cities buried by the eruption of Vesuvius in A.D. 79. As with our exploration of the Augustan period, the aim is to see how visual artists give form to sexual attitudes of Romans living in that time and in that place.

Plates

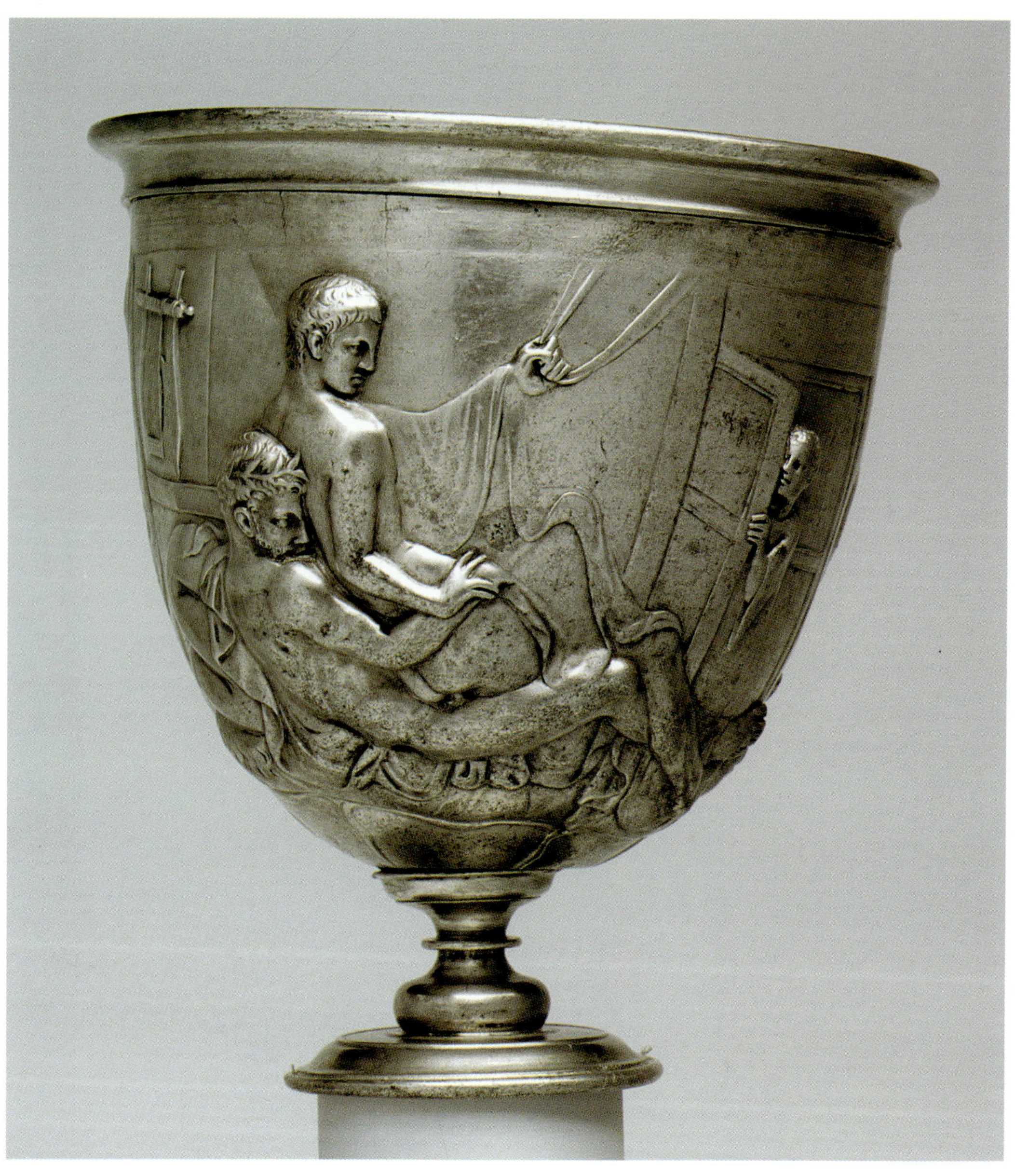

Plate 1. Male-male couple on bed, Warren cup, side A (30 B.C.–A.D. 30). New York, Metropolitan Museum of Art, anonymous loan L.1991.95. Photo courtesy of museum.

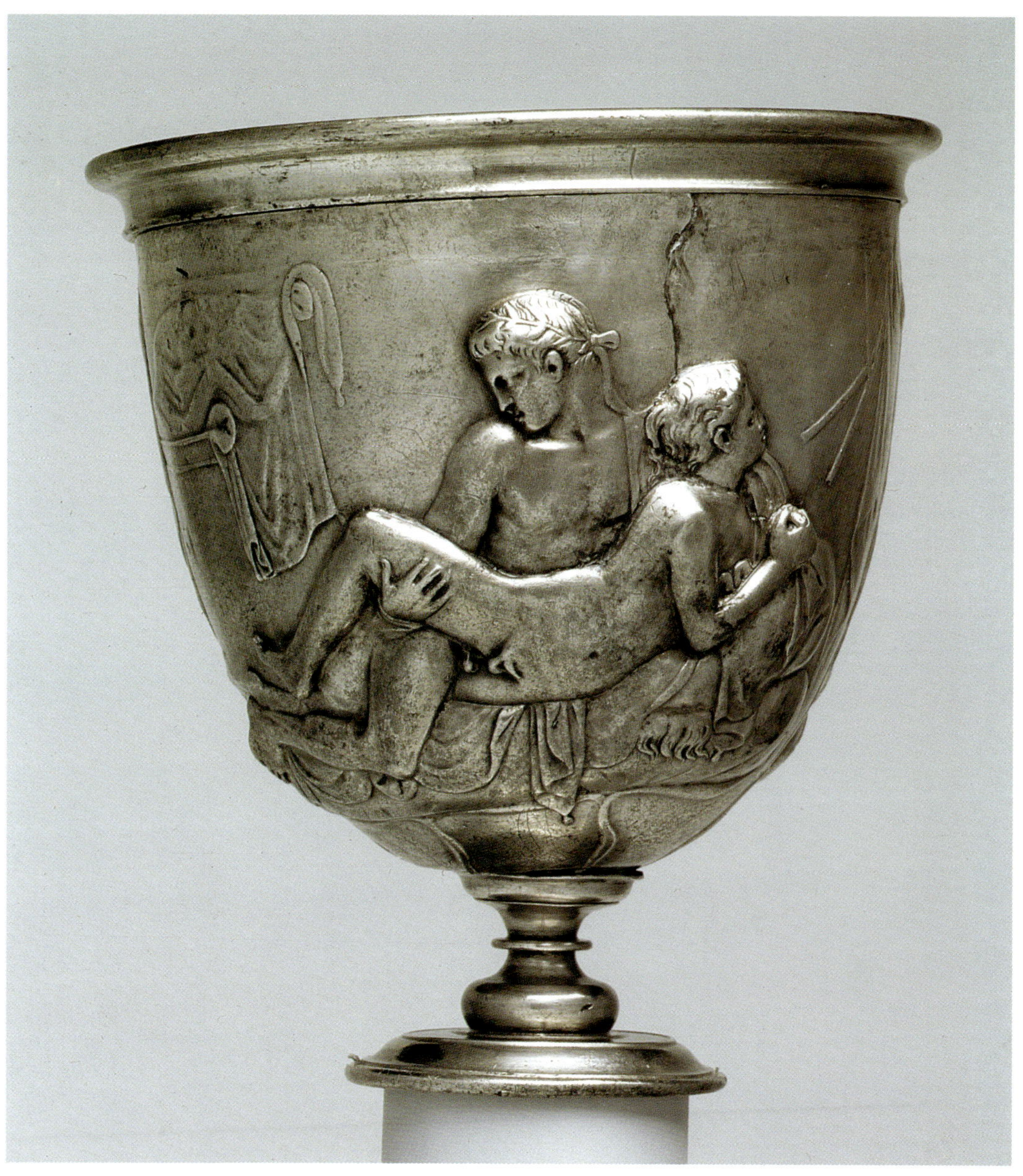

Plate 2. Man-boy couple on bed, Warren cup, side B (30 B.C.–A.D. 30). New York, Metropolitan Museum of Art, anonymous loan L.1991.95. Photo courtesy of museum.

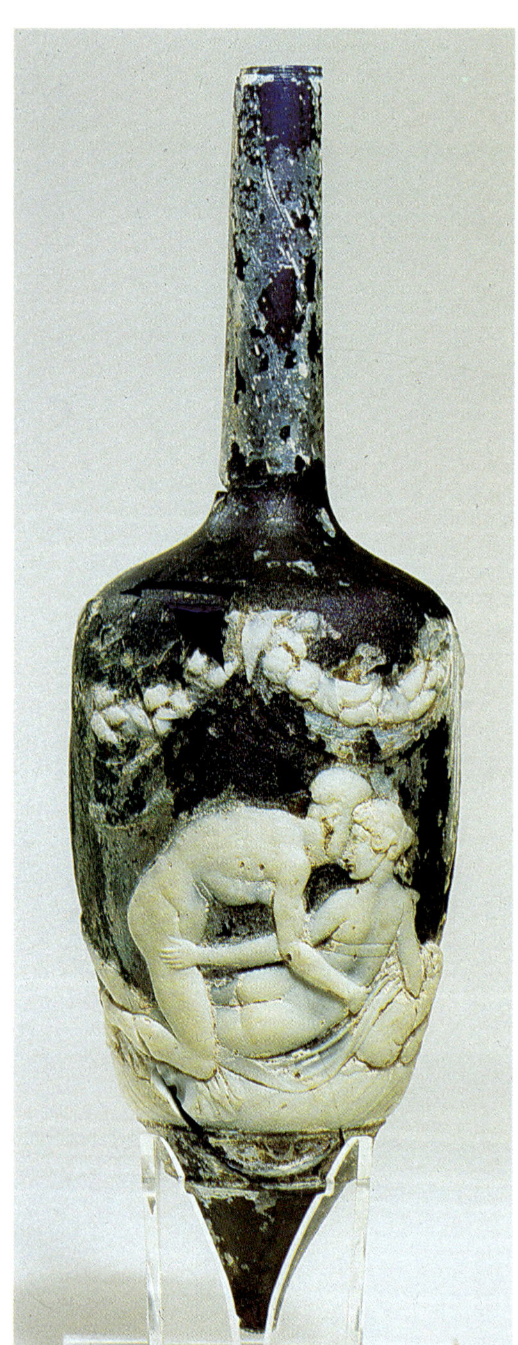

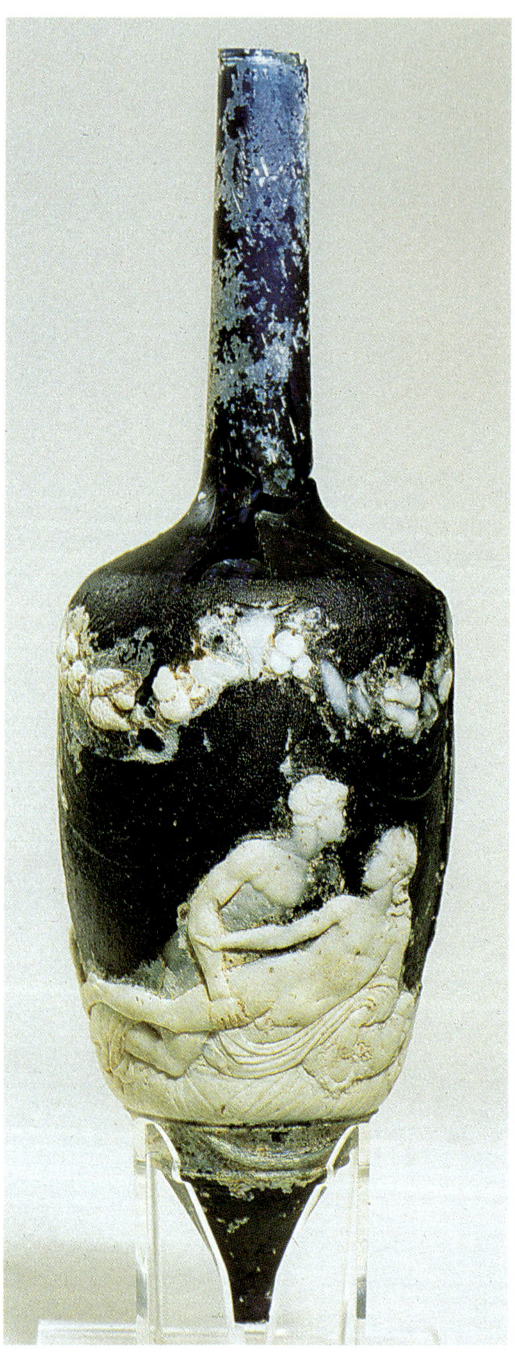

Plate 3. Male-female couple on bed, Ortiz flask, side A, from Estepa, Spain (30 B.C.– A.D. 30). Photo courtesy George Ortiz.

Plate 4. Man-boy couple on bed, Ortiz flask, side B, from Estepa, Spain (30 B.C.–A.D. 30). Photo courtesy George Ortiz.

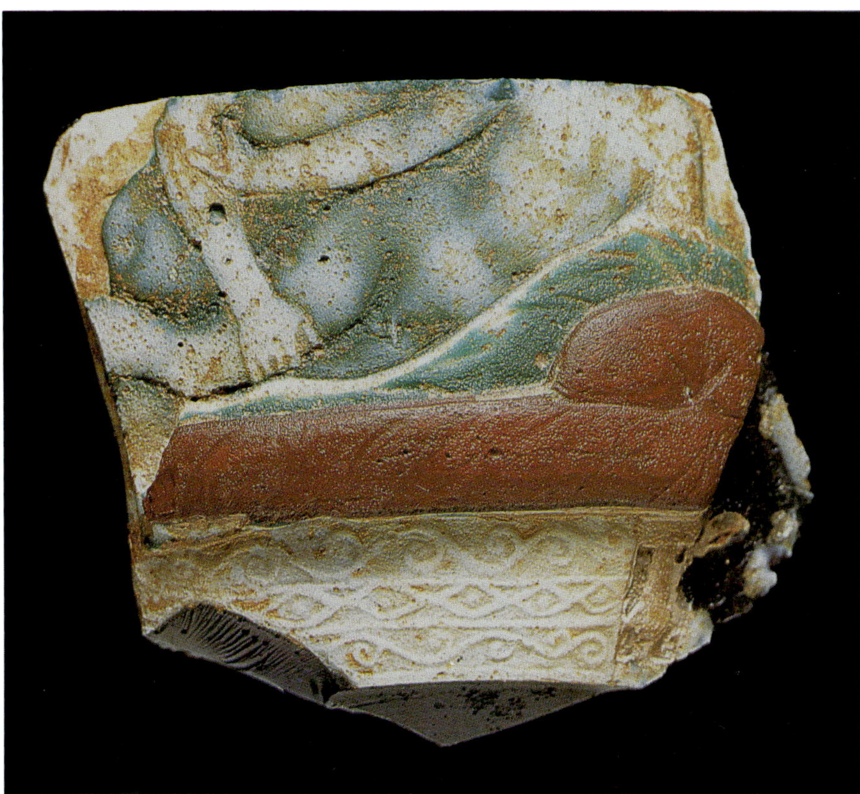

Plate 5. Man-boy couple on bed, fragment of multicolored cameo glass (30 B.C.– A.D. 30). London, British Museum, inv. GR 1956.3–1.5. Photo courtesy of museum. Copyright British Museum.

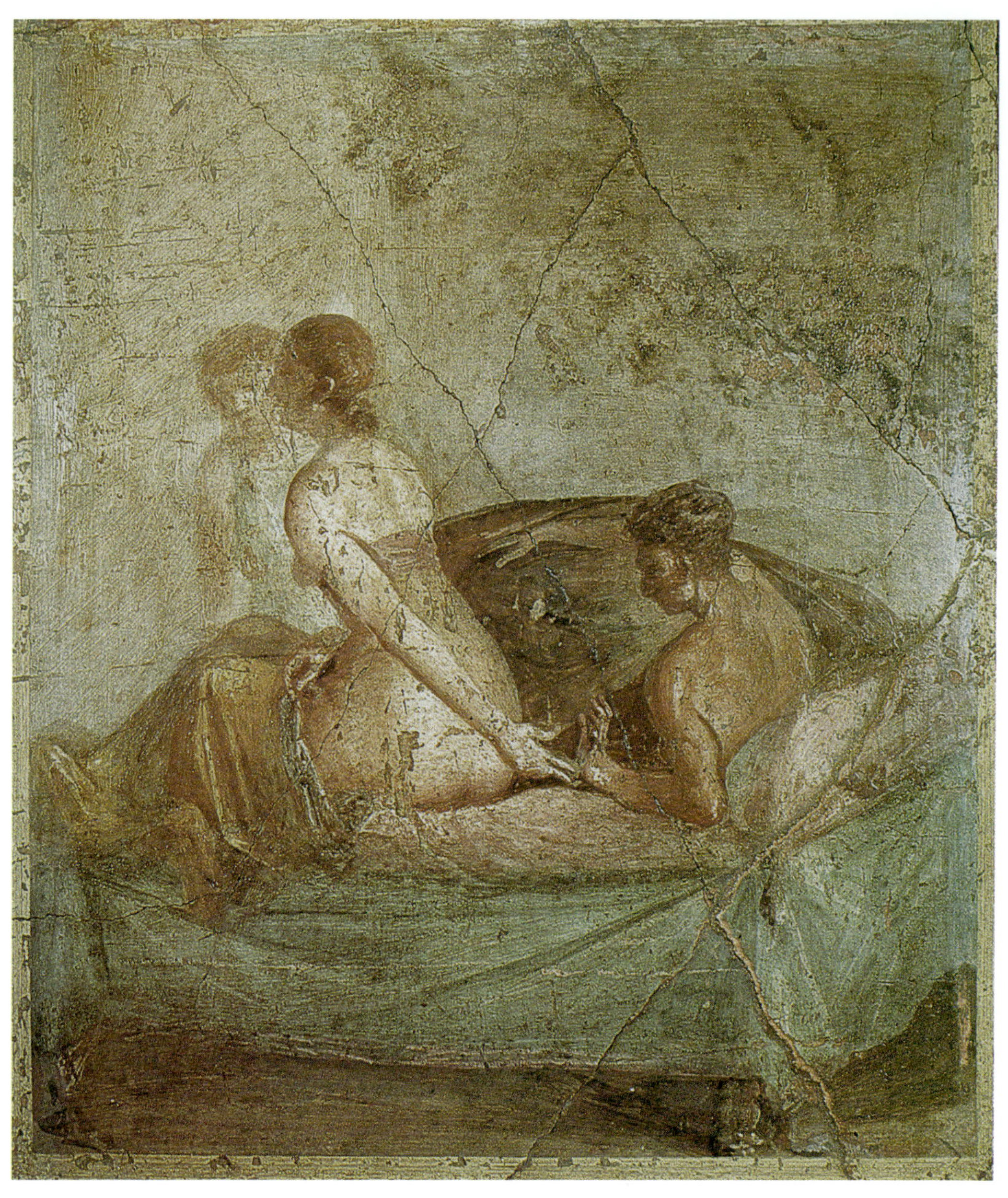

Plate 6. Male-female couple on bed with attendant, from Pompeii, House of Caecilius Iucundus (V, 1, 26) peristyle *l,* north wall, between triclinium *o* and cubiculum *p* (A.D. 62–79). Naples, Archaeological Museum, inv. 110569, W. 39.5 × H. 46 cm. Photo Michael Larvey.

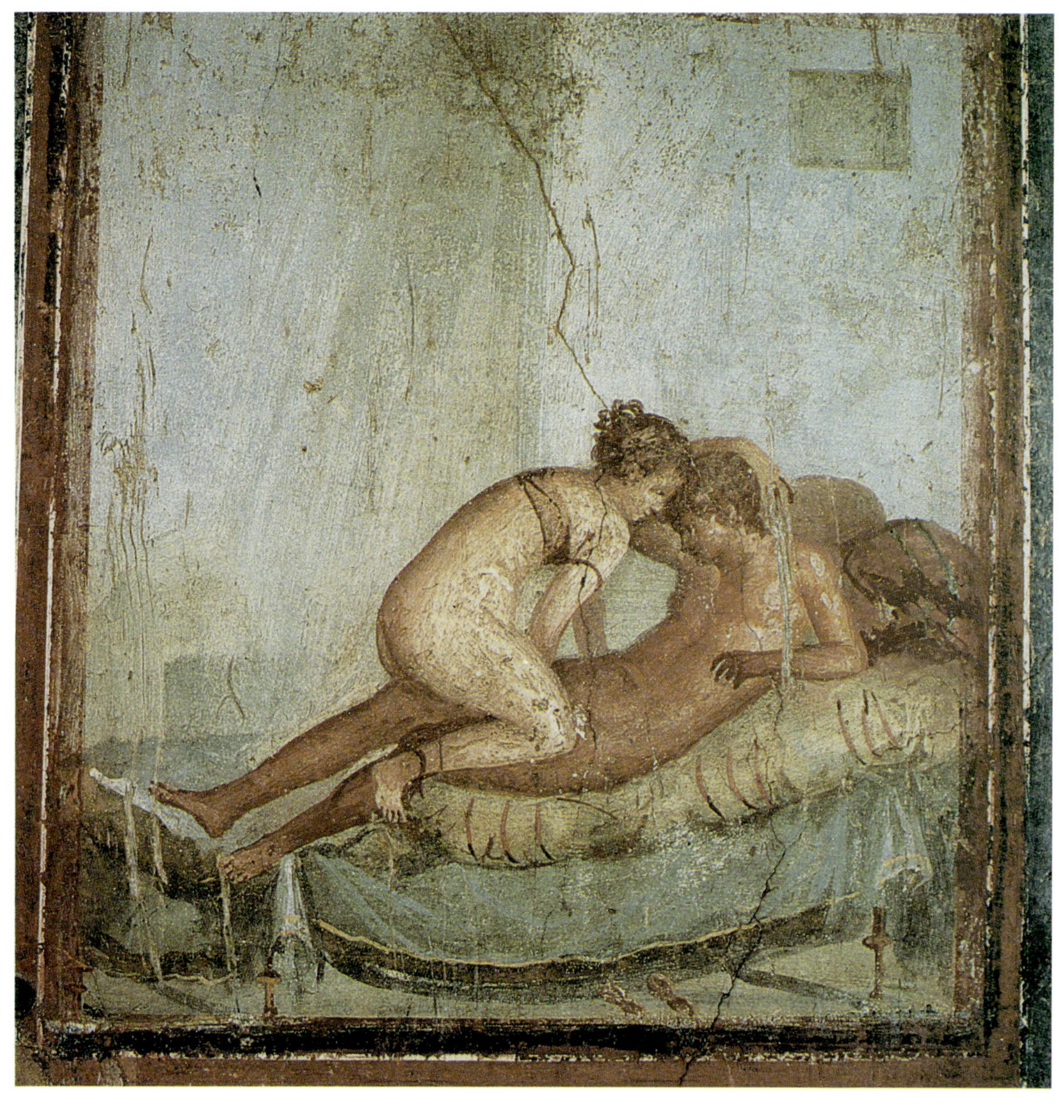

Plate 7. Male-female couple on bed, Pompeii, House of the Centenary (IX, 8, 6), room 43, south wall, central picture (A.D. 62–79). Photo Michael Larvey.

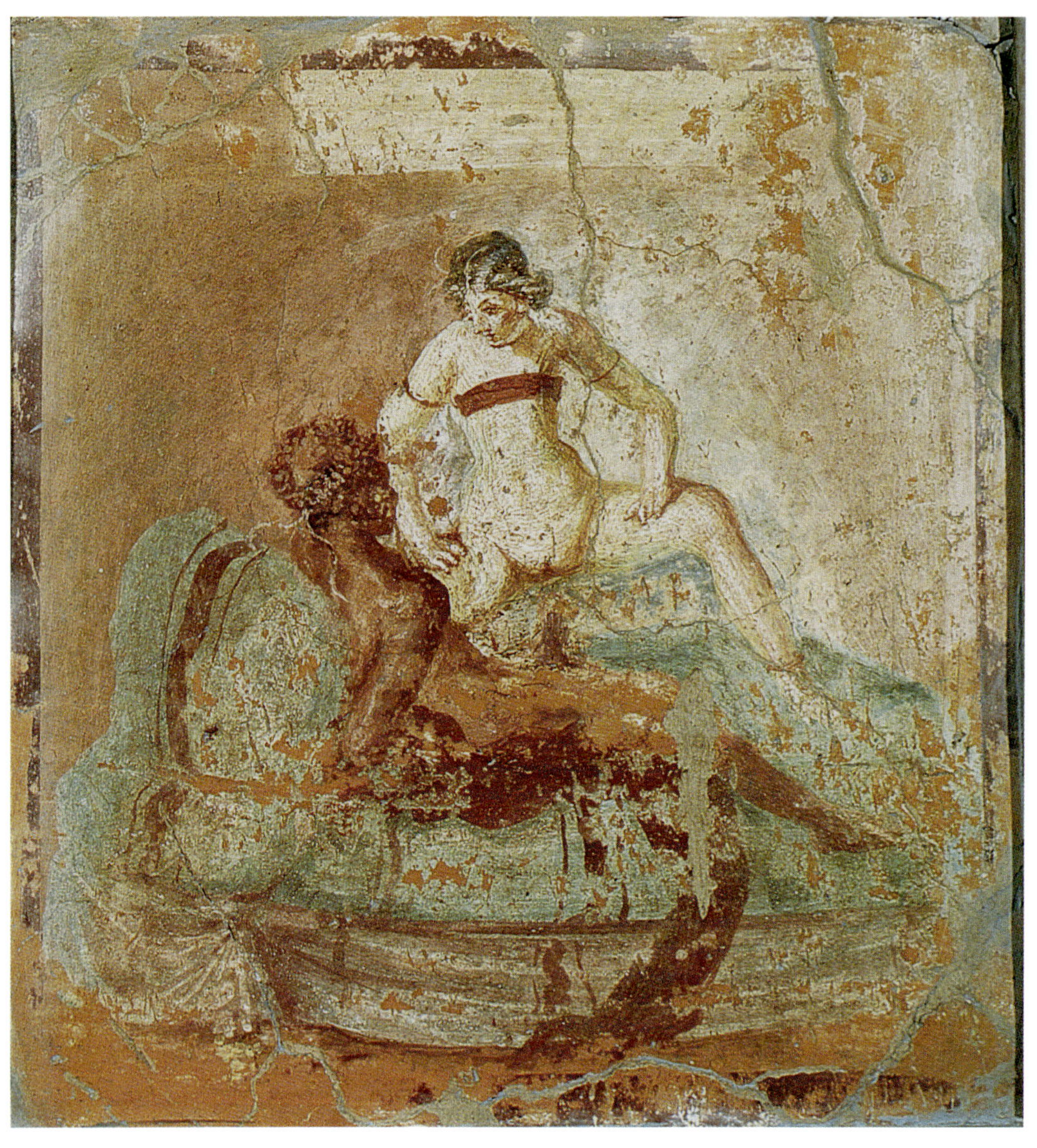

Plate 8. Male-female couple on bed, from Pompeii, unknown location (A.D. 62–79). Naples Archaeological Museum, inv. 27686, W. 38 × H. 39 cm. Photo Michael Larvey.

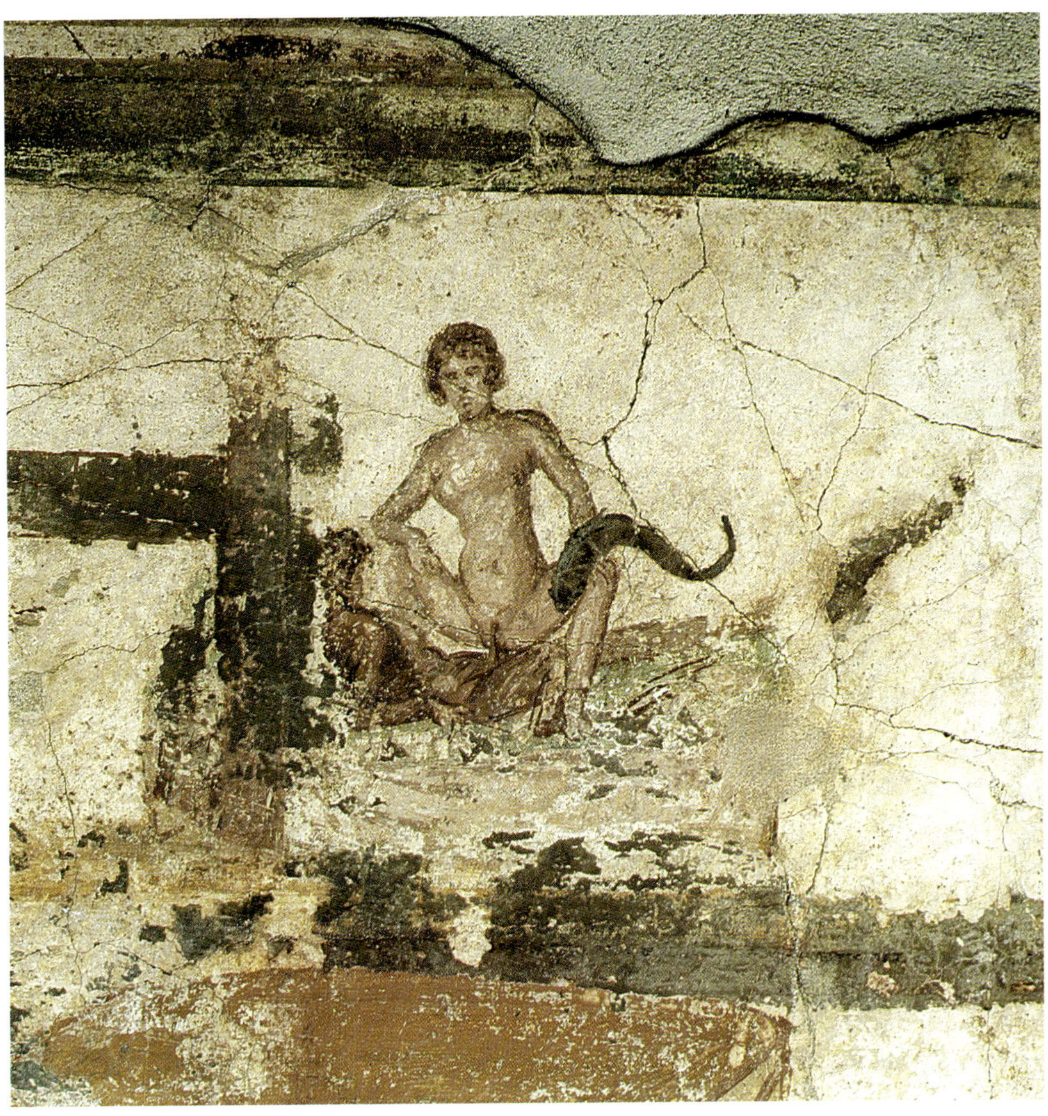

Plate 9. Male-female couple on bed, Pompeii, Suburban Baths, apodyterium 7, scene I (A.D. 62–79). Photo Michael Larvey.

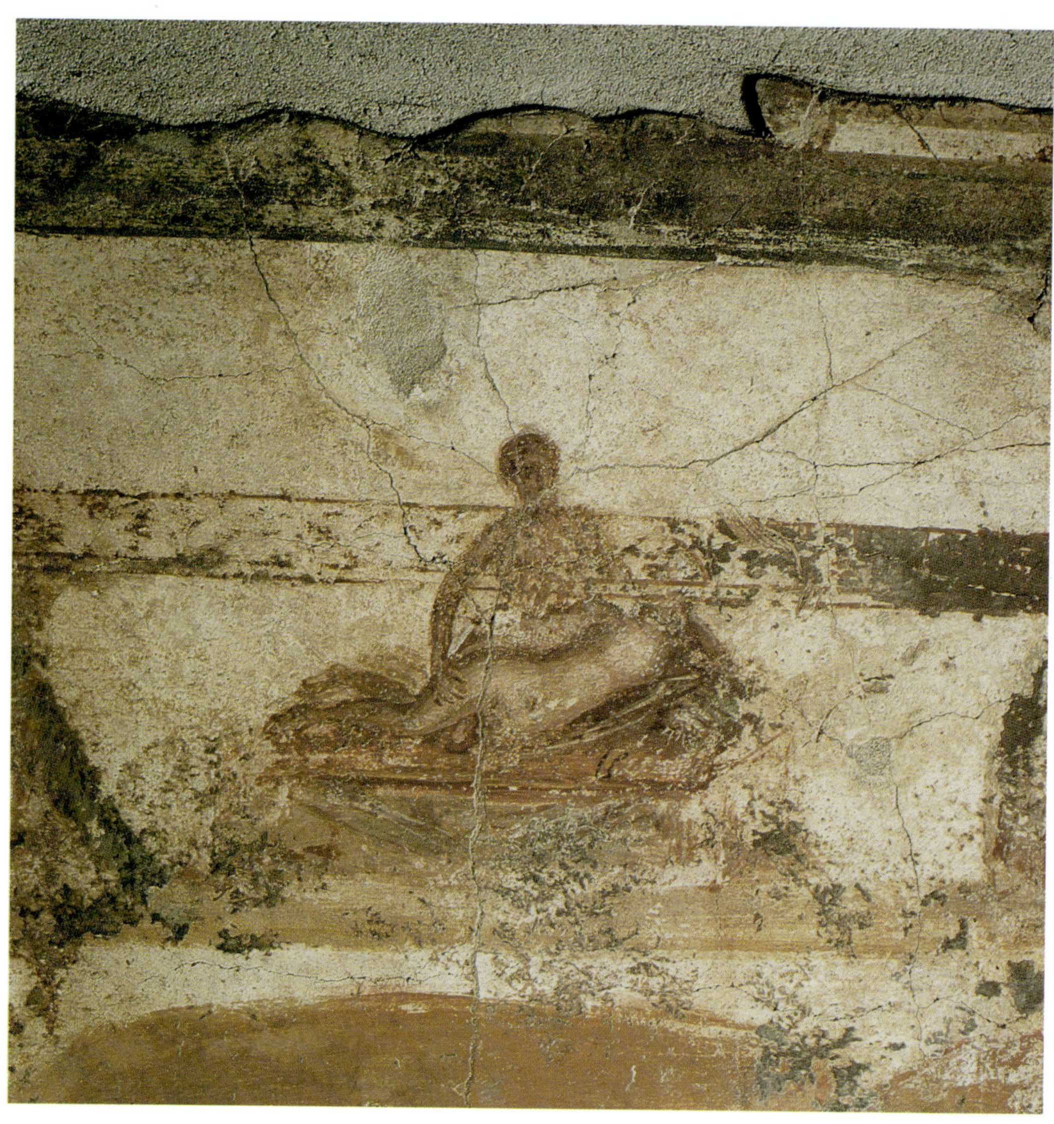

Plate 10. Male-female couple on bed, Pompeii, Suburban Baths, apodyterium 7, scene II (A.D. 62–79). Photo Michael Larvey.

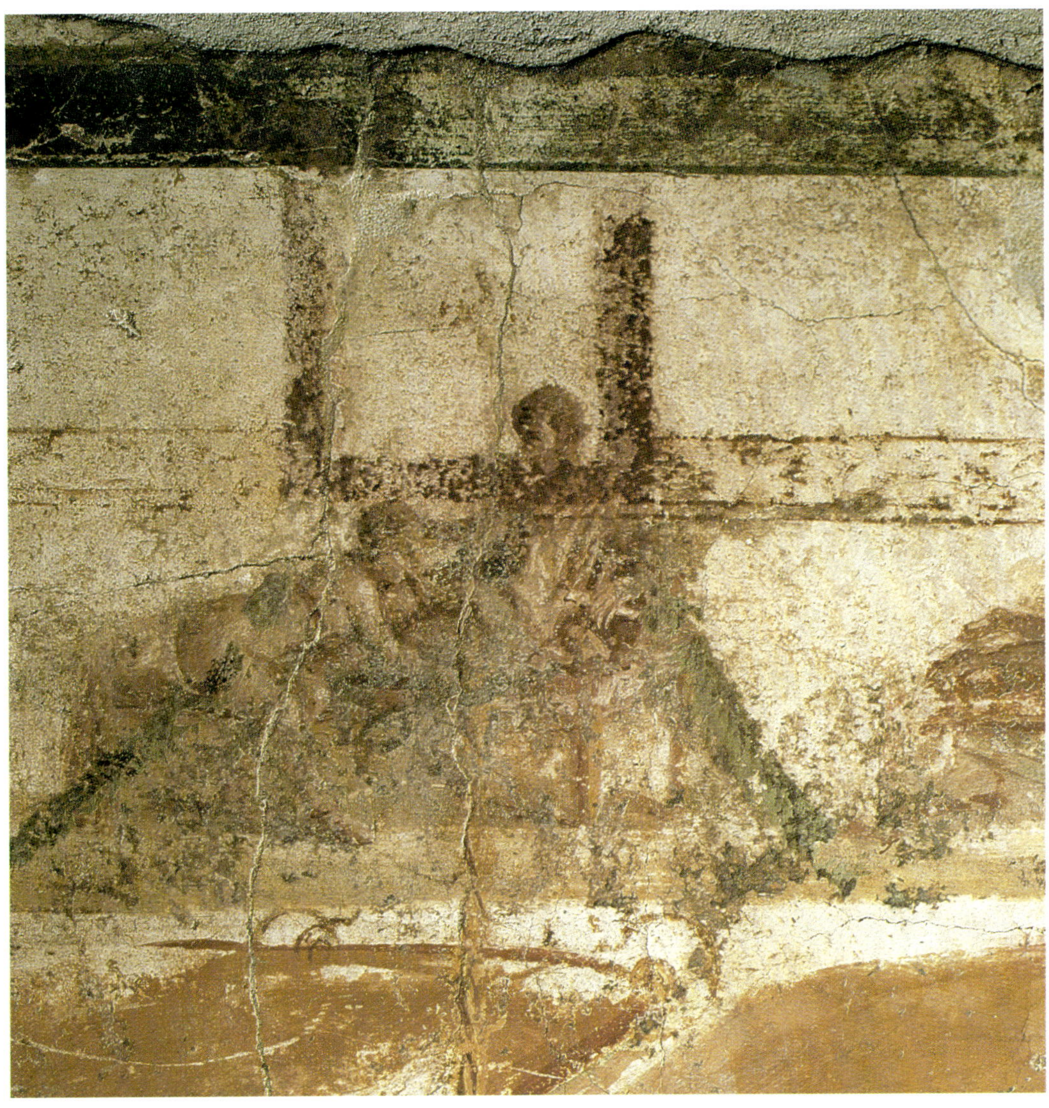

Plate 11. A woman fellating a man, Pompeii, Suburban Baths, apodyterium 7, scene III (A.D. 62–79). Photo Michael Larvey.

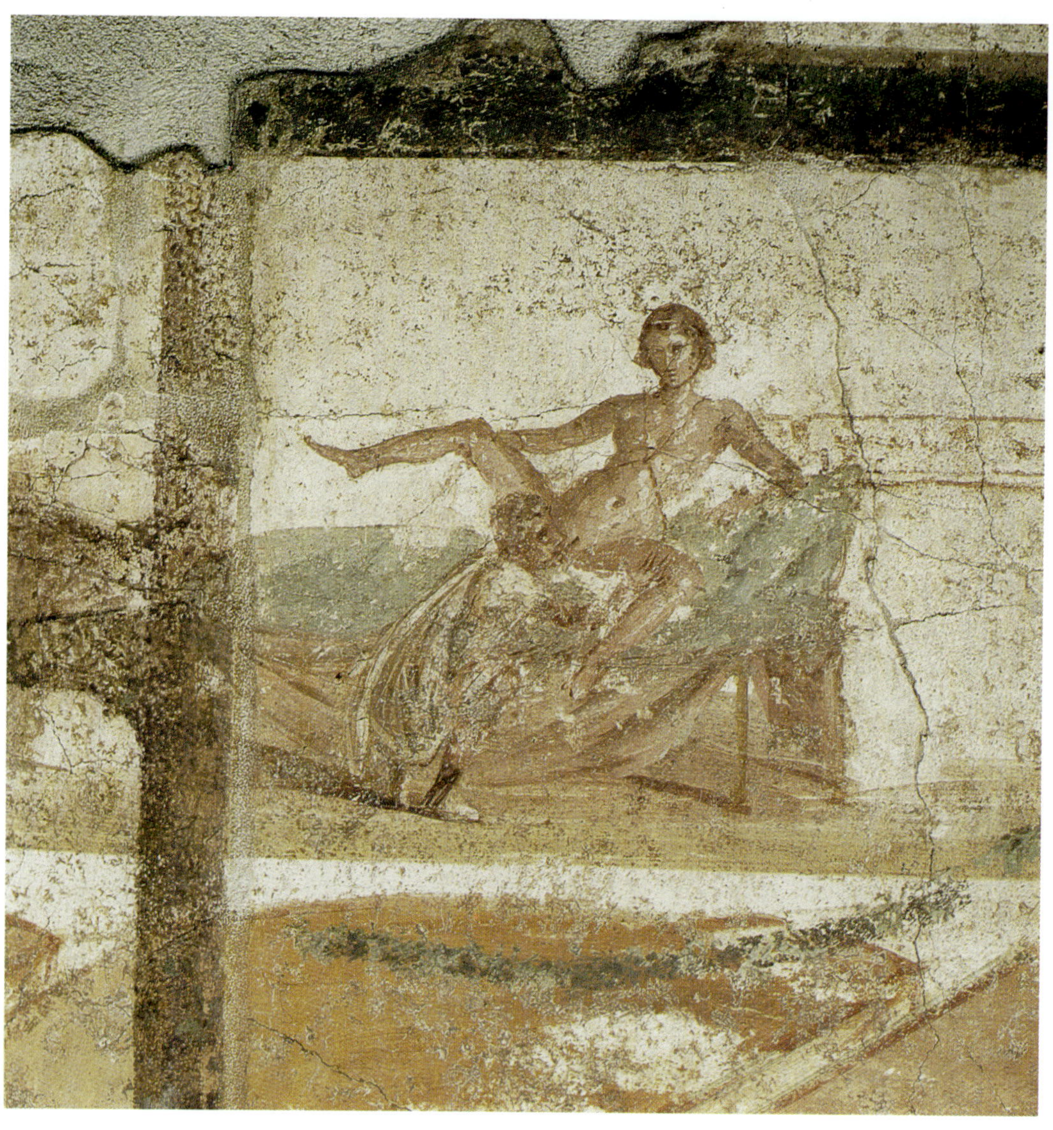

Plate 12. A man performing cunnilingus on a woman, Pompeii, Suburban Baths, apodyterium 7, scene IV (A.D. 62–79). Photo Michael Larvey.

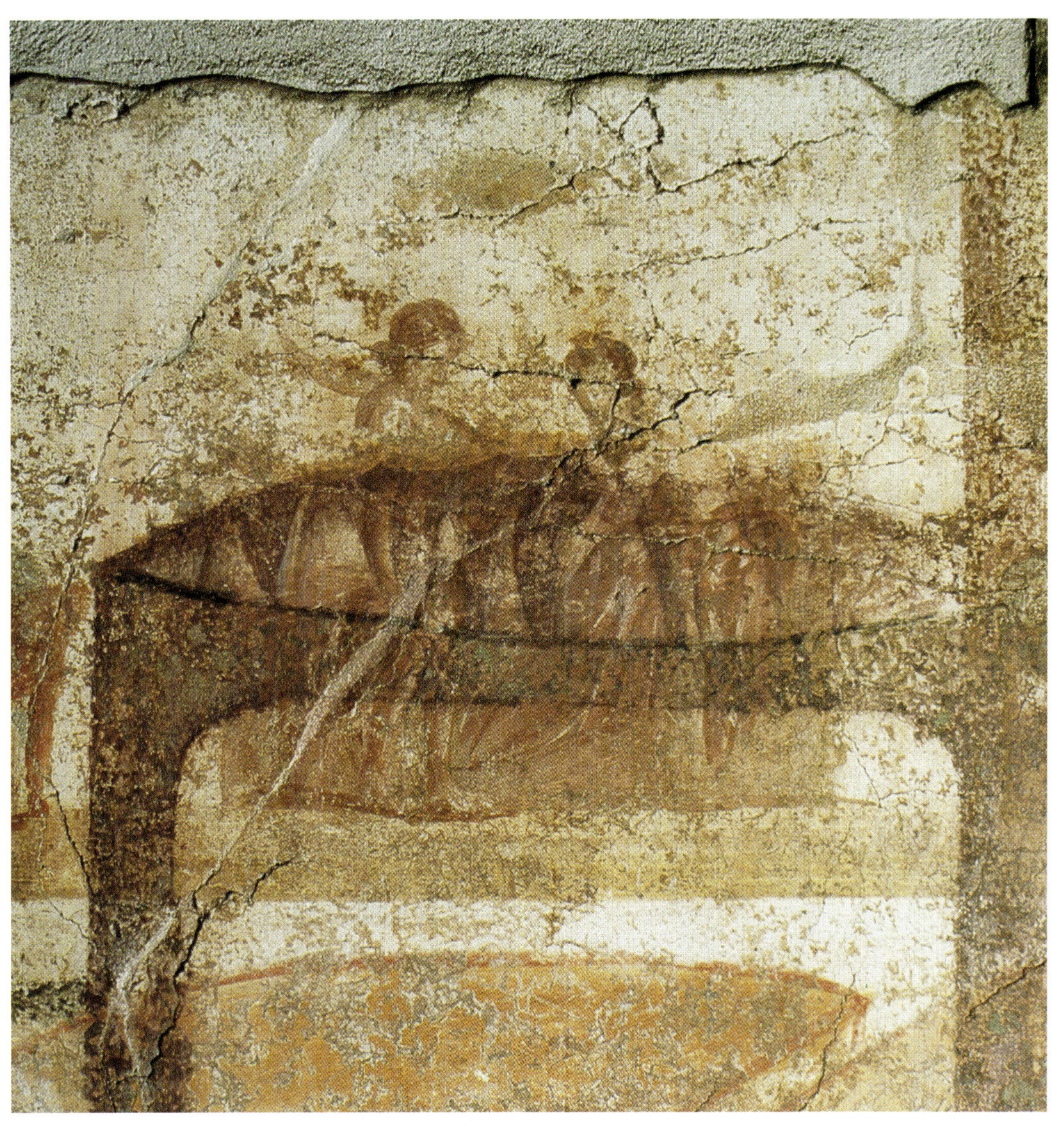

Plate 13. Two women copulating, Pompeii, Suburban Baths, apodyterium 7, scene V (A.D. 62–79). Photo Michael Larvey.

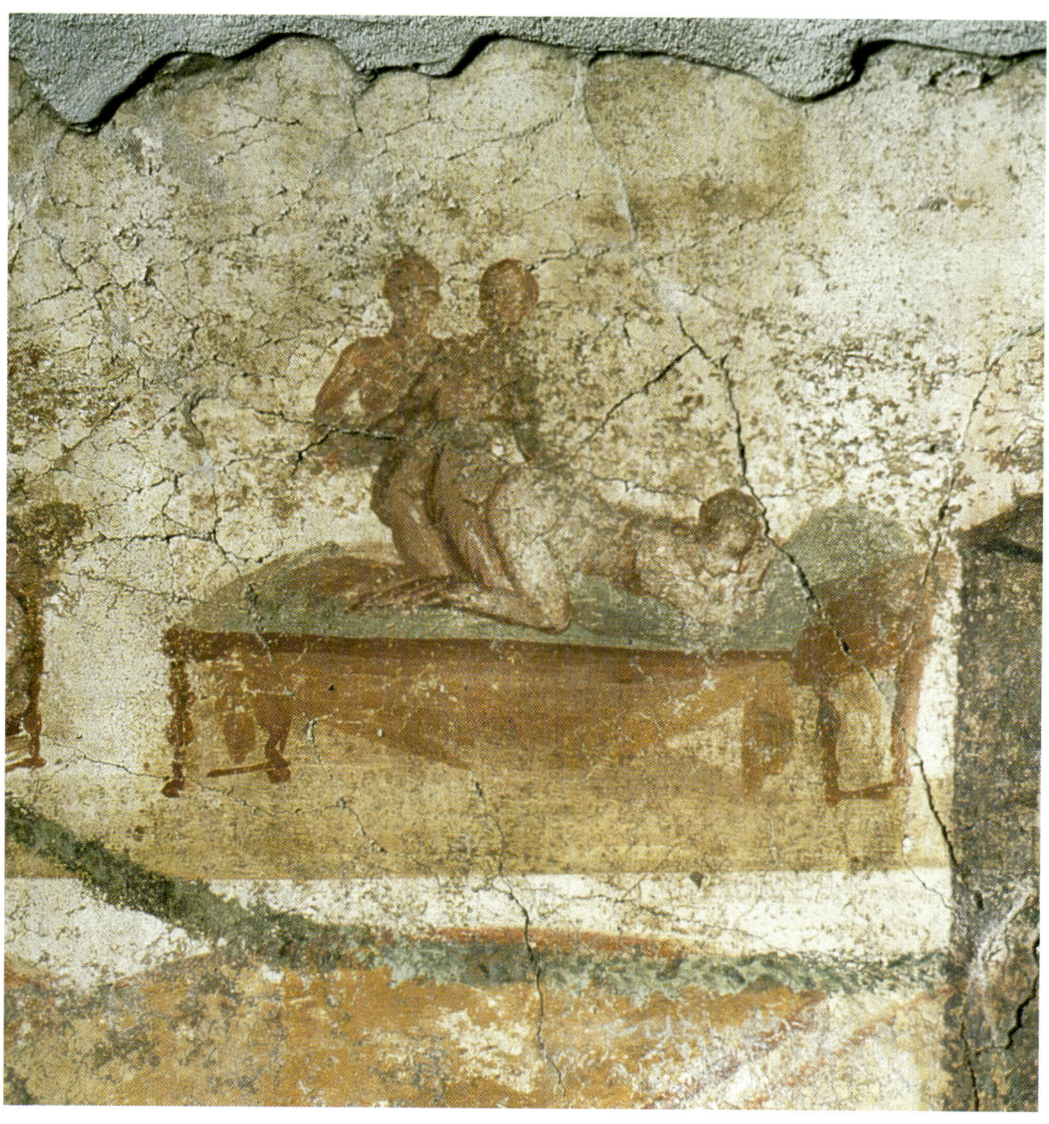

Plate 14. Threesome of two men and a woman, Pompeii, Suburban Baths, apodyterium 7, scene VI (A.D. 62–79). Photo Michael Larvey.

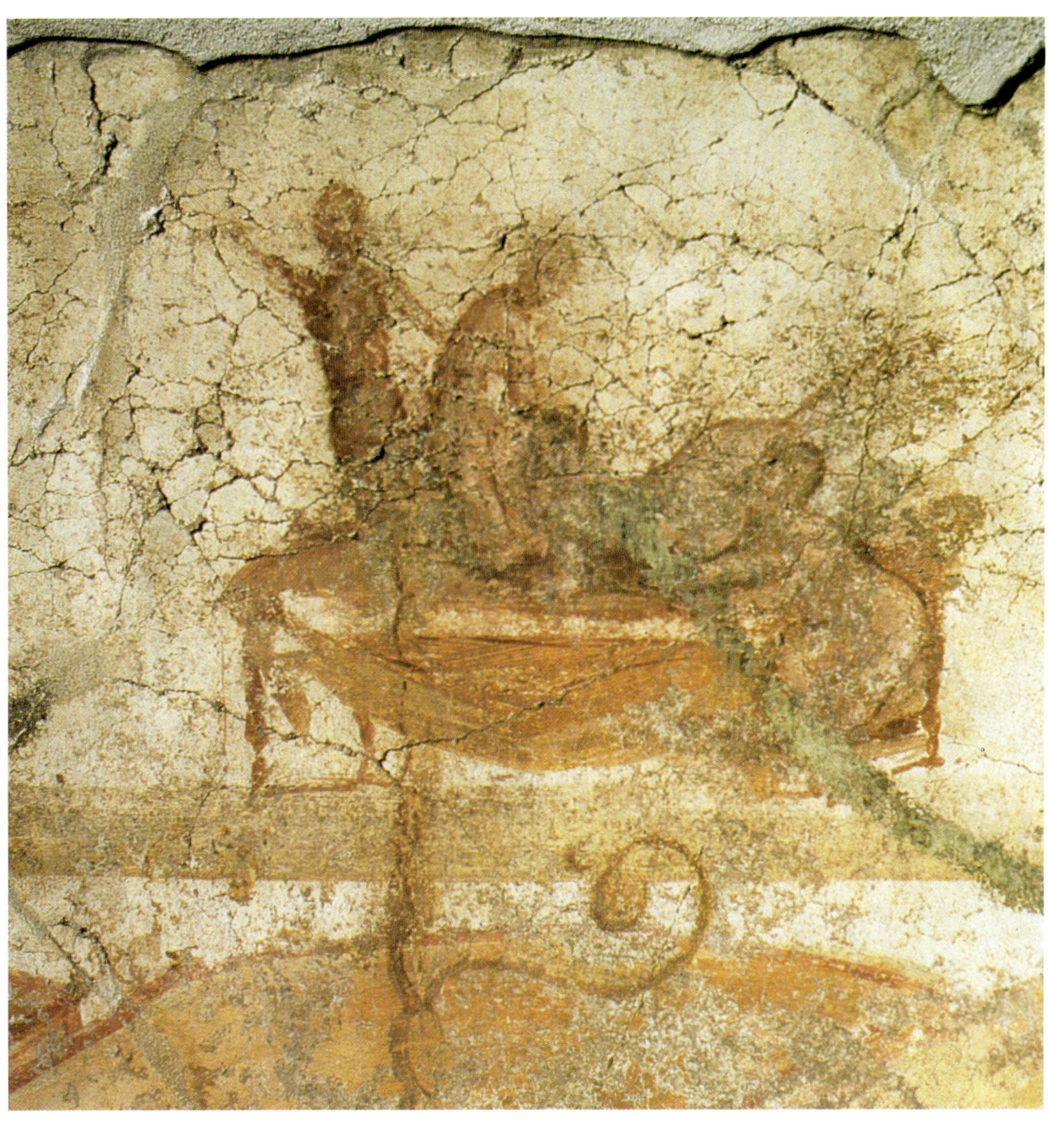

Plate 15. Foursome of two men and two women, Pompeii, Suburban Baths, apodyterium 7, scene VII (A.D. 62–79). Photo Michael Larvey.

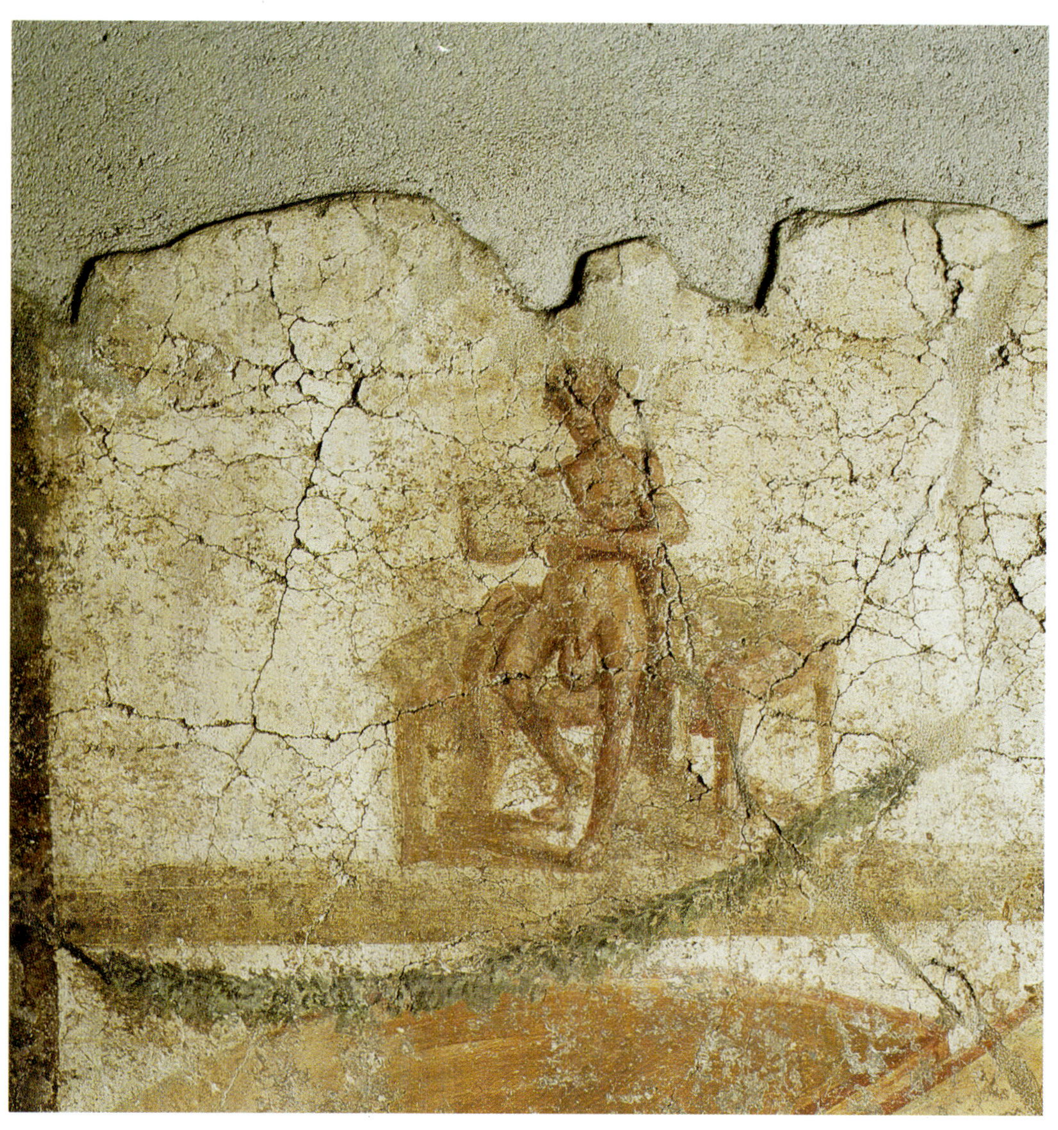

Plate 16. Poet with hydrocele, Pompeii, Suburban Baths, apodyterium 7, scene VIII (A.D. 62–79). Photo Michael Larvey.

POMPEII:
THE NERONIAN AND FLAVIAN PERIODS

A.D. 54–79

CHAPTER 6

The Display of Erotica and the Erotics of Display in Houses

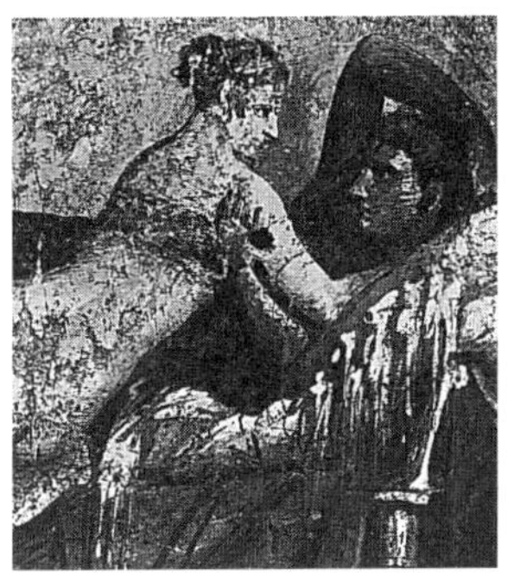

We owe the existence of wall paintings found in a variety of houses in Pompeii to the fact that artists painted them in fresco technique. The pigments, applied in a final thin layer of plaster, became incorporated into the wall itself through the process of carbonation. In many fresco paintings artists added details over the fresco when the plaster was partially dry; these areas in secco were less durable and deteriorated either during the centuries that the paintings were sealed under volcanic ash or—more usually—after their discovery when they were exposed to the elements. Even so, because excavators found them in their original architectural settings, as integral parts of the fresco decorations of whole rooms, we usually know at least where the so-called erotic paintings were displayed. In this sense the paintings are like those found in the Villa of the Farnesina (discussed in chapter 4).

Because the volcano's ashes preserved a great variety of evidence, in some cases we can name the owner of a house and even determine his or her social class and business. This information, along with analysis of the entire plan of the house—including considerations of size, probable uses of its various spaces, and the position of the room containing the erotic paintings—lets us set out a scenario for the use of those paintings and ask about their meanings for the ancient viewers. Who looked at the paintings? How did they relate to the rest of the decorative and iconographic program? Why did the owner choose to place the erotic painting or paint-

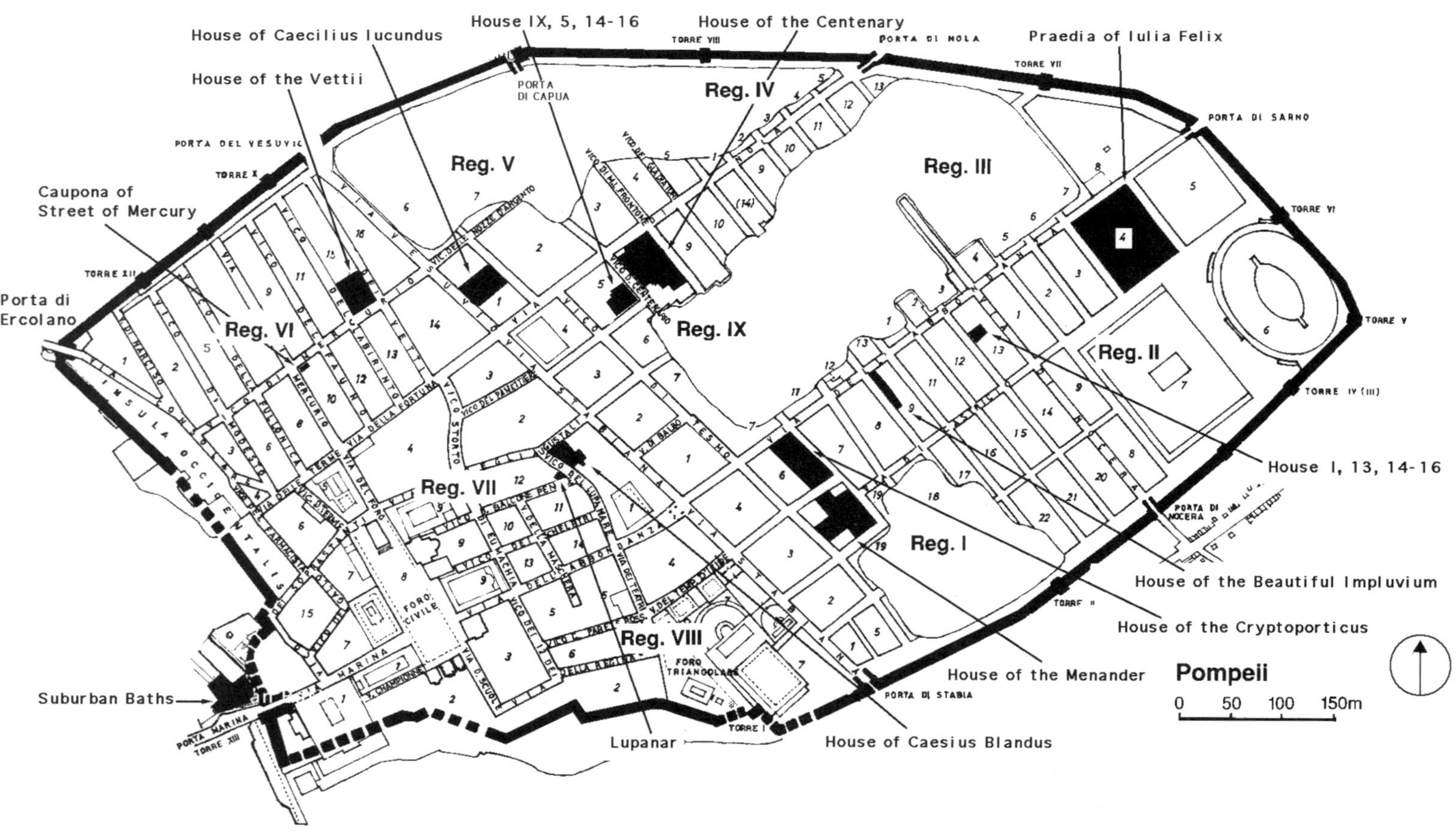

Map 1. Pompeii, plan with buildings discussed in this study indicated.

ings in that spot and no other? Taken together, these circumstances surrounding the creation and function of wall paintings that represent lovemaking define what I call the "erotics of display."

"Erotics" is a made-up word that helps us isolate ancient Roman sexual formulations from late twentieth-century associations that burden the word "erotic." If erotics signals cultural constructions of sexuality that rarely overlap with our own, the "erotics of display" builds on the concept of the incongruity of ancient and modern erotics to include the location, patronage, audience, and use of paintings of sexual intercourse found in the houses at Pompeii. When modern archaeologists and writers separate these images from their architectural contexts—by cutting them away from the walls or publishing them without reference to their architectural settings—the paintings become part of our twentieth-century ideas of what is erotic. Conversely, it becomes clear that, considered in their original settings, these same images often elicited responses in the Roman viewer that were very far from our constructions of the erotic.

In considering these paintings, I take into account not only the painting itself but also the patron who paid for it and planned its location in his or her house; it is important to consider the social class of both patron and viewers, for sex meant very different things for different social classes. We must consider both the availability and cost of sexual intercourse for women and men and for each social stratum from the elite to the servile, for like all societies, that of ancient Rome regulated sexual behavior along both class and gender distinctions. As we have seen, particularly in reference to the pygmy and the Ethiopian, ancient Romans had a strong sense of the Other.

Fortunately, we have an excellent standard for establishing the elite use of erotic painting in the painted panels from the cubicula of the Villa under the Farnesina in Rome. The owner of that villa was certainly a member of the elite class, and the representations of little panels that the artists painted on the walls of its cubicula indicate that in the Augustan period paintings of lovemaking *belonged* in the well decorated aristocratic bedroom. The panels do not set out sexual positions and keep company with a host of nonerotic images, illustrating the conceit of the picture gallery, or pinacotheca. In their decorative context the panels in the upper zone of the wall show that images of lovemaking belong in an art collection. Clearly the patron and the painter—like Ovid—knew that small erotic panels were at home in "proper"—and fashionable—bedroom decor.[1]

The houses and public buildings at Pompeii, because they were buried on a single day, offer much more contextual evidence than a building like the Farnesina villa. What modern archaeologists regret is that the excavations at Pompeii began in 1748, when excavators were really treasure hunters, looking for the best statues and most interesting wall paintings for royal collections. They often abandoned or willfully destroyed what did not interest them. On the subject of wall paintings of love-making, we note a terrible irony. Anything—sculpture, mosaic, or wall painting—that the excavators judged to be obscene was either destroyed on the spot or removed and locked up in the so-called Cabinet of Obscene Objects in the Naples Archaeological Museum. (Today the museum still keeps this room locked up but calls it the Pornographic Collection or the Erotic Collection.)[2] Even after scientific excavations began in the 1860s, the practice of removing "obscene" paintings continued. So did the practice of leaving the wall paintings of excavated houses exposed to the elements. Thus quite a few orphaned erotic paintings in the Pornographic Collection are still in good condition while the walls they were cut from have faded beyond recognition.

A Painting of Lovemaking in a Third-Style Jewel Box: The House of the Beautiful Impluvium

The fate of the only picture to survive intact from the House of the Beautiful Impluvium presents the worst-case scenario. It seems to be the last erotic painting to have been removed from its walls. Matteo Della Corte partially excavated the house in 1916. Subsequently someone had the picture photographed before its removal (Figs. 49 and 50). When Maiuri completed the excavation of the house in 1954, he returned the painting to its original place, but without providing for its conservation.[3] Today it is nearly illegible. This fact, added to the terrible state of conservation of the entire house, is all the more lamentable because the cubiculum that housed the painting of lovemaking, like the other principal rooms of this tiny house, belongs to a rare phase of wall painting at Pompeii. This is the late Third Style, dated to A.D. 40–45.[4]

The use of this erotic painting as part of a Third-Style decorative ensemble has significance for both social and cultural history at Pompeii.[5] It demonstrates that a practice first documented in Rome around 20 B.C. was thriving in Pompeii sixty years later, for when we last saw paintings of lovemaking it was in the little pinakes high up on the walls of cubicula in the Villa of the Farnesina. The Farnesina was a lavish villa in the capitol that boasted the best in fashionable decoration; the little House of the Beautiful Impluvium, located in an unimportant town near Naples, still reflected that taste. Furthermore, the erotic painting has moved from the upper zone to the center of the wall. The picture in the center of each wall in reception spaces focused the viewer's attention in a way that earlier painting had not. The rest of the wall became an elaborate setting for the gem in the middle: the central picture. What then does it mean when a cubiculum receives a central picture that details aspects of lovemaking? Such was the subject matter of the painting on south wall of cubiculum 11 in the House of the Beautiful Impluvium; the central pictures from the room's other three walls have not survived.

The plan reveals the house's small dimensions and the desire of the owner who remodeled it in A.D. 40–45 to make up for small size with elegant reception spaces (Fig. 51). He ordered precious marble decoration for the impluvium and expanded the *tablinum* (the main reception area, 7) to make it as deep as the atrium. Most important for our inquiry, he commissioned wall painters of no mean skill to decorate the entire house in a fine Third-Style manner that included, for instance, such features as intricate Ionic colonnades bearing shields with portrait heads in the tablinum.

A glance at the plan reveals that the location of cubiculum 11 is hardly that of a retreat for lovemaking. The atrium is the most public of the spaces in the Roman house, and cubiculum 11 is at the center of the atrium's left (east) wall. This cubiculum also communicates with the wing of the atrium itself via a door on its south wall. This wall had as its centerpiece the picture representing lovemaking (see Fig. 50).

Although the painter had difficulty in rendering the figures convincingly, his composition is unique. The man, reclining with his arm crooked over his head in erotic repose, welcomes the woman as she kicks off her sandals and climbs up on the bed. She wears the breast band, but her clothes have fallen from her torso to bunch in an arc around the circle of her buttocks. Drapery clings to her dangling left leg. She turns in profile to gaze intently at the man as she supports herself on

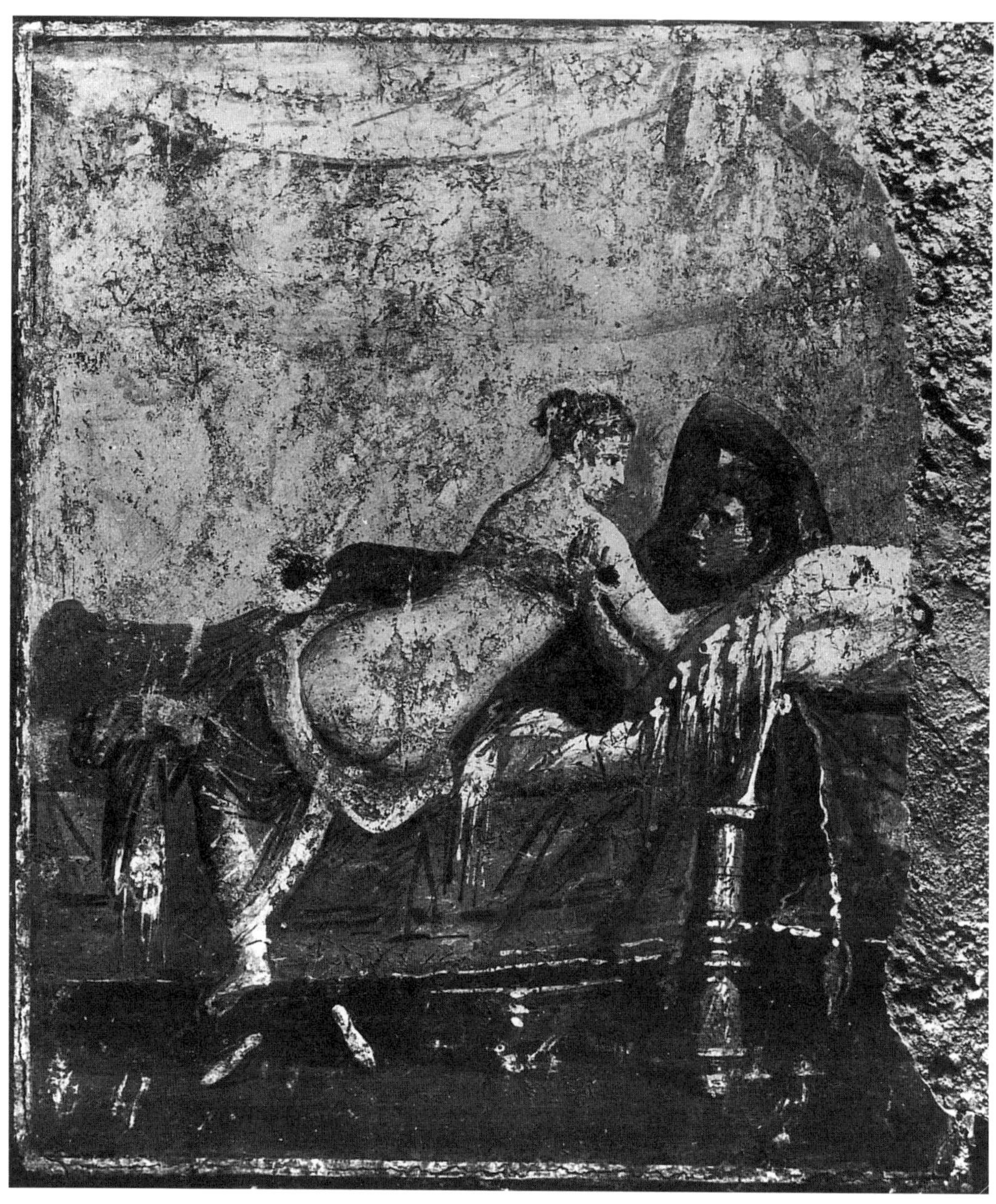

Figure 49. Male-female couple on bed, Pompeii, House of the Beautiful Impluvium (I, 9, 1), cubiculum 11, south wall, state at time of excavation (A.D. 40–45). By permission of the Ministero per i Beni Culturali e Ambientali, Istituto Centrale per il Catalogo e la Documentazione, N 66009.

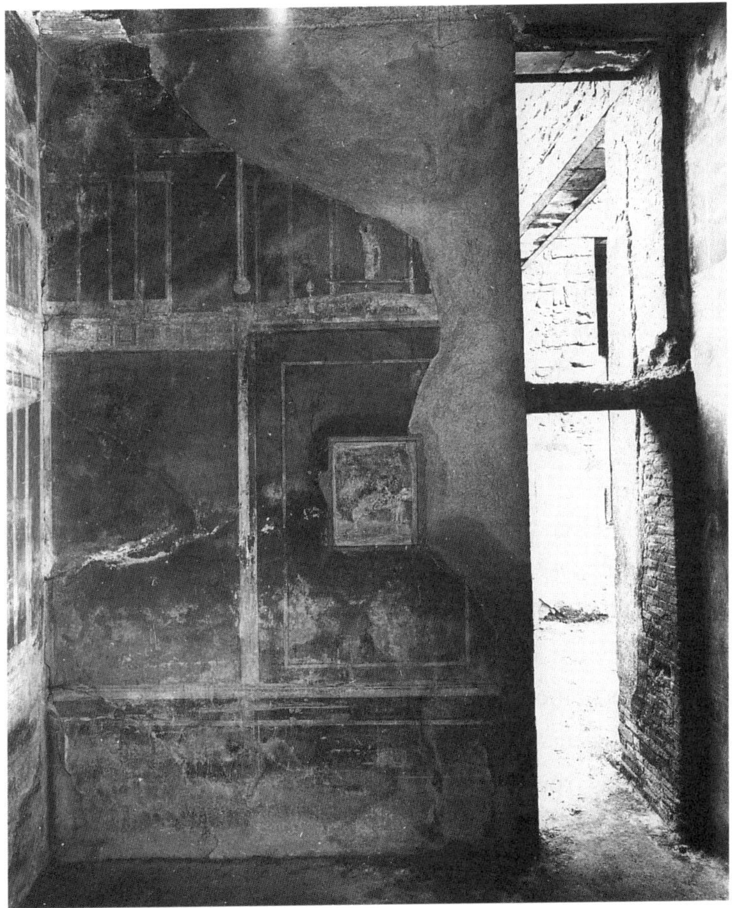

Figure 50. Pompeii, House of the Beautiful Impluvium (I, 9, 1), south wall of cubiculum 11 (A.D. 40–45). Photo Istituto Centrale per il Catalogo e la Documentazione N 34959.

her right arm, slipping her hand around his neck. He grasps her right shoulder with his left hand.

Were the artist more capable, and had the other three central pictures of this cubiculum survived, cubiculum 11 could shed considerable light on a phase in the artistic representation of lovemaking that is not well documented, the period between the paintings of the Farnesina sixty years before and the paintings of the late Fourth Style of A.D. 62–79 that constitute the bulk of the evidence from Pompeii

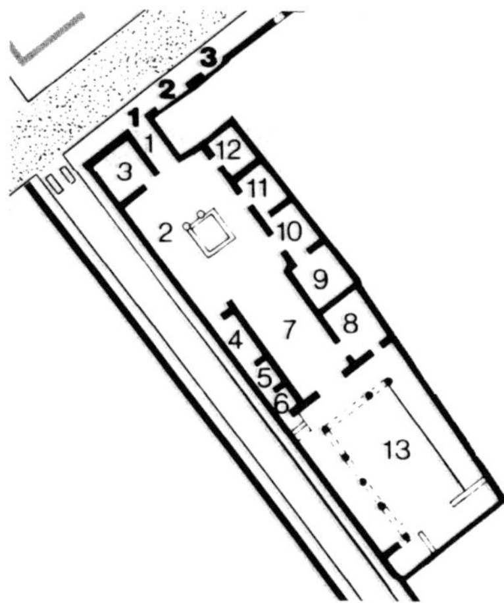

Figure 51. Pompeii, House of the Beautiful Impluvium (I, 9, 1), plan.

and Herculaneum. From what remains, however, we can make several observations. The woman's body does not fit the neo-Attic body type of the Augustan period. She is exaggeratedly tall and slim, with a tiny head, slight chest, and ample hips and buttocks. The artist's use of drapery to frame her buttocks—apparently using a compass to create a section of a circle—points to the female somatotype fashionable during the late Hellenistic period. Comparison with the terra-cotta statuette of two women from Myrina reveals the artist's allegiance to this particular manner of representing the beautiful female body; this body type first achieved widespread popularity in the second and first centuries B.C. (Fig. 52) and gradually regained prominence in representations of lovemaking after the death of Augustus.

In the absence of the other central pictures that the artist incorporated into this cubiculum we cannot determine the meaning that this single surviving painting of lovemaking had for the owner and for his guests. To judge from the refinement of the entire cubiculum's decorative scheme and its easy accessibility to the atrium, it was a room that the owner must have enjoyed using not only for sexual adventures but also for reception of guests who were more important or intimate than the clients he greeted in the tablinum or even those he entertained over a meal in the *triclinium* (dining hall). Its painting of lovemaking dated to the period of the Third Style gives us reason to believe that the fashion for decorating small rooms with pictures of lovemaking continued in the period between 20 B.C. and A.D. 45 in Pompeian houses both large and small. With the later and much more complete House of Caecilius Iucundus we can trace this trend into the period of the Fourth

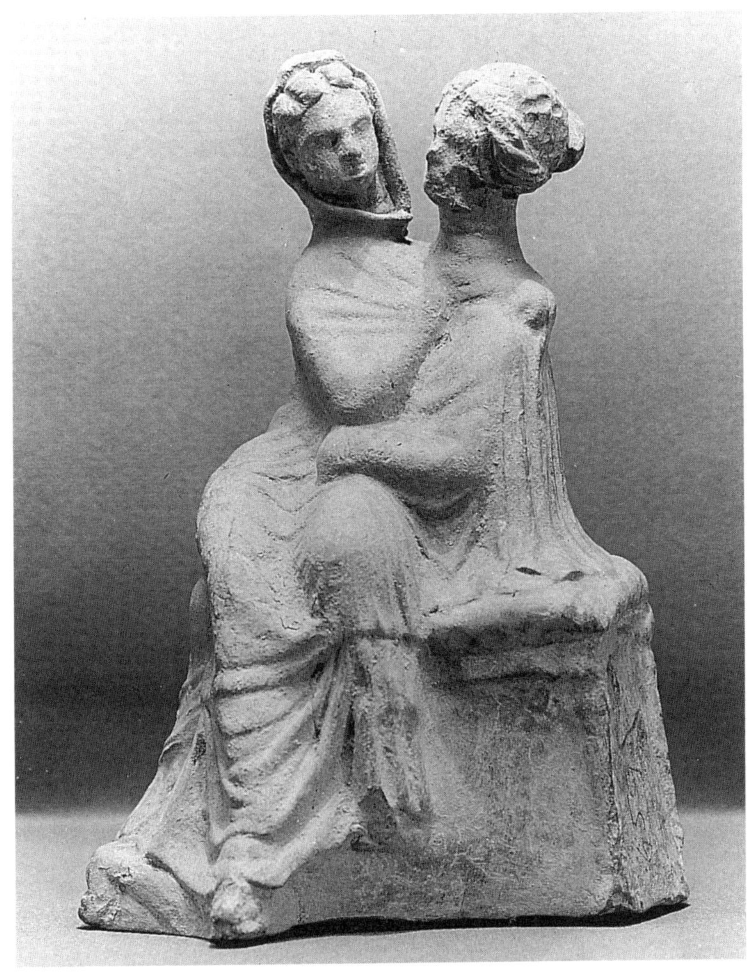

Figure 52. Two women, one seated on other's lap, terra-cotta figurine from Myrina (1st c. B.C.). Paris, Louvre, inv. MYR 659. © RMN.

Style (A.D. 45–79) and shed more light on what it meant to an owner to display erotic pictures in his or her house.

A Trophy of Elite Taste in a Freedman's House: The House of Caecilius Iucundus

The fine panel from the peristyle of the House of Caecilius Iucundus is still in the Pornographic Collection of Naples Museum (Plate 6).[6] On the plan the original

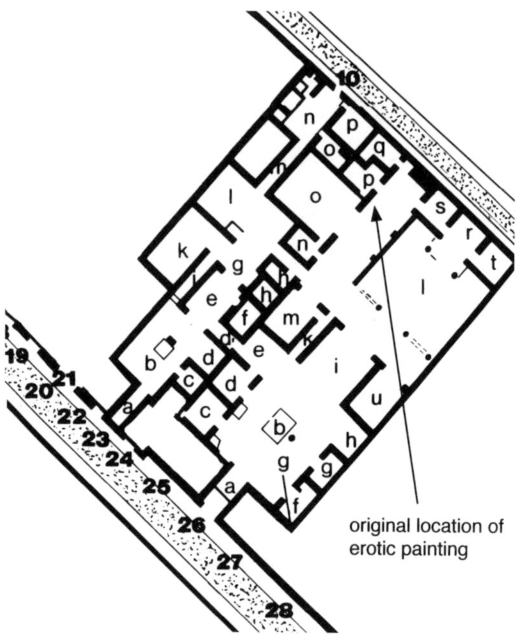

Figure 53. Pompeii, House of Caecilius Iucundus (V, 1, 26), plan.

location of the erotic painting is clearly indicated (Fig. 53). Several spectacular finds in this house permit us to understand the possible context for this painting. Sogliano, who excavated the house in the summer of 1875, found 154 wax tablets recording sums paid by the banker L. Caecilius Iucundus to persons for whom he had sold land, animals, and slaves between the years A.D. 52 and 60. He also collected taxes levied on the colony of Pompeii. Because the transactions involve small sums, scholars conclude that he was a person of average means, certainly a freedman.[7] Filling out the picture of the Caecilii is a herm portrait found at the left of the tablinum, dedicated by the freedman Felix. The inscription on the herm, "From Felix to our patron Lucius," indicates that Felix was a freedman whose family inherited the house and the business from a Lucius who lived in the early part of the first century of our era. The L. Caecilius Iucundus who lived in the house—and who presumably carried out the transactions recorded in the wax tablets—was probably a freedman descendant of Felix.[8] Finally, several marble reliefs adorning the domestic shrine on the north side of the atrium document the earthquake of 5 February A.D. 62. Aside from these rather unusual finds, the excavators found very few objects of value. There is evidence that shortly after ash from Vesuvius covered the house, treasure hunters carried off the most valuable objects, including the contents of the strongbox in the atrium.[9]

In the Augustan period the owner acquired and annexed the adjoining house at V, 1, 23; he then had the two houses redecorated with paintings of the Third Style. Scholars date the celebrated Third-Style frescoes of tablinum *i* to about A.D. 35–45.[10] The acquisition of the adjoining house meant that the owner could dispense with the service door at the back of peristyle *l* and install a symmetrical suite of rooms, *s*, *r*, and *t* to frame the house's visual axis—the sight line common in Roman houses that runs from the entryway passage through the atrium and tablinum to a feature at the back of the peristyle.[11] Complementing this group of rooms was another suite consisting of triclinium *o* with cubicula *n* and *p*.[12] Triclinium *o* is the largest of four triclinia resulting from this remodeling. Since it faced south, it would serve for winter entertainment, whereas triclinia *m*, *u*, and *k* (installed in V, 1, 23) faced east and would be appropriate for hot weather.[13]

After the earthquake of 62 the owner had the rooms around peristyle *l*—as well as the peristyle itself—redecorated, even though he was able to preserve the fine Third-Style tablinum as a "period" room. He had the doors between triclinium *o* and cubicula *n* and *p* closed. Cubiculum *n* apparently became a service room, since it received only plain plaster walls, whereas the artist concentrated his attention on the paintings in the triclinium and cubiculum *p*—and, in particular, on the erotic painting on the peristyle wall between these two rooms. Although most of the paintings of this suite were legible at the time of excavation, today we rely on the descriptions from 1876 by August Mau to reconstruct the iconographic program.[14] This is true, as well, for the paintings in the group of three rooms at the east of the peristyle and for the elaborate representation of a garden painted on the south wall of the peristyle—all gone today.[15]

Triclinium *o* received an unusually refined Fourth-Style scheme that won acclaim at the time of its discovery. In 1880 Presuhn included the arabesque frieze with griffins, centaurs, sphinxes on the right wall in his pattern book for decorative artists,[16] and anonymous artists from the German Archaeological Institute in Rome recorded the life-size roundels with "priestesses" that decorated the walls.[17] The main picture on the rear wall was a Judgment of Paris, illegible today. On the right (east) wall the central picture of Theseus Abandoning Ariadne, now in Naples, is an ambitious and dramatic interpretation of the myth.[18] Mau noted that before its removal there were clear traces of gilding detailing Ariadne's chain and her anklets.[19]

The same artist created the erotic painting in the peristyle. Today a hole in the north wall of peristyle *l* between triclinium *o* and cubiculum *p* records its original placement, since the excavator judged its subject matter to be obscene and had it cut from its wall and placed it in the Pornographic Collection in Naples. There the painting stands out by virtue of the refinement of its execution; it may be the finest erotic painting in the collection.

In its original setting the painting commanded pride of place; it established a pictorial link between the iconographic program of the triclinium and that of the cubiculum. Elements of the painting itself reward close scrutiny (see Plate 6). It is a delicate and nuanced scene of lovemaking in a cubiculum, painted with care and attentive to detail. An elegantly clothed *cubicularius* approaches a couple on a bed. The artist used gold even more lavishly than he had in the picture in the triclinium of Ariadne abandoned by Theseus. He applied gold to delineate the servant's hairnet and armlet as well as to define the jewelry that the seated woman wears, including her bracelets, earrings, and hairnet. An elegant yellow cloth covers her legs, it, too, decorated with applied gold. (Unfortunately, all the applied gold, visible at the time of excavation and reported by both Sogliano and Mau, disappeared because of the procedures used to detach the fresco.) The artist paid special attention to color and the opulence of fabrics throughout; the bed, for instance, has a pink coverlet with blue sham.

Models in high art must have inspired the artist, for this composition is complex. Far from being a frank scene of sexual intercourse, the conceit here is one of (male) desire and (female) resistance. The woman holds her hand behind her, whether to conceal her desire to touch the man or to locate him is not clear. He lifts his arm as though in entreaty, but she cannot see this gesture. A nice touch is the way his left hand curves up at the wrist, allowing the artist to show his virtuosity in depicting delicate fingers. The viewer sees these details but the woman does not, allowing the person who looks at this scene of lovemaking to understand the man's entreaty and the woman's hesitation in a way that the woman—and perhaps her lover also—cannot. This is a kind of privileging of the voyeur's perspective that also characterizes the refined representations of the Farnesina panels.

What meanings do the opulence of color and gold detail, coupled with the representation of sexual dalliance, have in their setting in the House of Caecilius Iucundus? To begin with, these qualities in the painting relate it to the elevated images of lovemaking that elite patrons favored in their homes. Apparently the patron wished to differentiate this erotic image from those franker and more shabbily painted ones that people saw in humbler settings like the brothel and bath that we examine in chapter 7. The fact that this was probably the only picture within this large peristyle's decorative scheme—and the fact that it is right next to the biggest room off the peristyle—indicates that L. Caecilius Iucundus wanted visitors to stop and look at it.

A glance at the plan confirms that he also wished the room to the right of the picture to be a special kind of cubiculum, with an anteroom and two barrel-vaulted alcoves. The masons made special indentations in the lower parts of the walls to accommodate the couches that stood in each alcove (Fig. 54). Cubicula like this one had begun to be popular in the wealthy villas of late-Republican Italy about a hundred years before, almost always as part of a suite that included a reception–dining space (called either a triclinium or an *oecus*). In the plan of the Villa of Oplontis, spaces 11 and 12 constitute a suite of double-alcoved cubiculum with its accompanying reception or dining room (Fig. 55). In the Villa of the Mysteries there were three double-alcove cubicula (rooms 4, 8, and 16).[20] Cubiculum 4 formed a suite with oecus 5—the famous Room of the Mysteries; cubiculum 8 with oecus 6. The Villa at Settefinestre boasted three double-alcove bedrooms, each connected with an oecus, as well as three other suites consisting of two adjoining rooms.[21] As Wallace-Hadrill shows, these villas set the dominant pattern in proliferation of space for entertainment: "The essence of the Roman suite is that it provides an ample context for a crowded social life, allows guests to pass in astonishment from one fine room to another, and enables the master to hold court wherever the whim of the season or moment takes him."[22] This pattern not only endured through the first century of the common era, it also spread to the smaller, humbler houses in towns like Pompeii. Finding such a suite in the House of Caecilius Iucundus underscores the extent of its diffusion.

The cubiculum in one of these suites was not an ordinary bedchamber but a carefully decorated room that an elite citizen might use as a reception space for a high-ranking guest. The elite regularly used cubicula for meetings with peers or people of slightly lower social standing. The ancient literature includes five instances

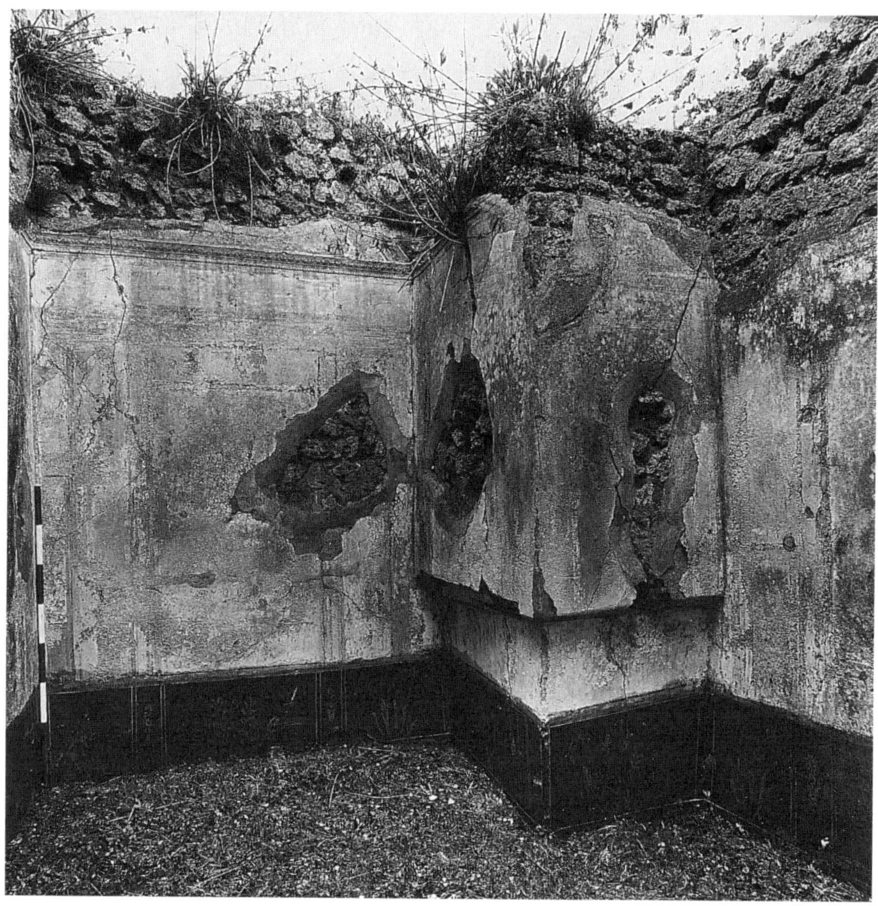

Figure 54. Pompeii, House of Caecilius Iucundus (V, 1, 26), cubiculum *p,* from entrance (A.D. 62–79). Photo Istituto Centrale per il Catalogo e la Documentazione N48400.

of Romans receiving friends *in cubiculo,* three instances of their conducting business there, and four of emperors holding trials *intra cubiculum.*[23] What use would L. Caecilius Iucundus make of his double-alcove bedroom?

Someone entering the cubiculum, presumably after studying the fine erotic painting in the peristyle, would see relatively large figures—averaging 25 cm in height—at the center of the walls in front, to the right, and to the left. The room's principal image, at the center of the north wall, was a group of Mars and Venus with a figure of Cupid standing in the panel to the right. Venus' upper body was nude, and she raised her right arm so that her hand was almost above her left shoulder.

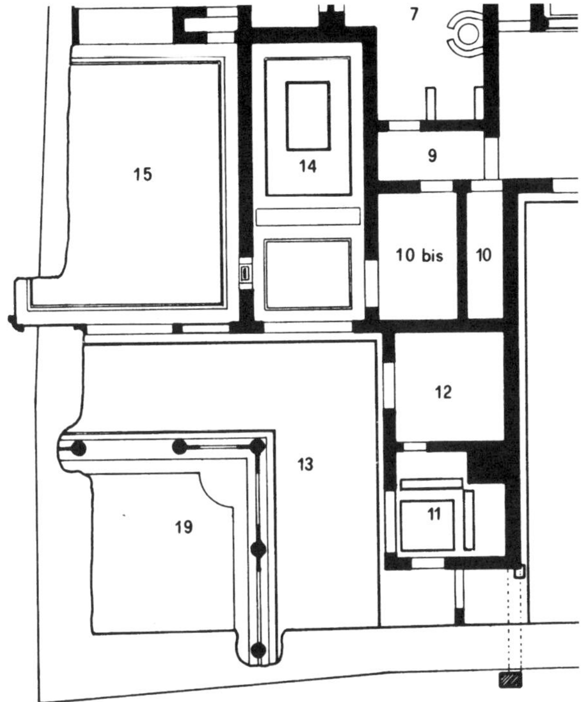

Figure 55. Torre Annunziata, Villa of Oplontis, plan, detail, suite 11–12–14.

In her fingers she held a green ribbon. Helmeted Mars was removing the purple garment that covered Venus' lower parts. Mau notes that its composition was almost the same as the central picture of room *t*, removed from its wall and now in the Naples Museum.[24] Bacchus, dressed in a purple chlamys and holding a thyrsus, presided over the east wall. In the upper part of the left wall stood a muse dressed in a long purple chiton, holding a lyre in her left hand with the plectrum in her right.

Even given the fragmentary nature of the evidence, it seems clear that the artist intended to expand the theme of lovemaking from the human to the divine. He did so by associating the vision of elite dalliance in the peristyle panel with an image of passion stirring the quintessential divine lovers, Mars and Venus, in the main panel of the cubiculum. Wine and song, personified by Bacchus and Erato, muse of love poetry, furthered this iconography of amorous pleasures.

But was this a room used for lovemaking?[25] The revelry of the dinner party in the triclinium might end with a sexual encounter—certainly not a very private one—in the cubiculum. But the refinement of the painting representing lovemaking, its location in the peristyle, the somewhat erudite nature of the program of images in the cubiculum itself, and the close architectural relation between triclinium and cubiculum indicate a different primary intent. We must think of the meanings that the architectural and decorative ensemble might have for the owner and his guests. The elements of this ensemble were mythological paintings in the largest triclinium, erotic painting in the peristyle, and love theme in the double-alcove bedroom.

As a middle-class man of only moderate means living in the Pompeii that was still in ruins in the aftermath of the earthquake of A.D. 62, L. Caecilius Iucundus fits the profile of the former slaves who embellished their houses with features of villas.[26] He took care to redecorate the all-important area around the peristyle—most likely damaged by the earthquake—in the style of the time even while carefully retaining the elegant Third-Style tablinum as a status symbol. He ordered up new paintings to emphasize the importance of the unit formed by triclinium *o* and cubiculum *p*, and he had the artist open up the south part of his big peristyle with elaborate paintings of a wild-animal park and fountains in the form of nymphs.[27] Seen in the context of the patron's redecorating effort, the purpose of the panel now in Naples seems to be to recall, in slightly pretentious references, the cubicula of the very wealthy that often featured refined representations of lovemaking. These associations become a bit obvious because this picture is literally displaced, displayed in the peristyle rather than within the cubiculum.

We imagine the owner explaining to his guests the unsubtle visual relations among the mythological paintings featuring nude beauties in the triclinium (Venus, Minerva, and Juno in the Judgment of Paris; Ariadne), the lovemaking of the human couple outside the triclinium, and the loves of the gods within the cubiculum. We even have a parallel in Petronius Arbiter's characterization of Trimalchio, the former slave, who now that he has won his freedom and wealth delights in nothing better than explaining imagery to his bored guests. Frescoes greet his guests—a trompe l'oeil painting of a dog (with the legend CAVE CANEM—Beware of the Dog) and the story of his life told through allegories of divine intervention (Petronius, *Satyricon* 29). Trimalchio interprets the zodiac in an elaborate dish served to his guests (39); offers a ridiculous iconographic explanation of the imagery in his silver vessels (52); and orders up the iconographic program for his tomb (71).

If Petronius' account of Trimalchio is any gauge of the attitudes of the freedman class toward art, the so-called erotic painting in the House of Caecilius Iucundus is far from our modern conception of a scene of sexual intercourse meant primarily to stimulate the viewer.[28] For in addition to its sexual message, the painting also functioned as a kind of trophy—a sign of the owner's elite pretensions and social climbing.

Pendant Display of Paintings of Lovemaking: The House of the Centenary

For the use and viewing of its two paintings of lovemaking, the House of the Centenary provides different contexts. Both are in a secluded room, numbered 43 on the plan (Fig. 56). *We* associate seclusion and privacy with sexual intercourse. Did the ancient Romans? And does the isolation of the room where the erotic paintings appear in the House of the Centenary make it—as some scholars would have it—a lovemaking chamber—a *camera d'amore?*[29] To answer these questions, we need to consider the possible functions of the room in the layout of the whole house. Then we need to ask what "privacy" might mean for the owner of the House of the Centenary. Finally, we need to look at the iconographic and decorative systems that the erotic paintings fit into.

The House of the Centenary is a wealthy one that takes up a whole city block; it is at least three times larger than the House of Caecilius Iucundus. It dates originally to the second century B.C. and underwent a complete remodeling in the period of the mature Third Style of about A.D. 15. At this time the owner put in a private bath with a swimming pool. In the last decades of its existence a redecorating campaign transformed a number of rooms, including a grandiose fountain house, with Fourth-Style decorative schemes.[30] The two erotic paintings that form part of the decoration of room 43 belong to this campaign, as does 42, the room that visitor or owner must walk through to get to 43. The painting of room 41, identified as a triclinium, kept most of its Third-Style decoration, even though the owner had new central pictures in the Fourth Style inserted into the centers of the walls.[31]

To get to room 43 a person had to pass through one of the atria. The visitor would proceed down a corridor at 39, through triclinium 41, and through room

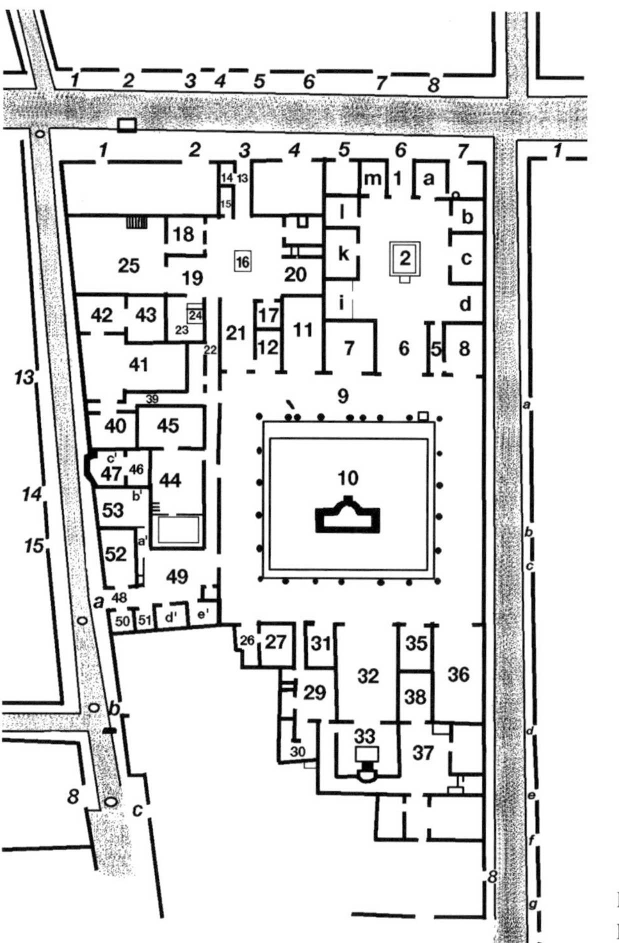

Figure 56. Pompeii, House of the Centenary (IX, 8, 6), plan.

42. We can see why to some modern scholars 42 was a room for lovemaking—tucked away, in what seemed to them to be a "private" part of the house. Yet this cubiculum was an integral part of an entertainment suite and in its context, I argue, had an entirely appropriate decorative system.

For one thing, the architectural configuration spells "luxury," not "lust." This is a variation on the configuration, discussed above in relation to the House of Caecilius Iucundus, that was prominent in the villas of the very rich during the first century B.C. In the House of the Centenary the owner inserted this kind of suite into his house as a sign of luxury. Seen in this light, it is similar to other features of the luxury villa that he had constructed, like the big fountain house at 32–33 in the plan.

For another thing, ancient Romans had practically no equivalent to our late twentieth-century conception of privacy. The concept is simply alien to their mentality.[32] Whereas the position of the cubiculum reads, to the modern viewer, like an attempt to create a "private" retreat, to the owner and visitors the combination of triclinium with the two adjoining rooms, one serving as an anteroom for the other, meant that its function could be either reception or sleeping. And when Romans used the cubiculum for sleeping or even for lovemaking, there were servants present. As we noted in chapter 4 in reference to the Farnesina paintings, the *cubicularius* was an invisible presence who even slept on a mat at the threshold to the cubiculum. In the picture from the House of Caecilius Iucundus the artist, following paintings like those from the truly aristocratic Farnesina villa, depicted such a servant precisely to add to its elite tone.

When we look at the context displayed in the wall painting of this suite, we find an intermingling of mythological pictures with the scenes of human lovemaking, a blend much like that of the House of Caecilius Iucundus. Interestingly, room 41 of the House of the Centenary is an elegant triclinium painted in the mature Third Style. Just as Caecilius Iucundus preserved his old tablinum, so the owner of the House of the Centenary kept his triclinium as a period room (except for its center pictures of the Fourth Style, inserted later). But he had rooms 42 and 43 painted in the current style. The decorative scheme of room 42 was rich in ornament and decorated with three pictures, all in terrible condition today. At the center of the north wall was Cassandra. Two pictures decorated the west wall on either side of the window: Endymion and Selene, and Venus as a fisherwoman. Venus had two companions: a swimming *amorino* and a fishing *amorino.* Having taken in this hardly salacious program, the visitor would then enter room 43.

In Roman decoration, the wall of a room opposite the entrance always carries the most important picture. Here the viewer would see in front of her—not an image of copulation, but one of Hercules sleeping. Although much damaged today, the hero is still visible, nude, surrounded by *amorini*. The erotic paintings are secondary, occupying the walls to the right and the left.

All three center pictures formed part of an ambitious Fourth-Style decorative system. The system is still partially visible on the right-hand wall (Fig. 57). There is

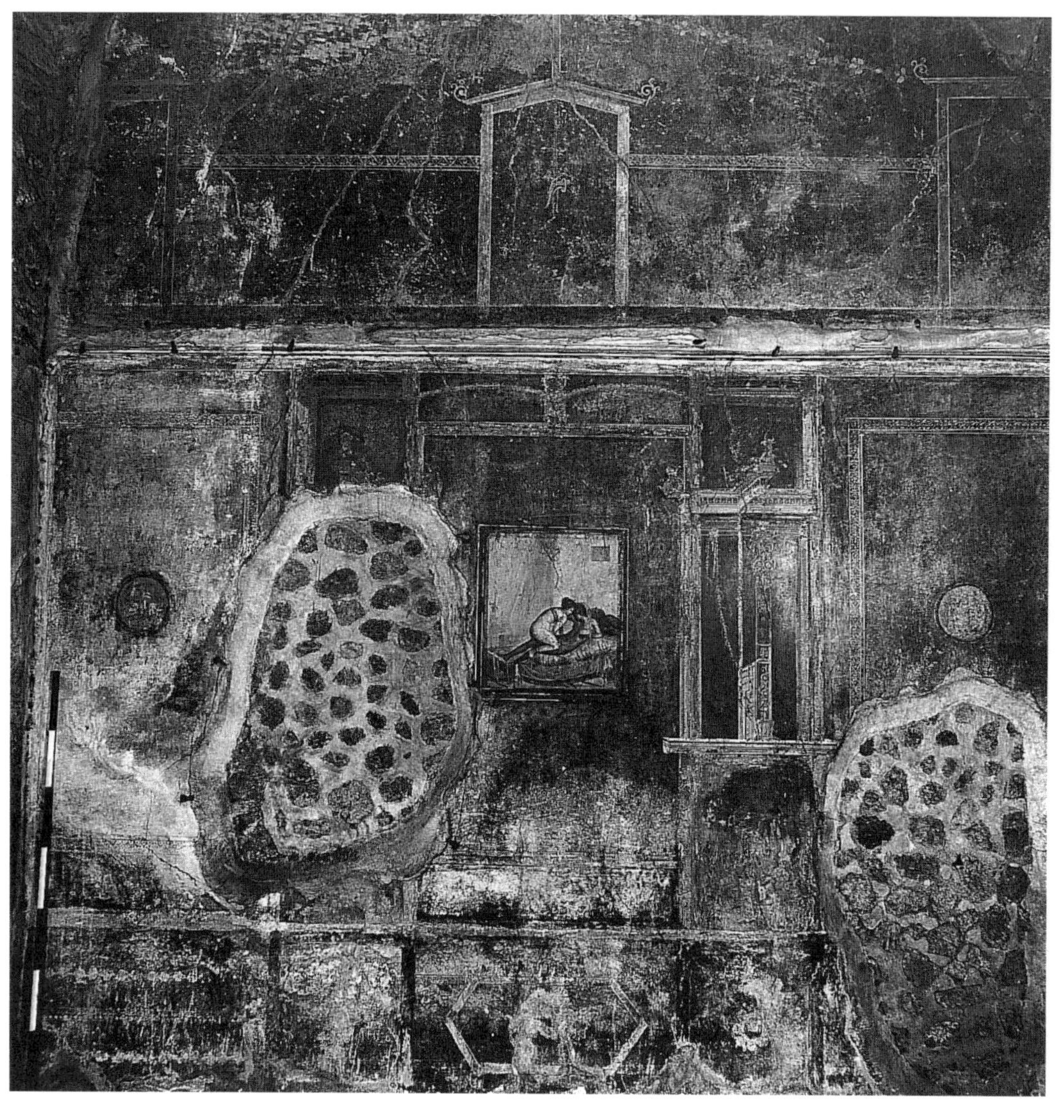

Figure 57. Pompeii, House of the Centenary (IX, 8, 6), room 43, south wall (A.D. 62–79). Photo Michael Larvey.

a black dado and black middle zone, with tall red panels framing the central picture. Many secondary figures filled these panels, so that the relative isolation of the erotic pictures that we see today is misleading. There was originally much more to look at than the central panels.

The central picture on the left wall is the more damaged of the two, but its subject is still legible (Fig. 58). The artist had the man reclining on a bed; he holds his head and torso up with on his left elbow, while the rest of his body trails off to the left. The woman has her back to the man and places her hands on her knees as she squats down on his penis. The man's right arm passes behind her hips, but paint losses make it impossible to know the position of that hand, whether on her back or around her waist. She is slim and tall—less substantial than the neo-Attic women in the Farnesina panels.

Remains of the underpainting provide a sense of the architecture of the chamber. Three differently colored zones suggest a space that is open to the light of a peristyle in the center. A garland hangs from a point slightly to the right of the top center of the picture, and there is a small, dark square panel on the wall, upper left. The light panel in the background is the artist's attempt to open up the scene to the landscape—or at least to a planted garden. A painting from an unknown house in Pompeii, now in the Pornographic Collection (Fig. 59), offers an interesting parallel: behind the couple on the bed there is a light panel framing a tree. The tree is now leafless, probably because the leaves, added in secco, were lost in the process of removing the painting from the wall. The artist represented a view from the lovemaking chamber to create an aura of upper-class sophistication and gentility: architects often took pains to site cubicula in the villas of the wealthy so that they looked out on special views—either to a planted garden or to special features in the landscape. Statius (ca. A.D. 45–96) and Pliny the Younger (ca. A.D. 61–112) make much of rooms, conceived as pavilions for viewing the landscape.[33] Although the artist merely reflected such elite pretensions in this rather ineptly painted representation, it is significant that he chose to locate the scene of lovemaking not in a closed chamber but in a room open to the pleasant landscape view.

Because the picture on the right wall is better preserved, it shows us more details (Plate 7). The artist used shadows to indicate a strong light coming in from the right. The woman, her hair arranged in a high helmet of curls, wears a breast band, as well as an anklet and an armband. She is astride the man, who leans on his left elbow while holding his right arm crooked around his head in the gesture of erotic repose. The woman's forehead slightly overlaps the top of the man's head as she leans forward. From this crouching position she supports herself with her extended left arm while reaching down with her right hand, most likely to grasp the man's

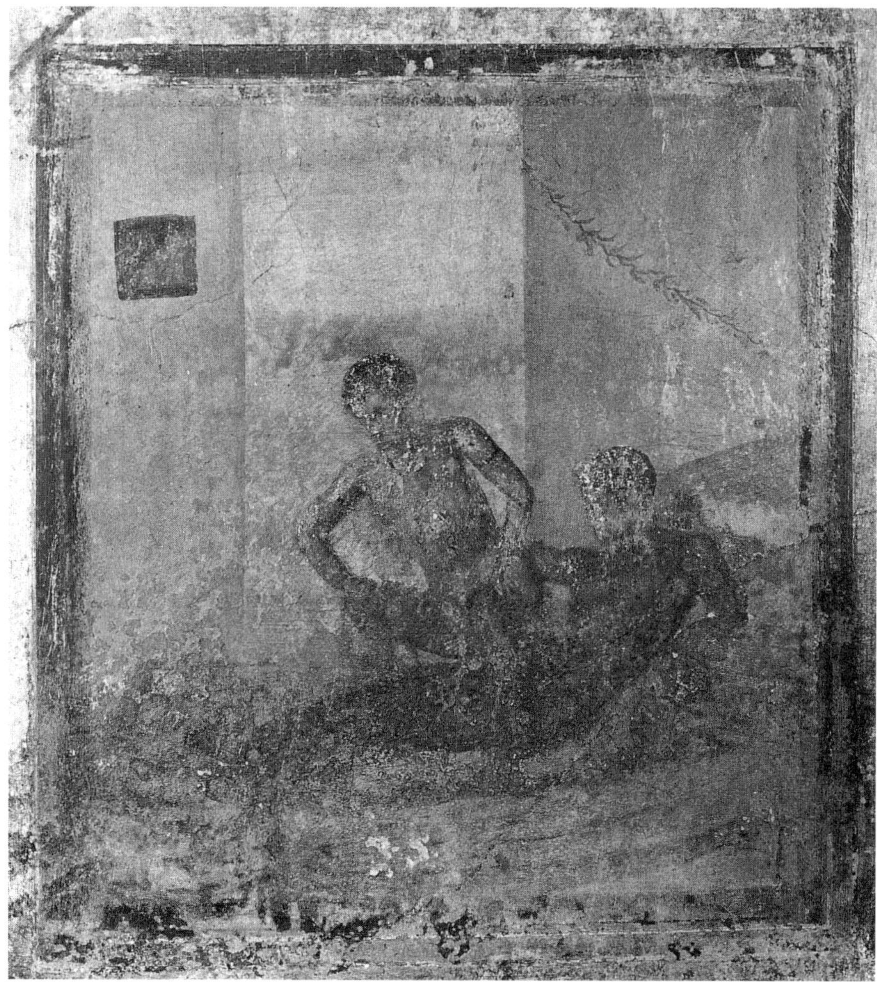

Figure 58. Male-female couple on bed, Pompeii, House of the Centenary (IX, 8, 6), room 43, north wall, central picture (A.D. 62–79). Photo Michael Larvey.

penis, hidden from view behind her right thigh. Here the background is less clear than in the left-hand picture, although we see a dark rectangle at upper right.

This, and the similar, nearly square shape in the central picture of the wall opposite, are the underpaintings for the *tabellae* mentioned by Ovid. A bronze mirror cover, found on the Palatine, suggests an excellent parallel (Fig. 60). Scholars date it to the Flavian period because of the woman's hairstyle.[34] The shuttered panel at the top of the mirror is so well articulated that its imagery is legible. In the paint-

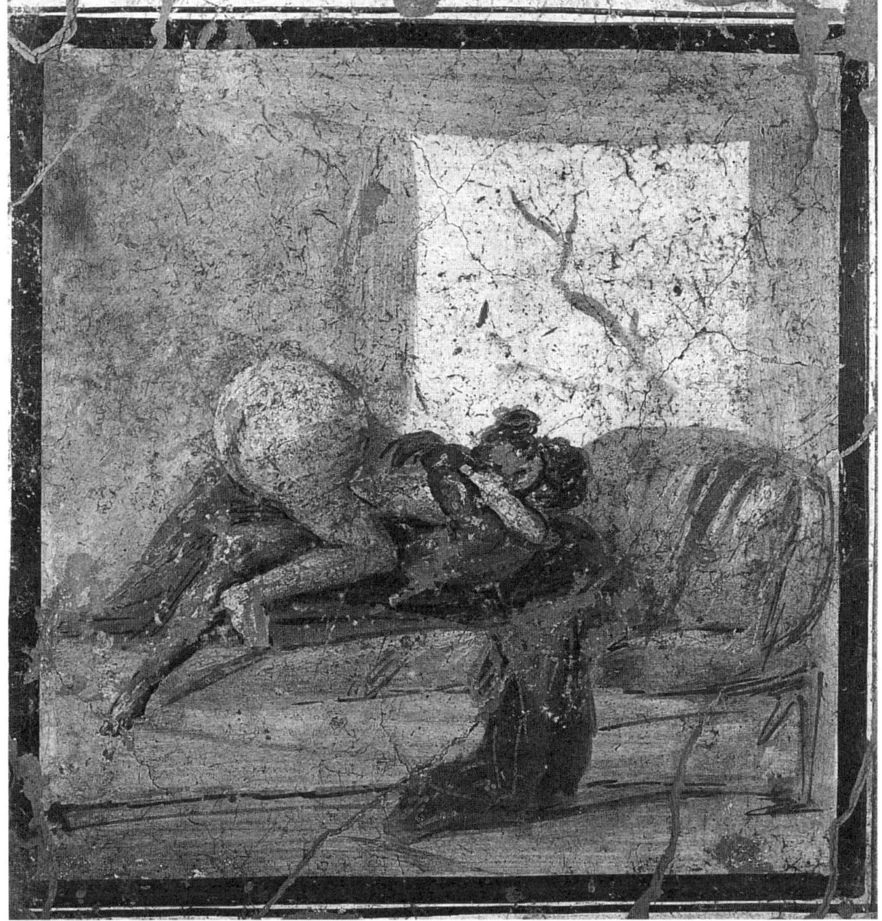

Figure 59. Male-female couple on bed, from Pompeii, unknown location, (A.D. 62–79). Naples, Archaeological Museum, inv. 27684, W. 33 × H. 33 cm. Photo Michael Larvey.

ings from the House of the Centenary losses of the applied secco have reduced what must be similar representations of erotic pinakes to the dark patches visible today.

Identifying the motifs is not enough, of course, if we are to understand the meaning of these paintings as part of the decoration of a secluded room in a private house. Obviously the situation is different from that of the House of Caecilius Iucundus, where the painting's placement in the peristyle probably meant that it would

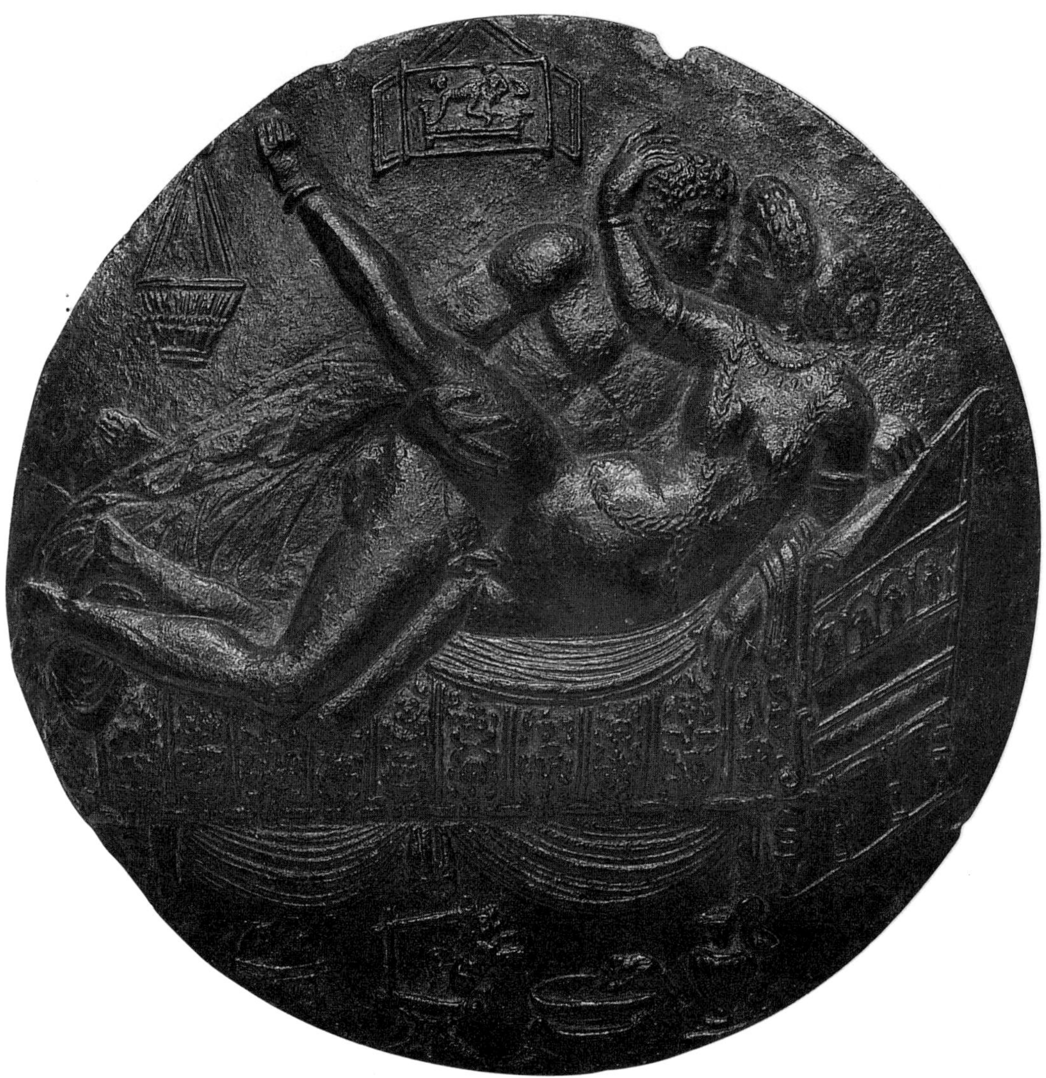

Figure 60. Male-female couple on bed, bronze mirror cover found on Palatine, Rome (A.D. 69–79). Rome, Antiquarium Comunale, photographic archive of the Antiquarium Comunale. Photo Antonello Idini.

be seen by more visitors than might enter room 43 to look at the two central pictures in the House of the Centenary. Furthermore, the use of gold and the presence of the *cubicularius* are references to the gentility of aristocratic paintings like those of the Farnesina; both scenes in the House of the Centenary represent more active lovemaking than the ambiguous scene from the House of Caecilius Iucundus. Yet the triclinium-anteroom-cubiculum configuration of the House of the Centenary closely parallels similar suites in wealthy villas considered above. In reality, it is a more elaborate imitation of such suites than the abbreviated version in the House of Caecilius Iucundus. It follows that the two pictures of lovemaking in room 43 of the House of the Centenary formed part of a decorative scheme that paralleled—even imitated—the display of such *tabellae* in the cubicula of the very wealthy. Their inclusion was correct for a space where the owner might receive and entertain his social peers—but we must not assume that sexual intercourse was the entertainment. As for the notion that this part of the house was set up as a brothel: if the owner were to set up a brothel in part of his house, he would make the path to the rooms as short as possible—and he certainly would *not* route the clients through his (grand)father's prize Third-Style triclinium!

The Vettii Brothers' Folly: A Cook's Bedroom?

One of the most spectacular houses preserved at Pompeii belonged to two freedmen brothers, A. Vettius Restitutus and A. Vettius Conviva (Fig. 61). Its complex programs of elegant Fourth-Style wall painting, complemented by a garden-peristyle adorned with twelve fountains and numerous marble and bronze sculptures, still delight thousands of tourists every day.[35] Both their hard-won civic status and the display of the wealth that brought them that status were important to the Vettii. A. Vettius Conviva, who appears as a witness in one of the wax tablets found in the House of Caecilius Iucundus, was an *augustalis;* to become an *augustalis* the former slave had to pay a considerable sum to finance public works.[36] In their atrium the Vettii had two money chests attached to the walls. Within the complex and sometimes baffling imagery of their lavishly painted rooms, images of commerce appear alongside themes from classical mythology. For instance, in the largest reception space, oecus *q,* the delicate frieze of cupids and psychai illustrates the manufacture and sale of wine, perfume, and flower garlands while the big central pictures presumably there, and in the nearby reception spaces, explore lofty themes of divine and mortal transgression and retribution.[37] Similarly, the patrons took pains to include throughout the house the imagery of the two deities who protected

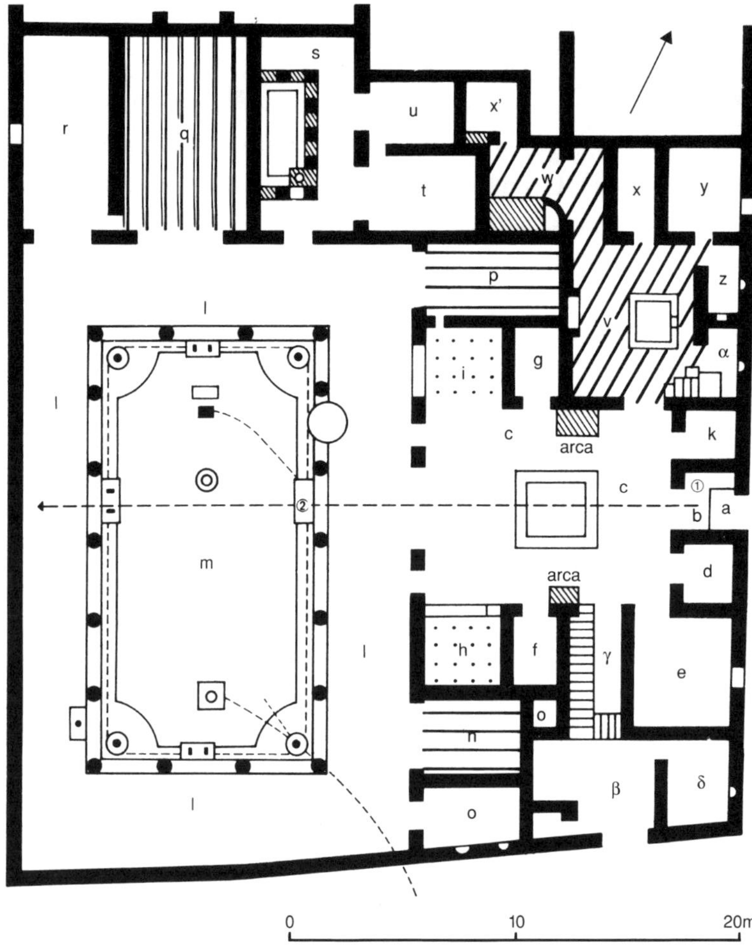

Figure 61. Pompeii, House of the Vettii (VI, 15, 1), plan.

commerce, Fortuna and Mercury. But even given this eccentric eclecticism, in view of both the quality of the house and its decoration, it comes as a surprise that these wealthy patrons commissioned an artist to decorate the ground-floor room next to the kitchen hearth with frank, shoddily painted scenes of couples making love.

The painter probably chose a white-ground scheme for room *x'* both for reasons of economy and to increase the light in the room, since its only source of light is its narrow doorway (Fig. 62). The artist painted its principal decoration—three pictures of male-female couples on beds—rapidly and with a very simple palette

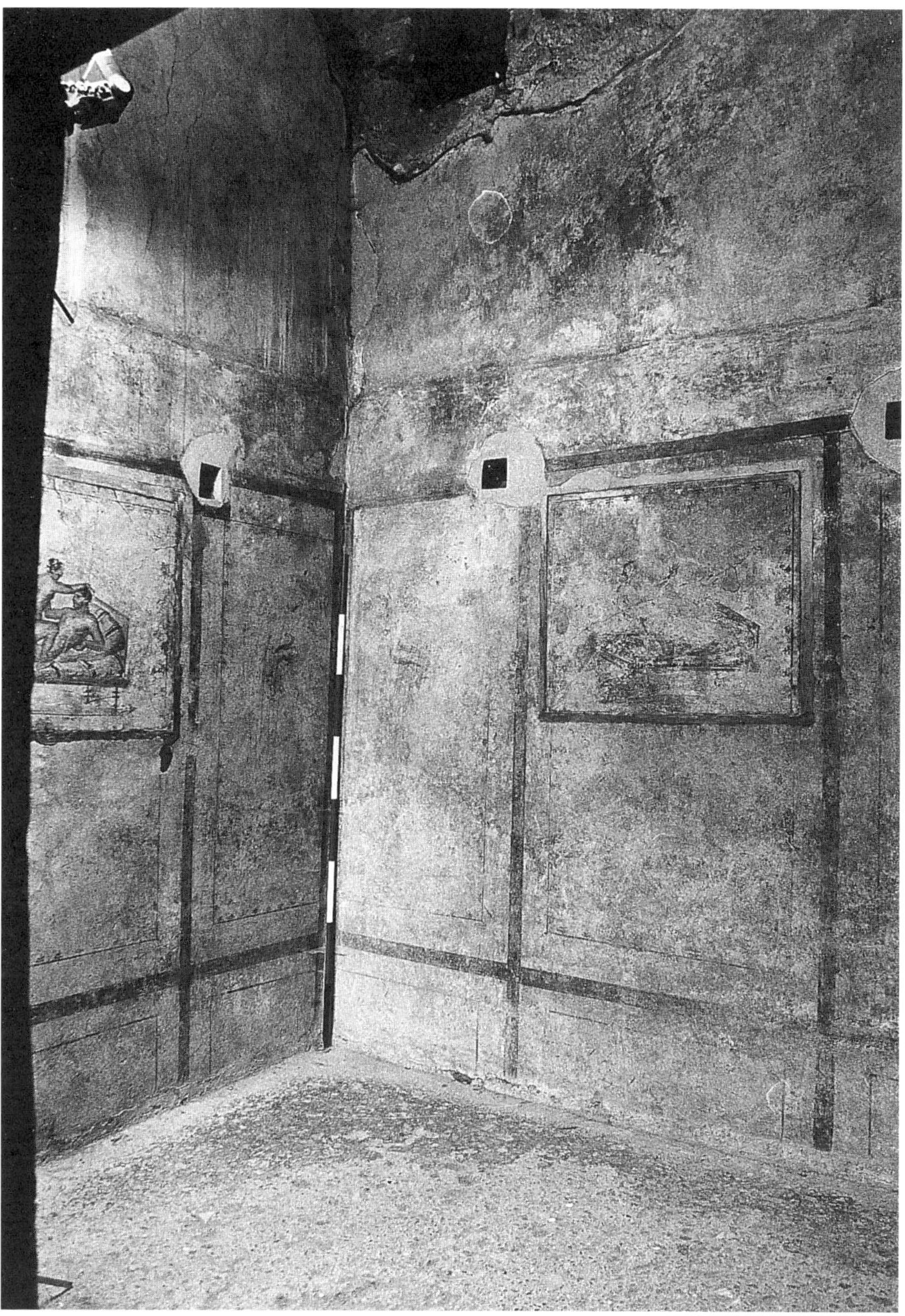

Figure 62. Pompeii, House of the Vettii (VI, 15, 1), room *x'*, view from doorway, north and west walls (A.D. 62–79). Photo Michael Larvey.

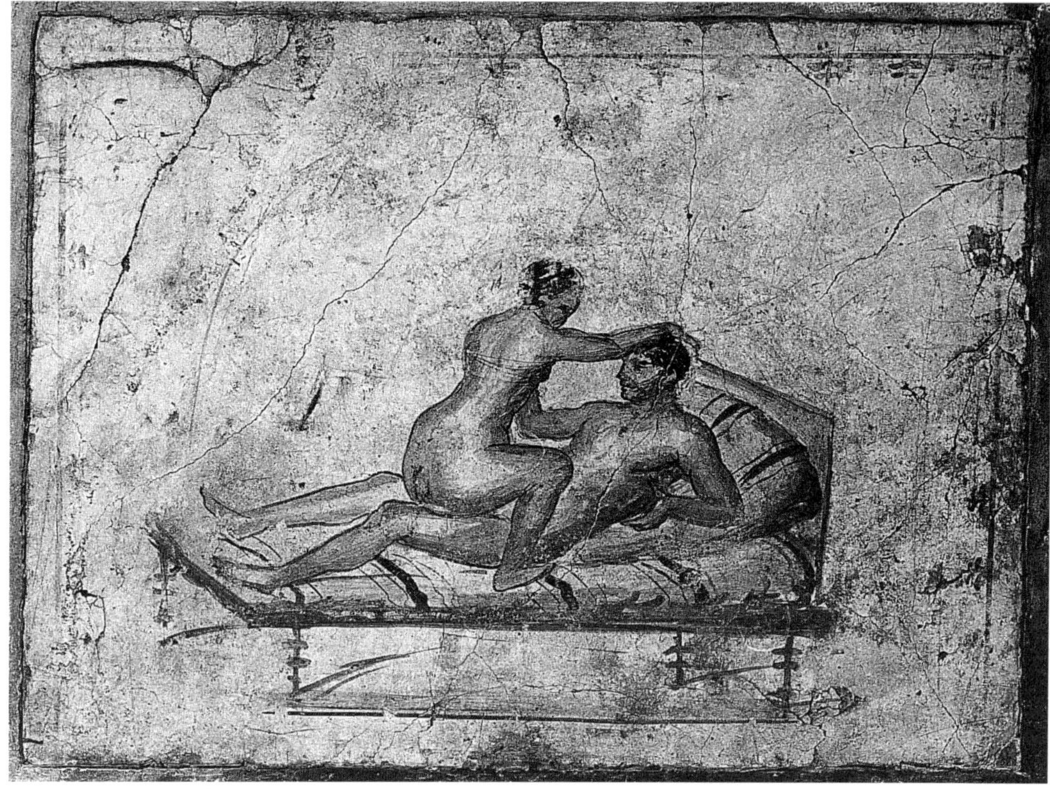

Figure 63. Male-female couple on bed, Pompeii, House of the Vettii (VI, 15, 1), room *x'*, west wall, central picture (A.D. 62–79). Photo Michael Larvey.

consisting of porphyry red, red ocher, and yellow ocher. Wide red bands divide the walls into three horizontal zones and three vertical ones, yet because the ceilings are so low the paintings take up nearly half the area of their panels. (In the photograph the meter marker, 1.60 m [62.4 in.] in height, provides an idea of the cramped nature of the space.) Square holes at the top of the middle-zone rectangles may have held beams to support a lightly constructed mezzanine.

At the center of the left (west) wall a man reclines on his back, resting on a heavy cushion and propped up on his left elbow (Fig. 63). The woman, clad only in a filmy breast band, faces him, her buttocks resting on the man's legs at mid-thigh. She leans forward slightly while resting her right hand on the man's head; the man reaches up to her unseen left shoulder with his right arm. In contrast to the paintings we have seen so far, the artist chose to eliminate all other elements of the set-

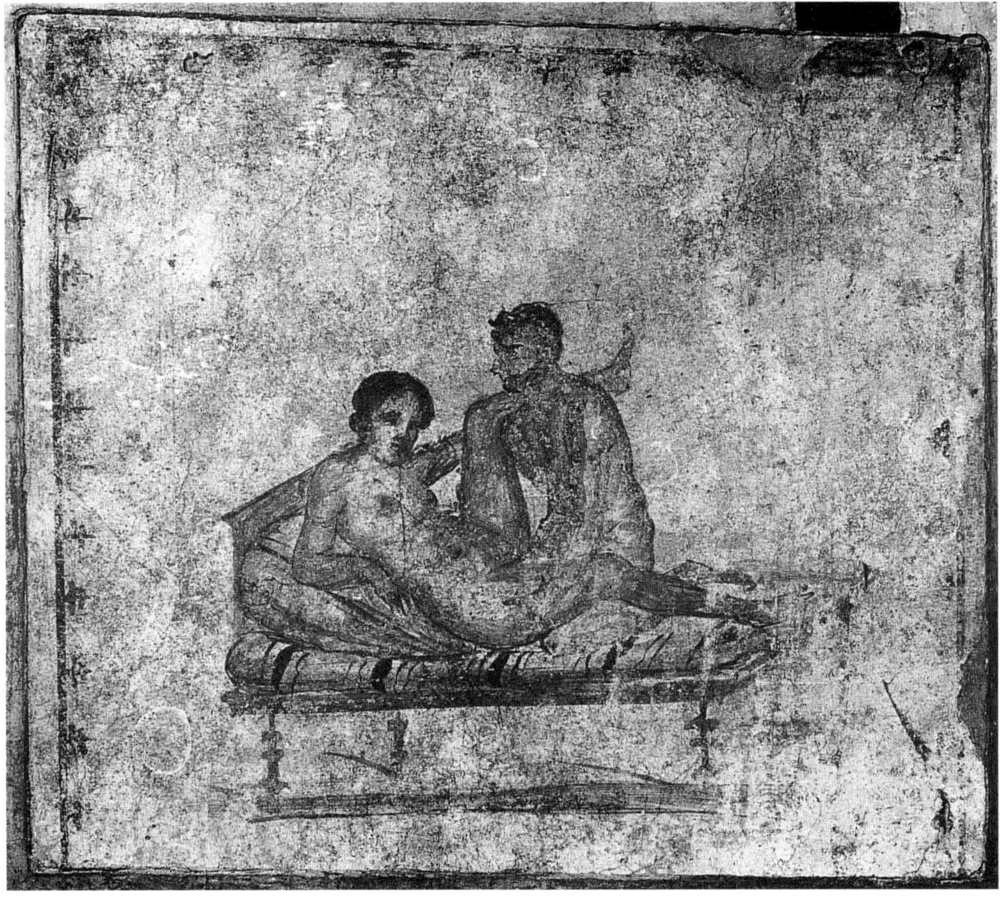

Figure 64. Male-female couple on bed, Pompeii, House of the Vettii (VI, 15, 1), room *x'*, east wall, central picture (A.D. 62–79). Photo Michael Larvey.

ting: everything is at its simplest, from the indication of the bed's legs and their shadows to the modeling of the figures themselves.

The central picture on the opposite wall inverts the position of the couple by presenting the woman reclining while the kneeling man faces her (Fig. 64). She stretches her right leg out along the bed but raises her left up over the man's right shoulder as he prepares to enter her. The artist depicted her face in three-quarters view and gave her a calm, even nonchalant expression; because of paint losses only the outlines of the man's profile are clear. Paint losses have nearly completely erased the painting on room *x*''s north wall. A final painted element is that of an owl perched on the short south wall; it probably stands for good fortune in lovemaking.[38]

Almost from the moment of its discovery scholars hypothesized that room *x*' was destined for the cook.[39] In favor of this supposition is its location, accessible only to someone who walked through the servants' atrium and past the large stove platform in the southwest corner of *w*. The odors and heat of cooking certainly permeated little room *x*'. In style, the paintings do not fit the profile of the paintings of lovemaking that adorned either the peristyle of the House of Caecilius Iucundus or the cubiculum of the House of the Centenary; they find their closest parallels in the relatively careless paintings of the brothel, or *lupanar,* at VII, 12, 18–20 (see Figs. 82–84). Yet it is highly unlikely that the Vettii set up a room in their servants' quarters as a brothel. For one thing, it was not a profitable business, considering the low prices commanded by the owners of the prostitutes at Pompeii, generally varying between one and sixteen asses: the usual cost is two asses, the price of a cup of common wine.[40] For another, wealthy and pretentious freedmen like the Vettii would avoid commerce of any sort within their house; this was precisely the kind of association that would remind people of their servile origins.

Rewarding a servant with a room that would remind him of the rough-and-ready lupanars would not be out of character for former slaves like the Vettii. In many ways the overburdened displays of complicated mythological cycles—and even the far-fetched mixtures of gods and demigods—indicate that the Vettii were adventurous and even quirky patrons. Take, for example, the unforgettable experience of entering the house: poised to the right of the door is a big painting of Priapus, god of fertility and abundance, weighing his enormous phallus against a sack of coins (Fig. 65). This bold and humorous image initiated a "Priapus axis" that culminated in the statue of the same deity in the peristyle: there he appeared as a fountain figure who spurted water from his enormous phallus into a basin. The patrons positioned him right on the line of vision established at the entryway: this visual axis went through the atrium and to the left of the jet of water spurting from the fountain-Priapus (Fig. 66; see plan, Fig. 61). Priapus belongs at both doorway and in the garden. At the all-important passageway into the house, Priapus' phallus wards away the Evil Eye. He has much the same apotropaic function as the ithyphallic Ethiopian placed at the entrance to the bath that we discussed in chapter 5. Priapus also belongs in the peristyle, there in his guise as god of fertility and custodian of

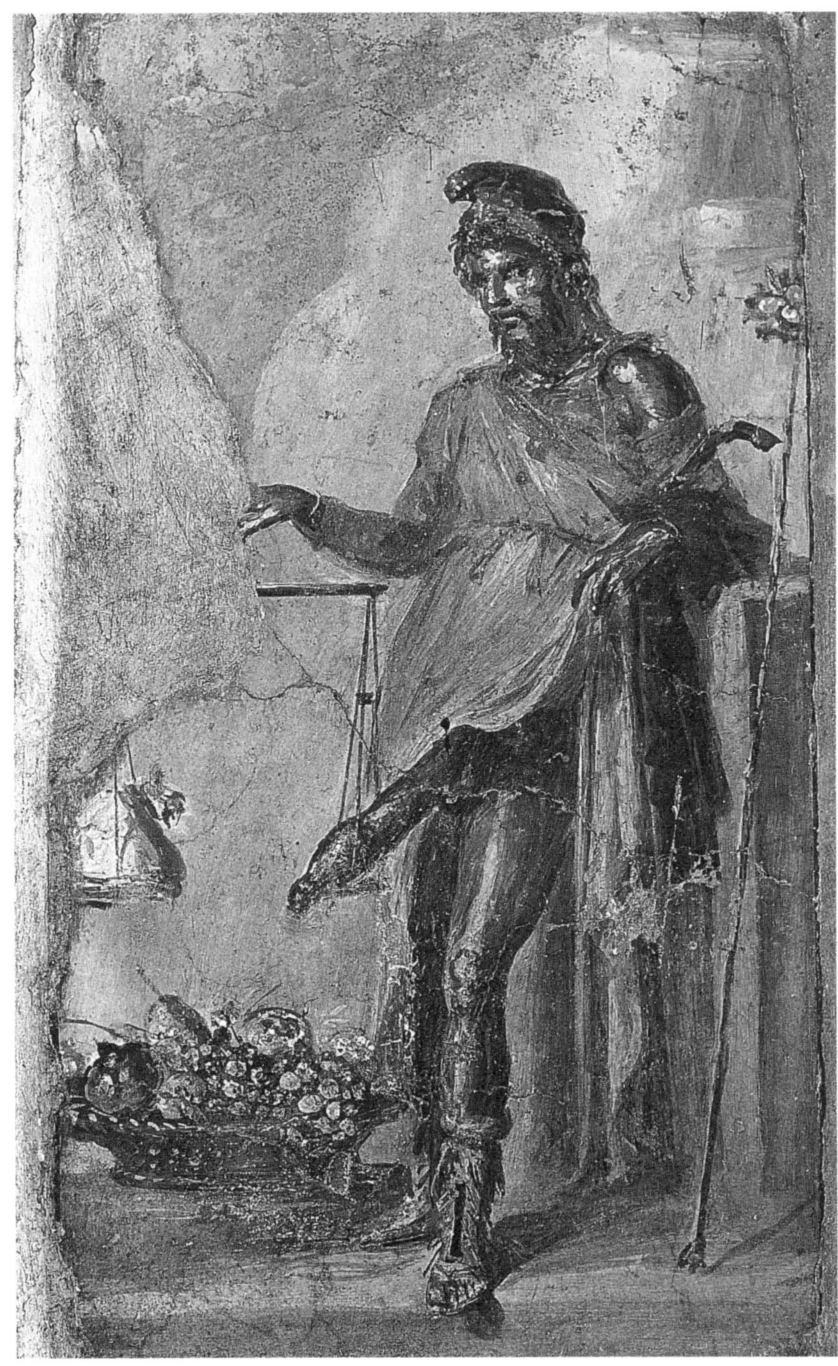

Figure 65. Priapus weighing his member against a sack of money, Pompeii, House of the Vettii (VI, 15, 1), fauces *b* (A.D. 62–79). Photo Michael Larvey.

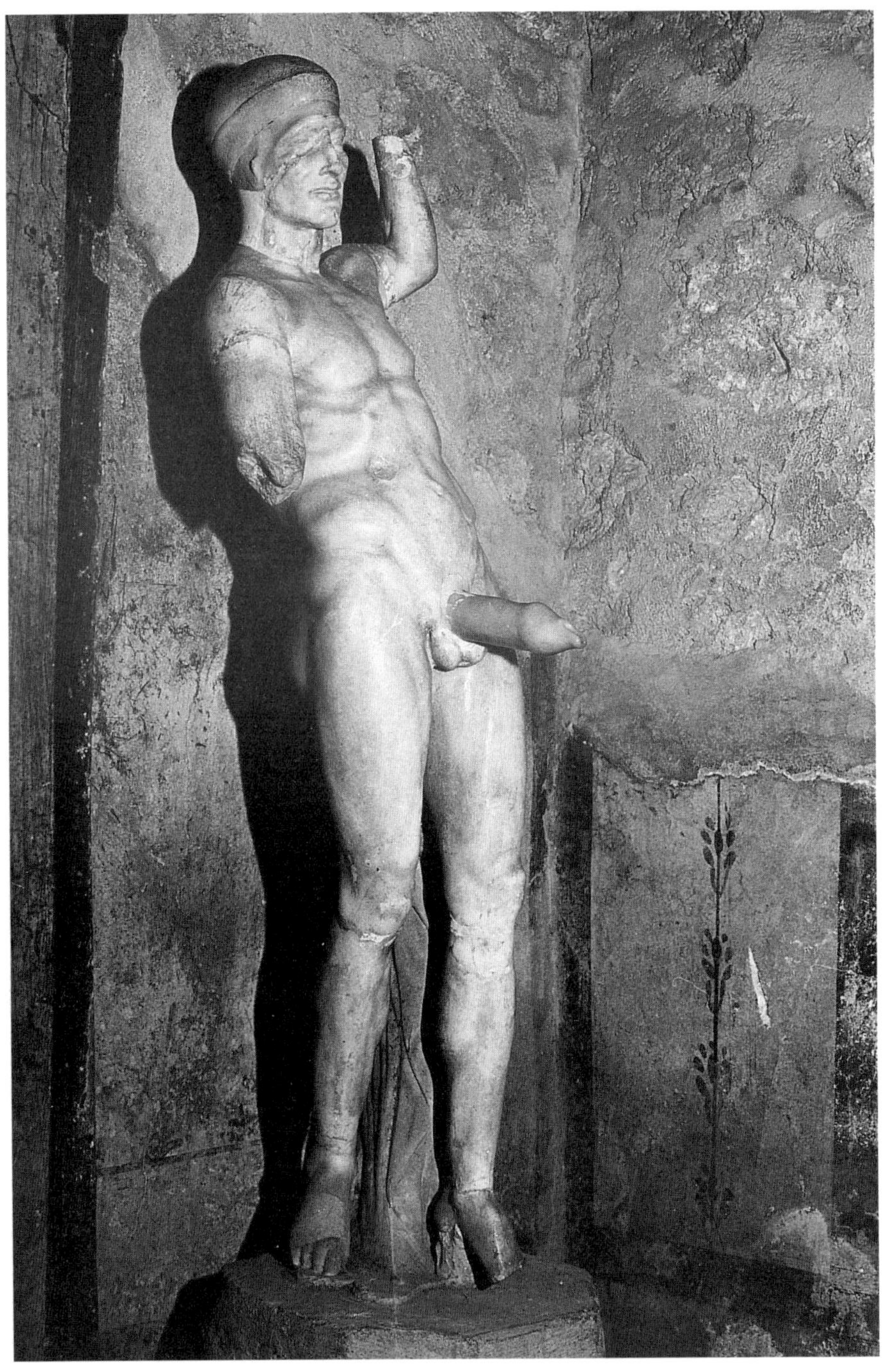

Figure 66. Fountain statue of Priapus, Pompeii, House of the Vettii (VI, 15, 1), from peristyle *l*, stored in room *x*' (A.D. 62–79). Photo Michael Larvey.

the fruits of that fertility in the garden. He joins a large Dionysian company, since the Vettii brothers filled the peristyle's garden with statues of Dionysus, Ariadne, maenads, Silenus, and satyrs.

The Vettii showed a fondness for another phallic demigod, Hermaphroditus. As we have seen, artists in the Hellenistic period elaborated many representations of this deity who displayed the sexual characteristics of both male and female. Pollitt suggests that the ancient viewer regarded such representations with a combination of superstitious anxiety and reverence.[41] Rather than a sexual curiosity, Hermaphroditus represented the unification of the two sexes in one deity as well as the dual nature of the individual's sexual psyche: the woman within every man and the man in every woman. In the late first century, the Vettii brothers placed images of Hermaphroditus at key positions near passageway spaces. In the house's principal oecus (*q*) the god appears in a little panel on the south wall, to the right of someone looking out to the garden. Silenus, a god in Dionysus' retinue, approaches her/him from behind; he registers surprise as he sees Hermaphroditus' prominent erection (see Fig. 15).[42] Another image of Hermaphroditus appears over the southern doorway of oecus *p;* this time it is Pan who discovers him/her.

It is not so much the appearance of Priapus and Hermaphroditus within the iconography of the House of the Vettii—but rather their prominence and emphasis—that strikes a special note. The more we study the iconography of the house, the more we perceive that the Vettii liked emphatic—even overburdened—imagery, and that they wanted to surprise and amuse their guests. How better to achieve this goal than to emphasize the humorous representation of the phallic god, or to insert two vignettes of the ambisexual god in prominent locations? The Vettii (like many other Pompeian house owners and Petronius' Trimalchio) wanted to make the experience of entering their house vivid—even while protecting the house and its occupants from the Evil Eye. Similarly, the images of Hermaphroditus in the major reception spaces could evoke both wonder and surprise in the ancient viewer. Knowing that the Vettii brothers were patrons with a taste for sexually outlandish representations, we see in the erotic paintings in room *x*' another aspect of their unconventional taste. And knowing that they themselves were once slaves, we advance the notion that they outfitted this room as a gift for a favorite slave, most probably the cook. Once again Petronius Arbiter's account of the wealthy freedman Trimalchio offers a useful parallel—this time in his lavish treatment of his slaves.[43]

A House-to-Brothel Makeover? The House at IX, 5, 16

If it is relatively easy to dismiss the notion that room *x'* of the House of Vettii saw use as a *cella meretricia,* or room used by a prostitute, it is because so much of the house's decoration survives. The case is much more difficult for the House at IX, 5, 16—precisely because so little survives. Sogliano excavated an entire city block (insula 5), located directly to the west of the House of the Centenary, in a rapid campaign of 1877–1878.[44] Today all the houses are in a deplorable state of repair. The only thing really left intact is a small room in the House at IX, 5, 16 decorated with pictures of lovemaking, since officials made sure that it received a modern roof and a heavy door to protect the morals of the curious. The few old photographs available concentrate on the much larger part of the house accessible from the doorway at number 14. Descriptions from Sogliano and Mau have to make up for what is today a veritable ruin; and from these descriptions emerges a house that required extensive redecoration after the earthquake of 62. As the plan reveals, there are really two houses here: one was a fairly large atrium house with a peristyle entered at 14 (Fig. 67). The letters *a* through *v* designate its rooms. The other house, accessible through a door at the back of the atrium but with a street entrance at 16, has only six rooms, lettered *a'* through *f'*.

August Mau supposed that this smaller house was a combination *caupona*-lupanar, that is, a tavern-brothel.[45] Some of his reasons are more convincing than others. He begins with the stove-platform found in the right-hand corner of the atrium near the street entrance, pointing out that it is of the type found in shops that sold heated wine. He notes that the wall with flower planter around the impluvium had scenes of pygmies painted on it. The scene that the viewer would encounter as he or she entered from the street showed a man and woman pygmy making love. This really means very little, when one considers how usual such scenes are: the elaborately painted masonry couches in the garden of the House of the Ephebe—certainly no brothel—present just this kind of scene to incoming guests.[46]

Mau's strongest point is his assertion that the four erotic paintings of room *f'* (a fifth is destroyed) could be put only in a room of a building where sex was for sale. He implies that no decent person would have such pictures in his bedroom. Mau's construction of "decency" for the Pompeian owner and his guests is, of course,

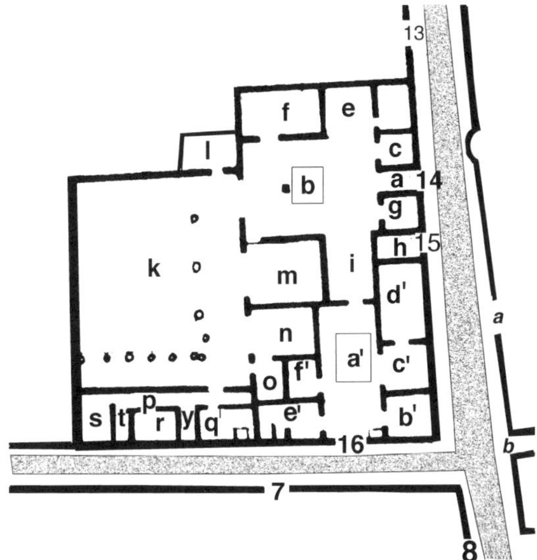

Figure 67. Pompeii, House at IX, 5, 14–16, plan.

highly suspect. As a nineteenth-century Christian gentleman of the Victorian period, Mau was the product of an acculturation with regard to sex that could find even the glimpse of a woman's ankles "indecent."

The room announced both its all-over decorative scheme and the erotic theme of its center pictures to someone entering the room from the atrium (Fig. 68). It is a pared-down version of the elegant Fourth-Style scheme of the House of the Centenary. The artist created his decoration on a white ground, probably for reasons of economy rather than for better light, since the room has both a window and a door opening on to the atrium. There are thin stripes in the socle beneath the uniform red bands that form the simple tripartite division of the median zone. Within the resulting three panels the artist created a second frame using interlaced garlands in the side panels with flying *amorini* at their centers; a carpet border frames the erotic picture at the center of the wall. Over the center of each panel two flowers hang upside down from a nail. The upper zone uses a single pattern, the swastika meander.

The central pictures of *f'*, like those of the House of the Vettii room *x'*, emphasize positions rather than the niceties of bedroom decor. They lack servants, elaborate gilded draperies, or views to the outdoors. They are not without nuance, however. The centerpiece of the wall opposite the door, although badly deterio-

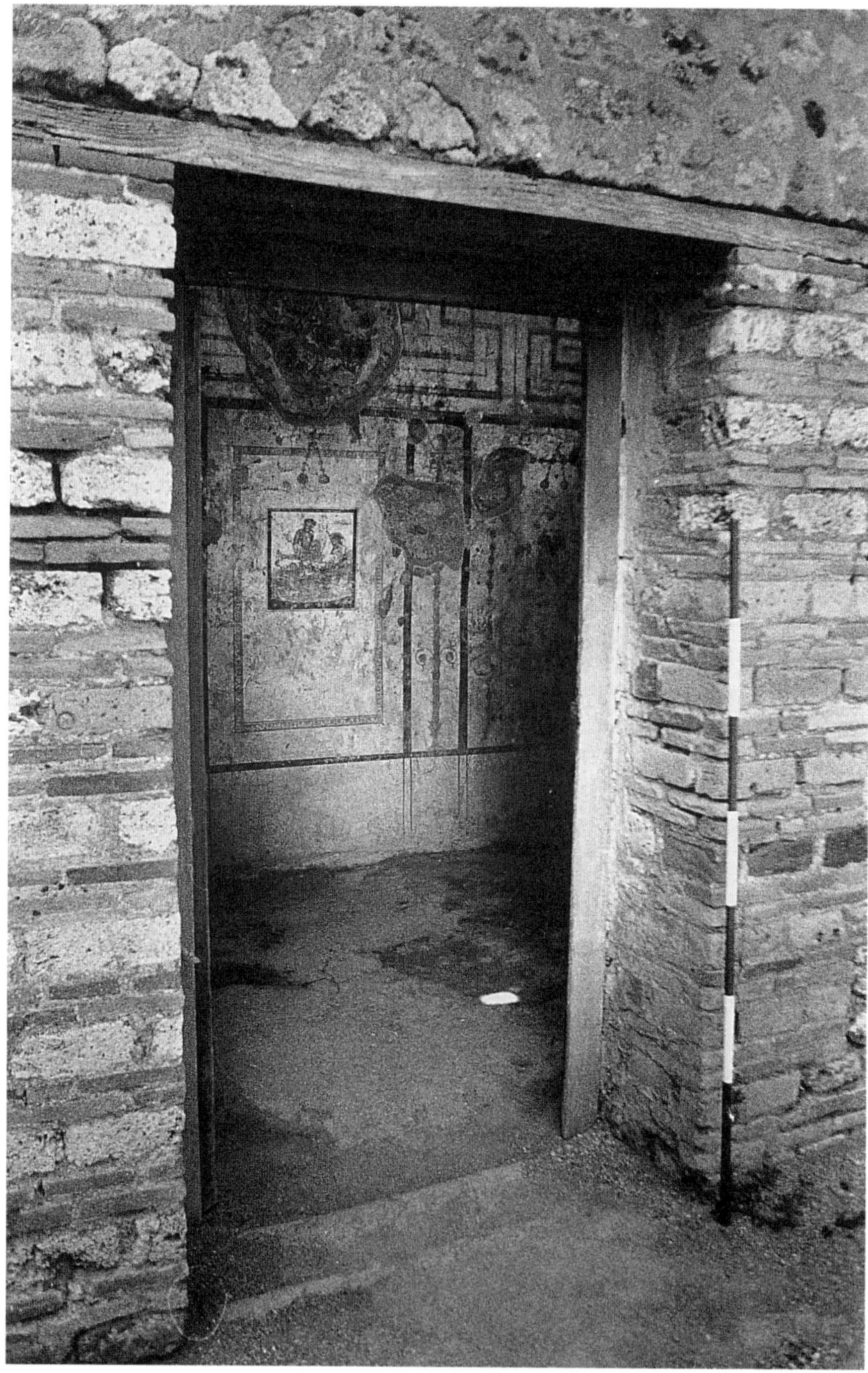

Figure 68. Pompeii, House at IX, 5, 16 room *f'*, doorway and west wall. Photo Michael Larvey.

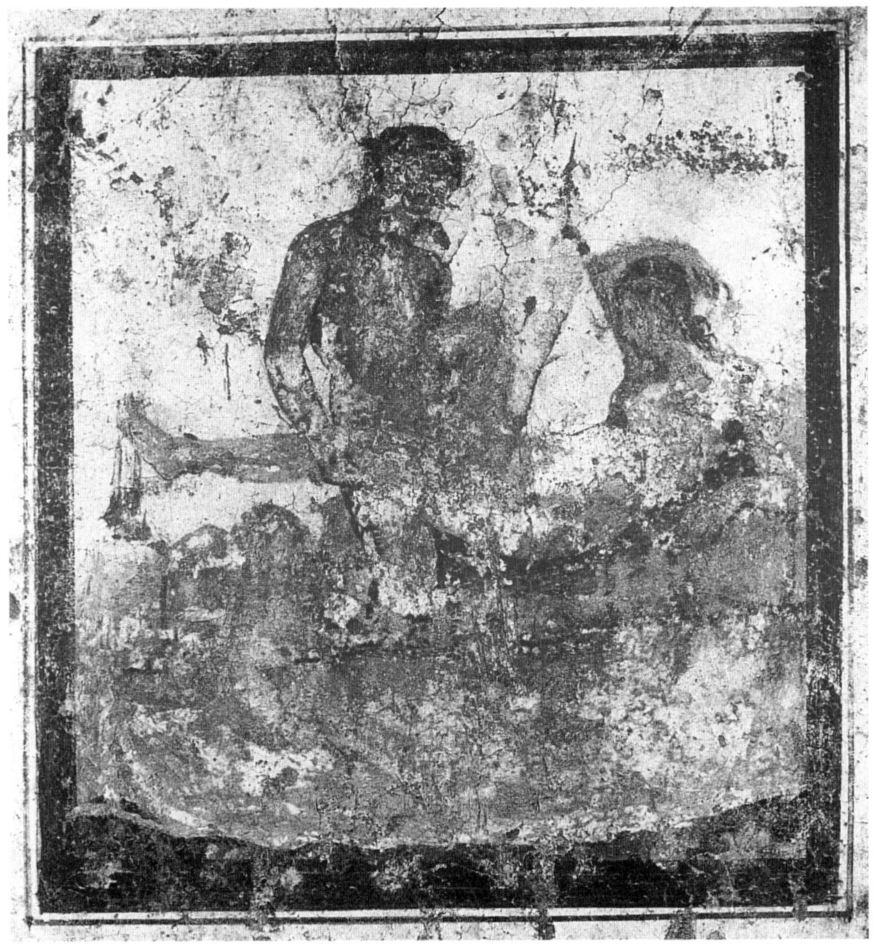

Figure 69. Male-female couple, Pompeii, House at IX, 5, 16, room *f'*, west wall, center picture (A.D. 62–79). Photo Michael Larvey.

rated, clearly attempts to emulate the grace of models that go back at least to Augustan-period Arretine ware (Fig. 69). Within the double frame the artist presented a closeup view of a couple on a bed. The woman reclines in a pose meant to emphasize her gracefulness and beauty. The gesture of her right arm, crooked over her head to frame her face, signifies—as we noted earlier—both repose and composed sexual readiness. The artist gave the woman a neoclassical profile. Her hair, pulled back away from her face and tucked under, has come loose at the back, like that of the woman on the Arretine bowl in Boston discussed above (see Fig. 38). The man

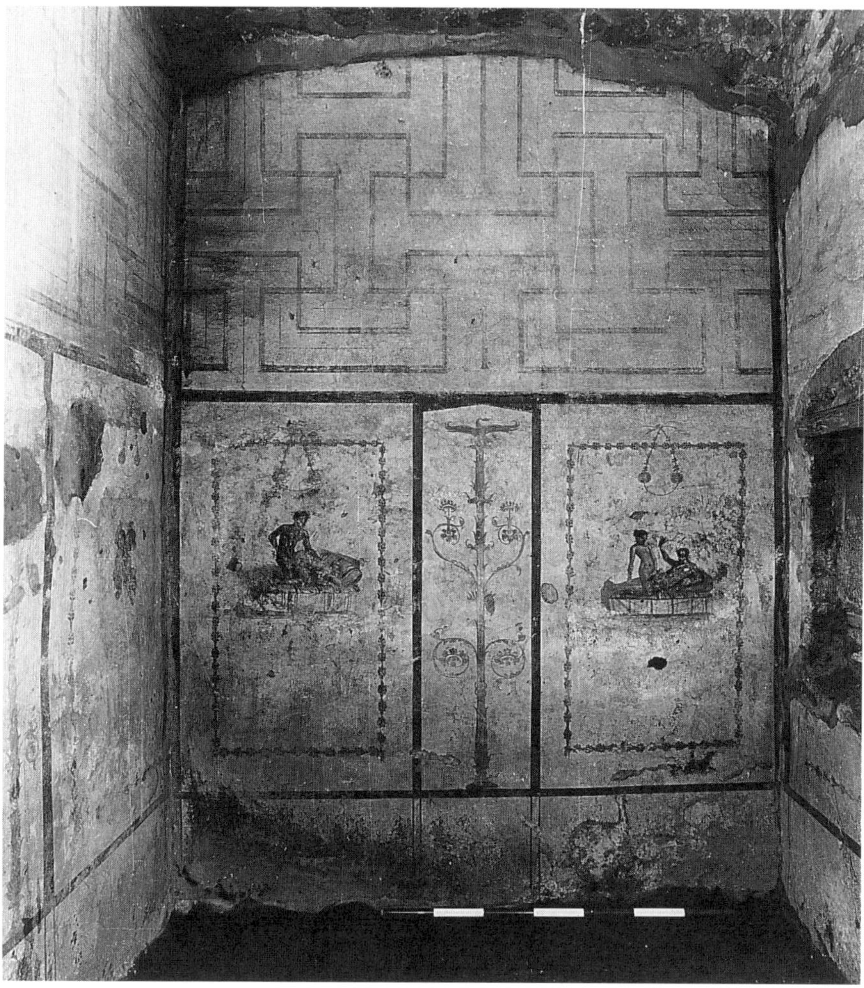

Figure 70. Pompeii, House at IX, 5, 16, room *f*', north wall (A.D. 62–79). Photo Istituto Centrale per il Catalogo e la Documentazione N 53023.

kneels on the bed and parts her legs to enter her. In keeping with the relative restraint of the scene the artist avoided the extreme sexual acrobatics of many similar depictions where the man holds his partner's legs high in the air (see Figs. 2, 40, and 64).

The decorative scheme of the north wall features two lateral panels with scenes of lovemaking that have for their frame the inner garland rather than the double

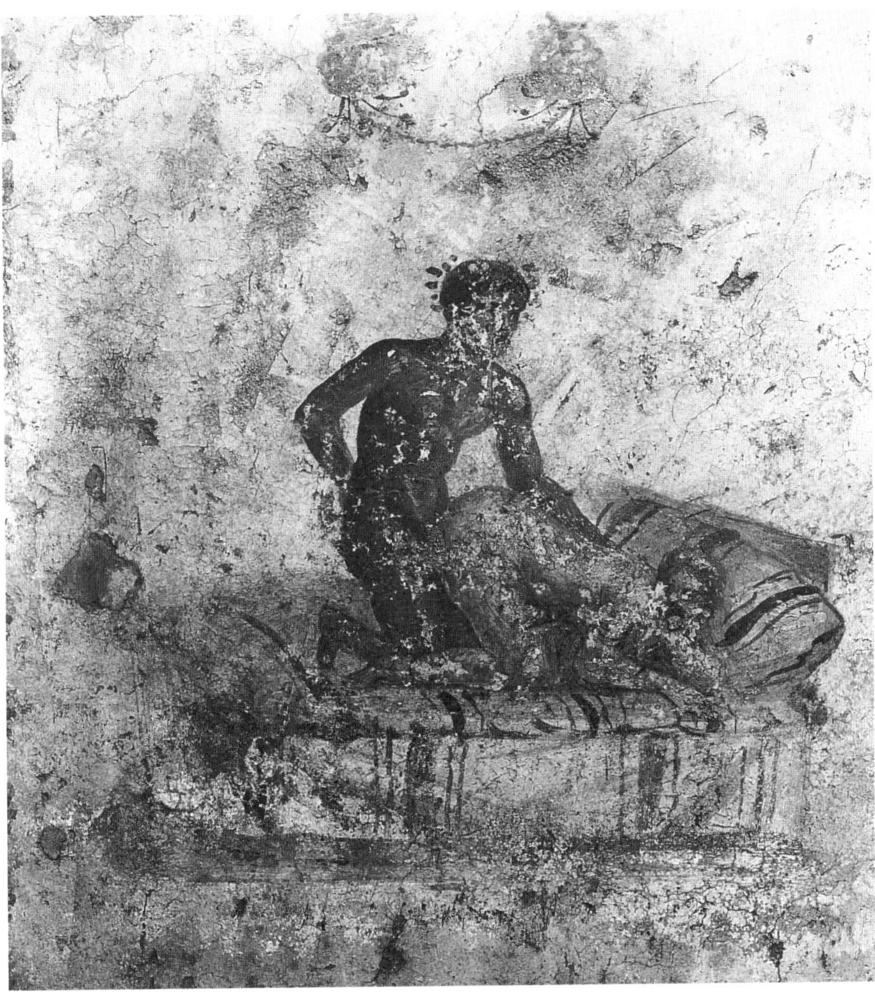

Figure 71. Male-female couple, Pompeii, House at IX, 5, 16, room *f'*, north wall, western picture (A.D. 62–79). Photo Istituto Centrale per il Catalogo e la Documentazione N 53016.

frame that defines the west-wall panel as a "picture" (Fig. 70). These two panels flank an elaborate candelabrum that marks the center of the wall. In the left-hand image, the man kneels facing right as does the woman, but she is crouching down; she supports her upper torso with her right elbow even while she raises her buttocks to receive the man's thrusts (Fig. 71). The couple is not unbeautiful, although paint losses unkindly erased the woman's mouth as well as much of the man's classically proportioned head, crowned with ivy and turned in three-quarters view. Another feature worth noting is that the large pillow, the mattress cover, and the sham—all decorated with a pattern of a wide stripe framed between small stripes—reveal the headboard but not the legs of the bed. Was this a platform—like the masonry ones in the lupanar at VII, 12, 18–20 (see Fig. 81)—rather than a wooden bed?

The couple depicted on the right-hand panel raise seemingly unanswerable questions about the meaning of sexual body language to the ancient viewer (Fig. 72). The woman kneels facing the man and straddling him so that her genitals are near his. The artist took some pains to depict her thin and well proportioned body and head in three-quarters view; she leans back away from the man and inclines her head—perhaps coyly, perhaps intimidated by the way the man waves his right hand toward her face. Paint losses make it impossible to understand what the woman is doing with her left hand. She is either grasping the man's penis or touching her own genitals. Similarly, it is unclear what the man's gesture means, since although his right hand seems to say "stop," the rest of his body seems quite relaxed as he leans back against the pillow while propping himself up with his left elbow. Did the artist use this gesture to express, rather, the man's amazement or delight?[47]

There are no images of lovemaking on the entryway wall, since the window (now walled up) and the door itself took up most of the space for wall painting. Only the right-hand panel of the south wall remains (Fig. 73). On another platform bed the woman, in profile, kneels straddling the man's hips as she leans forward to kiss him. He is reclining, his head resting on the pillow as he supports his upper torso with his left elbow. Even though this is the worst preserved of the paintings, it is perhaps the most tender, emphasizing the kiss as either prelude or accompaniment to actual copulation. The artist wanted to make the woman's profile attractive and paid special attention to her coiffure, with the hair pulled back from the forehead and gathered in curls at the back.

It is difficult to agree with Mau solely on the basis of the subject matter of the pictures in this room that this little house became a brothel when these paintings were executed. The strongest piece of evidence against Mau's interpretation is room *x'* of the House of the Vettii (see Fig. 62). Mau did not know this room at the time he decided that the House at IX, 5, 16 was a brothel, since the House of the Vettii was not discovered until 1892. In many ways room *x'* is just as humble as *f'*, if

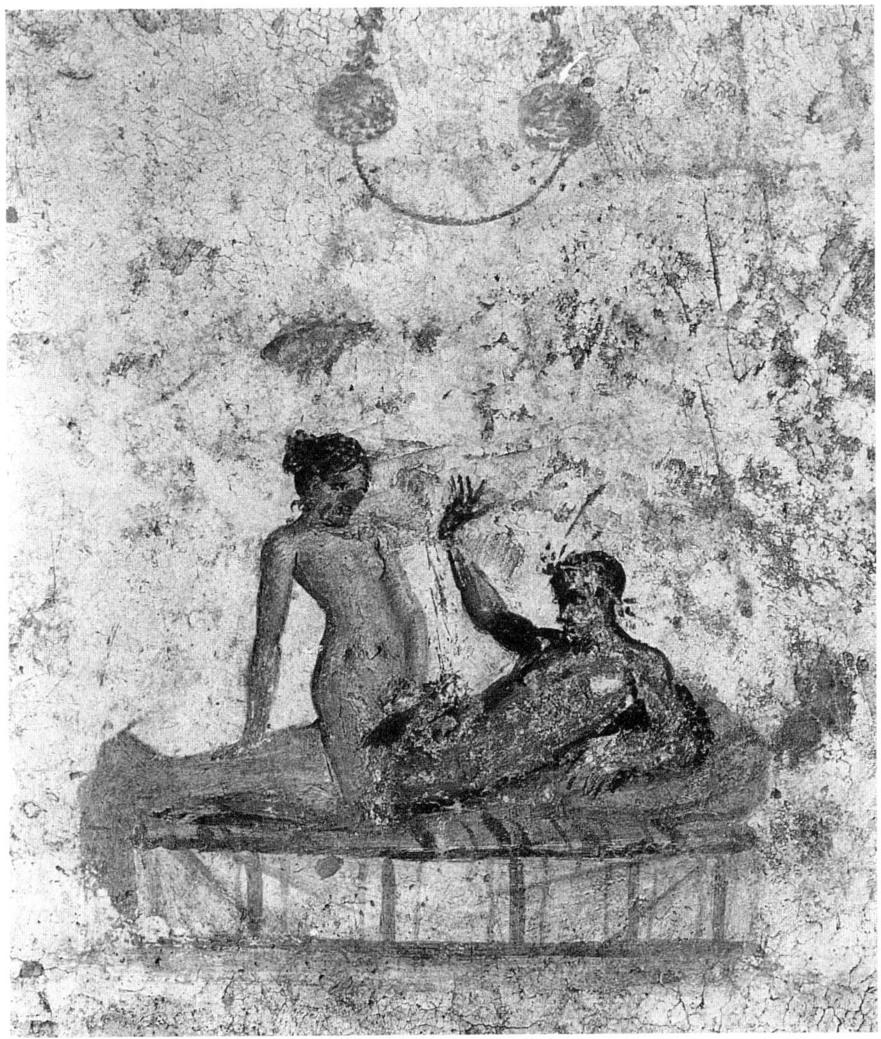

Figure 72. Male-female couple, Pompeii, House at IX, 5, 16, room *f*', north wall, eastern picture (A.D. 62–79). Photo Michael Larvey.

not more so. Both rooms are white-ground, with simple scenes of lovemaking painted in a slapdash fashion. Both are small rooms, with the difference that *f*' is highly visible from the atrium.

The House of the Vettii is one of the grandest of the period in Pompeii, yet even the modest House at IX, 5, 16 had large central pictures in its other rooms that looked up to high-art models. The wing *c*' seems to have had a rather ambi-

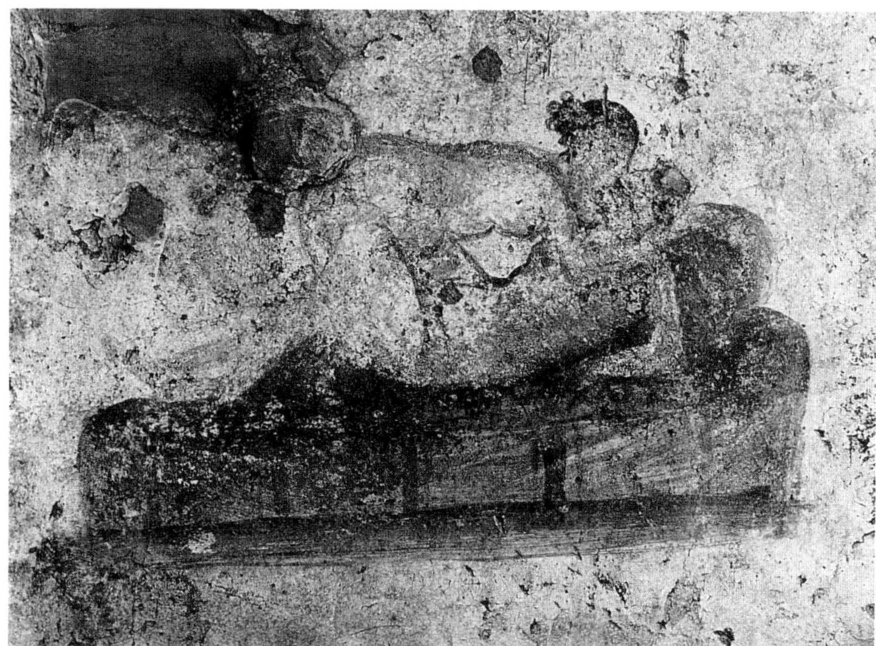

Figure 73. Male-female couple, Pompeii, House at IX, 5, 16, room *f'*, south wall, western picture (A.D. 62–79). Photo Michael Larvey.

tious painting program, to judge from the painting of Medea found on its back wall. Sogliano found it to be of such high quality that he had it cut from the wall and sent to the National Museum in Naples.[48] Triclinium *d'* had a number of pictures: in the center left wall was a seaport with warships. A painting of a sacred tree with a shield and two lances on it graced the center of the right wall. There were also four tiny pictures on each of these long walls.[49] Even the care taken to decorate the impluvium planter has parallels in the representations of Nilotic scenes in Pompeii's elegant houses.[50]

So is this a house-to-brothel makeover? Unfortunately the answer could rest only on evidence that is no longer there. The wine-heating stove for the shop that Mau identified is a little heap of rubble today; Sogliano, in fact, thought it was a staircase to the upper story.[51] Rubble is all that remains of the pygmy frieze around the impluvium-planter, and the small finds from the house were never published.[52] There are no graffiti and no evidence for either masonry or other types of beds in room *f'*. In the end, I think that House at IX, 5, 16 is simply a house-to-tavern makeover, with one of the attractions being a room that could be used—among other things—for the occasional tryst by willing (and sometimes paid) partners. This architectural configuration does not spell the kind of production-line sex-for-sale that we will encounter in the narrow rooms of the lupanar at VII, 12, 18–20.

Venus, Priapus, Phalluses, and Lovemaking in a Poor Man's Garden: The Summer Triclinium of the House at I, 13, 16

The tiny house at I, 13, 16, excavated in 1953 and published only in 1990, dates to the last period of the city's life (Fig. 74).[53] Yet the fact that more than half of its ground-floor area is a garden—and the care evident in outfitting that garden with an elaborate outdoor dining room—signals the importance that the idea of upper-class entertainment had for the owner. The house had only three fully enclosed rooms on the ground floor: two square ones (rooms 2 and 4) to the right and left of the entry, and room 5. The builder used the cheapest possible construction methods as he carved this house's spaces from what had been the back part of another house—the one facing north with its street entrance at number 1. He even used wattle-and-daub—known as *opus craticium* in antiquity—for the walls of room 4;[54] its Fourth-Style paintings were still not finished in A.D. 79. Room 2 had red plaster floors (*cocciopesto*) with two-tone walls: red plaster with yellow stripes below and white plaster above. Yet this obviously poor owner lavished his attention and meager means on a feature that—in refined form—belonged in the houses and villas of the wealthy: an outdoor dining room, or summer triclinium. It is significant that the imagery of this triclinium combines apotropaic phalluses with pictures of the goddess Venus, the god Priapus, and an erotic picture, for these are the elements that appear in subtler and interwoven pictorial and sculptural schemes in grand houses like that of the Vettii. This little summer triclinium presents late Pompeian attitudes toward sexual representation in their simplest and most transparent form.

Since the house lacks an atrium, the wide entryway from the street, room 1, also functioned as a circulation space. The visitor entered the summer triclinium directly after passing through room 1 and turning left. Although room 3 also opened to the garden at its eastern end, the masonry couches form a U that opens to the room's south door. Their arrangement follows that of the three portable couches (*klinai*) that gave the triclinium its Greek name. Despite the poor quality of the decoration, both artist and patron put considerable effort into the display. Unfortunately today we must rely on photographs taken at the time of excavation, for the walls are almost illegible today. An excavation photo shows that the artist wanted to create an impressive display for the entering guest, for he loaded the north wall with imagery (Fig. 75). Although he divided the wall into the three vertical panels typical of the Fourth Style (only two are visible), he abandoned all semblance of symmetry in his placement of pictures. The tall vertical picture in the left-hand panel is a naive representation of a statue of Venus on a pedestal (Fig. 76).[55] She is nude and combs her hair with her right hand while she holds a mirror out with her other. Since she is not actually looking into the mirror, the fact that her face appears in it is all the more remarkable. On the right Priapus stands atop an unusually tall pedestal, his erect phallus half as long as he is tall. In between the two appears a strutting peacock. This picture displaced what was to be the central picture of this panel: a small, summarily painted landscape. The artist improvised his scheme to fit two marble heads—probably from statues ruined in the earthquake of 62—into his bizarre decoration. On this wall he framed the marble head of a bearded man, perhaps a Hercules, with dark red paint; he painted a garland under the head to "support" it. He fit the other reused head, a crowned Dionysus, high up on the left-hand wall—but there for some reason he placed it off center.

In the extreme upper left corner of the back wall the artist painted four phalluses. One is much larger than the others; the red border of the wall rises at this point to make room for it. Beneath are three small phalluses in three different positions: the one on the right mimics the position of the large phallus, while the other two point downwards. Paint traces indicate that these two small phalluses were ejaculating, as was perhaps also the large one.

The final element of this unusual collection on the north wall is a picture of a man and a woman copulating on a bed (Fig. 77). Despite paint losses and the meager talents of the artist, this little picture provides details not seen elsewhere. The setting seems to have been important to the artist and patron, for not only is there a door to the extreme left of the picture, but the artist took pains to represent a elaborate drapery extending along the entire upper edge of the picture. To my knowledge, the only other representation of a door in the lovemaking chamber is the half-open one that a boy walks through on side A of the Warren cup (Plate 1).

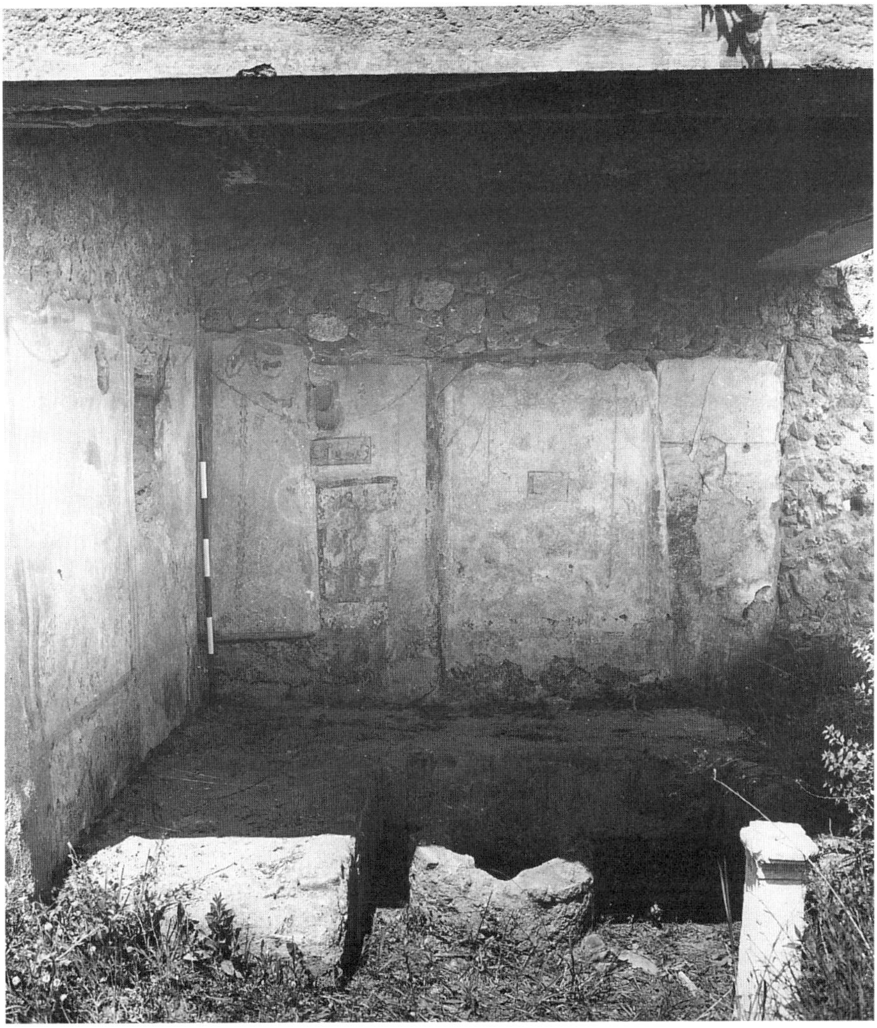

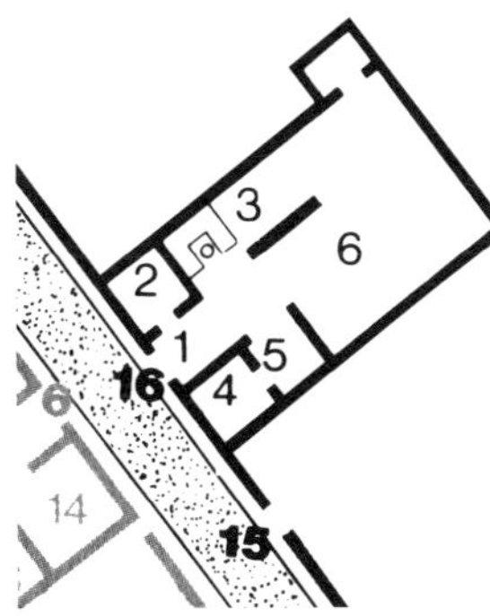

Figures 74–75. Pompeii, House at I, 13, 16. Figure 74: plan. Figure 75: Triclinium 3, north and west walls (A.D. 62–79). Photo Istituto Centrale per il Catalogo e la Documentazione N 36692.

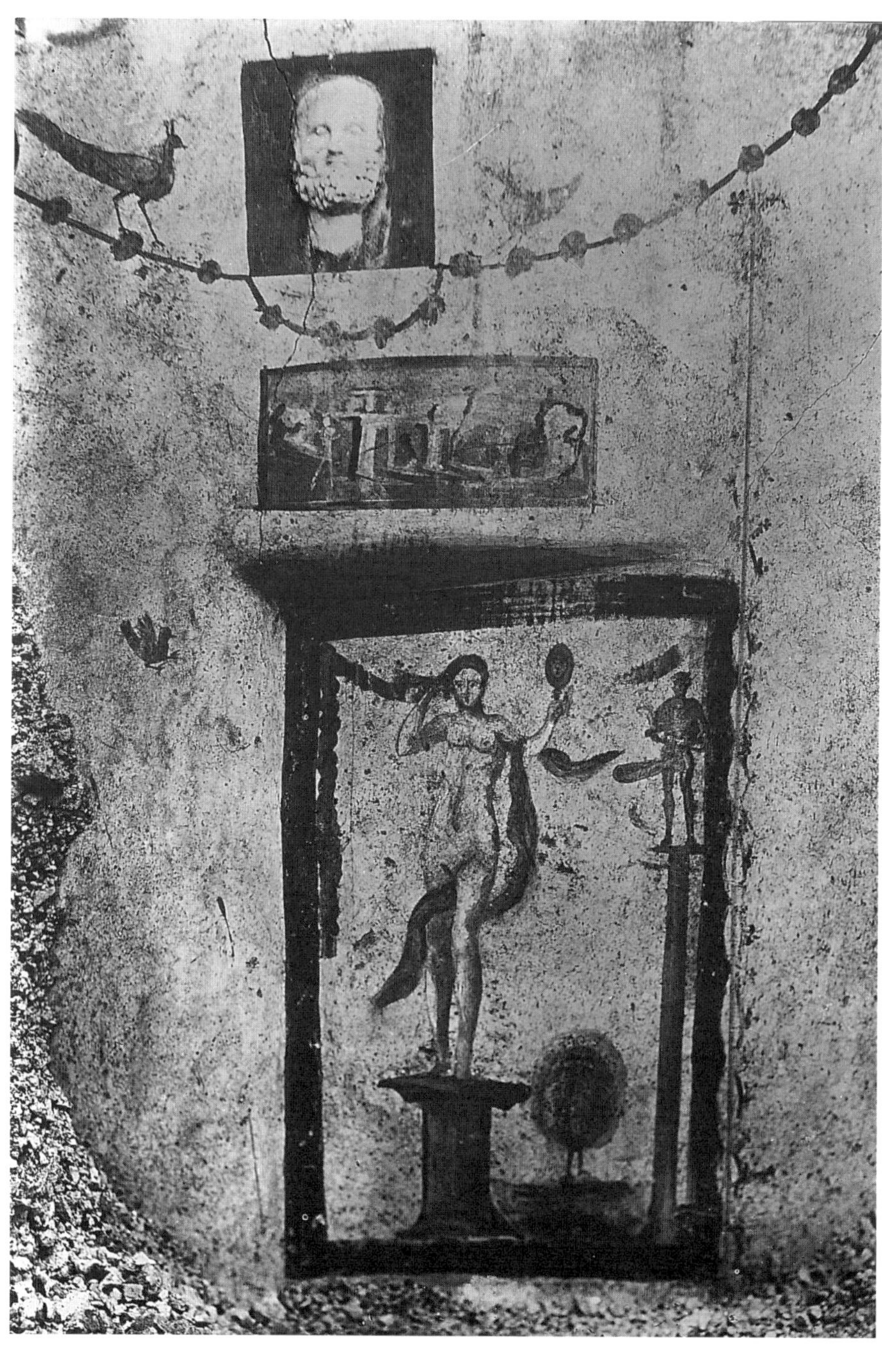

Figure 76. Paintings of Venus and Priapus and of landscape, marble head in niche, Pompeii, House at I, 13, 16, triclinium 3, north wall (A.D. 62–79). Photo Istituto Centrale per il Catalogo e la Documentazione E 108843.

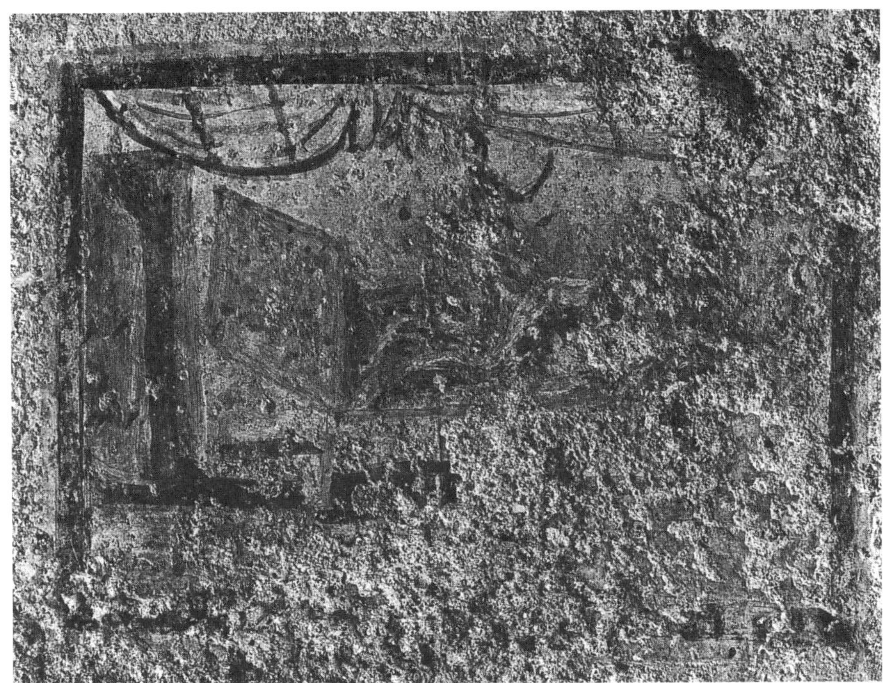

Figure 77. Male-female couple on bed, Pompeii, House at I, 13, 16, triclinium 3, north wall, central part (A.D. 62–79). Photo Istituto Centrale per il Catalogo e la Documentazione N 57636.

As for the swagged drapery, there is a parallel in a painting of unknown provenance in the Naples Museum, where the drapery is fuller and gathered at the top center of the panel (Fig. 78). Even the bed is unusual, in that it has an extremely high headboard. Rather than represent one of the pair resting against it, the artist turned both partners around on the bed and had the man kneeling while he enters the prone woman, whose upper body (now missing) must have rested on the foot of the bed. Beneath the picture of copulation—and taking up about as much space—is a vignette of a bird pecking at cherries.

What can this eclectic mixture of imagery tell us about cultural constructions of sexuality? The seating arrangement around the triclinium's couches was highly important to cultured Romans, so that the main image in this room appears, significantly, right at the place where the guest of honor would recline. It is the consular place, to the far left on the couch against the back wall, where the picture of

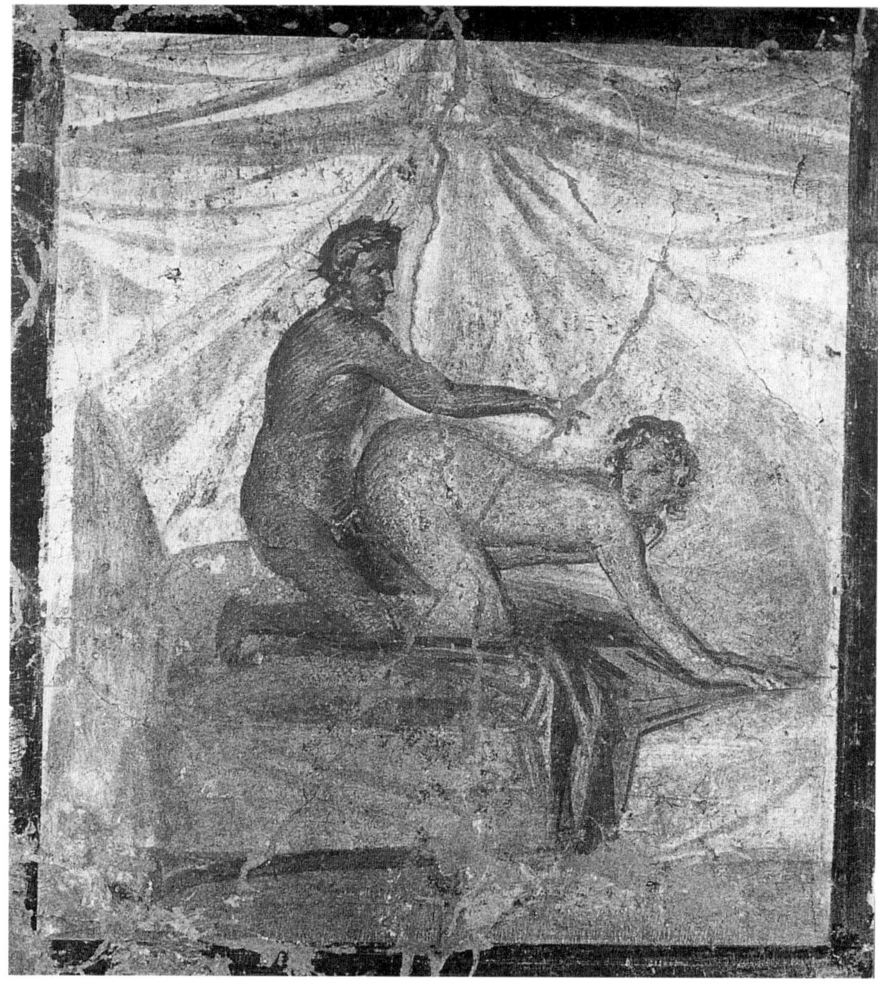

Figure 78. Male-female couple on bed, from Pompeii, unknown location (A.D. 62–79). Naples, National Archaeological Museum, inv. 27696, W. 42 × H 46 cm. Photo Michael Larvey.

Venus and Priapus appears.[56] From the top corner of the wall four phalluses protect this guest against the Evil Eye. The host would recline immediately to the right of the guest of honor, on the left-hand couch. To imagine the niceties of the elite dinner party with its ironclad etiquette in such a humble setting may seem somewhat ludicrous, but this is precisely the fantasy that its decoration implies. Dining in the Greek fashion separates the cultured from the loutish boors, who as Martial disparagingly notes, sit at stools to take their meals.[57] To emphasize his knowledge of the proper etiquette, the patron urged the artist to abandon the canonical symmetry of proper Fourth-Style wall decoration in order to emphasize the hierarchies in the seating arrangement.

The content of these representations reveals another naive reading of upper-class sign systems, for the artist contrived an artless compendium of the elements that belonged in the houses of the wealthy.[58] Even though this is technically a garden space, the heads inserted into the walls may allude to the portraits of illustrious ancestors that the elite displayed in the atriums of their houses. This coveted privilege, the so-called *ius imaginum,* never extended to the non-elite.[59] There are also many references to the gardens of the wealthy. Jashemski emphasizes the worship of Venus in gardens, documenting numerous instances at Pompeii.[60] In our picture she appears with phallic Priapus, who is protector of the garden from thievery as well as guarantor of fertility. The peacock who struts in the painting is the bird of Juno that makes its appearance frequently in the wall decoration of wealthy villas.[61] Two more perch on the garland to either side of the bearded head. The inclusion of multiple phalluses in the upper corner of the room's principal wall might seem excessive but certainly not improper or erotic to the ancient viewer. He or she would see in them a considerate attempt on the part of the host to bless this dining place with good luck even as they warded off the Evil Eye with a quadruple threat.

Finally, the representation of the couple making love on a big bed in a room was a clear reference to similar scenes in well-outfitted interiors that appeared in aristocratic houses and villas. Here the artist displaced this picture—as in the House of Caecilius Iucundus—to mark its importance, for it signaled high culture even in this unusually poor setting.

Consideration of the erotics of display in these six Pompeian houses underscores the dangers of applying modern moral or iconographic judgments to pictures that represent sexual activity. Rather than aid our attempts to understand them, the placement in locked rooms singles them out in such a way as to increase modern misunderstanding of their ancient function and meaning. Dangers of misinterpretation multiply in cases where excavators cut them out of their original architectural contexts.

It is clear that the whole class of pictures that modern excavators considered obscene had little or no such overtones for the ancient patron and viewer. Their attitudes toward the display of sex were quite different from ours. Pictures of humans making love could be a sign of upper-class pretensions, an invitation to enjoy a good meal and wine-drinking party, or a play on the sexual proclivities of a cook, depending on where they appeared and for whom they were meant. In the following chapter we see that the circumstances of display were all-important to the meanings of the paintings of sexual activity in public buildings as well.

CHAPTER 7

THE DISPLAY OF EROTICA AND THE EROTICS OF DISPLAY IN PUBLIC BUILDINGS

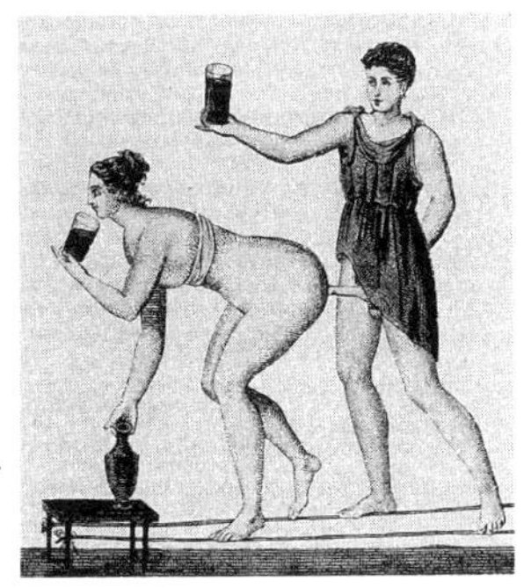

One of the great problems of Pompeian archaeology has been the vague and ad hoc reasoning that excavators have used to decide on the functions of buildings. Often the inclusion of erotic paintings in a decorative scheme led them to call the building a brothel. In the last chapter we examined the reasons why Mau believed that the House at IX, 5, 16 was a private residence made over into a lupanar and found his reasoning questionable in terms of both the architectural and iconographic evidence. Pompeian excavators applied equally debatable criteria to buildings that are clearly not houses, but eating and drinking establishments. If they found erotic paintings in them, the sites immediately became bordellos. If we believe these Pompeian archaeologists, we end up with an unusual statistic. According to their count, Pompeii had 35 brothels.[1] If the city had a population of about ten thousand inhabitants,[2] we get the extraordinary number of one brothel for each 286 persons, including women and children, or about one brothel for every 71 men in Pompeii. Scholars estimate that Rome itself had only about 45 lupanaria—and this in a city with a population of well over one million.[3] Wallace-Hadrill brings the number of brothels at Pompeii down to one certain lupanar with more than one room (the lupanar at VII, 12, 18–20) and to nine establishments consisting of a single room, or *cella meretricia*.[4] One of the consequences of this more realistic figure is that it leaves us with a great number of nondomestic spaces that were not brothels but that were decorated with images of people engaged in sexual intercourse. What did these representations, displayed in a whole range of public buildings, mean to the ancient viewer? Would the male viewer understand them differently from the female viewer? Why did the owners and their customers want to see them in these places? What was the nature of the pleasure they took in looking at them?

LOVE—AND FANTASY—FOR SALE: THE LUPANAR AT VII, 12, 18-20

Fortunately it is possible to study a building that both clearly functioned as a lupanar and still preserves its wall painting program. It is located in region VII, block 12, and occupies the triangle made by the meeting of an irregular north-south street and a narrow east-west one (Fig. 79). The brothel is tiny, especially when compared with the ample spaces of the houses we have considered: the House of the Centenary takes up a whole city block, and even the ground floor of the small House at IX, 5, 16 is twice as large. There were ten rooms in all in the lupanar—five on its upper story and five on the ground floor. A wooden staircase at number 20 led to the upstairs rooms, accessible from a balcony that ran along the perimeter of the building. There was a bell at the entrance to the staircase and a latrine under the stairs. The ground-floor plan is that of a corridor with cubicles opening off it (Fig. 80). Each cubicle has a raised masonry platform that served as a bed—with a pillow also in masonry (Fig. 81).

Before attempting to define the erotics of display in the lupanar, we need to ask a fundamental question: who were the viewers? Considerations of societal custom and analysis of graffiti let us sort out the brothel's clientele. Few Romans from elite or other ancient families wealthy enough to own slaves frequented brothels. Instead, they purchased love-slaves to fulfill their desires. There was no stigma attached to the sexual use of slaves, since they were the property of the owner.[5] The sources indicate that such sexual use was unexceptional. In Roman society people often assumed that former slaves had been sexual partners to their former masters and mistresses.[6] And yet Horace, writing in the late first century B.C. about the moralist Cato the Elder (234–149 B.C.), notes that Cato praised a man for frequenting a brothel.[7] The early third-century A.D. scholiast Porphyrio, commenting on Horace, explains that such behavior allows a man to check his lust without committing a

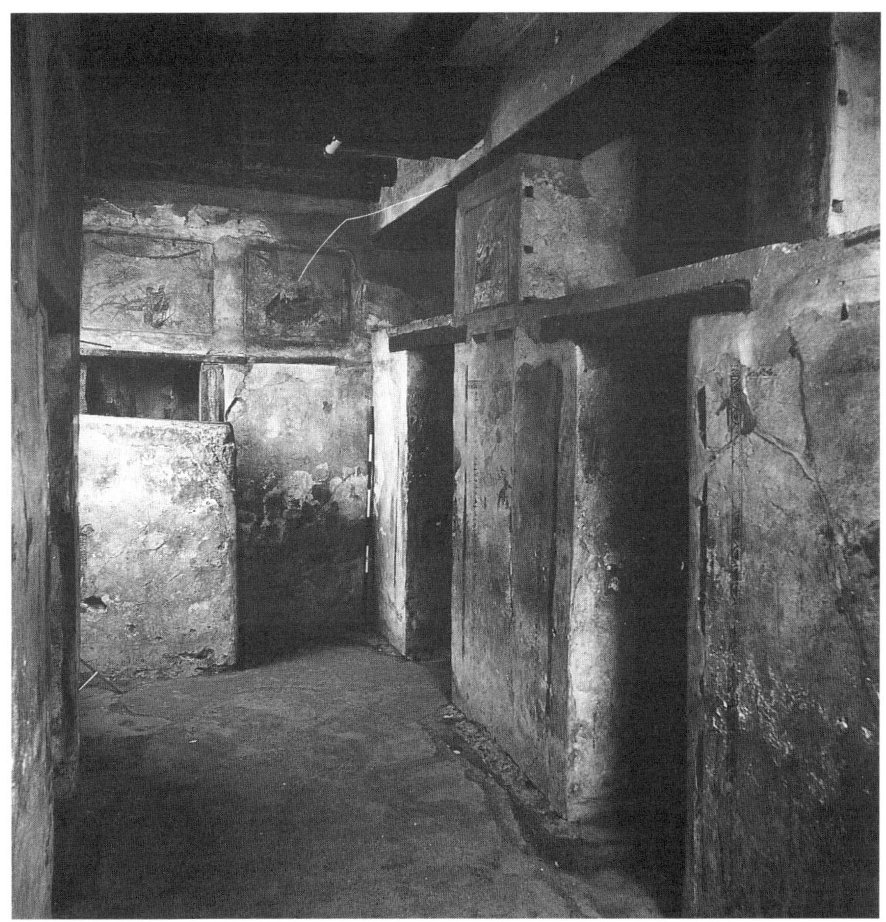

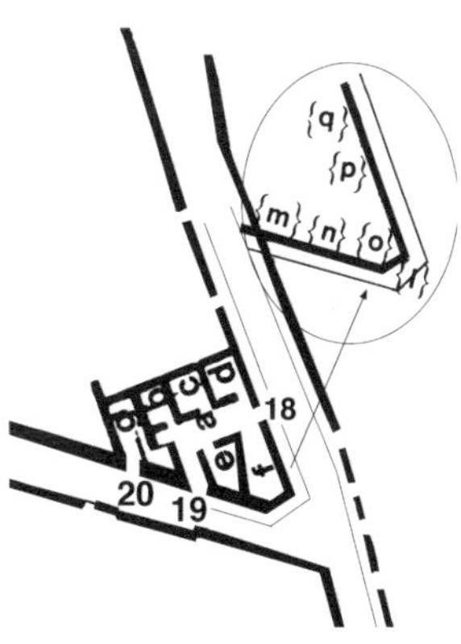

Figures 79–80. Pompeii, Lupanar at VII, 12, 18–20. Figure 79: Plan. Upper story indicated in the oval. Figure 80: View from eastern doorway, at 18. Photo Michael Larvey.

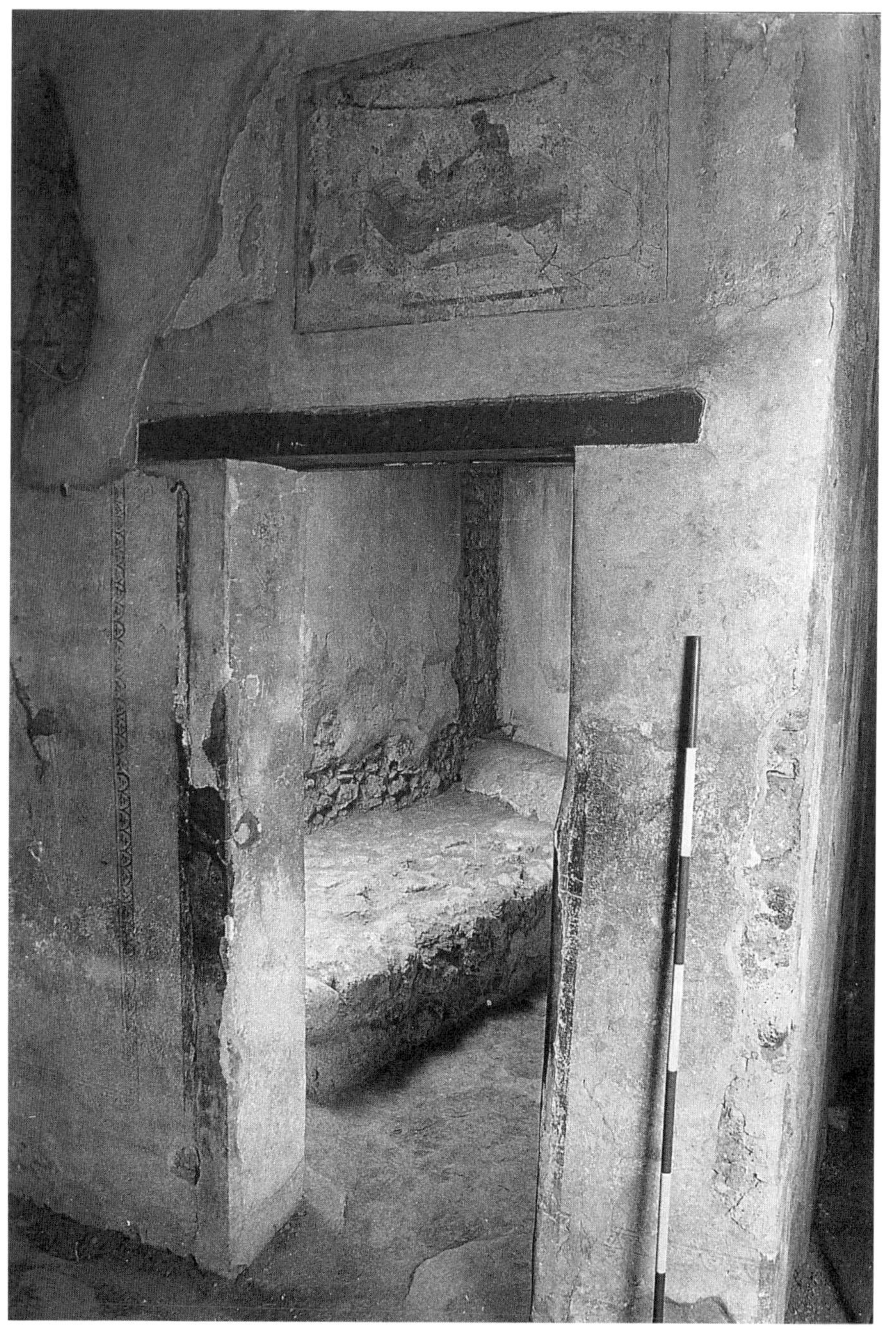

Figure 81. Pompeii, Lupanar at VII, 12, 18–20, view of cubicle and masonry platform that served as bed, south wall, west part (A.D. 72–79). Photo Michael Larvey.

crime;[8] pseudo-Acro adds to the story, saying that the man continued to visit the brothel afterward, whereupon Cato remarked to him, "I praised you for going there, not for living there."[9] Whether such use of bordellos by elite citizens was common in the latter half of the first century A.D. is difficult to say. At Pompeii the strongest argument against their use by persons of refinement is their very shabbiness—hardly places, it would seem, where anyone with money would want to have sex.[10]

Graffiti found both in this lupanar and elsewhere in Pompeii further define its clientele, for they record the names of prostitutes and their customers. Because ancient Romans used a strict system of nomenclature, we can sometimes distinguish names of people who are slaves or freedpersons from those of freeborn citizens.[11] Analysis of the graffiti uncovers no names of the local elite families among their clientele; instead they are names of foreign origin—typical of persons who are slaves—along with names indicating persons who were once slaves. Similar names turn up in graffiti that describe or advertise prostitutes; these appear in every type of building from the houses of the wealthy to streetside shops. The profile of the sex-for-sale business that emerges is one of freedmen buying slaves (both male and female) specifically for use as prostitutes. As we saw in chapter 6, the range of prices for these prostitutes' sexual services varied from 2 asses (the cost of a cup of common wine) to 16 asses. At Pompeii prostitutes were readily available and fairly cheap.

To clients of the lupanar—between the lower middle and the bottom of the social hierarchy and relatively poor—the wall painting begins to show their own fantasies. The owner had recently had the walls repainted: in the plaster of the first cubicle on the left, excavators found the imprint of a coin minted in A.D. 72.[12] Taken as a whole, the painting scheme is more than just the six erotic panels. Like the room of the House at IX, 5, 16, it is a white-ground decoration with the usual Fourth-Style divisions of the wall. The artist decorated the lower walls of the corridor in a simple scheme of panels defined by carpet borders; in the center of each panel is a winged animal. The erotic tabellae appear in the upper zone, defined by level of the lintels over the openings to the cubicles.

Presiding over the north wall is an image of the god Priapus (Fig. 82). This Priapus departs from the standard iconography, for he has two phalluses.[13] As we saw in considering the two representations of the Priapus in the House of the Vettii, he is protector of passageway spaces such as crossroads and doorways. His phallus protects the viewer from demons that the Romans believed inhabited such liminal

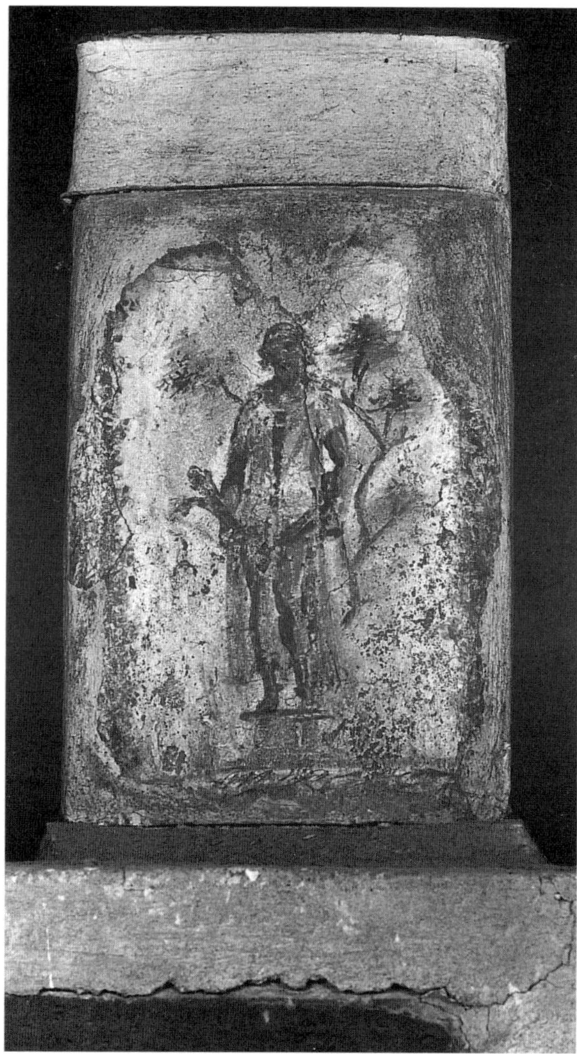

Figure 82. Priapus with two phalluses, Pompeii, Lupanar at VII, 12, 18–20, north wall, upper zone, center part (A.D. 72–79). Photo Michael Larvey.

spaces. And if one phallus is apotropaic, two should be doubly effective against the Evil Eye.[14] Like the four phalluses that an artist painted in the summer triclinium of the House at I, 13, 16, this image demonstrates the excessive superstition of the non-elite. Another aspect of Priapus is his role as agricultural deity who protects the fruits of the garden. The randy verses of the hymns to Priapus emphasize his readiness to punish the thief with sexual penetration, rendered all the more painful because of the enormous size of his member.[15] Here, in the lupanar, the image of Priapus promises the client good fortune in sexual pleasure. It seems likely that by

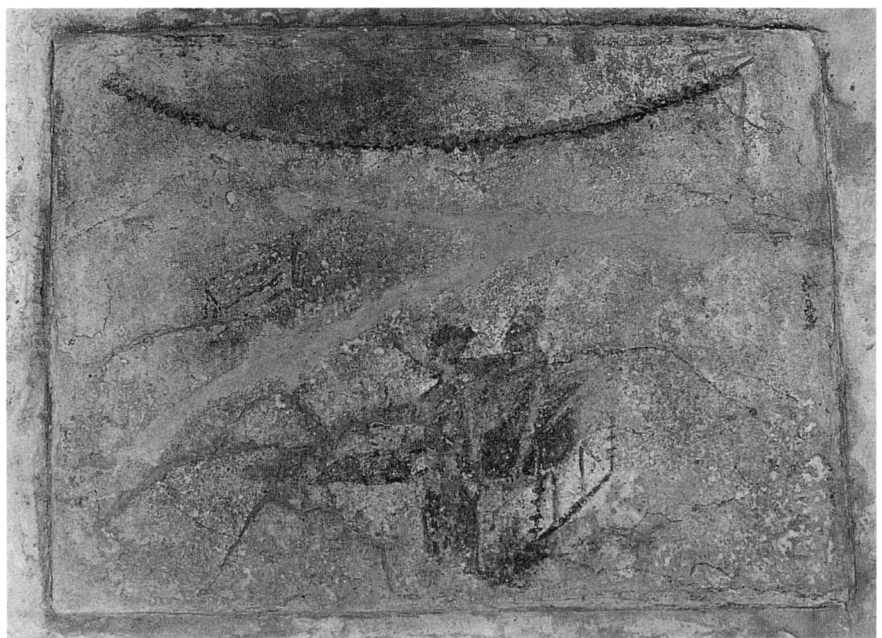

Figure 83. Male-female couple contemplating erotic pinax, Pompeii, Lupanar at VII, 12, 18–20, west wall, upper zone, south part (A.D. 72–79). Photo Michael Larvey.

representing him with two phalluses, the artist also gave Priapus a humorous aspect. His doubled phallic powers might even lead the male viewer to think about the pleasure of experiencing orgasm with two penises instead of one.

The fact that the seven pictures of lovemaking occur on beds complete with bedsteads, big round bolsterlike pillows, and colorful bedspreads already removes them from the reality of the narrow cubicles below where prostitute and customer actually met. In fact, despite many paint losses, we can still make out some bedroom accessories as well—items such as lamps on lampstands and vessels that would be hard to fit into the cubicles. The greatest discrepancy between a painting and the reality of the lupanar shows up in a panel on the west wall where the couple is not engaged in intercourse at all (Fig. 83). Rather, they are contemplating lovemaking, for they are looking at an erotic pinax in the upper left quadrant of the panel. Paint losses are such that only its outlines are visible. The artist set the pinax on a diagonal and rendered its two shutters in perspective. Unlike any of the known ancient paintings of lovemaking, only the man is actually in the bed. The woman, fully clothed, stands beside the bed, clad in a long green dress. Her head is in profile, revealing her hairdo of fashionable piled-up curls, a style popular in the seventies. She touches her left breast with her right arm while demurely lifting her dress with her extended left arm to reveal her turned-out foot. The man leans back against the cushion at the headboard in a relaxed pose, his left arm dangling off the bed, while he raises his right arm to point to the pinax.

Humble as it is, this painting represents a fantasy—one of imaginary social mobility: that the man and his intended sexual partner could calmly contemplate an erotic pinax as a prelude to actual lovemaking. As we observed in our study of paintings in houses, the higher the class of the patron the more sophisticated the display of erotica. In the Farnesina villa the erotic painting is one element in the collection of a connoisseur. Even though nothing could be farther from the aristocratic painting collection than both the quality of the representations themselves and the actual erotics of display in the lupanar, in this painting the artist offered an upper-class fantasy for the lower-class viewer. By encoding a world quite different from that of the lupanar, the representation becomes a sign of upper-class luxury. It is the luxury of the man lying in bed, with his intended sex partner standing attentively at his side to contemplate together a picture of lovemaking on the wall.

To customers of servile or freedman status who frequented the lupanar, this woman looks like a man's servant. Of course, she could be the prostitute in the cubicle, but her pretty dress, hairdo, and demure pose indicate that she is a fancier kind of woman. She seems to represent the hetaira, the sexual servant for upper-class lovemaking. Her characterization as a refined prostitute and the representation of the preliminaries to lovemaking rather than the act itself seem equally at odds with the actual conditions of the lupanar. Clearly, the erotics governing the display of this and the other six pictures representing lovemaking in the lupanar are quite different from the picture-gallery aesthetic of the elite bedroom. Rather than being part of a collection of works of art with diverse subjects, they preside from on high over what must have been intense traffic in the corridor below.

Yet they represent the couples in situations of comfort and isolation that were simply not possible in the lupanar's cramped booths, furnished only with unyielding masonry beds. The best preserved of these tabellae emphasizes—in its own humble way—the richness and comfort of the lovemaking chamber (Fig. 84). Compared with the picture of the couple looking at a pinax, where the figures are quite

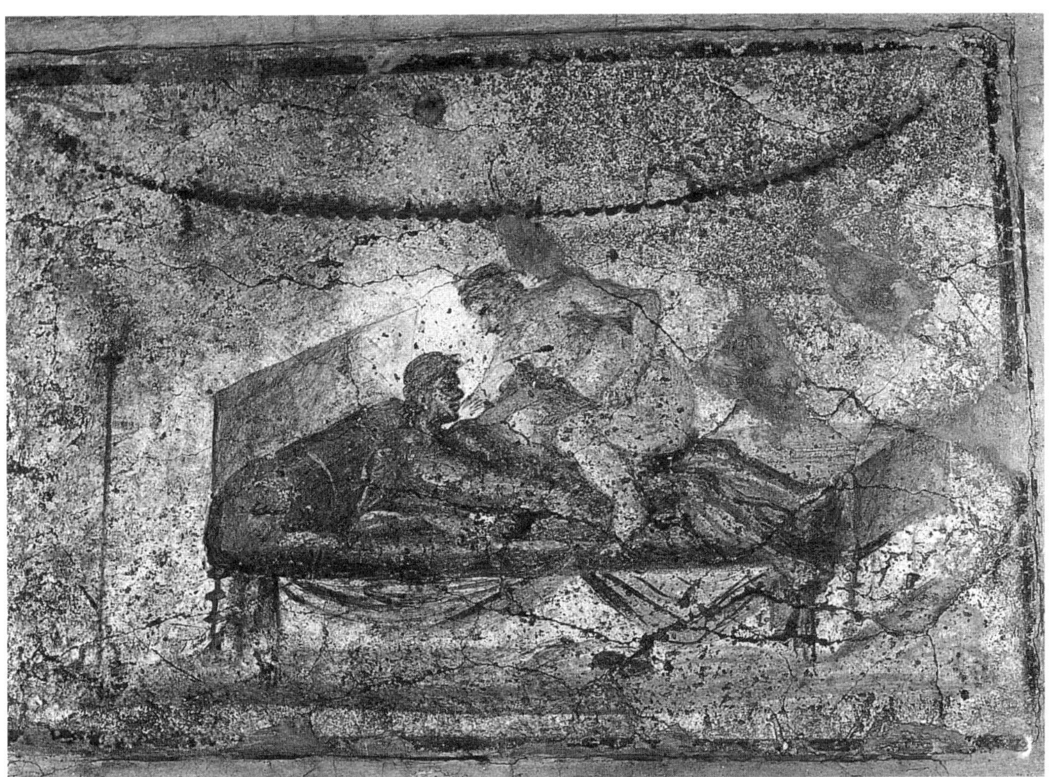

Figure 84. Male-female couple on bed, Pompeii, Lupanar at VII, 12, 18–20, south wall, upper zone, east part (A.D. 72–79). Photo Michael Larvey.

small in relation to the frame, here the artist enlarged the figures to fill most of the frame. He kept a space at the left edge of the picture for a lampstand, an accessory typical of a well-appointed bedchamber. He elaborated the bed quite fully, including bedstead and footboard, ample bolster at its head, and bedcovers swagged from the bottom of the mattress.

Examination of the couple's pose and facial features reveals further nuances that are somewhat surprising in a brothel painting. Rather than picturing intercourse, the artist represented an ambiguous moment. The man's pose is quite relaxed: he reclines on his back while raising up his head—but not his torso. He gazes straight ahead rather than at his partner. She straddles his outstretched legs, crouching to rest her buttocks on his left thigh. The artist rendered her in three-quarters view to reveal her upper torso as she leans forward sharply to gaze at her inattentive partner. Her profile is well enough preserved to see that the artist wanted her to be a sober beauty of classical profile, with a continuous straight line shared between brow and nose, a tiny closed mouth, and a square jaw. In contrast, the man has an unusually unclassical face, with convex forehead and short, curved nose. The woman extends her right arm behind the man's left shoulder while resting her left hand on her left thigh. Both body language and facial expression suggest a lull in the process of lovemaking, or perhaps the man's detachment and the woman's efforts to engage his attention. Here in the lupanar, where the modern viewer would expect explicit illustration of sexual positions, the painting expresses amorous dalliance and even detachment—fantasies, to be sure, in relation to the realities of the establishment.

Parallels with the refined representations on Arretine pottery of the Augustan period come to mind when we view the most beautiful of the paintings (Fig. 85). Although the woman's tall, slender body and small head fit with the revival of late Hellenistic aesthetics in the Flavian period, the artist took care to delineate her classical facial features. The couple's pose, with the man kneeling facing the woman while he parts her legs to enter her, is also one that recalls Augustan models (see Figs. 38 and 39). Once again, the couple's eyes do not meet. The woman seems to be absorbed in her own reverie—or pleasure—while the man inclines his head forward as if concentrating on his act of penetration. The artist showed details of the couple's faces, hair, and bodies, even though he painted them in a rapid technique that used daubs of paint to represent highlights. Was this attention to detail and pose another way of encoding upper-class luxury for the clientele of the lupanar?

The other three legible paintings—perhaps by the hand of another, less experienced artist—lack such nuances.[16] They portray variations on rear-entry sex, positions that give the artist few opportunities to distinguish between the man's and the woman's mental states. Of course, in a fine painting like that from the House of Caecilius Iucundus the artist found a way to communicate to the viewer the ambiguous emotions of the couple—even though the man faces the woman's back (see Plate 6).

If the erotics of display seem much clearer in the lupanar than in any of the buildings we examined so far, it is because its architecture and graffiti tell us unambiguously that it is a brothel meant for poor, lower-class clients: we know, in other words, who viewed them and why they were there. Less clear are the mean-

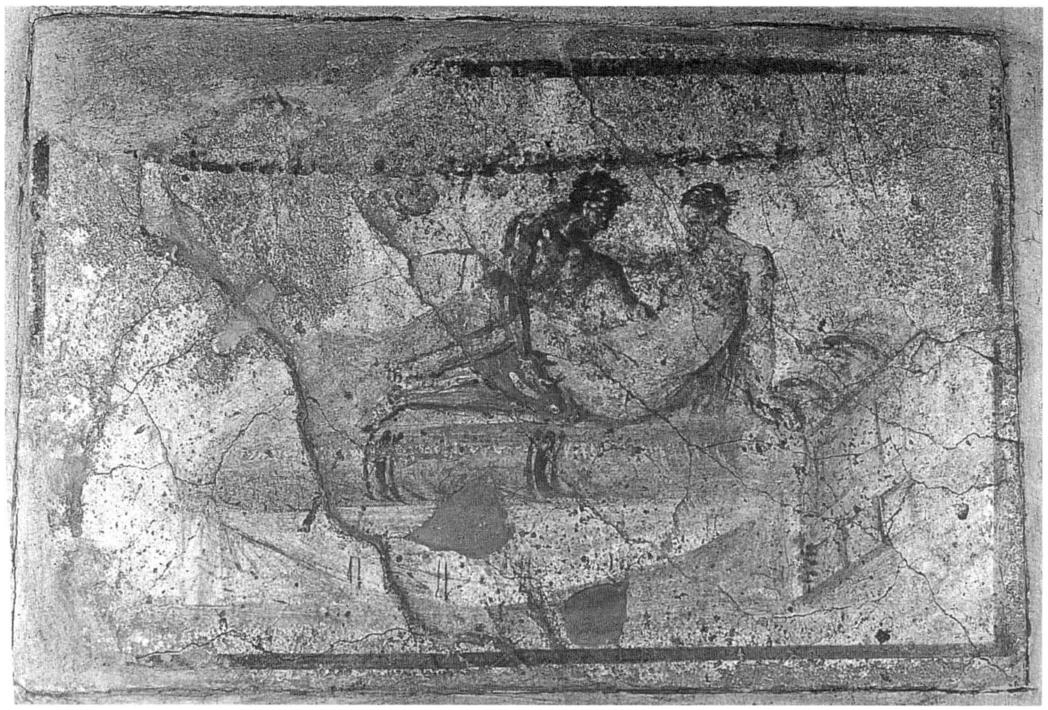

Figure 85. Male-female couple on bed, Pompeii, Lupanar at VII, 12, 18–20, south wall, upper zone, second panel from east (A.D. 72–79). Photo Michael Larvey.

ings that these paintings had for the intended viewers. On a very practical level, even though the corridor itself is a rather cramped space, the paintings would give clients something to look at while they were waiting their turn. Yet the imagery of the paintings hardly corresponds to the services they will receive. For one thing, the artist put his lovers on pretty beds with covers that are in rooms graced with pinakes and lampstands. For another, he created scenarios that emphasize the preliminaries to lovemaking (the couple looking at a picture of lovemaking) and underscored the contrasts between the emotional states of the man and the woman. These are all artistic constructions that point to environments far removed from the realities of the lupanar. In half the paintings in the lupanar, illustration of sexual positions was a secondary consideration. Instead, they encode fantasies of upper-class sexual luxuries for viewers who could not afford them.

Should we, with our twentieth-century Euro-American imaginations, be surprised that the humble pictures in the lupanar have as much to do with evoking elite values as they do with depicting sexual acts? Perhaps, because our consumer mentality colors our understanding: we assume that in the lupanar the paintings must "advertise" sexual services that a man could buy from one of the attending prostitutes. Rather than list specific services available, the artist's somewhat inept representations of erotic tabellae drew on a repertoire of imagery that could be appropriate in a variety of architectural contexts—from the cubicula of the super-rich to the peristyle of freedmen like Caecilius Iucundus. If we consider the actual conditions that surrounded lovemaking in the brothel, the paintings elevate to high ideals what was surely rough-and-ready sexual commerce.

Sex as Public Spectacle: The Paintings of the Caupona of the Street of Mercury

Whereas the lupanar's erotic paintings both illustrate and dignify the matters transacted there, several paintings from the Caupona of the Street of Mercury (VI, 10, 1) reveal the ancient Romans' fondness for sex shows as a form of entertainment. When the tavern's main room was excavated in 1823, the sexual subject matter of four of the thirteen paintings that decorated it (*b* on the plan, Fig. 86) was quite legible.[17] Today little remains of these erotic pictures—although some of the other scenes are in relatively good condition—so that we must rely on engravings done by Roux and published by Famin in 1836 to reconstruct their subject matter and their contribution to the whole iconographic program.[18] Discussion of this room generally ignores the images of sexual intercourse to focus on its genial scenes of everyday life as examples of the genre of so-called popular art. Even articles in recent publications are content to comment that the owner included the erotic paintings to designate sex-for-sale as one function of this establishment.[19] Yet the concept of advertising does not explain their content. Whereas many of the images in the lupanar emphasize upper-class values of physical beauty and leisurely sexual dalliance, the pictures in the caupona present sexual acrobatics as a form of entertainment that is much like the scenes of eating, drinking, and gambling that appear on the same walls.

The big counter that takes up most of *a* was for selling food and drink to passersby; room *b* was apparently reserved for customers who wanted to sit on rude stools—no high-class dining couches for them—and tarry. A glance at the subjects

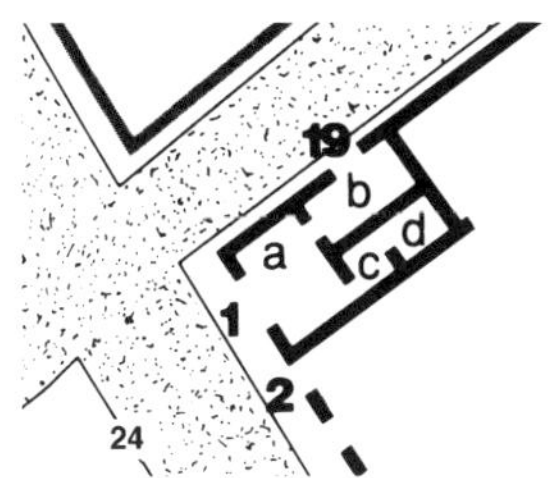

Figure 86. Pompeii, Caupona of the Street of Mercury (VI, 10, 1), plan.

of the various pictures on room *b*'s walls reveals that the owner wanted them to speak directly to his clientele about pleasures that they knew from their own experience. The artist inserted the paintings into a very simple system of panels framed by big red bands on a white ground.[20] On the east part of the north wall was a picture, now nearly illegible, showing a wine-transport cart. There was a similar picture in room *c*. Next to it is a picture of a servant who pours wine for a soldier. Someone put words in his mouth by scratching *da fridam pusillum*—"Give me a little cold water"—above his head. On the adjoining short east wall were two of the four scenes of sexual play that we discuss in a moment.

There were five pictures in all on the south wall (Fig. 87). Two pictures of sexual intercourse, in the panels adjoining the right and left corners, framed the three pictures—still preserved—with scenes of life in the tavern. This is a theme that also appears on the walls of the Caupona of Salvius (VI, 14, 36), painted perhaps by the same hand.[21] Men play dice in the second panel from east; in the picture in the middle of the wall is another vignette with dialogue written above it: the man on the left asks the man on the right to give him wine from Sentinum to drink. In the next picture we see a group of travelers sitting to eat under a pole hung with foodstuffs. Finally, on the north part of the west wall that separated room *b* from the front counter, the artist depicted four figures, two of them eating while a servant chats with a customer.

It is not difficult to guess why the four erotic pictures have not survived even though these simple scenes of tavern life have: some prudish hand destroyed them in the period after Roux drew and engraved them.[22] All that remain are traces of feet and heads on the left-hand panel of the east wall and on the west panel of the south wall. Even so, the pictures' relationship both to the person entering this room and to the other pictures included in the room's decorative scheme is clear. Some-

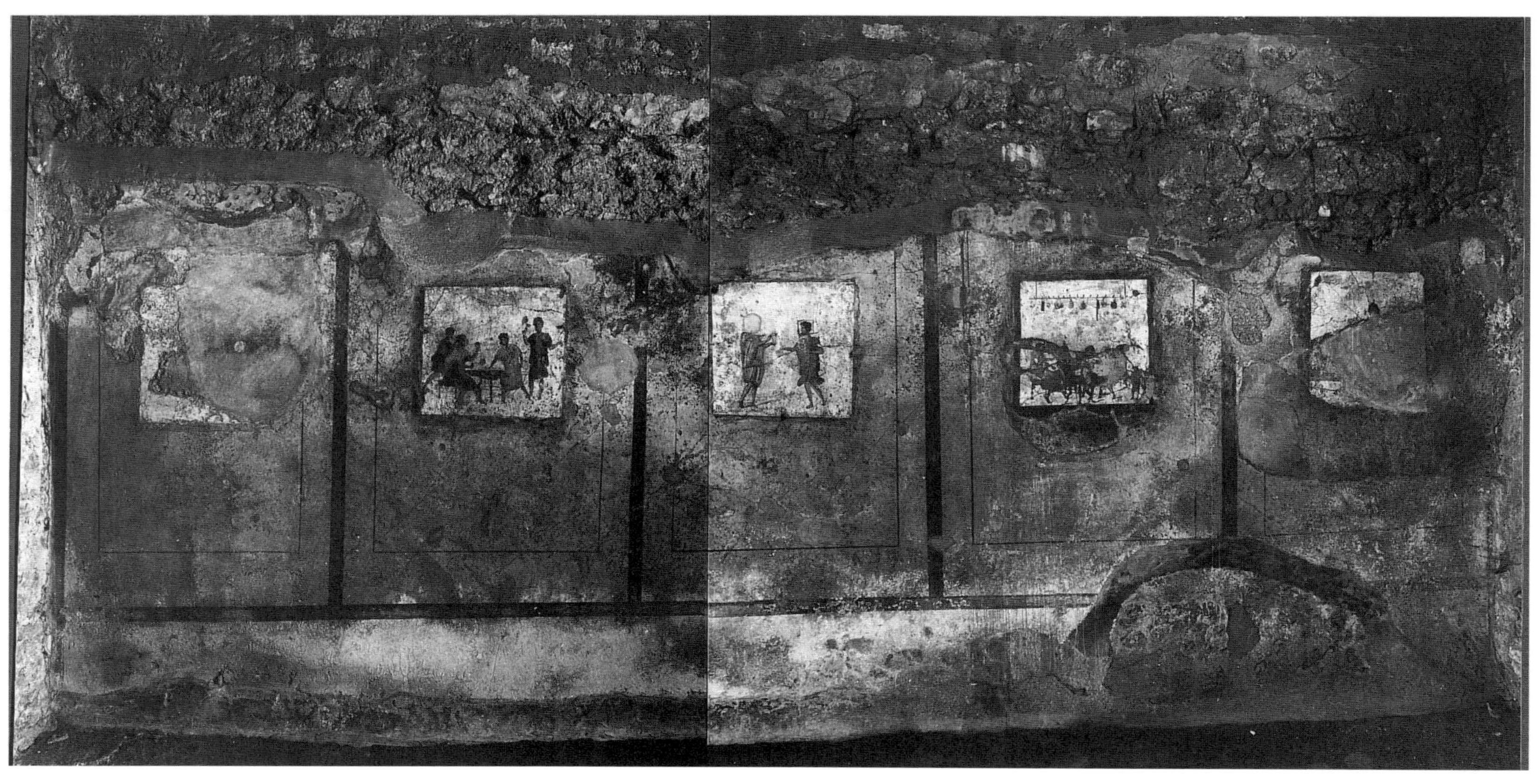

Figure 87. Scenes of gaming, drinking, and eating, Pompeii, Caupona of the Street of Mercury (VI, 10, 1), room *b*, south wall (A.D. 62–79). Photo Istituto Centrale per il Catalogo e la Documentazione N 56098–56099.

one coming in from the serving area (*a*) would see two erotic vignettes. They were probably the most important pictures in the room, for as we noted above in reference to room 43 of the House of the Centenary, the wall opposite a room's principal entrance carried the most important pictures. The other two erotic pictures, on the far right and left sides of the south wall, would greet someone entering from the secondary north doorway; they framed the three scenes of tavern life. From their positions in the room's decoration it seems clear that the owner wanted to highlight these four erotic vignettes: they were important to the theme that he wanted to establish.

A closer look at the imagery of the three scenes preserved in Roux's engravings reveals that they contributed substantially to the owner's concept of his establishment as a place for a little mischievous fun. The most outrageous and amusing picture graced the east wall opposite the principal entrance (Fig. 88). Today only the legs of the man on the right and a head remain.[23] A woman represented in profile bends deeply at the waist to perform several feats simultaneously. She reaches down with her right hand to place a wine pitcher on a low table while she raises a glass of wine to her lips. She has just filled both her glass and that of her companion, who seizes the opportunity as she bends over to penetrate her from the rear. He stands in a relaxed contrapposto, with his left leg extended and turned out in three-quarters view while supporting most of his weight with his flexed right. He tucks his left hand behind his hip while stretching out his right arm. The glass of wine that he holds in the palm of his right hand demonstrates an equilibrium almost equal to that of his partner.

The woman wears only the breast band, with her hair pulled back from the face and piled up in a crown of curls. The man's sleeveless tunic descends on a sharp diagonal to reveal his extraordinarily long penis and one of his testicles. These, of course, are details that we cannot verify today because of the painting's destruction. Nor can we verify the most curious element of all: the parallel ropes that appear beneath the couples' feet. Helbig went so far as to suggest that the principal subject was the performance of a tightrope act and that the modern draftsman added the man's erect penis simply to titillate the nineteenth-century viewer.[24] Fröhlich proposes a much likelier solution, that what the draftsman interpreted as ropes were merely the cast shadows that regularly appear in Pompeian paintings as thin lines behind the figures' feet.[25] Not only is there no evidence that ancient tightrope walk-

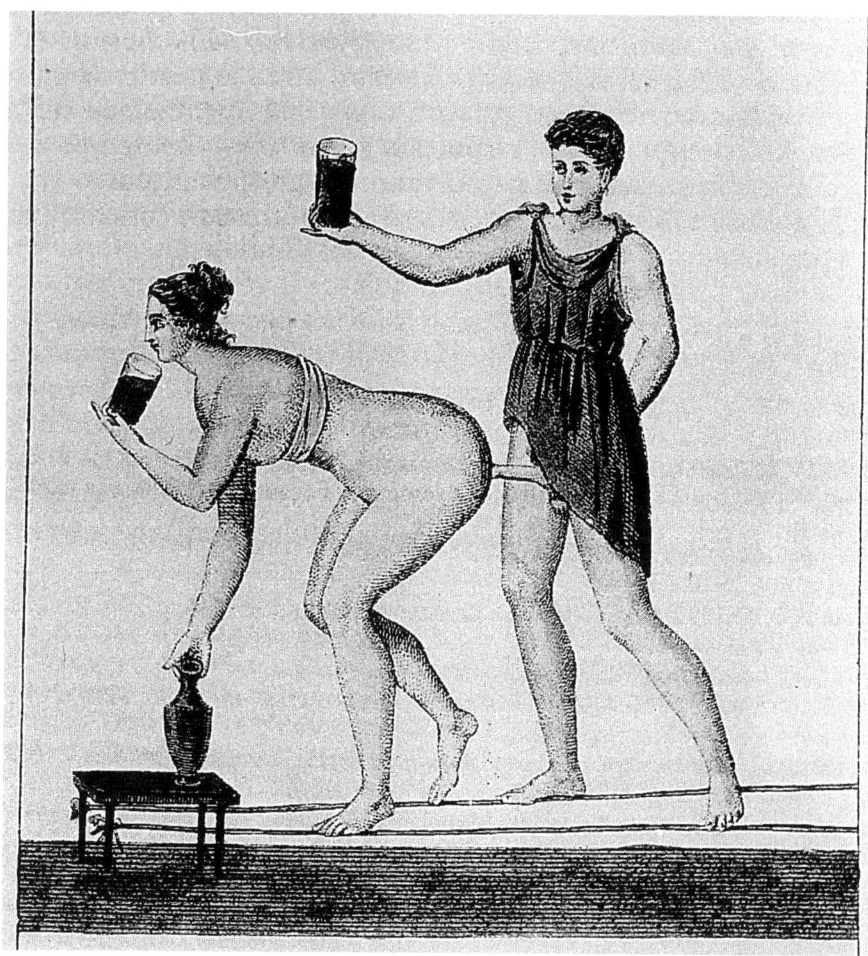

Figure 88. Male-female couple performing sexual acrobatics (destroyed), Pompeii, Caupona of the Street of Mercury (VI, 10, 1), room *b*, east wall, north part (A.D. 62–79). After Barré, *Herculaneum et Pompéi* (1827), pl. 35.

ers performed on two, rather than one, rope, but merely tying the ropes to the legs of an ordinary table would be unlikely to keep them taut enough to support the couple's weight.

The scene, then, far from being pure acrobatics—as Helbig would have it—becomes one of *sexual* acrobatics. Considering the cramped quarters of the tavern and the modest purses of owner and customers, it is unlikely that the painter was recording a floor show staged here to entertain the clientele. Nor would it be likely that the patron was "advertising" the services of a particularly talented prostitute.

This is an image from another context, that of sexual entertainments that the Roman populace so enjoyed.

Among the many different kinds of entertainment available to audiences were mimes that featured sexual intercourse. Research on the Roman theater underscores the importance of the obscene mimes as an integral part of productions that included the genres of tragedy and comedy. By the second century B.C. their original relation to cults of fertility had faded into obscurity while the performances of nude mimes became outlandish explorations of sexual play. Both Valerius Maximus and Martial repeat the story that Cato, that staunch upholder of old Republican values, always left the theater before the mimes (called *nudatio mimarum*) during the *Floralia:* he didn't want his stern presence to spoil the people's fun.[26] Having a picture in his caupona that evoked or recalled an outrageous sexual balancing-act from such a performance was one of the owner's ways of attracting viewers and potential customers into his little shop.

The two other pictures that we can locate on the walls of room *b,* while they do not directly invoke sex-as-public-performance, share one salient feature with this representation: the large size of the man's penis. One scene showed a standing man with a huge erection attempting to denude a resisting woman.[27] The other, located on the far right of the south wall, showed the equally phallic man lying down on a bed with the woman about to mount him. Behind the bed are a lamp and a servant.[28] Perhaps the draftsman exaggerated the size of the mens' members in all three drawings, but I am inclined to accept their unusual dimensions for two reasons. First, in the case of the sexual acrobats, a large penis allowed spectators to see the act of penetration—even from the back row. Second, among the established tropes in contemporary literature are tales of unusually well endowed men.

We addressed the Roman aesthetic preference for men with small penises in our investigation of images of hypersexual black men in chapter 5. Here the Roman sources—both textual and visual—follow Greek precedents. But in Petronius' *Satyricon,* a saga of the revenge of Priapus upon the character Encolpius, one vignette has a huge crowd of bathers gathering around Encolpius' friend and rival, Ascyltus, to admire his enormous penis (Petronius, *Satyricon* 92). They applaud him, as the bathers do in Martial 9.3: "If from the baths you hear a round of applause, Maron's giant prick is bound to be the cause."[29] Caelia covers her bath slave's large penis with a brass sheath to keep her prize a secret.[30] Here in the tavern, where the artist included the erotic paintings as part of a compendium of life's pleasures, he emphasized not only sexual acrobatics, but also the men's super-penises, to elicit a combination of dumbstruck admiration and laughter from viewers.

It is possible that little cubiculum *d,* where the artist tried—despite his meager skills—to produce a "proper" Fourth-Style decoration, saw use as a lovemaking chamber. The female—and probably also the male—waiters who served food and drink to customers commonly provided sexual services.[31] Yet there are no paintings of lovemaking in cubiculum *d:* rather they are pictures with erotic overtones. The center picture on the north wall has as its subject Venus fishing (the same subject used in room 42 of the House of the Centenary); in the center of the south wall appear Polyphemus and Galatea. These pictures, as well as the faux-marble socle, show that the owner wanted this little room—if it was used for making love—to recall the domestic sphere: its tone was far removed from that of the sexual spectacle in room *b.*

If the sexual feats pictured in the very modest Caupona of the Street of Mercury demonstrate that some Pompeians enjoyed representations of sexual performance for its comic value, the contrivances of sexual humor reach an unprecedented level of sophistication in the elaborately equipped Suburban Baths.

Sex and Laughter in the Suburban Baths

In 1986, the discovery of unique paintings representing sexual activity in a bath complex renewed the debate about whether the presence of erotic paintings meant that the building saw use as a brothel.[32] The baths are "suburban" in the sense that they lie just outside the city's walls, in a two-story structure located along the steep road that leads from the ancient river port up to Pompeii's Marine Gate. The large bath complex occupies the ground floor; three apartments fill the upper story. The principal approach to the upper story was from covered sidewalk, even though a stairway (to the south of room 7) connects the baths with this upper story (Fig. 89). The excavator, Luciana Jacobelli, found the erotic paintings in ground-floor room 7. Analysis of the entire bath complex establishes that this room was a dressing room, or apodyterium.

Comparison with other baths at Pompeii suggests that the owner of the Suburban Baths was an enterprising private individual whose establishment offered a

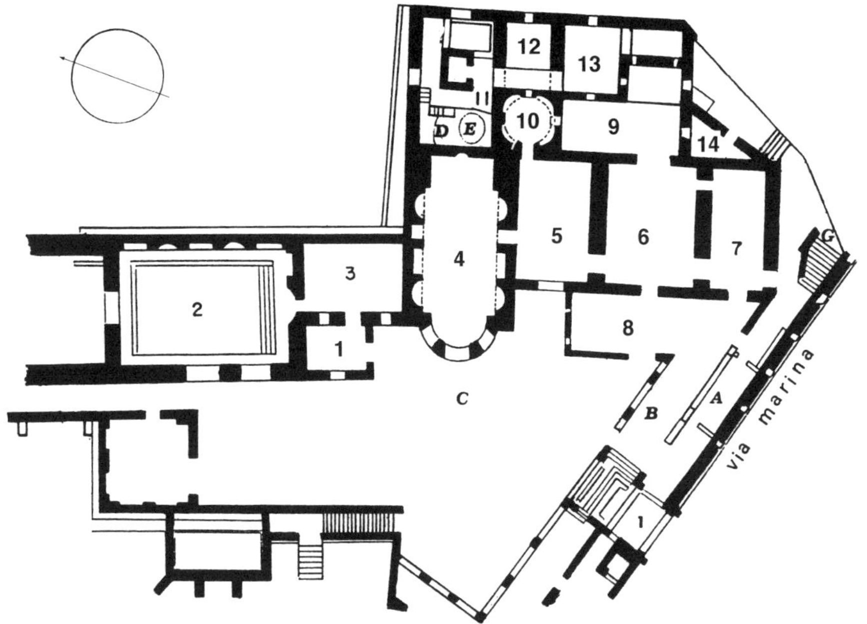

Figure 89. Pompeii, Suburban Baths, plan.

number of amenities unavailable in the old-fashioned public facilities at Pompeii.[33] Rooms were large and well lighted, and had many luxury features. There was an elaborate cold-plunge (*natatio,* 9), with a mosaic waterfall splashing cold water into it, and paintings with sea creatures on its sides. In addition to the usual heated rooms, bathers could also enjoy the dry heat in one room (*laconicum,* 10), and even a large heated swimming pool (2) flanked by richly decorated rooms (1 and 3). Significantly, the plan reveals a fact that makes these baths unlike all other baths functioning at Pompeii at the time of the eruption: the Suburban Baths are the only ones not divided into separate sections for men and women.[34] There is only one dressing room in the Suburban Baths, and whether the two sexes bathed at the same time, or at different times, this apodyterium had to serve all patrons. As will become clear, the fact that both women and men used this room and looked at the painted sexual vignettes that decorated it, has important implications for understanding the attitudes the two sexes had toward sexual representation.

Aside from the sexual vignettes, the apodyterium's Fourth-Style decorative scheme follows established practice. For instance, one of its functions was to differ-

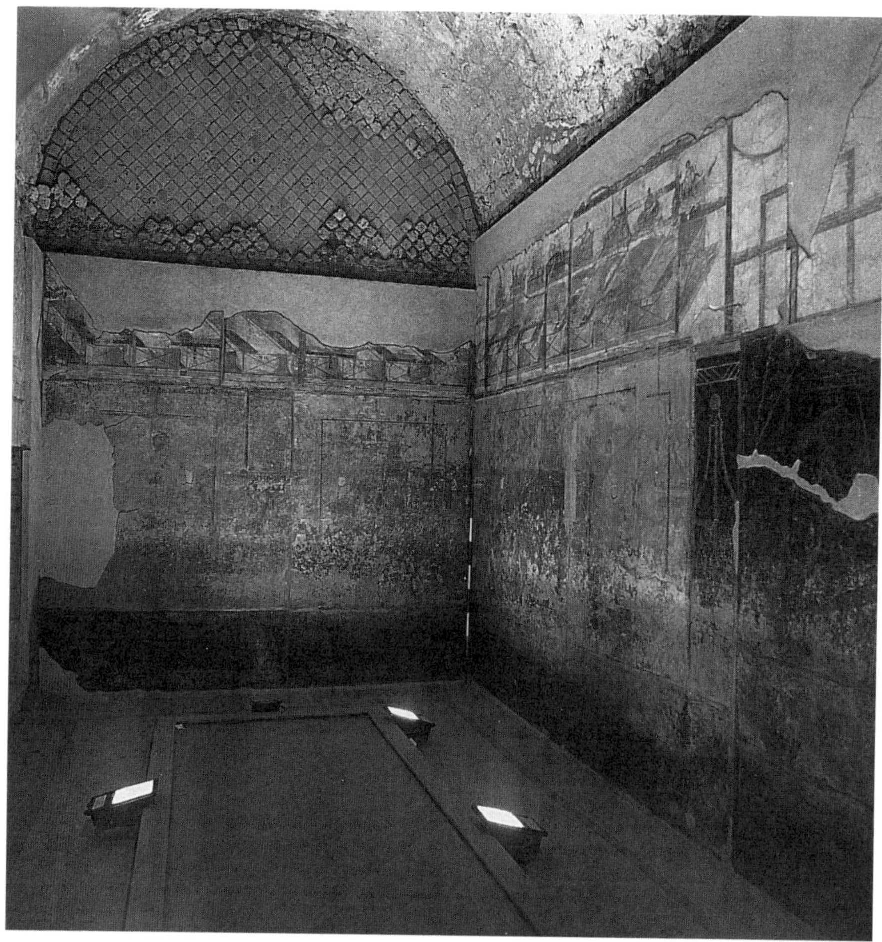

Figure 90. Pompeii, Suburban Baths, apodyterium 7, south and east walls (A.D. 62–79). Photo Michael Larvey.

entiate the circulation space from the space where bathers dressed by using different color schemes and different architectural representations (Fig. 90).[35] Simple motifs—a black socle with plants, a black middle zone with large rectangular panels, and a white upper zone with aediculae and garlands—decorate the western half of the space. This area would see the most traffic, since it encompassed three doorways: the entrance itself and two doors to right and left of the entry. A tall thin panel divides the wall at midpoint, signaling a dramatic change in the decorative scheme. Although the socle is still black, the middle zone switches to a yellow

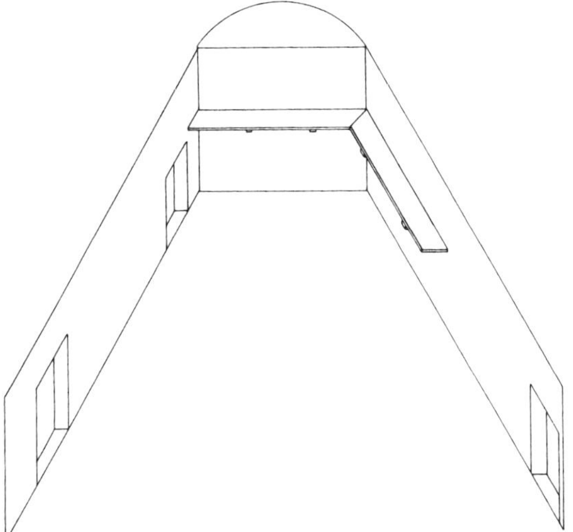

Figure 91. Pompeii, Suburban Baths, apodyterium 7, hypothetical restoration of wooden shelves. Drawing by Stephan Mols.

ground. Most striking of all is the white-ground decoration of the upper zone, preserved on the right and back walls:[36] here the artist represented a deep shelf that supports sixteen numbered boxes. Although only the boxes in perspective (numbers 9–16) survive on the rear wall, above those on the right wall appear the most audacious ancient erotic paintings found to date.

The sixteen boxes, Jacobelli explains, are two-dimensional representations of the real containers for bathers' clothing that would rest on wooden shelves directly below (Fig. 91).[37] These representations in perspective even reproduce accurately the dimensions of the masonry shelves with compartments for clothes preserved in apodyteria at Pompeii and Herculaneum. The excavator found holes in the right and rear walls for the brackets that held the wooden shelves and the boxes. The only remains of the boxes themselves, doubtless made of a lightweight wood, are little metal straps that served as reinforcing, designated in the paintings with an X at the front and along the side of each box.

Shortly before the eruption of A.D. 79, the owner had the inner part of the room repainted in a scheme that covered the erotic paintings of the upper zone with simple Fourth-Style motifs.[38] It is quite possible that a new owner or manager took over the baths. Whether he himself had more conservative tastes in decoration, or whether he thought he could attract a larger clientele without the erotic images, is difficult to judge. In any case, it seems clear that this repainting had as its sole purpose the canceling out of the erotic vignettes, since the artist, rather than repainting the whole room, painted over only the section of the wall containing the erotic vignettes and the zone immediately below.[39] Although this poorly executed painting that covered them to a certain extent preserved the erotic images, in some places it still adheres, making it difficult to read several of the scenes.

What was the purpose of the numerals? They appear on white labels in the upper center of each box, between the arms of the X straps. The sequence starts with number I, to the left of the right wall's midpoint, and continues to number VIII, located at the corner. The numbered boxes then continue on the rear wall, ending with XVI. By representing the boxes with numbers the artist also numbered the real containers below, where each bather deposited her or his things.

As if this were not enough, he added an unforgettable "label" atop each box in the form of an erotic representation. A careful look at these eight little paintings suggests that the artist had no intention of depicting the upper-class fantasies that we saw in paintings like the one in the House of Caecilius Iucundus—or even in some of the paintings in the lupanar. Rather he aimed, like the painter of the lost paintings of the Caupona of Mercury, to amuse the viewer with outrageous sexual spectacle.

The artist began the series with a representation that is explicit but fairly common in Roman erotic wall painting (Plate 9). The woman, facing the viewer in scene I, strikes a relaxed pose as she sits on the man's penis. She plants her feet squarely on the bed to right and left of the man's upper thighs. Her body is upright, but her position is unusually relaxed: she leans to her right to rest her wrist on her knee while extending her left arm to place her hand on her left knee. (Remains of a thick, green, curving element from the later overpainting cover parts of the woman's left arm, hand, and leg.) The woman's curly hair falls to cover her ears. Her slim body recalls that of the women in room *f'* of the House at IX, 5, 16 (see especially Fig. 72), although the artist had some difficulty in rendering her right breast in perspective. Overpainting covers the portion of the man's figure to the viewer's extreme left, yet enough remains to show us that the artist placed him obliquely on the bed: he reclines, propping himself up with his elbows, so that the viewer looks over his head, back, and shoulders to focus on his erect penis as it enters the woman's vagina. She has removed her pubic hair through depilation, a common practice for men as well as women in this period.[40] A few fluid lines near the man's hand and the woman's foot must indicate the striped bedcovers, otherwise erased by the overpainting.

Closest to this representation among fresco paintings is the panel, probably from Pompeii, now in the Naples Museum (Plate 8).[41] It is clearly the work of a more skillful artist than the painter of the Suburban Baths: he was better at placing the figures in space and depicting their interaction. Despite paint losses it is still possible to see how this artist used light and shadow to give the figures volume. He also animated the woman; her counterpart in the Suburban Baths painting looks quite bland and detached in comparison. In the Naples painting she turns her head sharply to engage the man's gaze even as she pushes up her body to poise her vagina over his waiting penis. The man's pose is also more active than that of the man in the Suburban Baths: he sits upright, his torso supported by a big striped cushion. The artist paid attention to details, such as the man's floral crown (tied at the back with ribbons) and the woman's hairdo. Yet the major contrast between the Naples picture and that from the Suburban Baths—a trait that appears in some other scenes of the baths—has to do with relative scale, not details: the artist underplayed the man's figure both in pose and in size to emphasize the woman. Her pose and body dominates the painting in the Suburban Baths.

There have been two tendencies in the modern literature interpreting this sexual position. Dover notes that it never appears in Greek vase painting,[42] and some scholars, most notably Catherine Johns, see the popularity of this representation in Roman art as a sign of the sexual emancipation of the Roman woman. Johns argues that when the woman is on top, riding the man, she has freedom of sexual expression, since whether facing him or with her back to him she can move around quite independently: the position requires "her very active cooperation."[43] Others take the opposite tack: Paul Veyne, for instance, sees the *mulier equitans* (woman riding) position in terms of the woman having to do all the work while serving the man who simply lies there.[44] Neither the visual evidence nor the ancient literature supports either of these essentially modern constructions of sexuality. Although both the ancient Greeks and the Romans discuss this position in some detail, and although it appears with great frequency in painting and in relief sculpture, nowhere do we get the sense that this position encoded the woman's domination over the man—or vice versa.[45]

A more fruitful approach is to think of the visual properties of this representation, since it above all was a way of showing the act of penetration—and the woman's beautiful face, breasts, torso, and legs—to best advantage. Ovid recommends this position for the small woman but cautions against it for a tall woman.[46] As Myerowitz points out, this and the other seven positions that Ovid specifies address the woman's act of presenting her best features to her lover. The woman, in effect, "composes" herself to look good—a self-conscious act.[47] What is interesting in the Suburban Baths image is that the artist depicted the woman riding as large—not small. In this sense he privileged the woman as aesthetic object. A Roman woman looking at this representation might understand it as showcasing feminine beauty and power at the expense of male. For the Roman man who enjoyed sex with women, the artist constructed a view that shows off the woman's beautiful face, breasts, and torso to her lover—just the effect that Ovid says she will have if she rides the man. By depicting this position, and by making the woman's figure loom large, the artist gave viewers of both sexes a way of looking at lovemaking that favors different, but complementary, points of view. For both sexes the artist assumed the viewer's interest in clearly seeing the penis penetrating the vagina. But it is also a representation that privileges the woman's body over the man's. It is only in this sense that the woman "dominates" the man. She dominates a visual composition that reveals the first-century Romans' avid interest in the beauty of the nude female body in all activities, including that of making love.

In scene II the woman reclines on her left side, her upper body resting on a big fringed cushion (Plate 10). She supports her head with her left hand, her elbow resting on the cushions, while her right arm curves around her head in the by now familiar gesture of sexual readiness. The man kneels upright on the bed, his right knee between the woman's legs as he grasps her right thigh with his right arm. He turns his head toward the woman. (Unfortunately the later decoration of this wall covered both the man's torso and the woman's face with a Fourth-Style carpet border.) Traces of red pigment show the spool-ornaments of one of the bed's legs; on the bed itself is a yellow coverlet. There is a green cushion with stripes and fringes at its head and a green sham swagged below the bed frame.

As in scene I, display of the woman's fashionable body seems uppermost in the artist's mind, for this pose turns her graceful torso, thighs, and legs to the viewer. Not only is it a variation of the many representations of male-female intercourse in the Arretine ware considered in chapter 4, it is also the preferred pose for representing a man penetrating a boy, and for similar reasons. Just as the pose permits the artist to show the woman's breasts, in male-male representations it allows him to feature the boy's genitals (see Plate 2 and Figs. 26 and 27). However, comparison with other representations of the woman or boy lying on the left side reveals an ambiguity in scene II. For some reason the artist, so intent on displaying penetration in scene I, placed the man's body too squarely behind the middle part of the woman's back to allow him to be in the act of penetrating the woman either anally or vaginally.

It may be that the artist simply miscalculated the man's position, or that he wanted to represent *approach* from the rear but not the act of penetration. The woman's pose, with her right arm raised to frame her head, is one that we have encountered before (see Fig. 23). Here it relays the woman's sexual readiness or at least sexual accessibility. As in scene I, the artist made the woman's body the subject of the picture and the object of the viewer's gaze. If she is available, it is as much to the spectator as to her partner's somewhat clumsy approach.

For the astute female viewer, this depiction of the woman's glamour coupled with the man's seeming ineptitude was probably quite funny. Her eyes would understand the clichés, especially that of the crooked-arm gesture, as well as the awkwardness of the moment pictured. It is less likely that the man looking at this scene would be very much aware of the clumsiness of the man in the picture—especially if he was intent on taking in the obvious display of the woman's anatomy that this pose offers.

Even though scenes I and II feature well known, common representations, the artist privileged the display of the woman's body in ways that might have elicited different responses from men and women viewers. Scene III takes a different tack by figuring a rarity in the Roman visual record, the act of a woman fellating a man—and that, to be sure, in a unique composition (Plate 11). The man sits upright on the bed, his left arm leaning on the headboard; he holds a scroll in his left hand. He wears a white tunic, indicated by the folds that descend to his waist, but he hikes it up to uncover his genitals. He extends his right arm to rest his hand on the head of the woman, who sits on the edge of the bed as she leans deeply forward to suck the man's penis. The artist took some care to depict the woman's act of balancing her body: she leans on her right elbow and rests her buttocks on the bed, but to maintain her position she must extend her right leg to the floor while demurely folding her left leg back. Paint traces outline her breast band. The man, his head in three-quarters view, does not look at the woman but seems to gaze into space. Nor does his partner look at him: her head, in profile, inclines downward as she places her mouth around the tip of his penis. (Remains of a green garland from the later painting campaign appear to left and right.)

Six representations of fellatio appear in Attic vase painting, but always in the context of the symposium, where it is a service rendered by hetairai. In these scenes, most involving a trio of two men and a woman, the artists represent the woman as unattractive (see Fig. 1). In two instances they show the man brandishing a sandal over the woman's body, as if to threaten her with a beating.[48] I know of no visual representations of fellatio in Hellenistic art; when such scenes begin to appear on Roman lamps of the first century A.D., they figure a man and a woman on a bed rather than the trios or the orgy-at-the-symposium scenario of the Attic vases. This is also the case with the one scene of fellatio found on the first-century coinlike tokens called spintriae (discussed in chapter 8).[49] Even in the second- and third-century relief medallions from the Rhône Valley (also considered in chapter 8), where in general all the sexual imagery is freer and more imaginative than in painting, scenes of fellatio are rare.[50]

The representation closest to scene III is on a lamp, now in the Naples Museum, of unknown provenance (Fig. 92).[51] Although in mirror reversal with respect to the painting, the essentials of the composition are the same: the man pulls his tunic up to expose his erect penis to the woman. She crouches down to poise her mouth over the man's member while he places his hand on her head as if to push her down on it. This gesture of the man resting his hand on the woman's head is common to all representations of fellatio. What might it indicate about ancient Roman attitudes toward this sexual practice?

Both ancient literature and graffiti tell us that fellatio was the province of prostitutes; it was a sexual act that no Roman man of the elite class could request of his wife—and with good reason. The Romans were particularly concerned about the purity and care of the mouth. It was the organ of speech and above all the organ of public oratory. Social interactions also focused on the clean mouth, since it was customary for social equals to kiss when greeting each other. Although no oratorical or forensic texts accuse women of having unclean mouths because of their acts of fellatio, such accusations against men do appear. In invective literature, the worst

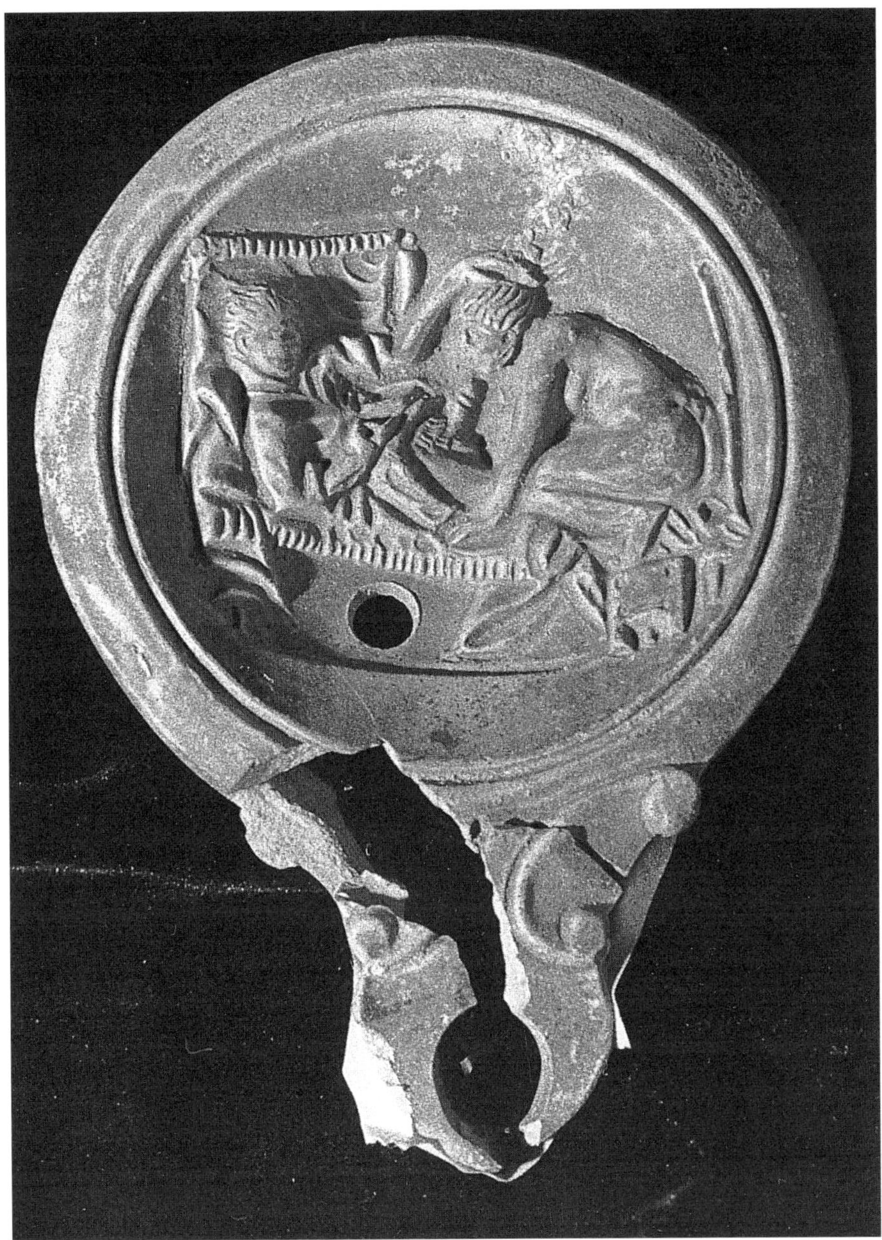

Figure 92. Lamp with scene of fellatio, from Pompeii. Naples Archaeological Museum inv. 27864, diameter 9.25 cm. Photo Michael Larvey.

possible insult is to accuse a man of fellating another man, and the worst possible threat against a man is that of forcing him to fellate someone. The verb that describes this forced fellatio, *irrumare,* places the fellator in the category of impurity.[52] The Romans believed that an unclean mouth (*os impurum*) affected not only the perpetrator of the fellatio but spread out to infect the whole of society.[53] They excluded such impure persons from society by placing them in the category of the outcast; they suffered the status of infamy, or *infamia,* and—along with prostitutes of both sexes, actors, and gladiators—could not act within the citizen body. It is logical to extend this Roman belief about the impurity of the male fellator to women; it is an act that any freeborn woman would avoid performing at all costs.[54] Slaves and freedwomen, of course, had little choice in the matter, yet the gesture of the man's hand on the woman's head—about to push her head down on his penis—seems to encode, in visual terms, the woman's expected reluctance to perform fellatio.

We should not assume that the threat of *infamia* kept men from seeking the pleasure of fellatio or that some women—whether highborn or servile—did not enjoy fellating their partners. They would simply dare not speak of the practice and hope that their partners would keep quiet as well. Even though Martial emphasizes that the *fellatrix* was a low prostitute (11.61), he satirizes the fact that men competed to have the services of an accomplished one (4.7). He calls attention to the hypocrisy of men wanting to be fellated but not wanting anyone to know about it: "Two bits of gold will get you Galla's cunt, and four will get you a lot more. Then why give her ten, Aeschylus? She will give you a blow job for much less. What is this? Hush money" (9.4).[55] He pushes his satire even further when he proposes that fellatio was a way for a girl to keep her virginity while still satisfying her lover.[56] Martial is certainly joking here, for no man would marry a freeborn woman known to have performed this act.[57] Graffiti from Pompeii, since they are written by ordinary, probably non-elite men, reveal outright enthusiasm for fellatio. They evaluate the relative merits of various *fellatrices.*[58]

A final element of scene III, the scroll that the man holds in his left hand, adds a further nuance to considerations of class and social status. A fragmentary terracotta relief medallion of the second century from the Rhône Valley reproduces a man who lifts his tunic up to his waist with the very hand that holds a scroll. Although the fragment with the figure of the woman is lost, it is likely that she was fellating him.[59] The scroll is the marker of literacy and of upper-class values associated with reading: mastery of oratory, literature, and especially poetry. As we will see in scene VIII, where a man represented as a poet is reading an open scroll, the attribute of the scroll adds considerably to the comic dimensions of the scene. If the demure prostitute's delicate posture as she prepares to fellate the man separates her from the hardly delicate positions of her counterparts on the lowly lamps, the scroll in the man's hand is a humorous send-up of elite literary pretensions.

Like scenes I and II, scene III seems to send its intended mixed audience different messages for male and female viewers. The artist constructed the comic trope of the literate, perhaps highborn, man enjoying a sexual pleasure that—because of Roman attitudes toward oral purity—was supposed to be somewhat difficult to obtain. The Roman man looking at this scene would be well aware of the irony in representing both an "intellectual" man and such a dainty—could she be elite?—woman. The freeborn woman would find the painting amusing as well, but probably for different reasons. She could laugh with impunity at the unfortunate woman—she certainly would have to be a prostitute or slave—who had to fellate the man in the picture. Certainly this was an act that she would rather her husband pay a woman of the servile ranks to do, thereby saving herself from the threat of oral impurity.

With scene IV the artist further explores questions of the pure versus the impure mouth—this time that of the man. A naked woman leans back on a bed and spreads her legs to reveal her depilated genitals to the man (Plate 12). Jewelry adorns her nude body: an anklet, a bracelet, an arm band, and a long gold chain that crosses between her breasts and trails off to the sides of her waist. This kind of crisscross chain appears in many representations of lovemaking, most notably in a mirror cover in Capitoline Museum (see Fig. 60) and in the painting on the east wall of room *x'* of the House of the Vettii (see Fig. 64).[60] The woman's hair is slightly curly and frames her face to just below the ears; she keeps it in place with a white headband. She sits on a high bed with a green coverlet and a pink sham that arcs upward at the corners to reveal the bed's legs. As in scene I, the artist did everything possible to focus the viewer's gaze on the woman's body. He set her nearly frontally, with the light delineating the left three-quarters of her body, and he dramatized the woman's act of spreading her legs: she grasps her right leg at the knee to hold it up in the air while resting the other on the edge of the bed.

The man, in contrast, seems insignificant. Not only is he much smaller than the woman, he is crouching down to lick the woman's vagina. He is fully clothed in a white tunic and wears ankle-high shoes.[61] His face is in profile, revealing his turned-up nose and large eyes, gazing, it would seem, up at the woman. As in the first two scenes, but even more noticeable here, the artist made the woman much larger than the man. He also emphasized the man's right hand, resting above the woman's left knee, by making it unusually large and by spreading the fingers.

This scene is unique among preserved wall paintings. It is true that Suetonius, as part of his famous account of Tiberius' sexual debauchery on Capri, describes a painting by Parrhasios that represented oral sex between Meleager and Atalanta. Most scholars interpret Suetonius' four-word description to mean that the picture showed Atalanta performing fellatio on her partner.[62] Judith Hallett proposes that Suetonius' words describe a scene of *mutual* oral stimulation, or "69," where Meleager was performing cunnilingus on Atalanta while she was fellating him. Even if Parrhasios' painting represented cunnilingus as well as fellatio, the meaning it would have for the ancient viewer was quite different from the *isolated* act of cunnilingus represented in scene IV.[63] Similarly, when cunnilingus appears on lamps, it is part of a reciprocal act, with the man licking the woman's vagina while the woman responds by sucking the man's penis (Fig. 93). Such representations—whether the hypothetical painting of Suetonius' description or the actual ones of the lamps—because they make both partners equal in their sexual activities, contrast markedly with the scene from the Suburban Baths. Scene IV is, in fact, entirely unlike the known representations of cunnilingus, where the man is the same size as the woman, on (not crouching beneath) the bed, nude, and—most important—receiving fellatio in return for his performance of cunnilingus. Why then did the artist of the Suburban Baths emphasize the woman—and the pleasure that the man is giving her—while making the man small and subservient?

The answer to this question lies in Roman attitudes toward men who performed cunnilingus. In their thinking, cunnilingus, like fellatio, brought about the disgrace of oral impurity on the person who performed it. In the Roman hierarchy of sexual debasement, the man suspected of performing cunnilingus was even more defiled than a man who was the passive partner in male-to-male sex.[64] In 4.43 Martial first accuses Coracinus of being penetrated by males, then switches his invective to something much worse: he practices cunnilingus on women. "I did not call you,

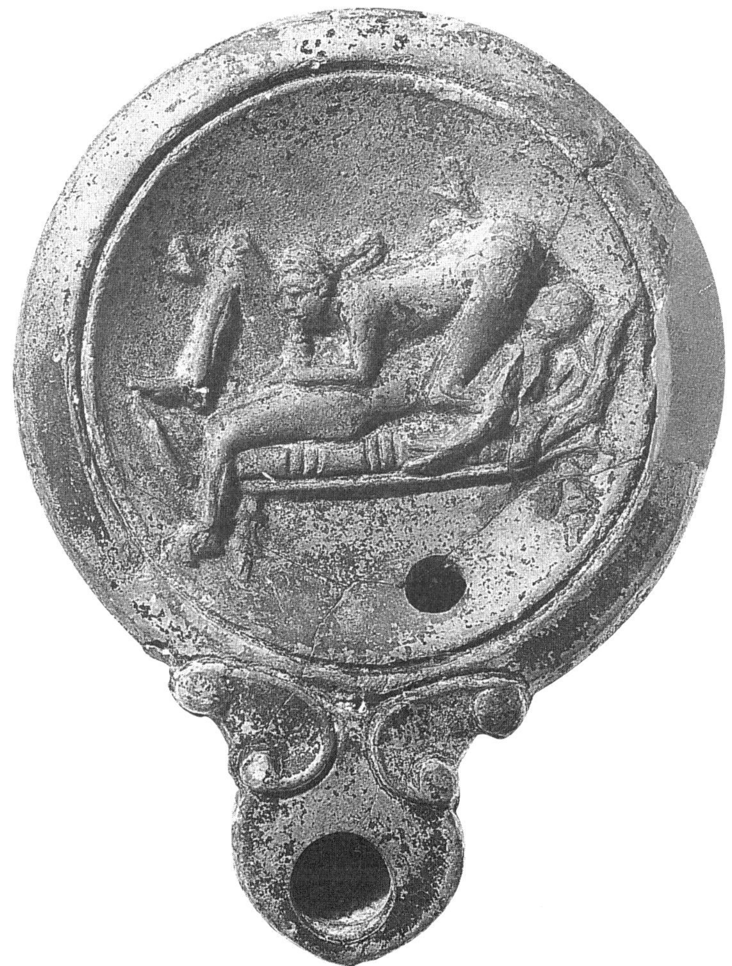

Figure 93. Male-female couple engaging in 69, terra-cotta lamp (1st c. A.D.). Cyprus Museum, inv. 2759. Photo courtesy of museum.

Coracinus, a passive homosexual; I am not so rash or daring, nor one willing to tell lies . . . yet what did I say? This light and insignificant thing—a known fact that you yourself will not deny. I said that you, Coracinus, were a cunt-licker."[65] The artist made the man in the painting of the Suburban Baths nothing more than a *cunnilinctor:* he is all hands, mouth, smaller than the woman—and not even receiving genital stimulation from the woman in return for his act of debasement.

Over against these male literary constructions, however, we find some evidence that women regularly hired male prostitutes to pleasure them with cunnilingus. Graffiti at Pompeii proclaim that male prostitutes were willing to perform cunnilingus on women for a price similar to that which female prostitutes requested for fellatio, between one and three asses.[66] Perhaps detractors wrote these graffiti to debase their male enemies by saying that their tongues were for hire, or perhaps these graffiti reveal actual sexual practices. If a woman could easily obtain cunnilingus from a male prostitute for little money, the scene in the Suburban Baths would reflect a service that was routinely available to Pompeian women. Even so, the artist's rendering is no straightforward documentation of a routine sexual practice. He pushed his image into the realm of parody to make his audience laugh.

It is the artist's very exaggeration of the man's "perversion" that would make him an extremely comic figure in the eyes of ancient Roman of both sexes. The artist knowingly played with a deeply ingrained Roman attitude toward a sexual practice to produce side-splitting comic parody. If the viewer doubled over with laughter—as I am sure many ancient visitors to the Suburban Baths did—it was because the artist manipulated the mechanisms of sexual taboo to produce an image of a man so enthusiastic about licking a woman's genitals that he eagerly served her, fully clothed—his eyes bugging with excitement—while the object of his enthusiasm, her face expressionless, obliged his perversion. For the male viewer, the fact that the man is clothed and the woman entirely naked—if we exclude her crisscross chain—signaled yet another reversal. In nearly all images of lovemaking, it was the man who was naked and the woman who was clothed—at least to the point of wearing the breast band.[67] His clothed status is inappropriate, just as the woman's nakedness signals that she is a brazen prostitute. The Roman man looking at this picture saw sexual etiquette turned upside down.

A Roman woman looking at scene IV would recognize the same reversals that would strike the male viewer, with the added thrill, perhaps, of seeing the woman having the upper hand. She is obviously in control of the sexual proceedings: it is the man who crouches and implores. The woman is the object of genital worship, not to mention the artist's focus on her body as the beautiful contrast to the man's ugliness. He depicts her with fine proportions, graceful gestures, and expensive jewelry; the man, in contrast, has no proportions at all: his gestures are comic and his expression desperate.

It is not only cunnilingus, but also the sex and status of the two people pictured, that make this scene so funny for Roman viewers of both sexes. That cunnilingus was a practice that was fair game for comic parody is clear not only from this representation but also from scene VII, considered below, where it is a woman who practices it.[68]

Scene V is so abraded and obscured by the remains of the overpainting (here the top of a pavilion) that the sex of the person on the left is unclear (Plate 13). This figure stands on the floor with the right hand at the side. The head is inclined downward, as if to gaze at the genitals of the woman on the bed. She reclines, supporting herself on her left elbow while raising her right leg high up to rest on the standing person's left shoulder. She also inclines her head, but it is rendered in three-quarters view rather than in profile like her partner; she wears the breast band.

It is lamentable that no amount of scrutiny will yield for certain the identification of the sex of the standing figure. Jacobelli interprets this standing figure as a man and links the composition with another wall painting from Pompeii.[69] She also cites numerous representations of this position in lamps and ceramics. I, however, propose a different reading of the scene for three reasons—none of them, I admit, entirely conclusive. First, the standing figure's hair is dressed in the same manner as that of the figure on the bed, pulled back from the face into a curly mass at the nape of the neck and probably tied with some sort of crown or band. It is a hairdo that we observe in a great number of sexual representations from the Augustan period on (for instance, Figs. 38, 39, Plate 8); it also matches that of the woman in scene VI. Second, the figure's body is distinctly pale; unlike the dark tones used consistently for the men throughout, the color matches that of the reclining woman. Beyond these indications in the scant remains of the painting itself, I argue, as does Melissa Kepke, that the artist increases the level of perversion/debasement with each successive scene.[70] In this interpretation, the relatively tame image of male-female intercourse of Jacobelli's reading seems out of place. Much more titillating—and completely without precedent in the visual record—would be a scene of a female-female couple imitating a well known heterosexual position.

The major difficulty in a female-to-female reading of the scene is reconstructing what kind of sexual act two women in this position might perform. Scene V could of course represent two women stimulating each other by rubbing their clitorides together. It is likely, however, that the ancient Roman male viewers would immediately assume that the standing woman had a dildo strapped to her genitals.

For one thing, the painting replicates a male-female pose where the man raises the woman's leg to increase the degree of penetration. For another, in all the preserved Greek and Roman literary constructions of woman-woman lovemaking—all fabricated, of course, by male authors—the "lesbian" is a phallic woman.[71]

In sexual intercourse she is literally a woman using a fake phallus so that she is "just like" a man. Roman authors rarely write about female-to-female lovemaking. Ovid's moral tale of Iphis, a girl raised as a boy who falls in love with a girl, requires that Iphis actually become a man before the two can consummate their love. The solution to Iphis' "unnatural" love is in her metamorphosis: the goddess Isis transforms her into a man on the day before the wedding (*Metamorphoses* 9.666–797). Seneca the Elder, when recounting the story of the man who caught his wife and another woman in bed and killed them both, emphasizes the feelings of the husband, who could make sense of the scenario only by casting one of the couple as the penetrator, or "man." He has the husband say: "But I looked at the man first, to see whether he was natural (*eggegénetai*) or artificial (*prosérraptai*)." The "artificial man" would be a woman with a dildo strapped on.[72]

Juvenal and Martial do construct scenarios focused on the phallic "lesbian." These authors make her into an deviant and intractable reversal of the phallic man whom the Romans considered the proper model of sexuality. For example, in Juvenal's sixth satire he writes of Tullia, a Roman matron, and her lover, Maura. Returning from a dinner party the two women "take turns riding each other." Tullia's husband, the object of this satire, does not realize that a woman has made him a cuckold.[73]

Although there are no extant visual representations of a woman wearing a dildo to penetrate another woman, scenes of hetairai fondling dildoes or even sucking on them are fairly common in Greek vase painting.[74] Martial, who—as Richlin points out—was fascinated with the mechanics of female-female sex, fills this gap in the visual record with several descriptions of the "lesbian" acting "like a man" by using a dildo to penetrate her partner.[75] In 7.67 he writes: "Abhorrent of all natural joys, Philaenis sodomizes boys," and in 1.90: "yet, Bassa—oh, monstrous—you were, it seems, a poker."[76]

Central to both the visual and verbal representations of female-to-female lovemaking is the cultural construction by males of the unnatural woman who has no need of a man to achieve sexual satisfaction. Martial, it seems, mirrors a widespread anxiety on the part of his class and sex about the independent woman. Changes in laws reflect the elite woman's emancipation during the course of the first century. Marriage law now allowed the woman to divorce easily and to have increasing control over her own property. By the second century a woman could take her property with her if she divorced her husband. Thus Martial in 8.12 says, "Why have I no desire to marry riches? / Because, my friend, I want to wear the breeches. / Wives should obey their husbands; only then / Can women share equality with men."[77] His depiction of Philaenis in 7.67 has her not only sodomizing boys but exercising, drinking, and eating like a man.

If one of the mechanisms of comedy is to laugh at the worse-case scenario, scene V as an image of female-to-female lovemaking would provoke mirth even while mirroring anxieties male viewers had about emancipated women pleasuring each other. Perhaps the female viewer found the image amusing specifically because it revealed the very male notion that a woman needs to be penetrated by a phallus to feel sexual pleasure. If both in this scene and in the scene of cunnilingus the artist overturned the power of the phallic male as dispenser of sexual pleasures to the passive female, in scene VI he further explored this comic mechanism of the (male) world turned upside down by adding the image of the passive male homosexual to the brew.

The artist depicted a sexual threesome: the man kneeling at the left is anally penetrating the kneeling man in the middle, who in turn penetrates the woman who crouches on the bed, her face in the pillow and her buttocks raised (Plate 14). The trio plays on a bed rendered in perspective, with a light green coverlet and a sham attached at either end of the bed frame so that it forms a swag along its length. The artist posed the woman carefully, putting her head in profile and crossing her arms beneath her face. She wears a breast band. Her hair, like that of the standing figure on the left in scene VI, is pulled back from her face toward the nape of her neck. Although the torso of the man who has entered her is nearly upright, he leans his lower body back, better to receive the penis of the man kneeling, upright, behind him. His left arm falls behind the woman's buttocks, but the artist had him reaching back with his right arm to clasp the hand of the man behind him. This man has a heavier physique than the man in the middle, and the artist turned his head so that he looks out at the viewer.

Once again the Suburban Baths add a unique visual representation of lovemaking. The most standard component is the woman's pose. In addition to the three paintings still in their architectural contexts considered so far (see Figs. 71, 80, and 81), three paintings from Pompeii, now in the Naples Museum, put the woman in this position.[78] Lamps often represent the woman in this crouching, rear-entry position.[79] In classical Greek constructions of sexuality, the pose seems to be reserved for sex-workers and low-life types. Dover documents a number of images of women assuming this position in Attic vase painting, hypothesizing that prostitutes preferred anal to vaginal intercourse to avoid pregnancy.[80] Snippets of Greek literature, including sources as diverse as the comedies of Aristophanes and the *Idylls* of Theocritus, seem to indicate that the ancient Greeks considered the crouching rear-entry position the province of prostitutes—both women and boys.[81] As we saw in chapter 2, the Greeks of the fourth century B.C. called this pose the "lioness;" it is the position assumed by the woman on the engraved side of the Boston mirror, but with the woman looking out at the viewer (see Fig. 3). Stewart suggests that by this time elite ideology with regard to sexual culture may have shifted, making it acceptable for the female owner of the mirror to contemplate this lovemaking position.[82] Later on, in the Augustan period, the fragment of a cameo-glass vessel in the Metropolitan Museum is a reminder that an artist used this pose for costly artwork meant for the elite classes.[83] Visual representations aside, it is more difficult to determine what it meant for a real Roman woman to assume this pose. The literature is as silent as visual representation is eloquent. Did the image of the woman crouching to raise her buttocks in the air still keep its association with prostitutes? It is hard, after all, to imagine Ovid recommending this position to the elite women whom he was advising on how to look their best in sexual encounters! And yet Roman artists and artisans freely figure women in this undignified way when they wanted to show the uninhibited woman, whether prostitute or not.

If from an elite point of view the woman in scene VI is debasing herself in the very act of assuming her position, the fact that she is being penetrated by a man who is also being penetrated by a man pushes her debasement to the absolute limit. We saw in chapter 3 how elite Roman authors heaped scorn upon the adult man who enjoyed being penetrated by other adult men; there we considered—in an attempt to explain the overwhelmingly positive images of sexual intercourse between men and boys in art—the possibility that artists were reflecting a social reality that the writers dared not speak of. We also considered the possibility that objects like the Warren cup, the Ortiz flask, and the Arretine bowls were purely artistic constructions meant to figure art rather than real life; they could be fantasies of sexual pleasures à la grecque—handed down through Hellenistic artistic culture to Augustan artists eager to revive and evoke the Greek Golden Age. With either of these interpretative strategies the modern viewer has to negotiate a blend of artistic representations that shuffle—deliberately—Greek and Roman contents. In the end the question must be: what filter will put these Augustan-age images into a credible cultural focus? Here, half a century later in the Suburban Baths, the question is different.

The artist is explicit; he expresses his ideas in Roman—not Greek or Hellenistic Greek—terms. He is out to show the viewer something that she would not see on her Augustan silver cups or Arretine bowls, something as much a sexual spectacle as anything she might see in the obscene nude mimes in the theater. Although there is a slight difference in physique between the two men in scene VI (the man who is doing the penetrating is brawnier than his partner), it would be very hard to make the middle man into a boy. He is the same height, stature, and dark color as the man who penetrates him. This is man-man, not man-boy lovemaking. The artist swept aside the conventions of boy-love that dominate the images of the Augustan period. If the partners often tenderly gaze at each other on the Arretine ware, here the positions of all three make it impossible for any of the partners to catch the other's eye. The artist used each person's view to emphasize his or her sheer pleasure in a bravura sexual performance. The artist allowed the woman to see only her crossed arms and the bedcovers, yet her expression is—to judge from the sketchy lines—one of pleasure. The women in several of the paintings from Pompeii mentioned above look out at the viewer, but here the artist has the man at the end of the chain looking out. Paint losses make it impossible to determine the gaze of the man in the middle; his head seems to be in a three-quarters view—in contrast to the nearly frontal pose of the man behind him—as he directs his gaze downward toward the woman's lower back or buttocks. The muscular end man turns to the spectator as if to say: "Look at me/us—see what we're doing!" His gaze is the link with the spectator, since the other two are fully engaged in their pursuit of pleasure; his gaze also implicates the viewer as a voyeur: it reveals that he knows that the viewer is looking at the trio.

While he gazes—or returns the viewer's gaze—this man also grasps the hand of the man he anally pleasures. This gesture increases in significance if we consider that every other option would emphasize the mechanics of lovemaking. If the artist had him grasp his partner around the waist or chest, the viewer would read this as an attempt to increase penetration or contact; a pose that detached all but his penis from his partner—his hands planted on his own hips or tucked behind his own buttocks—would emphasize detachment and the power of his phallic thrusts. Rather, he holds his partner's hand—the only tenderness, yet a significant one—in this otherwise acrobatic display of lovemaking skills.

The only parallel visual representation also emphasizes position, gaze, and bodily contact. It is a humble second-century A.D. terra-cotta relief medallion used as appliqué decoration on a Gaulish vase (Fig. 94).[84] Even within its tiny format (11 cm [4¼ in.] in diameter) the artist described a lovemaking chamber by including a bed with a swagged sham, two vessels, a hanging garland, and even a pinax. The threesome is standing in front of the bed rather than kneeling on it, yet the woman bends deeply like her counterpart in the Suburban Baths. The male in the middle grasps her at the waist with his right arm while he penetrates her. Behind him stands a man with a cloak over his right shoulder: he seems to have his right arm around the middle man's chest while his penis, clearly visible, slips between his buttocks. The artist took pains to differentiate both the faces and the gazes of the three protagonists. The woman in the medallion, unlike the woman in scene VI, sharply turns her head, indicated by a rendering that is as detailed as it is anatomically impossible. We see her classical profile and complicated hairdo. She attentively gazes at the two men gazing at each other. The man in the middle is beardless; he too has a Greek profile, with straight nose, deepset eyes, and generous, square jaw. Although mostly destroyed, the head of the man who is penetrating him seems to be that of a bearded man. As we noted, this is a convention for differentiating the adult male from the boy that goes back to sixth-century Attic pottery. Here it is unlikely to have the same weight as it did seven hundred years before.

What is significant about the fragmentary medallion is the emphasis on communication among the participants. Unlike the scene in the Suburban Baths, none of them addresses the viewer. This strict adherence to profile views creates a self-contained narrative, for although the woman is pleasuring the beardless man, he actually turns to gaze at the bearded man—not her. Did the artist use the mutual gaze of the two men to the exclusion of the woman to figure the superiority of the pleasure the man in the middle feels? Or to highlight the affection between the two men? Another possibility is that the bearded man is a transgressor who has

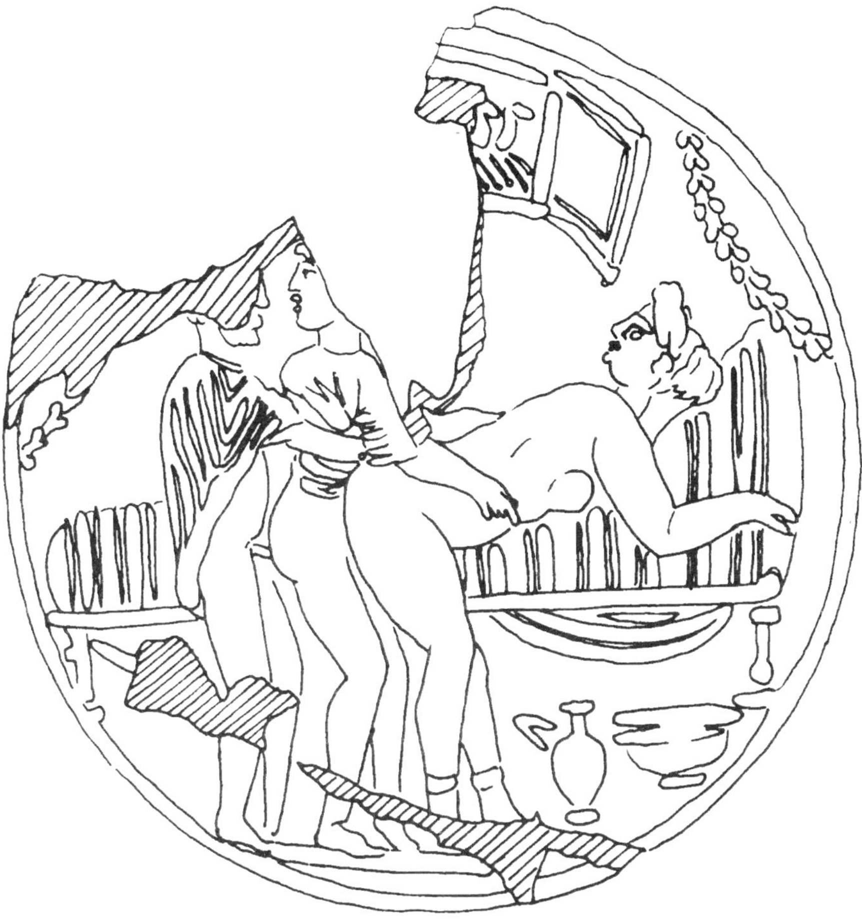

Figure 94. Threesome of two men and a woman in a bedchamber, relief medallion from Lyons, 11 cm. diameter (2d c. A.D.). After Desbat, *Figlina* 5–6 (1980–1981), no. E 032.

surprised the lovemaking couple as he attempts to enter the beardless man from the rear. What is important for comparative purposes is that the image exists in a cheap, mass-produced medium and that it appears later than the painting in the Suburban Baths. Despite its rarity in Pompeian painting discovered to date, the fact that such a close parallel turns up in pottery excavated in southern Gaul indicates that artists had been representing the male-male-female threesome in the visual arts of the first century with some frequency.

Literary sources hardly ignore this sort of threesome. There are mentions of group sex in Catullus, the *Palatine Anthology,* and in Propertius.[85] According to Martial, the poet Sabellus, in trying to outdo the sex manuals of Elephantis, describes love-making in "chains."[86] In *Tiberius* Suetonius describes a triple chain of girls and boys arranged in group sex for the emperor's entertainment. "In his retreat at Capri, he put together a bedroom that was the theater of his secret debauches. There he assembled from all over companies of male and female prostitutes, and inventors of the monstrous couplings (which he called spintriae), so that, intertwining themselves and forming a triple chain (*triplici serie connexi*), they mutually prostituted themselves in front of him to fire up his flagging desires."[87] Graffiti from Pompeii, Herculaneum, and from second-century Ostia Antica often refer to group sex, although none describes the pose of scene VI.[88]

A lamp from Kavoussi, Crete depicts a standing threesome, but the men's positions—one facing the woman and the other behind her—indicate that one is penetrating her anally while the other penetrates her vaginally.[89] Another medallion from the Rhône Valley is a graceful variant of the lamp, for the two men recline on a bed to the right and left, their legs extended beneath a woman who sits between the two while holding up a palm.[90] More humorous is a Rhône Valley medallion that has the woman riding on the reclining man's back—and holding a lamp—while a standing man parts her legs to enter her.[91] In all these compositions, however, penetrating the woman is both men's objective, a construction having nothing to do with the emphasis on male-to-male sex in both scene VI and in the Gaulish medallion. The problem—at least in terms of elite Roman texts and the sexual constructions that they pretend to uphold—is not that two men are having sex with one woman, but that one of the men is being penetrated by another man.

Although the expected response to scene VI was laughter, it must have provoked different responses from a woman or a man. For the Roman man the outrageous aspect of the scene was that of the penetrated man seeming to prefer his sensation of being penetrated to his own act of penetrating the woman: the fact that he holds his male partner's hand would tip the comic scale in that direction. For the Roman woman looking at this scene the outrage would be that a woman—even a prostitute—allowed herself to be penetrated by a man who has lost his phallic status by being penetrated himself. Viewers of both sexes would find another irony here. Texts often accuse the man who liked to be penetrated by other men (the *cinaedus*) of adultery with another man's wife.[92] This assumption that the cinaedus is capable of all kinds of sexual excess—with men or women—makes the man in middle a concrete illustration of a particularly perverse kind of bisexuality. He is perverse for Roman viewers of both sexes precisely because some writers see his effeminacy, part of the life of luxury that moralists rail against, as particularly attractive to women. The representation in the Suburban Baths would allow viewers of both sexes to laugh at the very enactment of the fears that moralists express. Those unaware of the literary tradition could simply compare their experiences with such men with what they saw depicted on the wall.

The apportionment of comic outrage on the one hand to male viewers, on the other to female viewers, follows through in scene VII. Although badly damaged by overpainting, it is a scene of four people making love (Plate 15). A nude man kneels at the left-hand side of a bed that is quite similar to the one in scene VI. He looks out at the viewer while he raises his right hand in the air and penetrates the man kneeling in front of him. The artist depicted the head of the man being penetrated in three-quarters view; he leans forward as a woman, kneeling on her left knee but with her right leg raised in the air, crouches on her elbows to fellate him. A second woman, kneeling on the floor, performs cunnilingus on her. (Remains of a green garland from the later painting campaign cover the back of the woman performing fellatio and the knees of the woman performing cunnilingus.)

This scene surpasses the other vignettes in its—to use a Roman term—"impurity." In addition to representing an adult man being penetrated by another man (the impurity is that of the man who is being penetrated), scene VII shows two forms of oral impurity, putting both the woman who is fellating the man and the woman who is performing cunnilingus on her into categories of utter depravity. As Jacobelli notes, after exploring all possible literary and visual parallels: "I know of no Roman figural expression of an orgy in which one observes male and female homosexual partners, and bisexual ones at that, who are engaged simultaneously—and at such a unabashed level of explicitness—in an action that places all of these inclinations paratactically on the same level."[93]

Of course, judgments about the relative debasement of the four would be the stuff of comic shock—and the occasion for laughter—for the ancient viewer. The man who liked to penetrate other men would see his counterpart's waving right arm as a gesture of triumph in attaining pleasure. Artists used this gesture of a man waving his right arm to single out the victorious general in battle reliefs; later they would use it to denote the deceased man's triumph over death on battle sarcophagi.[94] These associations would only add comic punch to this representation of sexual triumph. Like the women being pleasured in scenes I and IV, this male penetrator looks out, addressing the viewer's gaze. He is the winner in terms of Roman attitudes toward sex; he keeps his phallic status (unlike the man he penetrates) and performs neither cunnilingus nor fellatio (as do the two women in scene VII). To the Roman man or woman looking at this scene, his gesture would indicate a sexual tour-de-force: achieving maximum pleasure in a foursome without losing status by performing "debased" acts.

Not so the other three. The man simultaneously penetrated and fellated has an ambiguous status for the Roman viewer, for he loses status in being penetrated by a man and yet gains a perfectly legitimate phallic pleasure in being fellated. The shame and impurity of fellatio rested entirely on the person who took the penis in her or his mouth, not on the person who inserted his penis into the mouth. They expressed another aspect of the phallic construction of sexuality typical of ancient Roman thinking—the "socket" mentality mentioned by Richlin: as long as the man does the inserting of his penis into whatever orifice, be it the vagina, anus, or mouth of another, he is blameless. The owner of the orifice—the receptive or "passive" partner—is always to blame.[95]

In relation to scene III we discussed the status and meanings of the woman who performs fellatio, and for scene IV that of the man who performs cunnilingus. What then of image of a woman performing cunnilingus on her partner? This image is unique in the visual record; there are no representations—not even on Greek ceramics—of this sexual act. As we noted, the textual record on homosexual relations between woman gives us only men's opinions about relationships between women—all negative.[96] The late second-century A.D. author Artemidorus of Ephesos classifies erotic dreams in three categories. He considers sex between women, unlike that between men, to be against nature (*parà phùsin*).[97] In the range of acts that Martial calls up to characterize the "lesbian" Philaenis' debasement, her preference for performing cunnilingus on women rather than fellatio on men reveals that she assumes a "male" role not just physically but also psychologically.[98]

In connection with scene IV we mentioned graffiti advertising the availability of male prostitutes to perform cunnilingus on women. It may also be possible that some women in ancient Pompeii commonly paid *female* prostitutes to provide cunnilingus. If so, the female client of the Suburban Baths would find this aspect of the foursome amusing but not shocking. A woman performing cunnilingus on another woman might be an act that she was familiar with—perhaps from personal experience. For the woman viewer, scene VII presented a slice of sexual life where the women actors—both the woman performing cunnilingus and the one fellating a man—were clearly prostitutes. As sex-workers, they performed as they were paid to. The humor lay in the fact that *both* women were using their mouths to perform "impure" acts in a dual combination of oral debasement. The men who viewed this scene probably constructed the woman performing cunnilingus either as a prostitute, or, like Martial, as a entrenched "lesbian."

Since scenes I through VII constitute a steady crescendo of increasingly comic representations of sexual depravity, we might expect scene VIII to represent five on a bed, or an even more acrobatic coupling than scene VII. Instead the artist ended the sequence of the south wall with a single figure (Plate 16). A nude man stands in front of a table. The artist showed his body in exaggerated contrapposto, with his left leg bearing the weight of his body, while he places his right leg, bent sharply at the knee, behind him. The artist also expanded the space between his legs and the man's wide hips because they frame his enormous testicles: they descend nearly to his knees. As if to highlight conspicuous deformity, the artist exerted some care to make the man's upper body seem quite normal: his head, crowned with leaves, is in three-quarters view and he wears a pleasant expression as he reads the scroll that he holds in his left hand. At the moment of excavation traces of writing were visible on the scroll.[99]

The image is clearly a caricature—but of whom? For the ancient Roman, both the fact that the man is reading from a scroll and that he wears a leafy crown would have meant that he was a literary man, perhaps a poet. In the probably contemporary painting of the poet Menander in the House of the Menander the seated figure, crowned in ivy, reads from a similar scroll. Its writing—unlike that on the scroll held by the figure in the Suburban Baths—was legible at the time of discovery.[100] A mosaic from Hadrumentum presents Vergil with similar iconography: although the poet is clothed and has no ivy crown, he holds a scroll with writing on it.[101] Clearly the comic element in the "poet" from the Suburban Baths is the contrast between his supposedly high intellectual calling and the fact that the artist denuded him and afflicted him with a conspicuous deformity of his sexual organs.

If the representation of such a physical affliction for the sake of comedy seems puzzling or even upsetting to the modern viewer, it is because our modern Euro-American culture fosters attitudes of compassion toward people with physical deformities. Not so with the Hellenistic Greeks and the ancient Romans, who thought that it was entirely appropriate to laugh at a whole range of human beings. As we saw in chapter 5, they could laugh at people with somatotypes that did not fit their ideals, such as the Ethiopian or the northern European. Sources as diverse as Plutarch and Martial mention the fact that the wealthy paid especially high prices for slaves who were physically deformed or mentally handicapped.[102] Cicero, in instructing the orator on the mechanisms of humor, points out that people with physical deformities were fair game.[103] Given these social attitudes toward real people, it should come as no surprise that art from both the Hellenistic and Roman period frequently represented dwarfs, hunchbacks, or people with enlarged heads; such use of malformations in art for the sake of comedy is quite common.[104]

The affliction that the artist of the Suburban Baths gave to the poet also appears in a group of Hellenistic terra-cotta figurines.[105] Hydrocele is a well known medical condition that causes enlargement of the testicles.[106] To Roman viewers who were accustomed to being amused by figures of dancers with hydrocele, the representation of the Terme suburbane poet must have been outrageously funny. Jacobelli's hypothesis that scene VIII might be a caricature of an erotic poet is especially attractive in light of the fact that he reads an open scroll; the fact that the man being fellated in scene III also holds a scroll—in this case rolled up—adds a further comic context to the man of letters absorbed in sex.[107]

Could our erotic poet be reading from a sex manual? It seems likely, since central to the comic effect of scene VIII is the fact that of all the men and women represented on the south wall, only the poet is alone and not engaged in any ostensible sexual act. If it is a sex manual, he is reading about what the people in the other seven scenes are actually doing. Yet it is better that he is not engaged in sexual activity, for to the ancient viewer he would cut a ridiculous figure. The artist achieved his comic effect by encouraging the viewer to imagine what an outrageous figure a man with this deformity would make of himself while engaging in sexual acts.[108]

It seems likely that the artist planned another comic effect—this time a joke on the literate viewers. By putting writing on the scroll, the artist was tantalizing literate viewers, since the image of the poet is small and high up on the wall. It is easy to imagine curious readers craning their necks to decipher what was written on the scroll, even while the other clients in the apodyterium watched them straining their eyes—yet another demonstration of how, in the Suburban Baths, architectural context is as crucial as the pictures' content in structuring the apparatus of humor.

Because the eight vignettes of the east wall are lost, the preserved paintings constitute only half of the iconographic program. This means that we can only speculate what meanings the whole would have had. Furthermore, the fact that many of the preserved representations are unique makes it difficult to employ the usual comparative methods of art history. Jacobelli proposes that the artist had access to a special illustrated manuscript that might have been the treasured possession of the person who commissioned the paintings.[109] From our analysis of the content and context of the paintings that do remain, however, we can make several conclusions.

We must read the Suburban Baths paintings in terms of their intended audience. As we saw, it was not the elite class, but rather those various strata of Pompeian society who used a public bath. Most likely—but not necessarily—these were people who did not have private baths in their houses or villas. They were men and women, probably bathing at different times of the day.[110] Because the paintings were meant to be seen and enjoyed by both sexes, these vignettes provide an unusual opportunity to hypothesize the meaning that they would have for that elusive person, the Roman female viewer. Her presence in this apodyterium becomes all the more important in view of the exclusively male constructions of female sexuality in the extant ancient literature. Here, in a room decorated with many images entirely new within the preserved visual record, we can register some Roman women's probable understanding of scenes of lovemaking. Here we may have the only concrete space in the ancient world—specifically because its decoration was meant for both sexes—to reconstruct a female gaze.[111]

Since these paintings represent the very kinds of sexual activity that the upper classes frowned upon and denied doing—even though the central trope of both Martial and Juvenal is the hypocrisy of this class—they constitute an excellent case of visual artists giving the lie to literary constructions. As such, the paintings of the Suburban Baths add significantly to one of the central themes of this book, that of visual artists' gleefully representing the very sexual acts condemned by most Roman authors. The crescendo in the outrageousness of these activities, from the relatively commonplace male-female intercourse of scene I to the complex foursome of scene VII, is hard to interpret satisfactorily because we do not have the final eight scenes to complete the sixteen vignettes. The single figure of the erotic poet might be a pivot between the first seven and the last eight scenes, poised as he is in all his ridiculousness in the corner. Finally, if these tiny paintings were simply humorous locker labels, as I think they were, they were not intended to instruct people like sex manuals. Because of their very outrageousness in the face of Roman sexual constructions, the only proper response was laughter.

Our look at paintings of lovemaking in their various contexts in public buildings reveals images that were far from being instructions on sexual positions or advertisements for sexual services. They were meant to entertain the viewer. They could encode upper-class luxury for the lower-class customer of the lupanar, or they could evoke peals of laughter from women or men of various social levels in the Suburban Baths. They formed an integral part of ensembles of interior decoration. Seen in context, such "erotic" paintings show us conceptions of sex and humor quite different from our own.

ITALY AND THE PROVINCES

THE FIRST THROUGH THE THIRD CENTURIES

CHAPTER 8

The Invention and Spread of Sexual Imagery through the Roman World

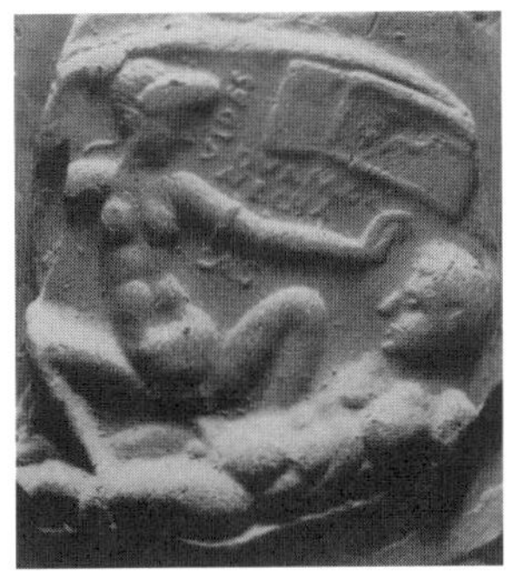

The aim of this book is to put the so-called erotic art of the Roman world back into its context. And we can do so most easily with art that carries a good deal of information. The unmistakable Augustan/Julio-Claudian traits of the Warren cup, for example, allow us to compare it with other objects—Arretine wares and cameo-glass vessels—dated to that period because of their style. Both date and architectural context are quite explicit in the three houses from Pompeii with mosaics of ithyphallic black men; such too is the case for nearly all the Pompeian paintings with erotic subject matter considered in chapters 6 and 7.

In contrast to artworks with full contexts are those that hold little specific information about their place within ancient Roman culture. For the most part these are relatively plain objects made with some sort of mold to allow easy replication of their sexual imagery. In the first century spintriae appear: they are coinlike objects each with a representation of lovemaking on the obverse and a number on the reverse that we consider as a popular manifestation of the Roman interest in sex manuals with numbered illustrations of sexual positions.

Terra-cotta lamps and vessels reproduce a broader range of scenes of lovemaking than either the spintriae or wall paintings. They have a long history, beginning in the second century B.C. at Pergamon and continuing through the fifth century. What can we learn about cultural constructions of sexuality from these mass-produced objects found throughout the ancient Roman world? If we try to interpret them in terms of the presumed culture of the owner, we must be content with rather general conclusions. Or we can look at studies of sexual imagery that arrange motifs into typological lists and tell us little about ancient attitudes toward sex. Our strategy will be to investigate a few images of lovemaking that fall *outside* the typological lists, appearing seemingly without precedent. With these we can ask what local cultural conditions might bring about a demand for "new" sexual imagery—and we can also inquire whether this imagery is really new or whether it stems from sources that we simply do not know.

Finally, we consider a mid-third-century painted room with erotic pictures excavated at Ostia Antica and apply to these paintings the same criteria as for the Pompeian examples, even though the dearth of comparative information and the paintings' poor state of preservation make it difficult to interpret them fully.

Numbers and Representations of Lovemaking: The Spintriae and Sex Manuals

In Jacobelli's discussion of the erotic vignettes in the Suburban Baths, she notes that the only other sexual representations connected with numbers appear on spintriae, bronze coinlike objects measuring about 20 mm in diameter.[1] Various compositions of male-female lovemaking decorate the figured sides of the spintriae; numbers between I and XVI fill the reverses (Fig. 95).[2] The firmest scholarship establishes that they first appeared under the emperor Tiberius, continuing to be coined through the end of the first century.[3] There are three main theories about their function: that they were brothel tokens with the number indicating the money value (in asses) of the token; that they were entryway tokens into imperially sponsored games; that they were gaming tokens. The first theory depends on Suetonius' statement that Tiberius forbade people to use coins with the imperial image in latrines and bordellos;[4] the spintriae would substitute for coins. Even if Suetonius' statement is correct, how could this law be enforced, and was it in use after Tiberius died? It was certainly out of use by the period of Vespasian, who instituted a public latrine tax (Suetonius *Vespasian* 23.4). The second hypothesis comes from a reading of Martial 8.78, written on the occasion of games to celebrate the triumph of Domitian over the Dacians in A.D. 88–89 or for the festival of the *Septimontia:* "Now come sportive

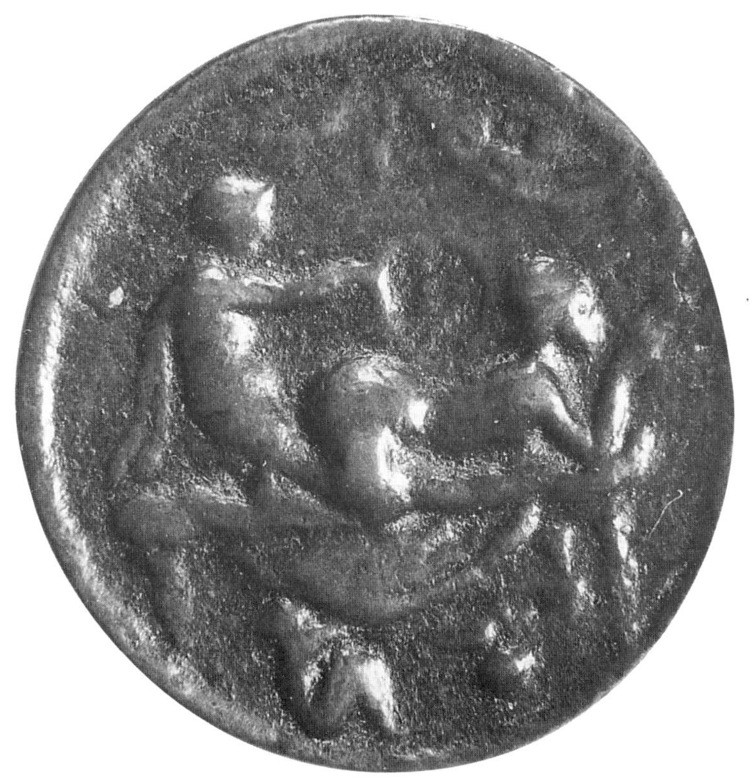

Figure 95. Couple on bed, obverse of spintria (A.D. 30–79). London, British Museum, inv. C.249.21. 1906.11–3–2928. Photo courtesy of museum. Copyright British Museum.

tokens [*lasciva nomismata*] in sudden showers."[5] Shackleton Bailey resolves this phrase by making the *nomismata* tokens that entitled the holder to receive presents-in-kind—not sexual services in local lupanars.[6] The third explanation, that the spintriae were pieces used in some sort of board game, is the most plausible. In favor of this hypothesis is the fact that different sexual representations might appear with a given number; the numbers themselves seem to be the important information and the erotic scene a sort of variable decoration for the piece.[7]

The numbers lead us from the scenes of the Suburban Baths to the most salient aspect of the spintriae: the fact that they relate numbers to representations of lovemaking. Twenty-five years ago Otto Brendel, noting that sexual representations become standard and nonnarrative in the late Hellenistic and Roman eras, made a good case for the existence of lost sex manuals, encyclopedic catalogs of sexual positions. Even without the evidence of the spintriae and the paintings of the Suburban Baths, Brendel cited the *Kama Sutra* (Aphorisms on love) as a reflection of illustrated sex manuals of Hellenistic origin that described male-female coital positions in words, numbered them, and illustrated them with pictures.[8] The fact that the *Kama Sutra,* a sophisticated Sanskrit text from the Gupta period (A.D. 320–540) attributed to Vâtsyâyana, is itself a collection and revision of earlier texts makes it a highly suggestive parallel for the Hellenistic and Roman world.

Illustrated sex manuals of Hellenistic origin would go a long way toward explaining not only the standard and highly schematic representations of male-female intercourse on the spintriae but also similar imagery on lamps and vases, replicated with little variation from the late Hellenistic period though the fifth century. The Hellenistic period saw the birth of the encyclopedia; scholars at centers of learning such as Pergamon and Alexandria devoted considerable effort to classifying and organizing knowledge. Their taxonomic interests extended into the realm of human sexuality, to judge from the scattered references in Greek and Latin literature to the sex manuals. Unfortunately, none of these sexual compendia survives intact; we must study the fragments in combination with ancient authors who mention the sex manuals to reconstruct their content and style. In a recent article Holt Parker points out that both authorship and audience for the sex manuals are problematic. The ancient sources attribute them to female authors, the most famous being the mythical founder of the genre, Astyanassa, followed by Philaenis (ca. 370 B.C.), Botrys (ca. 340 B.C.), and Elephantis (first century B.C.?). Parker points out that their Greek names and descriptions as famous prostitutes are most patently the inventions of male authors.[9] The fragments themselves detail sexual positions and preliminaries to lovemaking.

Ovid's *Art of Love,* as a parody of the ancient sex manuals, gives a good notion of the originals, particularly in the passage at the end of book three, considered in chapter 4, where Ovid gives advice specifically to women.[10] Among the "thousand ways of Venus" (*mille modi veneris*) Ovid only comments on eight. Ancient authors—both Christian and pagan—attack the sex manuals precisely because, rather than preach moderation (as did the Stoics and some Peripatetic philosophers), they laid out seemingly endless options for finding pleasure in sex.[11] Their very detail caused them "to be seen not as handbooks to pleasures but as inducements to luxury."[12] It is clear that the sex manuals were popular and to a certain extent controversial within ancient Hellenistic and Roman constructions of the use of sex as a pleasure.

The critical question for us, however, is whether these texts were illustrated. If so, they provided a ready source for artists. And if, as seems likely, the authors discussed sexual positions in an orderly fashion, they might arrange them by number or letter.[13] For the standard and endlessly repeated imagery to appear on lamps and terra-cotta vessels from the second century B.C. through the fifth century, it is sufficient to posit a moment in the late Hellenistic period when an artist or group of artists first copied illustrations from the sex manuals. Once they had made simple copies, artists would not need to return to these relatively expensive and rare sources each time they created a small variant on a sexual position. They simply used existing objects in terra-cotta as models.[14]

The best way to explain the numbers on the reverses of the spintriae is that the artist(s) who conceived them had the task of mass-producing numbered gaming pieces in metal. The most apt serial imagery available—and one traditionally associated with numbers—was that of the sexual positions that already decorated moldmade terra-cotta vessels and lamps. Instead of choosing other serial imagery surrounding a single theme, such as types of gladiators or species of animals that also decorated lamps, they chose sexual representations because numbers often appeared with them in the illustrated sex manuals. Probably the sexual imagery tied in with some aspect of the game, such as its name; in any case the images of lovemaking gave a stimulus for amusing banter among the players. The inscriptions on gaming pieces referring to amusing sexual practices and persons fit well with the thesis that the spintriae themselves were gaming pieces, where we find words such as *moice* (adulterer); *patice* (pathic); and even *cunulinge* (cunt licker).[15]

The Artists and His Models: Low- versus High-Art Sources

Discussions of illustrated sex manuals as models for erotic representations tend to assume that artists needed highly detailed sources to create their compositions, whether in painting or relief.[16] The two following case studies indicate that in actual working conditions artists often needed only summary models. Humble spintriae, like terra-cotta objects, were cheap and easily portable models for painting.

Analysis of a conspicuous parallel between spintriae and paintings, first pointed out by Simonetta and Riva, demonstrates this point.[17] Two unusual features strike the viewer of a painting from Pompeii now in the Naples Museum: its vertical format and its background, consisting of white drapery gathered at the top center to form deep folds radiating from that point (see Fig. 78).[18] Use of the vertical rectangle forced the artist to abbreviate the bed, rather than showing it in its full length, and to place the couple in the exact center of the pictorial space. The white drapery background further emphasizes this central placement, since all the folds fall from the point at the top center of the rectangle's upper edge. Although these peculiarities might come from a model in an illustrated sex manual, the source is probably a cheaper, more readily available one.

Among the images of lovemaking the one decorating the spintria of Fig. 95 is a likely source for the Naples painting. Not only does it provide the drapery configuration, it also accounts for the unusual vertical format and the central placement of the painting's composition. It goes without saying that the rear-entry position and even the man's extended arm match the composition of the spintria. The painting is certainly much more detailed than its crude model: the artist executed it at a much larger scale and in fresco since it formed the centerpiece of a (lost) wall-decorative composition. Yet such elaboration, such filling in of details, is precisely what a patron expects an artist to be able to do.

Review of another compositional type further reinforces the notion that artists looked at inexpensive artworks for their compositions rather than at expensive illustrated sex manuals. In discussing the Warren cup, we saw that the position of the man and boy on side B was a variation on a composition common in Arretine ware (see Plate 2 and Figs. 26 and 27). Known in the literature as Dragendorff Type XIV 8a, this rear-entry scene features the man, left, kneeling to enter the boy. By extending the boy's body across the bed, his head to the right, his legs parted between the man's knee at the left, the artist displays his upper torso and genitals. The significance of this pose for our discussion of sources and copies is that, as Dragendorff noted, the artist created the male-male lovemaking scene simply by removing the breasts and breast band and adding male genitals to the male-female composition. We could see Warren cup side B either as an elaboration of the contemporary composition on the Arretine ceramics or as a more faithful reflection of "the original." This supposed original composition of man-boy lovemaking would exist in an expensive source such as an illustrated sex manual or a famous lost painting by a Greek or Hellenistic master. Of the two possibilities, one positing a high-art model that filters down to the inexpensive media such as wall painting and ceramics, the other presuming that artists created variations on well-circulated compositions according to their own skills and the amount of money the patron was willing to pay, I think that the second was by far the more common practice. The degree of elaboration, complexity, and nuance within what are standard, infinitely repeated sexual compositions would seem to depend more on the artist than on the source.

What about representations that are unique in the preserved visual record? In this study, they include the Leiden gemstone (see Fig. 9), side A of the Warren cup (Plate 1), and scenes III–VIII of the Suburban Baths (Plates 11–16). Although aspects of these images find parallels in the standard canonical repertoire, they otherwise stand out from that repertoire by reason of their originality. For instance, one element of side A of the Warren cup, the strap that the man being penetrated holds on to, appears on Greek vases of the classical period, yet the couple's pose otherwise has no known parallels. Similarly, in Suburban Baths scene VI, the figure of the woman crouching down on her elbows to raise her buttocks in the air finds its counterpart in many representations of male-female lovemaking, but not in a situation where the man who penetrates her is in turn being penetrated by another man. To explain such images, must we posit out-of-the-ordinary models that outstripped the standard second-century B.C. sex manuals in their inventiveness?

It is true that both literary and artistic evidence point to a continual refinement and expansion of sexual imagery in the ensuing three centuries. Martial's epigram to Sabellus (discussed in chapter 7 in relation to the scenes of group sex in the Suburban Baths) accuses him of trying to outdo Elephantis' erotic manual; he shames him for proposing new positions for male-to-male coitus and for group sex.[19] Such expanded erotic manuals provide one attractive way of explaining unique images of lovemaking. As we saw, Jacobelli takes this approach to explain the imagery of the Suburban Baths; she hypothesizes a source in models from treasured manuscripts belonging to the owner of the baths that the artist was allowed to use.[20] A problem with this hypothesis is the low quality of the paintings themselves. Either the artist wasted refined images from an expensive sex manual, or the visual models themselves were on the simplest level.

Our alternative is to credit the artist with the invention of these outrageous compositions. For one thing, only an accident of preservation makes them unique. Future excavations may uncover parallels to scene A on the Warren cup or the otherwise unique scenes in the Suburban Baths. For another, the awkwardnesses of pose on the Leiden gemstone, Warren cup side A, and in the unique images of the Suburban Baths seem to indicate that the artist is unsure of himself. Does this mean he is working without a model at all? Invention rather than work from high-art sources might well explain a lack of balance between figures as on side A of the Warren cup; disparity of scale between figures, as between the man and woman in scene IV (cunnilingus); unresolved poses, as between the two woman in scene VII. Barring clear evidence of high-art sources for these unique images, my own preference is to attribute them to individual artists working for imaginative—if not particularly fussy—patrons.

Images of Lovemaking on Lamps: Questions of Acculturation and Sources

Hermet, a twentieth-century man of the cloth, when forced to confront the erotic imagery on pottery from La Graufesenque in southern France, predictably blamed Roman paganism for importing filthy art and morals into innocent Gaul: "When Roman civilization was not yet well established in Gaul, under the reigns of Tiberius, Claudius, and Nero, the potters made no erotic subjects lest they shock and lose their clientele. Only when Gaul was completely Romanized under Vespasian . . . did such scenes appear on the vases. This observation is a palpable proof that the Romans imported into Gaul, with civilization, the corruption of morals."[21] His statement, of course, reveals more about his own constructions of sexual morality than that of the ancient Gauls or their Roman conquerors. We cannot guess a people's attitudes toward sex from art with sexual subject matter because visual representation has myriad literal and symbolic meanings for any culture. An alternative scenario to Hermet's would be that the Gauls wished to possess ceramics with sexual scenes because that imagery stood for the luxury and high culture that they aspired to. It is equally possible that the imagery itself was unimportant, whether of lovemaking or gladiators or gods and goddesses; it was the possession itself of a ceramic piece with figural decoration that had meaning for the indigenous Gaul. Several methodological strategies can shed light on these questions of the acceptance—and even enthusiastic embrace—of sexual representation.

One approach is to compare the frequency of sexual imagery with that of other motifs to determine how common or popular erotic lamps and vases were within a culture. Leibundgut does this for the Roman lamps found in Switzerland. Her total of 1,121 lamps includes 159 with representations of lovemaking: erotic scenes make up the third largest of the subject categories, bested only by 233 representations of animals and 198 of gladiators and gladiatorial weapons.[22] In his study of Roman lamps in the British Museum, Bailey notes that the four largest categories of representation on the Italian lamps are myth and legend, animals, entertainment (gladiators, the circus, drama), and sex. He rightly points out that whereas there is a great degree of variation in the first three groups, "the more limited character of the erotic scenes can perhaps place the lamps which bear them into the largest single group. This probably reflects the proportions actually produced in antiquity, rather than the acquisition policy of the Museum."[23]

Beyond these brief notices, no scholar has undertaken the daunting task of charting all the motifs of ancient lamps. Whether erotic scenes constitute the most popular subject, as Bailey sees it, or whether they are only among the most popular also depends on how narrowly we define the other categories. For our purposes it is sufficient to note both the great popularity of lamps with erotic scenes and their long life. They attest to a large proportion of customers who chose representations of sexual imagery on lamps over other available motifs.

Who were these buyers? Leibundgut's analysis of the Swiss material shows the close connection of the oil lamps to the arrival of military personnel. Excavations reveal that civilians in the Romanized areas still used the pine-torches, pitch, and resin that the Greek geographer Strabo describes in the late first century B.C.[24] The greatest use of oil lamps, predictably, is on western Lake Geneva, near the province of old Gallia Narbonensis and in the big cities like Augst; these areas had a strong contingent of Italian-Roman business men. In the second century, with the increased isolation of the Rhineland armies, oil lamps declined sharply in military camps. Yet at this time lamps appeared increasingly in graves. Leibundgut concludes that in losing their functional use for lighting they gained symbolic power.[25]

This point takes on even more significance in light of the fact that Roman lamps required olive oil for fuel. Since this oil had to be imported to northern regions, burning it in a lamp there was a costly act.[26] If lamps as grave goods had symbolic meaning, current studies allow us only to speculate generally on that symbolism. For the indigenous provincial, I suggest, they symbolized the luxury of Roman culture. Whether the fact that lamps produced light had specific religious meaning in the context of burial is a moot point and would require specifics about the deceased's beliefs that we cannot know. Finally, are there any specific meanings that we can attach to erotic representations on lamps found in graves? Their choice of erotic versus nonerotic subject matter shows no clear pattern, and we cannot argue, as we could in the case of sarcophagi, that the ancient Romans attached special significance to erotic images on lamps found in tombs.[27] The important thing, at least in the northern and western provinces, seems to be that they were *Roman* lamps.

Another approach that provides information about acculturation is to trace the survival of a particular image of lovemaking over time. One example will suffice. In chapter 2 we examined a fine representation of male-to-male lovemaking in a fragment from Pergamon (see Fig. 7) and a mold found at Sardis (see Fig. 8). Such molds allowed ceramists to produce enormous quantities of terra-cotta vessels and lamps. Some excavations turn up an unusual number of lamps: for example, Vindonissa, near Basel, was a Roman military installation occupied for less than a century (from about A.D. 30 to 101), yet excavators found over sixteen hundred lamps.[28] The lampmakers used plaster or terra-cotta molds, making it easy to produce large quantities of lamps of the same shape and with the same figural decoration. The prevalence of lamps made from the more perishable plaster molds, however, also suggests that artists had to renew the molds fairly frequently. The fact that the composition of the Sardis mold has a long afterlife indicates the relative popularity of this highly original artistic invention. Nearly six hundred fifty years later it appears in simpler form on a lamp found at Ephesus and dated to A.D. 500–600 (Fig. 96). Variations and simplifications of the motif most likely relate to the process of repeatedly renewing molds.

Although Deubner maintains that the Ephesos lamp relief is still a male-to-male lovemaking scene, the artist seems to have elaborated the original composition to make the man's partner a woman.[29] He gave the "boy" an elaborate wiglike band of hair consisting of a double row of curls. As we saw, artists often changed the sex

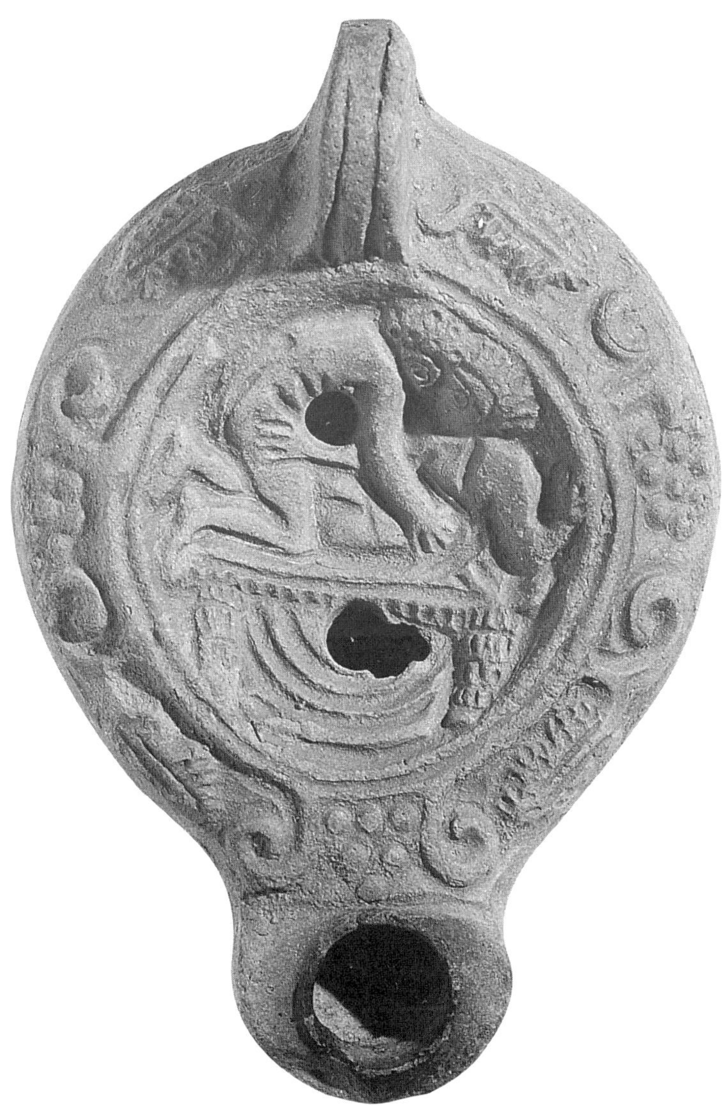

Figure 96. Male-female couple on bed, terra-cotta lamp from Ephesus (A.D. 500–600). British Museum 1867.11–22.232. Made in western Asia Minor. Photo courtesy of museum. Copyright British Museum.

of the receptive partner in terra-cotta production, usually by the addition or subtraction of breasts and male or female genitals.

Most important for this study is the long life of the motif in the area of modern-day western Turkey. The artist omitted many details from the lamp but clearly indicated the boy's (now woman's) position, lying on her right side, her framed buttocks, back toward the viewer, left hand on the man's thigh, and so on. Why would such a motif have an iconographic history going back six hundred fifty years? One part of the answer has to do with the demand for lamps; the other with the techniques used to produce them. Excavation of lamps reveals that their subject matter seems to have little connection to how the Romans used them.[30] The longevity of motifs showing lovemaking attests to their popularity for the consumer, but unfortunately finding a lamp with a scene of sexual activity on it does not mean that the ancient user connected it with lovemaking activities. Bailey notes: "Lamps with erotic scenes must have appealed to many ancient buyers (they cannot all have been used in brothels) over a long period of time and throughout the Roman Empire. They range in date from Augustan times to the fifth or sixth century A.D."[31]

Although interesting for what they tell us about workshop procedures, such motif-survival studies also tell us something about cultural attitudes. The fact that lamps with sexual representations appear in so many contexts makes it highly unlikely that they were used only in lovemaking chambers. Furthermore, it is clear that representations of lovemaking survived for seven centuries—well into the early Christian period—along with those of gladiators, gods and goddesses, and animals. To a certain extent we can go beyond these general conclusions by analyzing works of art that are either unique or that have reliable contexts. From these we can learn the most.

Uncommon Representations in Ceramics: Inventions or Copies?

It is refreshing to find instances of imagery that—even if artistically undistinguished—present sexual situations that fall outside or go beyond the usual and much repeated imagery. Here we consider several compositions that seem to be unique: one that originated in the workshop of Vitalis at La Graufesenque, several appliqué medallions from vessels found in the Rhône Valley, and finally a little figural group signed by the artist Pistillus.

Ceramic vessels from La Graufesenque saw exportation throughout the Roman empire.[32] Vitalis was certainly not alone in creating scenes of sexual intercourse for the decoration of this first-century Gaulish terra sigillata. A variety of compositions of human couples on beds reveals the potters' interest and that of their clients in scenes of lovemaking. Hermet refused to publish a particularly explicit scene of a standing ithyphallic satyr penetrating a maenad; he called it *la grande érotique* and cut the composition in two, printing the figure of the satyr on one plate and that of his partner on another.[33]

It was perhaps the composition of four people copulating that convinced Hermet that the Romans had corrupted the morals of the indigenous Gauls. Replicas survive on vases stamped with the name Vitalis. One of them was found at Bregenz, Austria (Figs. 97 and 98).[34] Vitalis was active between A.D. 65 and A.D. 80 at the site of La Graufesenque, located near modern-day Millau on the Dourbie river. The foursome takes place on a simple bed with a low headboard. To the right lies a woman, her torso and head propped up by two long, wedge-shaped cushions. Her buttocks rest on the bed while she draws her knees up, it seems, in preparation for penetration. She extends her left arm to the shoulder of another woman whose buttocks appear in three-quarters view. Behind her is a man who kneels at the extreme left side of the bed. He pushes his upper body toward the woman, his head in profile. Although he is clearly not on the bed at all, the man standing at the far left of the composition is penetrating the kneeling man. He grasps him by the shoulders with both of his hands.

This composition has several features in common with scene VII of the Suburban Baths (see Plate 15). Both artists, rather than divide the foursome into two male-female couples, placed the two women at the right and the two men at the left. Furthermore, both highlighted the position of the man on the far left. As we noted, this man, since he is merely penetrating another man and not being penetrated or otherwise debased, differs from the other three in his freedom from impurity. He is the victor who addresses the viewer directly by looking out, even waving, at her or him. Although the activity of the two women in Vitalis' composition does not involve the cunnilingus and fellatio of Suburban Baths scene VII, their gesture of embrace and the fact that they face each other, perhaps gazing into each other's

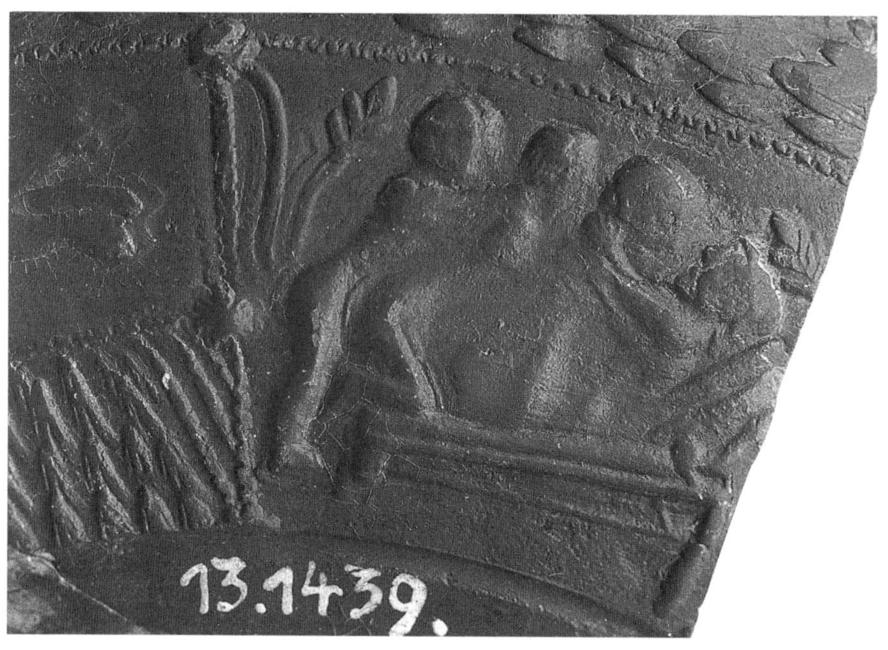

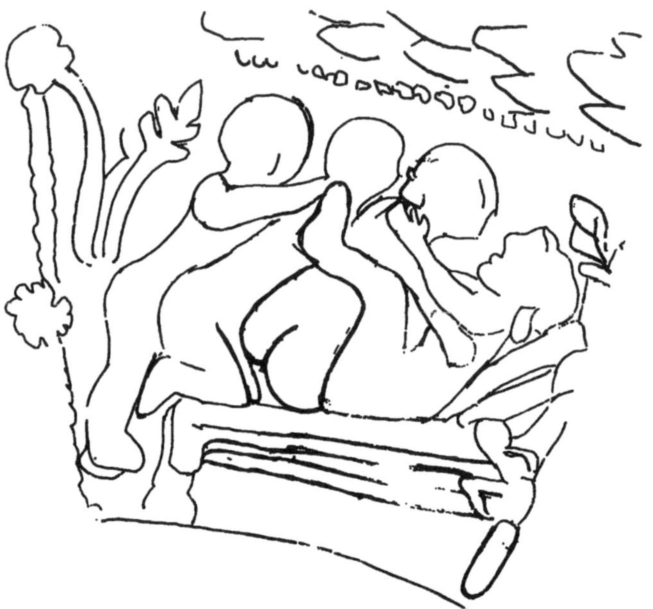

Figure 97. Foursome of two men and two women, terra-cotta vessel by Vitalis, found at Bregenz, Austria (A.D. 65–80). Photo courtesy of museum. Copyright Vorarlberger Landesmuseum, Bregenz.

Figure 98. Foursome of two men and two women, terra-cotta vessel by Vitalis found at Bregenz, Austria (A.D. 65–80). Drawing by Margaret Woodhull.

eyes, indicate that they are at least exchanging affections. Finally, the man who seems to be trying to persuade one of the women to accept his penis is himself being penetrated—like his counterpart in the Suburban Baths—by the man on the far left. In Roman thinking this man is the most "debased" of the foursome because of his passive role in anal intercourse.

We wonder, of course, whether Roman conceptions of impurity carried much weight with the people—both Roman soldiers and merchants and the indigenous Gauls—who bought the vases made by Vitalis and by other potters who included daring scenes of sexual intercourse in their repertoire. For one thing, such imagery appears in no particular pattern that would distinguish it from other subjects. For another, a vase, even a decorated one, is a utilitarian object meant for daily use rather than prolonged contemplation. It seems that Vitalis' creation was meant, like the little vignettes of the Suburban Baths, to amuse the viewer and perhaps provoke laughter—not to comment on the moral status of the four protagonists.

In chapter 7 we examined a relief medallion representing a threesome of two men and a woman as the only clear parallel to Suburban Baths scene VI (Fig. 94). Such medallions, like many others found in sites in the Rhône Valley, decorated simple terra-cotta vessels with bulbous bodies and narrow necks.[35] The medallions range in size from about 5 to 18 cm in diameter and attest to the inventiveness of individual ceramic artists working in this area during the second and early third centuries.[36] Analysis of all the new compositions—or new twists on old themes—is not possible here, but two further examples illustrate the approaches of artists to sexual subject matter. Two fragments found in southeastern France document a composition of a couple making love beneath a pinax (Fig. 99).[37] A man, reclining full length on a bed with his right arm curved around his head (in the gesture of sexual readiness that we remarked in many compositions), is looking at a woman who poises her vagina above his erect penis. She turns to her left to look at him; although her torso faces the viewer frontally, the artist depicted her head in profile, like the man's. She wears her hair in a three-part hairdo with a bonnet of high curls around her forehead and temples, hair pulled back and upwards behind the bonnet, with a bun at the back. This hairstyle is popular among the women in Trajan's court.[38] She wears an armband on her left arm, the same one that extends to touch the man's crooked right elbow.

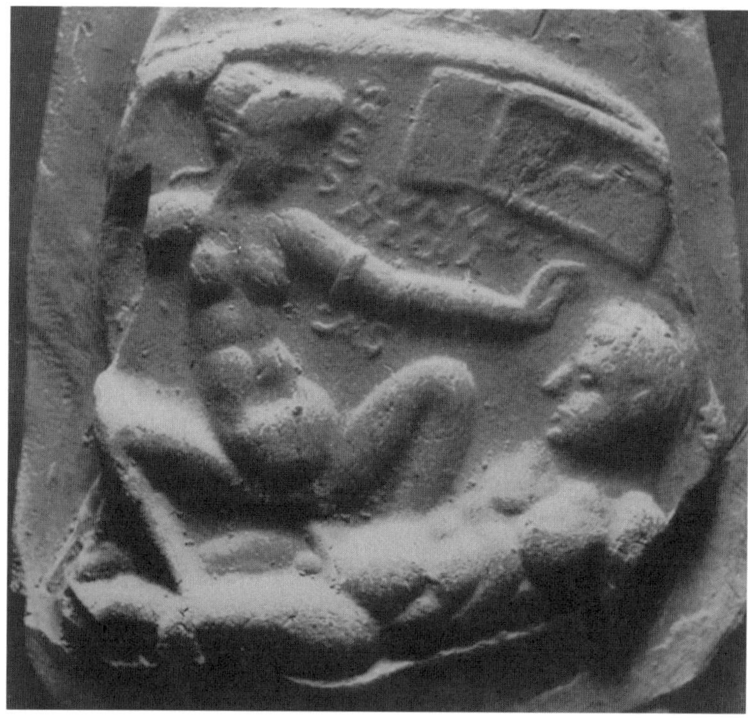

Figure 99. Male-female couple on bed beneath a pinax, terra-cotta appliqué medallion from Rhône Valley (2d–early 3d c. A.D.). Nîmes, Archeological Museum, ex. coll. E. Dumas. After Wuillemeier and Audin, *Médaillons d'applique,* no. 73.

There is a shuttered painting, or pinax, on the wall between the couple. It represents a four-horse chariot or quadriga galloping to the viewer's right. The painting proposes a witty visual pun, since the Romans called the woman's position *mulier equitans,* or the woman riding. Here of course the implication is that she is not just riding but galloping. As if not content with this clever word or image play, the artist put words in the woman's mouth that comment on the sexual performance of her partner. VA . . . VIDES QVAM BENE CHALAS. Aside from the missing first word, probably her partner's name in the vocative, this clearly translates "You see how well you fuck."[39] The use of captions, some referring to the sexual act depicted, is characteristic of the Rhône Valley appliqué medallions with sexual subjects.[40] Such captions are also common in nonsexual scenes on the appliqué medallions, like those depicting gladiators, divinities, and myths.

The only other clear parallel for this genial captioning, or putting words into

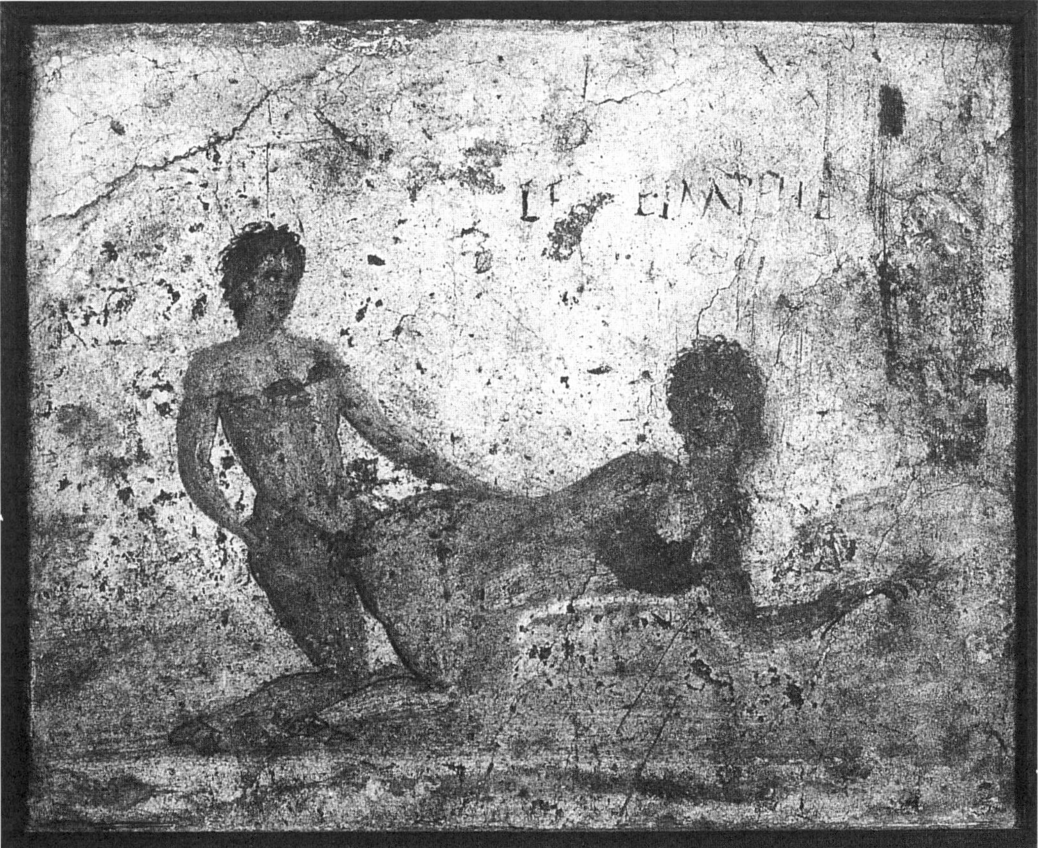

Figure 100. Male-female couple, from Pompeii, Caupona at VII, 9, 33 (A.D. 62–79). Naples Archaeological Museum, inv. 27690, W. 35.5 × H 38 cm. Photo Michael Larvey.

the sexual protagonists' mouths, is a painting removed from a room of the caupona at VII, 9, 33 at Pompeii (Fig. 100). The excavator naturally concluded that the entire tavern was a brothel, although it now seems clear that at most this was a single room for a prostitute, a *cella meretricia*.[41] In this picture the woman, who has assumed the position for rear-entry sex, turns to her partner, kneeling behind her, to say LENTE IMPELLE, or "Put it in slowly."

It is revealing that when the woman "speaks" in both the Rhône Valley ceramic and in the picture at Pompeii, her remarks focus on the man's virility or his sexual expertise. Her speech may, in fact, be an attempt to assuage male fears of poor performance through positive reinforcement. The woman addresses the man to tell him how well he makes love while she "rides" his penis, so that even though the mulier equitans position is one that gives the woman a great deal of control, it is the *man's* powers of lovemaking that she praises. In the Pompeian painting the implication of "Put it in slowly" is that the man should enter the woman slowly because his penis is especially big and/or he particularly eager. In short, the words that the artist put in the woman's mouth are ones any man would like to hear: that he performs well in bed. As we might expect, the artistic and textual construction is a male one that not only celebrates the beauty and desirability of woman but also emphasizes the man's successful performance.

It is also true that when the man speaks to the woman, sometimes it is to tell her how good *her* sexual performance is. For example, in another relief medallion by this same artist a man who holds the palm of victory in his left hand is about to crown the woman with a laurel wreath that he holds in his right (Fig. 101). The artist had him say to her: TU SOLA NICA or "You're the only victrix."[42] There may even be an implied narrative here, if we read the man with palm as a victorious charioteer, giving up his crown to the woman who has "conquered" him in sex. It is interesting that she seems to have just dismounted from the reverse position of the "woman riding," that is with her back to the man's gaze rather than facing him.[43] In fact, she is looking at her reflection in a mirror and not at the man at all. In other instances, the man's words are those of persuasion, trying to get the woman to yield to his sexual urge. One such legend reads FVTVO BENE VOLVI ME, or "I fuck well. Turn to me."[44]

The intent of the medallion showing a woman with sword and shield is clearly humorous (Fig. 102). The woman straddles the man, as if about to assume the mulier equitans position, but she leans back to brandish her weapons. The man registers some alarm by raising his right arm, bent at the elbow, his hand shielding his face. The words ORTE SCUTUS EST mean, literally, "What's that? It's a shield."[45] In a reversal of roles the woman has become the aggressor, the "soldier" in the battle of love. It is significant that the man's penis is flaccid. He *should* be armed with an erection ("sword") for the "battle" of lovemaking. But even with an erection, he is powerless to defend himself against the woman's real weapons. Given the fact that many such medallions decorated vessels used by the Roman military, the image takes on a further level of irony. The soldier looks at the "defenseless" woman

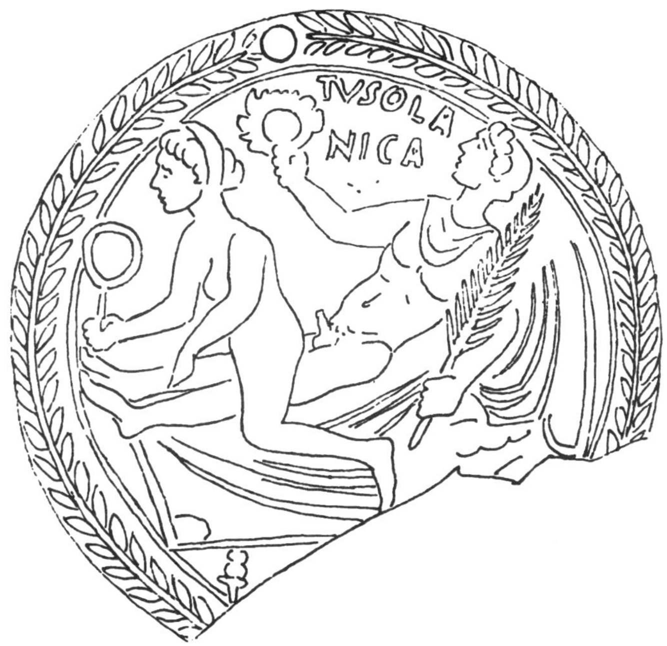

Figure 101. Male-female couple, terra-cotta appliqué medallion from Rhône Valley (2d–early 3d C. A.D.). After Wuillemeier and Audin, *Médaillons d'applique,* no. 71.

in a situation where she could easily defeat (castrate) the man—using the soldier's own weapons.

Different artists of the appliqué medallions develop humorous compositions in other ways.[46] In many scenes they make the woman (in one case the man) hold a lamp in her hand while making love,[47] a tactic similar to the female sexual acrobat in the painting from the caupona on the Street of Mercury discussed in chapter 8 (see Fig. 88). Such balancing acts become even more preposterous when the woman is reclining on the back of a bent-over man while being penetrated by another.[48] Other props achieve similar humorous effects, such as a net (the trap of love—and perhaps a reference to Hephaestus capturing Venus and Mars in a net),[49] or a scarf that the woman wraps around her lover's neck.[50] Finally there are scenes of the woman being penetrated not by a human male but by a rearing stallion.[51] It becomes clear that the buyers of vessels with humorous erotic imagery, like the viewers of the erotic vignettes in the apodyterium of the Suburban Baths, did not blush at any sexual invention that the artists produced.

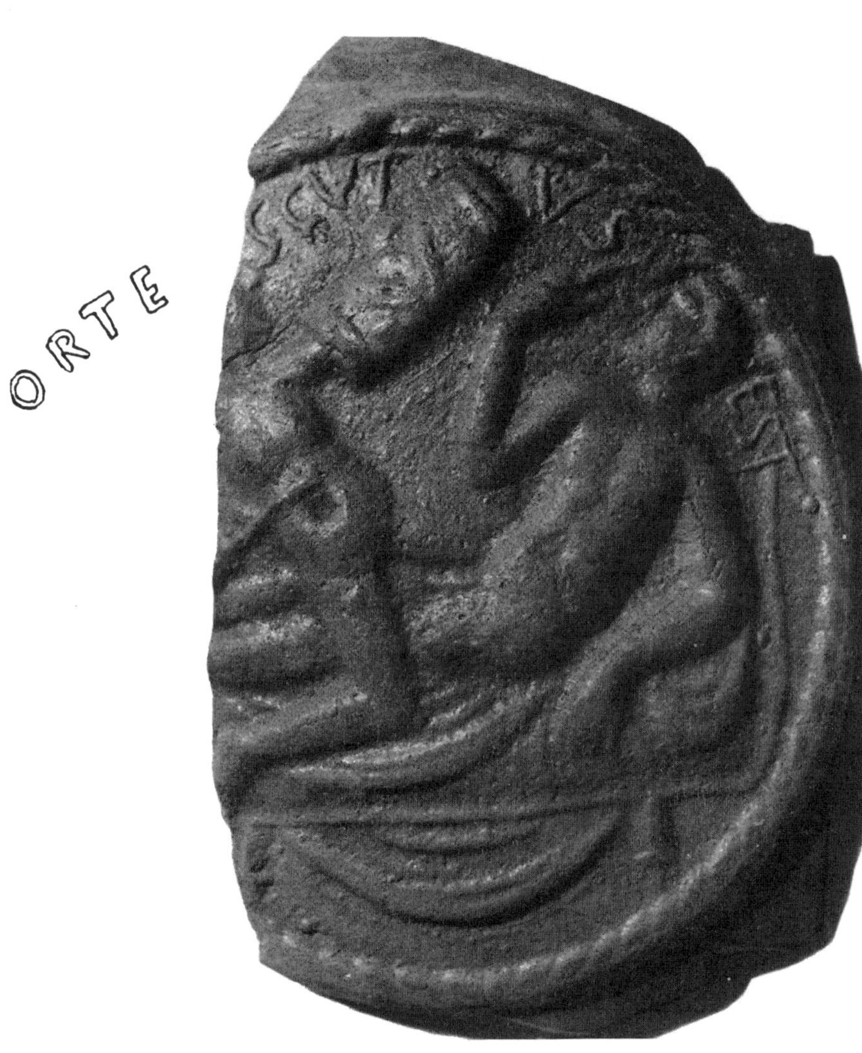

Figure 102. Male-female couple, terra-cotta appliqué medallion from Rhone Valley, found in Arles in 1951 (2d–early 3d c. A.D.). Arles, Lapidary Museum, After Wuillemeier and Audin, *Médaillons d'applique,* no. 74.

It is perhaps because the tiny statuette showing a couple embracing on a bed seems to exemplify the ideal of conjugal love that the piece has received a good deal of attention in the literature (Fig. 103).[52] Although the bed is only 12 cm long and 7 cm (4 ¾ × 2 ¾ in.) high, the artist took care to articulate its form: three legs support it along its front, or open side. A high, S-curved board encloses the mat-

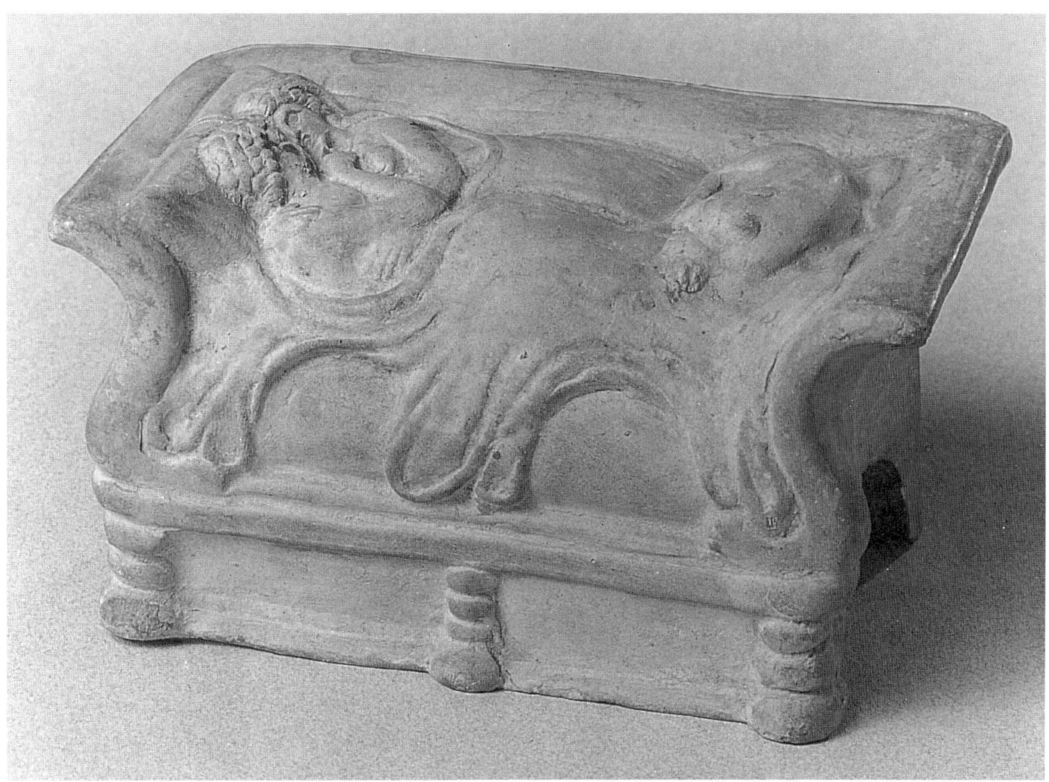

Figure 103. Male-female couple and dog on bed, terra-cotta statuette, signed PISTILLUS FECIT, found at Gironde, Bordeaux (2d C. A.D.). Louvre Museum, inv. 72474. © RMN.

tress on the other three sides, flattening at the top to form a kind of ledge. Within this enclosure lie the couple under heavy covers that part to reveal their nude torsos. The man and woman face each other, sharing a big pillow; at the other end of the mattress their faithful dog sleeps at their feet. The man is on the left, his hair short and curled in a netlike pattern. His face nearly touches the woman's, as he bends his right arm sharply so that he can touch her chin. This amorous gesture—the so-called chin-chuck—has a long history in Greek and Roman art.[53] The woman, her hair arranged in curving strands that part over her left shoulder, passes her left arm beneath the man's right to grasp him just above the waist. In contrast to the couple's amorous intensity, the dog lies curled up in a ball, his muzzle resting on his crossed front paws.

The artist, proud of his diminutive creation, signed it PISTILLUS FECIT. He seems to have been active in the early part of the second century A.D. Excavators unearthed the example in the Louvre toward the end of the nineteenth century at Bordeaux. A seemingly identical replica found in 1865 at the site of an important Roman villa at Montceau-les-Mines has disappeared.[54] Pistillus also signed a similar bas-relief found in 1872 in a field at Autun,[55] and was probably the author of a fragmentary medallion, also in the Louvre, showing the upper part of the couple and meant to be suspended from a cord.[56] It is interesting that none of the contexts seems to be funerary: so far all of Pistillus' creations come from Roman villas.

Precedents and parallels abound for Pistillus' little statuette. Etruscan sarcophagi in both terra-cotta and stone frequently portray male-female couples; an example remarkably similar in pose to the Louvre terra-cotta—but for its monumental size—represents a couple kissing.[57] Yet these are funerary monuments, and Pistillus' creation seems to have a different purpose. I believe that it represents the cozy conclusion to a banquet. It stands, like so many images in painting and sculpture from the Roman world, for the pleasures of lovemaking as a fitting conclusion to the convivial feast. Modern interpretations err in transferring bourgeois notions onto the piece when they interpret Pistillus' creation as the married couple in the nuptial bed.[58] Instead their nudity, the fact that the man is initiating lovemaking with the gesture of the chin-chuck, and the presence of the dog indicate that the artist portrayed the conclusion to an evening of merrymaking. We saw, especially in the Farnesina pinakes discussed in chapter 4, that the woman's nudity in scenes of sexual intimacy usually indicates that she is no longer a virgin; the virgin bride is always draped in some fashion. The chin-chuck gesture is inappropriate for a husband with his wife, since its context is nearly always that of courting or entreating the man's partner to assent to sexual union. Finally, the dog is a common feature of banquet scenes, usually pictured below the banquet couch or tables. In a rather brilliant stroke of invention Pistillus moved the dog up onto the bed itself and put him into a sound sleep—the very image of the torpor that comes with overindulgence in food and drink.

Seen in this light, the Louvre statuette begins to appear much less familiar for the modern viewer. Perhaps the bourgeois gentlemen who have written about the cozy charm of this Gallo-Roman creation were thinking about contemporary scenarios in the comfort of their own homes, with the cat or dog curled up at the foot of their own beds. To the ancient Roman Pistillus' composition would have different resonance as an image of sexual pleasure—the crowning pleasure of the convivial feast. It is a tiny monument to the Romanization of Gaul, where artists provided mass-produced terra-cotta statuettes not only of the gods and goddesses, gladiators, and exotic beasts, but also of Roman-style drinking, eating, and lovemaking.

Brothel or Luxury Bedroom in Third-Century Ostia?

Accidents of preservation seem to account for the lack of paintings of lovemaking in the period of the second century. Elsewhere I consider a related iconography, that of Jupiter's mortal lovers Ganymede and Leda, in a painting of the late second century at Ostia Antica. Located in the main reception space of the large House of Jupiter and Ganymede, this painting shows at most the prelude to lovemaking, since Jupiter is merely chucking Ganymede's chin.[59] At Ostia we look in vain for second-century wall paintings that show sexual intercourse. Yet a third-century decorative program that features erotic paintings—and this in a fine house at Ostia Antica—indicates that the tradition of decorating private houses with images of lovemaking continued unbroken from the time of Pompeii's destruction.

Today the images are hard to decipher. The visitor to Room 5 of the House of the Painted Vaults at Ostia Antica will find the wall decoration puzzling, for inserted into the rough plaster of the west wall is an isolated and nearly illegible painting of a couple on a bed. It bears no relation with the mid-second-century white-ground decoration of the room, divided by airy aediculae framing tiny landscape paintings. The official publication of the painting of this house, in addition to illustrating this puzzling wall in its present state, reproduces two grainy old photographs that document the *south* wall of this room, with a detail of a different erotic painting near its center. The author, Felletti Maj, states that both erotic pictures came from a later, mid-third-century painting phase that disappeared.[60] Archival photographs dated 17 November 1938 reveal that when this room first saw the light of day excavators found a nearly complete third-century decorative program with two well preserved erotic paintings (Fig. 104). It was a white-ground decoration applied on a very thin stratum of plaster over the existing second-century program.

As soon as systematic excavations began at Ostia Antica, the excavators ran into

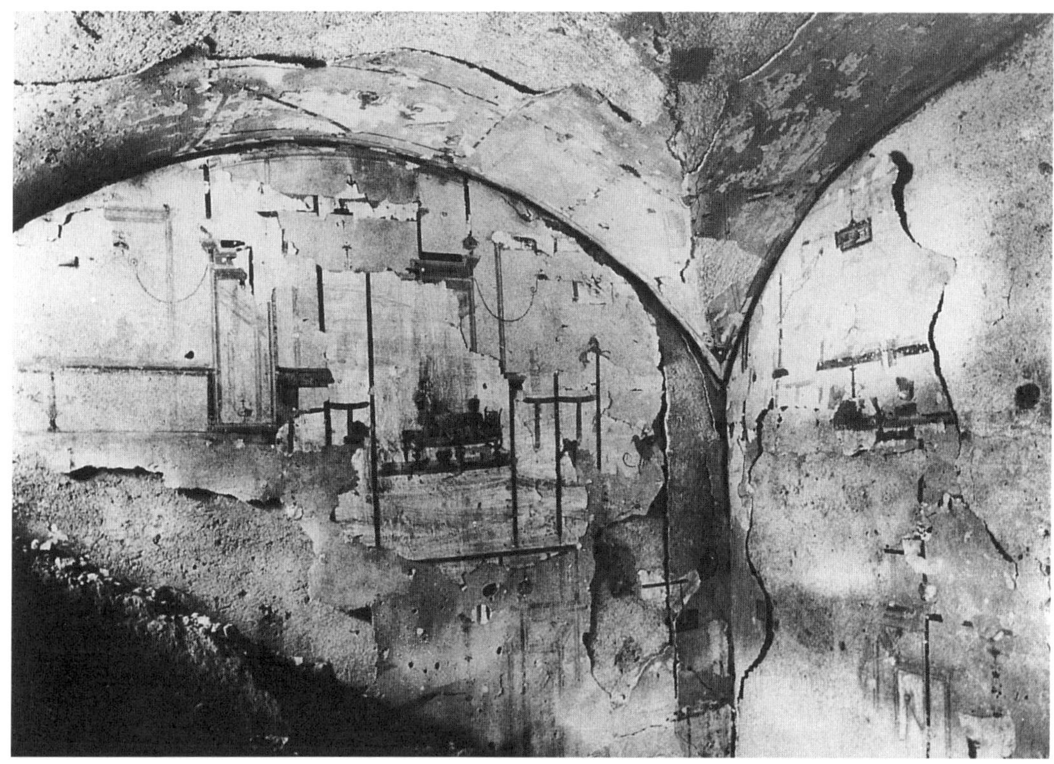

Figure 104. Ostia Antica, House of the Painted Vaults (III, 5, 1), room 5, west and south walls (A.D. 250). Excavation photo dated 17 November 1938. Courtesy Soprintendenza alle Antichità di Ostia Antica.

a problem with third-century repainting programs in the simple manner known as the "Stripe Style": the moment the plaster was exposed to air and dampness it inevitably began to peel off the wall.[61] Because third-century painters did not usually roughen the walls that they were covering but rather applied the new plaster directly on the smooth walls, the new stratum almost inevitably failed to adhere after excavation. The solution was simple and brutal. Except in rare cases, excavators let the third-century painting fall off the wall. In keeping with the decision of Guido Calza to give as much precedence as possible to Ostia at its heyday—in the second century—the third-century painting had served its purpose: to preserve the "better" second-century painting levels.

Although it was not possible to save all of the Stripe Style decoration of the "erotic" room of the House of the Painted Vaults, in the fifties a conservator at-

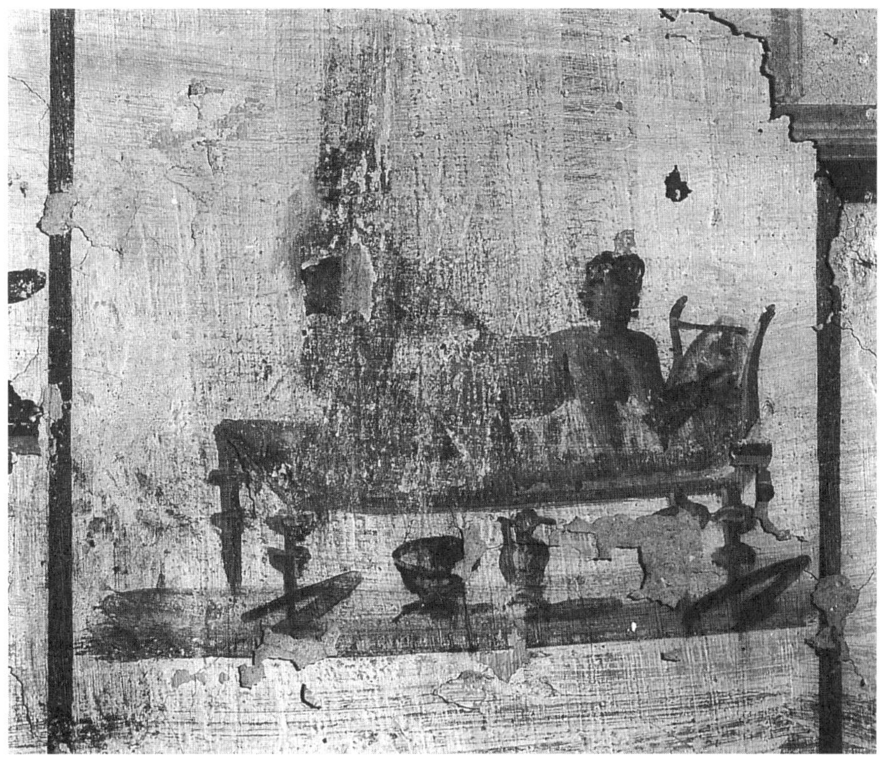

Figure 105. Male-female couple on bed, Ostia Antica, House of the Painted Vaults (III, 5, 1), room 5, central picture, south wall (A.D. 250). Excavation photo dated 17 November 1938. Courtesy Soprintendenza alle Antichità di Ostia Antica.

tempted to save the two erotic pictures, full of crisp detail at the time of excavation (Figs. 105 and 106). He detached both of them from the Antonine underlayer and reattached the painting of the south wall to a new panel; he plastered the image from the west wall into an empty spot about a meter away from the place it had originally occupied. Unfortunately, all of the details, fragile because the artist had added them when the fresco was partially dried, disappeared in this process of detachment (*strappo*). Today the erotic images are barely legible blurs.

Analysis of the now-lost decoration reveals that the owner who had this room repainted in about A.D. 250 wanted the latest style in interior decoration. Instead of the time-honored divisions of the wall into socle, middle zone, and upper zone, the artist divided the white ground with stripes of bright red and green that covered the entire wall like a fantastic net. Using vertical and horizontal stripes (some

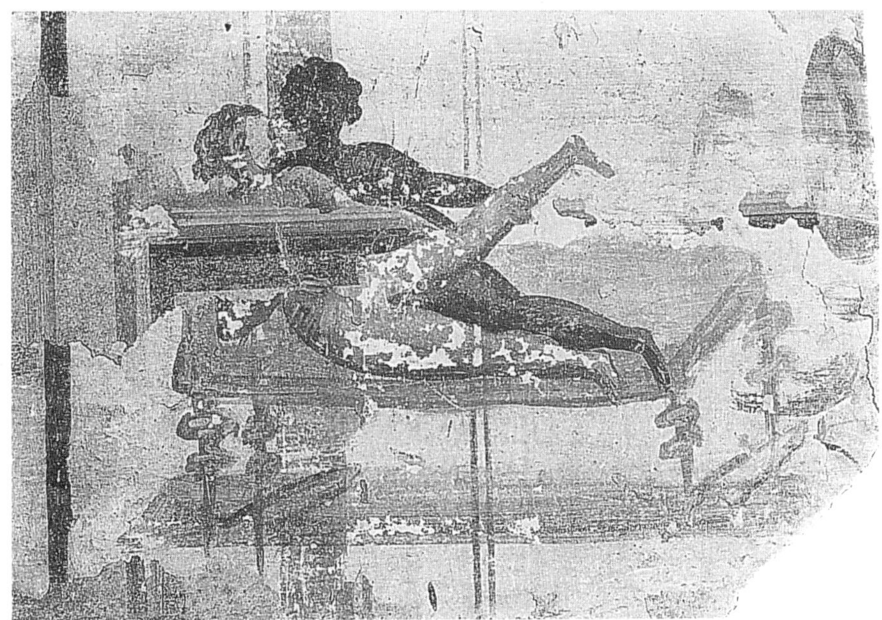

Figure 106. Male-female couple on bed, Ostia Antica, House of the Painted Vaults (III, 5, 1), room 5, central picture, west wall (A.D. 250). Excavation photo dated 17 November 1938. Courtesy Soprintendenza alle Antichità di Ostia Antica.

of these curved to suggest the tops of aediculae), he created a rhythmic but never rigidly geometric pattern that "opened up" at intervals to frame figural motifs. If earlier painting styles insist that figural scenes of lovemaking have frames—and sometimes shutters in perspective—and that they be treated like pictures on the wall, Stripe Style compositions lack frames so that the imagery floats within these open white spaces. And if the combinations of wildly vibrating stripes, painted for the most part freehand and with a heavily loaded brush, threaten to jump off the wall in their exuberance, the figural representations serve to stabilize the composition: they invite the viewer to come close to appreciate their subject matter and details. The two scenes of lovemaking in Room 5, although painted in a color key similar to that of the surrounding network of stripes, required a fuller gamut of colors: flesh tones (reddish brown for the man, pink for the woman), blue for the bedspread, brown for the bed, and bronze for the vessels.

Because there are few surviving examples, third-century Stripe-Style decorations receive little scholarly attention. Parallels for the Stripe-Style decoration of the House of the Painted Vaults suggest that it was not, as some scholars propose, a cheap alternative to traditional schemes based on representation of the fictive colonnade, aedicula, and central picture. In particular, the paintings of the Villa Piccola under San Sebastiano in Rome reveal the vitality and power of the new style.[62] The owner of the House of the Painted Vaults does not seem to have fallen onto hard times when he commissioned this redecoration program for Room 5 and adjacent Room 6 (where only the ceiling remains);[63] he was renewing his house in the style of the times. It seems that the House of the Painted Vaults maintained its status as a respectable mid-income dwelling until the later third century.

The House of the Painted Vaults was about one hundred thirty years old when the owner redecorated it in the Stripe Style. This quarter of Ostia was a residential one that took shape during the rapid-paced development following the construction of Trajan's harbor in the year 100. A variety of apartment buildings, constructed in the brick-faced concrete techniques that made vertical expansion possible, rose up in this area. The plan of the House of the Painted Vaults reveals but one of the many innovative solutions to the problem of increased population density (Fig. 107). Windows to the street, rather than a central atrium or courtyard, provide illumination for all the rooms. A long corridor provides circulation and divides reception spaces (entryway 1, rooms 2, 11, and 12) from sleeping spaces (rooms 4 and 5) and service spaces (room 6 and kitchen 7). Mosaics and wall painting also reveal functional hierarchies. An unusual feature designed to open out the house to light and air is the dining pergola situated at 10. Folding doors would open it to the street for summer dining. The partially preserved second floor repeats this plan in its main features.

In three subsequent redecoration campaigns the ground-floor rooms of the House of the Painted Vaults kept their original functions. Very little of the original Hadrianic decoration remains. Excavators attempted to preserve the painting of the subsequent phase, datable to about 150–160. In room 4 they were able to preserve—for a while—a rare ceiling decoration from the third phase; it is a "panel-style" scheme of the Severan period (about 200–220). This bold decorative scheme divided the ceiling into an octagon with spokes radiating out over the cross vault. In the lunettes that occupied the outer spokes the artist painted white-ground still lifes and Nilotic scenes. Compared to the second-phase Antonine program, the new decoration was showier, evincing a preference for dramatic color contrasts and

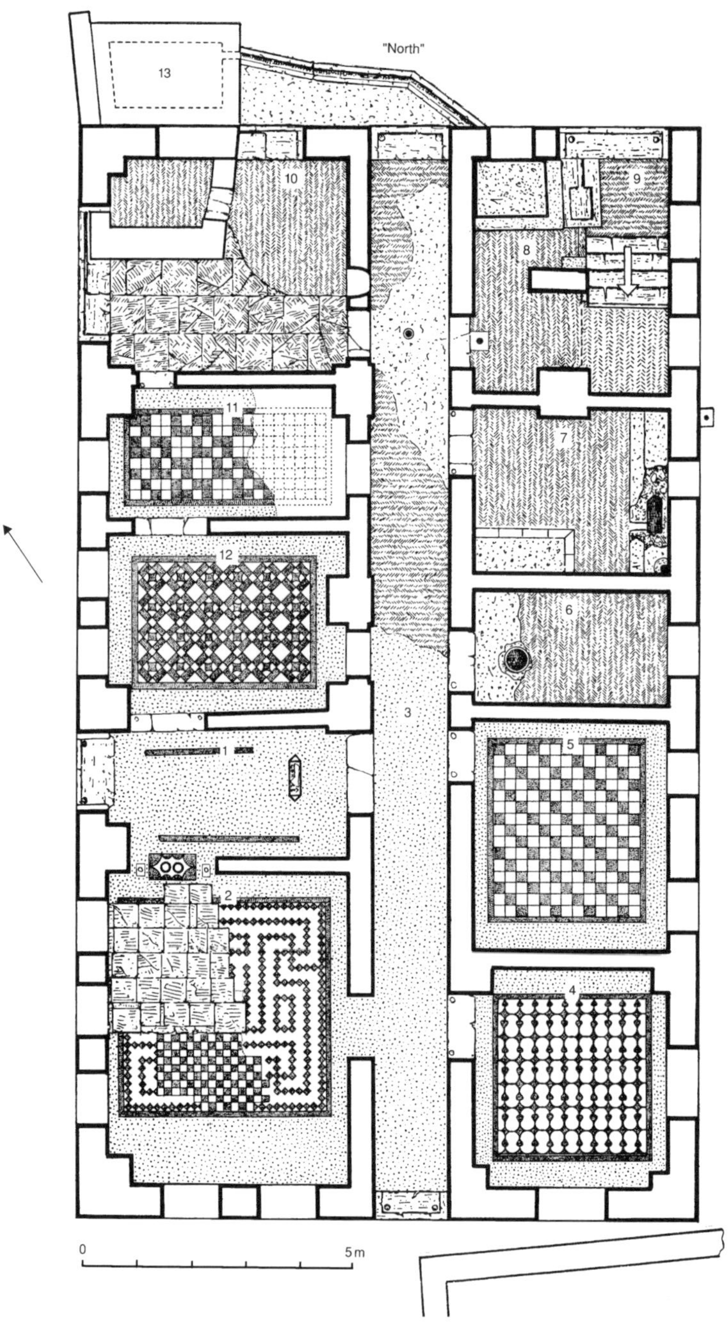

Figure 107. Ostia Antica, House of the Painted Vaults (III, 5, 1), plan.

boldly painted imagery rather than the sober miniature landscape with diminutive garlands and statues that it covered. Beyond this shift in taste, there is nothing in the Severan phase decoration to indicate a change in use of the house. This is also the case with the mid-third-century phase, the one that our erotic paintings belong to. It was not until the later third century that the house underwent a major change—the transformation of the dining pergola into a shop for selling heated wine, with a masonry counter and a cistern.[64]

The later third century was not kind to Ostia Antica. The particulars are not clear—especially given the haste of excavations and the decision not to save third-century materials—yet it is clear that commercial focus shifted to Portus, the city that grew around Trajan's harbor. Add to this the economic troubles of the century of the "soldier emperors" and we have ample explanation for the loss of population at Ostia, signaled by the abandonment of buildings and lowering of standards in painting and mosaics. Nevertheless, the owner of the House of the Painted Vaults had funds to remodel and redecorate his or her house in the 250s. Unfortunately the only major feature of this redecoration program that we can recapture is the repainting of Room 5. How, then, can we interpret the use of sexual representation as a salient feature of this redecoration program? One approach would be to date the installation of the wine-selling shop several decades earlier and posit the owner's transformation of the ground floor into a public house furnished with "back rooms" for prostitutes. Several problems attend such an explanation. Our analysis of houses and taverns at Pompeii having painted rooms decorated with scenes of lovemaking connects paintings of sexual intercourse between human beings to luxury rather than to the sex trade. There is no hard evidence that this equation of images of lovemaking with upper-class luxury changed in the third century.

The quality of the images of lovemaking themselves, to judge from the photographs, was fairly high. On the south wall, the artist situated the image of the bed with the couple on it, as well as the vessels beneath it, directly on a ground-line stripe that spans the width of a tall vertical rectangle (see Figs. 104 and 105). This rectangle's thin stripe borders constitute the only frame for the images of the couple on the bed. It is curious that the image of lovemaking is not at the center of the wall but to right of center, and placed rather higher than usual—just below the springing of the groin vaults. The artist signaled its importance in the Stripe-Styles scheme by elaborating two pairs of T-shaped forms to either side. Since the plaster bearing the rest of the decoration had already fallen by the time of excavation, we do not know whether there was another erotic vignette on this wall.

Within this decorative framework the artist depicted a rather elaborate bed using rapid, inaccurate brushstrokes. He used two conventional V-shapes to depict the shadows cast by the legs. There are two vessels beneath the bed: a basin to the left and a pitcher to the right. At the right side an elaborate, lyre-shaped headboard rises up, its curve interrupted where the plaster has fallen off in a jagged pattern with the earlier paint showing through. It is a rear-entry scene, with the woman kneeling and supporting her upper body on her elbows; she turns in full profile to face the man at her buttocks. Although kneeling, he sits back slightly as he poises his erect penis to enter her. Although his figure is quite abraded, his pose is clear. He holds his torso straight up while resting his right arm on the woman's waist. He looks straight ahead, in profile, not down at his partner. Because the secco detail adhered better on the right side of the image, it is possible to note some details of execution. In the woman's face and upper body the artist handled the tonal shading range to good effect, with the light source coming from the left (as the V-shaped shadows of the bed's legs indicate). The back of her head, as well as her somewhat clumsily delineated left shoulder are in shadow while her face and chest are in light. He indicated her forehead, eye, nose, and lips with calculated little strokes of the dark color. Less clear is the delineation of a breast that appears between her two arms, and the gesture of her left arm is less than successful: it seems to be slightly raised against the big cushion that appears—illogically—behind the bar that connects the two curving ends of the headboard.

The artist represented the bed in much the same way as on the west or entryway wall (see Fig. 106), although the loss of a large triangular-shaped flake of plaster prevents us from knowing whether the bed's headboard—this time on the left—had the same curved profile. (The form that cancels out the headboard and the couples' midsections is the top of an aedicula in the Antonine decoration underneath.) Three curious, half-abraded forms appear behind the bed to the right. Their round forms and apparent stripe patterns suggest that they are bed cushions, although it seems odd that they would stand upright. Another possibility is that the form directly behind the bed's leg is a table, and that the upright "cushions" are shields. The two people both rest their upper bodies against the headboard—presumably propped up on pillows as the man lifts the woman's left leg to penetrate her from behind. The man's hand is on her leg, just below the knee (notice that her foot points down), and she may be assisting this move with her extended left arm. Her right elbow appears on the bed just below the plaster loss.

As in the image on the south wall, here the artist demonstrated his skill in delineating figures and their features with the rapid, fluid brushstrokes that are the hallmark of the Stripe Style. The light falls on the couple from the right—even though the artist erred in showing the V-shaped shadows of the bed's legs going to the right. Working within the dark tonalities of the man's body the artist framed his face with a big crown of wavy hair, quite uncommon in the mid-third century. Contemporary portraits in marble show extremely short, military-style haircuts. The man faces out toward the viewer in a frontal pose, although it is impossible to make out his features. The woman, in contrast, looks to her right in near profile, her face framed by light and unruly hair. Although a plaster loss has erased the back of her head, it is clear that the artist gave her a lively profile by using light daubs for her brow, nose, and area above her lip—giving her a most unclassical appearance.

Even if the artist was using fairly common, inexpensive models (like lamps) for his composition, it is clear that his aim was to render them in the style of the time; he used a heavily loaded, large brush to good effect. The individual features of the figures' faces and bodies emerge from a skein of approximate dots, blobs, and patches of paint in a fascinating, fresh style. Once again—and at a distance of nearly two centuries from Pompeii—we find an artist attempting to please his patron with stylish representations of a subject that encoded upper-class values in two ways: both the representation of sexual pleasure and use of the most fashionable style in painting were signs of luxury.

Since less of the Stripe-Style plaster adhered to the entryway wall, and since the excavators neglected to photograph the entire wall at the time they cleared the room, it is difficult to relocate the image of a couple on a bed to its original place. To judge from the one archival photograph that documents the painting before its removal, it seems to have been located above and just to the left (south) of the entryway into Room 5. Since that doorway takes up northern fourth of the wall, it makes sense to imagine the image of the couple on the bed as one of two foci for the decorative scheme: there was probably another image of a couple on a bed—probably in a different position—on the southern side of the wall. Unfortunately there was nothing left of this half of the wall's Stripe-Style decoration.

Although it is impossible to know what the whole program of Room 5 would be in A.D. 250, it is reasonable to assume that its principal feature was the use of images of couples on beds making love in different positions. Although neither the north nor east walls preserve decoration from this phase, I would envision at least six—if not eight such vignettes—within the decorative scheme, two on each of the long walls and either one or two on each of the short ones.

This unique painted room from Ostia Antica is particularly valuable for this study because it shows us that the same conceptions of erotic paintings as signs of luxury that were so important to first-century Pompeians still kept their hold on patron and artist in the third. Other objects that we examined in this chapter reflect parallel attitudes toward sexual imagery. Among the mold-made, and therefore mass-produced, objects, the first-century spintriae reveal cognitive connections that ancient Romans made between numbers and representations of a variety of sexual positions, indirect evidence for encyclopedic catalogs of the *figurae veneris.* These simple, portable representations, like the infinitely replicated imagery on lamps, could easily serve as models for wall painters and artists working in other media. With lamps we have strong evidence for both the diffusion of sexual imagery throughout the Roman world and its ready acceptance as a sign of luxury among the Romanized peoples of the empire. Like the painted room at Ostia Antica, these humble but late mass-produced objects suggest that many cultural attitudes toward visual representations remained essentially the same until the fourth century, with one exception. Missing from the visual record are scenes of male-male love comparable to those from the period between Augustus and the end of the first century. Whether such representations existed but vanished either through accidents of preservation or deliberate destruction we cannot know. Considering the survival of so much male-female imagery, and even representations of orgies with several men and women, it seems likely—but not provable on the basis of the evidence available—that the visual tradition of male-to-male lovemaking scenes continued as well.

Conclusions

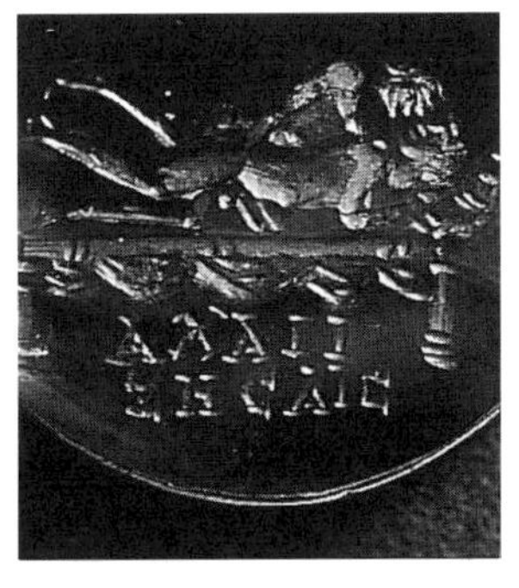

Perhaps the single most startling conclusion from this study is that—at least in matters of sex—the Romans were not at all like us. Hoping to reconstruct ancient Roman attitudes toward sex during three and a half centuries, I underscore the difficulties of looking at ancient Roman sexual acculturation from a contemporary Euro-American viewpoint on what we call sexuality. Even allowing for considerable cultural differences, Roman concepts of sex correspond in very few ways to ours.

The primary reason for these marked differences is that Roman attitudes toward sex are pre-Christian. Christianity's most extreme stance—still prevalent in many communities in the late twentieth century—allows people to practice sex only if married and for purposes of procreation. Such strictures on what is, after all, a guiltless and ubiquitous pleasure in other times and in other societies, shroud sexual acts in secrecy and foster associations of sex with guilt, sin, and punishment.

The works of art that we examined suggest that rather than hiding sexual representations, ancient Romans enjoyed seeing them, primarily because they associated sex with pleasure rather than sin. Although it was a sexuality conceived in terms of male dominance, Roman people of both sexes and of all classes seemed to enjoy looking at lovemaking. They could look at a wide range of sexual imagery that took in the debased behavior of outcasts such as the prostitute, the deformed, or the non-Roman other; many outrageous sexual representations protected the viewer from the Evil Eye. All these associations kept sexual imagery in plain sight.

The paintings, vessels, lamps, and coins picture sexual intercourse in a great variety of ways, ranging from the tastefully elegant to the outrageously parodic. On the one hand, the Roman viewer enjoyed looking at images of "perfect" sex—and not sex just for procreation. Procreation was a duty, but sex with the great variety of possible partners who would not bear legitimate offspring was the sex that artists portrayed for patrons: this was sex with the most beautiful male and female prostitutes, slaves, freedpersons, and foreigners. On the other hand, these same Roman viewers also enjoyed looking at images of outrageous sexual acts—ones no freeborn person would ever admit to enjoying, such as performing cunnilingus or fellatio, being the receptive partner in anal intercourse, threesomes and foursomes, and wild sexual acrobatics. The coexistence of both kinds of images underscores the view that sex—at least at the level of fantasy—was for fun and enjoyment, and that even acts one might not perform could be the subject matter of art that one would own.

Did Roman parents shield children—or even adult women—from sexual imagery? The fact that objects of everyday household use, such as ceramic lamps and vases, bore sexual imagery argues against the notion that their owners kept them hidden away (as our museums have done until recently). These same objects also often appear as part of burial offerings. Again, it would be a mistake to imagine that our Western prudery obtained in ancient Rome. According to Dio Cassius, when Augustus' wife, Livia, found out that some men were about to be executed for encountering her when they were naked, she saved their lives, saying that "to chaste women such men are no different from statues."[1] This story is hardly unambiguous, yet its purpose seems to be to convince the reader that proper Roman women didn't have sexual feelings for men other than their husbands. Livia's experience of seeing the men, far from being an erotic one, was so trivial to her that they seemed no more real to her—and had no more power to move her sexually—than statues.

Ovid's statement that erotic poetry never corrupted a person pure of heart should, it seems, be taken as characteristic of elite attitudes of the time. Furthermore, Propertius' quite negative, moralistic attitude toward erotic paintings seems to ring false in view of the evidence, particularly that of the wall painting considered in this book.[2] Recent study of moral legislation, particularly in the age of Augustus, points to the hypocrisy of the classes it addressed.[3] It seems that the ancient Romans did not in general fear that visual representations would corrupt morals. Even so, both Catullus and Martial call the reader's attention to the distinction between life and art, suggesting, perhaps, that representation was not entirely innocent.[4]

Our study of wall paintings pointed out not only their relative permanence but also the fact that the patrons wished guests to see them, whether in fancy cubicula attached to dining suites or in the peristyle. Nearly all seem to announce luxury, not to announce that a space was meant for sexual intercourse. Central to understanding such paintings in private houses is the cachet of the elite picture collection that they carried, since erotic *tabellae* formed an important part of the wealthy person's collection. Works of art that seem (to the modern viewer) to be erotic or meant to be sexually stimulating often had as their primary purpose the evocation of the life of culture and luxury. How else explain the fine gilded painting in the House of Caecilius Iucundus? Or the use of erotic vignettes in the third-century redecoration of the House of the Painted Vaults?

Careful examination of paintings of sexual intercourse in public buildings undermines the frequently repeated hypothesis that they "advertised" sexual-acts-for-sale. Instead, they serve a variety of purposes: to present fantasies of exalted erotic encounters in the brothel, where the environment suggests just the opposite; to create a mood of conviviality in the tavern by evoking the fun of popular entertainments that featured sexual acrobatics; or in the most complex space, the dressing room of the Suburban Baths, to make men or women who disrobed there roar with laughter.

It is clear that visual art tells us what literature does not. For one thing, the artistic remains are far more democratic and catholic than the texts that have come down to us. They range from objects of extreme luxury, such as the Ortiz flask and the Warren cup, to mass-produced Arretine ceramics or provincial Gallic relief medallions decorating humble utilitarian jars. Wall paintings cover a similarly broad range of quality, with the added advantage that many remain in their original architectural settings. The very fact that patrons commissioned artists to paint not only scenes of ideal lovemaking between beautiful couples but also acts that only persons who suffered the status of infamy would perform, reveals how far visual artists had to stray from the ideal to please their patrons. Although they could look to the more outrageous sex manuals for models and inspiration, it seems likely that they simply turned to mass-produced sexual imagery of the spintria and lamps and freely varied their schemes.

If we consider the conclusions of this book from a feminist perspective, it is clear that the ancient Roman viewer who looked at lovemaking was not just the elite male subject of texts written by elite males or others working for them. Women of all classes saw the lamps, vases, spintriae, and wall paintings that form the focus of this book. In my discussion of the apodyterium of the Suburban Baths, a space frequented by both men and women, I argue that the artist deliberately created images of lovemaking that had different messages for the female and male viewer. Knowing that the Roman elite woman of the first century of our era enjoyed a greater degree of emancipation than her forebears, we see without surprise that artists, and their patrons (many of whom might be women), created sexual imagery that specifically addressed the woman's role in lovemaking.

Another discovery that emerges from this study is the way that ancient Romans put humor into their visual representations of sex. Although such humor abounds in Roman literature, sexual humor in art, because it has a very different audience from that of literature, requires much more effort to understand. Here we encounter unusual difficulties of interpretation, since sexual humor seems to be extremely culture-bound. Many of the images in the Suburban Baths, for example, baffle the late twentieth-century Euro-American, even though our society proclaims and espouses a high degree of sexual freedom. Perhaps this is because our culture, still deeply tied to a Christian and Puritan ethic, tends to frame sex as such a serious pleasure that the sexual jokes of the Suburban Baths are lost on us. The Suburban Baths paintings, by representing every outrageous sexual act as glorified locker labels, introduce sex into the relatively uncharted territory of Roman humor in visual art.

A Variety of Roman Sexualities

In the ancient Roman world, not only an individual's attitudes toward sex, but even the sexual activities he or she would engage in, changed according to that person's social class, status, and ethnicity. The contrast with notions of sexuality in our Euro-American culture could not be greater. Whereas Christianity and Judaism promote the notion of a single moral standard for all people, rich and poor—a set of codes upheld by our legal system—it is immediately clear that what mattered to the ancient Roman when it came to sex was the status of the individual(s) engaging in sexual activity. Furthermore, Roman laws with regard to sex ignored most of the population, since its purpose was to defend the values of the elite, ruling class. These values include the production of legitimate heirs and the protection of people with freeborn status from debasement (*stuprum*). If, for example, we find injunctions against an adult, free male being penetrated by another man, these are aimed at maintaining the proper power structure. There is no problem with a free male penetrating another adult man, or for that matter, boy, woman, or girl, as long as the person he penetrates is of inferior status.

What investigation of works of art demonstrates is that artists, their patrons, and viewers avidly sought imagery of all manner of sexual activities that the elite citizen would *not* perform with his or her social equal. The question the art historian must ask, of course, is whether these many visual representations record life as it was lived or whether they remain entirely artistic inventions. What I try to show is that the contexts surrounding these artistic representations strongly suggest that art often reflected sexual life as it was actually lived.

Much of the art we examined is conventional visual representation, and yet many artists deliberately overturned convention to represent actual sexual practices. I would like to think that the artists who created the Leiden gem, the Warren cup, the paintings of the Suburban Baths, and perhaps even some of the ceramics from the Rhône Valley, created unconventional representations for patrons and buyers who found the standard sexual scenes uninteresting. Perhaps—and this is where we approach Roman attitudes toward sex most closely—they wanted the unconventional in art because that is what they wanted in real life. The fact that some ancient Romans bought and prized works of art with images of male-to-male lovemaking, threesomes and foursomes, cunnilingus, fellatio, or the ithyphallic Ethiopian tempts me to think that these objects in some way expressed their own attitudes toward sex: the kinds of sexual acts they engaged in or, at least, enjoyed looking at.

I return to the image of looking—looking at lovemaking. Men and women whom the artist represents as having sex gaze in various directions: into a partner's eyes, at a part of the partner's body, into the pillow, and sometimes out at the viewer. We moderns can gaze at ancient representations, but do we see what the ancient Roman viewer saw? I hope this book shows that we do not.

NOTES

CHAPTER 1

1. See Ann Snitow, Christine Stansell, and Sharon Thompson, eds., *Powers of Desire: The Politics of Sexuality* (New York, 1983); Judith Butler, *Gender Trouble: Feminism and the Subversion of Identity* (New York, 1990).

2. Even the biological "givens" are far from clear: see Anne Fausto-Sterling, "The Five Sexes," *New York Academy of Sciences* (March–April 1993): 20–26; Butler, *Gender Trouble,* 106–111; Amy Bloom, "The Body Lies," *New Yorker,* 18 July 1994, 38–49.

3. Michel Foucault, *An Introduction,* trans. Robert Hurley, vol. 1 of *The History of Sexuality* (New York, 1986); Michel Foucault, *The Use of Pleasure,* trans. Robert Hurley, vol. 2 of *The History of Sexuality* (New York, 1985); Michel Foucault, *The Care of the Self,* trans. Robert Hurley, vol. 3 of *The History of Sexuality* (New York, 1986).

4. John Boswell, *Christianity, Social Tolerance, and Homosexuality* (Chicago, 1980); in "Concepts, Experience, and Sexuality," *differences* 2, no. 1 (1990): 67–87 Boswell restated his position, noting that no one would really identify him- or herself as a strict essentialist. See also Diana Fuss, *Essentially Speaking* (New York, 1989); and Anthony Corbeill, *Controlling Laughter: Political Humor in the Late Republic* (Princeton, 1996), 14–16.

5. One exception is the poet Sulpicia, in the poems listed as Tibullus 4.7–12; scholars now agree that this poet is a woman rather than a man writing in a woman's persona. See Holt N. Parker, "Sulpicia, the *Auctor de Sulpicia,* and the Authorship of 3.9 and 3.11 of the Corpus Tibullianum," *Helios* 21 (1994): 39–62; Judith P. Hallett, "Feminist Theory, Historical Periods, Literary Canons, and the Study of Greco-Roman Antiquity," in *Feminist Theory and the Classics,* ed. Nancy Sorkin Rabinowitz and Amy Richlin (New York, 1993), 61, 64.

6. A further problem is that of literacy among the people of the non-elite classes. See Paul Zanker, *Pompeji: Stadtbilder als Spiegel von Gesellschaft und Herrschaftsform* (Mainz, 1995); William V. Harris, *Ancient Literacy* (Cambridge, Mass., 1989).

7. Several texts treat male-male lovers, in the love poems of Horace and Catullus and perhaps in the Nisus-Euryalus episode in book 9 of the *Aeneid*. These, however, are quite few in comparison to the very full visual record examined here.

8. Jean Marcadé, *Roma Amor: Essay on Erotic Elements in Etruscan and Roman Art* (Geneva, 1965); Jean Marcadé, *Eros Kalos: Essay on Erotic Elements in Greek Art* (Geneva, 1965); a particularly lamentable recent example of the text/image pastiche is the catalog for a 1989–1990 exhibition in Paris and Athens, *Eros grec: amour des dieux et des hommes* (Athens, 1989).

9. Whereas the symposium scenes on Greek vases commonly include scenes of sexual intercourse, usually between male drinkers and female sex-workers, in the Roman period free men and women dined and drank together. The Roman banquet often figures amorous couples but never outright sexual intercourse. For an recent discussion of paintings at Pompeii showing the drinking party, see Antonio Varone, "Scavi recenti a Pompei lungo via dell'Abbondanza (*Regio* IX, *ins.* 12, 6–7)," in *Ercolano 1738–1988: 250 anni di ricerca archeologica,* Atti del Convegno internazionale Ravello-Ercolano-Napoli-Pompei, 30 October–5 November 1988, ed. Luisa Franchi dell'Orto (Rome, 1993), 622–630.

10. Catherine Johns, *Sex or Symbol? Erotic Images of Greece and Rome* (Austin, 1982), 66–67; for apotropaic images in baths, see Katherine M. D. Dunbabin, "*Baiarum Grata Voluptas:* Pleasures and Dangers of the Baths," *Papers of the British School in Rome* 57 (1989): 6–49; and below, chapter 5, 129–136.

11. Otto J. Brendel, "The Scope and Temperament of Erotic Art in the Greco-Roman World," in *Studies in Erotic Art,* Theodore Bowie et al. (New York, 1970), 8.

12. John J. Winkler, *Constraints of Desire* (New York, 1990), 8–10.

13. Jeffrey Henderson, "Greek Attitudes Toward Sex," in *Civilization of the Ancient Mediterranean: Greece and Rome,* ed. Michael Grant and Rachel Kitzinger (New York, 1988), 2:1251.

14. Henderson, "Greek Attitudes," 1251.

15. Gilbert H. Herdt, ed., *Rituals of Manhood: Male Initiation in Papua New Guinea* (Berkeley, 1982); Gilbert H. Herdt, ed., *Ritualized Homosexuality in Melanesia* (Berkeley, 1984).

16. David M. Halperin, *One Hundred Years of Homosexuality* (New York, 1990), 54–71; see also Wayne R. Dynes and Stephen Donaldson, *Homosexuality in the Ancient World* (New York, 1992), ix–xiii.

17. Isabel Fonseca, "Among the Gypsies," *New Yorker,* 25 September 1995, 92–93.

18. Anne Sutherland, *Gypsies: The Hidden Americans* (New York, 1975).

19. Walter L. Williams, *The Spirit and the Flesh: Sexual Diversity in American Indian Culture* (Boston, 1988).

20. Paul Turner, "Novels, Ancient and Modern," *Novel* 2 (1968): 15–24; Winkler, *Constraints of Desire,* 101–126 on Longus, *Pastorals of Daphnis and Chloe;* David Konstan, *Sexual Symmetry: Love in the Ancient Novel and Related Genres* (Princeton, 1993).

21. For a guide to editions and translations of ancient Greek and Latin texts discussed in this book, see 331–336.

CHAPTER 2

1. See Michael Thomas, "Sexuality and Regeneration in the Tomb of the Bulls: Rites of Passage in Archaic Etruscan Tomb Painting" (master's thesis, Southern Methodist University, 1994); Larissa Bonfante, "Etruscan Sexuality and Funerary Art," in *Sexuality in Ancient Art,* ed. Natalie B. Kampen (New York, 1996), 155–169.

2. For a good general coverage see Henderson, "Greek Attitudes Toward Sex," 1249–1264.

3. Kenneth J. Dover, *Greek Homosexuality* (Cambridge, Mass., 1978); H. A. Shapiro, "Courtship Scenes in Attic Vase-Painting," *American Journal of Archaeology* 85 (1981): 133–143; Eva Keuls, *The Reign of the Phallus: Sexual Politics in Ancient Athens* (New York, 1985); Charles A. M. Hupperts, "Greek Love: Homosexuality or Paederasty? Greek Love in Black Figure Vase-Painting," in *Proceedings of the 3d Symposium on Ancient Greek and Related Pottery,* Copenhagen, 31 August–4 September 1987, ed. Jette Christiansen and Torben Melander (Copenhagen, 1988), 255–268; Robert F. Sutton, Jr., "Pornography and Persuasion on Attic Pottery," in *Pornography and Representation in Greece and Rome,* ed. Amy Richlin (New York, 1992), 3–35; H. A. Shapiro, "Eros in Love: Pederasty and Pornography in Greece," in *Pornography and Representation in Greece and Rome,* ed. Amy Richlin (New York, 1992), 53–72; Martin F. Kilmer, *Greek Erotica on Attic Red-Figure Vases* (London, 1993); Françoise Frontisi-Ducroux, "Eros, Desire, and the Gaze," in *Sexuality in Ancient Art,* ed. Natalie B. Kampen (New York, 1996), 81–100.

4. Aeschines *Against Timarchus;* Dover, *Greek Homosexuality.*

5. For a more pessimistic and problematic verison of Athenian sexuality that qualifies many of Dover's observations, see David Cohen, *Law, Sexuality and Society: The Enforcement of Morals in Classical Athens* (Cambridge, 1991).

6. Dover, *Greek Homosexuality,* 98–100.

7. Hupperts ("Homosexuality or Paederasty?" 255–268) argues that some vase paintings represent anal intercourse; Frontisi-Ducroux ("Eros, Desire, and the Gaze,"

85) suggests that the representation of intercrural intercourse—especially since the partners do not gaze at each other—is an artistic convention that stands for actual consummation through anal intercourse.

8. Alan H. Sommerstein, trans., Aristophanes, *Clouds* (Chicago, 1982), 107–108. Or more succinctly in William Arrowsmith's translation (Ann Arbor, 1962), 75: "To wit—*Demonstrating each attribute individually.* BUILD, Stupendous. COMPLEXION, Splendid. SHOULDERS, Gigantic. TONGUE, Petite. BUTTOCKS, Brawny. PECKER, Discreet. But follow my opponent here, and your reward shall be, as follows: BUILD, Effeminate. COMPLEXION, Ghastly. SHOULDERS, Hunched. TONGUE, Enormous. BUTTOCKS, Flabby. PECKER, Preposterous! (but thereby insuring you an enormous and devoted political following)." See John J. Winkler, "Phallos Politikos: Representing the Body Politic in Athens," *differences* 2, no. 1 (1989): 29–45.

9. Dover, *Greek Homosexuality,* 122–135; Henderson, "Greek Attitudes," 1259–1260.

10. Johns, *Sex or Symbol,* 120.

11. Andrew F. Stewart ("Reflections," in *Sexuality in Ancient Art,* ed. Natalie B. Kampen [New York, 1996], 145) notes that the Boston mirror is the only extant one with this subject matter, and in 152–153 n. 36 he updates the bibliography of W. Züchner (*Griechische Klappspiegel,* Jahrbuch des Deutsches Archäologisches Institut, Supplement 14 [Berlin, 1942], no. 95).

12. Mary B. Comstock and Cornelius C. Vermeule, *Greek, Etruscan, and Roman Bronzes in the Boston Museum of Fine Arts* (Boston, 1972), 257 no. 369: mirror and cover, ca. 325 B.C., from Corinth—gift of E. P. Warren, Res. 08.32c; Brendel, "Erotic Art," 42–46. Stewart ("Reflections," 153 n. 36) suggests that the man has the *anastolé* worn by Alexander the Great, positing a date after 330 B.C.

13. Brendel ("Erotic Art," 42–43) believes that this scene is a modern addition. In this he is alone among the authors who have studied the Boston mirror; in my judgment it is authentic.

14. Stewart, "Reflections," 147–149.

15. Alfred Brückner, *Anakalypteria,* Winckelmannsprogramm, 64, Archäologische Gesellschaft zu Berlin (Berlin, 1904), 12; Mairi Pandou, "Cat. no. 61," in *Eros grec,* 129–130.

16. Brendel's class-conscious analysis depends in many ways on Michael Rostovzeff, *The Social and Economic History of the Hellenistic World* (Oxford, 1941).

17. Aristotle *Politics* 1340a33.

18. Pliny (the Elder) *Naturalis Historia* 35.70, 35.72.

19. Suetonius *Tiberius* 44. For a full discussion of this passage see below, 315–316 (notes 62–63, chapter 7).

20. Brendel, "Erotic Art," 44–45 n. 47: "As the freedom of artists grew in one direction, it became narrowed in another by the social criticism it started to evoke."

21. Marcadé, *Eros Kalos,* 43; *Eros grec,* 132 no. 63: maximum height 15 cm, maximum width, 12 cm; Delos, Archaeological Museum, inv. B 7461, dated to the second century B.C.

22. Gift of Nicolas Koutoulakis, inv. 1995.86. Carlos A. Picón, "Fragment of a Dish with Erotic Scenes," *Metropolitan Museum of Art Bulletin* 53, 2 (1995): 14. I thank Dr. Picón for encouraging my research on this piece.

23. Picón, "Dish with Erotic Scenes," 14. David Whitehouse points out that there are no comparanda for the Metropolitan dish, since all known mold-made opaque white glass objects have imagery on one side only and that comparable objects date from the Augustan and early Julio-Claudian period (personal communication, 28 February 1996).

24. Michael Donderer, *Die Mosaizisten des Antike und ihre wirtschaftliche und soziale Stellung: Eine Quellenstudie,* Erlanger Forschungen Reihe A, Geisteswissenschaften, vol. 48 (Nuremberg, 1989).

25. Brendel, "Erotic Art," 54–57, with discussion of terra-cottas of the second century B.C. from Delos and Pergamon, and a third-century A.D. "Roman-Alexandrian" *lagynos* with serial sexual imagery. Picón ("Dish with Erotic Scenes," 14) also suggests the influence of the sex manuals.

26. Holt N. Parker, "Love's Body Anatomized: The Ancient Erotic Handbooks and the Rhetoric of Sexuality," in *Pornography and Representation in Greece and Rome,* ed. Amy Richlin (New York, 1992), 95–97.

27. *Eros grec,* 131 no. 62: fragment of a vase with red glaze, height 8.5 cm, width, 14 cm, Delos, Archaeological Museum, inv. 10706, 10684, dated to the late Hellenistic period.

28. Otfried R. Deubner, "Griechische Reliefkeramik in hellenistischer Zeit," *Archäologischer Anzeiger* 54 (1939): 348 fig. 10.

29. Jörg Schäfer, *Hellenistische Keramik aus Pergamon* (Berlin, 1968), 79–80.

30. Gerhild Hübner, *Die Applikenkeramik von Pergamon* (Berlin, 1993), 194, cat. 144 pl. 29.

31. Otfried R. Deubner, "Miszellen zur Hellenistische Reliefkeramik," *Archäologischer Anzeiger* 109 (1994): 90–92; Deubner also disagrees with Schäfer on his E 37, E 53, E 55, and E 56, identifying them as pederastic groups.

32. C. H. Greenwalt, Jr., "Sardis, 1979," *Türk arkeoloji dergisi* 26, no. 1 (1982): pl. 47 fig. 28.

33. Marianne Maaskant-Kleibrink, *Catalogue of the Engraved Gems in the Royal Cabinet, The Hague* (The Hague, 1978), 1:372 no. 1172. This collection was moved to Leiden in 1980.

34. The one exception to this rule is the mythological satyr, always erect—even when he is being penetrated (François Lissarrague, "The Sexual Life of Satyrs," in *Before Sexuality,* ed. David M. Halperin, John J. Winkler, and Froma I. Zeitlin [Princeton, 1990], 64–65 fig. 2.28).

35. Line by line, with accents and breathings:

1 *Πάρδαλα, πεῖ-*
2 *νε, τρύφα, περιλά-*
3 *μβανε. Θανεῖν σε*
4 *δεῖ. ὁ γὰρ χρόνος*
5 *ὀλίγος.*

6 *Αχαιέ,*
7 *ζήσαις.*

One exceptional letter use is:

6 *Αχαιέ ΑΧΑΙΙ*

In sentence form, the inscription reads:

Πάρδαλα, πεῖνε, τρύφα, περιλάμβανε. Θανεῖν σε δεῖ. ὁ γὰρ χρόνος ὀλίγος. Αχαιέ, ζήσαις.

Maaskant-Kleibrink (*Catalogue of the Engraved Gems,* 372) incorrectly gives OLITOC in line 5. I thank Malcolm Bell, Eric Moormann, and especially Andrew Riggsby for helping to translate this inscription.

36. Maaskant-Kleibrink, *Catalogue of the Engraved Gems,* 372 no. 1172.

37. Véronique Dasen, "Pygmaioi," *Lexicon Iconographicum Mythologiae Classicae,* vol. 8, part 1, 594–601.

38. Peter Fraser, *Ptolemaic Alexandria* (Oxford, 1972), with extensive bibliography; on the artistic culture, see J. J. Pollitt, *Art in the Hellenistic Age* (Cambridge, 1986), 250–263, and bibl. 300–301.

39. Jean Pierre Cèbe, *La caricature et la parodie dans le monde romain antique, des origines à Juvénal* (Paris, 1966), 351 and passim; Dasen, "Pygmaioi," vol. 8, part 1, 594–601.

40. Irene Bragantini, Mariette de Vos, and Franca Parise Badoni, *Pitture e pavimenti di Pompei,* Repertorio delle fotografie del Gabinetto Fotografico Nazionale, Istituto Centrale per il Catalogo e la Documentazione, vol. 3 (Rome, 1986), 352–353, with bibl.

41. Katherine M. D. Dunbabin, "Triclinium and Stibadium," in *Dining in a Classical Context,* ed. William J. Slater (Ann Arbor, 1991), 121–148.

42. Hesiod *Theogonia* 120–123. Loeb trans. by Hugh Evelyn White (Cambridge, Mass., 1927).

43. Edgar Lobel and Denys Page, *Poetarum lesbiorum fragmenta* (Oxford, 1955), 198. But Ares is his father according to Simonides (Denys Page, *Poetae melici graeci* [Oxford, 1962], 575).

44. Nicole Blanc and Françoise Gury, "Eros/Amor, Cupido," *Lexicon Iconographicum Mythologiae Classicae,* vol. 3, part 1, 952.

45. In addition to the common metonymy of Venus for sex, in Apuleius *Metamorphoses* 3.20 sex is described as a "rite of Venus." I owe this citation to Andrew Riggsby.

46. Pausanias 9.31.2.

47. Gérard Siebert, "Hermes," *Lexicon Iconographicum Mythologiae Classicae,* vol. 5, part 1, 300 no. 81.

48. Amy Richlin, *The Garden of Priapus: Sexuality and Aggression in Roman Humor* (New Haven, 1983), 116.

49. Richlin, *Garden of Priapus,* 122.

50. Richlin, *Garden of Priapus,* 125.

51. Brendel, "Erotic Art," 52.

52. Ovid *Metamorphoses* 4.300–350; see also Nicole Loraux, *The Experiences of Tiresias: The Feminine and the Greek Man,* trans. Paula Wissing (Princeton, 1995).

53. Ovid *Metamorphoses* 4.285–388.

54. Fausto-Sterling, "The Five Sexes," 20–26.

55. Aileen Ajootian, "Hermaphroditos," *Lexicon Iconographicum Mythologiae Classicae,* vol. 5, part 1, 268–285, bibl. 270.

56. Ajootian, "Hermaphroditos," 276–277, with bibl.; Pliny (the Elder) *Naturalis Historia,* 34.80.

57. Doro Levi, *Antioch Mosaic Pavements* (Princeton, 1947), 1:183–185.

58. Pliny (the Elder) *Naturalis Historia* 7.34.

CHAPTER 3

1. Hans Jucker, *Vom Verhältnis der Römer zur bildenden Kunst der Griechen* (Frankfurt, 1950); M. Pape, *Griechische Kunstwerke aus Kriegsbeute und ihre öffentliche Aufstellung in Rom: von der Eroberung von Syrakus bis in augusteische Zeit* (Hamburg, 1975); Pollitt, *Hellenistic Age,* 150–163.

2. Suetonius *Divus Augustus* 28.

3. Erika Simon, *Augustus: Kunst und Leben in Rom um die Zeitenwende* (Munich, 1986); Antikenmuseum Berlin, *Kaiser Augustus und die verlorene Republik* (exh. cat., 7 June–14 August 1988 [Berlin, 1988]).

4. Paul Zanker, *The Power of Images in the Age of Augustus* (Ann Arbor, 1988).

5. Ann L. Kuttner, *Dynasty and Empire in the Age of Augustus: The Evidence of the Boscoreale Cups* (Berkeley, 1995); David Castriota, *The Ara Pacis Augustae and the Imagery of Abundance in Later Greek and Early Roman Imperial Art* (Princeton, 1995); Charles Brian

Rose, *Commemoration and Imperial Portraiture in the Julio-Claudian Period* (New York, 1997); Diane Favro, *The Urban Image of Augustan Rome* (New York, 1996).

6. Brendel, "Erotic Art," 54.

7. Brendel, "Erotic Art," 55.

8. Zanker, *Power of Images,* 253.

9. The first modern owner of the cup was Edward Perry Warren (1860–1928), an American collector, who acquired it some time in the early twentieth century. Opinion is divided on the find spot of the Warren cup because Warren's meticulous records of all ancient objects that he either owned or sold do not include the cup. There are two published opinions: Gaston Vorberg (*Glossarium eroticum* [Stuttgart, 1932], 457) gives Syria as the find spot (without further explanation) in the caption beneath an image of the Warren cup. Donald E. Strong (*Greek and Roman Gold and Silver Plate* [London, 1966], 137) states: "A cup with scenes of homosexual love recently on the London Market is said to have been found in Palestine together with coins of Claudius," explaining in 137 n. 6, "R. V. Nicholls informed me about its provenance." One expert who prefers to remain anonymous has good grounds for a provenance from Pompeii. If and when Warren's own notes on the cup are found, more precise information may be available. After Warren's death the cup seems to have passed by inheritance to Asa Thomas, and thence to a dealer. In the late fifties the Warren cup was offered for sale but no museum bought it, presumably because its subject matter was considered too obscene for public display. Cornelius Vermeule, curator of ancient art at the Boston Museum of Fine Arts, included it in a brief article (Cornelius C. Vermeule, "Augustan and Julio-Claudian Court Silver," *Antike Kunst* 6, no. 1 [1963]: 33–46). The collector who bought the cup loaned it for some time to the Basel Art Museum. In 1992 the cup went on display as an anonymous loan to the Metropolitan Museum of Art in New York (Metropolitan Museum of Art, L.1991.95).

10. For shapes of silver drinking cups of the period, see Strong, *Gold and Silver Plate,* 134 fig. 27. The Warren cup corresponds most closely to the "deep ovoid" type "b." The foot and liner of the Warren cup are ancient. The cup does not stand fully perpendicular on its foot because one side of the foot has telescoped into the metal of the cup (a small wedge used in the current display corrects the problem). I thank Richard Stone of the Department of Conservation, Metropolitan Museum of Art, for allowing me to consult him and examine the Warren cup in April 1992.

11. For a recent review of the literature, see Catherine Johns, "Research on Roman Silver Plate," *Journal of Roman Archaeology* 3 (1990): 28–43; François Baratte, ed., *Argenterie romaine et byzantine,* Actes de la Table Ronde, Paris 11–13 October 1983 (Paris, 1988); François Baratte and Kenneth Painter, eds., *Trésors d'orfèvrerie gallo-romains,* exh. cat., 8 February–23 April 1989 (Paris, 1989); Simon, *Augustus,* bibl.

12. Amedeo Maiuri, *La casa del Menandro e il suo tesoro di argenteria* (Rome, 1933), 1:321–330 figs. 125 and 126; 2: pls. 31–36.

13. Peter J. Connor, "The Dead Hero and the Sleeping Giant by the Nikosthenes Painter at the Beginnings of a Motif," *Archäologischer Anzeiger* 99 (1984): 387–394; St. F. Schröder, *Römische Bacchusbilder in der Tradition des Apollon Lykeios* (Rome, 1989): 30. I thank Andrew Stewart for calling my attention to this and related bibliography.

14. Andrew F. Stewart, "Dionysos at Delphi: The Pediments of the Sixth Temple of Apollo and Religious Reform in the Age of Alexander," in *Macedonia and Greece in Late Classical and Early Hellenistic Times,* ed. Beryl Barr-sharrar and Eugene N. Borza (Washington, D.C., 1982), 213 n. 68, with bibl.

15. Pollitt, *Hellenistic Age,* 134 fig. 146 (third century B.C.).

16. Margarete Bieber, *Sculpture of the Hellenistic Age* (New York, 1961), fig. 624.

17. Hellmut Sichtermann, *Die mythologischen Sarkophage. Die Antiken Sarkophag-reliefs,* vol. 12, part 2 (Berlin, 1992), 33–35, with bibl.

18. In addition to Fig. 23, the cup from the House of the Menander, the gesture of "erotic repose" occurs [as noted] in Fig. 34, Rome, Villa under the Farnesina, cubiculum D, left wall, attic zone, to right of central aedicula [female]; Fig. 49, Pompeii, House of the Beautiful Impluvium (I, 9, 1), cubiculum 10, south wall [male]; Pl. 7, Pompeii, House of the Centenary (IX, 8, 6), room 43, south wall, central picture [male]; Fig. 69, Pompeii, House at IX, 5, 14, room *f*', west wall, center picture [female]; Pl. 10, Pompeii, Suburban Baths, apodyterium 7, Scene II [female]; Fig. 99, appliqué medallion in terra-cotta, couple making love beneath a pinax [male].

19. Maiuri, *Casa del Menandro,* 245–251. On the class and social status of the last owners of the House of the Menander, see John R. Clarke, *The Houses of Roman Italy, 100 B.C.–A.D. 250: Ritual, Space, and Decoration* (Berkeley, 1991), 170–193.

20. See Maiuri (*Casa del Menandro,* 241–245) for a rapid overview of silver finds in the area of Vesuvius.

21. Emeline Richardson, *The Etruscans: Their Art and Civilization* (Chicago, 1964), 134.

22. Henri de Villefosse, "Le trésor de Boscoreale," *Monuments Piot* 5 (1899): 1–290; Soprintendenza archeologica di Pompei, *Il tesoro di Boscoreale,* exh. cat., 20 August–30 September 1988 (Milan, 1988); François Baratte, *Le trésor d'orfèvrerie romain de Boscoreale* (Paris, 1986); Kuttner, *Dynasty and Empire.*

23. K. F. Johansen, "New evidence about the Hoby cups," *Acta archaeologica* 31 (1960): 185–190; Vermeule, "Court Silver," pls. 12, 1–4; 13, 1–2; Antikenmuseum Berlin, *Kaiser Augustus,* 569–571, cat. 396–397, with bibl.

24. Wolf-Rudiger Megow, *Kameen von Augustus bis Alexander Severus: antiken Münzen und geschnittene Steine* (Berlin, 1987), 11:9–11, pls. 3, 4.

25. Anne-Kathrein Massner, *Bildnißangleichung: Untersuchungen zur Entstehungs- und Wirkungsgeschichte der Augustusporträts (43 v. Chr.–68 n. Chr.)* (Berlin, 1982); Klaus Fittschen, "Die Bildnisse des Augustus," *Saeculum aureum* 3 (1991): 149–186; Dietrich Boschung, *Die Bildnisse des Augustus,* Das römische Herrscherbild, part 1, vol. 2 (Berlin, 1993).

26. A. C. Brown, *Catalogue of Italian Terra-Sigillata in the Ashmolean Museum* (Oxford, 1968), xix: "It has long been recognized that a close relationship exists between Italian terra-sigillata and contemporary silverware, so much so that the potters' work is often described as 'poor man's silver.' This correspondence is reflected not only in a community of vase shapes but also in the subject-matter of vase decoration." See also E. Ettlinger, "How Was Arretine Ware Sold?" *Rei cretariae romanae fautorum acta* 25–26 (1987): 5–19; G. Pucci, "La ceramica aretina: 'imagerie' e correnti artistiche," in *L'art décoratif à Rome à la fin de la république et au début du principat,* ed. X. Lafon and G. Sauron (Rome, 1981), 101–121.

27. The manuscript *Libro della Compositione del Mondo,* written by Ser Ristoro d'Arezzo and dated 1282, is quoted in full in A. Fabroni, *Storia degli antichi vasi fittili aretini* (Arezzo, 1841), 12 ff.; George H. Chase, *Catalogue of Arretine Pottery* (1916; enlarged ed., Boston, 1975), 4–5 provides an English translation of Ser Ristoro's description of the contemporary interest in Arretine ware.

28. Christine Alexander, *Arretine Relief Ware* (Cambridge, Mass., 1943).

29. Brown, *Ashmolean Museum.*

30. Chase, *Arretine Pottery.*

31. Francesca Porten Palange, "Fälschungen in der arretinischen Reliefkeramik," *Archäologisches Korrespondenzblatt* 19 (1989): 197–216. The author points out that the combination of maker stamp and workshop stamp (EPOC + C.ANNI) on molds with scenes of alternating male-female and male-male lovemaking is highly unlikely, a fact noted earlier by Hans Dragendorff and Carl Watzinger (*Arretinische Reliefkeramik mit Beschreibung der Sammlung in Tübingen* [Reutlingen, 1948], 89). On this basis, Porten Palange rejects the following molds depicting male-male lovemaking: Metropolitan Museum inv. no. 21.88.165 (Alexander, *Arretine Relief Ware,* pls. 34, 1 a–b; 38, 20) and Ashmolean Museum inv. no. 1966.251, cat. 62 (Brown, *Ashmolean Museum,* pls. 15, 16, and 19; figs. 1 and 3).

32. Brown (*Ashmolean Museum,* 28 pl. 18) published two fragments of the mold for this composition, the one in the Ashmolean, Oxford, cat. 77 joining with another in the Archaeological Museum, Arezzo, no. 10734.

33. A third composition, known through a dubious mold in the Ashmolean (Brown, *Ashmolean Museum,* 23, cat. 62, pls. 16 and 17), differs from this second composition only by virtue of the substitution of candelabra holding the garlands.

34. Margarete Bieber, "Strophium," *Pauly-Wissowa,* series 2, vol. 4, cols. 378–380.

35. Dragendorff and Watzinger (*Arretinische Reliefkeramik,* 89) note erotic types of the Perennius workshop: "Typus XIV 8. Das Mädchen, das eine Binde unter der Brust trägt, hat sich von dem Jüngling weg auf die linke Seite geworfen, so daß es dem Beschauer seine Vorderseite zukehrt. Es stützt sich dabei auf den linken Arm und faßt mit dem angestreckten rechten den Unterarm des Jünglings, der sich über es wirft und es herumzudrehen sucht, indem er es am Oberschenkel faßt. XIV 8a. Dieser Typus kommt dahin variiert vor, daß bei sonstiger genauer Übereinstimmung aus dem Mädchen ein Knabe gemacht ist. Die Brustbinde wird in diesem Falle natürlich fortgelassen."

36. Dover, *Greek Homosexuality,* 91–100; see also Shapiro, "Eros in Love," 55–58; Sutton, "Pornography and Persuasion," 14.

37. Sutton, "Pornography and Persuasion," 11–12 figs. 1.2 and 1.3. I thank Amy Richlin for pointing out this difference between the Greek and Roman representations.

38. It is difficult to determine how expensive silver vessels were in Roman terms. François Baratte ("Arts précieux et propagande impériale au début de l'empire romain: l'exemple des deux coupes de Boscoreale," *Revue du Louvre et des Musées de France* 41, no. 1 [1991]: 37) sees silver vessels as belonging to the minor arts, not on the same level of originality as imperial art. But we lack evidence for the mass production of silver vessels, such as exact repetition of motifs from molds.

39. S. M. Goldstein, L. S. Rakow, and J. K. Rakow, *Cameo Glass* (Corning, N.Y., 1982), 13–15 and 18: in addition to the sixteen complete cameo vessels, there are an estimated two hundred fragments.

40. Modern attempts to reproduce Roman cameo glass give an idea of the time and labor involved. It took John Northwood three years to make a replica of the Portland Vase, even though he used hydrofluoric acid to remove unwanted overlay (John Northwood, II, *John Northwood: His Contribution to the Stourbridge Flint Glass Industry, 1850–1902* [Stourbridge, 1958], 89–90). Northwood's son worked full-time for eighteen months to make a plaque depicting Aphrodite and her attendants (W. E. S. Turner, "Noteworthy Productions of the Glass Craftsman's Art, II: Mr John Northwood's Plaque of Aphrodite," *Journal of the Society of Glass Technology* 8 [1924]: 92–93).

41. Kenneth Painter and David Whitehouse, "Early Roman Cameo Glasses," *Journal of Glass Studies* 32 (1990): 139.

42. María del Pilar Caldera Castro ("Un balsamario de vidrio camafeo procedente de Ostippo [Estepa, Sevilla]," *Archivo español de arqueología* 59 [1986]: 211 n. 2) studied it in the collection of D. R. Machuca; she reports that it was later sold to an Italian collector. By 1990 it was listed as in the Ortiz collection: Painter and Whitehouse, "Early Roman Cameo Glasses," 162, cat. A15 figs. 124 and 125; David Whitehouse, "Cameo Glass," in *Roman Glass: Two Centuries of Art and Invention,* ed. Kenneth Painter and Mar-

tine Newby (London, 1991), 29–30, pls. VI, VII; George Ortiz, *In Pursuit of the Absolute: Art of the Ancient World: The George Ortiz Collection* (Bern, 1996), unpaginated, cat. 221, with two facing color plates.

43. See Mario Torelli, *Typology and Structure of Roman Historical Reliefs* (Ann Arbor, 1982), pl. 2.5; Castriota, *Ara Pacis Augustae,* figs. 40–41.

44. Hanns Gabelmann, "Römische Kinder in Toga Praetexta," *Jahrbuch des Deutschen Archäologischen Instituts* 100 (1985): 497–541; C. Brian Rose, "'Princes' and Barbarians on the Ara Pacis," *American Journal of Archaeology* 94 (1990): 456 n. 11 for long-haired Bosporan princes; 459–461 for barbarian princes from Gaul with long hair.

45. Generally the word *capillati* (long-haired) referred to slave boys (Petronius *Satyricon* 27, 29, 57). See also Nigel M. Kay, *Martial Book XI: A Commentary* (London, 1985), 89–92, for commentary on Martial 11.11.3. I disagree with Whitehouse ("Cameo Glass," 30), who cites from Martial 16.62.2, describing the schoolmaster's class of many long-haired boys (*frequentes capillati*), and 2.57.5, regarding an effeminate, extravagantly dressed man and his long-haired hangers-on (*grex togatus sequitur et capillatus*); furthermore Martial was writing in the final decades of the first century of our era.

46. Whitehouse, "Cameo Glass," 30 pl. 8b.

47. Halperin, *One Hundred Years of Homosexuality,* 8: "Homosexuality and heterosexuality, as we currently understand them, are modern, Western, bourgeois productions. Nothing resembling them can be found in classical antiquity." See also Foucault, *Use of Pleasure,* 187–246.

48. Amy Richlin, "The Meaning of *irrumare* in Catullus and Martial," *Classical Philology* 76 (1981): 40–46; Richlin, *Garden of Priapus,* 26–30; J. N. Adams, *The Latin Sexual Vocabulary* (London, 1982), passim; Vorberg, *Glossarium Eroticum,* passim.

49. For a rebuttal to this view, see Boswell, "Concepts, Experience, and Sexuality," 69–70.

50. Eva Cantarella, *Bisexuality in the Ancient World,* trans. C. O. Cuilleanáin (New Haven, 1992), 120–154.

51. Amy Richlin, "Not before Homosexuality: The Materiality of the *Cinaedus* and the Roman Law against Love between Men," *Journal of the History of Sexuality* 3, no. 4 (1993): 571; yet John D'Emilio ("Capitalism and Gay Identity," in *Powers of Desire: The Politics of Sexuality,* ed. Ann Snitow, Christine Stansell, and Sharon Thompson [New York, 1983], 100–113) argues that gay men have not always existed throughout history but constitute a recent phenomenon, a recent product of capitalism. Dick Hebdige (*Subculture: The Meaning of Style* [London, 1979]) even proposes that the concept of subculture is a historically specific notion.

52. Aline Rousselle, "Personal Status and Sexual Practice in the Roman Empire,"

Zone 5 (1989): 309. This issue was called *Fragments for a History of the Human Body* (part 3, ed. Michel Feher with Ramona Naddaff and Nadia Tazi).

53. Scriptores Historiae Augustae *Alexander Severus* 24.3–4: Alexander Severus decreed that the taxes on pimps, prostitutes, and male prostitutes (*exoleti*) should not go into the public coffers; Jasper Griffin, *Latin Poets and Roman Life* (Chapel Hill, 1986), 25: "boys employed in male prostitution had their own holiday, and this was duly recorded in the State calendar."

54. Halperin, *Homosexuality,* 165–166 n. 83, for definition of phallus, and 164–165 n. 67, for distinction between phallus and penis.

55. Gabelmann, "Toga Praetexta," 497–541; W. Gercke, *Untersuchungen zum römischen Kinderporträt* (Hamburg, 1968); H. R. Goette, *Studien zu römischen Togadastellungen* (Mainz, 1990); Richlin, "Not Before Homosexuality," 537–539.

56. "Dum ted abstineas nupta, vidua, virgine, / iuventute et pueris liberis, ama quidlubet" (Plautus *Curculio* 35–38; my translation in text).

57. Catharine Edwards, *The Politics of Immorality in Ancient Rome* (Cambridge, 1993), 70–73.

58. Richlin, "Not Before Homosexuality," 554–571.

59. Richlin, *Garden of Priapus,* 226.

60. Richlin, "Not Before Homosexuality," 572.

61. Gordon Williams, *Tradition and Originality in Roman Poetry* (London, 1968), 551.

62. Griffin, *Latin Poets,* 22: "As for homosexual relationships in poetry and in life, one of the chief arguments used by those who regard the poems as 'unreal' is that at Rome such practices were 'the object of penal legislation.' I do not find this such an obstacle as do its proponents." See also Jasper Griffin, "Augustan Poetry and the Life of Luxury," *Journal of Roman Studies* 66 (1976): 87–105; Cantarella, *Bisexuality,* 120–156; Richlin, "Not Before Homosexuality," passim.

63. Dover, *Greek Homosexuality,* 84–87.

64. Paul Veyne, "Homosexuality in Ancient Rome," in *Western Sexuality: Practice and Precept in Past and Present Times,* ed. Philippe Ariès and André Béjin, trans. Anthony Forster (Oxford, 1985), 28: "Should we really believe that the Romans learnt it from the Greeks, who taught them so much else? If the answer is yes, one might infer that homosexuality is such a rare perversion that one people can only have picked it up through another's bad example. If, on the other hand, it appears that pederasty was indigenous in Rome, the astonishing thing is not that a society should practise pederasty, but that it should not practise it. What needs explanation is not Roman tolerance but contemporary intolerance."

65. Ramsay MacMullen, "Roman Attitudes to Greek Love," *Historia* 31 (1982): 484–502.

66. Sara Lilja, *Homosexuality in Republican and Augustan Rome* (Helsinki, 1983).

67. Cantarella, *Bisexuality*, 97–186.

68. Craig Williams, "Homosexuality and the Roman Man: A Study in the Cultural Construction of Sexuality" (Ph.D. diss., Yale University, 1992), 9–10.

69. Brown, *Ashmolean Museum*, 8, cat. 6, pl. 6 figs. 1 and 2: "The companion (sex uncertain) lies on the left side, twisted round with the head in profile; looking up at the youth, the right arm outstretched. A lock of hair, perhaps suggesting the figure could be a girl, falls into the nape of the neck."

70. Dover, *Greek Homosexuality*, 86–87.

71. Hupperts, "Homosexuality or Paederasty?" 255–268.

72. Jiri Frel, "Euphronios and His Fellows," in *Ancient Greek Art and Iconography*, ed. Warren Moon (Madison, 1983), 147–151 figs. 10.2–10.6; Arezzo, Museo archeologico nazionale, *Capolavori di Euphronios: un pioniere della ceramografia attica*, exh. cat., 26 May–31 July 1990 (Arezzo, 1990), 192–193, cat. 43, attributed to Smikros by D. von Bothmer.

73. Illustrated in Brendel, "Erotic Art," fig. 19.

74. Keuls, *The Reign of the Phallus*, 293; Keuls's interpretation is not entirely convincing: see Peter von Blanckenhagen, "Puerilia," in *In Memoriam Otto Brendel*, ed. Larissa Bonfante and Helga von Heintze (Mainz, 1976), 37–41; see also the representation of a female lowering herself onto a male seated on a chair in Brendel, "Erotic Art," figs. 25 and 26.

75. Vermeule, "Court Silver," 39.

76. E.g., on the bronze relief from a mirror cover of the Flavian period in Rome, Palazzo dei Conservatori, *Bellezza e seduzione nella Roma imperiale*, exh. cat., 11 June–31 July 1990 (Rome, 1990), 99, cat. 145, color photo fig. 35 on 54; see also Molly Myerowitz, "The Domestication of Desire: Ovid's *Parva Tabella* and the Theater of Love," in *Pornography and Representation in Greece and Rome*, ed. Amy Richlin (New York, 1992), 145–147 fig. 7.10, and here Fig. 60.

77. A relief from the Sebasteion at Aphrodisias, securely dated by inscriptions to the later Julio-Claudian period, pictures a similar voyeur in the person of Eros watching Leda being penetrated by the swan (Pascale Linant de Bellefonds, "Leda," *Lexicon iconographicum mythologiae classicae*, vol. 6, part 1, 241 no. 99; vol. 6, part 2, 122). I owe this reference to Brian Rose.

78. Dorothea Michel, "Bemerkungen über Zuschauerfiguren in pompejanischen sogenannten Tafelbildern," in *La regione sotterrata dal Vesuvio: studi e prospettive*, Atti del Convegno internazionale 11–15 November 1979, ed. Alfonso de Franciscis (Naples, 1982), 537–598.

79. John R. Clarke, "The Decor of the House of Jupiter and Ganymede at Ostia

Antica: Private Residence Turned Gay Hotel?" in *Roman Art: The Private Sphere,* ed. Elaine Gazda (Ann Arbor, 1991), 89–104.

80. Jenifer Neils, personal communication, 1995.

81. Personal communication, December 1995.

82. References to beards are collected in August Mau, "Bart," *Pauly-Wissowa,* vol. 3, cols. 30–34; literary sources attest to three occasions when a Roman male of the first century A.D. would have facial hair: before the *depositio barbae;* as an indication of mourning; on the battlefield. The only bearded Julio-Claudian image conclusively associated with mourning is Caligula in the Louvre: Dietrich Boschung, *Die Bildnisse des Caligula,* Das römische Herrscherbild, part 1, vol. 4 (Berlin, 1989), 87 and 110 no. 13; K. de Kersauson, *Portraits de la République et d'époque Julio-Claudienne,* vol. 1 of *Musée du Louvre: Catalogue des portraits romains* (Paris, 1986), 186 no. 84. Suetonius (*Caligula* 24) notes that the emperor grew a beard following the death of his sister Drusilla. For bearded portraits of Gaius Caesar see John Pollini, *The Portraiture of Gaius and Lucius Caesar* (New York, 1987), 71–75, 91. For the beard in Greek portraits see R. R. R. Smith, *Hellenistic Royal Portraits* (Oxford, 1988). I thank Brian Rose for this reference.

83. Zanker, *Power of Images,* 101–166.

84. Griffin, *Latin Poets,* 18–26; Richlin, *Garden of Priapus,* 34–49; Cantarella, *Bisexuality,* 120–154.

CHAPTER 4

1.

scilicet in domibus vestris [nostris] ut prisca virorum
artificis fulgent corpora picta manu
sic quae concubitus varios venerisque figuras
exprimat, et aliquo parva tabella loco.
utque sedet vultu fassus Telamonius iram,
inque oculis facinus barbara mater habet
sic madidos siccat digitis Venus uda capillos
et modo maternis tecta videtur aquis.

Ovid *Tristia* 2.521–528; my translation in text.

2. Ovid *Ars Amatoria* 2.679–680, 3.771–788; Parker, "Love's Body Anatomized," 95–97; Myerowitz, "The Domestication of Desire," 135–136.

3. "Ad res Venerias intemperantior traditur; nam speculato cubiculo scorta dicitur habuisse disposita, ut quocumque respexisset ibi ei imago coitus referretur" (my translation in text, of Suetonius *De Poetis* 24.62–64). Suetonius emphasizes the act of looking at sex reflected in mirrors rather than represented in art in Horace's bedroom. Mirrors—and by extension the sexual acts they reflect—also figure strongly in the long

diatribe of Seneca the Younger (ca. 4 B.C.–A.D. 65) against a sexually obsessed aristocrat, Hostius Quadra (Seneca [the Younger] *Quaestiones naturales* 1.16).

4. Suetonius *Tiberius* is one of twelve books, beginning with *Julius Caesar* and ending with *Domitian,* known collectively as *De Vita Caesarum.* Robert Graves published an English translation in 1957 under the title *The Twelve Caesars* (Baltimore, Md., 1957). Suetonius inspired Graves's earlier novels, *I, Claudius* (New York, 1934) and *Claudius the God and His Wife Messalina* (New York, 1935).

5. Suetonius *Tiberius* 44: "Cubicula plurifariam disposita tabellis ac sigillis lascivissimarum picturarum et figurarum adornavit librisque Elephantidis instruxit, ne cui in opera edenda exemplar imperatae schemae deesset" (my translation in text).

6. Hendrik G. Beyen ("Les *domini* de la Villa de la Farnesine," *Studia varia Carolo Guilielmo Vollgraff a discipulis oblata* [Amsterdam, 1948], 3–21) attributes the villa to Agrippa and Julia, followed by Peter von Blanckenhagen and Christine Alexander (*The Paintings from Boscotrecase,* Römische Mitteilungen, Supplement 6 [1962]: 60), but Frédéric Bastet and Mariette de Vos (*Proposta per una classificazione del terzo stile pompeiano,* Archeologische Studiën van het Nederlands Instituut te Rome, 4 [The Hague, 1979], 8–9) question the date of the closely related Villa of Agrippa at Boscotrecase, and Robert B. Lloyd ("The Aqua Virgo, Euripus, and Pons Agrippa," *American Journal of Archaeology* 83 [1979]: 193–204) attributes the Villa under the Farnesina to A. Crispinus Caepio.

7. Andrew Wallace-Hadrill, *Houses and Society in Pompeii and Herculaneum* (Princeton, 1994) 17, 58; Andrew M. Riggsby, "'Public' and 'Private' in Roman Culture: The Case of the Cubiculum." *Journal of Roman Archaeology* 10 (1997): 1–20.

8. Mikhail Rostowzew, "A cubiculo, cubicularius," *Pauly-Wissowa,* vol. 4, cols. 1734–1737; see also Sandra Joshel, *Work, Identity, and Legal Status at Rome: A Study of the Occupational Inscriptions* (Norman, Okla., 1992), passim.

9. The drawing reproduced in Julius Lessing and August Mau (*Wand- und Deckenschmuck eines römischen Hauses aus der Zeit des Augustus* [Berlin, 1891], pl. 7) shows this stolen panel, which represented a man and woman alone on a bed. The same plate appears in *Monumenti inediti pubblicati dall'Instituto di corrispondenza archeologica,* vol. 12 (Rome, 1885), pl. 19.

10. The mature Second-Style walls of the Villa of Oplontis (ca. 40 B.C.) include four shuttered paintings: two of landscapes in one reception room (oecus 15, on east wall), two of statues in another (oecus 23, on west wall) (John R. Clarke, "Landscape Paintings in the Villa of Oplontis," *Journal of Roman Archaeology* 9 [1996]: 103–105, cats. 2, 3, 14; figs. 4, 5, 7).

11. Fourth-century Lucanian vase painting seems to reflect the effects of color and shading that artists employed in the panel paintings; see Paolo Moreno, *La pittura greca* (Milan, 1987), 169–198.

12. Karl Schefold, *Pompejanische Malerei: Sinn und Ideengeschichte* (Basel, 1952), 32–34, 167; Karl Schefold, *Vergessenes Pompeji: unveröffentlichte Bilder römischer Wanddekorationen in geschichtlicher Folge herausgegeben* (Munich, 1962), 65, passim; Karl Schefold, *La peinture pompéienne: essai sur l'évolution de sa signification* (Brussels, 1972), 50–52, 232, 241; Clarke, *Houses of Roman Italy,* 55, 367–368; Bettina Bergmann, "The Roman House as Memory Theater," *Art Bulletin* 76 (1994): 225–256; Bettina Bergmann, "Fictions of the Roman Picture Gallery," synopsis in *CAA Abstracts 1995* (New York, 1995), 150–151.

13. Wolfgang Helbig, "Musaici di Centocelle," *Bullettino dell'Instituto di corrispondenza archeologica* (1866): 170–173; Gerhard Rodenwaldt, "Mosaik in Wiener Hofmuseum," *Römische Mitteilungen* 25 (1910): 256–262; Ludwig Curtius, *Die Wandmalerei Pompejis* (Leipzig, 1929), 112–113 fig. 69. The mosaic was found in an ancient Roman villa at Centocelle on the via Labicana; it measures W 39.7 cm × H 38.6 cm.

14. Helbig and Rodenwaldt identify the statue on a base as Dionysus; Curtius, as Artemis.

15. This evidence recently reviewed, with the addition of a newly discovered painting in the House of the Chaste Lovers at Pompeii: Varone, "Scavi recenti a Pompei," 617–640; sixteen articles from the symposium "Mani di pittori e botteghe pittoriche nel mondo romano: tavola rotonda in onore di W. J. Th. Peters in occasione del suo 75.mo compleanno" (Dutch School, Rome 16–17 May 1994), Eric M. Moormann, ed., *Mededelingen van het Nederlands Instituut te Rome* 54 (1995): 61–298.

16. W. Ehlich, "Cornice," *Enciclopedia dell'arte antica,* 2:859.

17. Bartolomeo Nogara, *Le Nozze Aldobrandine* (Milan, 1907), 1–25; Nogara cites dating by August Mau to the early Augustan period; Frank G. J. M. Müller, *The Aldobrandini Wedding* (Amsterdam, 1994).

18. Bernard Andreae, "Stuckreliefs und Fresken der Farnesina," in Wolfgang Helbig, *Führer durch den öffentlichen Sammlungen Roms,* ed. Hermione Speier, 4th ed. (Tübingen, 1969), 3:448.

19. Licia Vlad Borelli, "Nozze Aldobrandini," *Enciclopedia dell'arte antica,* 5:569–570, with bibl.

20. Catullus 61.169–171; Propertius 4.3.29–30, 55–56; Martial 10.35, 38. I thank Andrew Riggsby for these references.

21. Andreae, "Farnesina," 3:440; followed by Bragantini in Irene Bragantini and Mariette de Vos, *Le decorazioni della villa romana della Farnesina,* vol. 2, part 1 of *Museo Nazionale Romano: Le pitture* (Rome, 1982), 286.

22. Ranuccio Bianchi-Bandinelli, *Rome: The Center of Power,* trans. Peter Green (New York, 1970), 121, followed by Paolo Moreno, "Seleukos 3°," *Enciclopedia dell'arte antica,* 7:175.

23. Bragantini and de Vos, *Farnesina,* 22–23.

24. Brendel, "Erotic Art," 58–59.

25. Cicero *Epistulae ad Familiares* 9.22 discussed in Richlin, *Garden of Priapus,* 18–26.

26. The old inventory number of "Warren h" is Boston Museum of Fine Arts, Res 08.33h; the new inventory number is Res 08.3314.

27. The female authorship of the sex manuals is highly dubious, as discussed in chapter 8, 240–250.

28. The situation described in Petronius *Satyricon* 63, 69, 75; see in general J. Kolendo, "L'esclavage et la vie sexuelle des hommes libres à Rome," *Index* 10 (1981): 288–297.

CHAPTER 5

1. For an earlier version of the first part of this chapter, on the *Aethiops* bath attendant, see John R. Clarke, "Hypersexual Black Men in Augustan Baths: Ideal Somatotypes and Apotropaic Magic," in *Sexuality in Ancient Art,* ed. Natalie B. Kampen (New York, 1996), 184–198.

2. The conventional address system for locating all buildings at Pompeii and Ostia Antica consists of three numbers: the region (Latin *regio*) in Roman numerals (there are nine at Pompeii), followed by the city-block or *insula* in Arabic numerals, followed by the number of its entrance(s) on that insula. Some buildings also have names based on some feature or the name of its owner. Thus I, 6, 2 is the house in region I, city-block 6, with its doorway at number 2, called the House of the Cryptoporticus because of its elaborate *cryptoporticus,* or underground vaulted corridor. Erich Pernice, *Pavimente und figürliche Mosaiken* (Berlin, 1938), 54, later Second Style; John R. Clarke, *Roman Black-and-White Figural Mosaics* (New York, 1979), 61, 30–10 B.C.; John R. Clarke, "The Origins of Black-and-White Figural Mosaics in the Region Destroyed by Vesuvius," in *La regione sotterrata dal Vesuvio: studi e prospettive,* Atti del Convegno internazionale 11–15 November 1979, ed. Alfonso de Franciscis (Naples 1982), 669 n. 28; Nathalie de Haan, "Dekoration und Funktion in den Privatbädern von Pompeji und Herculaneum," *Bulletin Antieke Beschaving,* suppl. 3, *Functional and Spatial Analysis of Wall Painting* (proceedings of the Fifth International Congress on Ancient Wall Painting, Amsterdam, 8–12 September 1992), ed. Eric M. Moormann (1993): 34–37.

3. Arnold de Vos and Mariette de Vos, *Pompei Ercolano Stabia,* Guida archeologica Laterza, no. 11 (Rome, 1982), 332–333.

4. Vittorio Spinazzola (*Pompei alla luce degli scavi nuovi di via dell'Abbonzanda* [Rome, 1953], 1:437 and 571) attributes ownership of the House of the Cryptoporticus to one of the branches of the *gens* (clan) Valeria, probably the Valerii Rufi, yet this name does

not appear in Castrén's list (Paavo Castrén, *Ordo Populusque Pompeianus: Polity and Society in Roman Pompeii* [Rome, 1975], 233). Maiuri (*Casa del Menandro,* 1:20–21) concludes that the bronze seal found in the *procurator*'s quarters with the name Q(VINTI) POPPAEI EROTIS identifies the owner of the House of the Menander as Q. Poppaeus, of the powerful *gens* Poppaea; Q. Poppaeus was aedile in A.D. 39–40 (?) (Castrén, *Ordo,* 209). If the four graffiti, three on columns of the peristyle and a fourth on the south wall of the shoemaker's shop dependent on the house, identify the owner of the house at VII, 1, 40 as belonging to Marcus Caesius Blandus, he was not of the decurion class but merely a centurion of the ninth praetorian cohort: see Amedeo Maiuri, *Pompei* (Rome, 1934), 51; Matteo Della Corte, *Case ed abitanti di Pompei,* 3d ed. (Naples, 1965), nos. 78, 305, and 354; Castrén, *Ordo,* 146.

5. For this motif before its destruction see Pernice, *Mosaiken,* 54 pl. 20, 1.

6. Clarke, "Origins," 669–670 fig. 12.

7. John R. Clarke, "Mosaic Workshops at Pompeii and Ostia Antica," in *Fifth International Colloquium on Ancient Mosaics,* Bath, England, 5–12 September 1987, ed. Peter Johnson, Roger Ling, and David J. Smith (Ann Arbor, 1994), 91–98 figs. 3–6.

8. The mythical sea dragon (*ketos*) appears on the "Tellus/Italia/Venus" panel of the Ara Pacis to represent the sea; see Diana E. E. Kleiner, *Roman Sculpture* (New Haven, 1992), 96–97, with bibl. 119. Ancient Roman viewers might see the mosaic representation of the black male spearing the *ketos* with a trident as a burlesque of Perseus dispatching it with his sword. Such a parody would parallel the painted caricatures of the exploits of the gods painted on the walls of the *atriolo* of the House of the Menander baths. See Clarke, *Houses of Roman Italy,* 185–187. I owe this observation to Ann Kuttner.

9. Maiuri, *Casa del Menandro,* 1:146.

10. Spinazzola, *Pompei,* 1:462–466 figs. 531–532; de Haan ("Dekoration und Funktion," 35) correctly points out that these are black men, not pygmies.

11. The Gargamantes of the Fezzan are "black warriors" for some modern scholars, even though ancient texts distinguish them from *Aethiops* as they do for Moors (Lloyd A. Thompson, *Romans and Blacks* [Norman, Okla., 1989], 50–51).

12. For the iconography of the pygmy in Greek myth see Veronique Dasen, *Dwarfs in Ancient Egypt and Greece* (Oxford, 1993), 182–191.

13. In the most comprehensive study of the image of the black in antiquity by Jean Vercoutter, Jean Leclant, Frank M. Snowden, Jr., and Jehan Desanges, *From the Pharaohs to the Fall of the Roman Empire,* vol. 1 of *The Image of the Black in Western Art* (New York, 1976); see also Frank M. Snowden, Jr., *Blacks in Antiquity* (Cambridge, Mass., 1970).

14. Clarke, *Mosaics,* 58–62.

15. Tightly curled, frizzy, or corkscrew hair is a visual signifier for so-called Ne-

groid features in both public and private art, portraits, and personifications such as *Africa* and *Libya*): see Rolf M. Schneider, *Bunte Barbaren: Orientalenstatuen aus farbigem Marmor in der römischen Repräsentationskunst* (Worms, 1986), esp. pls. 42–44; see also Vercoutter et al., *From the Pharaohs,* passim.

16. Suzanne Germain, *Les mosaïques de Timgad: étude descriptive et analytique* (Paris, 1969), 94 no. 129 pl. 42, Musée de Timgad inv. 89. Precise dating is impossible because the building was never fully excavated. For color illustration see Vercoutter et al., *From the Pharaohs,* 256 fig. 347.

17. Thompson, *Romans and Blacks,* 16–17; see also Jehan Desanges, review of *Romans and Blacks,* by Lloyd A. Thompson, *Révue des études latines* 68 (1990): 233; see also below, note 41.

18. Thompson, *Romans and Blacks,* 35–36.

19. Juvenal 2.21–28, 6.597–602; Martial 6.39.1–9.

20. See Nikolaus Himmelmann, *Alexandria und der Realismus in der griechischen Kunst* (Tübingen, 1983), esp. pls. 14, 18, 22 c–d, 23 b, 33 a, 50 a, c–d, 51, a–d, 52, 61; Luca Giuliani, "Der seligen Krüppel: zur Deutung von Mißgestalten in der hellenistischen Kleinkunst," *Archäologische Anzeiger* 102 (1987): 701–721.

21. Cèbe, *Caricature,* 351 and n. 9, 354.

22. Brendel, "Erotic Art," 50–51.

23. Thompson, *Romans and Blacks,* 107.

24. Philostratus *Vita Apollonii* 3.11; *Vitae Sophistarum* 2.558.

25. De Haan, "Dekoration und Funktion," 35 n. 6 points out that six centuries later Sidonius Apollinaris (*Epistulae* 2.6) provides evidence that nude images of wrestlers and athletes were still the rule, although, he boasts, not in his bath.

26. See Clarke (*Houses of Roman Italy,* 170–193) for construction history and possible ownership.

27. Janet DeLaine, "Recent Research on Roman Baths," *Journal of Roman Archaeology* 1 (1988): 11–32; Inge Nielsen, *Thermae et Balnea: The Architecture and Cultural History of Roman Public Baths,* 2 vols. (Aarhus, 1990); Fikret K. Yegül, *Baths and Bathing in Classical Antiquity* (New York, 1992).

28. Dunbabin, "Baths," 33–43.

29. J. Hellegouarch, *Le vocabulaire latin des relations et des partis politiques sous la république* (Paris, 1972), 195–199.

30. M. W. Dickie and Katherine M. D. Dunbabin, "*Invidia rumpantur pectora:* The Iconography of Phthonos/Invidia in Graeco-Roman Art," *Jahrbuch für Antike und Christentum* 26 (1983): 10–11.

31. Dunbabin, "Baths," 35–37.

32. Dunbabin ("Baths," 37–38) notes that although in North Africa there are many

instances of apotropaic images, it would be a mistake to think that the majority of those who constructed baths were so conscious of the danger of bath demons or hostile magic that they needed to introduce some permanent protection into the decoration.

33. Carlin A. Barton, *The Sorrows of the Ancient Romans: The Gladiator and the Monster* (Princeton, 1993), 171–172: "There were places and points of passage where one was especially vulnerable: corners, bridges, baths, doorways. The 'liminal' areas were highly charged, dangerous."

34. Dunbabin, "Baths," 42–44; these are the examples from Roman Africa: Timgad, North-West baths, threshold between two heated rooms, *Aethiops* with fire shovel, A.D. 200 pl. 15a; Kharba/Oued Atmenia baths, threshold, black grotesque with huge head, hooked nose, hump on shoulder, three large phalluses, pl. 15b; Thuburbo Maius, Labyrinth Baths, threshold between *caldarium* and *tepidarium,* nude man striding to right; Bir Chana, provenance unknown, nude black slave carrying fire shovel; Cherchel, Volto Baths, nearly nude man carrying "un objet allongé (balai?)" wearing a collar.

35. Dunbabin ("Baths," 43–44) does not distinguish between the macrophallic bath attendant and the ithyphallic swimmers, here treated separately.

36. Doro Levi, "The Evil Eye and the Lucky Hunchback," in *Antioch-on-the-Orontes,* ed. Richard Stillwell (Princeton, 1941), 3:225. Giuliani ("Der seligen Krüppel," 701–721) sees images of physically deformed people less as charms against the Evil Eye than as vehicles to remind people of their own good fortune and well being.

37. Barton, *Sorrows of the Ancient Romans,* 168–172, with a good review of ancient texts, but, curiously, no mention of the modern works of classical scholarship studies.

38. The Romans believed that the image of phallus warded off the Evil Eye. It could appear alone, as in the threshold of the House of Jupiter the Thunderer at Ostia Antica (Giovanni Becatti, *Mosaici e pavimenti marmorei* [Rome, 1961], 185 no. 344, pl. 12) or it could be attached to a human figure. Often the phallus is that of the hunchback, also considered to be a protection against the evil eye; see Levi ("Evil Eye," 220–232) for full discussion of this iconography. In the entryway to the House of Evil Eye at Antioch, the hunchback is not an *Aethiops.* The square containing the hunchback mosaic was accompanied by another square containing the image of the infant Hercules strangling the serpents; both mosaics adorned a vestibule and dated to before 115. Levi compares the hunchback directly with the mosaic of the bath boy from the House of Menander. Later the owner superimposed another apotropaic mosaic, that of the Evil Eye, upon the mosaics of Hercules and of the hunchback to increase its prophylactic value (Doro Levi, *Antioch Mosaic Pavements* [Princeton, 1947], 1:32–34). See also Dunbabin, "Baths," 37–46.

39. Thompson, *Romans and Blacks,* 179 n. 32.

40. Grace Beardsley, *The Negro in Greek and Roman Civilization: A Study of the*

Ethiopian Type (1929; New York, 1967), 117; the passage from *Rhetorica ad Herennium* 4.50.63 reads: "ab avunculo rogetur Aethiops qui ad balneas veniat."

41. See Snowden's discussion (*Blacks,* 2–3, 172–174) of the evidence for this environmental theory of color in Greek and Roman texts.

42. Mariette de Vos, "Camillo Paderni, la tradizione antiquaria romana e i collezionisti inglesi," in *Ercolano 1738–1988: 250 anni di ricerca archeologica,* Atti del Convegno internazionale Ravello-Ercolano-Napoli-Pompei, 30 October–5 November 1988, ed. Luisa Franchi dell'Orto (Rome, 1993), 108–109 pls. 21, 1–2, and 22; Mariette de Vos, "Paving Techniques at Pompeii," *Archaeological News* 16, nos. 1–4 (1991): 36 and n. 1 figs. 1–4. De Vos believes that the figure represents Iulia Felix's bath slave, who figures in one of the electoral notices on the facade of the Praedia (*Corpus Inscriptionum Latinarum* 4.1150). Another mosaic of a bath attendant with a fire shovel, found in Spoleto, has no clear archaeological context. The genitals are prominent but, since the head is missing, it is impossible to identify his racial type. On the basis of style I date the Spoleto mosaic to A.D. 180–220; see de Vos, "Paving Techniques," fig. 3 (Deutsches Archäologisches Institut, Rome, inst. neg. 59.1610).

43. Beneath every bath, large or small, workers fed wood to the furnaces that heated floors, walls, and water. The shovel, whether square, as here, or heart-shaped, was indispensable and became a widespread symbol of heat, most clearly revealed in the mosaics of the Mithraeum of Felicissimus at Ostia Antica (third century A.D.), where the fire shovel appears with lightning bolt and sistrum to symbolize Leo, the (fire) sign of the Zodiac and the fourth stage in the seven-step initiation into the cult of Mithras (Giovanni Becatti, *I mitrei* [Rome, 1954], 109–110 pl. 25, 4); see also the figure of Leo from the Mithraeum of the Animals with fire shovel and sickle (88 pl. 18, 1).

44. De Vos, "Paving Techniques," 50–52 fig. 22; the mosaic is at the entrance to *caldarium* 21. For an overview of the iconography, see Katherine M. D. Dunbabin, "*Ipsa deae vestigia* . . . Footprints Divine and Human on Graeco-Roman Monuments," *Journal of Roman Archaeology* 3 (1990): 99–102; de Haan ("Dekoration und Funktion," 36) notes that a sandal also appears on the floor of the *tepidarium* of the House of Caesius Blandus.

45. Approximate date, A.D. 200. Dunbabin ("Baths," 41–42 pl. 4a) points out that only some of the thirteen examples of pairs of sandals or footprints are practical warnings.

46. Thompson, *Romans and Blacks,* 26–38, with references to ancient and modern sources.

47. Plutarch *Vitae Parallelae, Brutus* 48.2; Appian *Bella Civilia* 4.17.134; Scriptores Historiae Augustae, *Alexander Severus* 22.4–5.

48. Johns, *Sex or Symbol,* 61–75; for the apotropaic *terminus,* see the *Priapea,* passim.

49. I owe this observation and reference to Anthony Corbeill. Illustrated in United

Nations Educational Scientific and Cultural Organization, *Tunisia: Ancient Mosaics* (New York, 1962), pl. 21. The inscription O CHARI is of uncertain meaning: "Oh delight"; an abbreviation of Charidotes (an ephithet of Zeus, Bacchus, or Hermes); an invocation of *charismion,* a famous aphrodisiac, 17.

50. That he is urinating rather than ejaculating, as Dunbabin asserts ("Baths," 42), is clear from the downward angle of the phallus/penis and the steadiness of the stream it produces.

51. Note the parallel with the popular Roman image of *Hercules mingens.*

52. The figure of Buticosus also shares with the House of the Menander bath attendant the function of directing the viewer to the most important doorway; the *Aethiops* with his left-to-right stride, Buticosus with his "directional" erection, pointing to the viewer's right. See Clarke, *Mosaics,* 25–26 figs. 28 and 30. For bath attendant of the Severan period at Ostia, see Becatti, *Mosaici,* 227, 350–351 pl. 109, no. 270; and Clarke, *Mosaics,* 90 fig. 22.

53. The cognomen Buticosus does not occur elsewhere. Anthony Corbeill suggests that it is Greek and may be a pun on the Greek verb *buo,* "to stuff"; *butikos* would then mean "involved in stuffing," and the Latin suffix *-osus* could give the meaning "the big stuffer" and designate a person (imaginary or real) renowned for the size of his penis.

54. Dover, *Greek Homosexuality,* 125–135.

55. Scriptores Historiae Augustae, *Heliogabalus* 8.6, 12.3, 26.5; different accounts in Dio Cassius *Historia Romana* 80.6, 80.14, 80.15.4; Herodian *Historiae* 5.3.7, 5.8.1.

56. Thompson, *Romans and Blacks,* 107–109, 210 n. 84.

57. Maiuri, *Casa del Menandro,* 1:84–85 fig. 42 on 87; John R. Clarke, "Form, Function, and Meaning of *Symplegmata* in Pompeian Mosaics: The Case for the 'Domestication' of Sex," in *Actes du VIIe Colloque international pour l'étude de la mosaïque antique,* Tunis 3–7 October 1994, ed. Mongi Ennaifer (forthcoming).

58. Comparison of these early Silhouette-Style images of swimmers with polychrome mosaics that represent water reveals how much the mosaicist simplified his task by using this trope. Whereas in polychrome marine mosaics the artist must represent bodies half above the water and half below it by creating "transparent" waves, here the viewer must imagine the watery setting. See Clarke, *Mosaics,* 59.

59. Clarke ("Origins," 669) details modern restorations to these features by comparing the photograph in Pernice (*Mosaiken,* pl. 20, 3), taken in the 1930s, with another taken in 1979.

60. Jean-Pierre Adam and Pierre Varène ("Une peinture romaine représentant un scène de chantier," *Revue archéologique* 2 [1980]: 235–236 fig. 19) show a relief from Pompeii with two men carrying an amphora suspended from a pole by cords wound around the handles.

61. Similar amphoras could also contain water, vinegar, oil, must, honey, or fish sauce (Staatliche Museen Preußischer Kulturbesitz, *Römisches im Antikenmuseum* [Berlin, 1978], 153–154).

62. A. Alfonsi, "Este: Scoperta di un pavimento a mosaico," *Notizie degli scavi* (1911): 313–315 fig. 1. The figural panel, at the entrance to a room about 11 × 7 m, is 2.07 × 0.67 m; the dolphins are 0.35 m in length; the crater is 0.38 m high. Marion E. Blake, "The Pavements of the Roman Buildings of the Republic and Early Empire," *Memoirs of the American Academy in Rome* 8 (1930): 80 and 123 pl. 48, 3; Clarke, "Origins," 670 fig. 7.

63. Pernice, *Mosaiken,* pl. 20, 1.

64. Constantine, Musée Gustave Mercier, illustrated in Vercoutter et al., *From the Pharaohs,* figs. 355 and 356.

65. André Berthier ("Une mosaïque solaire trouvée à Constantine," *Mélanges Carcopino* [1966]: 113–124) proposes that the panel with the swimming black men symbolizes the dawn; the eagle in the center of the squameate roundel would be the zenith and in the panel with two ships meeting, the diving bull would symbolize the sunset. Berthier incorrectly dates the mosaic to the second or third century A.D. In Vercoutter et al. (*From the Pharaohs,* 260 figs. 356 and 357) Jehan Desanges repeats Berthier's interpretation. Gilbert-Charles Picard ("Une mosaïque pompéienne à Constantine et l'installation des Sittii à Cirta," *Revue archéologique* [1980]: 185–187) provides a much looser interpretation, seeing the swimmers as alluding to the heat of the room, suspended on hypocausts, and to water. For him the diving bull on the prow of the ship is simply a fantastic figurehead. He dates the mosaic to the period 50–30 B.C.

66. Clarke, "Origins," 666–667.

67. Kurt Weitzmann, *Illustrations in Roll and Codex* (Princeton, 1947), 23–24, 32.

68. Richard Brilliant, *Visual Narratives* (Ithaca, 1984), 53–89.

69. Anna Sadurska, *Les tables iliaques* (Warsaw, 1964); G. Karl Galinsky, *Aeneas, Sicily, and Rome* (Princeton, 1969), 3–61; Nicholas Horsfall, "Stesichorus at Bovillae," *Journal of Hellenic Studies* 99 (1979): 26–48.

70. Katherine M. D. Dunbabin, "Sic Erimus Cuncti . . . The Skeleton in Graeco-Roman Art," *Jahrbuch des deutschen archäologischen Instituts* 101 (1986): 223–224, pl. 35, brown sard, Berlin, Antikenmuseum, SMPK inv. FG 6518; see also pl. 34, a chalcedony in the Kestner-Museum, Hanover, showing a single skeleton leaning on amphora and serving wine, inv. K. 1038.

71. Maiuri, *Casa del Menandro,* 152–158 figs. 72–75; Pernice, *Mosaiken,* 59–60; Clarke, *Mosaics,* 13–15, 26, 59–63; Eric M. Moormann, *La pittura parietale romana come fonte di conoscenza per la scultura antica* (Assen, 1988), 153–154.

72. Clarke, *Houses of Roman Italy,* 185–187; caricature of the Aeneas group in the

Forum of Augustus from a villa at Stabiae: Zanker, *Power of Images,* 208–210 fig. 162; see also Cèbe, *Caricature,* passim.

73. Mariette de Vos, *L'egittomania in pitture e mosaici romano-campani della prima età imperiale,* Etudes préliminaires aux religions orientales dans l'empire romain, no. 84 (Leyden, 1980); Bragantini and de Vos, *Farnesina,* 30–31.

CHAPTER 6

1. See Ovid's text in note 1, chapter 4.

2. In 1819, at the suggestion of Francis I, duke of Calabria and future king of Naples, the curator isolated 102 objects that were potentially offensive to the morality of the period. Access to this room varied over time. Today, with many more objects housed within its cramped space, a special permit from the director of the museum is necessary. For a brief history of the collection, see Antonio De Simone, "The History of the Museum and the Collection," in *Eros in Pompeii,* by Michael Grant (New York, 1975), 168–169. For the parallel history of the Museum Secretum of the British Museum, see Johns, *Sex or Symbol,* 15–35.

3. Matteo Della Corte, "Pompei: Reg. I, ins. IX, n. 1," *Notizie degli scavi* (1913): 34–35; Valeria Sampaolo, "I 9, 1: Casa del Bell'Impluvio," in *Pompei, pitture e mosaici* (Rome, 1990), 1:919–920, with bibl.

4. For a review of the dating see Eric M. Moormann, "Giardini ed altre pitture nella Casa del Frutteto e nella Casa del Bracciale d'Oro a Pompei," *Mededelingen van het Nederlands Instituut te Rome* 54 (1995): 223.

5. For further information on the Third Style, with relevant bibliography, see Clarke, *Houses of Roman Italy,* 54–65, 125–163.

6. Naples, Museo nazionale, inv. 110569.

7. Jean P. Andreau, *Les affaires de Monsieur Jucundus* (Rome, 1974), 25–32.

8. Willem Jongman, *The Economy and Society of Pompeii* (Amsterdam, 1988), 219–220. Since the inscription gives only the patron's first name (*praenomen*) and omits his middle name (*nomen,* which tells us his *gens*) and last name (*cognomen*), we cannot be sure that Lucius was a Caecilius. Slaves took their former master's names when freed.

9. For details of the activities of these adventurers, whose tunnels left numerous holes in the walls at various heights, see Arnold de Vos, "V 1, 26: Casa di L. Caecilius Iucundus e Casa annessa V 1, 23," in *Pompei, pitture e mosaici,* regiones II–III–V (Rome, 1991), 3:576.

10. See especially Caroline E. Dexter, "The Casa di L. Cecilio Giocondo in Pompeii" (Ph.D. diss., Duke University, 1975), and more recently de Vos, "Casa di L. Caecilius Iucundus," 574–620, with bibl. 577.

11. Heinrich Drerup, "Bildraum und Realraum in der römischen Architektur," *Römische Mitteilungen* 66 (1959): 147–174.

12. Doors near the entryway to triclinium *o* allowed direct communication with the cubicula to either side.

13. Vitruvius *De Architectura* 6.4.1–2.

14. August Mau, *Bullettino dell'Instituto di corrispondenza archeologica* (1876): 149–151, 161–168, 223–232, 241–242, with nos. 38–41 describing the paintings of the garden area (*viridarium*) enclosed by the peristyle.

15. Some of the main features, including two paintings removed from the walls and taken to the Naples Museum: Room *t,* middle of north (entryway) wall, Hermaphroditus and Silenus (Naples inv. 111213); west (left) wall, Narcissus; south (back) wall, Mars and Venus (Naples inv. 111214); tondi of a woman and a bust of a satyr. Garden area *l,* south wall, divided into three parts: in the middle a *paradeisos,* lion and deer attacked by a tiger; on the sides representations of gardens with nymph-fountains; above a frieze with battleships (Mau, *Bullettino dell'Instituto* [1876]: 231–232; Moormann, *Pittura parietale,* 164, cat. 186/2; Wilhelmina Jashemski, *Gardens of Pompeii* [New Rochelle, N.J., 1979–1993], 2:384–385).

16. Emil Presuhn, *Die pompejanische Wanddekorationen für Künstler und Kunstgewerbtreibende* (2d ed. Leipzig, 1882), reprinted in de Vos, "Casa di L. Caecilius Iucundus," 613 pl. 75.

17. De Vos, "Casa di L. Caecilius Iucundus," 609.

18. Naples, Archaeological Museum, inv. 115396, illustrated in de Vos, "Casa di L. Caecilius Iucundus," fig. 74.

19. Mau, *Bullettino dell'Instituto* (1876): 226.

20. Amedeo Maiuri, *La villa dei misteri* (Rome, 1931), pl. B.

21. Andrea Carandini, *Settefinestre: una villa schiavistica nell'Etruria romana* (Modena, 1985), 1:153, plan naming the rooms; vol. 2, numbered plan: the three double-alcove bedrooms are at 3, 25, and 55; they adjoin oeci 2, 23, and 51 respectively. Other interconnected suites with cubicula that have a single alcove are 10–11, 21–29, 45–46, 34–35. There is also a large main suite with a large Corinthian oecus (30) at its center, with rooms 28, 29 and 21 adjoining it.

22. Wallace-Hadrill, *Houses and Society,* 55.

23. Wallace-Hadrill, *Houses and Society,* 17 n. 2. Riggsby ("Role of the Cubiculum") greatly expands and refines Wallace-Hadrill's observations through analysis of all four hundred occurrences of the word in Latin literature. He concludes that Romans used the cubiculum for six purposes: rest, sex, adultery, display of art, murder and suicide, and reception.

24. Naples inv. 111214.

25. This is the unsubstantiated conclusion of de Vos, "Casa di L. Caecilius Iucundus," 575.

26. Paul Zanker, "Die Villa als Vorbild des späten pompejanischen Wohngeschmacks," *Jahrbuch des Deutschen Archäologischen Instituts* 94 (1979): 460–523.

27. On paintings of wild-animal parks, see W. J. Th. Peters, *La casa di Marcus Lucretius Fronto e le sue pitture* (Amsterdam, 1993), 348.

28. Trimalchio was not a "typical" freedman, since he had inherited his dead patron's estate; see John H. D'Arms, *Commerce and Social Standing in Ancient Rome* (Cambridge, Mass., 1981), 97–120. Jean P. Andreau ("The Freedman," in *The Romans,* ed. Andrea Giardina, trans. Lydia G. Cochrane [Chicago, 1993], 175–198) defines the social status of the *libertus* from texts; see also G. Fabré, *Libertus: recherche sur les rapports patron-affranchi à la fin de la république romain* (Rome, 1981).

29. Dexter ("Casa di L. Cecilio Giocondo," 150), who calls it a *camera d'amore,* says she is following Richardson in attributing its "three erotic scenes" as well as the three pictures in room 42 to his Iphigenia painter. Unfortunately she gives no reference for Richardson's attributions, and there are only *two* paintings of lovemaking in room 43. Volker Michael Strocka (*Casa del Laberinto [VI 11, 8–10]: Häuser in Pompeji* [Munich, 1991], 4:92) uses equally impressionistic reasons for calling rooms 42 and 46 of the House of the Labyrinth *Liebesnester* (love nests), a notion that Eric M. Moormann also rejects in his review of Strocka in *Gnomon* 66 (1994): 174.

30. De Vos and Vos, *Pompei Ercolano Stabia,* 213.

31. Bragantini et al., *Pitture e pavimenti,* 3:530–531 with bibl.

32. Wallace-Hadrill, *Houses and Society,* 118: "The Roman house was no island of privacy, protected by watertight barriers against the world of public life outside. It was porous, constantly penetrated by the outside world; and from its ability to control and exploit this penetration it drew power, status, and profit." Annapaola Zaccaria Ruggiu (*Spazio privato e spazio pubblico nella città romana,* Collection de l'Ecole française de Rome, no. 210 [Rome, 1995], 397–409) underscores the gradient of "privacy" for the different uses of the cubiculum. Riggsby ("Role of the Cubiculum") maintains that the cubiculum is a place of secrecy that has a special role in the properly *Roman* distinctions between public and private.

33. Clarke, *Houses of Roman Italy,* 19–22; Bettina Bergmann, "Painted Perspectives of a Villa Visit," in *Roman Art in the Private Sphere,* ed. Elaine Gazda (Ann Arbor, 1991), 49–70.

34. Rome, Palazzo dei Conservatori, *Bellezza e seduzione,* 99, cat. 145, color photo fig. 35; Antiquarium Comunale inv. 13694.

35. Excavation reports: August Mau, "Scavi di Pompei, 1894–95, Regione VI, Isola ad E della 11," *Römische Mitteilungen* 11 (1896): 3–97; Antonio Sogliano, "La casa dei

Vettii in Pompei," *Monumenti antichi dell'Accademia dei Lincei* 8 (1898): cols. 233–416, with careful descriptions of decoration and sculpture; Clarke, *Houses of Roman Italy,* 208–235; Valeria Sampaolo, "VI 15, 1: Casa dei Vettii," *Pompei, pitture e mosaici,* vol. 5 (Rome, 1994), 468–572, with bibl. 470.

36. Steven E. Ostrow, "*Augustales* along the Bay of Naples: A Case for Their Early Growth," *Historia* 334 (1985): 64–101.

37. The indentations in the walls of oecus *q,* found empty at the time of excavation, were for large central pictures on wood panels.

38. De Vos and de Vos, *Pompei Ercolano Stabia,* 170.

39. Mau, "Scavi di Pompei 1894–95," 30.

40. The graffito found next to the entrance to the upper story of the Suburban Baths records the highest price yet known at Pompeii, 16 asses (equal to 1 denarius): "Si quis hic sederit, legat hoc ante omnia. Si qui futuere voluit, Atticen quaerat a(ssibus) XVI" (*Corpus Inscriptionum Latinarum* 4.1751; cf. Della Corte, *Case ed abitanti,* 442 no. 995); the same price, one denarius, is what Arphocras paid for Drauca's services: "Arphocras hic cum Drauca / bene futuit denario" (*Corpus Inscriptionum Latinarum* 4.2193). See also Antonio Varone (*Erotica pompeiana: iscrizioni d'amore sui muri di Pompei* [Rome, 1994], 134–144) for discussion of the prices noted in the graffiti. A relief of the Augustan period from Isernia that must have served as a shop sign has a traveler paying 8 asses for a woman (Angelo Viti, "*Ad Calidium:* l'insegna del piacere nel rilievo di Lucio Calidio Erotico: saggio epigrafico con note critico-bibliografiche," *Almanacco del Molise* 2 [1989]: 115–135).

41. Pollitt, *Hellenistic Age,* 149.

42. Labeled incorrectly as "Pan" in Clarke, *Houses of Roman Italy,* fig. 123.

43. Petronius *Satyricon* 41 (manumission), 49 (specifically the cook), 54 (manumission), 64 (slave boy riding his master). It is worth noting that these displays of generosity are gestures of power, not of fellow-feeling for his slaves.

44. Antonio Sogliano, *Notizie degli scavi* (1878): 180–184.

45. Mau, *Bullettino dell'Instituto* (1879): 209–210.

46. Arnold de Vos, "I 7, 11: Casa dell'Efebo o di P. Cornelius Tages," in *Pompei, pitture e mosaici* (Rome, 1990), 1:727 color pl.

47. In Scene VII of the Suburban Baths one of the men uses a similar hailing gesture while looking out at the viewer, signaling his pleasure and victory in lovemaking (see Pl. 15).

48. National Museum Naples, inv. 111440: Antonio Sogliano ("Le pitture murali campane scoverte negli anni 1867–1879" in *Pompei e la regione sotterrata dal Vesuvio nell'anno LXXIX* [Naples, 1879], 160–161 no. 842) described this fragment but did not recognize it as Medea. Mau (*Bullettino dell'Instituto* [1879]: 209–210, 266 no. 41 [d],

"Medea"), along with Paul Herrmann and F. Bruckmann (*Denkmäler der Malerei des Altertums* [Munich, 1904-1931], ser. 1, 97 pl. 74b), recognize this fragment as a copy of the picture of Medea from the adjoining House of Jason (IX, 5, 18) cubiculum e, pl. 73.

49. Mau, *Bullettino dell'Instituto* (1879): 209–210, 267 nos. 46–54 (c).

50. Mau's description of the impluvium-planter: "The impluvium of this atrium is a basin (1.85 × 1.40) surrounded by a little wall, exterior height 0.35, interior 0.52, width about 0.47, which on its surface has a cavity to plant flowers in. It is covered with red plaster" (Mau, *Bullettino dell'Instituto* [1879]: 207); further description of pygmies on interior sides of impluvium podium: "West side: two armed pygmies, one of which battles a crocodile, the other follows a hippopotamus; north side, boat with two pygmies, man and woman, united in an obscene group; another pygmy, riding on the stern and armed with a javelin appears frightened at the sight of a crocodile following the boat. East side: two armed pygmies fighting in the presence of a woman with a harp in her hands, with an ibis nearby. South side: two aquatic birds" (265–266).

51. Antonio Sogliano, *Notizie degli scavi* (1878): 184.

52. Mau (*Bullettino dell'Instituto* [1879]: 210) reports on the few objects that he saw during his visit: a few bronze vases, one of which was a measure, terra-cottas, and three lamps.

53. Adele Lagi, "I 13, 16," in *Pompei, pitture e mosaici* (Rome, 1990), 2:928–934; Jashemski, *Gardens,* 1:128 fig. 202; Irene Bragantini, Franca Parise Badoni, and Mariette de Vos, *Pompei 1748–1980: i tempi della documentazione,* exh. cat. (Rome, 1981), 160 fig. 16; Jashemski, *Gardens,* 2:58 no. 29 with fig. 67.

54. Vitruvius *De Architectura* 2.8.20; Clarke, *Houses of Roman Italy,* 257–263.

55. Moormann, *Pittura parietale,* 156–157, cat. 173.

56. Aug. Hug., "Triclinium," *Pauly-Wissowa,* series 3, vol. 7A, part 1: cols. 92–101; and August Mau, "Convivium," *Pauly-Wissowa,* vol. 14, cols. 1201–1208. Seen from the room's entrance, the couch on the right was the *summus,* that against the back wall the *medius,* and that on the left wall the *imus.* Upper-class Romans dined like the Greeks, reclining on these couches while supporting themselves on their left elbows, so that the most desirable place, both for its convenience and view out of the space, would be on the central couch, at the left. The guest of honor received this *locus consularis* (the consular place, *imus in medio*), and the host reclined to his right (*summus in imo*). The boorish host Trimalchio reverses the rules and sits *summus in summo* (Petronius Arbiter, *Cena Trimalchionis,* ed. Martin S. Smith [Oxford, 1975], 66–67, commentary on ch. 31, 8).

57. Martial 5.70.

58. On the miniaturization of the features of luxury villas in modest Pompeian houses, see Zanker, "Villa als Vorbild," 460–523.

59. Polybius 6.53; Pliny (the Elder) *Naturalis Historia* 35.6; Herbert Meyer, "Imagines maiorum," *Pauly-Wissowa,* vol. 9, cols. 1097–1104.

60. Jashemski, *Gardens,* 1:124–131.

61. Moormann, *Pittura parietale,* 57; on peacocks represented in the Villa of Oplontis, Bernard Andreae, "I pavoni della villa di Oplontis," *La regione sotterrata dal Vesuvio: studi e prospettive,* Atti del Convegno internazionale 11–15 November 1979, ed. Alfonso de Franciscis (Naples, 1982), 531–533.

CHAPTER 7

1. *Pompei: l'informatica al servizio di una città antica* (Rome, 1988), 71, with synoptic table. Among the thirty-five brothels this source distinguishes are nine *cellae meretriciae,* nineteen buildings specially constructed as brothels, and seven installations annexed to living quarters.

2. Willem Jongman, *The Economy and Society of Pompeii* (Amsterdam, 1988), 108–112, with discussion of the literature. He concludes that Eschebach's estimate of eight to twelve thousand is plausible, but high.

3. Werner Jobst, "Das 'offentliche Freudenhaus' in Ephesos," *Jahreshefte des Österreichischen archäologischen Institutes in Wien* 51 (1976–1977): 61–62; Luciana Jacobelli, *Le pitture erotiche delle terme suburbane di Pompei* (Rome, 1995), 65 n. 119; L. Preller, *Die Regionen der Stadt Rom* (Jena, 1848); Gus Hermansen, "The Population of Imperial Rome: The Regionaries," *Historia* 27 (1978): 129–168.

4. Andrew Wallace-Hadrill, "Public Honour and Private Shame: The Urban Texture of Pompeii," in *Urban Society in Roman Italy,* ed. T. J. Cornell and Kathryn Lomas (London, 1995), 53; on 52 he erroneously gives the address in *regio* VIII.

5. Paul Veyne, "The Roman Empire," in *From Pagan Rome to Byzantium,* vol. 1 of *A History of Private Life,* ed. Paul Veyne, trans. Arthur Goldhammer (Cambridge, Mass., 1987), 63–64.

6. Seneca *Controversiae* 4.10 says that sexual passivity is a crime for a free man, a necessity for a slave, and a duty for the freedman.

7. Horace *Satires* 1.2.31–34: "Quidam notus homo, cum exiret fornice, 'macte virtute esto' inquit sententia dia Catonis: 'nam simul ac venas inflavit taetra libido, huc iuvenes aequum est descendere, non alienas permolere uxores'" (When a well-known individual was making his exit from a brothel, "Well done! So may you continue!" was the inspired verdict of Cato: "As soon as the bane of lust has swollen their members, it's right for young men to come down here rather than grinding away at other men's wives" [translated by P. Michael Brown, *Horace Satires I* (Warminster, 1993)]).

8. Porphyrio's commentary on Horace *Satires* 1.2.31–32: "Marcus Cato ille Censoris, cum uidisset hominem honestum e fornice exeuntem, laudauit existimans libidinem compescendam esse sine crimine" (Marcus Cato the Censor, when he saw a man of high rank coming out of the brothel, praised him thinking that lust must be checked without committing a crime [my translation]). Latin text: *Pomponi Porfyrionis commentum in Horatium Flaccum,* ed. Alfred Holder (1894; Hildesheim, 1967), 232–233. Porphyrio's interpretation of *notus* is incorrect; the fact that the man was *notus* means that his morals needed improvement.

9. Pseudo-Acro's commentary on Horace *Satires* 1.2.31–32: "Catone transeunte quidam exiit de fornice; quem, cum fugeret, reuocauit et laudauit. Postea cum frequentius eum exeuntem de eodem lupanari uidisset, dixisse fertur: adulescens, ego te laudaui, tamquam huc interuenires, non tamquam hi habitares" (Cato coming across the man when he saw him leaving the brothel called him back and praised him. Later when he saw him leaving the same lupanar more frequently, he said: "Young man, I praised you for coming here, not for living here" [my translation]). Latin text: *Pseudoacronis scholia in Horatium vetustiora,* ed. Otto Keller (Leipzig, 1902), 1:20. I thank Anthony Corbeil for these references to Horace and the scholiasts.

10. Ray Laurence (*Roman Pompeii: Space and Society* [New York, 1994], 70–87) hypothesizes that sexual use of servants might cause domestic problems that induced aristocrats to frequent bordellos. He does not adduce convincing ancient sources to support his argument, nor does his location of bordellos on "dark" streets away from large houses convince me.

11. J. E. Sandys, *Latin Epigraphy: An Introduction to the Study of Latin Inscriptions,* 2d ed. (Cambridge, 1927); A. E. Gordon, *Illustrated Introduction to Latin Epigraphy* (Berkeley, 1983), esp. 17–30.

12. Eugenio La Rocca, Arnold de Vos, and Mariette de Vos, *Guida archeologica di Pompei* (Milan, 1976), 303.

13. Moormann, *Pittura parietale,* 198–199, cat. 255; Moormann points out that the model is similar to that of the so-called statue of the Maripara in Formello. See also Horst Blanck, "Il maripara: eine Priapstatue in Formello," *Römische Mitteilungen* 86 (1979): 339–350.

14. Catullus 5, speaking of his lover Lesbia, does not want others to know how many kisses she gives him, lest they become jealous and inflict him with the Evil Eye (*malus invidere*). I owe this reference to Michael Thomas.

15. Richlin, *Garden of Priapus,* 122–125.

16. The third painting from the eastern entrance on the south wall is largely destroyed.

17. For a full treatment of the structure with bibliography through 1936, see Ta-

tiana Warsher, "Codex Topographicus Pompejanus, Regio VI, ins. 10, pars 1" (typescript, German Archaeological Institute, Rome, 1936).

18. Roux's engravings appeared for the first time in César Famin, *Musée royal de Naples: peintures, bronzes et statues érotiques du cabinet secret, avec leur explication* (Paris, 1836); they were reprinted in M. L. Barré, *Musée secret,* vol. 8 of *Herculanum et Pompéi, recueil général des peintures, bronzes, mosaïques, etc. découverts jusqu'à ce jour et reproduits d'après le antichità di Ercolano, il Museo Borbonico et tous les ouvrages analogues* (Paris, 1877); Barré's moralizing comments on the erotic imagery epitomize the attitude of the period in regard to sex; recently a facsimile of the Spanish edition was republished: Frente de Afirmación Hispanista, *Museo secreto del arte erótico de Pompeya y Herculano* (Mexico City, 1995).

19. Thomas Fröhlich, *Lararien- und Fassadenbilder in den Vesuvstädten,* Römische Mitteilungen, Supplement 32 (Mainz, 1991), 214–222, esp. 221–222; Irene Bragantini, "VI 10, 1: Caupona della Via di Mercurio," in *Pompei, pitture e mosaici* (Rome, 1993) 4:1005–1028, bibl. 1005.

20. Bragantini ("VI 10, 1," 1007) notes that this wall painting is undatable on stylistic grounds; association with the conventional late Fourth-Style painting in room *d* places it in the last years of Pompeii.

21. Caupona of Salvius (VI, 14, 36): Giuseppe Fiorelli, *Notizie degli scavi* (1876): 193–195; August Mau, *Bullettino dell'Instituto* (1878): 191–194; Warsher, "Codex," nos. 131–138; F. A. Todd, "Three Pompeian Wall-Inscriptions, and Petronius," *Classical Review* 53, no. 1 (1939): 5–9; Karl Schefold, *Die Wände Pompejis: topographisches Verzeichnis der Bildmotive* (Berlin, 1957), 135–136; James Packer, "Inns at Pompeii," *Cronache pompeiane* 4 (1978): 46–47; Irene Bragantini, "VI 14, 35.36: Caupona di Salvius," in *Pompei, pitture e mosaici* (Rome, 1994), 5:366–371.

22. Bragantini ("VI 10, 1," 1007) also suggests that their destruction was not casual.

23. Fröhlich (*Lararien- und Fassadenbilder,* 217–218) places Fig. 88, the "tightrope walkers," in this position; Bragantini ("VI 10, 1," 1012) places a different picture there, one shown by Salomon Reinach (*Répertoire des peintures grec et romain* [Paris, 1922], 267 no. 12).

24. Wolfgang Helbig, *Wandgemälde der vom Vesuv verschütteten Stadte Campaniens* (Leipzig, 1868), no. 1503.

25. Fröhlich, *Lararien- und Fassadenbilder,* 217–218.

26. Valerius Maximus 2.10.8; Martial 1.1; Valerius Maximus mentions C. Mosius as aedile, presumably the aedile of 55, making this Cato Uticensis (the Younger); Martial does not specify the Cato.

27. Famin, *Cabinet secret,* 100 pl. 38; Reinach, *Répertoire des peintures,* 267 no. 3; Helbig, *Wandgemälde,* no. 1505.

28. Famin, *Cabinet secret,* 124 pl. 48; Reinach, *Répertoire des peintures,* 267 no. 7; Bragantini, "VI 10, 1," 1017.

29. Martial 9.3, trans. James Michie, *Martial: The Epigrams Selected and Translated* (London, 1973), 127.

30. Martial 11.75.

31. Andrew M. Riggsby, "Lenocinium: Scope and Consequences," *Zeitschrift der Savigny-Stiftung für Rechtsgeschichte: Romanistische Abteilung* 112 (1995): 423–427.

32. Clara Valenziano, "E sotto la cenere l'eros . . . ," *Il Venerdì di repubblica,* 2, 31 (1988): 145, cites opinions of Antonio Varone, director of the excavations, and Baldassare Conticello, then superintendent of Pompeii, that the paintings advertised additional services that were available to male clients of the baths; Luciana Jacobelli (*Le Pitture erotiche delle terme suburbane di Pompeii* [Rome, 1995], 61, 65, 92–97) sustains that neither this part of the establishment nor the upper-story apartments saw use as a lupanar.

33. Jacobelli, *Terme suburbane,* 18–23.

34. Jacobelli, *Terme suburbane,* 18; although the Central Baths also lacked separate sections for men and women, the building was not in operation at the time of the eruption (P. Bargellini, "Le terme centrali di Pompei," in *Les thermes romains,* Collection de l'Ecole française de Rome, 142 [Rome, 1991], 115–128).

35. Such differentiation of circulation space from reception space within a single room is common in Romano-Campanian painting: see Daniela Corlàita Scagliarini, "Spazio e decorazione nella pittura pompeiana," *Palladio* 23-25 (1974-1976): 3-44; John R. Clarke, "Notes on the Coordination of Wall, Floor, and Ceiling Decoration in the Houses of Roman Italy, 100 BCE–235 CE," in *IL 60: Essays Honoring Irving Lavin on his Sixtieth Birthday,* ed., Marilyn Aronberg Lavin (New York, 1990), 1-29, with bibl.

36. The painting of the left (north) wall has not survived. Since there was already a closet set into that wall, it is unlikely that its decoration continued that of the right and rear walls; the excavator did not find holes to support shelves corresponding to those on the opposite wall (Jacobelli, *Terme suburbane,* 63-64).

37. Jacobelli, *Terme suburbane,* 61-64.

38. Jacobelli, *Terme suburbane,* 80. For an overview of the building's painting program, see Luciana Jacobelli, "Le pitture e gli stucchi delle terme suburbane de Pompei," *4. Internationales Kolloquium zur römischen Wandmalerei, Kölner Jahrbuch für Vor- und Frühgeschichte* 24 (1991): 147-152.

39. Jacobelli, *Terme suburbane,* 80-82.

40. Martin Kilmer, "Genital Phobia and Depilation," *Journal of Hellenic Studies* 102 (1983): 104-112; on depilation in pathic men and boys, see Richlin, *Garden of Priapus,* 41, 93, 137, 168, 188-189 (anal depilation); vaginal depilation, 49, 123, n. 23.

41. Naples Museum, inv. 27686 (Vittoria Sampaolo, s.v. "pitture," in *Le collezioni*

del Museo nazionale di Napoli [Rome, 1986], 1:172–173 no. 347); Jacobelli, *Terme suburbane,* fig. 29.

42. Dover, *Greek Homosexuality,* 107.

43. Johns, *Sex or Symbol,* 136–137.

44. Paul Veyne, "La famille et l'amour sous le haut empire romain," *Annales: économies, sociétés, civilisations* 33 (1978): 53–54.

45. Jacobelli (*Terme suburbane,* 38–40) underscores the importance, especially in Ovid, of the attainment of *reciprocal* sexual pleasure for both the man and the woman.

46. Ovid *Ars Amatoria* 3.777: "Parva vehatur equo; quod erat longissima, numquam / Tebais Hectoreo nupta resedit equo" (A small woman should ride astride; Andromache / was too tall ever to ride on Hector's horse [trans. by Myerowitz, "Domestication of Desire," 136]).

47. Myerowitz, "Domestication of Desire," 136–137.

48. Kilmer (*Greek Erotica,* 71–72) enumerates three certain examples: R516; R223; R518; four examples imply that fellatio is the next step: R47.1; R464; R490; R1188. The context is that of the orgy after the symposium: all but two of the scenes are trios, and all but two involve violence (usually spanking the hetaira with a sandal) or its threat.

49. Ashmolean Museum, Oxford, in Johns, *Sex or Symbol,* 150 fig. 122; the man has his crooked right arm over his head.

50. Lamps: Vorberg, *Glossarium eroticum,* 184–186; Donald M. Bailey, *Roman Lamps Made in Italy,* vol. 2 of *A Catalogue of Lamps in the British Museum,* (London, 1980), 64; *Eros grec,* 123–124 no. 56 (where the woman curves her legs back toward her head in an acrobatic position while fellating the man). Vases with appliqué medallions from the Rhône Valley: Pierre Wuilleumier and Amable Audin, *Les médaillons d'applique gallo-romains de la vallée du Rhône* (Paris, 1952), 125 no. 217, 128 fig. 217 ("Atalante et Meleagre"), 127 no. 218, 128 fig. 218, 127 no. 219, 129 fig. 219; A. Desbat, "Vases à médaillons d'applique des fouilles récentes de Lyon," *Figlina* 5–6 (1980–1981): 98 E 002, 110 E 026.

51. Giuseppe Fiorelli, *Catalogo del Museo nazionale di Napoli: raccolta pornografica* (Naples, 1866), 16 n. 16; Marinella Lista, s.v. "Gli oggetti di uso quotidiano," in *Le collezioni del Museo nazionale di Napoli* (Rome, 1986), 1:198 no. 180, Naples Museum inv. 27864.

52. Werner A. Krenkel, "Fellatio and Irrumatio," *Wissenschaftliche Zeitschrift der Wilhelm-Pieck-Universität Rostock* 29 (1980): 77–88; Richlin, "The Meaning of *irrumare,*" 40–46.

53. Richlin, *Garden of Priapus,* 26–27; Corbeill, *Controlling Laughter,* 99–127.

54. Andrew Riggsby points out (personal communication, January 1996), that *infamia* covers several varieties of civic disqualification, and that jurists never specifically

mention *fellatio.* The procedural rules for bringing suit have three levels of disqualification, the *infames* being the least restrictive. The middle level of disqualification (i.e., those who can file suit only on their own behalf) includes the man "qui corpore suo muliebria passus est" (who has suffered his body to be used like that of a woman) and would probably include *fellatores* and *fellatrices* (*Digesta Iustiniani,* ed. Theodor Mommsen [*The Digest of Justinian,* ed. Alan Watson (Philadelphia, 1985)], 3.1.1.6 [Ulpian]). Women, however, already fall into this class because of their sex (*Digest* 3.1.1.5 [Ulpian]). The *lex Iulia* does not seem to address specific sexual acts (*Digest* 23.2.42 [Ulpian], *Digest* 23.2.44 [Paul]).

55. Martial 9.4: "Aureolis futui cum possit Galla duobus / Et plus quam futui, si totidem addideris: / Aureolos a te cur accipit, Aeschyle, denos? / Non fellat tanti Galla. Quid ergo? Tacet" (my translation in text).

56. T. A. J. McGinn ("Prostitution and Julio-Claudian Legislation" [Ph.D. diss., University of Michigan, 1986], 23) points out that *fellatio*'s advantages (to a prostitute who wanted to avoid pregnancy) made it cheaper than vaginal intercourse.

57. Martial 4.84: "Non est in populo nec urbe tota, / A se Thaida qui probet fututam, / Cum multi cupiant rogentque multi. / Tam casta est, rogo, Thais? Immo fellat" (There's no one in the whole city who can say he's fucked Thais, even though a lot of guys want to and a lot of guys ask. I ask, is Thais so chaste? As long as I don't ask: Does she suck dick? [trans. by Krenkel, "Fellatio and Irrumatio," 81]).

58. Collected and translated into English by Krenkel, "Fellatio and Irrumatio," 85–87. Some examples: *Corpus Inscriptionum Latinarum* 4.2273 "Myrtis bene felas" (You fellate well, Murtis); 2421 "Rufa ita vale, qvare bene felas" (Rufa, may you live long, 'cause you suck so well); "Sabina felas non belle faces" (Sabina, you suck. You do not perform well).

59. Wuilleumier and Audin attribute this design to their "premier céramiste érotique" (*Médaillons d'applique,* 49 no. 60, 52 fig. 60; further discussed in chapter 8 and its note 38 below).

60. Jacobelli (*Terme suburbane,* 44 n. 51) points out that the goddess Venus also wears this kind of chain, for example, in the painting in the Naples Museum inv. 9248 (Sampaolo, *Le collezioni del Museo nazionale,* 1:144 no. 157); Jacobelli also cites a gold chain of this type found in the Vesuvian area, see *Riscoprire Pompei,* exh. cat. (Rome, 1993), 268 no. 198.

61. Unfortunately, paint losses hide the man's garment: if he was wearing a toga rather than a tunic, the humorous effect would be even greater, since togas were a sign of class and female prostitutes also wore them.

62. Suetonius *Tiberius* 44. "Quare Parrasi quoque tabulam, in qua Meleagro Atalanta ore morigeratur, legatam sibi sub condicione, ut si argumento offenderetur decies pro ea sestertium acciperet, non modo praetulit, sed et in cubiculo dedicavit" (Some-

one offered Tiberius a painting by Parrhasios, in which Atalanta is performing fellatio on Meleager, on the condition that if he found its subject offensive he could instead receive 10,000 sesterces for it. Not only did he accept it, he placed it in his bedroom [my translation]).

63. Judith P. Hallett, "*Morigerari:* Suetonius *Tiberius* 44," *Antiquité classique* 47 (1978): 196–200. The compound *morigeror,* applied to fellatio, literally means for a woman to submit to a man in a wifely manner (originally), but by Suetonius' time, in a sexual manner (Adams, *Latin Sexual Vocabulary*, 164 n. 7); see also Myerowitz, "Domestication of Desire," 137 n. 6. Jean-Michel Croisille (*Poésie et art figuré de Néron aux Flaviens* [Brussels, 1982], 259 n. 104) grossly misreads the passage in Diogenes Laertius 8.187–188 to mean that Chrysippus is describing a mythological painting of Zeus and Hera performing either cunnilingus or fellatio.

64. Richlin, *Garden of Priapus,* on the man who performs cunnilingus being more debased than the passive homosexual; Veyne, "Famille et l'amour," 53; Veyne, "The Roman Empire," 204; Edwards, *Politics of Immorality,* 71 n. 29 with references to Foucault's and Price's analysis of Artemidorus Daldianus, *The Interpretation of Dreams.* Holt N. Parker ("The Teratogenic Grid," in *Roman Sexualities,* ed. Judith P. Hallett and Marilyn Skinner [Princeton, forthcoming]) asserts that in Roman constructions of sexuality, cunnilingus makes the woman active and the man passive.

65. Martial 4.43: "Non dixi, Coracine, te cinaedum: / Non sum tam temerarius nec audax / Nec mendacia qui loquar libenter. / Si dixi, Coracine, te cinaedum, / Iratam mihi Pontiae lagonam, / Iratum calicem mihi Metili: / Iuro per Syrios tibi tumores, / Iuro per Berecyntios furores. / Quid dixi tamen? Hoc leve et pusillum, / Quod notum est, quod et ipse non negabis, / Dixi te, Coracine, cunnilingum" (my translation in text).

66. *Corpus Inscriptionum Latinarum* 4.3999: "Glyco cunnum / lingit a(ssibus) II" (Glyco licks cunt for two asses); *Corpus Inscriptionum Latinarum* 4.8940, "Maritimus / cunnu(m) li(n)get a(ssibus) II / II,/ virgines am- / mittit" (Maritimus licks cunt for four asses. He accepts virgins [the writer misspells *lingit* as *liget* and *admittit* as *ammittit*]: Varone, *Erotica pompeiana,* 138 with bibl.

67. Veyne ("The Roman Empire," 203) asserts, without documentation, that only "libertines" made love with a completely naked woman.

68. An inscription in a second-century mosaic in the Baths of the Trinacria at Ostia Antica reads *statio cunnilingorum.* This is a clever reference to the *stationes,* or offices, arranged around the Forum of the Corporations. Each *statio* represented a commercial enterprise, using inscriptions with formulae such as *statio sabratensium* with the figure of an elephant, representing ivory traders from Sabratha (Becatti, *Mosaici,* 141 fig. 277; Carlo Pavolini, *Ostia,* Guida archeologica Laterza, no. 8 [Rome, 1983], 68, 130).

69. Jacobelli, *Terme suburbane:* 47 fig. 37; Naples Archaeological Museum, inv. 27697, Sampaolo, *Le collezioni del Museo nazionale,* 1:138 no. 102.

70. Melissa Kepke, "Sexual Satire: The Suburban Baths at Pompeii" (master's thesis, University of Texas at Austin, 1994).

71. Judith Hallett, "Female Homoeroticism and the Denial of Roman Reality in Latin Literature," *Yale Journal of Criticism* 3 (1989): 209–227.

72. Seneca (the Elder) *Controversiae* 1.2.23: "Hybreas, inquit, cum diceret controversiam de illo qui tribadas deprehendit et occidit, describere coepit mariti adfectum, in quo non deberet exigi inhonesta inquisitio:

> ἐγὼ δ' ἐσκόπησα πρότερον τὸν ἄνδρα,
> <εἰ> ἐγγεγένηταί τις ἢ προσέρραπται.

(Hybreas, he said, speaking of the *controversia* about the man who caught his wife and another woman in bed and killed them both, proceeded to describe the feelings of the husband [after all the husband ought not to be asked to carry out so shameful an examination]: "But I looked at the man first, to see whether he was natural or artificial" [trans. by M. Winterbottom, *The Elder Seneca, Controversiae Books 1–6,* Loeb Classical Library (Cambridge, Mass., 1974), 86–87]).

73. Juvenal 6.306–313: "Go now, check it out, with what a sneer Tullia sniffs the air and what the milk-mate of the notorious Maura says, Maura, when she's passing the old altar of Chastity. At night they stop their litters here, they piss here, and fill the statue of the goddess with long squirts, and take turns riding each other, and are moved with the Moon for witness, and from there they go to their homes: you, when light's returned, tread your wife's urine on your way to visit your great friends" (trans. by Richlin, *Garden of Priapus,* 206).

74. Keuls, *The Reign of the Phallus,* 82–86 figs. 72–80.

75. Richlin, *Garden of Priapus,* 134.

76. Martial 7.67: "Pedicat pueros tribas Philaenis / Et tentigine saevior mariti" (trans. by George Augustus Sala, in J. P. Sullivan and Peter Whigham, eds., *Epigrams of Martial Englished by Divers Hands* [Berkeley, 1987], 279). Martial 1.90, Loeb trans. by Walter C. A. Ker (Cambridge., Mass., 1968), 87.

77. Martial 8.12: "Uxorem quare locupletem ducere nolim, / Quaeritis? Uxori nubere nolo meae. / Inferior matrona suo sit, Prisce, marito: / Non aliter fiunt femina virque pares" (trans. by James Michie, in *Martial Englished,* 291).

78. Sampaolo, *Le collezioni del Museo nazionale,* inv. 27696, 1:172–173 no. 348; lacking inv. number, 1:170–171 no. 344; and inv. 27690, 1:172–173 no. 350.

79. Johns, *Sex or Symbol,* pls. 23, 25 figs. 95, 108, 109, 111, and 114; Kilmer, *Greek*

Erotica, 33, with list of figures on 34; M. C. Gualandi-Genito, *Le lucerne antiche del Trentino* (Trento, 1986), 234 n. 45.

80. Dover, *Greek Homosexuality,* 105–106; the only certain representation of anal penetration is Dover's B51, 100, where the artist clearly depicted the vulva; Johns (*Sex or Symbol,* 133) rightly points out that in most cases we cannot tell if the artist is representing anal or vaginal intercourse.

81. Greek term *kúptein* for the partner leaning forward to raise the buttocks in the air for coitus *a posteriore*—either vaginal or anal, and in both heterosexual and homosexual relationships: *kúptein* for a woman adulterer described in the position in Aristophanes *Thesmophoriazusae* 488 ff.; for a boy in Theocritus *Idylls* 5.116–117. Aristophanes *Lysistrata* 231 and *Plutus* 149–152 indicate that this was an indecent position that only a prostitute would assume; cf. also Herodotus' story (*Historia* 1.61) of Peisistratos "baking his loaves in a cold oven," i.e., having anal intercourse with his wife.

82. Stewart, "Reflections," 148.

83. Metropolitan Museum of Art, Marquand Gift, 81.10.349.

84. Desbat, "Vases à médaillons," 112, E 032; Jacobelli, *Terme suburbane,* fig. 42.

85. Catullus 56; *Anthologia Palatina* 5.49; Propertius 4.8.

86. Martial 12.43. For text and translation, see chapter 8, note 19.

87. Suetonius *Tiberius* 32: "Secessu vero Capreensi etiam sellariam excogitavit, sedem arcanarum libidinum: in quam undique conquisiti puellarum et exoletorum greges, monstrosique concubitus repertores, quos spintrias appellabat, triplici serie connexi, invicem incestarent se coram ipso, ut aspectu deficientes libidines excitaret" (my translation in text).

88. Examples from the graffiti: Pompeii: *Corpus Inscriptionum Latinarium* 4.2450, 9848 suppl. 3935, 3941, 3942. Herculaneum: Matteo Della Corte, "Le iscrizioni di Ercolano," *Rendiconti della Accademia di archeologia, lettere e belle arti, Napoli* 33 (1958): 306–307. Ostia Antica, House of Jupiter and Ganymede: Guido Calza, "Scavi recenti nell'abitato di Ostia," *Monumenti antichi* 26 (1920): fig. 20; A.W. Van Buren, "Graffiti at Ostia," *Classical Review* 37 (1923): 164; Clarke, "House of Jupiter and Ganymede," 93.

89. Kavoussi, East Crete, Heraklion, Archaeological Museum, inv. 9284: *Eros grec,* 122–123 no. 53. Note the close parallel of this representation to Martial 10.81: "On Phyllis one morning a couple of bucks / paid a lecherous call: they were looking for fucks. / But each wants to strip her and have the first thrust, / While Phyllis is eager to seem and be just. / So one lifts up her legs for the tool's firm caress, / As the other lifts up the back of her dress" (trans. by J. P. Sullivan in *Martial Englished,* 395).

90. Wuilleumier and Audin, *Médaillons d'applique,* 49 no. 59, 50 fig. 59; reconstructed in Desbat, "Vases à médaillons," 96 fig. 4.

91. Wuilleumier and Audin, *Médaillons d'applique,* 133 no. 233, 134 fig. 233.

92. Edwards, *Politics of Immorality,* 83–84.

93. Jacobelli, *Terme suburbane,* 56–57.

94. Richard Brilliant, *Rank and Gesture in Roman Art* (New Haven, 1963), 184–188.

95. Richlin, "Not Before Homosexuality," 536. See also Parker, "Teratogenic Grid."

96. Seneca *Controversiae* 1.2.23; Lucian *Dialogi Meretricii* (Dialogues of the courtesans) 5; Pseudo Lucian *Amores* 28; Ovid *Metamorphoses* 9.666–797; Martial 7.67, 7.70; Juvenal 6.225–235 and 246–264.

97. Artemidorus (Daldianus) *The Interpretation of Dreams (Oneirocritica)* 1.80. See texts collected by Hallett, "Female Homoeroticism," 209–227; Bernadette Brooten, "Paul's Views on the Nature of Women and Female Homoeroticism," in *Immaculate and Powerful: The Female Sacred Image and Social Reality,* ed. C. W. Atkinson, C. H. Buchanan, and M. Miles (Boston, 1985), 61–87. See Corbeill (*Controlling Laughter,* 14–56) on the term *natura* in relation to physical peculiarities.

98. Martial 7.67: "Non fellat—putat hoc parum virile—, / Sed plane medias vorat puellas. / Di mentem tibi dent tuam, Philaeni, / Cunnum lingere quae putas virile" (Oh, you that think your sex to cloak / By kissing what you cannot poke, / May God grant that you, Philaenis, / Will yet learn to suck a penis [trans. by Sala, in *Martial Englished,* 279]).

99. Personal communication from Luciana Jacobelli; the process of removal unfortunately obliterated this writing.

100. Maiuri, *Casa del Menandro,* vol. 2, pl. 12.

101. Helga von Heintze, "Die antiken Bildnisse Vergils," *Gymnasium* 94 (1987): 481–497, fig. 18; Tunis, Bardo Museum, inv. Sousse 57.104.

102. Plutarch *Moralia* 520 ff.; Martial 8.13.

103. Cicero *De oratore* 2.239. Corbeill (*Controlling Laughter,* 14–56) provides a full discussion of this and related texts.

104. Luca Giuliani, "Der seligen Krüppel," *Archäologische Anzeiger* 102 (1987): 701; Robert Garland, *The Eye of the Beholder: Deformity and Disability in the Graeco-Roman World* (Cornell, 1995).

105. Simone Mollard-Besques, *Epoques hellénistique et romaine, Grèce et Asie Mineure,* vol. 3 of *Catalogue raisonné des figurines et reliefs en terre-cuite grecs, étrusques et romaine, au Musée national du Louvre* (Paris, 1972), 172 nos. 1203, 1204, 1215, 1224, 1242; see especially inv. 1150 from Smyrna, analyzed by D. and M. Gourevitch, "Terre cuites hellénistiques d'inspiration médicale au Musée du Louvre," *La Presse médicale* 25, no. 12 (1963): 2752 fig. 5.

106. Paolo Sambroia, "Note sulla diagnosi e l'invididuazione dell'idrocele dall'età antica all'età moderna," appendix III to *Terme suburbane,* by Jacobelli, 118–119.

107. Jacobelli, *Terme suburbane,* 60. Lucian of Samosata, a second-century rhetori-

cian, parodies the flamboyant orator who, in addition to being effeminate in dress, gestures, and walk, carries a scroll: *"Kai Biblion Aei"* (Lucian, *Praeceptor* 15), See Erik Gunderson, "Contested Subjects: Rhetorical Theory and the Body" (Ph.D. disseration, University of California, Berkeley, 1996), 168–170.

108. An interesting parallel for the artist suggesting, rather than picturing, the emotions of a protagonist is the painting by Timanthes (Quintilian *Institutio Oratoria* 2.13.13) in which various sad figures watch the sacrifice of Iphigenia and Agamemnon's veiled face encourages the viewer to fill in the emotions (*suo quique animo aestimandum*).

109. Jacobelli, *Terme suburbane,* 81.

110. Jacobelli (*Terme suburbane,* 94–97) argues for both sexes using the baths simultaneously.

111. On the difficulty of hypothesizing the female gaze in contemporary terms, see Mary Anne Doane, "Film and the Masquerade: Theorising the Female Spectator," *Screen* 23, no. 314 (1982): 74–88.

CHAPTER 8

1. Jacobelli, *Terme suburbane,* 70. The name spintria is completely without historical or philological basis; it appears in Suetonius *Tiberius* 43, to designate "monstrous couplings"; the full passage is discussed in the previous chapter (and see chapter 7, note 87).

2. Jacobelli wonders about a connection between the numbers from I to XVI on both the spintriae and the clothing compartments in the apodyterium of the Suburban Baths. As I suggest later, the most probable connection is a conceptual one.

3. T. V. Buttrey, "The Spintriae as a Historical Source," *The Numismatic Chronicle and Journal of the Royal Numismatic Society* 13 (1973): 55 between 22 and 37; on less conclusive evidence, Bono Simonetta and Renzo Riva (*Le tessere erotiche romane [spintriae]* [Lugano, 1981]) maintain that they were coined between 70 and 95.

4. Suetonius *Tiberius* 58: "nummo vel anulo effigiem impressam latrinae aut lupanari intulisse."

5. Martial 8.78: "Nunc veniunt subitis lasciva nomismata nimbis, / Nunc dat spectatas tessera larga feras, / Nunc implere sinus securos gaudet et absens / Sortitur dominos, ne laceretur, avis" (Now come sportive tokens in sudden showers, now the lavish coupon bestows the animals they have been watching, now birds are happy to fill safe laps and find masters in absence by lot, lest they be torn apart [trans. by D. R. Shackleton Bailey, *Martial Epigrams* (Cambridge, Mass., 1993), 2:227]).

6. Shackleton Bailey (*Martial Epigrams,* 2:227 n. "f"), in disagreement with Friedländer, who thought that *lasciva* referred to tokens giving free access to brothels

or to prostitutes in the theater. See also Regling, "Spintria," *Pauly-Wissowa,* series 2, vol. 3, col. 1814.

7. Jacobelli (*Terme suburbane,* 72–74) convincingly argues that the spintriae were gaming pieces.

8. Brendel, "Erotic Art," 63–64.

9. Parker, "Love's Body Anatomized," 92–94, list of ancient authors, 108. The *Suda,* or *Suidas,* a tenth-century lexicon, employs the name "Elephantine"; most scholars, including Parker, assume that she is the same person as Elephantis. I use the name Elephantis throughout this book. Jacobelli (*Terme suburbane,* 67 n. 136) cites a Baroque parallel in the *Satyra sotadica de arcanis Amoris et Veneris* of about 1600, published under the fictitious female name Aloysia Sigaea Toletana (critical edition, ed. B. Lavagnini [Catania, 1935]).

10. Ovid *Ars Amatoria* 3.769–88.

11. For a brief characterization of these texts see Jacobelli, *Terme suburbane,* 67–68 nn. 138–148; see also Parker, "Love's Body Anatomized," 92–94; Werner Krenkel, "Figurae veneris (I)," *Wissenschaftliche Zeitschrift der Wilhelm-Pieck-Universität Rostock* 34 (1985): 50–56.

12. Parker, "Love's Body Anatomized," 98.

13. Andrew Riggsby points out (personal communication) that by Cicero's time laws have numbered chapters and that books are numbered. Legions and units within legions are also numbered. These provide a reasonable precedent for using such numeration for sexual positions, although, he adds, the enumerated list was not such a taken-for-granted technology as it is for us.

14. The spintriae, in turn, were a source for Renaissance artists: see Bette Talvacchia, "L'erotismo in Giulio Romano, fra decoro, decorazione, e scandolo," *La Nuova Città* 5 (1994): 95–113; Bette Talvacchia, "Figure lascive per trastullo e l'ingegno," in *Giulio Romano* (Milan, 1989), 277–287.

15. Compiled in Christian Huelsen, "Miscellanea epigrafica," *Römische Mitteilungen* 11 (1896): 227–237. I thank Anthony Corbeill for this observation.

16. Brendel, "Erotic Art," 63–69; Jacobelli, *Terme suburbane,* 68, 81.

17. Bono Simonetta and Renzo Riva, *Le tessere erotiche romane (spintrae)* (Lugano, 1981), 28 pl. 6.

18. Naples Museum, inv. 27696; Grant, *Eros in Pompeii,* 154; Sampaolo, *Le collezioni del Museo nazionale,* 1:172, cat. 348, dated to Fourth Style.

19. Martial 12.43: "Facundos mihi de libidinosis / Legisti nimium, Sabelle, versus, / Quales nec Didymi sciunt puellae / Nec molles Elephantidos libelli. / Sunt illic Veneris novae figurae, / quales perditus audeat fututor, / Praestent et taceant quid exoleti, / Quo symplegmate quinque copulentur, / Qua plures teneantur a catena, / Extinctam liceat quid ad lucernam. / Tanti non erat esse te disertum" (You read me some

all too well-turned verses about debauchees, Sabellus, such as neither Didymus' girls know of nor the voluptuous little books of Elephantis. Therein are novel erotic postures such as only a desperate fornicator would venture, what male prostitutes provide and keep quiet about, in what combinations five persons are linked, by what chain are held more than five, what can go on when the lamp is out. You paid too high a price for your poetic skill [trans. by Shackleton Bailey]). See also Krenkel, "Figurae veneris (I)," 51.

20. Jacobelli, *Terme suburbane,* 81.

21. Frédéric Hermet, *Vases sigillés,* vol. 1 of *La Graufesenque (Condatomago)* (Paris, 1934), 284; my translation.

23. Annalis Leibundgut (*Die römischen Lampen in der Schweiz* [Bern, 1977], 190) lists the following numbers of finds according to subject:

233 animals
198 gladiators and gladiatorial weapons
159 erotic symplegmata [sexual couplings]
139 scenes of cult and daily life
138 goddesses and demigods
138 gods, heroes, and their attributes
92 animals attacking each other
92 amorini [cupids]
75 riders and racers
74 birds
68 masks and heads
49 fish
34 bacchic scenes
33 mythical beasts
30 plants
21 grotesques from the theater

The author notes (189) that the astoundingly high number of more than four hundred different molds makes the motif catalog representative and permits judgments not only for the Swiss material but for lamp images in general.

23. Bailey, *Roman Lamps Made in Italy,* 64.

24. Strabo *Geographia* 4.6.9.

25. Leibundgut, *Schweiz,* 128.

26. Leibundgut, *Schweiz,* 128–129.

27. Michael Koortbojian, *Myth, Meaning, and Memory on Roman Sarcophagi* (Berkeley, 1995).

28. Siegfried Loeschcke, *Lampen aus Vindonissa: Ein Beitrag zur Geschichte von Vindonissa und des antiken Beleuchtungswesens* (Zurich, 1919).

29. Deubner, "Hellenistische Reliefkeramik," 90–92; Donald M. Bailey, *Roman Provincial Lamps,* vol. 3 of *A Catalogue of Lamps in the British Museum* (London, 1988),

65 cat. Q 3104, with bibl., pl. 105: "L. 9.6 W. 6.6. Reg. 1867.11–22.232. Excavated for Museum: Wood. Ephesus. About AD 500–600." In his *Greek and Roman Pottery Lamps* (London, 1963), 32, Bailey dates the same lamp to the fourth or fifth century A.D. but in both cases identifies the reclining figure as a woman.

30. Bailey, *Pottery Lamps,* 12.

31. Bailey, *Roman Lamps Made in Italy,* 64.

32. Although most of the vessels from La Graufesenque went to sites in modern-day France, Hermet's list of find spots includes Italy, Switzerland, Austria, Germany, Holland, Great Britain, Scotland, Spain, and North Africa.

33. For the complete composition, see Johns, *Sex or Symbol,* 33 fig. 17.

34. Robert Knorr, *Töpfer und Fabriken verzierter Terra-Sigillata des ersten Jahrhunderts* (Stuttgart, 1919), 78 pl. 81A; Hermet, *Vases sigillés,* 283–284; Frédéric Hermet, *Vases graffites,* vol. 2 of *La Graufesenque (Condatomago)* (Paris, 1934), 17 pl. 124.

35. For the typology of their shapes see Desbat, "Vases à médaillons," 7–47.

36. For the most recent information on dating see Desbat, "Vases à médaillons," 175–181.

37. Wuilleumier and Audin (*Médaillons d'applique,* 49) dubbed the artist who created this and other compositions the "premier céramiste érotique" in their 1952 publication; Desbat ("Vases à médaillons," 97) contests their classification of ceramists by subject matter.

38. Especially Marciana and Matidia: see Max Wegner, *Hadrian, Plotina, Matidia, Sabina,* Das römische Herrscherbild, part 2, vol. 3 (Berlin, 1956), pls. 35, 39.

39. For the origins and nuances of this *chalas,* a loanword, perhaps introduced into Latin by Greek prostitutes, see Adams (*Latin Sexual Vocabulary,* 172–174). The word literally means to "open up" or "loosen" a woman or boy both by and for entry. VA . . . could also be the beginning of VALEAS.

40. For example, TENEO TE or "I've got you [in the sexual sense]" (Wuilleumier and Audin, *Médaillons d'applique,* 51 no. 64); ITA VALEAS DECET ME or "I like it like that" (Wuilleumier and Audin, *Médaillons d'applique,* 54, nos. 68 and 69), and other captions discussed below.

41. Giuseppe Fiorelli, *Pompeianarum antiquitatum historia nunc primum collegit indicibusque instruxit* (Naples, 1860–1864), 2:63–68.

42. Wuilleumier and Audin, *Médaillons d'applique,* 54–56 no. 71.

43. This is the *adversus* position; see Krenkel, "Figurae veneris (I)," passim.

44. Wuilleumier and Audin, *Médaillons d'applique,* 131 no. 231, by their "troisième céramiste érotique."

45. Desbat ("Vases à médaillons," 97) provides the literal translation, "Viens! c'est le bouclier," proposing that the words are part of a pun on the word *scutus* that eludes

us today. In his discussion of the captions on the paintings of the Inn of Salvius at Pompeii, Todd ("Three Pompeian Wall-Inscriptions," 7–8) convincingly argues that *orte* is a syncopated form of *oro te* with the meaning of "Come off it!" or "Here, stop it!" or a rude "What's that?"

46. These are the "second" and "third" erotic ceramists of Wuilleumier and Audin (*Médaillons d'applique,* 125 and 131).

47. Eric Moormann suggested to me that the lamp might allude to Psyche's lamp in the story of Amor and Psyche.

48. Wuilleumier and Audin, *Médaillons d'applique,* 133 no. 233.

49. Wuilleumier and Audin, *Médaillons d'applique,* 131 no. 232; Hephaestus' net: Homer *Odyssey* 8.266–366; Ovid *Metamorphoses* 4.174–189.

50. Wuilleumier and Audin, *Médaillons d'applique,* 133 no. 238.

51. Wuilleumier and Audin, *Médaillons d'applique,* 138 nos. 249–250.

52. Cited in Micheline Rouvier-Jeanlin, *Les figurines gallo-romaines en terre cuite au Musée des antiquités nationales, Gallia* Supplement 24 (Paris 1972), 236.

53. Leo Steinberg, *The Sexuality of Christ in Renaissance Art and in Modern Oblivion* (New York, 1983), 3; Gerhard Neumann, *Gesten und Gebärden in der griechischen Kunst* (Berlin, 1965), 67–69.

54. Rouvier-Jeanlin, *Figurines gallo-romaines,* 236 no. 566.

55. Harold de Fontenay, *Inscriptions céramiques gallo-romaines découvertes à Autun* (1874), no. 559; *Corpus Inscriptionum Latinarum* 13, 10.015 (84) x.

56. From Saint-Pourçain: Rouvier-Jeanlin, *Figurines gallo-romaines,* 236 no. 567.

57. Boston, Museum of Fine Arts, inv. 86.145. Illustrated in Cornelius C. Vermeule, *Greek, Etruscan and Roman Art: The Classical Collections of the Museum of Fine Arts, Boston* (Meriden, Conn., 1963), pl. 184.

58. 1892 work by Th. Amtmann cited in Rouvier-Jeanlin, *Figurines gallo-romaines,* 236.

59. Clarke, "Decor of House of Jupiter and Ganymede," 89–104; John R. Clarke, "New Light on the Iconography of Jupiter, Ganymede, and Leda in the House of Jupiter and Ganymede at Ostia Antica," *4. Internationales Kolloquium zur römischen Wandmalerei, Kölner Jahrbuch für Vor- und Frühgeschichte* 24 (1991): 171–175.

60. Bianca Maria Felletti Maj, *Le pitture della casa delle volte dipinte e della casa delle pareti gialle,* Monumenti della pittura antica scoperti in Italia, sec. 3, Ostia, fasc. 1–2 (Rome, 1961), 17–19: on 17, fig. 9 is the central picture of south wall; pl. 5a shows the west and south walls with erotic painting on the south wall in place.

61. This layer of plaster is no thicker than a millimeter, according to Felletti Maj (*Volte dipinte,* 18).

62. Fritz Wirth, *Römische Wandmalerei vom Untergang Pompejis bis ans Ende des drit-*

ten Jahrhunderts (Berlin, 1934), 165 fig. 83; Ranuccio Bianchi-Bandinelli, *Rome: The Late Empire* (New York, 1971), 86–88 figs. 77–78 for the Villa Piccola S. Sebastiano; parallels from the first half of the third century include the cubiculum of the multiplication of the loaves in the Catacomb of Domatilla (G. J. Wilpert, *Le pitture delle catacombe romane* [Rome, 1903], pl. 54) and the cubiculum of the Good Shepherd in the Catacomb of Domatilla (Wirth, *Römische Wandmalerei,* 176 fig. 90).

63. Felletti Maj, *Volte dipinte,* 17–19, 33.

64. Felletti Maj, *Volte dipinte,* 31.

CONCLUSIONS

1. Dio Cassius *Historia Romana* 58.2.4.

2. Propertius 2.6.27–36: "Quae manus obscenas depinxit prima tabellas / et posuit casta turpia visa domo, / illa puellarum ingenuos corrupit ocellos / nequitiaeque suae noluit esse rudis. / a gemat in te[ne]bris, ista qui protulit arte / turpia sub tacita condita laetitia! / non istis olim variabant tecta figuris: / tum paries nullo crimine pictus erat" (The hand that first painted obscene pictures and put unseemly images into the chaste house, that hand corrupted the innocent eyes of girls and made them proficient in vice like itself. Ah, cursed be the man who with this art produced unseemly things that the joy of love once concealed. Not with such figures were houses decorated in days of old; then the walls were not frescoed with scenes of shame [my translation]). Bettina Bergmann ("The Pregnant Moment: Tragic Wives in the Roman Interior," in *Sexuality in Ancient Art,* ed. Natalie B. Kampen [Cambridge, 1996], 211) agrees with George P. Goold (trans., *Elegies of Sextus Propertius* [Cambridge, Mass., 1990], 137–139) that these lines refer not to brothel scenes but to the depiction of the adultery of gods and goddesses like Mars and Venus.

3. Griffin, *Latin Poets,* 112–114; Amy Richlin, "Approaches to the Sources on Adultery at Rome," in *Reflections on Women in Antiquity,* ed. Helene P. Foley (New York, 1981), 389–393; Bergmann, "Pregnant Moment," 211 n. 29; G. Karl Galinsky, *Augustan Culture: An Interpretive Introduction* (Princeton, 1996), 128–138.

4. Catullus 16.5; Martial 1.4.8, 2.15.13.

Glossary

Latin words appear with their plurals; Greek and Italian terms are so labeled.

aedicula, -ae	painted representation of a pavilionlike structure, modeled on a temple front, used by itself, or to frame a picture or figure
amphora, -ae	conical storage vessel with two handles
apodyterium, -a	dressing room of the bath
atrium, -a	central hall of the Roman house (domus), usually having a single central opening in the roof to capture rain water (compluvium) with a corresponding catch basin in the floor beneath (impluvium)
caldarium, -a	the hot room of the bath
caupona, -ae	tavern serving food and drink, often with simple guest rooms
cella meretricia, -ae . . . -ae	room designated for use by prostitute, located either in a storefront shop or in a caupona
chiton	the garment worn next to the skin, usually reaching to the feet (Greek), the Roman *tunica*
cinaedus, -i	the insertive or passive partner in male-male sexual intercourse, from Greek *kínaidos*

cryptoporticus, -i	underground or partially interred corridor
cubiculum, -a	bedchamber in the Roman house
erastes	adult male lover of the eromenos (Greek)
eromenos	preadult male beloved of the erastes (Greek)
fresco	wall painting in which the pigment is applied to the wet plaster so that it is incorporated (carbonated) into the final layer of plaster (Italian)
furnacator, -es	worker who stokes the furnaces beneath the floors of the bath
gens, -tes	clan; extended family of the paterfamilias
herm	stone pillar topped by sculpted head or torso
hetaira, -ai	female companion, a courtesan, a concubine (opposite of lawful wife, Greek)
insula, -ae	city block
laconicum, -a	dry-heat sauna room in a bath
lunette	semicircular area of wall formed by vaulted ceiling
natatio, -nes	swimming pool, cold plunge of a bath
oecus, -i	reception room often used for dining and entertainment
paterfamilias	male head of the gens, or extended family
pathicus, -i	the receptive or passive partner in male-male sexual intercourse
peristyle	garden or courtyard surrounded by a colonnade
pinacotheca, -ae	picture gallery
pinax, -kes	panel painting, often with wooden shutters
rhyton, -a	horn-shaped drinking cup

secco	in contrast to fresco painting; pigment added after the plaster has partially dried (Italian)
socle	bottom zone of wall painting
spintria, -ae	coinlike gaming pieces with a sexual representation on one side and a numeral on the other
strigil, -es	curved bronze scraper used by Greeks and Romans, especially after the bath
strophium, -a	a woman's breast band
stucco	fine lime plaster (Italian)
tabella, -ae	painting on wood panel, also tablet, board for games, placard
tablinum, -a	main reception room of the domus, focal point of the axis running from entryway through the atrium
terra sigillata	modern archaeological term for terra-cotta ware with relief decoration produced in Gaul and Germany from the first century A.D. on
tessera, -ae	cube-shaped stone used to make a mosaic; also used of gaming pieces
thyrsus, -i	wand carried by devotees of Dionysus
triclinium, -a	dining hall with three couches (klinai) arranged against the side and rear walls

A Guide to Classical Texts

My references to ancient Greek and Latin texts, usually contained in the notes, employ the standard English-language citation system: the author's name, followed by the conventional Latin name for the work (here spelled out in full rather than abbreviated), followed by arabic numerals that guide the reader to chapter, paragraph, and line. For abbreviations, and discussions of authors and their texts, please see *The Oxford Classical Dictionary,* edited by N. G. L. Hammond and H. H. Scullard, 2d ed. (Oxford, 1970).

In the following list of ancient works cited in this book, I have cited the readily available volumes of the *Loeb Classical Library.* This ongoing series, begun early in this century, encompasses both Greek and Latin authors and provides the Greek or Latin text on the left-hand page, with a good English translation facing it. For texts not available in the Loeb series, I cite a standard critical edition of the text.

Aeschines *Against Timarchus*	Aeschines. *The Speeches of Aeschines.* Translated by Charles Darwin Adams. Loeb Classical Library. New York, 1919.
Anthologia Palatina	*The Greek Anthology.* Translated by W. R. Paton. Loeb Classical Library. 5 vols. New York, 1916–1918.
Appian *Bella Civilia*	Appianus of Alexandria. *Appian's Roman History.* Translated by Horace White et al. 4 vols. Loeb Classical Library. Cambridge, Mass., 1912–1913. [Includes the five books of *Bella Civilia.*]

Apuleius *Metamorphoses*	Apuleius. *Metamorphoses.* Edited and translated by J. Arthur Hanson. 2 vols. Loeb Classical Library. Cambridge, Mass., 1989.
Aristophanes	*Aristophanes.* Translated by Benjamin Bickley Rogers. 3 vols. Loeb Classical Library. New York, 1924. [Includes *Lysistrata, Plutus, Thesmophoriazusae.*]
Aristotle *Politics*	Aristotle. *The Politics of Aristotle.* Translated by Ernest Baker. Oxford, 1946.
Artemidorus Daldianus *Oneirocritica*	Artemidorus Daldianus. *The Interpretation of Dreams.* Translated by Robert J. White. Noyes Classical Studies. Park Ridge, N.J., 1975.
Catullus	*Catullus, Tibullus, Pervigilium Veneris.* The poems of Gaius Valerius Catullus translated by F. W. Cornish; Tibullus, by J. P. Postgate; Pervigilium Veneris, by J. W. Mackail. Loeb Classical Library. 2d ed. Cambridge, Mass., 1988.
Cicero *De Oratore*	Cicero, *De Oratore.* Books 1–3. Vols. 3–4 of *Cicero in Twenty-Eight Volumes.* Translated by E. W. Sutton and H. Rackham. Loeb Classical Library. Cambridge, Mass., 1942.
———. *Epistulae ad Familiares*	Cicero, *Letters to his Friends.* Vols. 22–24 of *Cicero in Twenty-Eight Volumes.* Translated by W. Glynn Williams. Loeb Classical Library. Cambridge, Mass., 1927.
———. *Rhetorica ad Herennium*	Cicero. *Ad C. Herennium.* Vol. 1 of *Cicero in Twenty-Eight Volumes.* Translated by Harry Caplan. Loeb Classical Library. Cambridge, Mass., 1954.
Corpus Inscriptionum Latinarum	17 Volumes. Edited by Theodor Mommsen, et al. Berlin, 1863–.

Digest	*Digesta Iustiniani. The Digest of Justinian.* Latin text edited by Theodor Mommsen, English translation by Alan Watson. Philadelphia, 1985.
Dio Cassius *Historia Romana*	Cassius Dio Cocceianus. *Dio's Roman History.* Translated by Earnest Cary. 9 vols. Loeb Classical Library. New York, 1914–1927.
Diogenes Laertius	Diogenes Laertius. *Lives of the Eminent Philosophers.* Translated by R. D. Hicks. 2 vols. Loeb Classical Library. New York, 1925.
Herodian *Historiae*	*Herodian.* Translated by C. R. Whittaker. 2 vols. Loeb Classical Library. Cambridge, Mass., 1969–1970.
Herodotus *Historia*	*Herodotus.* Translated by A. D. Godley. 4 vols. Loeb Classical Library. Cambridge, Mass., 1920–1925.
Hesiod *Theogonia*	Hesiod. *Theogony.* Translated by Hugh Evelyn White. Loeb Classical Library. Cambridge, Mass., 1927.
Homer *Odyssey*	Homer. *The Odyssey.* Translated by A. T. Murray. 2 vols. Loeb Classical Library. New York, 1919.
Horace *Satires*	Horace. *Satires, Epistles and Ars Poetica.* Translated by H. Rushton Fairclough. Cambridge, Mass., 1926.
Lucian *Dialogi Meretricii*	*Lucian.* Translated by A. M. Harmon, K. Kilburn, and M. D. McLeod. 8 vols. Loeb Classical Library. Cambridge, Mass., 1913–1967 [Includes *Dialogues of the Courtesans* and *Praeceptor Rhetorum.*]
Martial	Martial. *Epigrams.* Edited and translated by D. R. Shackleton Bailey. 2 vols. Loeb Classical Library. Cambridge, Mass., 1993.

Ovid *Ars Amatoria*	Ovid. *The Art of Love and other Poems.* Translated by J. H. Mozley. Loeb Classical Library. New York, 1929.
———. *Metamorphoses*	Ovid. *Metamorphoses.* Translated by Frank Justus Miller. Loeb Classical Library. 1916, Cambridge, Mass., 1977.
———. *Tristia*	Ovid. *Tristia. Ex Ponto.* Translated by Arthur Leslie Wheeler. Loeb Classical Library. 1924, Cambridge, Mass., 1988.
Pausanias	Pausanias. *Description of Greece.* Translated by W. H. S. Jones. 4 vols. with companion vol. of maps, plans, and indices. Loeb Classical Library. Cambridge, Mass., 1935.
Petronius *Satyricon*	Petronius Arbiter. *Satyricon.* Translated by Michael Heseltine, revised by E. H. Warmington. Loeb Classical Library. 2d ed. London, 1969.
Philostratus *Vita Apollonii*	Philostratus, Flavius. *The Life of Apollonius of Tyana, the Epistles of Apollonis and the Treatise of Eusebius.* Translated by F. C. Conybeare. 2 vols. Loeb Classical Library. New York, 1912.
———. *Vitae Sophistarum*	Philostratus, Flavius. *The Lives of the Sophists. Eunipius.* Translated by Wilmer Cave Wright. Loeb Classical Library. Cambridge, Mass., 1921.
Plautus *Curculio*	Plautus. *Casina, The Casket Comedy, Curculio, Epidicus, The Two Menaechmuses.* Translated by Paul Nixon. Vol. 2. Loeb Classical Library. Cambridge, Mass., 1917.
Pliny (the Elder) *Naturalis Historia*	Pliny the Elder. *Natural History.* Translated by Horace Rackham, W. H. S. Jones, and D. E. Eichholz. 10 vols. Loeb Classical Library. Cambridge, Mass., 1938–1963.

Plutarch *Moralia*	Plutarch. *Moralia.* Translated by Frank Cole Babbitt et al. 16 vols. Loeb Classical Library. Cambridge, Mass., 1927–1969.
———. *Vitae Parallelae*	Plutarch. *Plutarch's Lives.* Translated by Bernadotte Perrin. 11 vols. Loeb Classical Library. 2d ed. Cambridge, Mass., 1949–1959.
Polybius	Polybius. *The Histories.* Translated by W. R. Paton. 6 vols. Loeb Classical Library. New York, 1922–1927.
Porphyrio(n) *Scholia*	*Pomponi Porfyrionis commentum in Horatium Flaccum.* Edited by Alfred Holder. 1894; Hildesheim, 1967.
Priapea	*Catvlli, Tibvlli, Propertii Carmina. Accedvnt Laevii, Calvii, Cinnae, aliorum reliqviae et Priapea.* Edited by Lvcianvs Mveller. Leipzig, 1884.
Propertius	Propertius, Sextus. *Propertius.* Translated by H. E. Butler. Loeb Classical Library. Cambridge, Mass., 1939.
Pseudo-Acro *Pseudoacronis scholia*	*Pseudoacronis scholia in Horatium vetustiora.* Edited by Otto Keller. 2 vols. Leipzig, 1902–1904.
Quintilian *Institutio oratoria*	Quintilian. *The Institutio oratoria of Quintilian.* Translated by H. E. Butler. 4 vols. Loeb Classical Library. New York, 1921–1922.
Scriptores Historiae Augustae	*The Scriptores historiae Augustae.* Translated by David Magie and Ainsworth O'Brien-Moore. 3 vols. Loeb Classical Library. New York, 1922–1932. [Includes *Alexander Severus, Heliogabalus,* and *Severus.*]
Seneca (the Elder) *Controversiae*	The Elder Seneca. *Controversiae. Suasoriae.* Translated by M. Winterbottom. 2 vols. Loeb Classical Library. Cambridge, Mass., 1974.

Seneca (the Younger) *Questiones Naturales*	Seneca, Lucius Annaeus. *Naturales Questiones.* Translated by Thomas H. Corcoran. 2 vols. Loeb Classical Library. Cambridge, Mass., 1971.
Sidonius Apollinaris *Epistulae*	Sidonius Apollinaris, Saint. *Poems and Letters.* Translated by W. B. Anderson. Loeb Classical Library. Cambridge, Mass., 1936.
Strabo *Geographia*	Strabo. *The Geography of Strabo.* Translated by Horace Leonard Jones. 8 vols. Loeb Classical Library. New York, 1917–1933.
Suda (Suidas)	*Suidae Lexicon post Ludolphum Kusterum ad codices manuscriptos.* Edited by Thomas Gaisford. Oxford, 1834.
Suetonius *De Poetis*	*Svetonio De poetis e biografi minori.* Edited with commentaries in Italian by Augusto Rostagni. Turin, 1964.
———. *De Vita Caesarum*	Suetonius. *Lives of the Caesars.* Translated by J. C. Rolfe. 2 vols. Loeb Classical Library. 2d ed. Cambridge, Mass., 1950–1951. [Includes *Divus Augustus; Tiberius; Vespasian.*]
Tacitus *Annales*	Tacitus. *The Histories and the Annals.* Translated by Clifford H. Moore and John Jackson. 4 vols. Loeb Classical Library. New York, 1925–1937.
Theocritus *Idylls*	*The Greek Bucolic Poets.* Translated by J. M. Edmonds. Loeb Classical Library. Rev. ed. Cambridge, Mass., 1928.
Valerius Maximus	Valerius Maximus. *Factorum et dictorum memorabilium libri novem.* Edited by Karl Friedrich Kempf. New York, 1976. Reprint of Berlin 1854 edition.
Vitruvius *De Architectura*	Vitruvius Pollio. *On Architecture.* Translated by Frank Granger. 2 vols. Loeb Classical Library. Cambridge, Mass., 1962.

Bibliography

Adam, Jean-Pierre, and Pierre Varène. "Une peinture romaine représentant un scène de chantier." *Revue archéologique* 2 (1980): 213–238.

Adams, J. N. *The Latin Sexual Vocabulary.* London, 1982.

Ajootian, Aileen. "Hermaphroditos." *Lexicon Iconographicum Mythologiae Classicae,* vol. 5, part 1, 268–285.

Alexander, Christine. *Arretine Relief Ware.* Corpus Vasorum Antiquorum, U.S.A. fasc. 9, Metropolitan Museum of Art, New York, fasc. 1. Cambridge, Mass., 1943.

Alfonsi, A. "Este: Scoperta di un pavimento a mosaico." *Notizie degli scavi* (1911): 313–315.

Amtmann, Th. *Lit nuptial, terre cuite gallo-romaine.* Bordeaux, 1892.

Andreae, Bernard. "I pavoni della villa di Oplontis." In *La regione sotterrata dal Vesuvio: studi e prospettive,* Atti del Convegno internazionale 11–15 November 1979, edited by Alfonso de Franciscis, 531–533. Naples, 1982.

———. "Stuckreliefs und Fresken der Farnesina." In *Führer durch den offentlichen Sammlungen Roms,* by Wolfgang Helbig, edited by Hermione Speier. Vol. 3. 4th ed., 430–452. Tübingen, 1969.

Andreau, Jean P. *Les affaires de Monsieur Jucundus.* Collection de l'Ecole française de Rome, no. 19. Rome, 1974.

———. "The Freedman." In *The Romans,* edited by Andrea Giardina, translated by Lydia G. Cochrane, 175–198. Chicago, 1993.

Arezzo, Museo archeologico nazionale. *Capolavori di Euphronios: un pioniere della ceramografia attica.* Exhibition catalog, 26 May–31 July 1990. Arezzo, 1990.

Ariès, Philippe, and André Béjin, eds. *Western Sexuality: Practice and Precept in Past and Present Times.* Translated by Anthony Forster. Oxford, 1985.

Bailey, Donald M. *Greek and Roman Pottery Lamps.* London, 1963.

———. *Roman Lamps Made in Italy.* Vol. 2 of *A Catalogue of Lamps in the British Museum.* London, 1980.

———. *Roman Provincial Lamps.* Vol. 3 of *A Catalogue of Lamps in the British Museum.* London, 1988.

Baratte, François. "Arts précieux et propagande impériale au début de l'empire romain: l'exemple des deux coupes de Boscoreale." *Revue du Louvre et des Musées de France* 41, no. 1 (1991): 24–39.

———. *Le trésor d'argenterie gallo-romaine de Notre-Dame-d'Alençon.* Paris, 1981.

———. *Le trésor d'orfèvrerie romain de Boscoreale.* Paris, 1986.

———, ed. *Argenterie romaine et byzantine.* Actes de la Table Ronde, Paris, 11–13 October 1983. Paris, 1988.

Baratte, François, and Kenneth Painter, eds., *Trésors d'orfèvrerie gallo-romains.* Exhibition catalog, 8 February–23 April 1989. Paris, 1989.

Bargellini, P. "Le terme centrali di Pompei." In *Les thermes romains.* Collection de l'Ecole française de Rome, no. 142, 115–128. Rome, 1991.

Barré, M. L. *Musée secret.* Vol. 8 of *Herculaneum et Pompéi, recueil général des peintures, bronzes, mosaïques, etc. découverts jusqu'à ce jour et reproduits d'après le antichità di Ercolano, il Museo Borbonico et tous les ouvrages analogues.* Paris, 1877.

Barton, Carlin A. *The Sorrows of the Ancient Romans: The Gladiator and the Monster.* Princeton, 1993.

Bastet, Frédéric, and Mariette de Vos. *Proposta per una classificazione del terzo stile pompeiano.* Archeologische Studiën van het Nederlands Instituut te Rome, 4. The Hague, 1979.

Beardsley, Grace H. *The Negro in Greek and Roman Civilization: A Study of the Ethiopian Type.* 1929. New York, 1967.

Becatti, Giovanni. *I mitrei.* Vol. 2 of *Scavi di Ostia.* Rome, 1954.

———. *Mosaici e pavimenti marmorei.* Vol. 4 of *Scavi di Ostia.* Rome, 1961.

Bendinelli, G. *Le pitture del Colombario di Villa Pamphili.* Monumenti della pittura antica scoperti in Italia. Section 3, Roma, fasc. 5. Rome, 1941.

Berger, John. *Ways of Seeing.* London, 1977.

Bergmann, Bettina. "Fictions of the Roman Picture Gallery." Paper given at the annual conference of the College Art Association, 1995. Synopsis in *Abstracts 1995* (New York, 1995), 150.

———. "Painted Perspectives of a Villa Visit." In *Roman Art in the Private Sphere,* edited by Elaine Gazda, 49–70. Ann Arbor, 1991.

———. "The Pregnant Moment: Tragic Wives in the Roman Interior." In *Sexuality in Ancient Art,* edited by Natalie B. Kampen, 199–218. Cambridge, 1996.

———. "The Roman House as Memory Theater." *Art Bulletin* 76 (1994): 225–256.

Berlin, Antikenmuseum. *Kaiser Augustus und die verlorene Republik.* Exhibition catalog, Staatliche Museen Preußischer Kulturbesitz, 7 June–15 August 1988. Berlin, 1988.

———. Staatliche Museen Preußischer Kulturbesitz. *Römisches im Antikenmuseum.* Berlin, 1978.

Berthier, André. "Une mosaïque solaire trouvée à Constantine." In *Mélanges d'archéologie, d'épigraphie et d'histoire offerts à Jérôme Carcopino,* 113–124. Paris, 1966.

Beyen, Hendrik G. "Les *domini* de la Villa de la Farnesine." *Studia varia Carolo Guilielmo Vollgraff a discipulis oblata,* 3–21. Amsterdam, 1948.

Bianchi-Bandinelli, Ranuccio. *Rome: The Center of Power.* Translated by Peter Green. New York, 1970.

———. *Rome: The Late Empire.* Translated by Peter Green. New York, 1971.

Bieber, Margarete. *Sculpture of the Hellenistic Age.* New York, 1961.

Blake, Marion E. "The Pavements of the Roman Buildings of the Republic and Early Empire." *Memoirs of the American Academy in Rome* 8 (1930).

Blanc, Nicole, and Françoise Gury. "Eros/Amor, Cupido." *Lexicon Iconographicum Mythologiae Classicae,* vol. 3, part 1, 952.

Blanck, Horst. "Il maripara: eine Priapstatue in Formello." *Römische Mitteilungen* 86 (1979): 339–350.

Blanckenhagen, Peter von. "Puerilia." In *In Memoriam Otto Brendel,* edited by Larissa Bonfante and Helga von Heintze, 37–41. Mainz, 1976.

Blanckenhagen, Peter von, and Christine Alexander. *The Paintings from Boscotrecase.* Römische Mitteilungen, Supplement 6. Mainz, 1962.

Bloom, Amy. "The Body Lies." *The New Yorker,* 18 July 1994, 38–49.

Boardman, John, and Eugenio La Rocca. *Eros in Griechenland.* London, 1976.

Bonfante, Larissa. "Etruscan Sexuality and Funerary Art." In *Sexuality in Ancient Art,* edited by Natalie B. Kampen, 155–169. New York, 1996.

Boschung, Dietrich. *Die Bildnisse des Augustus.* Das römische Herrscherbild, part 1, vol. 2. Berlin, 1993.

Boswell, John. *Christianity, Social Tolerance, and Homosexuality.* Chicago, 1980.

———. "Concepts, Experience, and Sexuality." *differences* 2, no. 1 (1990): 67–87.

Bowen-Ward, R. "Women in Roman Baths." *Harvard Theological Review* 85 (1992): 125–147.

Bowie, Theodore, Otto J. Brendel, Paul H. Gebhard, Robert Rosenblum, and Leo Steinberg. *Studies in Erotic Art.* New York, 1970.

Bragantini, Irene. "VI, 10, 1: Caupona della Via di Mercurio." In *Pompei, pitture e mosaici,* 4:1005–1028. Rome, 1993.

———. "VI 14, 35.36: Caupona di Salvius." In *Pompei, pitture e mosaici,* 5:366–371. Rome, 1994.

Bragantini, Irene, Franca Parise Badoni, and Mariette de Vos. *Pompei 1748–1980: i tempi della documentazione.* Exhibition catalog. Rome, 1981.

Bragantini, Irene, and Mariette de Vos. *Le decorazioni della villa romana della Farnesina.* Vol. 2, part 1 of *Museo Nazionale Romano: Le pitture.* Rome, 1982.

Bragantini, Irene, Mariette de Vos, and Franca Parise Badoni. *Pitture e pavimenti di Pompei.* Repertorio delle fotografie del Gabinetto Fotografico Nazionale, Istituto Centrale per il Catalogo e la Documentazione. 4 vols. Rome, 1981–1992.

Brendel, Otto J. "The Scope and Temperament of Erotic Art in the Greco-Roman World." In *Studies in Erotic Art,* by Theodore Bowie et al. New York, 1970.

Brilliant, Richard. *Rank and Gesture in Roman Art.* New Haven, 1963.

———. *Visual Narratives.* Ithaca, 1984.

Brooten, Bernadette. "Paul's Views on the Nature of Women and Female Homoeroticism." In *Immaculate and Powerful: The Female Sacred Image and Social Reality,* edited by C. W. Atkinson, C. H. Buchanan, and M. Miles, 61–87. Boston, 1985.

Brown, A. C. *Catalogue of Italian Terra-Sigillata in the Ashmolean Museum.* Oxford, 1968.

Brückner, Alfred. *Anakalypteria.* Winckelmannsprogramm, 64. Archäologische Gesellschaft zu Berlin. Berlin, 1904.

Burdett, Osbert, and E. H. Goddard, *Edward Perry Warren: The Biography of a Connoisseur.* London, 1941.

Butler, Judith P. *Gender Trouble: Feminism and the Subversion of Identity.* New York, 1990.

Buttrey, T. V. "The Spintriae as a Historical Source." *The Numismatic Chronicle and Journal of the Royal Numismatic Society* 13 (1973): 52–63.

Caldera Castro, María del Pilar. "Un balsamario de vidrio camafeo procedente de Ostippo (Estepa, Sevilla)." *Archivo español de arqueología* 59 (1986): 211–218.

Calza, Guido. "Scavi recenti nell'abitato di Ostia." *Monumenti antichi* 26 (1920): 322–430.

Cantarella, Eva. "Adulterio, omocidio leggitimo e causa d'onore in diritto romano." In *Studi in onore di Gaetano Scherillo,* 1:243–244. Milan, 1973.

———. *Bisexuality in the Ancient World.* Translated by C. O. Cuilleanáin. New Haven, 1992.

———. *Pandora's Daughters: The Role and Status of Woman in Greek and Roman Antiquity.* Translated by Maureen B. Fant. Baltimore, 1987.

Cantilena, Renata. "Vizi privati e pubbliche virtù. Il 'Gabinetto degli oggetti riservati' del Museo di Napoli." In *L'amore: dall'Olimpo all'alcova,* 51–60. Exhibition catalog. Milan, 1992.

Carandini, Andrea. *Settefinestre: una villa schiavistica nell'Etruria romana.* 3 vols. Modena, 1985.

Castrén, Paavo. *Ordo Populusque Pompeianus: Polity and Society in Roman Pompeii.* Rome, 1975.

Castriota, David. *The Ara Pacis Augustae and the Imagery of Abundance in Later Greek and Early Roman Imperial Art.* Princeton, 1995.

Cataudella, Q. "Intiamenta Amoris." *Latomus* 33 (1974): 847–857.

Cèbe, Jean Pierre. *La caricature et la parodie dans le monde romain antique, des origines à Juvénal.* Paris, 1966.

Chase, George H. *Catalogue of Arretine Pottery.* Museum of Fine Arts, Boston, 1916. Enlarged edition with additions by Mary B. Comstock and Cornelius C. Vermeule. Cambridge, Mass., 1975.

Christiansen, Jette, and Torben Melander, eds. *Proceedings of the 3d Symposium on Ancient Greek and Related Pottery,* Copenhagen, 31 August–4 September 1987. Copenhagen, 1988.

Clarke, John R. "The Decor of the House of Jupiter and Ganymede at Ostia Antica: Private Residence Turned Gay Hotel?" In *Roman Art in the Private Sphere,* edited by Elaine Gazda, 89-104. Ann Arbor, 1991.

———. "Form, Function, and Meaning of *Symplegmata* in Pompeian Mosaics: The Case for the 'Domestication' of Sex." In *Actes du VIIe Colloque international pour l'étude de la mosaïque antique,* Tunis, 3–7 October 1994, edited by Mongi Ennaifer. Forthcoming.

———. *The Houses of Roman Italy, 100 B.C.–A.D. 250: Ritual, Space, and Decoration.* Berkeley, 1991.

———. "Hypersexual Black Men in Augustan Baths: Ideal Somatotypes and Apotropaic Magic." In *Sexuality in Ancient Art,* edited by Natalie B. Kampen, 184–198. New York, 1996.

———. "Landscape Paintings in the Villa of Oplontis." *Journal of Roman Archaeology* 9 (1996): 81–107.

———. "Mosaic Workshops at Pompeii and Ostia Antica." In *Fifth International Colloquium on Ancient Mosaics,* Bath, England, 5–12 September 1987, edited by Peter Johnson, Roger Ling, and David J. Smith, 91–98. Ann Arbor, 1994.

———. "New Light on the Iconography of Jupiter, Ganymede, and Leda in the House of Jupiter and Ganymede at Ostia Antica." *4. Internationales Kolloquium zur römischen Wandmalerei, Kölner Jahrbuch für Vor- und Frühgeschichte* 24 (1991): 171–175.

———. "Notes on the Coordination of Wall, Floor, and Ceiling Decoration in the Houses of Roman Italy, 100 BCE–235 CE." In *IL 60: Essays Honoring Irving Lavin on his Sixtieth Birthday,* edited by Marilyn Aronberg Lavin, 1–29. New York, 1990.

———. "The Origins of Black-and-White Figural Mosaics in the Region Destroyed by Vesuvius." In *La regione sotterrata dal Vesuvio: studi e prospettive,* Atti del Convegno internazionale 11–15 November 1979, edited by Alfonso de Franciscis, 661–688. Naples, 1982.

———. *Roman Black-and-White Figural Mosaics.* New York, 1979.

———. "The Warren Cup and the Contexts for Representations of Male-to-Male Lovemaking in Augustan and Early Julio-Claudian Art." *Art Bulletin* 75, 2 (June 1993): 275–294.

Cohen, David. *Law, Sexuality and Society: The Enforcement of Morals in Classical Athens.* Cambridge, 1991.

Coletti Strangi, A. *Cosmesi e seduzione in Ovidio e nel mondo romano.* Aquila, 1992.

Comstock, Mary B., and Cornelius C. Vermeule. *Greek, Etruscan, and Roman Bronzes in the Boston Museum of Fine Arts.* Boston, 1972.

Connor, Peter J. "The Dead Hero and the Sleeping Giant by the Nikosthenes Painter at the Beginnings of a Motif." *Archäologischer Anzeiger* 99 (1984): 387–394.

Corbeill, Anthony. *Controlling Laughter: Political Humor in the Late Roman Republic.* Princeton, 1996.

Croisille, Jean-Michel. *Poésie et art figuré de Néron aux Flaviens.* Brussels, 1982.

Curtius, Ludwig. *Die Wandmalerei Pompejis.* Leipzig, 1929.

D'Arms, John H. *Commerce and Social Standing in Ancient Rome.* Cambridge, Mass., 1981.

Dasen, Véronique. *Dwarfs in Ancient Egypt and Greece.* Oxford, 1993.

———. "Pygmaioi." *Lexicon Iconographicum Mythologiae Classicae,* vol. 8, part 1, 594–601.

de Haan, Nathalie. "Dekoration und Funktion in den Privatbädern von Pompeji und Herculaneum." *Bulletin Antieke Beschaving,* supplement 3, *Functional and Spatial Analysis of Wall Painting* (proceedings of the Fifth International Congress on Ancient Wall Painting, Amsterdam, 8–12 September 1992), edited by Eric M. Moormann (1993): 34–37.

DeLaine, Janet. "Recent Research on Roman Baths." *Journal of Roman Archaeology* 1 (1988): 11–32.

Delcourt, M. *Hermaphroodite: mythes et rites de la bisexualité dans l'antiquité classique.* Paris, 1955.

Della Corte, Matteo. *Case ed abitanti di Pompei.* 3d ed. Naples, 1965.

———. "Le iscrizioni di Ercolano." *Rendiconti della Accademia di archeologia, lettere e belle arti, Napoli* 33 (1958): 239–308.

D'Emilio, John. "Capitalism and Gay Identity." In *Powers of Desire: The Politics of Sexuality,* edited by Ann Snitow, Christine Stansell, and Sharon Thompson, 100–113. New York, 1983.

Desbat, A. "Vases à médaillons d'applique des fouilles récentes de Lyon." *Figlina* 5–6 (1980–1981): 1–205.

Deubner, Otfried R. "Griechische Reliefkeramik in hellenistischer Zeit." *Archäologischer Anzeiger* 54 (1939): cols. 333–350.

———. "Miszellen zur hellenistische Reliefkeramik." *Archäologischer Anzeiger* 109 (1994): 87–92.

de Vos, Arnold. "I 7, 11: Casa dell'Efebo o di P. Cornelius Tages." In *Pompei, pitture e mosaici,* 1:619–727. Rome, 1990.

———. "V 1, 26: Casa di L. Caecilius Iucundus e Casa annessa V 1, 23." In *Pompei, pitture e mosaici,* 3:574–620. Rome, 1991.

de Vos, Arnold, and Mariette de Vos. *Pompei Ercolano Stabia.* Guida archeologica Laterza, no. 11. Rome, 1982.

de Vos, Mariette. "Camillo Paderni, la tradizione antiquaria romana e i collezionisti inglesi." In *Ercolano 1738–1988: 250 anni di ricerca archeologica,* Atti del Convegno internazionale Ravello-Ercolano-Napoli-Pompei, 30 October–5 November 1988, ed. Luisa Franchi dell'Orto, 99–116. Rome, 1993.

———. *L'egittomania in pitture e mosaici romano-campani della prima età imperiale.* Etudes préliminaires aux religions orientales dans l'empire romain, no. 84. Leiden, 1980.

———. "Paving Techniques at Pompeii." *Archaeological News* 16, nos. 1–4 (1991): 36–60.

Dexter, Caroline E. "The Casa di L. Cecilio Giocondo in Pompeii." Ph.D. dissertation, Duke University, 1975.

Dickie, M. W., and Katherine M. D. Dunbabin. "*Invidia rumpantur pectora:* The Iconography of Phthonos/Invidia in Graeco-Roman Art." *Jahrbuch für Antike und Christentum* 26 (1983): 7–37.

Dierichs, Angelika. *Erotik in der Kunst Griechenlands.* Mainz, 1993.

Dixon, Suzanne. *The Roman Family.* Baltimore and London, 1992.

Doane, Mary Anne. "Film and the Masquerade: Theorising the Female Spectator." *Screen* 23, no. 314 (1982): 74–88.

Donderer, Michael. *Die Mosaizisten des Antike und ihre wirtschaftliche und soziale Stellung: Eine Quellenstudie.* Erlanger Forschungen Reihe A, Geisteswissenschaften, vol. 48. Nuremberg, 1989.

Dover, Kenneth J. *Greek Homosexuality.* Cambridge, Mass., 1978.

Dragendorff, Hans, and Carl Watzinger. *Arretinische Reliefkeramik mit Beschreibung der Sammlung in Tübingen.* Reutlingen, 1948.

Drerup, Heinrich. "Bildraum und Realraum in der römischen Architektur." *Römische Mitteilungen* 66 (1959): 147–174.

DuBois, Paige. *Sowing the Body: Psychoanalysis and Ancient Representations of Women.* Chicago, 1988.

Dunbabin, Katherine M. D. "*Baiarum Grata Voluptas:* Pleasures and Dangers of the Baths." *Papers of the British School in Rome* 57 (1989): 6–49.

———. "*Ipsa deae vestigia* . . . Footprints Divine and Human on Graeco-Roman Monuments." *Journal of Roman Archaeology* 3 (1990): 99–102.

———. "Sic Erimus Cuncti . . . The Skeleton in Graeco-Roman Art." *Jahrbuch des deutschen archäologischen Instituts* 101 (1986): 186-255.

———. "Triclinium and Stibadium." In *Dining in a Classical Context,* edited by William J. Slater, 121–148. Ann Arbor, 1991.

Dynes, Wayne R. *Homosexuality: A Research Guide.* New York, 1987.

Dynes, Wayne R., and Stephen Donaldson. *Homosexuality in the Ancient World.* New York, 1992.

Edwards, Catharine. *The Politics of Immorality in Ancient Rome.* Cambridge, 1993.

Elsner, Jaś. *Roman Art and the Viewer.* New York, 1995.

Ericsson, C. H. "The Great Nilotic Mosaic in Palestrina." *Sundries in Honour of T. Säve-Söndergergh,* 55–65. Uppsala, 1984.

Eros grec: amour des dieux et des hommes. Exhibition catalog. Paris, November 1989–February 1990; Athens, March–May 1990. Athens, 1989.

Ettlinger, E. "How was Arretine Ware Sold?" *Rei cretariae romanae fautorum acta* 25–26 (1987): 5–19.

Fabré, G. *Libertus: recherche sur les rapports patron-affranchi à la fin de la république romaine.* Collection de l'Ecole française de Rome, no. 50. Rome, 1981.

Fabroni, A. *Storia degli antichi vasi fittili aretini.* Arezzo, 1841.

Famin, César. *Musée royal de Naples: peintures, bronzes et statues érotiques du cabinet secret, avec leur explication.* Paris, 1836.

Fausto-Sterling, Anne. "The Five Sexes." *New York Academy of Sciences* (March–April 1993): 20–26.

Favro, Diane. *The Urban Image of Augustan Rome.* New York, 1996.

Felletti Maj, Bianca Maria. *Le pitture della casa delle volte dipinte e della casa delle pareti gialle.* Monumenti della pittura antica scoperti in Italia. Section 3, Ostia, fasc. 1–2. Rome, 1961.

Fiorelli, Giuseppe. *Catalogo del Museo nazionale di Napoli: raccolta pornografica.* Naples, 1866.

———. *Descrizione di Pompei.* Naples, 1875.

———. *Pompeianarum antiquitatum historia.* 3 vols. Naples, 1860–1864.

Fittschen, Klaus. "Die Bildnisse des Augustus." *Saeculum aureum* 3 (1991): 149–186.

Foley, Helene P., ed. *Reflections of Women in Antiquity.* New York, 1981.

Fonseca, Isabel. "Among the Gypsies." *New Yorker,* 25 September 1995, 92–93.

Foucault, Michel. *The Care of the Self,* translated by Robert Hurley. Vol. 3 of *The History of Sexuality.* New York, 1986. Original title, *Le souci de soi.* Vol. 3 of *Histoire de la sexualité* (Paris, 1984).

———. *An Introduction,* translated by Robert Hurley. Vol. 1 of *The History of Sexuality.* New York, 1986. Original title, *La volonté de savoir.* Vol. 1 of *Histoire de la sexualité* (Paris, 1976).

———. *The Use of Pleasure,* translated by Robert Hurley. Vol. 2 of *The History of Sexuality.* New York, 1985. Original title, *L'usage des plaisirs.* Vol. 2 of *Histoire del la sexualité* (Paris, 1984).

Fraschetti, Augusto. "A proposito di ex-schiavi e della loro integrazione in ambito cittadino a Roma." *Opus* 1 (1982): 97–103.

Fraser, Peter. *Ptolemaic Alexandria.* Oxford, 1972.

Fremersdorf, Fritz. *Römische Bildlampen.* Bonn and Leipzig, 1922.

Frente de Afirmación Hispanista. *Museo secreto del arte erótico de Pompeya y Herculano.* Reprint. Mexico City, 1995.

Fröhlich, Thomas. *Lararien- und Fassadenbilder in den Vesuvstädten.* Römische Mitteilungen, Supplement 32. Mainz, 1991.

Frontisi-Ducroux, Françoise. "Eros, Desire, and the Gaze." In *Sexuality in Ancient Art,* edited by Natalie B. Kampen, 81–100. New York, 1996.

Fuss, Diana. *Essentially Speaking.* New York, 1989.

Gabelmann, Hanns. "Römische Kinder in Toga Praetexta." *Jahrbuch des Deutschen Archäologischen Instituts* 100 (1985): 497–541.

Galinsky, Karl. *Aeneas, Sicily, and Rome.* Princeton, 1969.

———. *Augustan Culture: An Interpretive Introduction.* Princeton, 1996.

Garber, Marjorie B. *Cross-Dressing and Cultural Anxiety.* New York, 1992.

Garland, Robert. *The Eye of the Beholder: Deformity and Disability in the Graeco-Roman World.* Cornell, 1995.

Gassner, V. *Kaufläden in Pompeji.* Vienna, 1986.

Gercke, W. *Untersuchungen zum römischen Kinderporträt.* Hamburg, 1968.

Germain, Suzanne. *Les mosaïques de Timgad: étude descriptive et analytique.* Paris, 1969.

Gilmore, David D. *Honor and Shame and the Unity of the Mediterranean.* Washington, D.C., 1987.

Giuliani, Luca. "Der seligen Krüppel: zur Deutung von Mißgestalten in der hellenistischen Kleinkunst." *Archäologische Anzeiger* 102 (1987): 701–721.

Gleason, Maud W. *Making Men: Sophists and Self-Presentation in Ancient Rome.* Princeton, 1995.

Goette, H. R. *Studien zu römischen Togadastellungen.* Mainz, 1990.

Goldstein, S. M., L. S. Rakow, and J. K. Rakow. *Cameo Glass.* Corning, N.Y., 1982.

Gordon, A. E. *Illustrated Introduction to Latin Epigraphy.* Berkeley, 1983.

Gourevitch, D., and M. Gourevitch. "Terre cuites hellénistiques d'inspiration médicale au Musée du Louvre." *La Presse médicale* 25, no. 12 (1963): 2752.

Grant, Michael. *Eros in Pompeii.* New York, 1975.

Greenwalt, C. H., Jr. "Sardis, 1979." *Türk arkeoloji dergisi* 26, no. 1 (1982): 95–109.

Greifenhagen, Adolf. *Beiträge zur antiken Reliefkeramik.* Berlin, 1963.

———. "Smikros, Lieblingsinschrift und Malersignatur." *Jahrbuch Berliner Museen* 9 (1967): 5–25.

Griffin, Jasper. "Augustan Poetry and the Life of Luxury." *Journal of Roman Studies* 66 (1976): 87–105.

———. *Latin Poets and Roman Life.* Chapel Hill, 1986.

Gualandi-Genito, M. C. *Le lucerne antiche del Trentino.* Trento, 1986.

Gullini, Giorgio. *I mosaici di Palestrina.* Rome, 1956.

Gunderson, Erik. "Contested Subjects: Rhetorical Theory and the Body." Ph.D. dissertation, University of California, Berkeley, 1996.

Hallett, Judith P. *Fathers and Daughters in Roman Society: Women and the Elite Family.* Princeton, 1984.

———. "Female Homoeroticism and the Denial of Roman Reality in Latin Literature." *Yale Journal of Criticism* 3 (1989): 209–227.

———. "Feminist Theory, Historical Periods, Literary Canons, and the Study of Greco-Roman Antiquity." In *Feminist Theory and the Classics,* edited by Nancy Sorkin Rabinowitz and Amy Richlin, 44–72. New York, 1993.

———. "*Morigerari:* Suetonius, *Tiberius* 44." *Antiquité classique* 47 (1978): 196–200.

———. "Roman Attitudes Toward Sex." In *Civilization of the Ancient Mediterranean: Greece and Rome,* edited by Michael Grant and Rachel Kitzinger, 1265–1278. Vol. 2. New York, 1988.

Hallett, Judith P., and Marilyn Skinner, eds. *Roman Sexualities.* Princeton, forthcoming.

Halperin, David M. *One Hundred Years of Homosexuality.* New York, 1990.

Halperin, David M., John J. Winkler, and Froma I. Zeitlin, eds. *Before Sexuality: The Construction of Erotic Experience in the Ancient Greek World.* Princeton, 1989.

Harris, William V. *Ancient Literacy.* Cambridge, Mass., 1989.

Haynes, Sybille. "Drei neue Silberbecher im British Museum." *Antike Kunst,* 4, no. 1 (1961): 30–37.

Hebdige, Dick. *Subculture: The Meaning of Style.* London, 1979.

Hedreen, Guy. *Silens in Attic Black-figure Vase-painting.* Ann Arbor, 1992.

Heintze, Helga von. "Die antiken Bildnisse Vergils." *Gymnasium* 94 (1987): 481–497.

Helbig, Wolfgang. "Musaici di Centocelle." *Bullettino dell'Instituto di corrispondenza archeologica* (1866): 170–173.

———. *Wandgemälde der vom Vesuv verschütteten Stadte Campaniens.* Leipzig, 1868.

Hellegouarch, J. *Le vocabulaire latin des relations et des partis politiques sous la république.* Paris, 1972.

Henderson, Jeffrey. "Greek Attitudes Toward Sex." In *Civilization of the Ancient Mediter-*

ranean: Greece and Rome, edited by Michael Grant and Rachel Kitzinger, 1249–1264. Vol. 2. New York, 1988.

———. *The Maculate Muse: Obscene Language in Attic Comedy.* 2d ed. New York, 1991.

Herbert, Kevin. *Ancient Art in Bowdoin College: A Descriptive Catalogue of the Warren and Other Collections.* Cambridge, Mass., 1964.

Herdt, Gilbert H., ed. *Ritualized Homosexuality in Melanesia.* Berkeley, 1984.

———. *Rituals of Manhood: Male Initiation in Papua New Guinea.* Berkeley, 1982.

Heres, G. *Die römische Bildlampen der Berliner Antikensammlung.* Berlin, 1972.

Hermans, Lex. *Bewust von andere lusten: Homoseksualiteit in het Romeinse keizerrijk.* Amsterdam, 1995.

Hermansen, Gus. "The Population of Imperial Rome: The Regionaries." *Historia* 27 (1978): 129–168.

Hermet, Frédéric. *Vases graffites.* Vol. 2 of *La Graufesenque (Condatomago).* Paris, 1934.

———. *Vases sigillés.* Vol. 1 of *La Graufesenque (Condatomago).* Paris, 1934.

Herrmann, Paul, and F. Bruckmann, *Denkmäler der Malerei des Altertums.* Munich, 1904–1931.

Himmelmann, Nikolaus. *Alexandria und der Realismus in der griechischen Kunst.* Tübingen, 1983.

Hopkins, Keith. *Conquerors and Slaves.* New York, 1978.

Horsfall, Nicholas. "Stesichorus at Bovillae." *Journal of Hellenic Studies* 99 (1979): 26–48.

Hübner, Gerhild. *Die Applikenkeramik von Pergamon.* Pergamenische Forschungen, vol. 7. Berlin, 1993.

Huelsen, Christian. "Miscellanea epigrafica." *Römische Mitteilungen* 11 (1896): 227–237.

Huld-Zetsche, Ingeborg. *Trierer Reliefsigillata Werkstatt.* Vol. 1. Bonn, 1972.

Hupperts, Charles A. M. "Greek Love: Homosexuality or Paederasty? Greek Love in Black Figure Vase-Painting." In *Proceedings of the 3d Symposium on Ancient Greek and Related Pottery,* Copenhagen, 31 August–4 September 1987, edited by Jette Christiansen and Torben Melander, 255–268. Copenhagen, 1988.

Ioppolo, Giovanni. *Le Terme del Sarno a Pompei.* Rome, 1992.

Jacobelli, Luciana. "Le pitture e gli stucchi delle terme suburbane di Pompei." *4. Internationales Kolloquium zur römischen Wandmalerei, Kölner Jahrbuch für Vor- und Frühgeschichte* 24 (1991): 147–152.

———. *Le pitture erotiche delle terme suburbane di Pompei.* Rome, 1995.

Jashemski, Wilhelmina. *Gardens of Pompeii.* 2 vols. New Rochelle, N.J., 1979–1993.

Jobst, Werner. "Das 'offentliche Freudenhaus' in Ephesos." *Jahreshefte des Österreichischen archäologischen Institutes in Wien* 51 (1976–1977): 61–84.

Johansen, K. F. "An antique replica of the Priam bowl from Hoby." *Acta archaeologica* 1 (1930): 273–277.

———. "New evidence about the Hoby cups." *Acta archaeologica* 31 (1960): 185–190.

Johns, Catherine. "Research on Roman Silver Plate." *Journal of Roman Archaeology* 3 (1990): 28–43.

———. *Sex or Symbol? Erotic Images of Greece and Rome.* Austin, 1982.

Jongman, Willem. *The Economy and Society of Pompeii.* Amsterdam, 1988.

Joshel, Sandra. *Work, Identity, and Legal Status at Rome: A Study of the Occupational Inscriptions.* Norman, Okla., 1992.

Jucker, Hans. *Vom Verhältnis der Römer zur bildenden Kunst der Griechen.* Frankfurt, 1950.

Kampen, Natalie B., ed. *Sexuality in Ancient Art.* New York, 1996.

Käser, Max. "*Infamia* und *ignominia* in dem römische Rechtsquellen." *Zeitschrift der Savigny-Stiftung für Rechtsgeschichte: Römanistische Abteilung* 73 (1956): 220–270.

Kay, Nigel M. *Martial Book XI: A Commentary.* London, 1985.

Kepke, Melissa. "Sexual Satire: The Suburban Baths at Pompeii." Master's thesis, University of Texas at Austin, 1994.

Keuls, Eva. *The Reign of the Phallus: Sexual Politics in Ancient Athens.* New York, 1985.

Kilmer, Martin F. "Genital Phobia and Depilation." *Journal of Hellenic Studies* 111 (1991): 182–193.

———. *Greek Erotica on Attic Red-Figure Vases.* London, 1993.

Kleiner, Diana E. E. *Roman Sculpture.* New Haven, 1992.

Knorr, Robert. *Töpfer und Fabriken verzierter Terra-Sigillata des ersten Jahrhunderts.* Stuttgart, 1919.

Koch-Harnack, Gundel. *Erotische Symbole: Lotosblüte und gemeinsamer Mantel auf antiken Vasen.* Berlin, 1989.

Kolendo, J. "L'esclavage et la vie sexuelle des hommes libres à Rome." *Index* 10 (1981): 288–297.

Koloski-Ostrow, A. *The Sarno Bath Complex.* Rome, 1990.

Konstan, David. *Sexual Symmetry: Love in the Ancient Novel and Related Genres.* Princeton, 1993.

Koortbojian, Michael. *Myth, Meaning, and Memory on Roman Sarcophagi.* Berkeley, 1995.

Krenkel, Werner A. "Fellatio and Irrumatio." *Wissenschaftliche Zeitschrift der Wilhelm-Pieck-Universität Rostock* 29 (1980): 77–88.

———. "Figurae veneris (I)." *Wissenschaftliche Zeitschrift der Wilhelm-Pieck-Universität Rostock* 34 (1985): 50–56.

Künzl, Ernst. "Le argenterie." In *Pompei '79,* edited by Fausto Zevi, 211–228. Naples, 1979.

Kuttner, Ann L. *Dynasty and Empire in the Age of Augustus: The Evidence of the Boscoreale Cups.* Berkeley, 1995.

Lagi, Adele. "I 13, 16." In *Pompei, pitture e mosaici,* 2:928–934. Rome, 1990.

La Penna, A. "La legittimazione del lusso privato da Ennio a vitruvio. Momenti, problemi, personaggi." *Maia* 44 (1989): 3–34.

La Rocca, Eugenio, Arnold de Vos, and Mariette de Vos. *Guida archeologica di Pompei.* Milan, 1976.

Laurence, Ray. *Roman Pompeii: Space and Society.* New York, 1994.

Lefkowitz, Mary R., and Maureen B. Fant. *Women's Life in Greece and Rome: A Sourcebook in Translation.* 2d edition, Baltimore and London, 1992.

Leibundgut, Annalis. *Die römischen Lampen in der Schweiz.* Bern, 1977.

Lessing, Julius, and August Mau. *Wand- und Deckenschmuck eines römischen Hauses aus der Zeit des Augustus.* Berlin, 1891.

Levi, Alda. *Le terrecotte figurate del Museo nazionale di Napoli.* Florence, 1926.

Levi, Doro. *Antioch Mosaic Pavements.* 2 vols. Princeton, 1947.

———. "The Evil Eye and the Lucky Hunchback." In *Antioch-on-the-Orontes,* vol. 3, edited by Richard Stillwell, 220–232. Princeton, 1941.

Licht, Hans. (pseud. Hans Brandt). *Die Homoerotik in der griechischen Literatur: Lukanios vom Samosata.* Bonn, 1921.

———. *Sittengeschichte Griechenlands.* 3 vols. Dresden and Zürich, 1925–1928. Vol. 1. *Die griechische Gesellschaft;* vol. 2. *Das Liebeslebender Griechen;* vol. 3. *Die Erotik in der griechischen Kunst.* Translated by J. J. Freese, without plates, *Sexual Life in Ancient Greece.* London, 1934.

Lilja, Sara. "Homosexuality in Plautus' Plays." *Arctos: Acta philologica Fennica* 16 (1982): 57–64.

———. *Homosexuality in Republican and Augustan Rome.* Helsinki, 1983.

Lippold, Georg. *Antike Gemäldekopien.* Munich, 1951.

Lissarrague, François. "The Sexual Life of Satyrs." In *Before Sexuality: The Construction of Erotic Experience in the Ancient Greek World,* edited by David M. Halperin, John J. Winkler, and Froma I. Zeitlin. Princeton, 1990.

Lloyd, Robert B. "The Aqua Virgo, Euripus, and Pons Agrippa." *American Journal of Archaeology* 83 (1979): 193–204.

Lobel, Edgar, and Denys Page. *Poetarum lesbiorum fragmenta.* Oxford, 1955.

Loeschcke, Siegfried. *Lampen aus Vindonissa: Ein Beitrag zur Geschichte von Vindonissa und des antiken Beleuchtungswesens.* Zurich, 1919.

Loraux, Nicole. *The Experiences of Tiresias: The Feminine and the Greek Man.* Translated by Paula Wissing. Princeton, 1995.

Maaskant-Kleibrink, Marianne. *Catalogue of the Engraved Gems in the Royal Cabinet, The Hague.* 2 vols. The Hague, 1978.

MacMullen, Ramsay. "Roman Attitudes to Greek Love." *Historia* 31 (1982): 484–502. Reprinted in *Changes in the Roman Empire,* 177–189. Princeton, 1990.

Maiuri, Amedeo. *La casa del Menandro e il suo tesoro di argenteria.* 2 vols. Rome, 1933.

———. "Una nuova pittura nilotica a Pompei." *Memorie: atti della Accademia nazionale dei Lincei,* ser. 8, 7 (1956): 65–80.

———. "Picturae ligneis formis inclusae." *Rendiconti della Accademia di archeologia, lettere e belle arti, Napoli* 33 (1958): 203–218.

———. *Pompei.* Rome, 1934.

———. *La villa dei misteri.* Rome, 1931.

Marcadé, Jean. *Eros Kalos: Essay on Erotic Elements in Greek Art.* Geneva, 1965.

———. *Roma Amor: Essay on Erotic Elements in Etruscan and Roman Art.* Geneva, 1965.

Marini, Giuseppe L. *Il gabinetto segreto del Museo nazionale di Napoli.* Turin, 1971.

Marks, M. C. "Heterosexual Coital Position as a Reflection of Ancient and Modern Cultural Attitudes." Ph.D. dissertation, State University of New York, Buffalo, 1978.

Massner, Anne-Kathrein. *Bildnißangleichung: Untersuchungen zur Entstehungs- und Wirkungsgeschichte der Augustusporträts (43 v. Chr.–68 n. Chr.).* Berlin, 1982.

Mau, August. *Pompeji in Leben und Kunst.* Leipzig, 1900.

McGinn, T. A. J. "Prostitution and Julio-Claudian Legislation." Ph.D. dissertation, University of Michigan, 1986.

McLaren, Angus. *Reproductive Rituals.* New York, 1984.

McNiven, Timothy J. "The Unheroic Penis: Otherness Exposed." *Source* 15, no. 1 (1995): 10–16.

Megow, Wolf-Rudiger. *Kameen von Augustus bis Alexander Severus.* Vol. 11 of *Antiken Münzen und geschnittene Steine.* Berlin, 1987.

Melander, Torben. "Intaglio with Representation of an African: Portrait or 'Mask'?" In *Ancient Portraiture: Image and Message,* edited by Tobias Fischer-Hansen et al., *Acta hyperborea* 4 (1992): 73–88. Copenhagen, 1992.

Menzel, H. *Antiken Lampen.* Mainz, 1954.

———. *Die römischen Bronzen aus Deutschland.* Vol. 2. Mainz, 1966.

Meyboom, Paul G. P. *The Nile Mosaic of Palestrina: Early Evidence of Egyptian Religion in Italy.* Leiden, 1995.

Meyer-Schlechtmann, Carsten. *Die pergamenische Sigillata aus der Stadtgrabung von Pergamon, Mitte 2. Jh. v. Chr.-Mitte 2 Jh. n. Chr.* Berlin, 1988.

Michel, Dorothea. "Bemerkungen über Zuschauerfiguren in pompejanischen sogenannten Tafelbildern." In *La regione sotterrata dal Vesuvio: studi e prospettive,* Atti del Convegno internazionale 11–15 November 1979, edited by Alfonso de Franciscis, 537–598. Naples, 1982.

Michie, James. *Martial: The Epigrams Selected and Translated.* London, 1973.

Mollard-Besques, Simone. *Epoques hellénistique et romaine, Grèce et Asie Mineure.* Vol. 3 of *Musée national du Louvre: catalogue raisonné des figurines et reliefs en terre-cuite grecs, étrusques et romaine.* Paris, 1972.

Montero Cartelle, E. *El·latìn eròtico.* Seville, 1991.

Monumenti inediti pubblicati dall'Instituto di corrispondenza archeologica, vol. 12. Rome, 1885.

Moormann, Eric M. "Giardini ed altre pitture nella Casa del Frutteto e nella Casa del Bracciale d'Oro a Pompei." *Mededelingen van het Nederlands Instituut te Rome* 54 (1995): 214–228.

———. *La pittura parietale romana come fonte di conoscenza per la scultura antica.* Assen, 1988.

———, ed. *Functional and Spatial Analysis of Wall Painting.* Supplement 3, *Bulletin Antieke Beschaving.* Proceedings of the Fifth International Congress on Ancient Wall Painting. Leiden, 1993.

———. "Mani di pittori e botteghe pittoriche nel mondo romano: tavola rotonda in onore di W. J. Th. Peters in occasione del suo 75.mo compleanno" (Dutch School, Rome 16–17 May 1994), *Mededelingen van het Nederlands Instituut te Rome* 54 (1995): 61–298.

Moreno, Paolo. *La pittura greca: da Polignoto ad Apelle.* Milan, 1987.

Mulvey, Laura. *Visual and Other Pleasures.* Basingstoke, 1989.

Myerowitz, Molly. "The Domestication of Desire: Ovid's *Parva Tabella* and the Theater of Love." In *Pornography and Representation in Greece and Rome,* edited by Amy Richlin, 145–147. New York, 1992.

Naples, Museo Nazionale. *I mosaici, le pitture, gli oggetti di uso quotidiano, gli argenti, le terrecotte invetriate, i vetri, i cristalli, gli avori.* Vol. 1 of *Le collezioni del Museo Nazionale di Napoli.* Rome, 1986.

Neudecker, Richard. *Die Pracht der Latrine.* Munich, 1994.

Neumann, Gerhard. *Gesten und Gebärden in der griechischen Kunst.* Berlin, 1965.

Nielsen, Inge. *Thermae et Balnea: The Architecture and Cultural History of Roman Public Baths.* 2 vols. Aarhus, 1990.

Noack, Ferdinand, and Karl Lehmann-Hartleben. *Baugeschichtliche Untersuchungen am Stadtrand von Pompeji.* Berlin, 1936.

Nogara, Bartolomeo. *Le nozze Aldobrandine.* Milan, 1907.

Northwood, John, II. *John Northwood: His Contribution to the Stourbridge Flint Glass Industry, 1850–1902.* Stourbridge, 1958.

Oliver, Andrew, Jr. *Silver for the Gods: 800 Years of Greek and Roman Silver.* Exhibition catalog. Toledo, 1977.

Ortiz, George. *In Pursuit of the Absolute: Art of the Ancient World: The George Ortiz Collection.* Berne, 1996.

Ostrow, Steven E. "*Augustales* along the Bay of Naples: A Case for Their Early Growth." *Historia* 334 (1985): 64–101.

Oswald, F. *Index of Figure-Types on Terra Sigillata.* 2d ed. London, 1964.

Packer, James. "Inns at Pompeii." *Cronache pompeiane* 4 (1978): 5–53.

Page, Denys. *Poetae melici graeci.* Oxford, 1962.

Painter, Kenneth, and David Whitehouse. "Early Roman Cameo Glasses." *Journal of Glass Studies* 32 (1990): 138–165.

Pape, M. *Griechische Kunstwerke aus Kriegsbeute und ihre öffentliche Aufstellung in Rom: von der Eroberung von Syrakus bis in augusteische Zeit.* Hamburg, 1975.

Parker, Holt N. "Heterosexuality." In *Oxford Classical Dictionary,* edited by Simon Hornblower and Antony Spawforth. 3d ed. New York, forthcoming.

———. "Love's Body Anatomized: The Ancient Erotic Handbooks and the Rhetoric of Sexuality." In *Pornography and Representation in Greece and Rome,* edited by Amy Richlin, 90–107. New York, 1992.

———. "Sulpicia, the *Auctor de Sulpicia,* and the Authorship of 3.9 and 3.11 of the Corpus Tibullianum." *Helios* 21 (1994): 39–62.

———. "The Teratogenic Grid." In *Roman Sexualities,* edited by Judith P. Hallett and Marilyn Skinner. Princeton, forthcoming.

Parlasca, Klaus. "Zur Problematik des Nilmosaiks von Palestrina." In *Fifth International Colloquium on Ancient Mosaics,* Bath, England, 5–12 September 1987, edited by Peter Johnson, Roger Ling, and David J. Smith, 41–44. Ann Arbor, 1994.

Pavolini, Carlo. *Ostia.* Guida archeologica Laterza, no. 8. Rome, 1983.

Pernice, Erich. *Pavimente und figürliche Mosaiken.* Vol. 6 of *Die hellenistische Kunst in Pompeji.* Berlin, 1938.

Peters, W. J. Th. *La casa di Marcus Lucretius Fronto e le sue pitture.* Amsterdam, 1993.

Phillips, Kyle M., Jr. "The Barberini Mosaic: Sunt hominum animaliumque complures imagines." Ph.D. dissertation, Princeton University, 1962.

Picard, Gilbert-Charles. "Une mosaïque pompéienne à Constantine et l'installation des Sittii à Cirta." *Revue archéologique* (1980): 185–187.

Picón, Carlos A. "Fragment of a Dish with Erotic Scenes." *Metropolitan Museum of Art Bulletin* 53, no. 2 (1995): 14.

Pollitt, J. J. *Art in the Hellenistic Age.* Cambridge, 1986.

Pomeroy, Sarah B., ed. *Women's History and Ancient History.* Chapel Hill, 1991.

Pompei: l'informatica al servizio di una città antica. Rome, 1988.

Porten Palange, Francesca Paola. *La ceramica arretina a rilievo nell'Antiquarium del Museo Nazionale in Roma.* Florence, 1966.

———. "Fälschungen in der arretinischen Reliefkeramik." *Archäologisches Korrespondenzblatt* 19 (1989): 197–216.

Preller, L. *Die Regionen der Stadt Rom.* Jena, 1848.

Presuhn, Emil. *Die pompejanische Wanddekorationen für Künstler und Kunstgewerbtreibende.* 2d ed. Leipzig, 1882.

———. *Pompeji: die neuesten Ausgrabungen von 1874 bis 1881*. 2d ed. Leipzig, 1882.
Progetto Pompei: Primo stralcio, un bilancio. Naples, 1988.
Pucci, G. "La ceramica aretina: 'imagerie' e correnti artistiche." In *L'art décoratif à Rome à la fin de la république et au début du principat,* edited by X. Lafon and G. Sauron, 101–121. Rome, 1981.
———. "Per una storia del lusso nella cultura materiale fra Tarda Repubblica e Alto Impero." *Index* 13 (1985): 573–587.
Rabinowitz, Nancy Sorkin, and Amy Richlin, eds. *Feminist Theory and the Classics.* New York, 1993.
Radt, Wolfgang. "Lampen und Beleuchtung in der Antike." *Antike Welt* 17, no. 1 (1986): 40–58.
Reinach, Salomon. *Répertoire des peintures grec et romain.* Paris, 1922.
———. *Répertoire de reliefs grecs et romains.* Vol. 1. Paris, 1909.
Richardson, Emeline. *The Etruscans: Their Art and Civilization.* Chicago, 1964.
Richlin, Amy. "Approaches to the Sources on Adultery at Rome." In *Reflections on Women in Antiquity,* edited by Helene P. Foley, 379–404. New York, 1981.
———. *The Garden of Priapus: Sexuality and Aggression in Roman Humor.* New Haven, 1983. Revised edition, New York, 1992.
———. "The Meaning of *irrumare* in Catullus and Martial." *Classical Philology* 76 (January 1981): 40–46.
———. "Not before Homosexuality: The Materiality of the *Cinaedus* and the Roman Law against Love between Men." *Journal of the History of Sexuality* 3, no. 4 (1993): 523–573.
———, ed. *Pornography and Representation in Greece and Rome.* New York, 1992.
Richter, G. M. A. "Grotesques and the Mime." *American Journal of Archaeology* 17 (1913): 149–156.
Riggsby, Andrew M. "Lenocinium: Scope and Consequences." *Zeitschrift der Savigny-Stiftung für Rechtsgeschichte. Romanistische Abteilung* 112 (1995): 423–427.
———. "'Public' and 'Private' in Roman Culture: The Case of the Cubiculum." *Journal of Roman Archaeology,* 10 (1997): 1–20.
Riscoprire Pompei. Exhibition catalog. Rome, 1993.
Robert, J. N. *Les plaisirs à Rome.* Paris, 1963.
Rodenwaldt, Gerhard. "Mosaik in Wiener Hofmuseum." *Römische Mitteilungen* 25 (1910): 256–262.
Rome, Palazzo dei conservatori. *Bellezza e seduzione nella Roma imperiale.* Exhibition catalog, 11 June 11–31 July 1990. Rome, 1990.

Rome, Palazzo delle esposizioni. *Invisibilia: rivedere i capolavori, vedere i progetti.* Exhibition catalog. Rome, 1992.

Rose, Charles Brian. *Dynastic Commemoration and Imperial Portraiture in the Julio-Claudian Period.* New York, 1997.

———. "'Princes' and Barbarians on the Ara Pacis." *American Journal of Archaeology* 94 (1990): 453–467.

Rostovzeff, Michael. *The Social and Economic History of the Hellenistic World.* Oxford, 1941.

Rousselle, Aline. "Personal Status and Sexual Practice in the Roman Empire." *Zone* 5 (1989): 301–333.

———. *Porneia: On Desire and the Body in Antiquity.* Translated by Felicia Pheasant. New York, 1988.

Rouvier-Jeanlin, Micheline. *Les figurines gallo-romaines en terre cuite au Musée des Antiquités nationales.* Supplement 24, *Gallia.* Paris, 1972.

Ruggiu, Annapaola Zaccaria. *Spazio privato e spazio pubblico nella città romana.* Collection de l'Ecole française de Rome, no. 210. Rome, 1995.

Sadurska, Anna. *Les tables iliaques.* Warsaw, 1964.

Salmon, P. "'Racisme' ou refus de la différence dans le monde gréco-romain." *Dialogues d'histoire ancienne* 10 (1984): 75–98.

Sampaolo, Valeria. "I 9, 1: Casa del Bell'Impluvio." In *Pompei, pitture e mosaici,* 1:919–941. Rome, 1990.

———. "VI 15, 1: Casa dei Vettii." In *Pompei, pitture e mosaici,* 5:468–572. Rome, 1994.

Sandys, J. E. *Latin Epigraphy: An Introduction to the Study of Latin Inscriptions.* 2d ed. Cambridge, 1927.

Saslow, James M. *Ganymede in the Renaissance: Homosexuality in Art and Society.* New Haven, 1986.

Sauron, Gilles. *QVIS DEVM? L'expression plastique des idéologies politiques et religieuses à Rome.* Rome, 1994.

Scagliarini, Daniela Corlàita. "Spazio e decorazione nella pittura pompeiana." *Palladio* 23–25 (1974–1976): 3–44.

Schäfer, Jörg. *Hellenistische Keramik aus Pergamon.* Berlin, 1968.

Schefold, Karl. *La peinture pompéienne: essai sur l'évolution de sa signification.* Collection Latomus, 108. Brussels, 1972.

———. *Pompejanische Malerei: Sinn und Ideengeschichte.* Basel, 1952.

———. *Vergessenes Pompeji: unveröffentlichte Bilder römischer Wanddekorationen in geschichtlicher Folge herausgegeben.* Munich, 1962.

———. *Die Wände Pompejis: topographisches Verzeichnis der Bildmotive.* Berlin, 1957.

Schneider, Rolf M. *Bunte Barbaren: Orientalenstatuen aus farbigem Marmor in der römischen Repräsentationskunst.* Worms, 1986.

Schrijvers, P. H. *Eine medizinische Erklärung der männlichen Homosexualität aus der Antike.* Amsterdam, 1985.

Schröder, F. *Römische Bacchusbilder in der Tradition des Apollon Lykeios.* Rome, 1989.

Screen Reader 1: Cinema/Ideology/Politics. London, 1977.

Shackleton Bailey, D. R., trans. *Martial Epigrams.* 2 vols. Loeb Classical Library. Cambridge, Mass., 1993.

Shapiro, H. A. "Courtship Scenes in Attic Vase-Painting." *American Journal of Archaeology* 85 (1981): 133–143.

———. "Eros in Love: Pederasty and Pornography in Greece." In *Pornography and Representation in Greece and Rome,* edited by Amy Richlin, 53–72. New York, 1992.

Sichtermann, Hellmut. *Die mythologischen Sarkophage.* Vol. 12, part 2 of *Die Antiken Sarkophagreliefs.* Berlin, 1992.

Siebert, Gérard. "Hermes." *Lexicon Iconographicum Mythologiae Classicae,* vol. 5, part 1, 285–387.

Siems, Andreas Karsten, ed. *Sexualität und Erotik in der Antike.* Darmstadt, 1988.

Simon, Erika. *Augustus: Kunst und Leben in Rom um die Zeitenwende.* Munich, 1986.

———. *Die Portlandvase.* Mainz, 1957.

Simonetta, Bono, and Renzo Riva. *Le tessere erotiche romane (spintriae).* Lugano, 1981.

Smith, R. R. R. *Hellenistic Royal Portraits.* Oxford, 1988.

Snitow, Ann, Christine Stansell, and Sharon Thompson, eds. *Powers of Desire: The Politics of Sexuality.* New York, 1983.

Snowden, Frank M., Jr. *Before Color Prejudice.* Cambridge, Mass., 1983.

———. *Blacks in Antiquity.* Cambridge, Mass., 1970.

Sogliano, Antonio. "Le pitture murali campane scoverte negli anni 1867–1879." In *Pompei e la regione sotterrata dal Vesuvio nell'anno LXXIX,* part 2, 87–243. Naples, 1879.

Soprintendenza archeologica della Toscana. *M. Perennius Bargathes.* Exhibition catalog, Museo archeologico di Arezzo. Florence, 1984.

Soprintendenza archeologica di Pompei. *Il tesoro di Boscoreale.* Exhibition catalog, 20 August–30 September 1988. Milan, 1988.

Spinazzola, Vittorio. *Pompei alla luce degli scavi nuovi di via dell'Abbonzanda.* 2 vols. Rome, 1953.

Steinberg, Leo. *The Sexuality of Christ in Renaissance Art and in Modern Oblivion.* New York, 1983.

Steinmeyer-Schareika, A. *Das Nilmosaik von Palestrina und eine ptolemäische Expedition nach Äthiopien.* Bonn, 1978.

Stenico, Arturo. *La ceramica arretina.* Vol. 1, *Museo archeologico di Arezzo, Rasinius.* Vol. 2, *Collezioni diverse, punzoni, modelli, calchi.* Milan, 1960–1966.

Stevenson, William Edward, III. "The Pathological Grotesque Representation in Greek and Roman Art." Ph.D. dissertation, University of Pennsylvania, 1975.

Stewart, Andrew F. "Dionysos at Delphi: The Pediments of the Sixth Temple of Apollo and Religious Reform in the Age of Alexander." In *Macedonia and Greece in Late Classical and Early Hellenistic Times,* edited by Beryl Barr-Sharrar and Eugene N. Borza, 205–228. Vol. 10 of *Studies in the History of Art.* Washington, D.C., 1982.

———. "Reflections." In *Sexuality in Ancient Art,* edited by Natalie B. Kampen, 136–154. New York, 1996.

Stillwell, Richard, ed. *Antioch: The Excavations.* Vol. 3. Princeton, 1941.

Strocka, Volker Michael. *Casa del Laberinto (VI 11, 8–10). Häuser in Pompeji,* vol. 4. Munich, 1991.

Strong, Donald E. *Greek and Roman Gold and Silver Plate.* London, 1966.

Strong, Donald E., and P. E. Corbett. "Three Roman Silver Cups." *British Museum Quarterly* 23 (1961): 68–83.

Sullivan, J.–P. "Martial's Sexual Attitudes." *Philologus* 123 (1979): 288–302.

Sullivan, J. P., and Peter Whigham, eds. *Epigrams of Martial Englished by Divers Hands.* Berkeley, 1987.

Sutherland, Anne. *Gypsies: The Hidden Americans.* New York, 1975.

Sutton, Robert F., Jr. "Pornography and Persuasion on Attic Pottery." In *Pornography and Representation in Greece and Rome,* edited by Amy Richlin, 3–35. New York, 1992.

Talvacchia, Bette. "L'erotismo in Giulio Romano, fra decoro, decorazione, e scandolo." *La Nuova Città* 5 (1994): 95–113.

———. "Figure lascive per trastullo e l'ingegno." In *Giulio Romano,* 277–287. Milan, 1989.

Tatum, James, ed. *The Search for the Ancient Novel.* Baltimore, 1994.

Thomas, Michael. "Sexuality and Regeneration in the Tomb of the Bulls: Rites of Passage in Archaic Etruscan Tomb Painting." Master's thesis, Southern Methodist University, 1994.

Thompson, Lloyd A. *Romans and Blacks.* Norman, Okla., 1989.

Todd, F. A. "Three Pompeian Wall-Inscriptions, and Petronius." *Classical Review* 53, no. 1 (1939): 5–9.

Torelli, Mario. *Typology and Structure of Roman Historical Reliefs.* Ann Arbor, 1982.

Turner, P. "Novels, Ancient and Modern." *Novel* 2 (1968): 15–24.

United Nations Educational Scientific and Cultural Organization. *Tunisia: Ancient Mosaics.* New York, 1962.

Valenziano, Clara. "E sotto la cenere l'eros . . . ." *Il Venerdì di repubblica* 2, no. 31 (1988): 145.

Varone, Antonio. *Erotica pompeiana: iscrizioni d'amore sui muri di Pompei.* Rome, 1994.

———. "Scavi recenti a Pompei lungo via dell'Abbondanza (*Regio* IX, *ins.* 12, 6–7)." In *Ercolano 1738–1988: 250 anni di ricerca archeologica,* Atti del Convegno internazionale Ravello-Ercolano-Napoli-Pompei, 30 October–5 November 1988, edited by Luisa Franchi dell'Orto, 622–630. Rome, 1993.

Vercoutter, Jean, Jean Leclant, Frank M. Snowden, Jr., and Jehan Desanges. *From the Pharaohs to the Fall of the Roman Empire.* Vol. 1 of *The Image of the Black in Western Art.* New York, 1976.

Vermeule, Cornelius C. "Augustan and Julio-Claudian Court Silver." *Antike Kunst* 6, no. 1 (1963): 33–46.

———. *Greek, Etruscan and Roman Art: The Classical Collections of the Museum of Fine Arts, Boston.* Meriden, Conn., 1963.

Vermeule, Cornelius C., and Mary B. Comstock. *Sculpture in Stone and Bronze in the Museum of Fine Arts, Boston: Additions to the Collections of Greek, Etruscan, and Roman Art, 1971–1988.* Boston, 1988.

Vermeule, Emily. "Some Erotica in Boston." *Antike Kunst* 12 (1969): 9–15.

Vertet, H. "Observations sur les vases à médaillons d'applique de la vallée du Rhône." *Gallia* 27 (1969): 93–127.

Veyne, Paul. "La famille et l'amour sous le haut empire romain." *Annales: économies, sociétés, civilisations* 33 (1978): 35–63.

———. "L'homosexualité à Rome." *Communications* 35 (1985): 26–33.

———. "Homosexuality in Ancient Rome." In *Western Sexuality: Practice and Precept in Past and Present Times,* edited by Philippe Ariès and André Béjin, translated by Anthony Forster, 26–35. Oxford, 1985.

———. "*Humanitas:* Romans and Non-Romans." In *The Romans.* Edited by Andrea Giardina, translated by Lydia G. Cochrane, 342–369. Chicago, 1993.

———. *La poesia, l'amore, l'occidente: l'elegia erotica romana.* Bologna, 1985.

———. "The Roman Empire." In *From Pagan Rome to Byzantium.* Vol. 1 of *A History of Private Life,* edited by Paul Veyne, translated by Arthur Goldhammer, 5–234. Cambridge, Mass., 1987.

Vickers, Michael. "Artful Crafts: The Influence of Metalwork on Athenian Painted Pottery." *Journal of Hellenic Studies* 105 (1985): 108–128.

Vickers, Michael, Oliver Impey, and James Allen. *From Silver to Ceramic: The Potter's Debt to Metalwork in the Graeco-Roman, Oriental and Islamic Worlds.* Oxford, 1986.

Villefosse, Henri de. "Le trésor de Boscoreale." *Monuments Piot* 5 (1899): 1–290.

Viti, Angelo. "*Ad Calidium:* l'insegna del piacere nel rilievo di Lucio Calidio Erotico: saggio epigrafico con note critico-bibliografiche." *Almanacco del Molise* 2 (1989): 115–135.

Vorberg, Gaston. *Ars erotica veterum: ein Beitrag zum Geschlechtsleben der Altertums.* Stuttgart, 1926.

———. *Die Erotik der Antike in Kleinkunst und Keramik.* Munich, 1921.

———. *Glossarium eroticum.* Stuttgart, 1932.

———. *Über das Geschlechtsleben im Altertum.* Stuttgart, 1925.

Wace, A. J. B. "Grotesques and the Evil Eye." *Annual of the British School of Athens* 10 (1903–1904): 103–114.

Wallace-Hadrill, Andrew. *Houses and Society in Pompeii and Herculaneum.* Princeton, 1994.

———. "Public Honour and Private Shame: The Urban Texture of Pompeii." In *Urban Society in Roman Italy,* edited by T. J. Cornell and Kathryn Lomas, 39–62. London, 1995.

———. "The Social Structure of the Roman House." *Papers of the British School at Rome* 56 (1988): 43–97.

Walters, H. B. *Catalogue of the Silver Plate (Greek, Etruscan and Roman) in the British Museum.* London, 1921.

Warsher, Tatiana. "Codex Topographicus Pompejanus, Regio VI, ins. 10, pars 1." Typescripts in American Academy and German Archaeological Institute, Rome, 1936.

Weeks, Jeffrey, "Discourse, Desire and Sexual Deviance: Some Problems in a History of Homosexuality." In *The Making of the Modern Homosexual,* edited by Kenneth Plummer, 76–111. London, 1981.

Wegner, Max. *Hadrian, Plotina, Matidia, Sabina.* Das Römische Herrscherbild, part 2, vol. 3. Berlin, 1956.

Weitzmann, Kurt. *Illustrations in Roll and Codex.* Princeton, 1947.

Whitehouse, David. "Cameo Glass." In *Roman Glass: Two Centuries of Art and Invention,* edited by Kenneth Painter and Martine Newby, 19–32. London, 1991.

Whitehouse, H. *The Dal Pozzo Copies of the Palestrina Mosaic.* British Archaeological Reports, supplementary series 12 (1976).

Wilkinson, L. P. "From the point of view of antiquity." (Classical approaches, IV: Homosexuality). *Encounter* 51, no. 3 (1978): 20–31.

Williams, Craig. "Homosexuality and the Roman Man: A Study in the Cultural Construction of Sexuality." Ph.D. disssertation, Yale University, 1992.

Williams, Gordon. *Tradition and Originality in Roman Poetry.* London, 1968.

Williams, Walter L. *The Spirit and the Flesh: Sexual Diversity in American Indian Culture.* Boston, 1988.

Wilpert, G. J. *Le pitture delle catacombe romane.* Rome, 1903.

Winkler, John J. *The Constraints of Desire.* New York, 1990.

Wirth, Fritz. *Römische Wandmalerei vom Untergang Pompejis bis ans Ende des dritten Jahrhunderts.* Berlin, 1934.

Wuilleumier, Pierre, and Amable Audin. *Les médaillons d'applique gallo-romains de la vallée du Rhône.* Paris, 1952.

Yegül, Fikret K. *Baths and Bathing in Classical Antiquity.* New York, 1992.

Zanker, Paul. *Die Bildnisse des Augustus: Herrscherbild und Politik im Kaiserlichen Rome.* Exhibition catalog. Munich, 1979.
———. *Pompei.* Turin, 1993.
———. *Pompeji: Stadtbilder als Spiegel von Gesellschaft und Herrschaftsform.* Mainz, 1995.
———. *The Power of Images in the Age of Augustus.* Ann Arbor, 1988.
———. "Die Villa als Vorbild des späten pompejanischen Wohngeschmacks." *Jahrbuch des Deutschen Archäologischen Instituts* 94 (1979): 460–523.
Zevi, Fausto. "L'arte 'popolare.'" In *La pittura di Pompei,* 267–273. Milan, 1991.
———, ed. *Pompei.* Naples, 1992.
Züchner, W. *Griechische Klappspiegel.* Jahrbuch des Deutsches Archäologisches Institut, Supplement 14. Berlin, 1942.

INDEX

Designer: *Barbara Jellow*
Compositor: *Integrated Composition Systems*
Text: *10/15 Bembo and Bembo Italic*
Display: *Bauer Text Initials*
Printer: *Data Reproductions Corporation*
Binder: *John H. Dekker & Sons*